HERE IS A MAGNIFICENT opportunity
to peer over the shoulders of those
who have made and lived the story of
our nation in all its adventure and variety over nearly five centuries. You will
find the vivid, intimate diaries of the
great and of the obscure, of public figures aware that they were recording crucial events and of private people who
confided to their ledgers and notebooks
their longings and concerns (including
love, the weather, and the passing of
time), the rhythm, texture, and excitement of their daily lives.

There are one hundred diarists represented. Some are famous people: Columbus, Washington, Lewis and Clark, John
Quincy Adams, Horace Greeley, Harold
L. Ickes. Some have written the classic
American diaries: Samuel Sewall (the
witch-burning judge of Salem), John
Woolman (the gentle Quaker who went
among the Indians), Thoreau, Walt
Whitman, and, from our own day, F. P. A.
and Will Rogers. Some live for us today
only through their diaries: a Massachu-

setts farmer determined to earn a £300 bounty for the scalp of an Indian, a prankish college student of 1853, a pioneer woman making the overland journey to Oregon, a member of the Donner Party. Some, like English actress Fanny Kemble and Simone de Beauvoir, were simply visitors, both appreciative and critical of the American phenomenon.

From the landing of the Pilgrims to the landings at Normandy in World War II, from the Continental Congress to New Deal Washington, from the Gold Rush to Wall Street in the '20s, from log cabin to metropolis and suburbia, the sweeping story of America is told by the people who wrote, at the time, of the life they saw and touched and breathed.

The selections in this book represent the fruit of years of searching and sifting through libraries, archives, and private collections. Each diary is prefaced by an editorial note which sets the scene and places the selection in the context of national events and the writer's life.

For a note about the editors, Josef and Dorothy Berger, see last page of book.

DIARY OF AMERICA

AMERICA

*The intimate story of our nation, told by 100
diarists — public figures and plain citizens,
natives and visitors — over the five centuries
from Columbus, the Pilgrims, and George
Washington to Thomas Edison, Will Rogers,
and our own time* ☆ ☆ ☆ EDITED BY
JOSEF AND DOROTHY BERGER

1957
SIMON AND SCHUSTER ★ NEW YORK

SOURCES AND ACKNOWLEDGMENTS

Adams, Franklin Pierce. Diary of Our Own Samuel Pepys. New York, 1935. Copyright 1935 by Franklin Pierce Adams.

Barron, Clarence W. They Told Barron, 1930; and More They Told Barron, 1931; both edited by Arthur Pound and Samuel T. Moore. By permission of Harper and Brothers. Copyright 1930, 1931 by Arthur Pound and Samuel Taylor Moore.

Blake, Dorothy. Diary of a Suburban Housewife. New York, 1936. By permission of William Morrow and Co. Copyright 1935, 1936 by Dorothy Blake.

Cresswell, Nicholas. Journal of Nicholas Cresswell, edited by Samuel Thornely. New York, 1924. By permission of the Dial Press, Inc. Copyright 1924, 1928 by Dial Press, Inc.

Forten, Charlotte L. Journal of Charlotte L. Forten, edited by Ray Allen Billington. By permission of The Dryden Press. Copyright 1953 by The Dryden Press, Inc.

Ickes, Harold L. The Secret Diary of Harold L. Ickes. New York, 1953. Copyright 1953 by Simon and Schuster, Inc.

Newberry, Julia. Julia Newberry's Diary, edited by Margaret Ayer Barnes and Janet Ayer Fairbank. New York, 1933. By permission of W. W. Norton & Co. Copyright 1933 by W. W. Norton & Co., Inc.

Stilwell, Joseph W. The Stilwell Papers, edited by Theodore H. White. New York, 1948. By permission of William Sloane Associates. Copyright 1948 by Winnifred A. Stilwell.

(Other sources and acknowledgments on page 618.)

To
our dear friend
Inez Hogan

INTRODUCTION

★

FOR THE MEASURE of America's greatness, read the historians. They are the reviewers, the provers. Expertly they search and sift the record, keep the checkup of a nation, test the validity of an ideal and give the weight and blood count of a heritage.

But for the heartbeat, go to the people. To be transported into the past, raw and free of the processing of later-day handlers, to be swept off-page into life as our forebears lived it—for this we must turn to those who wrote, at the time, of the America they saw and touched and breathed.

Our country has become a bulging storehouse of this personal record-keeping, published and unpublished—autobiographies, collected letters, memoirs, diaries. Some of the writing is professional; but much more is by persons who would not have called themselves writers—the doers, the amateurs, spare-time authors who were full-time subjects of their own writing.

This collection, made up of diaries, draws on both kinds of writers. In offering it we hope it will do for the reader, in some measure, what the gathering of it has done for us—enhance his feeling for the country's past, and here and there make it come astonishingly alive.

There are many kinds of diaries. Mostly they record individual experience—family matters, personal conduct, love affairs, business, travel, entertainment, adventure. Others focus on the larger picture—politics, public affairs, the headlines that emerge from many walks of life. Some—like Franklin P. Adams' "Our Own Samuel Pepys," Heywood Broun's "It Seems to Me," or the rope-spinning patter of Will Rogers—are the running comment of observers who themselves seldom step from the sidelines into the arena of action. Others—for example the diary of William Maclay or of John Quincy Adams or of Harold L. Ickes—record the diarist's own part in public life.

All, because they are contemporaneous and continuous, are journals—the story of the day—and their authors, in the large sense, journalists. The words diary and journal mean exactly the same thing and derive from the same Latin root—diary from diarium from dies (day), journal from diurnal, again from dies.

America's story-of-the-day goes back nearly five centuries. It leads us into

vii

the uncharted sea, takes us over trails no white man has ever trod, thrusts into our hands the rifle, the ax and the hoe, and makes overwhelming demands of performance with each. In the taprooms and coffeehouses, far from home in stagecoach or sailing packet, on the battlefront, or trudging beside the wagon trains, we meet men whose names will be the bywords of following generations; and we chat with others who would be forgotten except for one precious possession—a little notebook. With a dateline, a sentence or two, they bring us down-to-date. "Then" becomes "now" and "there" is "here."

We like this now-ness of diaries. Each unturned page is a tomorrow, heavy with hopes and fears, each entry a collaboration with destiny. And we, instead of being on the outside by an age or a century—suddenly we are among those present. We are In.

Also, and not least among our reasons for liking diaries, almost every one of them reveals more than its writer intended. This is of the very nature of diary-keeping. Try or not, none can avoid it. Sometimes, indeed, the diary goes full circle and reveals precisely what the diarist had hoped to conceal.

"O rare and excellent being!" writes one, addressing the adored entity which lives with him from page to page in his little book and which is, of course, himself, "My diary, truest of friends, who never talks back; agrees with everything I say; appreciates to the point of worship the good things I do and forgives at once the bad; and who, above all, will never, never betray me . . ."

How lucky that so many unsuspecting souls make the same mistake! Were they ever to stop trusting that rare and excellent being, how much delectable self-betrayal would be lost to us, how much less we should have remaining of them to laugh at, to admire, to condemn, to love!

Thousands of American diaries have been published and many more thousands, unpublished, are preserved. Out of the yellowing stacks of manuscript the state, county and local historical societies from time to time select for the press those that seem most interesting or valuable. Without these, a large part of this book would not have been possible.

Other diaries are privately printed by relatives or descendants as family keepsakes. And through the years a great many important ones have been picked up by historians and other professionals and edited into fascinating and valuable additions to the general library.

To the anthologist, digging into these mountains of material is as exciting as searching for rich veins of gold in the hills of the West must have been a century ago. Only here one can scarcely miss. There are rich veins everywhere one turns.

As the act of a human being revealing himself, a diary may be "gold" whether well written or ill. These works cannot be judged by standards that apply to other forms of writing. Thus the researcher, striking pay dirt almost anywhere he scratches the surface, is soon overwhelmed with the sheer weight of his treasures.

Years ago, in the beginning of our undertaking, we were puzzled that so little had been done with this avalanche of material. Here was America, the America of an unending procession of eyewitnesses, America in their own words, of the people, by the people. And for whom? Apparently for a few historians who quoted paragraphs here and there to illustrate or document their own works, and for antiquarians, genealogists, a handful of readers with special interests. And a whole people's story was gathering the sad dust of infinite disuse.

It wasn't very satisfying to know that a few diaries of important persons were widely distributed. Who is an unimportant person? The reader of diaries soon learns to be an ignorer of reputation. The story an Iowa housewife tells of herding her seven children over the Oregon Trail made far better reading to us than the Western diary of Washington Irving.

After a few such surprises we realized that for the book we wanted, we should have to count in, along with big-name writers, people like Sergeant John Smith, soldier in General Washington's army who was fighting hunger and cold as well as the British; or like little Elizabeth Fuller, who finally got round to making a new coat for Pa; or like Joseph Cleaver, Jr., college student of a century ago who loses all his debates, including the one on that shiny, brand-new issue, capital punishment.

And there they were—our pick of thousands of them—waiting to be brought back to the people by anyone who cared to say, "Here, this is you, writing about yourselves. This is your people, your ancestors, your neighbors, picturing your country."

Well, why not? Were we overvaluing this material? Had it really been neglected—or was there a catch?

We ran into the catch as soon as we started work. The catch was that in real life much happened to a human being about which other human beings couldn't care less. Diaries, being records of real life, were hopelessly cluttered with this miscellaneous much.

> Monday, August 6. I am so happy. Last night Davy came the closest yet to proposing. After all these years! Naturally, today I am walking on air. I am pretty sure he will propose next time, and we have a date on Friday. I can't wait. This morning Uncle Jason came down with awful pains in his stomach and the doctor says he can't eat any more fried clams.

We too are all a-twitter to learn what will happen next time Davy comes over. But that will be on Friday. Meanwhile, how much must we go through —and read through—if on Tuesday, Wednesday or Thursday Uncle Jason should again yield to temptation?

In addition to the Uncle Jasons that flit in and out of diaries, there is always the weather. More space is given to this topic than to any other. Yet unless it sets the scene for a boy and a girl or otherwise makes itself useful and relevant, all old weather leaves us cold.

But it is one thing to clear away the picnic-basket litter from a diary and another to strike out all the color. The minutiae, seemingly unrelated, are many times the grace notes, little touches that mean the difference between bare narrative and a scene re-created or a personality in all its dimensions. What, then, to strike out and what to keep?

There was no ready-made answer to that question. Those who have edited diaries from manuscript have followed no rules except their own. Some have tried meticulously to account for every slip of the diarist's pen, whether it makes sense to do so or not—which it usually doesn't. Some editors have put brackets around their own insertions of commas and periods. Others eliminate words, paragraphs, whole sections of manuscript, with no indication of the omission beyond a prefatory note.

Neither, of course, were there any rules for editing an anthology of diaries. The only standard had to be common sense. After much experiment we decided to stop bailing out the ocean and just go fishing—that is, we gave up trying to x out the parts that made a diary too dull for the casual reader and instead selected from it the parts that we thought would be most interesting to him.

In these pages there are no dots to indicate omissions. We have left them out for the same reason that the editors of the original manuscripts have done so. Here the device of dots would have not only intruded and annoyed; too often it would have been actually misleading. Thus faced with the choice of sacrificing conventions dear to the heart of the researcher or coming out with something too painfully bandaged, splinted and bedecked with editorial wound-stripes to offer the casual reader any sort of decent companionship, we decided against an overuse of bookish appurtenances and in favor of a book.

For easier reading we have modernized the spelling in the diaries of the sixteenth and seventeenth centuries. However, it is our feeling that in the individualistic spelling, grammar and phrasing of subsequent diaries there is character that should not be edited out. These we have preserved.

Any anthology worth publishing must necessarily have been a greater experience to the compiler, it seems to us, than it can possibly be to the reader. The editor reads the whole book represented by each selection he makes. A successful anthology ought to make the reader wish to go and do likewise.

Time and again, in the preparation of this book, we have felt like prefacing an excerpt with "But you really ought to read more of this. Please, we don't have room for all of it here, but there are so many good parts—just forget our anthology and go get the book!"

In the attics, basements and household catchalls of America there is an unknown number of old diaries. We believe the aggregate of these would amount to an important cultural treasure. How many have been burned or thrown away is also unknown, but this number doubtless would be even larger.

All such manuscripts ought to be given to the keeping of those best equipped to preserve them and put them to use—that is, the historical societies and public and institutional libraries. We urge any reader who owns an old family diary to do this. Otherwise, sooner or later, it probably will be destroyed.

If you feel hesitant about entrusting your family history to other hands, you can stipulate to the librarian that the manuscript is not to be made available to readers, or for publication, until fifty or a hundred years have passed. Time is a sure cosmetic for the softening of odd angles and unorthodox contours in the family skeleton. What your ancestors of a hundred years ago might have shuddered to make known will, a hundred years hence, only amuse, perhaps become a favorite conversation piece among your descendants.

The editors of this book would like to know, for possible future reference, about any such manuscripts. Don't, for heaven's sake, send your treasured family diary to us! But we shall welcome information as to its whereabouts, its author, the years it covers, the locale, the major events.

For their many kindnesses while we were working on this book, our thanks are due the officers and library workers of historical societies, state, county, and local, from coast to coast. We are deeply indebted to Edna Huntington, Theresa N. Swezey, Harriet M. Rodda and Edward Place, of the Long Island Historical Society; to Robert W. Hill, Edward B. Morrison and Jean R. McNiece of the New York Public Library's manuscript division and Shirley L. Spranger, Moritia-Leah Frederick and Leon Weidman of the New York Public Library's history room; Fred H. Forrest of the Columbia University Library; Archibald Hanna, Jr. of Yale University Library; Charles E. Baker and Wayne Andrews of the New York Historical Society; Louise Turpin, Theodore Avery, Jr. and Philip Evans of the Brooklyn Public Library, and many others.

We also wish to express our admiration of the work of William Matthews in the field of American diaries and to acknowledge the assistance we received from his excellent bibliography, American Diaries, published in 1945 by the University of California Press.

Among other works that we have found especially helpful are New England Diaries, a catalogue compiled by Harriette M. Forbes, privately printed in 1923; and A Catalogue of Manuscripts in the Western Americana Collection, Yale University Library, compiled by Mary C. Withington, Yale University Press, 1952.

To the editors and publishers of the diaries on which we have drawn for this anthology go our thanks for their generous permissions.

Finally, we are most deeply indebted to Justin D. Kaplan of Simon and Schuster, whose high editorial standards and enthusiasms prodded, inspired and induced us into harder work—and a better book—than we ourselves had expected.

JOSEF AND DOROTHY BERGER

Littleton, New Hampshire

CONTENTS

★

2. *THE NEW NATION*

3. WESTWARD THE COURSE

4. DEDICATION TO A PROPOSITION

5. NEW FRONTIERS FOR OLD

I.

THE

NEW

WORLD

THE DIARY of Christopher Columbus is the only day-to-day eyewitness account of the discovery of America.

Penned "with guileless simplicity," as Washington Irving describes it, it records the great adventure in meticulous detail from the sailing from Palos, Spain, on August 3, 1492, to the landfall of October 12; then the many peoples and places visited in three months of exploration among the West Indies; the departure for home on January 4, 1493, and the assortment of hair-raising hazards before the caravel Nina finally dropped anchor back in Palos on March 15—in all, 32 weeks of the most momentous venture in history. Samuel Eliot Morison, in his biography Admiral of the Ocean Sea, declares this diary to be "the source of about 98 per cent of our information about the actual discovery of America."

In the new world, from first sight to farewell, the diary is like one prolonged gasp, full of wonder at everything on these shores across the Atlantic; and full, too, of a devout awareness that what is happening will change the world so vastly that at every turn the hand of God must be very, very close.

The original manuscript of the diary is lost. What comes down to us is not a perfect copy; but that anything at all has come down to us is a piece of quite wonderful luck. On his return to Spain Columbus forwarded the diary to Ferdinand and Isabella at Barcelona. They consigned it to the royal archives. When or how it subsequently disappeared, nobody knows; but fortunately, before that happened it was copied. Later the copy, or copies, were lost too. Again fortunately, two accounts had been written from that draft.

One of these is included in a story of Columbus' life written by his son Ferdinand, who follows the diary very closely and quotes at length from it. After Ferdinand's death his manuscript lay ignored for nearly thirty years, until a grandson of the explorer took it to Italy. There, translated into Italian, it was published in 1571.

The other version is by Bartolome de Las Casas—a very full abstract of the diary, which puts the story into third person but often shifts to first person with the editorial note, "These are the Admiral's own words." Las Casas, who crossed the Atlantic himself in 1500 and was the first to be ordained a priest in the new world, was a dedicated scholar. Many writers with pet theories about the discovery of America have tried to break down the authenticity of Las Casas' abstract of the diary, which stood in their own disproof. So it still stands—widely regarded as the most important historical document of the Western Hemisphere.

3

What did destroy its usefulness for nearly 300 years was indifference. For the abstract, a small volume in parchment cover of 76 pages closely written in Las Casas' hand, was left unprinted until 1825! The wanderings of the price-less little book through those centuries, and such narrow escapes as it may have had, are unknown. It was discovered at length in the library of the Duke of Infantado at Madrid and printed by Martin Fernandez de Navarrette, a zealous editor in a country where the saving of knowledge was generally a thankless job.

But the tribulations of the diary were as nothing compared to those of the diarist. On the westward crossing, almost within sight of land, Columbus staved off failure of the whole venture only by a matter of hours when the threat of mutiny arose among his ninety frightened men.

The outward passage has been much celebrated in song and story. Events on the way back to Spain, though not so often recounted, were quite as suspenseful. Storms beset the tiny ships so fiercely that Columbus was afraid they would never get back to give the world their great news. Finally, it was touch and go whether credit for the discovery would be wrested from Columbus by the am-bitious Captain Pinzon of the Pinta, who was trying to beat the Nina home, pretty obviously with that idea in mind.

The first of these crises—the near mutiny—came when the caravels were westbound with the new world only 200 miles away.

"I shall shape a course for Japan . . ."
CHRISTOPHER COLUMBUS (1451-1506)

Wednesday, October 10 [1492]

The course was west-southwest. Here the people could endure no longer. They complained of the length of the voyage. But the Admiral cheered them up in the best way he could, giving them good hopes of the advantages they might gain from it. He added that, however much they might complain, he had to go to the Indies, and that he would go on until he found them, with the help of our Lord.

Of this crisis, the first official historian of the new world, Fernandez de Oviedo, who was a close friend of Columbus, wrote: "Columbus gave heart to those who were about to resort to something shameful, especially the three Pinzon brothers (Martin Alonso, Francisco Martin and Vicente Yanez) who were his captains, and they agreed to sail three days and no more."

Thursday, October 11

The course was west-southwest, and there was more sea than there had been during the whole of the voyage. They saw sandpipers, and a green reed near the ship. Those of the caravel *Pinta* saw a cane and a pole, and they took up another small pole which appeared to have been worked with iron; also another bit of cane, a land plant, and a small board. The crew of the caravel *Nina* also saw signs of land, and a small branch covered with berries. Everyone breathed afresh and rejoiced at these signs. After sunset the Admiral returned to his original west course.

Columbus does not say what led him to order this change in the course from west-southwest to due west. Other than to call it a sailor's hunch, there is no explanation. But certainly, had he not done so, he would have missed the land-fall at the island now called San Salvador.

Up to two hours after midnight they had gone ninety miles [since sunset] equal to twenty-two and a half leagues. As the caravel *Pinta* was a better sailer and went ahead of the Admiral [who was aboard the *Santa Maria*], she found the land [2 A.M., Friday, October 12] and made the signals ordered by the Admiral.

The land was first seen by a sailor named Rodrigo de Triana at a distance of two leagues.

The vessels were hove to, waiting for daylight; and on Friday they arrived at a small island of the Lucayos called, in the language of the Indians, Guanahani [San Salvador].

Presently they saw naked people. The Admiral went on shore in the armed boat, and Martin Alonso Pinzon [captain of the *Pinta*] and Vicente Yanez, his brother, who was captain of the *Nina*.

The Admiral took the royal standard, and the captains went with two banners of the green cross, which the Admiral took in all the ships as a sign, with an F and a Y [for Fernando and Ysabel].

Having landed, they saw trees very green, and much water, and fruits of diverse kinds.

The Admiral called to the two captains, and to the others who leaped on shore, and said that they should bear faithful testimony that he, in presence of all, had taken, as he now took, possession of the said island for the King and for the Queen.

Presently many inhabitants of the island assembled. What follows is in the actual words of the Admiral.

"I," he says, "that we might form great friendship, for I knew that they

were a people who could be more easily freed and converted to our holy
faith by love than by force, gave to some of them red caps, and glass
beads to put round their necks, and many other things of little value,
which gave them great pleasure, and made them so much our friends that
it was a marvel to see.

"They afterward came to the ship's boats where we were, swimming
and bringing us parrots, cotton threads in skeins, darts, and many other
things.

"It appeared to me to be a race of people very poor in everything. They
go as naked as when their mothers bore them, and so do the women,
although I did not see more than one young girl. All I saw were youths,
none more than thirty years of age. They are very well made, with very
handsome bodies, and very good countenances.

"They neither carry nor know anything of arms, for I showed them
swords, and they took them by the blade and cut themselves through
ignorance.

"They should be good servants . . ."

At once begins the search for Japan, for Cathay, for spices, and more than
anything else, for gold. Columbus took—without asking—six of the natives with
him and went on to the island now known as Rum Cay, then to Long Island,
another in the group now called the Bahamas. No Japan, no towered cities of
Cathay, no Grand Khan—but still the hope of finding gold. At Crooked
Island he went ashore again.

October 21

"At ten o'clock I arrived here, off this islet, and anchored. After breakfast I went on shore, and found only one house, in which there was no
one, and I supposed they had fled from fear, because all their property
was left in the house. I would not allow anything to be touched, but set
out with the captains and people to explore the island.

"If the others already seen are very beautiful, green, and fertile, this
is so much more so, with large trees and very green. Here there are large
lagoons with wonderful vegetation on their banks. Throughout the island
all is green, and the herbage like April in Andalusia. The songs of the
birds were so pleasant that it seemed as if a man could never wish to
leave the place. The flocks of parrots concealed the sun; and the birds
were so numerous, and of so many different kinds, that it was wonderful.
There are trees of a thousand sorts, and all have their several fruits; and
I feel the most unhappy man in the world not to know them, for I am

well assured that they are all valuable. I bring home specimens of them, and also of the land.

"I wished to fill up all the ships with water at this place, and, if there should be time, I intended to search the island until I had had speech with the king, and seen whether he had the gold of which I had heard. I shall then shape a course for another much larger island, which I believe to be Cipango [Japan] judging from the signs made by the Indians I bring with me. They call it Cuba, and they say that there are ships and many skillful sailors there."

November 12 [Puerto Gibara, Cuba]

"I saw and knew," (says the Admiral) "that these people are without any religion, not idolaters, but very gentle, not knowing what is evil, nor the sins of murder and theft, being without arms, and so timid that a hundred would fly before one Spaniard, although they joke with them."

November 21 [Tanamo Bay, Cuba]

This day Martin Alonso Pinzon parted company with the caravel *Pinta* in disobedience to and against the wish of the Admiral, and out of avarice, thinking that an Indian who had been put on his caravel could show him where there was much gold. So he parted company, not owing to bad weather, but because he chose.

December 12 [Moustique Bay, Haiti]

The Admiral set up a great cross on the west side of the entrance, on a very picturesque height, "in sign," he says, "that Your Highnesses hold this land for your own, but chiefly as a sign of our Lord Jesus Christ."

This being done, three sailors strolled into the woods to see the trees and bushes. Suddenly they came upon a crowd of people, all naked like the rest. They called to them, and went toward them, but they ran away.

At last they caught a woman; "for I had ordered that some should be caught, that they might be treated well, and made to lose their fear."

So they took the woman, who was very young and beautiful, to the ship, where she talked to the Indians on board; for they all speak the same language. The Admiral caused her to be dressed, and gave her glass beads, hawks' bells, and brass ornaments; then he sent her back to the shore very courteously, according to his custom.

He sent three of the crew with her, and three of the Indians he had on board, that they might open communications with her people. The sailors in the boat, who took her on shore, told the Admiral that she did not want to leave the ship.

December 16 [Port de Paix, Haiti]

Presently more than five hundred natives with their king came to the shore opposite the ships, which were anchored very close to the land. The Admiral sent him a present, which he received in great state.

He was a youth of about 21 years of age, and he had with him an aged tutor, and other counselors who advised and answered him, but he uttered very few words. One of the Indians who had come in the Admiral's ship spoke to him, telling him how the Christians had come from Heaven, and how they came in search of gold.

This king, and all the others, go naked as their mothers bore them, as do the women, without any covering, and these were the most beautiful men and women that had yet been met with.

December 18

The Admiral learned from an old man that there were many neighboring islands within a hundred leagues or more in which gold was produced; he even told him of an island that was all gold, and in the others so great a quantity that they gather it and sift it as in a sieve, and smelt it and make bars and a thousand works of art. This old man indicated to the Admiral the route and position where it was. The Admiral determined to go there.

December 22 [Acul Bay, Haiti]

As the Indians are so simple, and the Spaniards so avaricious and grasping, it does not suffice that the Indians should give them all they want in exchange for a bead or a bit of glass, but the Spaniards would take everything without any return at all.

December 23

These are the Admiral's words. He says that, according to his reckoning, a thousand people had visited the ship, all of them bringing something. Before they come alongside, at a distance of a crossbow's shot, they stand up in the canoe with what they bring in their hands, crying out, "Take it! Take it!"

The Admiral ordered something to be given to all, because such gifts were all well employed. "May our Lord favor me by his clemency, that I may find this gold, I mean the mine of gold, which I hold to be here, many saying that they know it."

On Christmas Day the Santa Maria was wrecked on a reef in Caracol Bay, off the coast of Santo Domingo. This was a heavy blow, but Columbus, now on board the Nina, quickly forgot his troubles when he saw natives coming alongside in canoes and holding up bits of gold which they were eager to trade for the little hawks' bells the Spanish had brought with them. They were "a loving people, without covetousness," but their king was "virtuous above all." He came aboard, begged Columbus not to grieve over the wreck, and promised to bring four pieces of gold as big as a hand if Columbus would save one of those little bells for him.

December 30

The Admiral went on shore to dinner. On landing, he was received by the king, who led him by the arm to the house where there were chairs, and a couch on which the Admiral sat.

Presently the king took the crown off his head and put it on the Admiral's.

January 10 [1493]

As soon as he heard from the Indians that the Admiral was on the coast of the same island of Espanola, and that he could not avoid him, Pinzon came to him. He wanted all the people of the ship to swear that he had not been there more than six days. But his treachery was so public that it could not be concealed. He had made a law that half of all the gold that was collected was his. When he left this port he took four men and two girls by force. But the Admiral ordered that they should be clothed and put on shore to return to their homes.

January 15

The Admiral now wished to depart [for Spain] for there was nothing to be gained by further delay.

January 16

They got under way three hours before daylight and left the gulf, which was named Golfo de las Flechas [Bay of Samana] with the land-breeze.

February 14

This night the wind increased, and the waves were terrible, rising against each other, and so shaking and straining the vessel [Nina] that she could make no headway, and was in danger of being stove in.

At sunrise the wind blew still harder, and the cross sea was terrific. They continued to show the closely reefed mainsail to enable her to rise from between the waves, or she would otherwise have been swamped.

The Admiral ordered that a pilgrimage should be made to Our Lady of Guadalupe, carrying a candle of 6 lbs. of weight in wax, and that all the crew should take an oath that the pilgrimage should be made by the man on whom the lot fell. As many chick-peas were got as there were persons on board, and on one a cross was cut with a knife. They were then put into a cap and shaken up. The first who put in his hand was the Admiral, and he drew out the chick-pea with a cross, so the lot fell on him; and he was bound to go on the pilgrimage and fulfill the vow.

Here the Admiral writes of the causes which made him fear that he would perish, and of others that gave him hope that God would work his salvation, in order that such news as he was bringing to the Sovereigns might not be lost.

"Although on the one hand I was comforted by the faith that I had that our Lord would never suffer a work which would highly exalt his Church, which at length after so much opposition and such labors I had brought to the last stage, to remain unaccomplished and that I should be broken; on the other hand, I thought that, either on account of my demerits or to prevent my enjoying so much glory in this world, it was His pleasure to take it away from me, and so while thus in perplexity I bethought myself of the venture of Your Highnesses who even if I should die and the ship be lost, might find means of not losing a victory already achieved, and that it might be possible in some way for the news of the success of my voyage to come to your ears; wherefore I wrote on a parchment, with the brevity that the time demanded, how I had discovered the lands that I had promised to, and in how many days; and the route I had followed; and the goodness of the countries, and the quality of their inhabitants and how they were the vassals of Your Highnesses who had possession of all that had been found by me.

"This writing folded and sealed I directed to Your Highnesses with the superscription or promise of a thousand ducats to him who should deliver it thus unopened, in order that, if some foreigners should find it, the truth of this superscription might prevent them from disposing of the information which was inside. And I straightway had a large cask brought, and having wrapped the writing in a wax cloth and put it into a kind of tart or cake of wax, I placed it in the barrel which, stoutly hooped, I then threw into the sea.

"All believed that it was some act of devotion. Then because I thought it might not arrive safely and the ships were all the while approaching Castile I made another package like that and placed it on the upper part of the poop in order that if the ship should sink the barrel might float at the will of fate."

Neither of these letters was ever found. In the certain knowledge that they would be worth a fortune, several forgeries have been attempted.

March 4

During the night they were exposed to a terrible storm [cyclone], expecting to be overwhelmed by the cross-seas, while the wind seemed to raise the caravel into the air, and there were rain and lightning in several directions. The Admiral prayed to our Lord to preserve them, and in the first watch it pleased our Lord to show land, which was reported by the sailors.

As it was advisable not to reach it before it was known whether there was any port to which he could run for shelter, the Admiral set the mainsail, as there was no other course but to proceed, though in great danger.

Thus God preserved them until daylight, though all the time they were in infinite fear and trouble. When it was light, the Admiral knew the land, which was the rock of Cintra, near the river of Lisbon, and he resolved to run in because there was nothing else to be done.

So terrible was the storm, that in the village of Cascaes, at the mouth of the river, the people were praying for the little vessel all that morning.

At the third hour they passed Rastelo, within the river of Lisbon, where they were told that such a winter, with so many storms, had never before been known, and that 25 ships had been lost in Flanders, while others had been wind-bound in the river for four months.

March 15

Yesterday, after sunset, she [the *Nina*] went on her course with little wind, and at sunrise she was off Saltes. At noon, with the tide rising, they crossed the bar of Saltes, and reached the port [Palos, Spain] which they had left on the 3rd of August of the year before [225 days before].

The Admiral says that so ends this journal.

The Pinta, under command of Martin Alonso Pinzon, parted company with the Nina during the storm in mid-February. Bypassing the Azores, the Pinta escaped the cyclone that almost sank the Nina. The overly ambitious Martin Alonso, as soon as he reached Spain at the port of Bayona, rushed a message overland to the King and Queen at Barcelona, claiming the discovery for himself and asking for an appointment. They sent back word that they preferred to hear the news from the Admiral. Still hopeful that by getting home first he could spread his story and make his claim stick, Pinzon raced on to his home port at Palos. There he beheld the Nina, already at anchor.

---★

1587-90: THE LOST COLONY OF ROANOKE

---☆

IN 1578 seven ships sailed to plant the first British colony in America. They failed to cross the ocean. But an English America remained a persistent vision in the mind of one of the captains. His name was Walter Raleigh.

Handsome, brilliant, "with a bold and plausible tongue," Raleigh won the favor of Queen Elizabeth and got from her a charter to colonize "heathen and barbarous lands," plus a grant of "all privileges of free persons native of England" to any such colonists. This latter, incidentally, was a promise not forgotten two centuries later when Americans were demanding those very privileges.

In 1584 Raleigh sent scouts across to explore the country north of Florida. They went to Roanoke Island, just inside Cape Hatteras. The soil there, they reported, was "the most plentiful of all the world" and the natives "as mannerly and civill as any of Europe."

The Virgin Queen was pleased and named the country Virginia after her own established condition. There followed two more of Raleigh's expeditions to Virginia, but they failed, first because the mother country was too slow in following up with shipment of necessary supplies for the settlers and second because, after a petty quarrel in which the British had vengefully and wantonly burned the corn of the Indians, the latter were no longer "mannerly and civill."

In 1586 Sir Richard Grenville left fifteen men to hold down a fort which had been built on Roanoke Island. The following year Raleigh sent over another contingent, 150 settlers, men and women, with an artist named John White as governor. But he gave White orders to stop at Roanoke only to pick up the fifteen who had been left there, then go on to settle on the friendlier shores of Chesapeake Bay.

About John White the record is nearly blank except for a diary he kept. Why Raleigh chose him for leadership is not explained. That the choice was a mistake is suggested in a series of strange failures on White's part to act with the boldness and force that might have saved his little band from becoming "the lost colony of Roanoke."

The first of these failures occurred when the three ships arrived at Hatteras ("Hatorask"). The commander of the fleet, a Spaniard named Simon Ferdinando, got into a quarrel with White and refused to take the people on to Chesapeake Bay. So they were forced to remain at Roanoke Island.

"We found no man nor sign . . ."
JOHN WHITE (latter part sixteenth century)

[Bahamas, July 7, 1587]

Early in the morning we weighed anchor, leaving Caycos with good hope that the first land that we saw next should be Virginia.

16 of July

We fell with the main of Virginia, which Simon Ferdinando took to be the island of Croatoan, where we came to anchor, and rode there two or three days; but finding himself deceived, he weighed, and bare along the coast, where in the night, had not Captain Stafford been more careful in looking out than our Simon Ferdinando, we had been all cast away upon the beach, called the Cape of Fear, for we were come within two cables length upon it; such was the carelessness and ignorance of our Master.

The two and twentieth of July

We arrived safely at Hatorask, where our ship and pinnace anchored. The Governor went aboard the pinnace, accompanied with forty of his best men, intending to pass up to Roanoke forthwith, hoping there to find those fifteen Englishmen which Sir Richard Grenville had left there the year before, with whom he meant to have conference concerning the state of the country and savages, meaning after he had so done to return again to the fleet and pass along the coast to the Bay of Chesapeake where we intended to make our seat and fort, according to the charge given us among other directions in writing under the hand of Sir Walter Raleigh.

But as soon as we were put with our pinnace from the ship, a gentleman, on orders from Ferdinando, who was appointed to return for England, called to the sailors in the pinnace, charging them not to bring any of the planters back again, but to leave them in the island, except the Governor and two or three such as he approved, saying that the summer was fair spent, wherefore he would land all the planters in no other place.

Unto this were all the sailors, both in the pinnace and ship, persuaded by the Master, wherefore it booted not the Governor to contend with them, but passed to Roanoke, and the same night at sunset went a-land on the island, in the place where our fifteen men were left, but we found none of them, nor any sign that they had been there, saving only we found the bones of one of those fifteen, which the savages had slain long before.

The three and twentieth of July

The Governor with divers of his company walked to the north end of the island, where Master Ralph Lane had his fort, with sundry necessary and decent dwelling houses, made by his men about it the year before, where we hoped to find some signs, or certain knowledge of our fifteen men.

When we came thither, we found the fort razed down, but all the houses standing unhurt, saving that the nether rooms of them, and also of the fort, were overgrown with melons of divers sorts, and deer within them, feeding on those melons. So we returned to our company, without hope of ever seeing any of the fifteen men living. ·

The same day order was given that every man should be employed for the repairing of those houses which we found standing and also to make other new cottages for such as should need.

The eight and twentieth

George Howe, one of our twelve assistants, was slain by divers savages, which were come over to Roanoke, either of purpose to espy our company and what we were, or else to hunt deer, whereof were many in the island.

These savages being secretly hidden among high weeds, where oftentimes they find the deer asleep and so kill them, espied our man wading in the water alone, almost naked, without any weapon save only a small forked stick, catching crabs therewithal, and also being strayed two miles from his company, and shot at him in the water, where they gave him sixteen wounds with their arrows; and after they had slain him with their wooden swords, they beat his head in pieces, and fled over the water to the main.

On the thirtieth of July

Master Stafford and twenty of our men passed by water to the island of Croatoan, with Manteo [an Indian who had been taken to England and then brought back] who had his mother and many of his kindred dwelling in that island, of whom we hoped to understand some news of our fifteen men, but especially to learn the disposition of the people of the country toward us and to renew our old friendship with them.

At our first landing they seemed as though they would fight with us. But perceiving us begin to march with our shot towards them, they turned their backs and fled.

Then Manteo, their countryman, called to them in their own language, whom, as soon as they heard, they returned, and threw away their bows and arrows, and some of them came unto us, embracing and entertaining us friendly, desiring us not to gather or spill any of their corn, for that they had but little.

We answered them that neither their corn nor any other thing of theirs should be diminished by any of us, and that our coming was only to renew the old love that was between us and them at the first and to live with them as brethren and friends; which answer seemed to please them well, wherefore they requested us to walk up to their town, who there feasted us after their manner and desired us earnestly that there might be some token or badge given them of us, whereby we might know them to be our friends when we met them any where out of the town or island.

They told us further that for want of some such badge divers of them were hurt the year before, being found out of the island by Master Lane, his company, whereof they showed us one, which at that very instant lay lame and had lain of that hurt ever since.

[July 31]

We had conference further with them that if they [the Indians of other towns nearby] would accept our friendship, we would willingly receive them again, and that all unfriendly dealings past on both parts should be utterly forgiven and forgotten.

To this the chief men of Croatoan answered that they would gladly do the best they could and within seven days bring the chief governors of those towns with them to our Governor at Roanoke, or their answer.

We also understood of the men of Croatoan how that the fifteen Englishmen left at Roanoke the year before by Sir Richard Grenville were suddenly set upon, that the Englishmen were forced to take the house wherein all their victuals and weapons were; but the savages forthwith set the same on fire; by means whereof our men were forced to take up such weapons as came first to hand, and without order to run forth among the savages, with whom they skirmished about an hour.

The place where they fought was of great advantage to the savages, that our men being some of them hurt, retired fighting to the water side, where their boat lay, with which they fled towards Hatorask. By that time they had rode but a quarter of a mile, they espied their four fellows coming from a creek thereby, where they had been to fetch oysters. These four they received into their boat, leaving Roanoke, and landed on a little island on the right hand of our entrance into the harbor of Hatorask, where they remained a while, but afterwards departed, whither as yet we know not.

The 18 [August]

Eleanor, daughter to the Governor [White himself] and wife to Ananias Dare, one of the assistants, was delivered of a daughter in Roanoke, and the same was christened there the Sunday following, and because this child was the first Christian born in Virginia, she was named Virginia.

At this time some controversies arose between the Governor and assistants about choosing two out of the twelve assistants which should go back as factors for the company into England.

The 22 of August

The whole company both of the assistants and planters came to the Governor and with one voice requested him to return himself into England, for the better and sooner obtaining of supplies and other necessaries for them.

[August 27]

The Governor being at the last through their extreme entreating constrained to return into England, departed from Roanoke and set sail for England.

John White left behind him 119 persons, including 17 women and 11 children. One might suppose that a man on whom so many others were dependent for very life in that wild spot, among them his own daughter and infant granddaughter, would have made every effort to rush back with the food and other things they needed.

John White did not rush back. Eight months after he left Roanoke he prevailed on Raleigh to send two ships for the relief of the colony. But these, instead of going about their business, "betook themselves wholly to hunt after pillage upon the Spanish coast" and returned without having gone anywhere near Virginia.

There followed another long, mysterious delay. All told, John White was

gone from the colony three years. Why, nobody knows. England was at war
with Spain, ships were urgently needed, and Sir Walter Raleigh was up to his
neck in planning the nation's defense against the Spanish Armada. But the great
defeat of the Armada came in July of 1588, and John White was still in England nearly two years later.

When at last he did go again to Roanoke, he was merely a lone passenger on
a London merchantman rather than master of his own fleet. Over those in
command of the ships he had no authority and apparently very little power of
persuasion.

The 20 of March in the year 1590

The three ships, the *Hopewell,* the *John Evangelist* and the *Little John,*
put to sea from Plymouth [England] with two small shallops.

The 15 of August

Towards evening we came to an anchor at Hatorask. We saw a great
smoke rise in the isle Roanoke near the place where I left our colony in
the year 1587, which smoke put us in good hope that some of the colony
were there expecting my return out of England.

The 16

Our 2 boats went ashore, and Captain Cook and Captain Spicer, and
their company with me, with intent to pass to the place at Roanoke where
our countrymen were left.

But before we were halfway between our ships and the shore we saw
another great smoke to the southwest; we therefore thought good to go to
that second smoke first; but it was much further from the harbor where
we landed than we supposed it to be, so that we were very sore tired before we came to the smoke.

But that which grieved us more was that when we came to the smoke,
we found no man nor sign that any had been there lately, nor yet any
fresh water in all this way to drink.

Being thus wearied with this journey, we returned to the harbor where we
left our boats, who in our absence had brought their casks ashore for fresh
water, so we deferred our going to Roanoke until the next morning.

17 of August

Our boats and company were prepared again to go up to Roanoke, but
Captain Spicer had then sent his boat ashore for fresh water, by means

whereof it was ten of the clock after noon before we put from our ships which were then come to anchor within two miles of the shore.

The admiral's boat was halfway towards the shore when Captain Spicer took off from his ship. The admiral's boat first passed the breach, but not without some danger of sinking, for we had a sea break into our boat which filled us half full of water, but by the will of God and careful steerage of Captain Cook we came safe ashore, saving only that our furniture, victuals, match and powder were much wet and spoiled. For at this time the wind blew at northeast and direct into the harbor so great a gale that the sea brake extremely on the bar and the tide went very forcibly at the entrance.

By that time our admiral's boat was hauled ashore, and most of our things taken out to dry, Captain Spicer came to the entrance of the breach and was half passed over, by the rash and undiscreet steerage of Ralph Skinner, his master's mate, a very dangerous sea brake into their boat and overset them quite; the men kept the boat, some in it and some hanging on it, but the next sea set the boat on ground, where it beat so that some of them were forced to let go their hold, hoping to wade ashore; but the sea still beat them down so that they could neither stand nor swim, and the boat twice or thrice was turned the keel upward, whereon Captain Spicer and Skinner hung until they sunk and were seen no more.

But four that could swim a little kept themselves in deeper water and were saved by Captain Cook's means, who so soon as he saw their oversetting, stripped himself and four others that could swim well and with all haste possible rowed unto them, and saved four.

There were 11 in all and 7 of the chiefest were drowned. This mischance did so much discomfort the sailors that they were all of one mind, not to go any further to seek the planters. But in the end by the commandment and persuasion of me and Captain Cook, they prepared the boats; and seeing the captain and me so resolute, they seemed much more willing.

Our boats and all things fitted again, we put off from Hatorask, being the number of 19 persons in both boats; but before we could get to the place where our planters were left, it was so exceeding dark that we overshot the place a quarter of a mile. There we espied toward the north end of the island the light of a great fire through the woods, to which we presently rode. When we came right over against it, we let fall our grapnel near the shore and sounded with a trumpet a call, and afterwards many familiar English tunes of songs, and called to them friendly. But we had no answer. We therefore landed at daybreak, and coming to the fire, we found the grass and sundry rotten trees burned about the place.

From hence we went through the woods, and from thence we returned by the waterside, round about the north point of the island, until we came to the place where I left our colony in the year 1587.

In all this way we saw in the sand the print of the savages' feet of two or three sorts trodden the night, and as we entered up the sandy bank, upon a tree, in the very brow thereof, were curiously carved these fair Roman letters *CRO;* which letters presently we knew to signify the place where I should find the planters seated, according to a secret token agreed upon between them and me at my last departure from them, which was that they should not fail to write or carve on the trees or posts of the doors the name of the place where they should be seated; for at my coming away they were prepared to remove from Roanoke 50 miles in the main.

Therefore at my departure from them in 1587 I willed them that if they should happen to be distressed in any of those places, that then they should carve over the letters or name a cross; but we found no such sign of distress. And having well considered of this, we passed towards the place where they were left in sundry houses, but we found the houses taken down, and the place very strongly enclosed with a high palisado of great trees, with curtains and flankers, very fort-like, and one of the chief trees or posts at the right side of the entrance had the bark taken off, and five foot from the ground in fair capital letters was graven *CROATOAN* without any cross or sign of distress; this done, we entered into the palisado, where we found many bars of iron, two pigs of lead, four iron fowlers, iron sacker-shot [for large cannon] and such like heavy things, thrown here and there, almost overgrown with grass and weeds.

From thence we went along by the waterside, towards the point of the creek to see if we could find any of their boats or pinnace, but we could perceive no sign of them, nor any of the last falcons and small ordnance which were left with them at my departure from them.

At our return from the creek, some of our sailors meeting us, told us that they had found where divers chests had been hidden, and long since digged up again and broken up, and much of the goods in them spoiled and scattered about, but nothing left of such things as the savages knew any use of, undefaced.

Presently Captain Cook and I went to the place, which was in the end of an old trench made two years past by Captain Amadas, where we found five chests that had been carefully hidden of the planters, and of the same chests three were my own, and about this place many of my things spoiled and broken, and my books torn from the covers, the frames of some of my pictures and maps rotten and spoiled with rain, and my armor almost eaten through with rust.

This could be no other but the deed of the savages our enemies.

And so the ships turn homeward, and John White turns with them. Why he gives up completely at this point; why he is unable to persuade the company to carry the search just a little further, notwithstanding the bad weather and the various other discouragements; or failing that, why he does not remain and undertake to go himself to Croatoan, to get there somehow and look for his daughter and her child—these are matters that perhaps could be explained, but are not. And not a word more is heard of the lost colony until a new group of Englishmen come, more than twenty years later, to settle at Jamestown. The Indians tell these later comers that white people have been living with Indians for some years at another place, but only recently the whites were massacred on orders from Powhattan. All but seven of the whites—four men, two boys, and a young girl—were killed. Those seven remain under the protection of a friendly chieftain.

There is no more of the story until, many years later, at the beginning of the eighteenth century, travelers to Carolina are astonished to find a tribe of Indians in the vicinity of Hatteras—Indians with gray eyes.

1620:   THE PILGRIMS FIND A HOME

AMONG THE fallacies that school children are taught about the Pilgrims—and there are many—is the idea that those 102 passengers of the Mayflower came to America to find freedom of worship.

This is something less than a half-truth. Actually only 41 were religious separatists. The others, like millions who were to follow them across the Atlantic, came to make a better living.

In his major contribution to Pilgrim history, Saints and Strangers, George F. Willison depicts them as a bold, earthy lot "from the cottages and not the castles of England"; and there was a difference of objectives that made for many an argument.

"*Friend*," writes Robert Cushman, their agent, before they sailed, "*if ever we make a plantation, God works a miracle, especially considering how scant we shall be of victuals and most of all ununited amongst ourselves.*"

The miracle was worked. But not without a "Mayflower Compact" to put down quarrels and possible rebellion; not without gunplay to drive off attacking savages; and not without a theft of Indian corn for seed amounting to grand larceny.

Although Cape Cod had been many times visited by Europeans—explorers and fishermen—the Mayflower's people found few traces of these predecessors. They picked up a big iron ship's kettle and a bottle of oil, and they saw some planks of an old shelter, possibly built by Breton fishermen. They uncovered a grave containing the skeletons of a man and a child. On the man's skull there was "fine yellow hair." A possible explanation lies in the fact that three or four years before, a French ship had run aground nearby in a storm.

The fullest account of the Pilgrims' adventure is William Bradford's *Of Plimoth Plantation*, a history which he began writing in 1630; but the earliest is *A Relation or Journall of the beginnings and proceedings of the English Plantation at Plimoth in New England by certaine English Adventurers*. This, published under the pen name "G. Mourt," was written by Bradford and Edward Winslow in what they themselves call their "plain and rude manner." It was printed in London in 1622.

Here are excerpts from the only firsthand, on-the-spot account of what the Pilgrims did and saw when they were faced with the problem of finding a home in the "hideous and desolate wilderness, full of wild beasts and wild men."

"*. . . so goodly a land.*"

WILLIAM BRADFORD (1590-1657)

EDWARD WINSLOW (1595-1655)

Upon the ninth of November [1620]

After many difficulties in boisterous storms, at length by God's providence, by break of the day we espied land which we deemed to be Cape Cod, and so afterward it proved. And the appearance of it much comforted us, especially, seeing so goodly a land, and wooded to the brink of the sea, it caused us to rejoice together and praise God.

11th of November [Provincetown Harbor]

We came to an anchor in the bay, which is a good harbor.

And every day we saw whales playing hard by us, of which in that place, if we had instruments and means to take them, we might have made a very rich return, which to our great grief we wanted. Our master and his mate professed we might have made three or four thousand pounds [$18,000 to $24,000] worth of oil.

This day before we came to harbor, observing some not well affected to unity and concord, but gave some appearance of faction, it was thought good there should be an association and agreement, that we should combine together in one body, and to submit to such government and governors as we should by common consent agree to make and choose, and set our hands to this that follows:

In the name of God, amen. We whose names are underwritten, the loyal subjects of our dread sovereign lord King James by the grace of God of Great Britain, France and Ireland, King, Defender of the Faith, etc.

Having undertaken for the glory of God, and advancement of the Christian faith and honor of our King and country, a voyage to plant the first colony in the northern parts of Virginia, do by these presents solemnly and mutually in the presence of God and one of another, covenant, and combine our selves together into a civil body politic, for our better ordering and preservation, and furtherance of the end aforesaid; and by virtue hereof to enact, constitute, and frame such just and equal laws, ordinances, acts, constitutions and offices from time to time as shall be thought most meet and convenient for the general good of the colony; unto which we promise all due submission and obedience. In witness whereof we have hereunder subscribed our names. Cape Cod, 11th of November in the year of the reign of our sovereign lord King James, of England, France and Ireland and of Scotland anno Domini 1620.

15th of November

They were set ashore, and when they had ordered themselves in the order of a single file and marched about the space of a mile, by the sea, they espied five or six people, with a dog, coming towards them, who were savages, who when they saw them ran into the wood and whistled the dog after them.

[November 16]

About ten o'clock we came into a deep valley, full of brush and long grass, through which we found little paths or tracts, and there we saw a deer, and found springs of fresh water, of which we were heartily glad, and sat us down and drunk our first New England water with as much delight as ever we drunk drink in all our lives.

We went on further and found where a house had been, and four or five old planks laid together. Also we found a great kettle which had been some ship's kettle and brought out of Europe. There was also a heap of sand, which we digged up, and in it we found a little old basket full of fair Indian corn, and digged further and found a fine great new basket full of very fair corn of this year, with some thirty-six goodly ears of corn, some yellow, and some red, and others mixed with blue, which was a very goodly sight. The basket was round, and narrow at the top. It held about three or four bushels, which was as much as two of us could lift up from the ground, and was very handsomely and cunningly made.

We were in suspense what to do with it, and the kettle, and at length after much consultation, we concluded to take the kettle, and as much of the corn as we could carry away with us; and when our shallop came, if we could find any of the people, and come to parley with them, we would give them the kettle again, and satisfy them for their corn. So we took all the ears and put a good deal of the loose corn in the kettle for two men to bring away on a staff. Besides, they that could put any into their pockets filled the same. The rest we buried again, for we were so laden with armor that we could carry no more.

We returned that night to the fresh water pond and there we made our rendezvous, making a great fire, and a barricado to windward of us, and kept good watch with three sentinels all night.

[November 17]

In the morning we took our kettle and sunk it in the pond, and trimmed our muskets, for few of them would go off because of the wet, and so coasted the wood again to come home, in which we were shrewdly puzzled, and lost our way.

As we wandered we came to a tree, where a young sprit was bowed down over a bow, and some acorns strewn underneath. Stephen Hopkins said it had been to catch some deer, so, as we were looking at it, William Bradford being in the rear, when he came looked also upon it, and as he went about, it gave a sudden jerk up, and he was immediately caught by the leg. It was a very pretty device, made with a rope of their own making, and having a noose as artificially made as any roper in England can make, and as like ours as can be, which we brought away with us.

[November 29]

We marched to the place where we had the corn formerly, which place we called Corn Hill [North Truro, Cape Cod]; and digged and found the rest, of which we were very glad; so as we had in all about ten bushels, which will serve us sufficiently for seed.

We sent home our weakest people, and some that were sick, and all the corn, and 18 of us stayed still and lodged there that night.

[November 30]

Having discovered this place, it was controversial amongst us, what to do touching our abode and settling there. Some thought it best for many reasons to abide there.

Robert Coppin, our pilot, made relation of a great navigable river and good harbor in the other headland of this bay, almost right over against Cape Cod, not much above eight leagues distant, in which he had been once; and because that one of the wild men with whom they had some trucking stole a harping iron from them, they called it Thievish Harbor [Plymouth, Massachusetts] and beyond that place they were enjoined not to go, whereupon, a company was chosen to go out upon a third discovery.

Whilst some were employed in this discovery, it pleased God that Mistress White was brought to bed of a son, which was called Peregrine.

Wednesday the sixth of December

We sailed six or seven leagues by the shore but saw neither river nor creek. At length we met with a tongue of land [in Wellfleet Bay]. As we drew near to the shore we espied some ten or twelve Indians, very busy about a black thing—what it was we could not tell—till afterwards they saw us and ran to and fro as if they had been carrying something away. We landed a league or two from them, and had much ado to put shore anywhere, it lay so full of flat sands.

When we came to shore we made us a barricado and got firewood and set our sentinels and betook us to our lodging, such as it was. We saw the smoke of the fire which the savages made that night, about four or five miles from us.

[December 7]

In the morning we divided our company, some eight in the shallop and the rest on the shore went to discover this place. We saw two becks of fresh water, which were the first running streams that we saw in the country, but one might stride over them.

We found also a great fish, called a grampus, dead on the sands. They in the shallop found two of them also in the bottom of the bay, dead in like sort. They were cast up at high water and could not get off for the frost and ice. They were some five or six paces long, and about two inches thick of fat, and fleshed like a swine. They would have yielded a great deal of oil, if there had been time and means to have taken it. So we finding nothing for our turn, both we and our shallop returned.

We then directed our course along the sea sands to the place where we first saw the Indians. When we were there we saw it was also a grampus which they were cutting up.

We fed upon such victuals as we had, and betook us to our rest, after we had set out our watch. About midnight we heard a great and hideous cry, and our sentinel called *Arm, Arm!*

So we bestirred ourselves and shot off a couple of muskets, and the noise ceased. We concluded that it was a company of wolves or foxes, for one told us he had heard such a noise in Newfoundland.

About five o'clock in the morning we began to be stirring. Anon, all upon a sudden, we heard a great and strange cry, which we knew to be the same voices, though they varied their notes.

One of our company being abroad came running in and cried, *They are men! Indians! Indians!* And withal, their arrows came flying amongst us. Our men ran out with all speed to recover their arms, as by the good providence of God they did.

In the meantime, Captain Miles Standish, having a snaphance [gun] ready, made a shot, and after him another. After they two had shot, other of us were ready, but he wished us not to shoot till we could take aim, for we knew not what need we should have, and there were four only of us which had their arms there ready.

The cry of our enemies was dreadful, especially when our men ran out to recover their arms. Their note was after this manner: *woath, woach, ha ha hach, woach.*

A lusty man, and no wit less valiant, who was thought to be their captain, stood behind a tree within half a musket shot of us, and there let his arrows fly at us; he was seen to shoot three arrows, which were all avoided, for he at whom the first arrow was aimed saw it and stooped down and it flew over him; the rest were avoided also. He stood three shots of a musket. At length one took full aim at him, after which he gave an extraordinary cry, and away they went all.

We followed them about a quarter of a mile. Then we shouted all together two several times and shot off a couple of muskets, and so returned. This we did that they might see we were not afraid of them nor
discouraged.

Thus it pleased God to vanquish our enemies and give us deliverance.
By their noise we could not guess that they were less than thirty or forty,
though some thought that they were many more. We took up eighteen
of their arrows, which we have sent to England by Master Jones [captain
of the *Mayflower*] some whereof were headed with brass, others with
harts horn, and others with eagle claws. Many more no doubt were
shot, yet by the especial providence of God none of them either hit or
hurt us, though many came close by us, and on every side of us, and
some coats which hung up in our barricado were shot through and
through.

So after we had given God thanks for our deliverance, we took our
shallop and went on our journey.

Thursday the 28th of December [Plymouth]

So many as could went to work on the hill where we proposed to build
our platform for our ordnance and which doth command all the plain
and the bay and from whence we may see far into the sea, and might be
easier empaled, having two rows of houses and a fair street.

So in the afternoon we went to measure out the ground, and first we
took notice how many families they were, willing all single men that had
no wives to join with some family as they thought fit, that we might
build fewer houses, which was done, and we reduced them to 19 families.
To greater families we allowed larger plots, to every person half a pole
[about eight feet] in breadth and three in length, and so, lots were cast
where every man should lie, which was done and staked out.

Our former discoveries in frosts and storms and the waiting at Cape
Cod had brought much weakness amongst us, which increased every day
more and more, and after was the cause of many of their deaths. [Within
three months more than fifty died.]

Tuesday, the 9 January [1621]

A reasonable fair day, and we went to labor that day in the building
of our town.

Friday the 16 [March]

There presented himself a savage, which caused an alarm. He very
boldly came all alone and along the houses straight to the rendezvous

where we intercepted him, not suffering him to go in, as undoubtedly he would, out of his boldness.

He saluted us in English, and bade us welcome, for he had learned some broken English amongst the Englishmen that came to fish at Monchiggon [the island of Monhegan, Maine].

He was a man free in speech, so far as he could express his mind, and of a seemly carriage. We questioned him of many things. He was the first savage we could meet withal.

The wind beginning to rise a little, we cast a horseman's coat about him, for he was stark naked. He asked some beer, but we gave him strong water and biscuit and butter and cheese and pudding and a piece of a mallard, all of which he liked well, and had been acquainted with such amongst the English.

He told us the place where we now live is called Patuxet, and that about four years ago all the inhabitants died of an extraordinary plague, and there is neither man, woman nor child remaining, as indeed we have found none, so as there is none to hinder our possession or to lay claim unto it.

These people are ill affected towards the English, by reason of one Hunt, a master of a ship, who deceived the people and got them under color of trucking [trading] with them, twenty out of this very place where we inhabit, and seven men from the Nausites, and carried them away, and sold them for slaves, like a wretched man (for £20 a man) that cares not what mischief he doth for the profit.

Thursday the 22 of March

About noon we met again about our public business, but we had scarce been an hour together but Samoset [the Indian] came again and Squanto, the only native of Patuxet, who was one of the twenty captives that by Hunt were carried away, and had been in England and dwelt in Cornehill with Master John Slanie, a merchant, and could speak a little English, with three others, and they brought with them some few skins to truck, and some red herrings newly taken and dried, but not salted, and signified unto us that their great sagamore Masasoit was hard by, with Quadequina, his brother, and all their men.

They could not well express in English what they would, but after an hour the King came. The Governor called for some strong water and drunk to him, and he drunk, a great draught that made him sweat all the while after.

Then they treated of peace, which was:

1. That neither he nor any of his should injure or do hurt to any of our people.

2. And if any of his did hurt to any of ours, he should send the offender that we might punish him.

3. That if any of our tools were taken away when our people were at work, he should cause them to be restored, and if ours did any harm to any of his, we would do the like to them.

4. If any did unjustly war against him, we would aid him; if any did war against us, he should aid us.

5. He should send to his neighbor confederates to certify them of this, that they might not wrong us, but might be likewise comprised in the conditions of peace.

6. That when their men came to us, they should leave their bows and arrows behind them, as we should do our pieces when we came to them.

So after all was done, the Governor conducted him to the brook, and there they embraced each other and he departed.

We cannot yet conceive but that he is willing to have peace with us, especially because he hath a potent adversary, the Narowhiganseis, that are at war with him, against whom he thinks we may be some strength to him, for our pieces are terrible unto them.

1679: THE CITY OF NEW YORK

FROM A REFUGE IN HOLLAND, *a little sect of seventeenth-century religious dissenters called the Labadists after their leader, Jean de Labadie, sent two of its members to America to look around for a place of permanent settlement. Jasper Danckaerts and Peter Sluyter toured the eastern seaboard and went back with a favorable report. In 1683 the group came over and settled in Maryland.*

Nearly 200 years after Danckaerts made the trip, his diary was picked up in a bookshop in Holland by Henry C. Murphy, secretary of the Long Island Historical Society. Murphy brought it back to America, translated it, and presented it to the Society, which treasures it today.

Danckaerts' account, though long-winded and moralistic, was the work of a sharp observer. It offers one of the most minutely detailed word-pictures we have today of the city of 3,500 inhabitants that was New York.

"Truly a wild worldly world . . ."
JASPER DANCKAERTS (born 1639)

[September 23, 1679]

Having then fortunately arrived, by the blessing of the Lord, before the city of New York, we stepped ashore about 4 o'clock in the afternoon, in company with Gerrit, our fellow passenger, who would conduct us in this strange place. He had lived here a long time.

We went to Gerrit's father-in-law's, a very old man named Jacob Swart [now 255 Pearl Street, Manhattan].

24th, Sunday

In order to avoid scandal and for other reasons we went to church and found there truly a wild worldly world. I say wild, not only because the people are wild but because almost all the people who go there to live, or who are born there, partake somewhat of the nature of the country.

We heard a minister preach, who had come from the up-river country. He used such strange gestures and language that I think I never in all my life have heard anything more miserable.

As it is not strange in these countries to have men as ministers who drink, we could imagine nothing else than that he had been drinking a little this morning. His text was, "Come unto me, all ye," etc., but he was so rough that even the roughest and most godless of our sailors were astonished.

The church being in the fort, we had an opportunity to look through the latter. It is not large; it has four points or batteries; it has no moat outside, but is enclosed with a double row of palisades. It is built from the foundation with quarry stone. The parapet is of earth. It is well provided with cannon, for the most part of iron, though there were some brass pieces, still bearing the mark of arms of the Netherlanders. The garrison is small.

Along the edge of the water below the fort there is a very large rock extending apparently under the fort, which is built upon the point formed by the two rivers, namely, the East River, which is the water running between the Mahatans and Long Island, and the North River, which runs straight up to Fort Orange [Albany].

In front of the fort, on the Long Island side, is a small island called Noten Island [Nut Island, now Governor's Island] around the point of

which vessels must go in sailing out or in, whereby they are compelled
to pass close by the point of the fort, where they can be flanked by several of the batteries.

It has only one gate, and that is on the land side, opening upon a broad
plain or street, called the Broadway or Beaverway. Over this gate are
the arms of the Duke of York.

The good old people with whom we lodged begged we would go with
their son Gerrit to one of their daughters, who lived in a delightful place
and kept a tavern, where we would be able to taste the beer of the
Netherland, inasmuch as it was also a brewery, but when we arrived
there we found ourselves much deceived. It was resorted to on Sundays
by all sorts of revelers, and was a low pot-house.

29th, Friday

We started at 2 o'clock for Long Island. The outer shore of this island
has before it several small islands and broken land, such as Coninen
[Coney] Island, a low sandy small island of about three hours' circuit, its
westerly point forming with Sandy Hook, on the other side, the entrance
from the sea. It is oblong in shape, and is grown over with bushes. Nobody lives upon it, but it is used in winter for keeping cattle, horses,
oxen, hogs and others. There is a ferry for the purpose of crossing over
[the East River] which is farmed out by the year, and yields a good income, as it is a considerable thoroughfare, this [Long Island] being one
of the most populous places in this vicinity.

A considerable number of Indians live upon it. The fare is 3 stuivers
for each person [less than half a cent].

We went on, up the hill, along open roads and a little woods, through
the first village, called Breukelen, which has a small and ugly little
church standing in the middle of the road. We went upon several plantations where Gerrit was acquainted with almost all the people, who made
us very welcome, sharing with us bountifully whatever they had, whether
it was milk, cider, fruit or tobacco, and especially, and first and most of
all, miserable rum or brandy which had been brought from Barbadoes
and other islands, and which is called by the Dutch *kill-devil*. All these
people are very fond of it, and most of them extravagantly so, although it
is very dear and has a bad taste.

We proceeded on to Gouanes where we arrived in the evening at one
of the best friends of Gerrit, named Symon. He took us into the house,
and entertained us well. We found a good fire, halfway up the chimney,
of clear oak and hickory, which they made not the least scruple of
burning profusely.

There had been already thrown upon it, to be roasted, a pailful of Gouanes oysters. They are large and full, some of them not less than a foot long.

30th, Saturday

We came to the plantation of the Najack Indians, which was planted with maize, or Turkish wheat. We found the whole troop together, consisting of seven or eight families, and twenty or twenty-two persons, I should think.

Their house was low and long, about sixty feet long and fourteen or fifteen feet wide. The bottom was earth, the sides and roof were made of reed and the bark of chestnut trees; the posts or columns were limbs of trees stuck in the ground, and all fastened together. The top, or ridge of the roof, was open about half a foot wide from one end to the other, in order to let the smoke escape.

October 1st, Sunday

We went into one house where there were two children lying dead [of smallpox] and unburied, and three others sick, and where one had died the week before. This disease was more fatal this year than usual.

6th, Friday

Went out about 2 o'clock to explore the island of [Manhattan]. This island runs east and west, or somewhat more northerly. On the north side of it is the North River, by which it is separated from the main land on the north; on the east end it is separated from the main land by a creek, or rather a branch of the North River, emptying itself into the East River.

They can go over this creek at dead low water upon rocks and reefs, at the place called Spyt den Duyvel. This creek coming into the East River forms with it the two Barents Islands [now called Ward's and Randall's islands].

At the west end of these two running waters, that is, where they come together to the east of these islands, they make, with the rocks and reefs, such a frightful eddy and whirlpool that it is exceedingly dangerous to pass through them, especially with small boats, of which there are some lost every now and then, and the persons in them drowned. There are two places where such whirling of the stream occurs, which are on account of the danger and frightfulness called the Great and Little Helle Gadt.

This island [Manhattan] is about seven hours' distance in length, but it is not a full hour broad. The sides are indented with bays, coves and creeks. It is almost entirely taken up, that is, the land is held by private owners, but not half of it is cultivated. Much of it is good wood land. The west end on which the city lies, is entirely cleared for more than an hour's distance, though that is the poorest ground; the best being on the east and north side.

There are many brooks of fresh water running through it, pleasant and proper for man and beast to drink, as well as agreeable to behold, affording cool and pleasant resting places, but especially suitable places for the construction of mills.

A little eastward of Nieu Haerlem there are two ridges of very high rocks, with a considerable space between them, displaying themselves very majestically, and inviting all men to acknowledge in them the majesty, grandeur, power and glory of their creator, who has impressed such marks upon them. Between them runs the road to Spyt den Duyvel.

Traced along streets of today, the road ran up Broadway, Park Row, the Bowery, Fourth Avenue, to Union Square, Broadway to Madison Square, and then irregularly to the Harlem River at Third Avenue and 130th Street. The "two ridges of very high rocks" eastward of New Harlem were the present Mount Morris and Mott Haven.

We went from the city, following the Broadway. Upon both sides of this way were many habitations of negroes, mulattoes, and whites. These negroes were formerly the proper slaves of the West India Company, but, in consequence of the frequent changes and conquests of the country, they have obtained their freedom.

We left the village called the Bowery [so called because its main street ran through the farm or *bouwery* of Peter Stuyvesant] lying on the right hand, and went through the woods to New Harlem, a tolerably large village about three hours' journey from New Amsterdam. As our guide, Gerrit, had some business here, and found many acquaintances, we remained overnight. This house was constantly filled with people, all the time drinking, for the most part, that execrable rum.

7th, Saturday

This morning, about half-past six, we set out from the village, in order to go to the end of the island; but before we left we did not omit supplying ourselves with peaches which grew in an orchard along the road.

The whole ground was covered with them and with apples, lying upon the new grain with which the orchard was planted.

10th, Tuesday

Finding no opportunity of going to Staten Island, we asked our old friend Symon what was the best way for us to get there, when he offered us his services to take us over in his skiff, which we accepted.

11th, Wednesday

We embarked early this morning in his boat and rode over to Staten Island, where we arrived at 8 o'clock. It is the usual place where ships, ready for sea, stop to take in water, while the captain and passengers are engaged in making their own arrangements and writing letters previous to their departure.

The woods are used for pasturing horses and cattle, for being an island, none of them can get off. Each person has marks upon his own, by which he can find them when he wants them. When the population of the country shall increase, these places will be taken up.

18th, Wednesday

I must here remark, in passing, that the people in this city who are almost all traders in small articles, whenever they see an Indian enter the house, who they know has any money, they immediately set about getting hold of him, giving him rum to drink, whereby he is soon caught and becomes a fool. If he should then buy anything, he is doubly cheated, in the wares and in the price. He is then urged to buy more drink, which they now make half water, and if he cannot drink it, they drink it themselves. They do not rest until they have cajoled him out of all his money, or most of it; and if that cannot be done in one day, they keep him, and let him lodge and sleep there, but in some out-of-the-way place, down in the ground, guarding their merchandise and other property in the meantime, and always managing it so that the poor creature does not go away before he has given them all they want. And these miserable Christians are so much the more eager in this respect because no money circulates among themselves, and they pay each other in wares, in which they are constantly cheating and defrauding each other. Truly, our hearts grieved when we heard of these things.

1697:   A JUDGE ATONES FOR THE
SIN OF SALEM

THE STORY of the Salem witchcraft trials has been many times retold and re-enacted, but not yet with the spotlight on perhaps the most poignant figure in the whole long cast of characters—Judge Samuel Sewall of Boston.

The Judge was neither hard of heart nor ill-willing toward his fellow-man. When he sat as one of the court at Salem that condemned to death nineteen helpless, aging human beings on the charge of witchcraft, he sincerely hoped he was carrying out the will of the Almighty.

The proceedings were strange and disturbing. The accused were prosecuted on "supernatural evidence"—hysterical girls shrieking in court and pointing at defendants who, they said, were inflicting invisible torments on them. To the mind of a practical, level-headed lawyer, what kind of jurisprudence was this?

And yet, thousands of "witches" had been executed in England on the same kind of proof. And had not the Reverend Cotton Mather, greatest authority in America on matters supernatural, assured the Judge that this was the only way to defeat the devil? Did not Mather stand at his side and watch the hangings, one by one, and with noticeable satisfaction pronounce them "righteous"?

That was in the summer of 1692. But as the leaves turn in Boston Common, the dreadful spectacle on Salem's Gallows Hill sticks in the Judge's mind. Who is qualified to weigh and interpret "spectral evidence," who authorized to take the life of another on the strength of it? Before the snow falls, the Judge is on his knees, asking God for vindication.

The diary of Samuel Sewall covers a span of nearly fifty-six years. It has been regarded by many critics as the greatest of all American diaries. Be that as it may, certainly it offers one of the best contemporary pictures of seventeenth-century New England. In it Judge Sewall has little to say about the proceedings at Salem, but much about what he himself comes to regard as the terrible sequel to that tragedy in his own life.

34

"Ye would not have condemned the guiltless . . ."
SAMUEL SEWALL (1652-1730)

April 11 [1692]

Went to Salem, where, in the meeting-house, the persons accused of witchcraft were examined. Was a very great assembly. 'Twas awful to see how the afflicted persons [hysterical young girls who alleged they had been bewitched] were agitated.

August 19

[In the margin appear the words, "Doleful Witchcraft!"]

This day George Burroughs, John Willard, John Procter, Martha Carrier and George Jacobs were executed at Salem, a very great number of spectators being present. Mr. Cotton Mather was there, Mr. Sims, Hale, Noyes, Cheever and others. All of them [the accused] said they were innocent, Carrier and all. Mr. Mather says they all died by a righteous sentence. Mr. Burroughs, by his speech, prayer, protestation of innocence, did much move unthinking persons, which occasions their speaking hardly concerning his being executed.

September 19

About noon, at Salem, Giles Cory was pressed to death for standing mute [refusing to plead to an indictment on the charge of witchcraft]. Much pains was used with him two days, one after another, by the court and Captain Gardner of Nantucket who had been of his acquaintance, but all in vain.

September 21

A petition is sent to town in behalf of Dorcas Hoar, who now confesses. Accordingly an order is sent to the sheriff to forbear her execution, notwithstanding her being in the warrant to die tomorrow. This is the first condemned person who has confessed.

November 22

I prayed that God would pardon all my sinful wanderings and direct me for the future; that God would bless the Assembly in their debates, and that he would assist our judges and save New England as to enemies and witchcrafts and vindicate the late judges.

December 22

Betty being sick, lies abed and sweats.

December 23

She takes a vomit and brings up two worms, one about six inches and the other above eight inches long; a third about eleven inches in length.

March 9 [1693]

Joseph puts his grandmother and mother in great fear by swallowing a bullet which for a while stuck in his throat. He had quite got it down before I knew what the matter was. When I come home my wife shows me the bullet Joseph swallowed, which he voided in the orchard. The Lord help us to praise him for his distinguishing favor.

August 7

About 4 in the morning I go for the midwife. About 4 P.M. my wife is brought to bed of a daughter. Thanks be to God.

September 9

I return from Point Judith, having been gone from home ever since the 28 of August. At my return find Jane [his new daughter] not well.

September 12

Call Mr. Willard [Rev. Samuel, of Old South Church, Boston] to pray with little Jane. Went to Roxbury lecture. Mr. Hobart came home with me, who also prayed with Jane. Both excellently. By Dr. Oakes's advice I gave her a little manna. The good Lord prepare her and us for the issue and help us to choose the things that please him. Nurse Judd watches.

September 13

Between 12 and 1 at night following that day, Jane expires in neighbor Smith's lap, Nurse Hill and I being by.

November 21 [1694]

My wife is brought to bed of a daughter between 9 and 10 of the clock in the morn.

March 18 [1695]

Last night I dreamed that all my children were dead except Sarah [the infant daughter] which did distress me sorely with reflections on my omission of duty towards them, as well as breaking oft the hopes I had of them. The Lord help me thankfully and fruitfully to enjoy them and let that be a means to awaken me.

April 29

The morning is very warm and sunshiny. In the afternoon there is thunder and lightning, and about 2 P.M. a very extraordinary storm of hail, so that the ground was made white with it, as with blossoms when fallen. 'Twas as big as pistol and musket bullets. It broke of the glass of the new house about 480 quarrels [squares] of the front.

Mr. Cotton Mather dined with us and was with me in the new kitchen when this was. He had just been mentioning that more ministers' houses than others proportionably had been smitten with lightning, inquiring what the meaning of God should be in it.

Many hailstones broke through the glass and flew to the middle of the room or farther. People afterward gazed upon the house to see its ruins.

I got Mr. Mather to pray with us after this awful providence. He told God he had broken the brittle part of our house and prayed that we might be ready for the time when our clay tabernacles should be broken.

'Twas a sorrowful thing to me to see the house so far undone again before 'twas finished.

June 21

About one at night, Jane comes up with an unusual gate and gives us an account of mother's illness, not being able to speak a considerable time.

I went to Captain Davis' and fetched some treacle water and syrup of saffron. Dame Ellis made a cake of herbs to strengthen mother's stomach. In the morn Roger Judd is sent to Cambridge for Dr. Oliver, mother choosing to speak with him and no other. When he comes he advises to a plaster for the stomach, which is applied, and a potion made of bezar [a concretion from the alimentary tract of an animal, thought to be an antidote for poisoning] to be taken in syrup of saffron and treacle water, of which she took once or twice.

About 8 or 9 I called Mr. Willard at her desire, who prays with her. Finding the room free once, and observing her very great weakness, I took the opportunity to thank her for all her labors of love to me and mine and asked her pardon for our undutifulness. She, after a while, said,

God pity 'em; which was the last prayer I heard her make. A little before sunset she expired.

July 26

Poor little Mary falls down into the cellar of Matthias Smith's house and cuts her head against the stones, making a large orifice of more than two inches long. 'Twas about six past meridian. The Lord sanctify me to this bloody accident.

August 8

About 9 P.M. little Sarah has a convulsion fit. I and Mr. Torrey were sent for to see it. It lasted not long. When all quiet, Mr. Torrey went to prayer. A little after lecture Sarah has another sore fit. My wife and I take her to bed with us.

August 9

About six in the morn Sarah has another sore fit in her mother's arms presently after she was brought down.

August 13

We have a fast kept in our new chamber. Mr. Willard begins with prayer and preaches from II Chron. 34:27. Mr. Allen prays. P.M., Mr. Bayley begins with prayer, preaches from Luke 1:50 and then concludes with prayer. Sung the 27 Psalm 7-10. I set the tune and burst so into tears that I could scarce continue singing.

From this attack Sarah recovers.

October 12

Little Mary grows a little better after very sore illness.

January 6 [1696]

Kept a day of fasting with prayer for the conversion of my son [Samuel] and his settlement in a trade that might be good for soul and body.

January 13

About 10 o'clock. When I came in, past 7 at night, my wife met me in the entry and told me Betty [daughter, 14 years old] had surprised them. I was surprised with the abruptness of the relation. It seems that Betty Sewall had given some signs of dejection and sorrow. But a little after dinner she had burst into an amazing cry, which caused all the family to cry too. Her mother asked her the reason. She gave none. At last she said she was afraid she should go to hell; her sins were not pardoned.

She was first wounded by reading a sermon of Mr. Norton's about the 5th of January, text John 7:34 ["Jesus answered them, Verily, verily, I say unto you, Whosoever committeth sin is the servant of sin."]. And those words in the sermon, John 8:21, "Ye shall seek me and shall die in your sins," ran in her mind and terrified her greatly. And staying home January 12 she read out of Mr. Cotton Mather, "Why hath Satan filled thy heart," which increased her fear.

Her mother asked her whether she prayed. She answered Yes, but feared her prayers were not heard because her sins were not pardoned.

Mr. Willard, though sent for timelier, yet not being told of the message, came not till after I came home. He discoursed with Betty, who could not give a distinct account but was confused, as his phrase was.

Mr. Willard prayed excellently. The Lord bring light and comfort out of this dark and dreadful cloud and grant that Christ's being formed in my dear child may be the issue of these painful pangs.

February 7

Last night Sam could not sleep because of my brother's speaking to him of removing to some other place, mentioning Mr. Usher's. I put him to get up a little wood, and he fainted, at which my brother was much startled and advised to remove him forthwith and place him somewhere else.

February 10

The good Lord finally give rest unto my dear son and put him into some calling wherein he will accept of him to serve him.

February 16

I was very sorrowful by reason of the unsettledness of my Samuel.

February 22

Betty comes unto me almost as soon as I was up and tells me the disquiet she had when waked. Told me she was afraid she should go to hell. Asked her what I should pray for. She said [to pray] that God would pardon her sin and give her a new heart. I answered her fears as well as I could, and prayed with many tears on either part. Hope God heard us. I gave her solemnly to God.

May 3

Betty can hardly read her chapter for weeping. Tells me she is afraid she is gone back. Does not taste that sweetness in reading the Word which once she did. Fears that what was once upon her is worn off. I said what I could to her and in the evening prayed with her alone.

May 7

The Lord help me not to do, or neglect, anything that should prevent the dwelling of brethren together in unity. And Oh, most bountiful and gracious God, who givest liberally and upbraidest not, let thy Grace with me and in me be sufficient for me in making myself ready. And out of thy infinite and unaccountable compassions, place me among those who shall not be left but shall be accepted by thee here and taken into glory hereafter. Though I am beyond conception vile, who may say unto thee, What doest thou? Thou canst justify thyself in thy proceedings.

May 11

Joseph falls down and breaks his forehead so as bleeds pretty much.

May 18

I am forced to go to Ipswich Court; and being to go, my wife desired me to go on to Newbury. I went with brother on Wednesday night. Visited father, mother, friends, returned to Salem, got thither about nine. Supped well with the fish brought out of Wenham Pond.

Between eleven and noon Thomas comes in and brings me the amazing news of my wife's hard time and my son's being stillborn.

We get up our horses from the ship and set out by starlight about 12, yet the bells rung for five before we got over the ferry.

Found my wife as well as usually. But I was grievously stung to find a sweet desirable son dead, who had none of my health to succor him and save his life. The Lord pardon all my sin and wandering and neglect, and sanctify to me this singular affliction. These tears I weep over my abortive son.

September 16

Keep a day of prayer in the east end of the town-house, Governor, Council and Assembly. Mr. Morton begun with prayer, Mr. Allin prayed, Mr. Willard preached—if God be with us who can be against us? Spake smartly at last about the Salem witchcrafts, and that no order had been suffered to come forth by authority to ask God's pardon.

November 12

I set Betty to read Ezekiel 37, and she weeps so that she can hardly read. I talk with her and she tells me of the various temptations she had; as that she was a reprobate, loved not God's people as she should.

December 12

A very great show of snow in on the ground. I go in the morn to Mr. Willard to entreat him choose his own time to come and pray with little Sarah. He comes a little before night and prays very fully and well. Mr. Mather, the president, had prayed with her in the time of the court's sitting.

December 22

Being catechising day, I give Mr. Willard a note to pray for my daughter publicly, which he did. This day I remove poor little Sarah into my bedchamber, where about break of day December 23 she gives up the ghost in Nurse Cowell's arms. Born November 21, 1694.

Neither I nor my wife were by, nurse not expecting so sudden a change, and having promised to call us. I thought of Christ's words, "Could you not watch with me one hour!" and would fain have sat up with her, but fear of my wife's illness, who is very valetudinarious, made me to lodge with her in the new hall, where she was called by Jane's cry, to take notice of my dead daughter.

Nurse did long and pathetically ask our pardon that she had not called us, and said she was surprised.

Thus this very fine day is rendered foul to us by reason of the general sorrow and tears in the family.

Master Cheever was here the evening before. I desired him to pray for my daughter. The chapter read in course was Deuteronomy 22, which made me sadly reflect that I had not been so thoroughly tender of my daughter, nor so effectually careful of her defense and preservation, as I should have been. The good Lord pity and pardon and help for the future as to those God has still left me.

December 24

Sam recites to me in Latin, Matthew 12 from the 6th to the end of the 12th verse. The 7th verse did awfully bring to mind the Salem tragedy. ["If ye had known what this meaneth, I will have mercy and not sacrifice, ye would not have condemned the guiltless."]

December 25

We bury our little daughter. 'Twas wholly dry, and I went at noon to see in what order things were set; and there I was entertained with a view of, and converse with, the coffins of my six children.

On January 4, 1697, Pastor Willard and other friends of Sewall caused the General Court to proclaim a solemn day of fasting and prayer to atone for the miscarriage of justice at Salem "in the late tragedy raised among us by Satan and his instruments."

Judge Sewall, to his everlasting credit, used the opportunity to "put up a bill"—that is, to hand a written statement to the minister for reading aloud. That afternoon, before the congregation of Boston's Old South Church, Judge Sewall stood with bowed head while Pastor Willard read the eminent jurist's confession of shame for his part in the condemnation of those charged with witchcraft five years before at Salem:

> Samuel Sewall, sensible of the reiterated strokes of God upon himself and family; and being sensible that as to the guilt contracted . . . at Salem he is, upon many accounts, more concerned than any that he knows of, desires to take the blame and shame of it, asking pardon of men, and especially desiring prayers that God, who has an unlimited authority, would pardon that sin . . .

By this act Judge Sewall set in motion widespread healing of a sorely chafed New England conscience. As the news of it went out, it was like a fresh breath, long overdue, of the air that already had in it the first tang and promise of freedom from old-world religious inquisition. There followed a public acknowledgement of error by those who had served on the jury at Salem.

One lone dissident tried to keep the old hysteria alive. Cotton Mather, angry, determined to vindicate himself, attempted to engineer still another witchcraft scare. He produced a woman as witness who showed some of the familiar symptoms of the "bewitched," but it turned out that she was merely an alcoholic with delirium tremens.

But even Mather was secretly unsure of himself. While Sewall was making his confession public, Mather was confiding to his own diary that he was "afflicted last night with discouraging thoughts, as if unavoidable marks of the divine displeasure might overtake my family for my not appearing with vigor to stop the proceedings of the judges when the inexplicable storm from the invisible world assaulted the country."

1704: *VENTURESOME JOURNEY OF A BOSTON SCHOOLMA'AM*

It took courage and stamina to make the trip from Boston to New York on which 38-year-old Madam Knight set out, alone and without advance arrangements for an escort, in the autumn of the year 1704. Her route, which was that now traversed by the New Haven Railroad, lay alongshore through country where the Indians were "the most salvage of all the salvages."

But there was business to be looked after, and this salty schoolma'am considered herself quite up to the rigors of the journey. Besides, as she points out, the people of New England were very strict in punishing violations of their laws, "even to a harmless Kiss or Innocent merriment among Young people." Madam Knight had been indicted herself for selling liquor to the Indians in her father's store.

Daughter of a Charlestown shopkeeper, she had been married to the agent for a London merchandising firm. Her husband died while on a business trip to England. Madam Knight lived in her father's house and added to her earnings by copying court records, taking in boarders, and teaching. Among her pupils of later years, according to a Boston tradition, was a boy named Benjamin Franklin.

Her business on the trip included a stop at New Haven to look after the estate of a wealthy cousin who had just died, and a shopping sojourn in New York. Her account of her travels is one of the best known and best liked of all American diaries.

Between the writing of this diary and its first appearance in print—there have since been many reprintings—more than a hundred years elapsed. It was published in 1825 by Timothy Dwight, President of Yale University. He obtained a copy from a descendant of the diarist and at once appreciated its unique literary flavor and historical value.

In his preface Editor Dwight asks his readers to "compare the state of things in the time of our author with that of the present period (1825)." Over the same route from Boston to New York which took Madam Knight two weeks to cover, he proudly points out, "we now proceed at our ease in a day and a half!"

Let us leave him to his reckless ways and breakneck speeds and accompany Madam Knight as far as New Haven.

"Wee went pretty briskly forward . . ."

SARAH KEMBLE KNIGHT (1666-1727)

Monday, Octb'r ye second, 1704

About three o'clock afternoon, I begun my Journey from Boston to New-Haven; being about two Hundred Mile. My Kinsman, Capt. Robert Luist, waited on me as farr as Dedham, where I was to meet ye Western post.

I vissitted the Reverd. Mr. Belcher, ye Minister of ye town, and tarried there till evening, in hopes ye post would come along. But he not coming, I resolved to go to Billingses where he used to lodg, being 12 miles further.

Madm Billings, seing no persuasions of her good spouses or hers could prevail with me to Lodg there that night, Very kindly went wyth me to ye Tavern, where I hoped to get my guide, And desired the Hostess to inquire of her guests whether any of them would go with mee.

But they being tyed by the Lips to a pewter engine, scarcely allowed themselves time to say.

The manuscript is torn here, but evidently the hostess has offered her son as guide for a certain number of pieces of eight.

I told her no, I would not be accessary to such extortion.

Then John shan't go, sais shee. No, indeed, shan't hee; And held forth at that rate a long time.

Upon this, to my no small surprise, son John arrose, and gravely demanded, what I would give him to go with me?

Give you, sais I, are you John?

Yes, says he, for want of a Better; And behold! this John look't as old as my Host, and perhaps had bin a man in the last Century.

Well, Mr. John, sais I, make your demands.

Why, half a pss. of eight and a dram, sais John.

I agreed, and gave him a dram (now) in hand to bind the bargain.

My hostess catechis'd John for going so cheep, saying his poor wife would break her heart.

His shade on his Hors resembled a Globe on a Gate post.

Thus, jogging on with an easy pace, my Guide telling mee it was dangero's to Ride hard in the Night, (whch his hors had the sence to

avoid) Hee entertained me with the Adventurs he had passed by late
Rideing, and eminent Dangers he had escaped, so that, Remembring the
Hero's in Parismus and the Knight of the Oracle, I didn't know but I had
mett wth a Prince disguis'd.

When we had ridd about an how'r wee come into a thick swamp, wch.
by Reason of a great fogg, very much startled mee, it being now very
Dark. But nothing dismay'd John; Hee had encountered a thousand and
a thousand such Swamps, having a Universall Knowledge in the woods;
and readily Answered all my inquiries wch. were not a few.

In about an how'r or something more, after we left the Swamp, we
come where I was to Lodg. My Guide dismounted and very Complasantly
help't me down and shewd the door, signing to me wth his hand to Go
in; wch I Gladly did—But had not gone many steps into the Room, ere
I was Interogated by a young Lady I understood afterwards was the
Eldest daughter of the family, with these, or words to this purpose, (viz.)
Law for mee—what in the world brings You here at this time a night?—
I never see a woman on the Rode so Dreadfull late, in all the days of
my versall life. Who are You? Where are You going? I'me scar'd out of
my witts—with much now of the same Kind. I stood aghast, Prepareing to
reply, when in comes my Guide—to him Madam turn'd, roreing out: Law-
full heart, John, is it You?—how de do! Where in the world are you
going with this woman? Who is she?

John made no Ansr. but sat down in the corner, fumbled out his black
Junk [pipe] and saluted that instead of Debb; she then turned agen to
mee and fell anew into her silly questions, without asking me to sitt
down.

I told her shee treated me very Rudely, and I did not think it my duty
to auswer her unmannerly Questions. But to get ridd of them, I told her
I come there to have the post's company with me to-morrow on my
Journey, &c.

Miss star'd awhile, drew a chair, bid me sitt, And then run up stairs and
putts on two or three Rings, (or else I had not seen them before,) and
returning, sett herself just before me, showing the way to Reding, that I
might see her Ornaments, perhaps to gain the more respect.

But her Granam's new rung sow, had it appeared, would affected me
as much. I paid honest John wth money and dram according to contract,
and Dismist him, and pray'd Miss to shew me where I must Lodg.

Shee conducted me to a parlour in a little back Leanto, wch was almost fill'd wth the bedsted wch was so high that I was forced to climb on
a chair to gitt up to ye wretched bed that lay on it; on wch having

Stretcht my tired Limbs, and lay'd my head on a Sad-coloured pillow, I began to think on the transactions of the past day.

Tuesday, October ye third

About 8 in the morning, I with the Post proceeded forward. And about two, afternoon, Arrived at the Post's second stage, where the western Post mett him and exchanged Letters.

Here, having called for something to eat, ye woman bro't in a Twisted thing like a cable, but something lighter; and laying it on the bord, tugg'd for life to bring it into a capacity to spread; wch having wth great pains accomplished, shee serv'd in a dish of Pork and Cabage, I suppose the remains of Dinner. The sause was of a deep Purple, wch I tho't was boil'd in her dye Kettle; the bread was Indian, and every thing on the Table service Agreeable to these.

I, being hungry, gott a little down; but my stomach was soon cloy'd, and what cabbage I swallowed serv'd me for a Cudd the whole day after.

Having here discharged the Ordnary for self and Guide (as I understood was the custom), About Three afternoon went on with my Third Guide, who Rode very hard; and having crossed Providence Ferry, we come to a River wch they Generally Ride thro'. But I dare not venture; so the Post got a Ladd and Cannoo to carry me to tother side, and hee rid thro' and Led my hors.

The Cannoo was very small and shallow, so that when we were in she seem'd redy to take in water, which greatly terrified mee, and caused me to be very circumspect, sitting with my hands fast on each side, my eyes stedy, not daring so much as to lodg my tongue a hair's breadth more on one side of my mouth then tother, nor so much as think on Lott's wife, for a wry thought would have oversett our wherey: But was soon put out of this pain, by feeling the Cannoo on shore, wch I as soon almost saluted with my feet; and Rewarding my sculler, again mounted and made the best of our way forwards.

The rode here was very even and ye day pleasant, it being now near Sunsett. But the Post told mee we had neer 14 miles to Ride to the next Stage, (where we were to Lodg). I askt him of the rest of the Rode, foreseeing wee must travail in the night.

Hee told mee there was a bad River we were to Ride thro', wch was so very firce a hors could sometimes hardly stem it: But it was narrow, and wee should soon be over.

I cannot express the concern of my mind this relation sett me in: no thoughts but those of the dang'ros River could entertain my Imagination, and they were as formidable as varios, still Tormenting me with the blackest Ideas of my Approaching fate—Sometimes seing my self drowning, otherwhiles drowned, and at the best like a holy Sister Just come out of a Spiritual Bath in dripping Garments.

Now was the Glorious Luminary wth his swift Coursers arrived at his Stage, leaving poor me wth the rest of this part of the lower world in darkness, with which *wee* were soon Surrounded. The only Glimering we now had was from the spangled Skies Whose Imperfect Reflections rendered every Object formidable. Each lifeless Trunk, with its shatter'd Limbs, appear'd an Armed Enymie; and every little stump like a Ravenous devourer. Nor could I so much as discern my Guide, when at any distance, which added to the terror.

Thus, absolutely lost in Thought, and dying with the very thoughts of drowning, I come up wth the post, who I did not see till even with his Hors: he told mee he stopt for mee; and wee Rode on Very deliberatly a few paces, when we entred a Thickett of Trees and Shrubbs, and I perceived by the Hors's going, we were on the descent of a Hill, wch, as wee come neerer the bottom, 'twas totaly dark wth the Trees that surrounded it.

But I knew by the Going of the Hors wee had entred the water, wch my Guide told mee was the hazzardos River he had told me of; and hee, Riding up close to my Side, Bid me not fear—we should be over Imediatly.

I now ralyed all the Courage I was mistriss of, Knowing that I must either Venture my fate of drowning, or be left like ye Children in the wood. So, as the Post bid me, I gave Reins to my Nagg; and sitting as Stedy as Just before in the Cannoo, in a few minutes got safe to the other side, which hee told mee was the Narragansett country.

Here Wee found great difficulty in Travailing, the way being very narrow, and on each side the Trees and bushes gave us very unpleasant welcomes wth their Branches and bow's, wch wee could not avoid, it being so exceeding dark.

Being come to mr. Havens', I was very civilly Received, and courteously entertained, in a clean comfortable House; and the Good woman was very active in helping off my Riding clothes, and then ask't what I would eat.

I told her I had some Chocolett, if shee would prepare it; which with the help of some Milk, and a little clean brass Kettle, she soon effected to my satisfaction. I then betook me to my Apartment, wch was a little Room parted from the Kitchen by a single bord partition; where, after I had noted the Occurrances of the past day, I went to bed, which, tho' pretty hard, Yet neet and handsome.

But I could get no sleep, because of the Clamor of some of the Town tope-ers in next Room.

I heartily fretted, and wish't 'um tongue tyed; I set my Candle on a Chest by the bed side, and setting up, fell to my old way of composing my Resentments, in the following manner:

> *I ask thy Aid, O Potent Rum!*
> *To Charm these wrangling Topers Dum.*
> *Thou hast their Giddy Brains possest—*
> *The man confounded wth the Beast—*
> *And I, poor I, can get no rest.*
> *Intoxicate them with thy fumes:*
> *O still their Tongues till morning comes!*

And I know not but my wishes took effect; for the dispute soon ended with 'tother Dram; and so Good night!

Wedensday, Octobr 4th

About four in the morning, we set out for Kingston with a french Docter in our company. Hee and ye Post put on very furiously, so that I could not keep up with them, only as now and then they'd stop till they see mee.

This Rode was poorly furnished wth accommodations for Travellers, so that we were forced to ride 22 miles by the post's account, but neerer thirty by mine, before wee could bait [refresh] so much as our Horses, wch I exceedingly complained of. But the post encourag'd mee, by saying wee should be well accommodated anon at mr. Devills a few miles further.

But I questioned whether we ought to go to the Devil to be helpt out of affliction. However, like the rest of Deluded souls that post to ye Infernal denn, Wee made all possible speed to this Devil's Habitation; where alliting in full assurance of good accommodation, wee were going in.

But meeting his two daughters, as I suposed twins, they so neerly resembled each other, both in features and habit, and look't as old as the Divel himselfe, and quite as Ugly, we desired entertainm't, but could hardly get a word out of 'um, till with our Importunity, telling them our necesity, &c. they call'd the old Sophister, who was as sparing of his words as his daughters had bin, and no, or none, was the reply's hee made us to our demands.

Hee differed only in this from the old fellow in to'ther Country; hee let us depart.

Thus leaving this habitation of cruelty, we went forward; and arriving at an Ordinary about two mile further, found tollerable accommodation. But our Hostes being a pretty full mouth'd old creature, entertain'd our fellow travailer, ye french Docter, wth Inumirable complaints of her bodily infirmities; and whisperd to him so lou'd, that all ye House had as full a hearing as hee: which was very divirting to ye company, (of which there was a great many,) as one might see by their sneering.

But poor weary I slipt out to enter my mind in my Jornal, and left my Great Landly with her Talkative Guests to themselves.

From hence we proceeded (about ten forenoon) through the Narragansett country [Rhode Island], pretty Leisurely; and about one afternoon come to Paukataug River, wch was about two hundred paces over, and now very high, and no way over to to'ther side but this. I darid not venture to Ride thro, my courage at best in such cases but small, And now at the Lowest Ebb, by reason of my weary, very weary, hungry and uneasy Circumstances.

So takeing leave of my company, tho' wth no little Reluctance, that I could not proceed wth them on my Jorny, Stop at a little cottage Just by the River, to wait the Waters falling, wch the old man that lived there said would be in a little time, and he would conduct me safe over.

I had scarce done thinking, when an Indian-like Animal come to the door, on a creature very much like himselfe, in mien and feature, as well as Ragged cloathing; but hee being, as I understood, going over the River, as ugly as hee was, I was glad to ask him to show me ye way to Saxtons, at Stoningtown [Connecticut]; wch he promising, I ventur'd over wth the old mans assistance; who having rewarded to content, with my Tattertailed guide, I ridd on very slowly thro' Stoningtown.

Here I heard there was an old man and his Daughter to come that way, down to N. London; and being now destitute of a Guide, gladly waited for them, being in so good a harbour, and accordingly, Thirsday, Octobr ye 5th, about 3 in the afternoon, I sat forward with neighbour Polly and Jemima, a Girl about 18 Years old, who hee said he had been to fetch out of the Narragansetts, and said they had Rode thirty miles that day, on a sory lean Jade, wth only a Bagg under her for a pillion, wch the poor Girl often complain'd was very uneasy.

Wee made Good speed along, wch made poor Jemima make many a sow'r face, the mare being a very hard trotter; and after many a hearty and bitter Oh, she at length Low'd out: Lawful Heart father! this bare mare hurts mee, I'me direfull sore I vow; with many words to that purpose: poor Child sais Gaffer—she us't to serve your mother so. I don't care how mother us't to do, quoth Jemima, in a pasionate tone. At which the old man Laught, and kick't his Jade o' the side, which made her Jolt ten times harder.

About seven that Evening, we come to New London Ferry: here, by reason of a very high wind, we mett with great difficulty in getting over— the Boat tos't exceedingly, and our Horses capper'd at a very surprizing Rate, and set us all in a fright; especially poor Jemima, who desired her father to say so jack to the Jade, to make her stand. But the careless parent, taking no notice of her repeated desires, She Rored out in a Passionate manner: Pray suth Father, are you deaf? Say so Jack to the Jade, I tell you. The Dutiful Parent obey's; saying so Jack, so Jack, as gravely as if hee'd bin to saying Catechise after Young Miss, who with her fright look't of all coullers in ye Rain Bow.

Being safely arrived at the house of Mrs. Prentices in N. London, I treated neighbour Polly and daughter for their divirting company, and bid them farewell; and between nine and ten at night waited on the Revd Mr. Gurdon Saltonstall, minister of the town, who kindly Invited me to Stay that night at his house, where I was very handsomely and plentifully treated and Lodg'd; and made good the Great Character I had before heard concerning him: viz. that hee was the most affable, courteous, Genero's and best of men.

Friday, Octor 6th

I got up very early, in Order to hire somebody to go with mee to New Haven, being in Great parplexity at the thoughts of proceeding alone; which my most hospitable entertainer observing, himselfe went, and soon return'd wth a young Gentleman of the town who he could confide in to Go with mee; and about eight this morning, wth Mr. Joshua Wheeler my new Guide, takeing leave of this worthy Gentleman, Wee advanced on towards Seabrook.

The Rodes all along this way are very bad, Incumbred wth Rocks and mountainos passages, wch were very disagreeable to my tired carcass; but we went on with a moderate pace wch made ye Journy more pleasent.

But after about eight miles Rideing, in going over a Bridge under wch the River Run very swift, my Hors stumbled, and very narrowly 'scaped falling over into the water; wch extreemly frightened mee. But through God's Goodness I met with no harm, and mounting agen, in about half a miles Rideing, come to an ordinary, were well entertained.

From hence wee went pretty briskly forward, and arriv'd at Saybrook ferry about two of the Clock afternoon; and crossing it, wee call'd at an Inn.

Landlady come in, with her hair about her ears, and hands at full pay scratching. Shee told us shee had some mutton wch shee would broil, wch I was glad to hear; But I supose forgot to wash her scratchers; in a little time shee brot it in; but it being pickled, and my Guide said it smelt strong of head sause, we left it, and pd sixpence a piece for our Dinners, wch was only smell.

So wee putt forward with all speed, and about seven at night come to Killingsworth, and Lodgd there that night.

Saturday, Oct. 7th

We sett out early in the Morning, and about two a clock afternoon we arrived at New Haven, where I was received with all Posible Respects and civility.

Madam Knight stayed in New Haven until December 6, then proceeded in company with a kinsman, Thomas Trowbridge, to New York, via Stratford Ferry, Fairfield, "Norowalk," Rye, and "New Rochell, a french town." In New York she attended a "vendue," or auction sale, and bought about a hundred reams of paper imported from Holland "and sold very Reasonably here." Presumably she wanted it for her work as a copyist in Boston.

Unlike the moralistic Jasper Danckaerts, Madam Knight found New York very much to her taste, business dealings and all. "They have Vendues very frequently and make their Earnings very well by them, for they treat with good Liquor Liberally, and the Customers Drink as Liberally and Generally pay for't as well, by paying for that which they Bidd up Briskly for, after the sack has gone plentifully about, tho' sometimes good penny worths are got there."

After a fortnight in the city she left for home on December 21. Visits en route delayed her homecoming until March 3. Back in Boston, after an absence of five months, she desires "sincearly to adore my Great Benefactor for graciously carying forth and returning in safety his unworthy handmaid."

1744: COFFEEHOUSE CHARACTERS

DR. ALEXANDER HAMILTON (not to be confused with his namesake of Revolutionary times) was a young physician who came to America from Edinburgh in 1739 and settled in Annapolis, Maryland. In his early thirties he built up a well-paying practice among the Chesapeake tobacco aristocracy, but contracted tuberculosis himself. In 1753 he was elected to the Maryland Assembly. Three years later he died at the age of 44.

In 1744, in an effort to regain his health, he had gone on a 1600-mile ramble to New Hampshire and back. The places he visited, the people he met, are fully recorded in his diary, which has won its long life because of the picture it gives of Colonial society at the coach-stop stratum.

On his return, Hamilton thought so little of the diary that he tossed it into the lap of a friend and forgot it once and for all. The recipient, an Italian, took it to his native land, and there it remained in obscurity for 150 years. Early this century a London dealer picked it up in a bookshop in Rome. After going through two more British firms, it was bought by an American collector, William K. Bixby, of St. Louis.

Bixby had it edited by historian Albert Bushnell Hart, but ordered only 487 copies printed for his friends. It was made available to the public in a new and larger edition in 1948.

"To drink stoutly . . ."
ALEXANDER HAMILTON (1712-1756)

Thursday, May 31 [1744]

I put up att one Tradaway's about 10 miles from Joppa [Maryland].

Just as I dismounted att Tradaway's, I found a drunken club dismissing. Most of them had got upon their horses and were seated in an oblique situation, deviating much from a perpendicular to the horizontal plane, a posture quite necessary for keeping the center of gravity within its propper base for the support of the superstructure; hence we deduct the true physicall reason why our heads overloaded with liquor become too ponderous for our heels.

Their discourse was as oblique as their position; the only thing intelligible in it was oaths and God dammes; the rest was an inarticulate sound like Rabelais' frozen words a thawing, interlaced with hickupings and belchings. I was uneasy till they were gone, and my landlord, seeing me stare, made that trite apology—that indeed he did not care to have such disorderly fellows come about his house; he was always noted far and near for keeping a quiet house and entertaining only gentlemen or such like, but these were country people, his neighbours, and it was not prudent to dissoblige them upon slight occasions. "Alas, sir!" added he, "we that entertain travelers must strive to oblige every body, for it is our dayly bread."

While he spoke thus, our bacchanalians, finding no more rum in play, rid off helter skelter as if the devil had possessed them, every man sitting his horse in a see-saw manner like a bunch of rags tyed upon the saddle.

I found nothing particular or worth notice in my landlord's character or conversation, only as to his bodily make. He was a fat pursy man and had large bubbies like a woman.

I supped upon fry'd chickens and bacon, and after supper the conversation turned upon politicks, news, and the dreaded French war. This learned company consisted of the landlord, his overseer and miller, and another greasy-thumbed fellow who, as I understood, professed physick and particularly surgery. In the drawing of teeth, he practiced upon the housemaid, a dirty piece of lumber, who made such screaming and squalling as made me imagine there was murder going forwards in the house. However, the artist got the tooth out att last with a great clumsy pair of black-smith's forceps; and indeed it seemed to require such an instrument, for when he showed it to us, it resembled a horsenail more than a tooth.

After having had my fill of this elegant company, I went to bed att 10 o'clock.

Tuesday, June 5 [Wilmington]

After dinner we fell upon politicks, and the expected French war naturally came in, whence arose a learned dispute which was about settling the meaning of the two words, declaration and proclamation.

Mr. Smith asserted that a proclamation of war was an impropper phraze, and that it ought to be a declaration of war, and on the other hand a proclamation of peace.

Mr. Morison affirmed with a bloody oath that there might be such a thing as a proclamation of a declaration and swore heartily that he knew it to be true both by experience and hearsay. They grew very loud upon it as they put about the bowl, and I retired into a corner of the room to laugh a little, handkerchief fashion, pretending to be busied in blowing my nose; so I slurd a laugh with nose blowing as people sometimes do a fart with coughing.

Saturday, June 9th [Philadelphia]

At six in the evening I went to my lodging, and looking out att the window, having been led there by a noise in the street, I was entertained by a boxing match between a master and his servant. The master was an unwieldy, pott-gutted fellow, the servant muscular, rawbon'd, and tall; therefor tho he was his servant in station of life, yet he would have been his master in single combat had not the bystanders assisted the master and holp him up as often as the fellow threw him down. The servant, by his dialect, was a Scotsman; the names he gave his master were no better than little bastard, and shitten elf, terms ill apply'd to such a pursy load of flesh.

Friday, June 15 [New York]

After supper they set in for drinking, to which I was averse and therefor sat upon nettles. They filled up bumpers att each round, but I would drink only three which were to the King, Governour Clinton, and Governour Bladen, which last was my own.

Two or three toapers in the company seemed to be of opinion that a man could not have a more sociable quality or enduement than to be able to pour down seas of liquor and remain unconquered while others sunk under the table. I heard this philosophical maxim but silently dissented to it.

I left the company att 10 att night pritty well flushed with my three bumpers and, ruminating on my folly, went to my lodging att Mrs. Hogg's in Broadstreet.

Sunday, June 17th [The Battery, New York]

Mr. Jefferys told me that to walk out after dusk upon this platform was a good way for a stranger to fit himself with a courtezan, for that place was the generall rendezvous of the fair sex of that profession after sun set. He told me there was a good choice of pritty lasses among them, both Dutch and English. However, I was not so abandoned as to go among them but went and supped with the Club att Todd's.

It appeared that our landlord was drunk, both by his words and actions. When we called for one thing he hastily pulled the bell rope, and when the servants came up, Todd had by that time forgot what was called for. Then he gave us a discourse upon law and gospell and swore by God that he would prove that law was founded upon gospell and gospell upon law, and that reason was depending upon both and therefor to be a good lawer it was substituted to be a good gospeller. We asked him what such a wicked dog as he had to do with gospell. He swore by God that he had a soul to be saved as well as the King, and he would neither be hang'd nor damn'd for all the Kings in Christendome.

We could not get rid of him till we put him in a passion by affirming he had no soul and offering to lay him a dozen of wine that he could not prove he had one. Att which, after some taggs of incoherent argument, he departed the room in wrath, calling us heathens and infidels. I went home att 12 a'clock.

Friday, July 6

I dined at Todd's, where there was a mixed company. After dinner they went to the old trade of bumpering.

In this company there was one of these despicable fellows whom we may call court spies, a man, as I understand, pretty intimate with Governour Clinton who might perhaps share some favour for his dexterity in intelligence. This fellow I found made it his business to foist himself into all mixed companies to hear what was said and to inquire into the business and character of strangers.

After dinner I happened to be in a room near the porch fronting the street, and overheard this worthy intelligencer a-pumping of Todd, the landlord. Todd informed him who I was, upon his asking the question. "You mean the pockfretten man," said he, "with the dark-coloured silk coat. One Hamilton from Maryland. They say he is a doctor, and traveling for his health."

Just as the inquisitor was desiring Todd to speak lower (he was not deaf) I bolted out upon them and put an end to the inquiry, and the inquisitor went about his business.

At five I went to the coffeehouse, and there meeting with Mr. Dupeyster, he carried me to the tavern, where in a large room were convened a certain club of merry fellows.

But the most remarkable person in the whole company was one Wendall, a young gentleman from Boston. He entertained us mightily by playing on the violin the quickest tunes upon the highest keys, which he accompanied with his voice, so as even to drown the violin, with such nice shakings and gracings that I thought his voice outdid the instrument.

I sat for some time immovable with surprise. The like I never heard, and the thing seemed to me next a miracle. The extent of his voice is impossible to describe or even to imagine unless by hearing him.

The whole company were amazed that any person but a woman or eunuch could have such a pipe, and began to question his virility; but he swore if the company pleased he would show a couple of as good witnesses as any man might wear.

Sunday, July 8th

I spent the morning att home and att one o'clock went to dine with Mr. Bayard. Among some other gentlemen there was my old friend Dr. Mc-Graa who to day seemed to have more talk and ostentation than usuall, but he did not shine quite bright till he had drunk half a dozen glasses of wine after dinner. He spoke now in a very arbitrary tone as if his opinion was to pass for an ipse dixit.

He and I unhappily engaged in a dispute which I was sorry for, it being dissonant to good manners before company, and what none but rank pedants will be guilty of. We were obliged to use hard physicall terms, very discordant and disagreeable to ears not accustomed to them. I wanted much to drop it, but he keept teizing of me.

The subject of this dispute, effect which the moon has upon all fluids, as well as the ocean, in a proportionable ratio by the law of gravitation or her attractive power, and even upon the fluids in the vessels of animals.

The thing that introduced this was an action of McGraa's which exceeded every thing I had seen for nastiness, impudence, and rusticity. He told us he was troubled with the open piles and with that, from his breeches, pulled out a linnen handkercheff all stained with blood and showed it to the company just after we had eat dinner.

After my astonishment att this piece of clownish impudence was over, I asked him if that evacuation att any particular times was greater or less such as the full or change of the moon in the same manner as the catamene in women. I intended only to play upon him. He answered with a sneer that he did not believe the moon had anything to do with us or our distempers and said that such notions were only superstitious nonsense, wondering how I could give credit to any such stuff.

There was another doctor at dinner with us who went away before this dispute began. His name was Ascough. When he came first in he told Mr. Bayard he would dine with him provided he had no green pease for dinner. Mr. Bayard told him there were some, but that they should not come to table, upon which, with some entreaty, the doctor sat down and eat pritty heartily of bacon, chickens, and veal, but just as he had begun upon his veal, the stupid wench, forgetting her orders to the contrary, produced the pease, att which the doctor began to stare and change colour in such a manner that I thought he would have been convulsed, but he started up and ran out of doors so fast that we could never throw salt on his tail.

Mr. Bayard was so angry that he had almost oversett the table, but we had a good dish of pease by the bargain which otherwise we should not have tasted. This was the oddest antipathy ever I was witness to.

Monday, July 9th

The people of New York att the first appearance of a stranger are seemingly civil and courteous but this civility and complaisance soon relaxes if he be not either highly recommended or a good toaper. To drink stoutly with the Hungarian Club, who are all bumper men, is the readiest way for a stranger to recommend himself, and a sett among them are very fond of making a stranger drunk. To talk bawdy and to have a knack att punning passes among some there for good sterling wit. Govr. Clinton himself is a jolly toaper and gives good example and, for that one quality, is esteemed among these dons.

1744:   DIVERSIONS OF A DIPLOMAT

THOUGH THE colonies were British, the vast Mississippi Valley that lay to the west of them was claimed by France. The French contended that their explorers had been the first to venture down the Mississippi River—Marquette and Joliet in 1673 and La Salle in 1682—and that these "firsts" entitled France to the land.

But the Iroquois Indians had a claim too. If this was the law, the red men argued, then obviously the land belonged to them; their people were "first" by uncounted ages.

The British quickly saw the justice of the Indian claim. They also saw in it an opportunity to outsmart the French and acquire the huge expanse themselves. The governors of Virginia, Maryland and Pennsylvania appointed commissions, and in July 1744, the commissioners came together to treat jointly with the Indians. For the equivalent of $2,400 they bought off the Iroquois claim to all the land west of the frontier—a far better bargain than Peter Minuit's famous $24 purchase of Manhattan Island.

The secretary of the Virginia Commission was young William Black, lately come from Scotland. If Black's diary deals more with pleasure than business, he seems to have had an uncommon talent for mixing the two.

"I butted against some posts on the pavement . . ."
WILLIAM BLACK (born about 1720)

Chester in Pennsylvania, Sunday the 26th [of May, 1744]

We found waiting for us Richard Peters Esq. Secretary of the Province and several other Gentlemen of Philadelphia, who Receiv'd us very kindly and Welcom'd us into their Province with a Bowl of fine Lemon Punch big enough to have Swimmed half a dozen young Geese; after pouring four or five glasses of this down our throats we cross'd the river about two hundred yards over, and riding three short miles on the other side brought us into sight of the famous city of Philadelphia.

Philadelphia, Wednesday the 30th

I went to spend the Evening with a Merchant and Townsman of mine; I had not seen him for some years before till that Forenoon, when he In-vited me to his House. I found him at Home according to Promise, & there I spent the forepart of the Night very Agreeably. He kept Batchellor House, and Consequently more Freedom than when a Wife and Children is to be Conform'd to.

I staid till after 11, and parted, he making me Promise to be no Stranger while I staid in Town, of which there was no great fear, as he kept a Glass of Good Wine, and was as free of it as an Apple-tree of its Fruit on a Windy Day in the month of July. I grop'd my way to where I Lodged, after having Butted against some Posts on the Sides of the Pavement, who kept me in my Road; about the mid hour I got to Bed, where I inclined to let myself rest till morning.

June the 8th

The Beautiful young Lady (the Morning) being Risen from her Bed, and with a Countenance blooming with fresh Youth and Sprightliness like Miss M——y S——r with soft Dews hanging on her pouting lips, be-gan to take her early walk over the Eastern Woods, when I Rose from my Bed and pass'd two Hours in writting, the rest of the time till Breakfast I spent with my Fiddle and Flute.

After Dinner I return'd to my Room and made out a fair copy of the Speech the Comm'rs designed to make at the opening the Treaty; In the Evening I made haste to the Rendezvous of the Fair.

On coming to the Place I found the Lady had been punctual to the

Appointment; I was lucky enough not to be Engaged with any more but the young Lady of the House, and her Acquaintance my Favorite; In a very little time I found myself alone with the latter. On which to Improve my Acquaintance and the Opportunity, I broached a Serious Discourse with her, which was not carried on long before I found her a person to whom Nature had been as bountifull in Regard to her Mind, as I before observ'd she had been Carefull of her Body; to be short, what with her Wit and Quickness of Expression, Join'd to the Influence of her Beauty and a manner of Behaviour, I was possess'd with a Pleasure much easier felt than describ'd, and can only be Imagin'd by those who know what it is to Enjoy the Company of a Woman Every way Agreeable.

As for my Self I have more of what Shakespeare calls the Milk of Human Kind than not to have a particular Pleasure in the Company of the Fair Sex, and I have few leisure hours but what I would Devote to the Charms of their Conversation did Opptys offer.

But, to Return to my Company, which I left for the sake of this little Digression, I found them so Agreeable that I staid till the Young Lady was oblig'd to go Home, where I Conveyed her, and took leave for the Night.

Philadelphia, Saturday the 9th

This Morning rose by 6 and Carried the Public Journal to the Commissioners for their perusal, and Breakfasted at their Lodgings.

An Express from New York with His Majesty's Declaration of Warr against France.

Philadelphia, Sunday, June the 10th

We went with Solemn Pace to the Market Place, where Secretary Peters Proclaim'd War against the French King and all his subjects. [The "Old French War" which terminated in 1748 with the peace of Aix-la-Chapelle.]

Then two Drums Beat the Point of Warr, and then the Ceremony Concluded with God Save the King, and three loud Huzza's! The Comm'rs return'd with the Governor in his Coach to his House, where we follow'd and Drunk Tea from thence to the Coffee House, and then the Commissioner went with his Honor to the Club. I Crowded away for Mr. Levy's, where I found Miss Levy alone, but I was not long there before I was Bless'd with the Agreeable Company of Miss Molly, which Seem'd to enter the Room like a Goddess, Smiling and all Cheerful, as I always found her; I am no Painter, Neither do I pretend any thing that way, yet I cannot pass by this Lady, without giving you a Rough Draught of her.

I cannot say that she was a Regular Beauty, but she was Such that few cou'd find any Fault with what Dame Nature had done for her. She was of the Middle Size (which I think is the Stature that best becomes the sex) very well Shap'd: her eyes were Black, full of Fire, and well Slit, they had something in them Remarkably Languishing, and seem'd to Speak the Softness of a Soul Replete with Goodness, her Eye-brows black and finely arch'd, her Nose was well turn'd, and of a Just Bigness, and her Mouth was Neither wide nor very little, with Lips of a fine Red, and when they moved discovered two Rows of Teeth white as Ivory and Regularly well Set; her Forehead round and Smooth, as for her Hair, it was a Shining black, but no ways harsh. Her Neck, her Arms, and Hands, seem to have been made and fitted for her Face, which was of a Complection made up of the Lilly and the Rose.

Such was her Person, and I assure you the Charms of her Mind and Conversation was not less Amiable; but I must Confess my Self unable to say Anything Adequate to this Lovely Young Creature; the Bloom of Roses and Lillies might a little Illustrate her Countenance, or their Smell her Sweetness. But to Comprehend her entirely, Conceive—Youth, Health, Beauty, Neatness, and Innocence, Imagine all those in their utmost Perfection, any way, place the Charming Molly's Picture before your Eyes.

To Return I had the Pleasure of her Company till after 9, in which time I had no small satisfaction; My Eyes was my Greatest Sense; when I view'd her, I thought all the Statues I ever beheld, was so Inferior to her in Beauty that she was more capable of Converting a man into a Statue, than of being Imitated by the Greatest Master of that Art, and I surely had as much delight in Surveying her, as the Organs of Sight are Capable of Conveying to the Soul: as usual, I seed her Safe home, and return'd to Mine, and about 11, went to Bed full of pleasing Reflections.

The reflections were passing. Black did not marry Molly. Shortly afterward, he did marry another girl, an event that brought his diary to an abrupt close. He settled in Manchester, Virginia, grew rich as a merchant, and left a great estate in Falls Plantation on the James River near Richmond.

1753: MAJOR WASHINGTON EARNS A
PROMOTION

ON THE reasonable calculation that 80,000 Frenchmen could not hold the American West against 1,300,000 land-hungry British, twenty of the latter joined in a speculative enterprise in 1747 to acquire land in the Ohio Valley. One of the stockholders was Governor Dinwiddie of Virginia. He forthwith granted his own company half a million acres of the land claimed by France.

But the Frenchmen—trappers, traders, soldiers—were stubborn. They had built many forts. They were planning a new one on the point of land where the Monongahela and Allegheny rivers fell together—where the city of Pittsburgh stands today. Whoever held that peninsula might also hold the fate of a nation, certainly that of the Ohio Company.

Another stockholder was Lawrence Washington of Mount Vernon, farmer and adjutant in charge of the local militia with the rank of major. In 1752 Lawrence died and his brother George succeeded to the estate and the military majority.

In October 1753, Governor Dinwiddie summoned George to Williamsburg. He wanted a message delivered to the French commander at Fort Le Boeuf, now Waterford, Pennsylvania, to the effect that everybody knew the English had the right to the Ohio Valley, and that whatever the French had in mind there, they had better just forget it.

It was a hard trip in bitter weather over mountains and through 300 miles of wilderness. But worse than the physical ordeal for the 21-year-old Washington was the delicate task of dealing with the Seneca Indians through their head man with the curious title of Half-King, to prevent an alliance with the French.

So well did Washington carry out the mission—even though the French brushed off the warning—that on his return a month later, he was promoted to a colonelcy. The incident foreshadowed the Seven Years' War, which decided the case for English rather than French domination of the American continent. It also set a young man on a path to greatness beyond his own farthest imaginings.

"*I endeavor'd to frustrate their Schemes . . .*"
GEORGE WASHINGTON (1732-1799)

October 31 [1753]

I was commissioned and appointed by the Honorable Robert Dinwiddie, Esq., Governor etc. of Virginia, to visit and deliver a Letter to the commandant of the French forces on the Ohio, and set out on the intended journey the same day.

November 30 [Loggs Town, center of the Six Nations Indians on the Ohio]

Last Night the great Men assembled to their Council-House to consult further about this Journey, and who were to go: the Result of which was that only three of their Chiefs with one of their best Hunters should be our Convoy.

We set out about nine o'Clock with the Half-King Jeskakake, White Thunder, and the Hunter; and travelled on the Road to Venango [now Franklin, in northwestern Pennsylvania].

December 4, Venango

We found the French Colors hoisted at a House from which they had driven Mr. John Frazier, an English subject. I immediately repaired to it, to know where the Commander resided. There were three Officers, one of whom, Capt. Joncaire, informed me, that he had the Command of the Ohio: But that there was a General Officer at the near Fort, where he advised me to apply for an Answer.

He invited us to sup with them; and treated us with the greatest Complaisance. The Wine, as they dosed themselves pretty plentifully with it, soon banished the Restraint which at first appeared in their Conversation; and gave a Licence to their Tongues to reveal their Sentiments more freely.

They told me That it was their absolute Design to take Possession of the Ohio, and, by G——, they would do it: For that, altho' they were sensible the English could raise two Men for their one; yet they knew, their Motions were too slow and dilatory to prevent any undertaking of theirs.

They pretend to have an undoubted Right to the River, from a Discovery made by one La Salle 60 Years ago; and the Rise of this Expedition is, to prevent our settling on the River or Waters of it, as they had heard of some Families moving-out in Order thereto.

6th

The Half-King came to my Tent, quite sober, and insisted very much that I should stay and hear what he had to say to the French. I fain would have prevented speaking any Thing, till he came to the Commandant, but could not prevail.

He told me, that at this Place of Council, Fire was kindled, where all their Business with these People was to be transacted; and that the Management of the Indian Affairs was left solely to Monsieur Joncaire.

As I was desirous of knowing the Issue of this, I agreed to stay. About 10 o'Clock they met in Council. The King spoke much the same as he had before done to the General; and offered the French Speech-Belt, which had before been demanded, with the Marks of four Towns on it, which Monsieur Joncaire refused to receive; but desired him to carry it to the Fort of the Commander.

7th

At 11 o'Clock we set out for the Fort.

12th

I prepared early to wait upon the Commander, and was received and conducted to him by the second Officer in Command. I acquainted him with my Business, and offered my Commission and Letter.

13th

The chief Officers retired to hold a Council of War; which gave me an opportunity of taking the Dimensions of the Fort and making what observations I could.

I could get no certain Account of the Number of Men here: But according to the best Judgment I could form, there are an Hundred exclusive of Officers, of which there are many.

I also gave Orders to the People who were with me to take an exact Account of the Canoes which were hauled-up to convey their Forces down in the Spring.

This they did, and told 50 of Birch Bark and 170 of Pine, besides many others which were blocked-out, in Readiness to make.

14th

As I found many Plots concerted to retard the Indians Business and prevent their returning with me, I endeavor'd all that lay in my Power to frustrate their Schemes, and hurry them on to execute their intended Design. They accordingly pressed for Admittance this Evening, which at Length was granted them, privately, with the Commander and one or two other Officers.

The Half-King told me that he offer'd the Wampum to the Commander, who evaded taking it, and made many fair Promises of Love and Friendship; said he wanted to live in Peace and trade amicably with them, as a Proof of which he would send some Goods immediately down to the Logg's-Town for them.

But I rather think the Design of that is to bring away all our straggling Traders they meet with, as I privately understood they intended to carry an Officer &c. with them. And what rather confirms this Opinion—I was enquiring of the Commander, by what Authority he had made Prisoners of several of our English Subjects. He told me that the Country belong'd to them; that no Englishman had a Right to trade upon those Waters; and that he had Orders to make every Person Prisoner who attempted it on the Ohio, or the Waters of it.

15th

The Commandant ordered a plentiful Store of Liquor, Provision, &c. to be put on Board our Canoe; and appeared to be extremely complaisant though he was exerting every Artifice which he could invent to set our own Indians at Variance with us, to prevent their going 'till after our Departure—Presents, Rewards, and every Thing which could be suggested by him or his Officers. I can't say that ever in my Life I suffered so much Anxiety as I did in this Affair: I saw that every Strategem which the most fruitful Brain could invent was practiced to win the Half-King to their Interest; and that leaving him here was giving them the Opportunity they aimed at.

16th

I urged and insisted with the Half-King so closely upon his Word that he set-off with us as he had engaged.

27th

Just after we had passed a Place called the Murdering-Town, we fell-in with a Party of French Indians who had lain in Wait for us. One of them fired at Mr. Gist or me, not 15 Steps off, but fortunately missed. We took this Fellow into Custody, and kept him till about 9 o'Clock: Then let him go, and walked all the remaining Part of the Night without making any Stop; that we might get the Start, so far, as to be out of the Reach of their Pursuit the next Day, since we were well assured that they would follow our Track as soon as it was light.

On the 11th of January, 1754

I got to Belvoir, where I stopped one Day to make necessary Rest; and then set out, and arrived in Williamsburgh the 16th; when I waited upon his Honor the Governor with the Letter I had brought from the French Commandant, and to give an Account of the Success of my Proceedings.

─── ★

1758:   FOR ONE INDIAN SCALP, £300

─── ☆

IN 1676 the white men triumphantly displayed the head of Indian King Philip on a pole in Boston, thus ending the fierce "war of extermination" that bore his name. The grisly exhibit was kept up for twenty-five years. Boston had a reason.

The Indians of New England, driven from their ancient hunting grounds by men who measured off the land, put fences around it, and then said this gave them the right to keep others out, retaliated in the only ways they could. One of these was to ally themselves with the French in Canada. Another was to lash out directly at the British—to raid, burn, kill; and this they did, with a brutality that matched the white man at his worst.

In 1744, following a declaration of war against the Indians of Nova Scotia, the Massachusetts General Court declared open season on red men and offered a reward for scalps; and in 1757 it increased this bounty from £250 to £300. This made Indian-killing a profitable sport—just how profitable may be gauged from the fact that in the same year the town of Boston voted to Schoolmaster Peleg Wiswall as his salary for one year, £120.

To seek the blood money, a man need only take gun in hand, sign up with the military authority, go out to kill on sight, keep a diary of his project, and turn it in to the Secretary's office. In the Massachusetts Historical Society there is such a diary, kept by one Captain James Cargill, of Newcastle, Maine, who got his man and his money.

"I shot . . . killed and scalped him . . ."
JAMES CARGILL (1725-1812)

May the 2d [1758]

Went to Whisacasick and Got Nathan Gove to go with me so we Gave in our Names and Intentions to Captain Williams But we had no proper Weather for Seting out Before the 8th.

The 10th

Marched to Samarescotta Pond and about Nine a Clock Came upon Some Moggzeen [moccasin] trackes. So went from hill to hill to try to Discover their Smook But Could See none and on our way Saw many tracks and Places where men had Layed.

The 11th

In the morning Left my Partnar with our Packes. So went as Privitly about as I Could to try to Make Some Discovery and Saw Many Signs where they had Been not Long before and about Nine a Clock went away again on to a hill to Indavour to Discoveour the Smook But Saw Nothing Remarkable untill I was within a Quarter of a Mile of my Partnar when I Saw an Indian which Came within about Ten Yards of me before he Saw me. But as Soon as I Saw he had Discovered me I Shot and killed him. So Charged my Gun But Could See no More.

So went and Scalped him and was Going off But Saw two Indians att about Eighty Yards Distance and as I was Looking at them before I was aware I was Shot at by a French Man which was behind me that I had not Seen, which Shot Struck my Powderhorn and Broke it and before I Could Get Clear of the Danger of my horn and turn to him he was So Close in upon me that Just as I Shot at him he Struck my gun aside and took Hold of me and Speaking in Good English offered me good Quarters.

But not Being willing to Submit to his Proposals I Claped my Pistol to his Breast and Snaped her. But She flashed by which Means I Got out of his hands and Got hold of my own Gun again and Struck him on the head and Broke my Gun.

But their was an Indian by, Alltho he never offered to help him when he had a hold of me, and as I run I saw two Indians follow me, and When I had Got about half way to my Partnar I Hallowed as loud as I Could and when he answered they Quit following me and Run Another way and as they turned I thought I heard one of their Guns Snap and as I Run I Droped the Scalp, So we Set off for home as fast as we Could and I Spat Blood all the way, Being Strained with the Scuffel I had with the French Man.

When we got home we Got ten Men more to Go with us to Look for the Scalp But I was not able to Go before the 15th when we went and found it.

Cargill collected his blood money. In the Massachusetts Archives there is a note that "the Committee are unanimously of opinion that the said James is intitled to £300 for killing said indian and that said sum be allowed and paid out of the Publick Treasury."

--- ★

1761:   WHEN PITTSBURGH WAS A TRADING
POST

--- ☆

WHERE PITTSBURGH IS NOW, James Kenny bought furs from "Sennica wariors" two centuries ago at a store established by the provincial government's Commission of Indian Affairs. Kenny, a Quaker, was a member of a prominent family in Chester, Pennsylvania. He accompanied the noted naturalist John Bartram on some of his botanical excursions. What makes this diary unique is that despite the thieving and other misdemeanors that Kenny expects of the Indians as a matter of course, he maintains in his dealings with them a tolerance and good humor shared by few other white men of his time.

"The Indians want to stay in ye House . . ."
JAMES KENNY (latter part of 18th century)

6 mo 12th [1761]

Some of ye Indians I was acquaint'd with before come, was Glad to see me, one of which Call'd Jammy Willson had some Bundles of Skins & some fur. He dealt here; this man has Curled black hair & never went to

War by report, but having obtained a White Woman & Boy, he kept ye Woman as his Wife, using her kindly; on finding she inclined to return to her own People he brought her & ye Boy with ye Amount of his Estate to our Store & told ye Woman notwithstanding He Loved her, as she want'd to leave him, would let her go, so he divided his substance equally with her, giving half of ye remaind^r to ye Boy & set them both free & went with ye Woman home giving her a Horse to Ride; an Instance of more self denial than many men of great Christian professions shews their poor Negros.

7 mo 15th

A Cousen of Delaware Georges, a Young Man born at Oley, had some trade here, seemed very good Nature'd & having no English Name I gave him my Name which he said he would keep, went out a Hunting.

8 mo 9th

My Namesake Indian returned from his Hunt last Night having brought thirty Skins with him & dealt them with me.

10th

The Indians that deal at our Store often want to stay in ye House at Nights while they remain here, & often want Victuals; they also want to bring their Squas to lie with at Night, which I Object against, letting them know that they shall bring none such to Sleep in our House, & Having shut out two Squas last Night, they kept throwing Stones on ye House & Door after we went to bed, untill we went out & threatcn'd them away.

10 mo 8th

There is a Proclamation from Col. Johnson Pasted up here for all ye Indian Traders to Adhere to, ye Prices of ye Goods that is now fix'd at a more benefishal profit than here before; all ye Traders to have a Pass else ye Commanding officers at each Post are forbid to let them Trade.

15th

About this time I went to get Coal over ye Mountain South side of ye Monongahela about 1¼ miles from ye sd River. With four men & 3 Horses carried them in bags to ye River & brot home at night in a flat boat 40 Bushel fine coal being dug out before. I killed a Turkey.

11 mo to 12th

Many Traders gone with Goods to Trade at ye Indians Towns. One Thos Cape that was Prisoner amongst ye Shawanas in Virginia, being set free, we have taken him to live with us.

16th

I am inform'd by Thos Cape that when ye Indians Kill a Deer in ye Woods & being in haste to follow ye Game, they leave a Cap or some part of their Clothing on ye killed Game until they return, which hinders ye Buzzards & Vermin to Eat it, also that if they intend to leave it all night where its kill'd they Bark or Blase 3 or four Trees round it & then wets some Powder in their Hand untill it is dissolved then dips their finger in it & Sprinkles it on ye Blaszes, which in ye Night will look like sparks of fire all round, & no Vermin would touch ye Carcase untill it would rot there.

12 mo 1st

Many of ye Inhabitants here have hired a School Master & Subscrib'd above Sixty Pounds for this Year to him, he has about Twenty Schollars, likewise ye Soberer sort of People seemes to long for some publick way of Worship, so ye School Master Reads ye Littany of Common Prayer on ye First Days to a Congregation of different Principels (he being a Prisbi-terant) where they behave very Grave (as I hear), on ye occasion ye Children also are brought to Church as they Call it.

7th

Ye Sennica Wariors have got ye last provissions allow'd them this Day with orders to go, being Supply'd with all they ask'd; they are very troublesome by crowding into ye Houses & thronging our fire Places, but behaves Civell, ye Indians in General being so theevish that we are under ye necessity to watch them with ye utmost care & must be Lossers after in some things unless we had as many spyes as they have thieves; this makes them fare ye worse amongst us, as we are affraid to let them Sleep in our Houses, or indulge them to tarry any longe time, but many of them are so good natured that they won't be affronted readily.

12 mo 8th

The Head Sennica Warior dealt Seven large Buckins with me, when many of them Croud'd in ye Store being very thievish (ye Agent being out) ye Warior seem'd not easy pleas'd with his full Pay which he took in

Powdr, so I gave him a Loaf of Bread which was satisfactory to them; one of them bringing a small Skin want'd Brass Wire for it, but could hardly please himself amongst a variety of sorts, telling me to hand more. I looked upon it as a Stratagem to keep me bussie that ye others might have oppertunity to Steal something. Several of 'em want'd to get behind ye Counter but I always turn'd 'em back & all they got was a Handful of salt. One took out a Kegg that stood behind ye door, whilst my Brother just step'd out, so I turn'd them all out & ye Hindmost stop'd by ye door & begg'd for a Little Salt, so I gave him a handful he being disappoint'd in Stealing of it.

12 mo 24th

Many of ye Indians have been inquiring when Christmass would come & one young Man a Cossen of Delaware George's ask'd me ye Reason of it. I told him that ye white people took notice of ye time on account of what happen'd then that ye Son of ye Good Spirit came in ye form of a man & liv'd many Days amongst ye people, done Many Maricles & suffer'd the Jews to put him to death, shewing Men by his example that they should not War nor fight but suffer as he did, & on ye third Day that he rose & assend'd, he having power over Death, Men &c., & would also raise good men again;—at which he seem'd much Affected.

25th

A young Indian Man brought us four Turkeys saying he was recommended by severals of his acquaintance to come to ye Quaker who would use him very well & having bought them & paid him Six Shillings Cash besides Victuals & drink, he going out heard of a better Market so came back & got the Turkeys, delivering ye Money again, but his second Chap not pleasing him in dealing he brought them back to us & had his money again, but he said Dam it several times at ye Second Chap.

1762 1 mo. 13th

I was inform'd some time ago by some Pack Horse Men that was at Tuscorawas that ye Indians there spoke very well of me (to them) & some Young Delawares that was here signified that was report'd amongst ye Indians that all ye Traders here would Cheat them but me & John Hart.

2 mo 4th

Frederick Post says that ye Indians are Voide of Reason, but I find that in many cases they will hear to reason & allow it to be right; many of them

will have theire Peltry too wet; its like some on purpose & others by accident & to reason with most of them in that case to make a reasonable
allowance in weight, they will grummel much & be for carrying them to
some other trader, but it's easy to make a reasonable allowance & not tell
them of it; all will go smooth enough & scarcely any of them but may be
easily Cheat'd, which I doubt they too often meet with.

1763:   A QUAKER DISARMS THE WARRIORS

To JOHN WOOLMAN the Christian ethic was a code of love to be practiced ex-
quisitely and preached incidentally. In this he reversed the order of the majority of ministers of his day. This man's purity of heart, his strong humility, his
patience and tenderness, as they come through in the brave and gentle words
of his journal, are closer to the good absolute attained in the teachings of Jesus
than are the writings of any other American known to these editors.

He was born into a Quaker family in Rancocas, New Jersey, in 1720. Educated in a Friends school "pretty well for a planter," he made his first appearance as preacher at the age of 20 but immediately felt that he had talked
too much and so kept silent for six weeks after. He taught school and studied
law but earned his way through most of his life as a tailor, serving the while also
as itinerant minister.

Poet John G. Whittier, himself a Quaker and editor of one of the more than
fifty editions of Woolman's journal, gives this description of him:

"A figure only four and a half feet high, hunchbacked, with projecting chest,
legs small and uneven, arms longer than his legs, a huge head, showing only
beneath the enormous white hat, large solemn eyes and a prominent nose, the
rest of his face covered with a snowy semicircle of beard falling low on his
breast."

Woolman waged a lifelong campaign to end slavery and was the most effective power against it of his time. After a tour of Virginia he wrote:

"I saw in these southern provinces so many vices and corruptions increased by
this trade [in slaves] and this way of life that it appeared to me as a dark
gloominess hanging over the land; and though now many willingly run into it,
yet in future the consequence will be grievous to posterity."

His method was "to persuade and entreat, and simply give hints of my way of thinking." And although others had gone before him bent on the same mission, he was the first to make any great headway. During his lifetime, and largely as a result of his efforts, most Pennsylvania Quakers freed their slaves.

Woolman's journal understates his own achievements—so much so that, as the famous British diarist Henry Crabb Robinson said of him, "Had he not been so very humble he would have written a still better book; for, fearing to indulge in vanity, he conceals the events in which he was a great actor."

The fault, if such it is, has not barred the journal from wide readership nor from undoubted status as an American classic. It has been used in Princeton University as a textbook for the purity of its language. In 1920 the state of Pennsylvania required a reading of it of all those preparing to take examinations for teaching jobs.

While Woolman's fight against slavery was a major concern and the one with which he is most often identified, his role as a peacemaker with the Indians was important too; and it so happens that the story he tells of his ten-day journey to the Indian settlement on the Susquehanna River in 1763, because of its narrative fullness, makes better reading than the generally terse, undetailed references to his fight to free the slaves.

Woolman knew the Indians had just declared new war on the white man when he set out toward them. The chances of his coming out of it alive were not of the best. A soldier who had fallen into the Indians' hands and then escaped told him that he had seen two of his fellow-captives "tortured to death in a very cruel manner." The story, Woolman added, "affected me with sadness." Still, he had to risk a visit with those same Indians, "that I might feel and understand their life, and the spirit they live in, if haply I might receive some instruction from them."

Contrast this with the reaction of Boston's Reverend Cotton Mather to similar circumstances fifty years earlier: "A great body of Indians were on their way to make a descent on our frontiers; but our army happily must meet 'em and beat 'em." Yet in the discrimination he used in the exercise of the Christianity of his own preaching Mather was neither better nor worse than most New England religious leaders—only louder.

Here is Christianity of another kind.

"The Indians would choose to shake hands."
JOHN WOOLMAN (1720-1772)

[June 9, 1763]

Having for many years felt love in my heart towards the natives of this land who dwell far back in the wilderness, whose ancestors were formerly the owners and possessors of the land where we dwell, and who for a small consideration assigned their inheritance to us, and being at Philadelphia in the eighth month, 1761, on a visit to some Friends who had slaves, I fell in company with some of those natives who live on the east branch of the river Susquehanna, at an Indian town called Wehaloosing, two hundred miles from Philadelphia.

At times I felt inward drawings towards a visit to that place, which I mentioned to none except my dear wife until it came to some ripeness. In the winter of 1762 I laid my prospects before my friends at our Monthly and Quarterly, and afterwards at our General Spring Meeting; and having the unity of Friends, and being thoughtful about an Indian pilot, there came a man and three women from a little beyond that town to Philadelphia on business.

Being informed thereof by letter, I met them in town in the fifth month, 1763; and after some conversation, finding they were sober people, I, with the concurrence of Friends in that place, agreed to join them as companions in their return, and we appointed to meet at Samuel Foulk's, at Richland, in Bucks County, on the 7th of sixth month.

Thus in true love and tenderness I parted from Friends, expecting the next morning to proceed on my journey. Being weary I went early to bed. After I had been asleep a short time I was awoke by a man calling at my door and inviting me to meet some Friends at a public house in our town, who came from Philadelphia so late that Friends were generally gone to bed.

These Friends informed me that an express had arrived the last morning from Pittsburg, and brought news that the Indians had taken a fort from the English westward and had slain and scalped some English people near the said Pittsburg and in divers places.

Some elderly Friends in Philadelphia, knowing the time of my intending to set off, had conferred together and thought good to inform me of these things before I left home, that I might consider them and proceed as I believed best.

Going to bed again, I told not my wife till morning. My heart was turned to the Lord for His heavenly instruction; and it was an humbling time for me. When I told my dear wife she appeared to be deeply concerned about it; but in a few hours' time my mind became settled in a belief that it was my duty to proceed on my journey, and she bore it with a good degree of resignation.

I took leave of my family and neighbors in much bowedness of spirit, and went to our Monthly Meeting at Burlington. After taking leave of friends there, I crossed the river accompanied by my friends Israel and John Pemberton; and parting the next morning with Israel, John bore me company to Samuel Foulk's, where I met the before-mentioned Indians, and we were glad to see each other.

Here my friend Benjamin Parvin met me and proposed joining me as a companion—we had before exchanged some letters on the subject—and now I had a sharp trial on his account; for, as the journey appeared perilous, I thought if he went chiefly to bear me company, and we should be taken captive, my having been the means of drawing him into these difficulties would add to my own afflictions; so I told him my mind freely and let him know I was resigned to go alone; but after all, if he really believed it his duty to go on, I believed his company would be very comfortable to me.

It was indeed a time of deep exercise, and Benjamin appeared to be so fastened to the visit that he could not be easy to leave me, so we went on, accompanied by our friends John Pemberton and William Lightfoot of Pikeland.

We lodged at Bethlehem, and there parting with John, William and we went forward on the 9th of the sixth month, and got lodging on the floor of a house about five miles from Fort Allen.

Here we parted with William, and at this place we met with an Indian trader lately come from Wyoming [a valley in eastern Pennsylvania along the Susquehanna River]. In conversation with him I perceived that many white people often sell rum to the Indians, which I believe is a great evil.

While my mind this evening was thus employed I also remembered that the people on the frontiers, among whom this evil is too common, are often poor, and that they venture to the outside of a colony in order to live more independently of the wealthy, who often set high rents on their land.

I was renewedly confirmed in a belief that if all our inhabitants lived according to sound wisdom, laboring to promote universal love and righteousness, and ceased from every inordinate desire after wealth and from all customs which are tinctured with luxury, the way would be easy for our inhabitants, though they might be much more numerous than at present, to live comfortably on honest employments, without the temptation they are so often under of being drawn into schemes to make settlements on lands which have not been purchased of the Indians, or of applying to that wicked practice of selling rum to them.

Tenth

We set out early this morning and crossed the western branch of Delaware, called the Great Lehie, near Fort Allen.

The water being high, we went over in a canoe. Here we met an Indian, had friendly conversation with him, and gave him some biscuit; and he, having killed a deer, gave some of it to the Indians with us.

After traveling some miles we met several Indian men and women with a cow and horse and some household goods, who were lately come from their dwelling at Wyoming and were going to settle at another place. We made them some small presents, and, as some of them understood English, I told them my motive for coming into their country, with which they appeared satisfied.

We pitched our tent near the banks of the river, having labored hard in crossing some of those mountains called the Blue Ridge. The roughness of the stones and the cavities between them, with the steepness of the hills, made it appear dangerous.

Near our tent, on the sides of large trees peeled for that purpose, were various representations of men going to and returning from the wars, and of some being killed in battle. This was a path heretofore used by warriors, and as I walked about viewing those Indian histories, which were painted mostly in red or black, and thinking on the innumerable afflictions which the proud, fierce spirit produceth in the world, also on the toils and fatigues of warriors in traveling over mountains and deserts—on their miseries and distresses when far from home and wounded by their enemies; of their bruises and great weariness in chasing one another over the rocks and mountains; of the restless, unquiet state of mind of those who live in this spirit, and of the hatred which mutually grows up in the minds of their children—the spirit of love and peace among these people arose very fresh in me.

This was the first night that we lodged in the woods, and being wet with traveling in the rain, as were also our blankets, the ground, our tent, and the bushes under which we proposed to lay, all looked discouraging; but

I believed that it was the Lord who had thus far brought me forward, and that He would dispose of me as He saw good, and so I felt easy.

We kindled a fire, with our tent open to it, then laid some bushes next the ground and put our blankets upon them for our bed, and, lying down, got some sleep.

In the morning, feeling a little unwell, I went into the river; the water was cold, but soon after I felt fresh and well.

About eight o'clock we set forward and crossed a high mountain supposed to be upward of four miles over.

Twelfth

Being the first of the week and a rainy day, we continued in our tent, and I was led to think on the nature of the exercise which hath attended me. Love was the first motion, and thence a concern arose to spend some time with the Indians, that I might feel and understand their life and the spirit they live in, if haply I might receive some instruction from them or they might be in any degree helped forward by my following the leadings of truth among them; and as it pleased the Lord to make way for my going at a time when the troubles of war were increasing and when, by reason of much wet weather, traveling was more difficult than usual at that season, I looked upon it as a more favorable opportunity to season my mind and to bring me into a nearer sympathy with them.

Thirteenth

The sun appearing, we set forward, and as I rode over the barren hills my meditations were on the alterations in the circumstances of the natives of this land since the coming in of the English. The lands near the sea are conveniently situated for fishing; the lands near the rivers, where the tides flow, and some above, are in many places fertile and not mountainous, while the changing of the tides makes passing up and down easy with any kind of traffic. The natives have in some places, for trifling considerations, sold their inheritance so favorably situated, and in other places have been driven back by superior force; their way of clothing themselves is also altered from what it was, and they being far removed from us have to pass over mountains, swamps, and barren deserts, so that traveling is very troublesome in bringing their skins and furs to trade with us.

By the extension of English settlements, and partly by the increase of English hunters, the wild beasts on which the natives chiefly depend for subsistence are not so plentiful as they were.

My own will and desires were now very much broken, and my heart was with much earnestness turned to the Lord, to whom alone I looked for help in the dangers before me. I had a prospect of the English along the coast for upwards of nine hundred miles where I traveled, and their favorable situation and the difficulties attending the natives as well as the Negroes in many places were open before me.

A weighty and heavenly care came over my mind, and love filled my heart towards all mankind, in which I felt a strong engagement that we might be obedient to the Lord while in tender mercy He is yet calling to us, and that we might so attend to pure universal righteousness as to give no just cause of offense to the Gentiles who do not profess Christianity, whether they be the blacks from Africa or the native inhabitants of this continent.

Here I was led into a close and laborious inquiry whether I, as an individual, kept clear from all things which tended to stir up or were connected with wars, either in this land or in Africa; my heart was deeply concerned that in future I might in all things keep steadily to the pure truth, and live and walk in the plainness and simplicity of a sincere follower of Christ.

I felt in that which is immutable that the seeds of great calamity and desolation are sown and growing fast on this continent. Nor have I words sufficient to set forth the longing I then felt, that we who are placed along the coast and have tasted the love and goodness of God might arise in the strength thereof, and like faithful messengers labor to check the growth of these seeds, that they might not ripen to the ruin of our posterity.

On reaching the Indian settlement at Wyoming we were told that an Indian runner had been at that place a day or two before us, and brought news of the Indians having taken an English fort westward and destroyed the people, and that they were endeavoring to take another; also that another Indian runner came there about the middle of the previous night from a town about ten miles from Wehaloosing, and brought the news that some Indian warriors from distant parts came to that town with English scalps and told the people that it was war with the English.

Our guides took us to the house of a very ancient man. Soon after we had put in our baggage there came a man from another Indian house some distance off. Perceiving there was a man near the door I went out; the man had a tomahawk wrapped under his match-coat out of sight. As I approached him he took it in his hand. I went forward and, speaking to him in a friendly way, perceived he understood some English.

My companion joining me, we had some talk with him concerning the nature of our visit in these parts; he then went into the house with us and, talking with our guides, soon appeared friendly, sat down and smoked his pipe. Though taking his hatchet in his hand at the instant I drew near to him had a disagreeable appearance, I believe he had no other intent than to be in readiness in case any violence were offered to him.

On hearing the news brought by these Indian runners, and being told by the Indians where we lodge that the Indians about Wyoming expected in a few days to move to some larger town, I thought, to all outward appearance it would be dangerous traveling at this time.

After a hard day's journey I was brought into a painful exercise at night, in which I had to trace back and view the steps I had taken from my first moving in the visit; and though I had to bewail some weakness which at times had attended me, yet I could not find that I had ever given way to willful disobedience.

Believing I had, under a sense of duty, come thus far, I was now earnest in spirit, beseeching the Lord to show me what I ought to do. In this great distress I grew jealous of myself, lest the desire of reputation as a man firmly settled to persevere through dangers, or the fear of disgrace from my returning without performing the visit might have some place in me.

Full of these thoughts, I lay great part of the night while my beloved companion slept by me, till the Lord, my gracious Father, who saw the conflicts of my soul, was pleased to give quietness. Then I was again strengthened to commit my life, and all things relating thereto, into His heavenly hands, and got a little sleep towards day.

Fifteenth

We proceeded forward till the afternoon, when, a storm appearing, we met our canoe at an appointed place and stayed all night, the rain continuing so heavy that it beat through our tent and wet both us and our baggage.

The next day we found abundance of trees blown down by the storm yesterday. We were much hindered by the trees and in some swamps our way was so stopped that we got through with extreme difficulty.

This afternoon Job Chilaway, an Indian from Wehaloosing who talks good English and is acquainted with several people in and about Philadelphia, met our people on the river.

Job told us that an Indian came in haste to their town yesterday and told them that three warriors from a distance lodged in a town above Wehaloosing a few nights past, and that these three men were going against the English at Juniata.

The news of these warriors being on their march so near us, and not knowing whether we might not fall in with them, was a fresh trial of my faith; and though, through the strength of Divine love I had several times been enabled to commit myself to the Divine disposal, I still found the want of a renewal of my strength, that I might be able to persevere therein; and my cries for help were put up to the Lord, who, in great mercy, gave me a resigned heart, in which I found quietness.

Parting from Job Chilaway on the 17th, we went on and reached Wehaloosing about the middle of the afternoon. The first Indian that we saw was a woman of a modest countenance, with a Bible, who spake first to our guide and then with an harmonious voice expressed her gladness at seeing us, having before heard of our coming.

By the direction of our guide we sat down on a log while he went to the town to tell the people we were come. My companion and I, sitting thus together in a deep inward stillness, the poor woman came and sat near us; and, great awfulness coming over us, we rejoiced in a sense of God's love manifested to our poor souls.

After a while we heard a conch shell blow several times, and then came John Curtis and another Indian man, who kindly invited us into a house near the town, where we found about sixty people sitting in silence. After sitting with them a short time I stood up, and in some tenderness of spirit acquainted them, in a few short sentences, with the nature of my visit, and that a concern for their good had made me willing to come thus far to see them; which some of them understanding, interpreted to the others, and there appeared gladness among them.

On the evening of the 18th I was at their meeting, where pure gospel love was felt, to the tendering of some of our hearts. The interpreters endeavored to acquaint the people with what I said, in short sentences, but found some difficulty, as none of them were quite perfect in the English and Delaware tongues, so they helped one another, and we labored along, Divine love attending.

Afterwards, feeling my mind covered with the spirit of prayer, I told the interpreters that I found it in my heart to pray to God and believed, if I prayed aright, He would hear me; and I expressed my willingness for them to omit interpreting; so our meeting ended with a degree of Divine love.

Before the people went out I observed Papunehang (the man who had

been zealous in laboring for a reformation in that town, being then very
tender) speaking to one of the interpreters, and I was afterwards told
that he said in substance as follows:

"I love to feel where words come from."

[June 21]

I was at two meetings on the 20th, and silent in them. The following
morning, in meeting, my heart was enlarged in pure love among them,
and in short plain sentences I expressed several things that rested upon
me, which one of the interpreters gave the people pretty readily.

The meeting ended in supplication, and I had cause humbly to acknowledge the loving-kindness of the Lord toward us; and then I believed that a door remained open for the faithful disciples of Jesus Christ
to labor among these people. And now, feeling my mind at liberty to
return, I took my leave of them in general at the conclusion of what I
said in meeting, and we then prepared to go homeward.

But some of their most active men told us that when we were ready
to move, the people would choose to come and shake hands with us.
Those who usually came to meeting did so; and from a secret draught
in my mind I went among some who did not usually go to meeting,
and took my leave of them also.

We expected only two Indians to be of our company, but when we
were ready to go we found many of them were going to Bethlehem with
skins and furs and chose to go in company with us. So they loaded two
canoes in which they desired us to go, telling us that the waters were so
raised with the rains that the horses should be taken by such as were
better acquainted with the fording places.

We, therefore, with several Indians went in the canoes, and others
went on horses, there being seven besides ours.

Twenty-fifth

The troubles westward, and the difficulty for Indians to pass through
our frontier, were, I apprehend, reasons why so many came, expecting
that our being in company would prevent the outside inhabitants being
surprised.

We reached Bethlehem on the 25th, taking care to keep foremost and
to acquaint people on and near the road who these Indians were. This
we found very needful, for the frontier inhabitants were often alarmed
at the reports of the English being killed by Indians westward.

Among our company were some whom I did not remember to have

seen at meeting, and some of these at first were very reserved; but we being several days together, and behaving in a friendly manner towards them, and making them suitable return for the services they did us, they became more free and sociable.

Twenty-sixth

Having carefully endeavored to settle all affairs with the Indians relative to our journey, we took leave of them, and I thought they generally parted from us affectionately.

We went forward to Richland and had a very comfortable meeting among our friends, it being the first day of the week. Here I parted with my kind friend and companion Benjamin Parvin, and, accompanied by my friend Samuel Foulk, we rode to John Cadwallader's, from whence I reached home the next day, and found my family tolerably well.

People who have never been in such places have but an imperfect idea of them; and I was not only taught patience, but also made thankful to God, who thus led about and instructed me, that I might have a quick and lively feeling of the afflictions of my fellow creatures whose situation in life is difficult.

★

1771:   A WHIMSICAL "DAUGHTER OF
LIBERTY"

☆

As a young officer, Joshua Winslow served king and country in the army of New Englanders that went to Cape Breton in 1745 and took the fortress of Louisburg from the French. Twenty-five years later, when the American colonies were talking defiance of England, Joshua sided with his king. To the mind of Tory Joshua, this meant exile; and long before actual war broke out, he and his wife went to live in Nova Scotia. Meanwhile, he wanted his eleven-year-old daughter Anna to "finish" in the Boston schools. So she was left in the home of her aunt in that city and told to keep a diary for Mama and Papa.

"Laughterre is apt to seize me . . ."

ANNA GREEN WINSLOW (1759-1779)

30th Nov. [1771]

My company yesterday made four couple [all young girls] at country dansing; danceing I mean. In the evening young Mr. Waters hearing of my assembly, put his flute in his pocket and played several minuets and other tunes, to which we danced mighty cleverly. But Lucinda [her aunt's slave] was our principal piper.

I am to leave off my black ribbins tomorrow, & am to put on my red cloak & black hatt—I hope aunt wont let me wear the black hatt with the red Dominie—for the people will ask me what I have got to sell as I go along street if I do, or, how the folk at New guinie do?

Dec 14th

My aunt says that till I come out of an egregious fit of laughterre that is apt to sieze me & the violence of which I am at this present under, neither English sense nor anything rational may be expected of me.

Jany 4th [1772]

I was dress'd in my yellow coat, my black bib & apron, my pompedore shoes, the cap my aunt Storer sometime since presented me with (blue ribbins on it) & a very handsome loket in the shape of a hart she gave me—the paste pin my Hond Papa presented me with in my cap, My new cloak & bonnet on, my pompedore gloves, &c. &c.

And I would tell you, that *for the first time, they all lik'd my dress very much.* My cloak & bonnett are really very handsome & so they had need be. For they cost an amasing sight of money, not quite £45 tho' Aunt Suky said, that she suppos'd Aunt Deming would be frightened out of her Wits at the money it cost. I have got *one* covering, by the cost, that is genteel, & I like it much myself.

Jany 11th

I have attended my schools every day this week except wednesday afternoon. I made a setting up visit to aunt Suky, & was dress'd just as I was to go to the ball. It cost me a pistoreen [a Spanish coin worth about 17 cents] to nurse Eton for tow cakes, which I took care to eat before I paid for them. I heard Mr Thacher preach our Lecture last evening Heb. II:3. I remember a great deal of the sermon, but a'nt time to put it down.

It is one year last Sepr since he was ordain'd & he will be 20 years of age next May if he lives so long.

I forgot that the weather want fit for me to go to school last thursday. I work'd at home.

Jany 17th

I told you the 27th Ult that I was going to a constitation with Miss Soley. I have now the pleasure to give you the result, viz. a very genteel well regulated assembly which we had at Mr Soley's last evening, miss Soley being mistress of the ceremony. Mrs Soley desired me to assist Miss Hannah in making out a list of guests which I did some time since, I wrote all the invitation cards.

There was a large company assembled in a handsome, large, upper room in the new end of the house. We had two fiddles, & I had the honor to open the diversion of the evening in a minuet with miss Soley.

Our treat was nuts, raisins, Cakes, Wine, punch, hot & cold, all in great plenty. We had a very agreeable evening from 5 to 10 o'clock. For variety we woo'd a widow, hunted the whistle, threaded the needle, & while the company was collecting, we diverted ourselves with playing of pawns.

I was dress'd in my yellow coat, black bib & apron, black feathers on my head, my paste comb, & all my paste garnet, marqueset & jet pins, together with my silver plume—my loket, rings, black collar round my neck, black mitts & 2 or 3 yards of blue ribbin (black & blue is high tast), striped tucker and ruffles (not my best) & my silk shoes compleated my dress.

Feb. 9th

I am disabled by a whitloe on my fourth finger & something like one on my middle finger from using my own pen; but altho' my right hand is in bondage, my left is free; & my aunt says, it will be a nice oppertunity if I do but improve it to perfect myself in learning to spin flax. I am pleased with the proposal & am at this present exerting myself for this purpose. I hope, when two or at most three months are past, to give you occular demonstration of my proficiency in this art, as well as several others.

My fingers are not the only part of me that has suffer'd with sores within this fortnight, for I have had an ugly great boil upon my right hip & about a dozen small ones—I am at present swathed hip & thigh, as Samson smote the Philistines, but my soreness is near over. My aunt thought it highly proper to give me some cooling physick, so last tuesday I took 1-2 oz Globe Salt (a disagreeable potion) & kept chamber. Since which, there has been no new eruption, & a great alteration for the better in those I had before.

I have read my bible to my aunt this morning (as is the daily custom) & sometimes I read other books to her. So you may perceive, I *have the use of my tongue.*

Feb. 10th

This day I paid my respects to Master Holbrook [her writing teacher] after a week's absence, my finger is still in limbo as you may see by the writeing.

I have not paid my compliments to Madam Smith [her sewing teacher] for, altho' I can drive the goos quill a bit, I cannot so well manage the needle. So I will lay my hand to the distaff, as the virtuous woman did of old.

Feb. 12th

Yesterday afternoon I spent at unkle Joshuas. Aunt Green gave me a plaister for my fingure that has near cur'd it, but I have a new boil, which is under poultice, & tomorrow I am to undergo another seasoning with globe Salt.

Feb. 13th

Everybody says that this is a bitter cold day, but I know nothing about it but hearsay for I am in Aunt's chamber (which is very warm always) with a nice fire, a stove, sitting in Aunt's easy chair, with a tall three leaved screen at my back, & I am very comfortable.

I took my second (& I hope my last) potion of Globe salts this morning.

Valentine day

My cousin Sally reeled off a 10 knot skane of yarn today. My valentine [first man she saw that day] was an old country plow-jogger. The yarn was of my spinning. Aunt says it will do for filling. Aunt also says niece is a whimsical child.

Feb. 21

My Grandmamma sent Miss Deming, Miss Winslow & I one eighth of a Dollar a piece for a New Years gift. I have made the purchase I told you of a few pages agone, that is, last Thursday I purchas'd with my aunt Deming's leave, a very beautiful white feather hat, that is, the out side, which is a bit of white hollond with the feathers sew'd on in a most curious manner, white & unsullyed as the falling snow; this hat I have long been saving my money to procure. As I am (as we say) a daughter of liberty I chuse to wear as much of our own manufactory as pocible. But my aunt says, I have wrote this account very badly.

Feb. 22d

I have spun 30 knots of linning yarn, and (partly) new footed a pair of stockings for Lucinda, read a part of the pilgrim's progress, coppied part of my text journal (that if I live a few years longer, I may be able to understand it, for aunt sais, that to her the contents as I first mark'd them, were an impenetrable secret). Play'd some, tuck'd a great deal (Aunt Deming says it is very true) laugh'd enough, & I tell aunt it is all human *nature*, if not human reason.

March 9th

After being confined a week, I rode yesterday afternoon to & from meeting in Mr Soley's chaise. I got no cold and am pretty well today. This has been a very snowy day today. Any body that sees this may see that I have wrote nonsense but Aunt says, I have been a very good girl to day about my work however—I think this day's work may be called a piece meal for in the first place I sew'd on the bosom of unkle's shirt, mended two pair of gloves, mended for the wash two handkerchiefs (one cambrick), sewed on half a border of a long apron of aunt's, read part of XXIst chapter of Exodus, & a story in the Mother's gift.

It's now tea time—as soon as that is over, I shall spend the rest of the evening in reading to my aunt. It is near candle lighting.

March 11

Boast not thyself of tomorrow; for thou knowest not what a day may bring forth. Thus king Solomon inspired by the Holy Ghost, cautions, Pro. XXVII: I. My aunt says, this is a most necessary lesson to be learn'd & laid up in the heart. I am quite of her mind. I have met with a disappointment to day, & aunt says, I may look for them every day—we live in a changing world—in scripture call'd a veil of tears.

March 19

By the way, I must inform you (pray dont let my Honor'd papa see this), that yesterday I put on No I of my new shifts, & indeed it is very comfortable. It is long since I had a shift to my back. I dont know if I ever had till now—It seem'd so strange too, to have any linen below my waist.

My aunt Deming says it is a grief to her that I don't always write as well as I can, I can write pretily.

March 28

This minute I have receiv'd my queen's night cap from Miss Caty Vans. [A seamstress. The "queen's night cap" was large and full, with plaited ruffles. Martha Washington wears one in her portraits.] We like it. Aunt says that if the materials it is made of were more substantial than gauze it might serve occationally to hold any thing mesur'd by an ½ peck, but it is just as it should be, & very decent, & she wishes my writing was *as* decent. But I got into one of my frolicks upon sight of the Cap.

April 9

My Papa inform'd me in his last letter that he had done me the honor to read my journals & that he approv'd of some part of them, I suppose he means that he likes some parts better than other, indeed it would be wonderful, as aunt says, if a gentleman of papa's understanding & judgment cou'd be highly entertain'd with every little saying or observation that came from a girl of my years.

June 4

Today the whole regiment muster'd upon the common. We went into King street where we saw all of them prettily exercise & fire.

September 22

The king's coronation day. In the evening I went to King Street to see the fireworks.

May 25 [1772]

After making a short visit with my Aunt at Mrs. Green's, over the way, yesterday towards evening I took a walk with cousin Sally to see the good folks in Sudbury Street & found them all well. I had my HEDDUS roll on [a fashionable and elaborate hair-do which consisted of a roll sometimes weighing as much as fourteen ounces]. Aunt Storer said it ought to be made less. Aunt Deming said it ought not to be made at all. It makes my head itch, & ach, & burn like anything Mamma.

This famous roll is not made wholly of a red Cow Tail, but is a mixture of that & horsehair (very course) & a little human hair of yellow hue, that I suppose was taken out of the back part of an old wig. But D—— made it all carded together and twisted up.

When it first came home, aunt put it on [me] & my new cap on it, she then took up her apron & mesur'd me, & from the roots of my hair on my forehead to the top of my notions, I mesur'd above an inch longer than I did downwards from the roots of my hair to the end of my chin. Nothing renders a young person more amiable than virtue & modesty without the help of fals hair.

Now all this mamma, I have just been reading over to my aunt. She is pleas'd with my description & grave (half grave) improvement, & hopes a little fals English will not spoil the whole with Mamma. Rome was not built in a day.

1773: *THE FACTS OF GRACIOUS LIVING IN VIRGINIA*

A FEW GENERATIONS after the failure of the Jamestown colony, which was finally burned and abandoned in 1698, Virginia planters began realizing in earnest the dream of riches that had been denied to the first comers. Among those who prospered were the Carters of the lush tidewater area. When young Philip Fithian came down from his home in New Jersey to fulfill a year's engagement as tutor to the seven children of Robert Carter, he found an estate of 330,000 acres, 500 slaves, and a great mansion a-glitter with light and a-tinkle with the music of the dance. At Nomini Hall the Carters lived graciously and hospitably. Fithian was deeply impressed—until he learned the formula underlying this opulence, as disclosed in his diary.

"Good God! Are these Christians?"
PHILIP VICKERS FITHIAN (1747-1776)

Monday 13 [December 1773]

The people are extremely hospitable, and very polite, both of which are most certainly universal Characteristics of the Gentlemen in Virginia—some swear bitterly, but the practice seems to be generally disapproved—I have heard that this Country is notorious for Gaming; however this be, I have not seen a Pack of Cards, nor a Die, since I left home, nor gaming nor Betting of any kind except at the Richmond Race. Almost every Gentleman of Condition keeps a Chariot and Four; many drive with six Horses.

Saturday 18

When the candles were lighted we all repaired, for the last minute, into the dancing Room; first each couple danced a Minuet; then all joined as before in the country Dances, these continued till half after Seven when we played *Button,* to get Pauns for Redemption; here I could join with them, and indeed it was carried on with sprightliness, and Decency; in the course of redeeming my Pauns, I had several Kisses of the Ladies! —Early in the Evening came colonel Philip Lee, in a traveling Chariot from Williamsburg—Half after eight we were rung into Supper; The room looked luminous and splendid; four very large candles burning on the table where we supp'd, three others in different parts of the Room; a gay, sociable Assembly, & four well instructed waiters!

Thursday 23

This Evening, after I had dismiss'd the Children, & was sitting in the School-Room cracking Nuts, none present but Mr. Carter's Clerk, a civil, inoffensive, agreeable young Man, who acts both in the character of a Clerk and Steward, when the Woman who makes my Bed asked me for the key of my Room, and on seeing the young Man, sitting with me, she told him that her Mistress had this afternoon given orders that their [the slaves'] Allowance of Meat should be given out to them to-morrow.

She left us; I then asked the young man what their allowance is? He told me that excepting some favourites about the table, their weekly allowance is a peck of Corn, & a pound of Meat a Head! And Mr. Carter is allow'd by all, & from what I have already seen of others, I make no Doubt at all but he is, by far the most humane to his Slaves of any in these parts! Good God! are these Christians?

When I am on the Subject, I will relate further, what I heard Mr George Lees Overseer, one Morgan, say the other day that he himself had often done to Negroes, and found it useful; He said that whipping of any kind does them no good, for they will laugh at your greatest Severity; But he told us he had invented two things, and by several experiments had proved their success.

For Sulleness, Obstinacy, or Idleness, says he, Take a Negro, strip him, tie him fast to a post; take then a sharp Curry-Comb, & curry him severely til he is well scrap'd; & call a Boy with some dry Hay, and make the Boy rub him down for several Minutes, then salt him, & unlose him. He will attend to his Business (said the inhuman Infidel) afterwards!

But savage Cruelty does not exceed His next diabolical Invention—To get a Secret from a Negro, says he, take the following Method—Lay upon your Floor a large thick plank, having a peg about eighteen Inches long, of hard wood, & very Sharp, on the upper end, fixed fast in the plank—then strip the Negro, tie the Cord to a staple in the Ceiling, so that his foot may just rest on the sharpened Peg, then turn him briskly around, and you would laugh (said our informer) at the Dexterity of the Negro, while he was releiving his Feet on the sharpen'd Peg!

Philip Fithian died three years later while serving as a chaplain in the Revolutionary Army. When it was learned in March 1776, that British General Howe was withdrawing his forces from Boston, Washington gave orders to rush every available man to New York to ward off the attack he anticipated there. Thousands of Yankee soldiers were sent into the city and its environs. With little knowledge or facilities to cope with the dangers of overcrowding, the American Army lost more men to sickness than to British bullets.

Fithian was quartered at Red Hook, in the western part of Brooklyn. For the whole regiment there were only one house and a barn, "so that many chose rather to sleep in their blankets on the ground." Later they were given tents but these didn't help much against the cold and wet. Fithian gave up his place in the house to another man. "Our tent is not very pleasant," he wrote in September. "But we must grow inured to these necessary hardships."

Three weeks later he was dead of dysentery.

── ★

1774:   FARE OVERSEAS: FOUR YEARS
OF A MAN'S LIFE

── ☆

MANY AN early immigrant to America, lacking the price of the passage, borrowed it by pledging or "indenting" his services for a period of years, sometimes four, sometimes more. These indentures could be bought and sold like any other commodity. At the beginning of the eighteenth century there were more indentured white servants in Virginia than there were Negro slaves.

John Harrower left his wife and children in Scotland to seek a spot in the world where life wasn't so hard. His diary is one of the few existing records of this curious form of semislavery.

"Like a parcell of Sheep . . ."
JOHN HARROWER

Jan. 23d [1774]

> Now in London in a garret room I am,
> here friendless and forsaken;
> But from the Lord my help will come
> Who trusts in him are not mistaken.

26th

This day I being reduced to the last shilling I had was obliged to engage to go to Virginia for four years as a schoolmaster for Bedd, Board, washing and five pounds during the whole time. I have also wrote my wife this day a particular accot. of everything that has happened to me since I left her untill this date; at 3 pm this day I went on board the *Snow Planter,* Capt. Bowers Comr., for Virginia, now lying at Ratcliff Cross, and imediately as I came On bd. I recd. my Hammock and Bedding.

February 6th

At 7 am got under way with a fair wind and at 11 am came to an anchor off Gravesend and immediately the Mercht. came onboard and a Doctor and clerk with him and while the Clerk was filling up the Indentures the doctor search'd every servt. to see that they were sound. Seventy-five were Intend [indentured] to Capt. Bowres for four years.

7th

This forenoon imployed in getting in provisions and water. At 4 pm put a servant ashore extreamly bade in a fever, and then got undere saile for Virginia.

13th

At noon the Indented servants was like to mutiny against the Capt. for putting them to Allowance of bread and Mate [a beverage resembling tea], but it was soon quelled.

March 13th

At 3 pm there was two servants put in Irons for wanting other than what was served. But they were soon released on their asking pardon and promising to behave better.

28th

At 7 am the Pillot wegh'd Anchor and wrought the ship up to Hampton Roads [Virginia] where we came to an Anchor at 10 am.

May 2d

At 2 pm the Capt. Carried 5 servts ashore to Hampton in order to sell their Indentures, But returned again at Midnight without selling any more but one Boat Builder.

10th

Got to our Moorings at 6 pm at the Town of Fredericksburgh.

11th

At night one Daniel Turner a serv. returned onbd from Liberty so drunk that he abused the Capt. and chief Mate and Boatswan to a very high degree, which made to be horse whipt put in Irons and thumb screwed. On houre afterward he was unthumbscrewed, taken out of the Irons, but then he was handcuffed, and gagged all night.

16th

This day severall came onbd. to purchase servts. Indentures and among them there was two Soul drivers. They are men who make it their business to go onbd. all ships who have either Servants or Convicts and buy sometimes the whole and sometimes a parcell of them as they can agree, and then they drive them through the Country like a parcell of Sheep untill they can sell them to advantage, but all went away without buying any.

17th

This day Mr. Anderson the Mercht. sent for me into the cabin and verry genteely told me that on my recomendations he would do his out-most to get me settled as a Clerk or bookeeper if not as a schoolmaster which last he told me he thought wou'd turn out more to my advantage upon being settled in a good famely.

18th

One Cooper, one Blacksmith and one Shoemaker were settled with Masters this day.

21st

This day one Mr. Cowly a man 'twixt fifty and sixty years of age, a servt., also three sons of his, their ages from eight to fourteen, were all settled with one McDonald a Scotchman.

23d

This morning a great number of Gentlemen and Ladies driving into Town it being an annuall Fair day and tomorrow the day of the Horse races. At 11 am Mr. Anderson begged me to settle as a schoolmaster with a friend of his one Colonel Daingerfield and told me he was to be in Town tomorrow, or perhaps tonight, and how soon he came he shou'd aquant me. At same time all the rest of the servants were ordered ashore to a tent at Frederickbg. and severall of their Indentures were then sold. About 4 pm I was brought to Colonel Daingerfield, when we imediately agreed and my Indenture for 4 years was then delivered him and he was to send for me the next day.

1777:   A BRITISH LOTHARIO GOES HOME

IN A sleepy hamlet in Derbyshire, England, Nicholas Cresswell helped manage his father's sheep farm. The job palled and parental rule was stern. At 24 Nicholas cut loose to seek his fortune in America. But the venture was ill-timed. Daring, resourceful, full of charm, Nicholas was every inch an Englishman, and he found himself among a people seething with defiance of his government. Three years he waited for the tide of rebellion to ebb. Instead it boiled up into war. Finally, "because they call me a tory" and because they suspected him of being a spy—which he wasn't—he went home. Not only was America a land of opportunity; here were adventure, romance, and other makings of a sprightly diary which is still in possession of Nicholas' descendants in Derbyshire.

"Squaws are very necessary . . ."
NICHOLAS CRESSWELL (1750-1804)

Friday, January 6, 1775, Alexandria, Virginia

Mr. Kirk and Mr. Sydebottom have got shares in a large purchase of land in the Illinois Country and have offered me one third part of it at the first cost if I choose to accept it, or they will give me 5000 acres to go and take a view of it for them and to be left to my choice, to take the third of their share at my return. They tell me their influence is pretty considerable with a great many of the other proprietors and they will endeavour to get me a Surveyor's Warrant. As I am not much acquainted with the situation of this country they have give me their Deeds to peruse, and I am to give them my answer in a week.

Indian Country, Saturday, August 26th

Set out early this morning, traveled very hard till noon, when we passed through the largest Plum Tree Thicket I ever saw. I believe it was a mile long, nothing but the Plum and Cherry Trees. Killed a Rattlesnake.

Just as the Sun went down we stopped to get our Supper on some Dewberries (a small berry something like a Gooseberry). Mr. Anderson had gone before me and said he would ride on about two miles to a small run where he intended to camp, as soon as I had got sufficient. I mounted my Horse and followed him till I came to a place where the road forked. I took the path that I supposed he had gone and rode till it began to be dark, when I imagined myself to be wrong, and there was not a possibility of my finding my way back in the night.

Determined to stay where I was till morning, I had no sooner alighted from my horse, but I discovered the glimmering of a fire about 400 yards from me. This rejoiced me exceedingly, supposing it was Mr. Anderson. When I got there, to my great disappointment and surprise found three Indian women and a little boy. I believe they were as much surprised as I was. None of them could speak English and I could not speak Indian. I alighted and marked the path I had come and that I had left, on the ground with the end of my stick, made a small channel in the earth which I poured full of water, laid some fire by the side of it, and then laid myself down by the side of the fire, repeating the name of Anderson which I soon understood they knew.

The youngest Girl immediately unsaddled my Horse, unstrapped the Belt, Hoppled him, and turned him out, then spread my blankets at the fire and made signs for me to sit down. The Oldest made me a little hash of dried Venison and Bear's Oil, which eat very well, but neither Bread or Salt.

After supper they made signs I must go to sleep. Then they held a consultation for some time which made me very uneasy, the two eldest women and the boy laid down on the opposite side of the fire and some distance away.

The youngest (she who had taken so much pains with my horse) came and placed herself very near me. I began to think she had some amorous design upon me. In about half an hour she began to creep nearer me and pull my Blanket. I found what she wanted and lifted it up. She was young, handsome, and healthy. Fine regular features and fine eyes, had she not painted them with Red before she came to bed.

Sunday, August 27

This morning my Bedfellow went into the woods and caught her horse and mine, saddled them, put my Blanket on the saddle, and prepared everything ready, seemingly with a great deal of good nature. Absolutely refused my assistance. The Old Woman got me some dried venison for Breakfast.

When I took my leave returned the thanks as well as I could by signs. My Bedfellow was my guide and conducted me through the woods, where there were no signs of a road or without my knowing with certainty whither I was going.

She often mentioned John Anderson and talked a great deal in Indian. I attempted to speak Indian, which diverted her exceedingly. In about an hour she brought me to Mr. Anderson's camp, who had been very uneasy at my absence and employed an Indian to seek me. I gave my Dulcinea a match coat, with which she seemed very well pleased.

Proceeded on our journey and about noon got to an Indian Town called Wale-hack-tap-poke, or the Town with a good Spring, on the Banks of the Muskinghan and inhabited by Dellawar Indians. Christianized under the Moravian Sect. It is a pretty town consisting of about sixty houses, and is built of logs and covered with Clapboards.

Wednesday, August 30th

My bedfellow very fond of me this morning and wants to go with me. Find I must often meet with such encounters as these if I do not take a Squaw to myself. She is young and sprightly, tolerably handsome, and can speak a little English. Agreed to take her. She saddled her horse and went with us to New Hundy about 3 miles off, where she had several relations who made me very welcome to such as they had. From there to Coashoskin, where we lodged in my Squaw's Brother's, made me a compliment of a young wolf but I could not take it with me.

Friday, September 1st

At Coashoskin Mr. Anderson found his horse. Saw an Indian Dance in which I bore a part. Painted by my Squaw in the most elegant manner. Divested of all my clothes except my calico short breech-clout, leggings, and Mockesons. A fire was made which we danced round with little order, whooping and hallooing in a most frightful manner. I was but a novice at the diversion and by endeavouring to act as they did, made them a great deal of sport and ingratiated me much in their esteem.

This is the most violent exercise to the adepts in the art I ever saw. No regular figure, but violent distortion of features, writhing and twisting the body in the most uncouth and antic postures imaginable. Their music is an old Keg with one head knocked out and covered with a skin and beat with sticks which regulates their times.

The men have strings of Deer's hoofs tied round their ankles and knees, and gourds with shot and pebblestones in them in their hands which they continually rattle.

The women have Morris bells or Thimbles with holes in the bottom and strung upon a leather thong tied round their ankles, knees and waists. The jingling of these Bells and Thimbles, the rattling of the Deer's hoofs and gourds, beating of the drum and kettle, with the horrid yells of the Indians, render it the most unharmonious concert, that human idea can possible concieve. It is a favorite diversion, in which I am informed they spend a great part of their time in Winter.

Saw an Indian Conjuror dressed in a Coat of Bearskin with a Visor mask made of wood, frightful enough to scare the Devil. The Indians believe in conjuration and Witchcraft.

Left the Town, went about 2 miles. Camped by the side of a run. A young Indian boy, son of one Baubee, a Frenchman, came after us and insists on going with us to Fort Pitt. Find myself unwell this evening, pains in my head and back. Nancy [his name for his "bedfellow"] seems very uneasy about my welfare. Afraid of the Ague.

Tuesday, Sept. 12th

Our Squaws are very necessary, fetching our horses to the Camp and saddling them, making our fire at night and cooking our victuals, and every other thing they think will please us. Traveled over several barren mountains, some of them produce great plenty of wild Grapes. Lodged in an old Indian Camp. Bad water.

Wednesday, Sept. 20th

N. [Nancy] uneasy at parting with me. Obliged to promise her to return in two moons.

Saturday, September 30th

Went over the River and bought a Porcupine Skin of an Indian. It is something like our Hedgehog at home, only the quills are longer, the Indians dye them of various colours and work them on their trinkets. N. very uneasy, she weeps plentifully. I am unhappy that this honest creature has taken such a fancy to me.

Monday, Oct. 2nd

Settling my affairs with Mr. John Anderson, who has behaved more like a Father than a common acquaintance. Made him a compliment of my silver buckles and agreed to keep up a correspondence. Parting with N. was the most affecting thing I have ever experienced since I left home. The poor creature wept most plentifully. However base it may appear to conscientious people, it is absolutely necessary to take a temporary wife if they have to travel amongst the Indians. Left Fort Pitt.

August 31, 1776

Waited on Mr. Francis Lightfoot Lee and Mr. Thos. Jefferson with my letters, who behaved with the greatest complaisance and politeness, proffered to get me a pass from the Congress by virtue of which I may travel where I please.

April 13, 1777

I am happy and unhappy to leave this Country. I am happy in leaving a Country where almost everyone looks upon me with an eye of jealousy and distrust and where I have lived for a long time in a miserable and perpetual state of suspense.

All these summed together are not half so grating as the thought of returning to my native country in poverty and rags and then be obliged to beg like a criminal to get my debts paid which I am now contracting. The bitter reflections, taunts, and sarcasms of my friends will be submitted then upon my conduct. No matter whether it be right or wrong, I have been unfortunate, therefore everyone thinks they have a right to find fault with my proceedings. I believe their reproofs will be tinctured with a good deal of acrimony, as I took this journey entirely against their consent.

I might turn soldier and get a good living by cutting the throats of my Friends and countrymen. But this my plaguing, squeamish conscience forbids and I must, and will, obey its dictates or I am forever miserable.

July 9

Went to New York in the boat with Colnl. Cotton to purchase stores for the voyage. Dined with Captn. Scott on board the Brig *Harriet*. Drunk tea at Mrs. Bennett's with Major L's Lady and several other ladies. After Tea I waited upon Mrs. L to her lodgings.

She insisted upon me staying to sup and spend the evening with her and I did not need much solicitation to spend an evening with a handsome and polite young lady.

After supper and a cheerful glass of good wine we entered into a very agreeable *tete-a-tete* and then O! Matrimony, matrimony, thou coverest more female frailties than charity does sin! Nicholas, if ever thou sinned religiously in thy life, it has been this time.

This kind, affable, and most obliging lady in public was most rigidly religious. At Mrs. Bennett's she had treated the character of a poor lady in the neighbourhood, who had made a slip and unfortunately been caught in the fact, in a most barbarous and cruel manner. She ran over the Scriptures from Genesis to Revelations. In that strain she continued till after supper and then I soon found she was made of warm flesh and blood.

Recommend me to the Girl who has compassion upon those who in an unguarded moment may have given way to the weakness of human nature, with honesty enough in her composition to confess that she has all her natural feelings, but philosophy enough to deny improper requests with good humor and with little levity or wantonness in her disposition (perfection I do not expect to find in a human being).

Such a one I think would make me very happy, but rather than I would marry one who overacts the part of religion, pretends to so much chastity and is in appearances a stiff, prudish, formal lump of mortality, I would go into Lapland and be dry nurse to a bear.

On board the Brig, July 10

This morning returned to the Ship. Ruminating upon last night's adventure most of this day, it will not bear reflection.

July 11

A note, or rather billet-doux from Mrs. L. I am determined to go. It would be ungrateful to refuse so kind an offer. My Shipmates begin to smell a Rat, I am rated by them confoundedly, but let them go on. While I fare well at no expense to myself I care not. Should like her better if she were not so religious.

II.

THE

NEW

NATION

ENGLAND CAME out of the French and Indian War in 1763 with all of America east of the Mississippi under her belt. It was a big bite, and the rough American frontier proved a highly indigestible morsel. Besides, hard times were spreading deep unrest among working people throughout the colonies. Many were moving west. Then, to keep down trouble with the Indians, a royal proclamation forbade the colonials to settle across the frontier. This unrealistic ruling came in a long series of oppressive acts—the hated Writs of Assistance (blanket search warrants), the Sugar Act, Townshend Acts (duties on imported manufactures), Stamp Act, Mutiny Act, the moving of British troops into Boston, and the symbolic tax on tea.

All these abrasions, plus the fiery agitation against them by drumbeaters like Sam Adams, helped speed uprising. But the American Revolution was more than any one of them and more than the sum of them. There was revolt in the very soul of a people against inequity wherever they found it—and that included home—but it was outwardly and consciously directed against the British.

It was in this setting that, five years before the "shot heard round the world" at Concord, a Boston street urchin threw a snowball. His target was a British guard at the customhouse. There were shouts. Other redcoats came on the double. A crowd gathered, spoiling for riot. Mistaking a bystander's cry for an order from their officers, the soldiers fired into the mob. Five men were killed, four outright. The British regretted the error; but to 25,000 townspeople and 2,000,000 colonists, it was dramatized as the "Boston Massacre."

Deacon John Tudor, a leading townsman, had no sympathy for mobs. But his diary, in which is given one of the fullest contemporary accounts of the shooting, shows how deeply even the soberest Bostonians were moved.

"A most horrid murder was committed . . ."
JOHN TUDOR (1709?-1795)

March [1770]

On Monday Evening the 5th current, a few Minutes after 9 O'Clock a most horrid murder was committed in King Street before the Customhouse [corner of State Street and Change Avenue] by 8 or 9 Soldiers under the Command of Capt Thos Preston drawn from the Main Guard on the South side of the Townhouse.

March 5th

This unhappy affair began by Some Boys & young fellows throwing Snow Balls at the sentry placed at the Customhouse Door. On which 8 or 9 Soldiers Came to his assistance. Soon after a Number of people collected, when the Capt commanded the Soldiers to fire, which they did and 3 Men were Kil'd on the Spot & several Mortaly Wounded.

The Capt soon drew off his Soldiers up to the Main Guard, or the Consequencis mite have been terable, for on the Guns fiering the people were alarm'd & set the Bells a Ringing as if for Fire, which drew Multitudes to the place of action.

Leut. Governor Hutchinson, who was commander in Chefe, was sent for & Came to the Council Chamber, were som of the Magistrates attended. The Governor desired the Multitude about 10 O'Clock to sepperat & go home peaceable & he would do all in his power that Justice shold be don &c.

The 29 Regiment being then under Arms on the south side of the Townhouse, but the people insisted that the Soldiers should be ordered to their Barracks 1st before they would sepperat, Which being don the people sepperated about I O'Clock.

Capt Preston was taken up by a warrent given to the high Sherif by Justice Dania [Richard Dana, a Boston lawyer] & Tudor [the diarist] and came under Examination about 2 O'clock & we sent him to Goal soon after 3, having Evidence sufficient to committ him, on his ordering the soldiers to fire: so aboute 4 O'clock the Town became quiet.

The next forenoon the 8 Soldiers that fired on the inhabitants was allso sent to Goal.

Tuesday A.M. the inhabitants mett at Faneuil Hall & after som pertinant speches, chose a Committee of 15 Gentlemn to waite on the Leut. Governor in Council to request the immediate removeal of the Troops.

The message was in these Words. That it is the unanimous opinion of this Meeting that the inhabitants & soldiery can no longer live together in safety; that nothing can Ratonaly be expected to restore the peace of the Town & prevent Blood & Carnage but the removal of the Troops: and that we most fervently pray his Honor that his power & influance may be exerted for their instant removal.

His Honor's Reply was. Gentlmen I am extreemly sorry for the unhappy difference & expecially of the last Evening, & Signifieng that it was not in his power to remove the Troops &c &c.

March 6

The Above Reply was not satisfactory to the Inhabitants, as but one Rigiment should be removed to the Castle Barracks.

In the afternoon the Town Adjourned to Dr Sewill's Meetinghouse, [Old South Church] not larg enough to hold the people, their being at least 3,000, som supos'd near 4,000, when they chose a Committee to waite on the Leut. Governor to let him & the Council Know that nothing less will satisfy the people than a total & immediate removal of the Troops oute of the Town.

His Honor laid before the Council the Vote of the Town. The Council thereon expressed themselves to be unanimously of opinion that it was absolutely Necessary for his Majesty service, the good order of the Town &c that the Troops Should be immeditly removed oute of the Town.

His Honor communicated this advice of the Council to Col Dalrymple & desir'd he would order the Troops down to Castle William. After the Col. had seen the Vote of the Council He gave his Word & honor to the Town's Committee that both the Rigiments should be remov'd without delay.

The Com^te return'd to the Town Meeting & Mr Hancock, chairman of the Com^te Read their Report as above, which was Received with a shoute & clap of hands, which made the Meetinghouse Ring: So the Meeting was dessolved and a great number of Gentlemen appear'd to Watch the Center of the Town & the prison, which continued for 11 Nights and all was quiet again, as the Soldiers was all moved off to the Castle.

March 8

Agreeable to a general request of the Inhabitants, were follow'd to the Grave in succession the 4 Bodies of Saml Gray, Saml Maverick, James Caldwell & Crispus Attucks, the unhappy Victims who fell in the Bloody Massacre.

On this sorrowfull Occasion most of the shops & stores in Town were shut, all the Bells were order'd to toll a solom peal in Boston, Charleston, Cambridge & Roxbery.

The several Hearses forming a junction in King Street, the Theatre of that inhuman Tradgedy, proceeded from thence thro' the main street, lengthened by an immence Concourse of people, So numerous as to be obliged to follow in Ranks of 4 & 6 abreast and brought up by a long Train of Carriages.

The sorrow Visible in the Countenances, together with the peculiar solemnity, Surpass description; it was suppos'd that the Spectators & those that follow'd the corps amounted to 15000, som supposed 20,000.

Note: Capt Preston was tried for his Life on the affare of the above Octob^r 24 1770. The Trial lasted 5 Days, but the Jury brought him in not Guilty.

John Adams, later to become one of the solidest exponents of independence, served in this trial as attorney for the defense of Captain Preston.

★

1775:   HOW PATRICK HENRY MADE THE

SPEECH

☆

HIS NEIGHBORS in Hanover County, Virginia, doubted if young Patrick Henry would ever come to much. The boy had plenty of big talk in him, but he was shy on work. Twice he failed as storekeeper, once as farmer. Then, going into law, he found himself. He was only 27 when, as attorney for a poor parson who was suing for his pay, he made a speech that endeared him far and wide to the common folk of Virginia.

In 1765 he was elected to the legislature. There he fought for the right of the colonies to make their own laws, independently of England, and ended a powerful exhortation with the line that has since been quoted and adapted without end: "If this be treason, make the most of it!"

For the next ten years he helped to fire the forge of American liberty. As a member of the Continental Congress, he was a leader of the "radicals." In 1775, while other men were still holding back and seeking remaining avenues to peace, Henry made an impassioned appeal to the Virginia convention to arm the militia. His conclusion of that speech, ". . . give me liberty or give me death!" has become a by-phrase of American history, but there is only one eyewitness account of the dramatic manner of his delivery. The picture is preserved and relayed to us through this diary.

"Give me liberty or give me death!"

WILLIAM WINSTAN FONTAINE

(born about 1835)

Saturday, February 19th, 1859, Williamsburg

I met an old friend of my father, Mr. Hugh Blair Grigsby, the Historian of the Virginia Convention of 1776. He introduced me to Ex-President John Tyler, as the great-grandson of Patrick Henry. Mr. Tyler asked me if I was the son of Colonel Wm. Spotswood Fontaine, of King William; and on my saying yes, he invited me to call at his room, as he wished to tell me something about Colonel Henry, which, perhaps, I had never heard. I accompanied Mr. Tyler to the house where he was staying.

On reaching his room, he said that his father had given him the following account of Colonel Henry's address delivered in March, 1775, in which he said: "Give me liberty, or give me death."

There were, said Mr. Tyler, many in the Convention who opposed the resolution of Mr. Henry to organize the militia and put the colony into a posture of defense; these gentlemen by some were unjustly called submissionists.

Mr. Henry was holding a paper-cutter in his right hand; and when he came to that part of his speech in which he said, "I know not what course others may take," he cast a glance at these gentlemen, and bending his head forward, and with stooping shoulders, and with submissive expression of countenance, he crossed his wrists, as if to be bound; then suddenly straightening up, a bold, resolute purpose of soul flashed over his countenance and then, struggling as if trying to burst his bonds, his voice swelled out in boldest, vibrant tone; "Give me liberty!" Then wrenching his hands apart, and raising aloft his hand with the clenched paper-cutter, he exclaimed: "Or give me death!" And aimed at his breast, as with a dagger, and dropped to his seat.

The effect, continued Mr. Tyler, was electrical. There was more in the tones and the action than in the words. The house was still as death. The members felt as if they had witnessed a real tragedy of the noblest days of the Roman Republic.

Then the members started from their seats. "The cry 'to arms' seemed to quiver on every lip and gleam in every eye."

I told Mr. Tyler that I had the very paper-cutter which the orator held in his hand, and afterwards gave to his daughter.

1775:   WASHINGTON IS NAMED TO COMMAND

HISTORY RECORDS *the election of George Washington to head the American Army as unanimous. But a unanimous election does not always reflect unanimity of opinion. There were several aspirants to the job, and they had friends who believed them to be better men for it than Washington. Behind the decision of the Continental Congress at Philadelphia in June 1775 is a story of personal ambitions, sectional rivalries, and political wirepulling. It is hinted at in the diary of John Adams, who became second President.*

"We were embarrassed . . ."
JOHN ADAMS (1735-1826)

[Undated]

The New England army investing Boston, the New England legislatures, congresses and conventions, and the whole body of the people were left without munitions of war, without arms, clothing, pay, or even countenance and encouragement. Every post brought me letters from my friends, urging in pathetic terms the impossibility of keeping their men together without the assistance of Congress.

I was urging all these things, but we were embarrassed with more than one difficulty, not only with the party in favor of the petition to the King and the party who were jealous of independence, but a third party, which was a Southern party, against a Northern, and a jealousy against a New England army under the command of a New England general.

Whether this jealousy was sincere, or whether it was mere pride and a haughty ambition of furnishing a Southern general to command the Northern army, the intention was very visible to me that Colonel Washington was their object, and so many of our staunchest men were in the plan that we could carry nothing without conceding to it.

Another embarrassment, which was never publicly known, and which was carefully concealed by those who knew it, the Massachusetts and other New England delegates were divided. Mr. Hancock and Mr. Cushing hung back; Mr. Paine did not come forward, and even Mr. Samuel Adams was irresolute.

Mr. Hancock himself had an ambition to be appointed commander-in-chief. Whether he thought an election a compliment due to him and intended to have the honor of declining it, or whether he would have accepted it, I know not. To the compliment he had some pretensions, for, at that time, his exertions, sacrifices, and general merits in the cause of his country had been incomparably greater than those of Colonel Washington.

But the delicacy of his health, and his entire want of experience in actual service, though an excellent militia officer, were decisive objections to him in my mind.

In canvassing this subject, out of doors, I found too that even among the delegates of Virginia there were difficulties. The apostolical reasonings among themselves, which should be greatest, were not less energetic among the saints of the ancient dominion than they were among us of New England.

In several conversations, I found more than one very cool about the appointment of Washington, and particularly Mr. Pendleton was very clear and full against it. Full of anxieties concerning these confusions, and apprehending daily that we should hear very distressing news from Boston, I walked with Mr. Samuel Adams in the Statehouse yard, for a little exercise and fresh air, before the hour of Congress, and there represented to him the various dangers that surrounded us.

He agreed to them all, but said, "What shall we do?" I answered him, that he knew I had taken great pains to get our colleagues to agree upon some plan, that we might be unanimous; but he knew that they would pledge themselves to nothing; but I was determined to take a step which should compel them and all the other members of Congress to declare themselves for or against something.

"I am determined this morning to make a direct motion that Congress should adopt the army before Boston and appoint Colonel Washington commander of it."

Mr. Adams seemed to think very seriously of it but said nothing.

Accordingly, when Congress had assembled, I rose in my place, and in as short a speech as the subject would admit, represented the state of the Colonies, the uncertainty in the minds of the people, their great expectation and anxiety, the distresses of the army, the danger of its dissolution, the difficulty of collecting another, and the probability that the British army would take advantage of our delays, march out of Boston, and spread desolation as far as they could go.

I concluded with a motion, in form, that Congress would adopt the army at Cambridge, and appoint a general; that though this was not the proper time to nominate a general, yet, as I had reason to believe, this was a point of the greatest difficulty, I had no hesitation to declare that I had but one gentleman in my mind for that important command, and that was a gentleman from Virginia who was among us and very well known to all of us, a gentleman whose skill and experience as an officer, whose independent fortune, great talents, and excellent universal character, would command the approbation of all Americans, and unite the cordial exertions of all the Colonies better than any other person in the Union.

Mr. Washington, who happened to sit near the door, as soon as he heard me allude to him, from his usual modesty, darted into the library-room, Mr. Hancock—who was our President which gave me an opportunity to observe his countenance while I was speaking on the state of the Colonies, the army at Cambridge, and the enemy—heard me with visible pleasure; but when I came to describe Washington for the commander, I never remarked a more sudden and striking change of countenance. Mortification and resentment were expressed as forcibly as his face could exhibit them.

Mr. Samuel Adams seconded the motion, and that did not soften the President's physiognomy at all. The subject came under debate, and several gentlemen declared themselves against the appointment of Mr. Washington, not on account of any personal objection against him, but because the army were all from New England, had a general of their own, appeared to be satisfied with him, and had proved themselves able to imprison the British army in Boston, which was all they expected or desired at that time.

Mr. Pendleton, of Virginia, Mr. Sherman, of Connecticut, were very explicit in declaring their opinion; Mr. Cushing and several others more faintly expressed their opposition and their fears of discontents in the army and in New England. Mr. Paine expressed a great opinion of General Ward and a strong friendship for him, having been his classmate at college, or at least his contemporary; but gave no opinion upon the question.

The subject was postponed to a future date. In the meantime, pains were taken out of doors to obtain a unanimity, and the voices were generally so clearly in favor of Washington, that the dissentient members were persuaded to withdraw their opposition, and Mr. Washington was nominated, I believe, by Mr. Thomas Johnson, of Maryland, unanimously elected, and the army adopted.

1776: THE REDCOATS END A VISIT TO
BOSTON

AFTER NEARLY A YEAR of holding Boston and trying to crush the revolution at the "hub," the British found themselves in trouble and had to switch their whole strategy. They had lost heavily in men and morale at Bunker Hill; they had come up against tough, dedicated harassment from every direction by the Yankees; and now Washington, in a besieging maneuver, had an important contingent of their army nearly hemmed in. In March 1776, General Howe gave the order to evacuate the town.

The diary of Deacon Timothy Newell, one of Boston's selectmen, depicts the British occupation as it looked to those who had to endure it.

"A siege of unparrolled wickedness . . ."
TIMOTHY NEWELL (1718-1799)

April 19th [1775]

At 10 of the clock last night, the King's Troops marched out from the bottom of the Common, crossed over to Phips farm, marched on till they came to Lexington, where they fired and killed *eight* of our people and proceeded to Concord where they were sent to distroy Magazines of Provisions.

After doing some damage by spiking up and destroying cannon &c they halted and were soon attacked by our People, upon which they retreated, being about 800 Men commanded by Major Pitcairn of the Marines. Upon their retreat they were joined by a Brigade commanded by Lord Piercy who continued the retreat and were beat by our People from thence down to Charlestown, which fight was continued till sunset.

Our People behaved with the utmost bravery—about thirty of our People were killed and wounded, and fifty of the Kings Troops. The next day they came over to Boston. (Double the number of Kings Troops to our People were in action that day) and blessed be God who most remarkably appear in our favor.

June 17

The Provincials last night began an Entrenchment upon Charlestown (Bunker's Hill) before sunrise. The *Tartar* Man of War and the battery from Corps hill began a cannonade about 2 o clock AM.

Gen¹ Howe with Cannon and three thousand Men landed on Charlestown point and marched up to the Redoubt after a great slaughter of Thirteen-hundred and twenty-five of the Regulars killed and wounded—one hundred twelve officers included—and of Provincials fifty killed and one hundred and eighty wounded and missing.

The Garrison gave way—A constant fire from the Men of War &c. all the night following—only three from one company and fourteen from another of the Regulars brought off.

September 27

These several days past have been tolerably quiet. The works at the Southward go on. Yesterday the *Cerberus* Man of war arrived in seven weeks from London—brings advices of coercive measures by Administration—5 Regiments—one thousand Marines, another Admiral with a fleet of men of war &c. and General Gage called home.

October 10

A negro man wheeling a barrow load of —— in the Streets, the Provost came up to him and caned him to a great degree. The negro conscious of his innocence asked him why he did so—he was told it was for wheeling his barrow at the side of the street and not in the middle. General Gage sailed this day for London and left several thousand Inhabitants in town who are suffering the want of Bread and every necessary of life.

13th [October]

Colonel Birch of the Lighthorse Dragoons went to view our Meeting-house which was destined for a Riding School for the Dragoons. It was designed to clear the floor, to put two feet of tan [bark] covered with horse dung to make it elastic. But when it was considered that the Pillars must be taken away,—so that the Pillars saved us.

25th

Several nights past the whole army was ordered not to undress—the cannon all loaded with grape shot from a full apprehension the Provincials would make an attack upon the town. The streets paraded all night by the Light Horse.

27th

The spacious *Old South Meeting house* taken possession of by the Light horse 17th Regiment of Dragoons commanded by Lieut. Colo. Samuel Birch. The Pulpit, pews and seats, all cut to pieces and carried off in the most savage manner as can be expressed and destined for a riding school. The beautiful carved pew with the silk furniture of Deacon Hubbard's was taken down by an officer and made a hog sty. The above was effected by the solicitation of General Burgoyne.

November 16th

Many people turned out of their houses for the troops to enter. The keys of our Meeting house cellars demanded of me by Major Sheriff by order of General Howe. Houses, fences, trees &c pulled down and carried off for fuel. My wharf and barn pulled down by order of General Robinson.

19th

A large ship arrived from Plymouth in England with almost every kind of provisions dead and alive, hogs, sheep, fowls, ducks, eggs, mince meat &c. Ginger-bread &c. *Memorandum* 25 Regiments of Kings Troops now in this distressed town.

2nd March, 1776

Saturday night half past 11, began from the Country, Bombardment and cannonade which continued on both sides till morning and then ceased and began again *Lord's day* evening at 9 and so continued all the night, and tho' several houses were damaged and persons in great danger, myself *one*, no one as I can learn received any hurt.

6th March

This day the utmost distress and anxiety is among the Refugees and associators [Tories] &c. orders being given to embark the Kings Troops and evacuate the Town. Blessed be God our redemption draws nigh.

7th Thursday

The last night and this day the Troops are very busily employed in removing their stores, cannon, ammunition—some of the Dragoons on board, the Refugees &c, in shipping their goods &c.

March 8th

The town all hurry and commotion, the troops with the Refugees and Tories embarking.

9th Saturday

Saturday evening 9 o'clock began the cannonade, which continued the whole night—One 18 pound shot came thro' our house, another thro' the fence and summer house into the Garden, and several shot thro' my neighbor's Houses.

12th

This day and night quiet—the Soldiers shut up in their Barracks, except some who were about, plundering. The wind high at N.W. The Inhabitants greatly distressed thro' fear the Town would be set on fire by the Soldiers.

13th Wednesday

The inhabitants in the utmost distress, thro' fear of the Town being destroyed by the Soldiers, a party of New York Carpenters with axes going thro' the town breaking open houses. Soldiers and sailors plundering of houses, shops, warehouses—Sugar and Salt &c. thrown into the River, which was greatly covered with hogsheads, barrels of flour, house furniture, carts, trucks &c.—One Person suffered four thousand pounds sterling, by his shipping being cut to pieces—Another five thousand pounds sterling, in salt wantonly thrown into the river.

14th March Thursday

The same as above except somewhat restrained by the General [Howe].

15th Friday

The General sent to the Selectmen and desired their immediate attendance, which we did accordingly. It was to acquaint us that as he was about retreating from the Town, his advice was for all the Inhabitants to keep in their houses and tho' his orders were to injure no person, he could not be answerable for any irregularities of his troops, that in case the King's troops met with any obstruction in their retreat he should set fire to the Town, which he wished to avoid—That he thought it his duty to destroy much of the property in the Town to prevent it being useful to the support of the Rebel army.

The General further said to us, that whoever had suffered in this respect (who were not Rebels) it was probable upon application to Government, they would be considered—that Letters had passed between him and *Mr.* Washington. That he had wrote to him in the style of *Mr* Washington. He observed the direction of our Letters to him was—To *his excellency General Washington,* which he did not approve and whatever Intelligence had been given to the Rebels, tho' in his letters to him, he did not charge him with being a Rebel.

He further said he had nothing against the Select-men, which if he had he should certainly have taken notice of it—The General told us the Troops would embark this day and was told by General Robertson it would be by three o clock.

The Regiments all mustered, some of them marched down to the wharf. Guards and Chevaux De Freze [spiked barriers] were placed in the main streets and wharves in order to secure the retreat of Out Centinels. Several of the principle streets through which they were to pass were filled with Hogsheads filled with horse-dung, large limbs of trees from the Mall to prevent a pursuit of the Continental Army. They manifestly appeared to be fearful of an attack. The wind proved unfavorable, prevented their embarking. They returned to their quarters. Soon after several houses were on fire. The night passed tolerably quiet.

16th Saturday

Great distress, plundering &c.

17th Lord's day

This morning at 3 o'clock, the troops began to move—Guard Chevaux de Freze, Crow feet strewed in the streets to prevent being pursued. They all embarked at about 9 o clock and the whole fleet came to sail. Every vessel which they did not carry off, they rendered unfit for use. Not even a boat left to cross the River.

Thus was this unhappy distressed town (thro' a manifest interposition of divine providence) relieved from a set of men, whose unparrolled wickedness, profanity, debauchery, and cruelty, is inexpressible, enduring a siege from the 19th April, 1775 to the 17th March 1776.

1776: TORY ON A TIGHTROPE

CONSIDERING HOW MANY Americans were against it, the winning of this country's independence was a phenomenon which historians can explain only by citing the commanding genius of George Washington, the assistance given by the French, and an uncommon lack of brilliance in the British Parliament. Be that as it may, the truth was that at least one-third of the American colonists were opposed to revolution. In Pennsylvania the proportion was more than half.

The rich and influential Allen family of Philadelphia, like most of their kind, sided with the King. Before the war, when Britain began cracking down on the Colonial economy, Chief Justice William Allen and his four sons had warmly espoused the American cause. The old judge was credited with influencing a year's delay in passage of the Stamp Act.

However, it was one thing to oppose British measures which hurt American businessmen, and which were later repealed; but to turn on the Royal Government for the sake of a principle declaring all men to be created equal—that was something else. The Allens made known that if the colonies went to war for independence, they would not go along.

Accordingly, in December 1776, John and Andrew Allen, the latter a member of the Continental Congress, put themselves under protection of the British Army. William, another brother, resigned his lieutenant-colonelcy in a Pennsylvania regiment and went over to the British.

James, richest of all the Allens, was a leading lawyer in Philadelphia. In 1776 he was sent to the Assembly from Northampton County. Few writers have stripped their souls more completely naked than he manages to do in this diary of a reluctant dissenter.

"America has seen its best days."
JAMES ALLEN (1742-1778)

July 26 [1775]

The Congress is now sitting here and have just published their Declaration & address to the inhabitants of Great Britain. Hitherto our arms have been successful; but God knows what will be the event of this war, as there seems to be a thorough determination on both sides to prosecute it. Many thinking people believe America has seen its best days.

The inconveniences are already sensibly felt; Debts as yet are paid & suits commenced, but it cannot last long; as people already plead it is no longer useful, I shall suffer considerably. My last year's profits were £600 & this year would have increased.

We have no hopes but that the struggle will be soon over: if it continues, America is ruined whoever gets the better. We however keep up our spirits & gloomy as things appear, prefer our situation to a mean acquiescence. It is a great and glorious cause. The Eyes of Europe are upon us; if we fall, Liberty no longer continues an inhabitant of this Globe.

Oct. 14

Last Thursday & the preceding Tuesday I appeared in Battalion in my uniform, as a private man in Captn Shees company. I have no opinion that this association will be very useful in defending the City. My Inducement principally to join them is that a man is suspected who does not; & I chuse to have a Musket on my shoulders, to be on a par with them; & I believe discreet people mixing with them, may keep them in order. With all my zeal for the great cause we are engaged in, I frequently cry out—Dreadful times!

May 15, 1776

Yesterday the Resolve of Congress was read by Bradford at the Coffeehouse [proposing to the colonies the establishment of new forms of government]. One man only Huzzaad; in general it was ill received. We stared at each other. My feelings of indignation were strong, but it was necessary to be mute. I am very obnoxious to the independants; having openly declared my aversion to their principles & had one or two disputes at the coffee house with them.

June 16

This day I set off with my family for Northampton, [near Philadelphia] with the Chariot, Phaeton, and Sulky. I have met the Assembly & sat from 20th May to this time & have been very active in opposing Independence & change of Government; but the tide is too strong.

Jany. 25, 1777

A long interval in my Diary to fill up.

Having let my house with a great part of my Furniture at £150 pr Anm. and left Phila which from the current of Politics, began to grow disagreeable; I thought myself happy in having so good a Retreat in Northampton County.

I went to Fort Lee commanded by our old Acquaintance Gen¹ Ewing, with whom I dined, & same day crossed the River to Head Quarters. Gen¹ Washington received me with the utmost politeness; I loged with him.

During October & November I remained at Trout-hall a calm spectator of the civil War, but occasionally gave great offence to the violent whigs in Northampton by entertaining the regular officers, our prisoners, & was often threatened on that account.

December produced Events that have given me great uneasiness. A persecution of Tories (under which name is included every one disinclined to independance tho' ever so warm a friend to constitutional liberty and the old cause) began; houses were broken open, people imprison'd without any colour of authority by private persons, & a list of 200 disaffected persons made out, who were to be seized, imprisoned & sent off to North Carolina; in which list, it was said, our whole family was set down; My Brothers under this dreadful apprehension fled from Philadª to Union, where I went over to them. Soon after, against my Judgmt, they all went to Trenton, & claimed protection from Gen¹ Howe's [British] army.

Thursday 19 Decʳ 1776 at 7 o'clock A.M. my house was surrounded by a Guard of Soldiers with fixed Bayonets; I got up & when I came down stairs the officer who was at the front door produced a Warrant from the Council of Safety to seize me & bring me before them.

I accordingly went to Philadª & appeared before them, & opened the scene by saying, that they had drawn me from my retirement unexpectedly; Mr Owen Biddle then said, that they had received accounts of the unwillingness of the Militia of Northampton County to march, that they knew my influence and property there, & were afraid of my being the cause of it, & added that my brothers being gone over to the enemy the publick would expect that I should be put up on my parole & hoped I wou'd have no Objection to stay within six miles of Philad[a].

I told them that my political principles were well known, to be unfriendly to the present views of Independance. I had not interfered in publick matters further than in confidential conversations with my friends & I wished always to remain so during the present unhappy war. In the afternoon they produced a certificate, which they hoped I would not object to; wherein they set forth, my brother's departure, & the backwardness of our Militia as reasons for sending for me, that I had given them satisfaction respecting my prudent conduct, that my conduct did not appear unfriendly to the cause of Liberty, nor inconsistent with the character of a Gentleman; & I in return pledged my honor verbally not to say or do any thing injurious to the present cause of America. So we parted amicably, as we began, with great politeness on both sides.

This disagreeable business over I spent five or six days in Philad[a] & near it with great pleasure at being in company with my relations and friends after so long absence.

Philad[a] seemed almost deserted & resembled a Sunday in service time. The Quakers are almost the only people determined to remain there. They press all persons walking the streets to work in trenches surrounding the town; I was stopt & with difficulty got off by walking on and taking no notice of 'em.

Feby 17, 1777

My particular situation has been of late very uneasy, owing to the Battalion of Militia of this district assembling in the town of Northampton to the number of 600 men. I never knew how painful it is to be secluded from the free conversation of one's friends.

July 30

I have not been at Philadelphia these six weeks & tho' I long to see my friends there, do not think it prudent to venture.

Septr. 5

In short, this Country is agitated to its foundations, & will probably soon be overturned.

Octobr. 1

Many people who disapprove Independance have no other wish than to remain at peace, & secure their persons without influencing the minds of others.

This some of the members of Congress have acknowledged to be the temper of most of the disaffected Gentlemen of Philad[a] & yet they are sent into banishment to a remote part of the country, exposed to the insult of the rabble, wherever they go.

October 15

Gen[l] Washington has issued orders to take the blankets, shoes, stockings &c of private families for the use of the army. This together with the licentiousness, plundering, stealing & impressing of the military, will sink this country to perdition. Misery begins to wear her ghastliest form. It is impossible to endure it. Three fourths of my income arises from my estate in Philad[a], from which I am cut off. My tenants whose rents are due in sterling, often pay off arrears of six or seven years in continental money at the old Exchange, and yet I dare not object, tho' I am as much robbed of 5/6ths of my property, as if it was taken out of my Drawer.

2 November

This last fortnight has totally changed the face of things and shewes the uncertainty of war; the Whigs who a little while ago were ready to give all for lost now think their affairs never wore a better aspect. My situation continues as before living in perpetual fear of being robbed, plundered and insulted. I sincerely wish myself out of the country, till this convulsion is over, and if my wife & children go into Philad[a] as she is anxious to be with her parents, I will endeavour to get to Europe, where I will live for a while with great economy. Any situation is preferable to my present one.

18 January, 1778

Hard is the fate of those poor people, whose only crime is, thinking differently from their oppressors.

11th May

The military have lived a very gay life the whole winter, & many very expensive entertainments given, at most of which I have been.

15 July

A fatality seems to attend Great-Britain in all her operations. In the midst of this scene of politics & triumphs of Independancy, I have had my share of distress. As to myself I also took the Oath (abjuring the King & swearing allegiance to the mob-government of Pennsylvania & the united states to prevent the confiscation of property) but to my surprise am called upon in a proclamation of the executive Council to surrender myself and stand a trial for high Treason. I have accordingly given bail for my appearance; but am under no fear of consequences, as I came into Philad^a with the Gen¹ pass and have repeatedly applied for leave to return; so that it is one of those instances of private malice which influences our publick councils. My health is much impaired. The disorder appears to be a collection of wind in the upper part of the Chest. My whole income this year will not pay my taxes.

1776:   SERGEANT SMITH'S SUBVERSIVE
TURKEYS

HE WAS A SOLDIER in Washington's army. He came from Bristol, Rhode Island. After the crushing loss of Fort Washington, key to New York City, he went through the despairing retreat across New Jersey into Pennsylvania. Then he campaigned in Washington's brilliant counteroffensive in the closing days of 1776 at Trenton and Princeton. He knew well enough that he was fighting for liberty—his own and that of generations to come after—but his greater concern most of the time was necessarily where to get something to eat and a place to sleep; for he was cold and hungry and far from home, and many times his own countrymen turned him away from their doors.

"they was tryd By fire & Excuted . . ."
JOHN SMITH (latter half of eighteenth century)

The 28th [September 1776]

We march'd to Norwark thiss Day. The houses Being much Crouded we was obligd to teak Up our Quarters in an old shop amongst the Rubbish & about mid Night I was Awaked By something Puling me & a Voice Crying turn out Dam you, Look here see and Behold. I Looked & saw five fat Geese. Some was fit for the Cook. The others was a Dressing By the fire side & Some Good Potatoes for sauce for Goos that Came to our Loging. I Eat a hearty meal, Asking no Questions with the Rest of my Brother Soldiers who Seamed Hearty in the Cause of Liberty. By the Rhoad in the morning we Eat the fragments & Rested in our hut or Rather Den of Th——fs.

The 29th Day was Lords Day. We Keept Somthing Close, Being obligd to for it Raind some part of the Day. This morning Came in to the River of Norwark m^r william Brown of swansey [Swansea, Mass.] in a sloop Loaded with shugar & Rum, By whome we sent Letters home. This Evening our Visiting Rounds went out on a Patrole again & took Up a Sheep & two Large fat turkeys, not Being able to Give the Countersign, & Brought to our Castel, where they was tryd By fire & Excuted By the whole Division of the free Booters. Then whilst the feast was Geting Ready two of our Party went out & found a Boat & Crosed over the River to the other Side and found a Boat, a float Loaded with Oisters, out of which they took about two Bushels of her freight & Brought it over to our store.

After this I Lay Down & Sleep a Little But was soon Awaked By sombody Saying it is Ready, Uncle Smith, turn out. Which Call I soon obeyd & made an Exelent meal of soupe.

The Wind Blew N:E all Night. In Morning Arose Early. The Leiut & Ensign Came to see Us how we had faird. We took up the Rest of our fare, which was the two turkey Prisoners, out of their Confinment and Set them Befor them & Befor the whole Assembly Present to Be Examined further, & Behold they were spechless. Then we Consumed them Befor the sun arose Upon them.

Munday morning the 30th Day

We Loaded our Baggage again & set out on our way from our Den towards york. We Breakfasd on the Rhoad & Dined at Stamford. In the afternoon march'd from this town to Horse neck & Loged in the Meeting house.

In the morng October the first

It Raind a Little in the morning. But we set out again after Breakfast & Came to Rey [Rye, N.Y.] where we halted a Little & here I saw Capt Charles D wolf & Simon By whom I sent home a nother Letter & then put forward again & Came to New Rochel.

We over Run our Reconing & got Beyond any Loging & was obligd to Return Back about a mile & Loged in a toreys Barn on hay. About Break of Day Next morn I heard a Voice saying Look here Dam you, & Behold I saw a pal of milk that was milked from Cows Belonging to our Landlord, of which was made a Pot of good Chocolat for Breakfast. Here we Cleand our Arms & Drew provisions & marched about noon for Head Quarters at Harlem, & marching thro E. Chester over Kings Brig we arived about Sun Down at harlem the second of October, & General Washington sent some tents for us to Loge under for we Brought none with us from Newport for they was not made when we Came away. Dismisd our team & sent it home.

Saturday the 12th

We was alarm'd again on hearing that the Enemy was Landing at East Chester. The General orders us to Cook three Day Provision & to hold our selevs in Readiness at one munites notice. About 2000 Pensilvania troops was ordred to East Chester to Reenforce our troops at that Place & marchd this afternoon. Also several Regements Came Over from the Jersey side to Goe Also to that Place.

The 13th October

We all turnd out Under Arms Befor it was Day, Expecting the Enemy to Come out against Us. At 9 a Clock at Night the Seargeant Major of our Rege^t Ordred us to turn out all the fategue Party Belonging to our Respective Companies Under armes & we Did. They march'd to General washingtons Quarters [near present-day 161st Street, New York City] & were Dismisd. It was a Blunder made in the Date of the Orders By some Under Officer. They Returned all of them safe to their tents again in Peace & Rested.

Munday the 14th

Receivd Orders to march to East Chester.

In the Morning of the 15th

Being tusday & somthing Pleaseant, I walked out to see the Country & found Plenty of fruit, Aples & Peaches, & went as far as our Lower Lines & Saw the Enemy on frogs Point where they was at an house over a Creek A Little Beyond Musquet Shot of our Guard. One who Appeard Like an Officer Venturd Down to the Creek & was shot Down By one of our men & was Caried Up By them to the house.

Sunday 20th

In the morning a Seargent Belonging to our Party, Being out on a flank Guard, Discovered a party of Regulars about 3 Quarters of a mile from our main Body & was a Going to fire upon them on seeing But 2 of them at first. But about a Dozen more starting up, he put Back & Joind us at the Crotch of the Rhoad.

Last night a Party went Down to East Chester & took By strategem 14 Toreys & Brought them to Head Quarters to Gen Lee, 3 white men & one Black & 4 white women & one Black one & a Boy & Garle & a Relation of one that Came Down on a Visit out of the Country who was set at Liberty again. The other was confind & halters Put about their Necks to terefy them & to Deter others from Being Guilty of the Like. The misirable wretches was Caried to white Plains & Confind in the Prison Under the State house. This Evening the Col. Confind 9 Drumers & fifers for not attending their Duty Better & Releasd them again in the morn after that they Promisd to Doe Beter for the futur.

Munday 21st october

ToDay we heard that the Enemy had advanced as far as the Boston Post Rhd. In the Evening Capt Baley with his Party Went Down to the Enemys advancd Guard so near as to hear them talk & found them too warm for him. He Came away home with out meaking any Noise & Got to Camp about two in the morning.

The 22 Day

Amaziah Blackmore, a Seargeant, went to Eastchester amongst the Diserted houses to see what he Could Plunder. Was surrounded in the house with a Lieu^t & a fifir & was made Prisioner By about 30 Hesians & Plunderd of his Shoe & Knee Buckles & 18 Dollers in Paper money & Caried away with them By a file of men with their Swords, for they had no Other arms. He watchd an opertunity & Sprang from Betwen them & Kicked away his shoes that was Loose on his feet & Got Clear of them & Came into Camp again.

Last Night Capt Baley & Leiu^t Richmond went Down & plundred Some houses at E:Chester of household furniture to the Value of 4 hundred Dollers & one Colt which the Gen made a Present of to Capt Baley for his seervice don.

Wensday the 23^d

I heaving not much Business, I went out of the Camp with Searg^t Hearvy

& a Lad to teak a walk to Get, If I Could, somthing for my self, as most of the others had Done Befor, & we went over a hill about 2 Miles from our Camp & Going Down the hill I Espied a Number of Hesians in an Orchard Geting aples, which we took for our own Men. But seing one who was Close By the hill, on seeing us, stept Behind some Bushes that was By the Path, Gave us some Suspition of their Being Enemies. We turnd Back & Ran up the hill again for we had no arms with us, & as soon as we Got to the top of the hill we heard a Voley of small armes Beyond the orchard. An affray soon Began which Lasted about 2 houres.

We Killd 9 & took 2 Hesians Prisioners. One, we hear, was a major, & took his horse & 10 Gunies in Money. We had a Rifle man Killd & an Indian wounded in the action. The two Prisioners was Brought Befor Gen[ll] Lee. I made all the Expedition to Get home I was able for fear I should Come under Blame for Leaving the Camp as it was Against Gen[ll] orders to Crose over the River without a pass. I Got into Camp without Being Discoverd By any Body their.

The 25th

Wc halted about two miles from the white Plains & Posted our selves as a Picquet. We were 250 in Number. It was Very Cold Loging on the Grownd without tents & But Little fire.

The Next Morning Being the 28th of October

Early in the morning we had orders from our General to strike tents & Clear away for a Battle—the Enemy was Advancing towards us—which Order was Obeyd Emeadetly & Every man under Arms that was Able.

We Verey soon Began to Discover the Enemys Aproach By the feild Peces firing below & soon Appeard on the Plain the Light horse & a host of our Enimies that made a Verey ware Like Appearance.

Our Rege[t] Being Posted on an Emenance that over looked all the Plain from East to west N & South [Fort Washington] the Kings troops apeard & Gave us Battle & our troops Being Hearty Seconded their Motion & a Verey Blody Battle Commenc'd & Continiued for some time, & then our men Being Obligd to Quit their Posts as they was superiour in Numbers to us. I saw the wounded on the Rhoad Verey many, & from a Disserter we Learnd they Lost Between 3 & 4 hundred Killd & Wounded & we Lost as many.

By what I saw my self this Battle Lasted from 9 in the morning till Night, tho the hotest of the Battle on the hill was But about 20 or 30 munits.

Wensday

Was teaken up a foolish Rogue who was a going to the Enemy & was Brought here. I heard he was to Be hanged.

Next Day was tried two Prisoners at Capt Loring Pecks tent, one for horse stealing, the other for Stealing a gun & Cloths. The horse theif was whipt at Night 25 Lashes & sent about his Business.

The Next morning [December 5]

After we had all Eat our Brakfasts, Paked up our things, it Began to Rain, & after we had Paraded our men, all the Lame & Lasey & the Faint Hearted & all that had no shoes nor Clothes to Keep them warm was Drafted out to Be Left Be hind. We marched in the Rain to Kings ferey & Crosed over & march'd thro mud & water as far as haverstraw, about 3 miles from the ferey & halted where we Drew fresh Beef & flower & had no salt to Season it. We was Obligd to Lie on the Cold wet Ground all night. It Being a Verey Blustring night & our tents not Being Come, we was Obligd to meak Us huts with Rails & Coverd with Straw for Us to Sleep Under this Night.

[December 7]

Here at this place [Ramapo, N.Y.] we Stopt to Refresh our selves a Little About noon & the inhabitents Abusd us, Caling us Damd Rebels, & would not sell Us any thing for money. The Soldiers Killd their fowles & one Stole a hive of Bees at Noon Day & Caried it off with him.

8th

We marchd forward & Pasd thro Pomton Plains [N.J.] a fine Level Country. All the inhabitents were Dutch & Cheifly torys. We Loged in the woods where the water was scarce & mud Plenty. Went forward thro Hanover town, where we met a Gentleman from the westward who informd us that about 7 or Eight thousand Hesians And toreys had march'd from Brunswick to Cut us off from the main body of our army that was at trenton.

The 10th

We turnd out and after we had form'd our whole Division, march'd to Chatham. Here the houses was all full & we Loged in the woods this night, it Being a Verey Cold Loging Place.

The 11th

About Sun Set ariv'd at Morisstown & march'd out into the wood where

we Loged on a Verey high hill. The People here & at Chatham are English
& Verey Kind in a General way as any strangers Could be Expected.

The 13th

We Loaded our Baggage into the Waggons & Carts & Paraded in the
Rhoad. Here we Left our sick and about 11 oclock march'd forward. The
Snow Melting Made the traveling Exceding Bad, the Rhoads Being of a
Clay Kind, was Become Morter & many of our Soldiers had no shoes to
wair, was obligd to Lace on their feet the hide of the Cattle we had kill'd
the Day Befor. We march'd in this Pleight about 10 or 11 miles to a
township Called Bedminster where we was overteaken by Willm Bradford
who was Sent to stop us from Gene^ll Lee who had stoped Back about 5
miles at a Place he Design'd we Should halt this night. But our Officers
Leading us as if the Devil had Sent for them Caried Us thro thick & thin
Untill Dark.

We march'd into a wood on a hill Where we Pitch'd our tents & Drew
Provisions to Cook & Lay Down to Sleep at this wood.

Honey was Brought to our tent By one or two of our Company that was
out on a Patrole for somthing to Eate.

One of them went to Teak a pece of the Comb out of the hive was stung
in the Eye & to Be Reveng'd took the whole family of bees & Put them to
Death & shard the Spoil amongst Us.

The 14th

The whole Division marchd forward to Germantown & Logd in the
woods. This Days march was Exceding tirsom as the Road was full of
Stones & Verey mudy. We Crosed over one small River. Here the inhabitents Refus'd to Give us Straw to Lie on But we took what we wanted
from them.

The 16th

About Day Break the Adgutent Came & ordred our tents Struck, Saying
that the Enemy was a Coming after us & were Almost Round us. We were
oblig'd to thro away our Broth that we had made for our Breakfasts &
Load our Kittles into the waggons and march without Breakfast. This Day
I was sent forward to Get Something Hot for Breakfast for three Officers
for it was a Verey Cold Day.

I went to Every house in my way for 10 or 11 miles But Got none till
noon. Then we Came to Bethlehem to Mr Delers who gave Vitules to
Near 70 men, Officers & Soldiers, saying they had Rather we should have

it then the Enemy who was Expected their as soon as we had Crosed over Deleware.

They gave us Cyder & Aples as Long as they had any Left. Tho they Appeard to Be But Poor people, they refus'd to teak any Pay for what we had.

I Crosed over the ferey to Easton in the Evening & went to Several houses to Get Liberty to Lay By the fire But Could not & So was Oblig'd to Lay my self Down on the frozen Grownd & snow for we Could not Pitch our tent. The Ground was frose so hard we made a Little fire with Some Railes that we took, for their was no other wood here about to Be had. The ferey men was Oblig'd to work all night to Get our Baggage over the Deleware & all the Next Day, But Did not Get it all over untill the Day after.

Monday morning

Early turn'd out But Eat no Breakfast, having not thing But Bread & fresh beaf & no salt to season it, nor Could we Get any here. The inhabitents were all Dutch & not the Kindest in the world.

About noon the Quartermaster Got two Barrels of salt Pork that was teaken from the toreys the Day Befor over to the Jerseys & Deleiverd one Days Alowance to Us. Afterwards we went to seek for Quarters amongst the houses But had some Dificulty, their Being no Room for Us. Some Companies was Oblig'd to Lie out again on the Ground.

I had a fine warm Room with a Stove in it where our Company all Stoed in this night. This was the first house I Sleept in Since I Left Conecticut. Here we Cook'd all our Provisions that we had. Some two or three of the Company Sleept in the Kitchen, their Being no Rome in the Stove Rooms.

After the Dutchman & his frow had gone to sleep, went Down in the Selor & got some Cyder & Aples and Potatoes & held a feast this nit. In the morning the old woman, heaving Ocasion to Draw Cyder, missing the Aples & Cyder, made a Great Gabber about it But got no satisfaction for it, & some other of her Neighbours Lost their Bees that made the Honey, But Could not tell where to find them for they Swarm in the night And flew from their Quarters to ours where they had Care teaken of them.

The 18th

We march'd from Easton for Bethlehem in Pensilvania.

The 19th

We Pased thro Springfeild township & Pitched in the woods & Sleep on the frozen Ground. This was an Extream Cold night to be here.

The 20th

Arose By Day & Struck tents & Got Ready for to march & no Bread for Us yet. The Sun about an hour high, went forward to Buckinham township. This Day we Pased thro Plumton where some of the Soldiers were infor^d that a Rich Torey or two Lived.

They went to him to Get Somthing to Eat. He Refused to Give them any thing to Eat, Where upon they took what they Could find in his house to Eat & Drink & went their way, he heaving Plenty of Cyder & other Sort of Liquor & honey & Butter which they took away, & Destroy'd several hives of Bees for him Befor his face.

I could Get But one Drink of his Cyder. We went from this house 7 or 8 mile further & Pitched in the woods where two of the Pad Rounds went on Patrole & took 2 hives of Bees & two Geese & Brought to our tents. I was Called up to Eat some honey with them for my Cold, it Being Verey toothsom for that, & then turnd in again.

The 21st of December

We march'd from Buckinham township about 4 miles to a towns Ship Called Macksfeild where we Stay'd in the woods until night waiting for our Officers to Get us into houses which they Could not, they Being all teaken up here abouts. Then we Pitched tents & Drew Provisions & Cooked it all.

This Evening our Pad Rounds went off and took 29 fowles that had not Got the Countersign & Brought them here where they were secur'd. After that two more went off again to see what they Could see & in their way they Kill'd a turkey & hid it then went towards the house where a Gun went off at them & a white man on a white horse Chased them a Grat way. But By turning and twisting about, Got Clear from him & Got home By midnight & turnd in to Sleep in Peace.

The 23d

This Day I had a Pair of Stockings & shoes from the Col. Cost 19/& 6 pence. This was a Cold Day But Plesant.

December the 26th

News Came that General Washington had a Battle at Trenton with the Kings Troops or Hesians this morning & had teaken 9 or 10 hundred of them Prisoners & took their stores & Baggage & intirly Routed the whole Nest of them. This afternoon Mr. Bourn, our Quarter Master, went to

Look for Better Quarters for Us & Return'd after he had Provided an house about 4 mile from here towards Philedelphia.

We was ordred to Goe their this Night, But our Collonel thinking we should Be as Comfortable in our tents as we Could Be any wher, told us we may stay if we had a mind for to stay & Goe in the morning Early as Posible, & ordred us to turn out Early & Get our Breakfast in order to march.

Munday the 30th

In the Afternoon our Brigade was sent for into the feild where we Paraded Befor the General who was present with all the feild Officers & after meaking many fair promises to them he Begged them to tarey one month Longer in the Scervice & Almost Every man Consented to stay Longer who Received 10 Doler Bounty as soon as Signd their names.

Then the Genll with the soldiers gave three Huzzas, with Claping of hands for Joy amongst the Specttators, & as soon as that was over the Genell ordered us to heave a gill of Rum pr man & set out to trenton to acquaint Genll Washington with his Good success as he termd it to Meak his heart Glad Once more. We was Dismisd to Goe to our Quarters with great Applause, the inhabitents & others saying we had Done honour to our Country.

1778: JOHN PAUL JONES INVADES
GREAT BRITAIN

"IF YOU want a thing done, do it yourself."

So said Poor Richard (Benjamin Franklin) and so impressed was Captain John Paul Jones of the just-born U.S. Navy that he took it as his motto for life. More than a year before the battle in which, as captain of the little Bonhomme Richard he slugged it out with the Serapis and came off with two British men-o'-war in the bag and everlasting fame for himself, Jones decided to cross the Atlantic and twist the tail of the British lion in its own den—that is, stage a raid, by himself, against the British on British soil.

Not least among his reasons was the hope of raising American prestige in the eyes of France, then a most important potential ally whose navy later fulfilled a crucial role in the war.

In the spring of 1778, in the Ranger, Jones made an incredibly bold descent on the coast of Scotland and England, a venture that called for as much daring as any sea fight in his career. And the nerve and spunk of this tiny invasion did win the respect of the French.

Dr. Ezra Green, of Dover, New Hampshire, whose diary starts off this joint account, was ship's surgeon on the Ranger. Despite his association with Jones, he lived to be 101.

"I stood with a pistol in my hand . . ."
EZRA GREEN (1746-1847)

Wednesday, 16th [April 1778]

Made some part of Ireland in the morning suppos'd to be the high Land of Dungarvin.

Saturday, 19th

Made a warm attempt to take a Cutter mounting 8 Guns; she slipped through Our Fingers; had the Captain [Jones] have permitted the Marines to fire on them when they first came under our lee Quarter, might have taken Her with great Ease.

Sunday, 20th

In the morning near the Isle of Man sunk a Schooner laden with Barley & Oats about 60 Tons burthen from some part of Scotland; in the Evening sunk a sloop in ballast from Ireland.

Wednesday, 23rd

Weather somewhat more moderate & our people a little recruited, Our enterprising Capt. with about 30 men went on shore about 11 p.m. with a Design to fire the Town of Whitehaven.

Jones's account of this affair is as follows:

JOHN PAUL JONES (1747-1792)

The 22d introduced fair weather, though the three kingdoms were, as far as the eye could reach, covered with snow. I now resolved once more to attempt Whitehaven; but the wind became very light, so that the ship would not in proper time approach so near as I intended. At midnight I left the ship with two boats and thirty-one volunteers; when we reached the outer pier the day began to dawn; I would not, however, abandon my enterprise, but despatched one boat under the direction of Mr. Hill and Lieut. Wallingford, with the necessary combustibles to set fire to the shipping on the north side of the harbor, while I went with the other party to attempt the south side.

I was successful in scaling the walls and spiking up all the cannon in the first fort; finding the sentinels shut up in the guard house, they were secured without being hurt. Having fixed sentinels, I now took with me one man only (Mr. Green) and spiked up all the cannon in the southern fort, distant from the others a quarter of a mile.

On my returning from the business, I naturally expected to see the fire of the ships on the north side, as well as to find my own party with every thing in readiness to set fire to the shipping on the south; instead of this, I found the boat under the direction of Mr. Hill and Mr. Wallingford returned, and the party in some confusion, their light having burnt out at the instant when it became necessary.

By the strangest fatality, my own party were in the same situation, the candles being all burnt out. The day too came on apace, yet I would by no means retract while any hopes of success remained. Having again placed sentinels, a light was obtained at a house disjoined from the town, and a fire was kindled in the steerage of a large ship, which was surrounded by at least one hundred and fifty others, chiefly from two to four hundred tons burden, and lying side by side, aground unsurrounded by the water.

There were, besides, from seventy to a hundred large ships on the north arm of the harbor, aground clear of the water, and divided from the rest only by a stone pier of a ship's height.

I should have kindled fires in other places if the time had permitted; as it did not, our care was to prevent the one kindled from being easily extinguished. After some search, a barrel of tar was found, and poured into the flames, which now ascended from all the hatchways. The inhabitants began to appear in thousands, and individuals ran hastily towards us. I stood between them and the ship on fire, with a pistol in my hand, and ordered them to retire, which they did with precipitation.

The flames had already caught in the rigging, and began to ascend the mainmast; the sun was a full hour's march above the horizon, and as sleep no longer ruled the world, it was time to retire. We re-embarked without opposition, having released a number of prisoners, as our boats could not carry them.

After all my people had embarked, I stood upon the pier for a considerable space, yet no person advanced; I saw all the eminences around the town covered with the amazed inhabitants.

When we had rode to a considerable distance from the shore, the English began to run in vast numbers to their fort; their disappointments may easily be imagined when they found, I suppose, at least 30 heavy cannon rendered useless.

At length, however, they began to fire, having as I apprehend, either brought down ships' guns or used one or two cannon which lay on the beach at the foot of the walls, dismounted, and which had not been spiked.

They fired with no direction, and the shots falling short of the boats, instead of doing us any damage afforded some diversion: which my people could not help showing, by discharging their pistols &c. in return of the salute.

Had it been possible to have landed a few hours sooner, my success would have been complete. Not a single ship, out of more than 200, could possibly have escaped, and all the world would not have been able to save the town. What was done, however, is sufficient to show that not all their boasted navy can protect their own coasts; and that the scenes of distress which they have occasioned in America may soon be brought home to their own door.

One of my people was missing; and must, I fear, have fallen into the enemy's hands after our departure. I was pleased that in this business we neither killed nor wounded any person. I brought off three prisoners as a *sample*.

Green's diary resumes:

Thursday, 24th

After watching the night and all the morning till broad day light in expectation of seeing the smoke of the Town and Shipping (ascend as the smoke of a Furnace) began to fear that our People had fallen into the Enemy's Hands; however, about half an hour after sun rise we discovered two small Boats at a great Distance coming out of the River's mouth, and clouds of smoke rising from the Shipping, soon after we saw them fire on the Boats from the Shore, but most of the Cannon being spiked up by our people they could do but very little; the Boats were soon out of their Reach and came along-side with 3 prisoners for one left behind.

The same Day crossed over to the other side of the Bay to the Mull of Galway. Capt. Jones with Lt. Wallingford and about 12 Men went on shore [at St. Mary's Isle] with design to take Ld. Selkirk Prisoner. As he was not at Home and no man in the House, for the sake of his Lady & her Company they came off without doing any further Damage than plundering Him of Plate to the amount of (as near as I can judge) 160 lb. weight of Silver.

Jones later bought the plate from his men and sent it back to the Countess of Selkirk.

1781:   CORNWALLIS SURRENDERS AT
YORKTOWN

At Dobbs Ferry, General Washington was preparing to attack the British in New York City. But on August 14, 1781, a letter reached him that changed the whole course of the war. It was from the Marquis de Grasse, commander of the great French fleet, announcing that he would sail for Chesapeake Bay. At Yorktown, on the Virginia Peninsula, Cornwallis had dug in with 7,000 British regulars. De Grasse hoped to be of help in a joint assault by the Americans and French on Cornwallis.

Washington at once changed plans, rushed his army southward, and reuniting with the forces of Lafayette, skillfully maneuvered the entrapment from Williamsburg, twelve miles from Yorktown. Cornwallis' only hope was help from the nineteen British ships commanded by Admiral Graves. But De Grasse's powerful fleet of twenty-four ships, now at Cape Henry, prevented the British re-enforcement. On the morning of October 17 a drummer boy appeared on the parapet and beat the signal for a parley. The surrender that followed virtually ended the Revolutionary War.

Dr. James Thacher, a surgeon in the American infantry, was from Barnstable, on Cape Cod. His diary gives us this eyewitness picture of the surrender.

"The soldiers manifested a sullen temper . . ."
JAMES THACHER (1754-1844)

October 18 [1781]

At an early hour this forenoon General Washington communicated to Lord Cornwallis the general basis of the terms of capitulation, which he deemed admissable, and allowed two hours for his reply. Commissioners were soon afterward appointed to prepare the particular terms of agreement. The gentlemen appointed by General Washington are Colonel Laurens, one of his aide-de-camps, and Viscount Noailles of the French army. They have this day held an interview with the two British officers on the part of Lord Cornwallis; the terms of capitulation are settled, and being confirmed by the commanders of both armies, the royal troops are to march out tomorrow and surrender their arms.

19th

This is to us a most glorious day; but to the English, one of bitter chagrin and disappointment. Preparations are now making to receive as captives that vindictive, haughty commander and that vanquished army who, by their robberies and murders, have so long been a scourge to our brethren of the Southern states. Being on horseback, I anticipate a full share of satisfaction in viewing the various movements in the interesting scene.

At about twelve o'clock, the combined army was arranged and drawn up in two lines extending more than a mile in length. The Americans were drawn up in a line on the right side of the road, and the French occupied the left. At the head of the former, the great American commander, mounted on his noble courser, took his station, attended by his aides. At the head of the latter was posted the excellent Count Rochambeau and his suite. The French troops, in complete uniform, displayed a martial and noble appearance; their band of music, of which the timbrel [a small hand drum] formed a part, is a delightful novelty, and produced while marching to the ground a most enchanting effect.

The Americans, though not all in uniform, nor their dress so neat, yet exhibited an erect, soldierly air, and every countenance beamed with satisfaction and joy. The concourse of spectators from the country was prodigious—in point of numbers was probably equal to the military—but universal silence and order prevailed.

It was about two o'clock when the captive army advanced through the line formed for their reception. Every eye was prepared to gaze on Lord Cornwallis, the object of peculiar interest and solicitude, but he disappointed our anxious expectations; pretending indisposition, he made General O'Hara his substitute as the leader of his army. This officer was followed by the conquered troops in a slow and solemn step, with shoulder arms, colors cased, and drums beating a British march.

Having arrived at the head of the line, General O'Hara, elegantly mounted, advanced to his Excellency the Commander-in-Chief, taking off his hat, and apologized for the non-appearance of Earl Cornwallis.

With his usual dignity and politeness, his Excellency pointed to Major General Lincoln for directions, by whom the British army was conducted into a spacious field, where it was intended they should ground their arms. The royal troops, while marching through the line, formed by the allied army, exhibited a decent and neat appearance, as respects arms and clothing, for their commander opened his store, and directed every soldier to be furnished with a new suit complete, prior to the capitulation.

But in their line of march we remarked a disorderly and unsoldierly conduct, their step was irregular, and their ranks frequently broken. But it was in the field, when they came to the last act of the drama, that the spirit and pride of the British soldier was put to the severest test: here their mortification could not be concealed. Some of the platoon officers appeared to be exceedingly chagrined when given the word, "Ground arms," and I am a witness that they performed this duty in a very unofficerlike manner, and that many of the soldiers manifested a *sullen temper,* throwing their arms on the pile with violence, as if determined to render them useless. This irregularity, however, was checked by the authority of General Lincoln.

After having grounded their arms and divested themselves of their accoutrements, the captive troops were conducted back to Yorktown, and guarded by our troops till they could be removed to the place of their destination.

SCARCELY MENTIONED IN HISTORY, yet one of the most effective guardians of democracy during the formative months of the new government of the United States, was a peppery Pennsylvania farmer named William Maclay.

In the spring of 1789 the first Congress organized under the Constitution met in New York. There were many pressures to bedeck the government in the trappings of royalty. The issue was joined on the invention of titles. The House of Representatives sensed danger, and as one of its first acts, adopted a resolution against all fancy titles.

But the Senate, under the leadership of John Adams, seemed bemused by the glint of titular handles like "highness" and "majesty." An alert and gallant little group led by Maclay fought long and hard to put down this insidious toying with the political foppery of the Old World—and in the end won out.

When the new government was formed, Jefferson was in France. It had been in operation eleven months when he returned to America. Maclay's admirers hold that because of the political warfare he waged during that interval he deserves to be known as the real founder of the Democratic party. But if he was not the party's father, certainly he was its Dutch uncle. Because of the irreverent and often impish descriptions he gives of many of the founding fathers—including Washington, who found his first opposition in Maclay—the Senator's diary was kept under close wraps by his family for a hundred years.

Incidentally, this diary, running to more than 400 printed pages, is the only existing continuous report of the proceedings of the first United States Senate organized under the Constitution.

"... the servants, not the lords ..."
WILLIAM MACLAY (1737-1804)

April 25 [1789]

The Vice-President [John Adams] as usual, made us two or three speeches from the Chair. I will endeavor to recollect one of them. It was on the reading of a report which mentioned that the President should be received in the Senate chamber and proceed thence to the House of Representatives to be sworn:

"Gentlemen, I feel great difficulty how to act. I am Vice-President. In this I am nothing, but I may be everything. But I am president also of the Senate. When the President comes into the Senate, what shall I be? I can not be president then. No, gentlemen, I can not, I can not. I wish gentlemen to think what I shall be."

Here, as if oppressed with a sense of his distressed situation, he threw himself back in his chair. A solemn silence ensued. God forgive me, for it was involuntary, but the profane muscles of my face were in tune for laughter.

29th April

I have observed ever since we began to do business that a Jehu-like spirit has prevailed with a number of gentlemen, and with none more than with the member from the Ancient Dominion [Richard Henry Lee of Virginia] who is said to be a notorious anti-Federalist (a most expensive and enormous machine of a Federal Judiciary, pompous titles, strong efforts after religious distinctions, coercive laws for taking the oaths, etc.).

I have uniformly opposed, as far as I was able, everything of this kind, and I believe have sacrificed every chance of being popular and every grain of influence in the Senate by so doing. But be it so. I have the testimony of my own conscience that I am right. High-handed measures are at no time justifiable, but now they are highly impolitic. Never will I consent to straining the Constitution, nor never will I consent to the exercise of a doubtful power. We come here the servants, not the lords, of our constituents.

30th April

This is a great, important day. Goddess of etiquette, assist me while I describe it. The Senate stood adjourned to half after eleven o'clock. About ten dressed in my best clothes; went for Mr. [Robert] Morris' lodgings, but met his son, who told me that his father would not be in town until Saturday.

Turned into the Hall. The crowd already great. The Senate met. The Vice-President rose in the most solemn manner. This son of Adam seemed impressed with deeper gravity, yet what shall I think of him? He often, in the midst of his most important airs—I believe when he is at loss for expressions (and this he often is, wrapped up, I suppose, in the contemplation of his own importance) suffers an unmeaning kind of vacant laugh to escape him. This was the case to-day, and really to me bore the air of ridiculing the farce he was acting.

"Gentlemen, I wish for the direction of the Senate. The President will, I suppose, address the Congress. How shall I behave? How shall we receive it? Shall it be standing or sitting?"

Mr. Lee began with the House of Commons (as is usual with him), then the House of Lords, then the King, and then back again. The result of his information was that the Lords sat and the Commons stood on the delivery of the King's speech.

Mr. Izard got up and told how often he had been in the Houses of Parliament. He said a great deal of what he had seen there. He made, however, this sagacious discovery, that the Commons stood because they had no seats to sit on.

Mr. Carrol got up to declare that he thought it of no consequence how it was in Great Britain; they were no rule to us. But all at once the Secretary, who had been out, whispered to the Chair that the Clerk from the Representatives was at the door with a communication.

Gentlemen of the Senate, how shall he be received?

Mr. Lee brought the House of Commons before us again. He declared that the Clerk should not come within the bar of the House; that the proper mode was for the Sergeant-at-Arms, with the mace on his shoulder, to meet the Clerk at the door and receive his communication; we are not, however, provided for this ceremonious way of doing business, having neither mace nor sergeant.

Here we sat an hour and ten minutes before the President arrived.

The President advanced between the Senate and Representatives, bowing to each. He was placed in the chair by the Vice-President; the Senate with their president on the right, the Speaker and the Representatives on his left. The Vice-President rose and addressed a short sentence to him. The import of it was that he should now take the oath of office as President. He seemed to have forgot half what he was to say, for he made a dead pause and stood for some time, to appearance, in a vacant mood. He finished with a formal bow, and the President was conducted out of the middle window into the gallery, and the oath was administered by the Chancellor.

As the company returned into the Senate chamber, the President took the chair and the Senators and Representatives their seats. He rose, and all arose also, and addressed them.

This great man was agitated and embarrassed more than ever he was by the leveled cannon or pointed musket. He trembled, and several times could scarce make out to read, though it must be supposed he had often read it before. He put part of the fingers of his left hand into the side of what I think the tailors call the fall of the breeches, changing the paper into his right hand. After some time he then did the same with some of the fingers of his right hand.

When he came to the words *all the world,* he made a flourish with his right hand, which left rather an ungainly impression. I sincerely, for my part, wished all set ceremony in the hands of the dancing-masters, and that this first of men had read off his address in the plainest manner, without ever taking his eyes from the paper, for I felt hurt that he was not first in everything.

Our Vice-President called it *his most gracious speech.* I can not approve of this.

May 1st

Attended at the Hall at eleven. The prayers were over and the minutes reading. When we came to the minute of the speech it stood, *his most gracious speech.* I looked all around the Senate. Every countenance seemed to wear a blank. The Secretary was going on: I must speak or nobody would.

"Mr. President, we have lately had a hard struggle for our liberty against kingly authority. The minds of men are still heated: everything related to that species of government is odious to the people. The words prefixed to the President's speech are the same that are usually placed before the speech of his Britannic Majesty. I know they will give offense. I consider them as improper. I therefore move that they be struck out, and that it stand simply address or speech, as may be judged most suitable."

The question was put and carried for erasing the words.

That the motives of the actors in the late Revolution were various can not be doubted. The abolishing of royalty, the extinguishment of patronage and dependencies attached to that form of government were the exalted motives of many revolutionists, and these were the improvements meant by them to be made of the war which was forced on us by British aggression—in fine, the amelioration of government and bettering the condition of mankind.

These ends and none other were publicly avowed, and all our constitutions and public acts were formed in this spirit. Yet there were not wanting a party whose motives were different. They wished for the loaves and fishes of government, and cared for nothing else but a translation of the diadem and sceptre from London to Boston, New York, or Philadelphia; or, in other words, the creation of a new monarchy in America, and to form niches for themselves in the temple of royalty.

I will endeavor (as I have hitherto done) to use the resentment of the

Representatives to defeat Mr. Adams and others on the subject of titles. The pompous and lordly distinctions which the Senate have manifested a disposition to establish between the two Houses have nettled the Representatives, and this business of titles may be considered as part of the same tune. While we are debating on titles I will, through the Speaker, Mr. Muhlenberg, and other friends, get the idea suggested of answering the President's address without any title, in contempt of our deliberations, which still continue on that subject. This once effected, will confound the Senators completely, and establish a precedent they will not dare to violate.

May 2d

After Senate adjourned, I saw the Vice-President standing disengaged. I stepped up to him, asked for his health, and fell into commonplace chat. He is not well furnished with small talk, more than myself, and has a very silly kind of laugh.

May 4

I learned this day that the title selected from all the potentates of the earth for our President was to have been taken from Poland, viz., *Elective Majesty*. What a royal escape!

May 6th

I have been a bird alone. I have had to bear the chilling cold of the North and the intemperate warmth of the South, neither of which is favorable to the Middle State from which I come. Lee and Izard, hot as the burning sands of Carolina, hate us. Adams with all his frigid friends, cool and wary, bear us no good-will. I could not find a confidant in one of them, or say to my heart, "Here is the man I can trust."

What has been my conduct, then? Spirit of Rectitude, bear witness for me. Have I trimmed to one of them? Or have I withheld a single sentiment that my judgment approved of? I trust I have not. Regardless of consequences, with no eye to emolument, without desire for reappointment, I meant to act as if I were immortal, and yet I wish to give satisfaction and content to the State that sent me here. Never, however, will I purchase that with discontent in my own bosom, nor does my dear country demand such a sacrifice at my hands.

May 7th

The committee reported an answer to the President's speech. It was read. One part was objected to, which stated the United States to have been in *anarchy* and *confusion,* and the President stepping in and *rescuing* them. A very long debate.

I rose, more in consequence of a kind of determination that I have adopted of saying something every day than from any fondness of the subject. I thought the whole clause improper; that to state the whole Union as being in anarchy or under impending ruin was sanctifying the calumnies of our enemies, who had long labored in the foreign gazettes to represent us as a people void of government. It was fixing a stain on the annals of America for future historians would appeal to the transactions of this very day as a proof of our disordered circumstances. I therefore was against the whole clause.

It was reconsidered and amended, and afterward recommitted to the same committee.

May 8th

Mr. Elsworth moved for the report of the Joint Committee to be taken up on the subject of titles. Mr. Lee led the business. He took his old ground—all the world, civilized and savage, called for titles; that there must be something in human nature that occasioned this general consent; that, therefore, he conceived it was right. Here he began to enumerate many nations who gave titles—such as Venice, Genoa, and others.

Mr. Elsworth rose. He had a paper in his hat, which he looked constantly at. He repeated almost all that Mr. Lee had said, but got on the subject of kings—declared that the sentence in the primer of *fear God and honor the king* was of great importance; that kings were of divine appointment; that Saul, the head and shoulders taller than the rest of the people, was elected by God and annointed by his appointment.

I sat, after he had done, for a considerable time, to see if anybody would rise. At last I got up and first answered Lee as well as I could. I mentioned that within the space of twenty years back more light had been thrown on the subject of governments and on human affairs in general than for several generations before; that this light of knowledge had diminished the veneration for titles, and that mankind now considered themselves as little bound to imitate the follies of civilized nations as the brutalities of savages; that the abuse of power and the fear of bloody masters had extorted titles as well as adoration, in some instances from the trembling crowd; that the impression now on the minds of the citizens of these States was that of horror for kingly authority.

Izard got up. He dwelt almost entirely on the antiquity of kingly government. He could not, however, well get further back than Philip of Macedon. He seemed to have forgot both Homer and the Bible. He urged for something equivalent to nobility having been common among the Romans, for they had three names that seemed to answer to honorable, or something like it, before and something behind. He did not say Esquire.

Mr. Carrol rose and took my side of the question. He spoke against kings. Mr. Lee and Mr. Izard were both up again. Elsworth was up again. Langdon was up several times, but spoke short each time. Patterson was up, but there was no knowing which side he was of. Mr. Lee considered him as against him and answered him, but Patterson finally voted with Lee.

The Vice-President repeatedly helped the speakers for titles. Elsworth was enumerating how common the appellation of President was. The Vice-President put him in mind that there were presidents of fire companies and of a cricket club. Mr. Lee at another time was saying he believed some of the States authorized titles by their Constitutions. The Vice-President, from the chair, told him that Connecticut did it. At sundry other times he interfered in a like manner.

I had been frequently up to answer new points during the debate. I collected myself for a last effort. I read the clause in the Constitution against titles of nobility; showed that the spirit of it was against not only granting titles by Congress, but against the permission of foreign potentates granting *any titles whatever;* that as to kingly government, it was equally out of the question, as a republican government was guaranteed to every State in the Union; that they were both equally forbidden fruit of the Constitution.

I called the attention of the House to the consequences that were like to follow; that gentlemen seemed to court a rupture with the other House. The Representatives had adopted the report and were this day acting on it, or according to the spirit of the report. We were proposing a title. Our conduct would mark us to the world as actuated by the spirit of dissension, and the characters of the Houses would be as aristocratic and democratical.

The report [of the Committee on Titles] was, however, rejected. "Excellency" was moved for as a title by Mr. Izard. It was withdrawn by Mr. Izard, and "highness" with some prefatory word, proposed by Mr. Lee.

Now long harangues were made in favor of this title. "Elective" was placed before. It was insisted that such a dignified title would add greatly to the weight and authority of the Government both at home and abroad. I declared myself totally of a different opinion; that at present it was impossible to add to the respect entertained for George Washington; that if you gave him the title of any foreign prince or potentate, a belief would follow that the manners of that prince and his modes of government would be adopted by the President. (Mr. Lee had, just before I got up, read over a list of the titles of all the princes and potentates of the earth, marking where the word "highness" occurred. The Grand Turk had it, all the princes of Germany had it, sons and daughters of crown heads, etc.)

That particularly "elective highness," which sounded nearly like "electoral highness" would have a most ungrateful sound to many thousands of industrious citizens who had fled from German oppression; that "highness" was part of the title of a prince or princes of the blood, and was often given to dukes; that it was degrading our President to place him on a par with any prince of any blood in Europe, nor was there one of them that could enter the list of true glory with him.

But I will minute no more. The debate lasted till half after three o'clock, and it ended in appointing a committee to consider of a title to be given to the President. This whole silly business is the work of Mr. Adams and Mr. Lee; Izard follows Lee, and the New England men, who always herd together, follow Mr. Adams. I had, to be sure, the greatest share in this debate, and must now have completely sold (no, sold is a bad word, for I have got nothing for it) every particle of court favor, for a court our House seems determined on, and to run into all the fooleries, fopperies, fineries, and pomp of royal etiquette; and all this for Mr. Adams.

May 9th

Attended the Hall at ten o'clock to go on the Judicial Committee. Met many of the members. I know not the motive, but I never was received with more familiarity, not quite so much, before by the members. At length the committee came in and reported a title—*His Highness the President of the United States of America and Protector of the Rights of the Same.*

Up now got the Vice-President, and for forty minutes did he harangue us from the chair.

"Gentlemen, I must tell you that it is you and the President that have the making of titles. Suppose the President to have the appointment of Mr. Jefferson at the court of France. Mr. Jefferson is, in virtue of that appointment, the most illustrious, the most powerful, and what not. But the President must be himself something that includes all the dignities of the diplomatic corps and something greater still. What will the common people of foreign countries, what will the sailors and the soldiers say, 'George Washington, President of the United States'? They will despise him to all eternity. This is all nonsense to the philosopher, but so is all government whatsoever."

I rose. Mr. President, the Constitution of the United States has designated our Chief Magistrate by the appellation of the President of the

United States of America. This is his title of office, nor can we alter, add to, or diminish it without infringing the Constitution. In like manner persons authorized to transact business with foreign powers are styled Ambassadors, Public Ministers, etc. To give them any other appellation would be an equal infringement. As to grades of orders or titles of nobility, nothing of the kind can be established by Congress.

Can, then, the President and Senate do that which is prohibited to the United States at large? Certainly not. Let us read the Constitution: *No title of nobility shall be granted by the United States.* The Constitution goes further. The servants of the public are prohibited from accepting them from any foreign state, king, or prince. So that the appellations and terms given to nobility in the Old World are contraband language in the United States, nor can we apply them to our citizens consistent with the Constitution.

As to what the common people, soldiers, and sailors of foreign countries may think of us, I do not think it imports us much. Perhaps the less they think, or have occasion to think of us, the better.

Postponement was carried.

May 11th

Mr. Izard and sundry gentlemen of the Senate were dissatisfied with our Vice-President. He takes on him to school the members from the chair. His grasping after titles has been observed by everybody. Mr. Izard, after describing his air, manner, deportment, and personal figure in the chair, concluded with applying the title of *Rotundity* to him.

I have really often looked at him with surprise mingled with contempt when he is in the chair and no business before the Senate. Instead of that sedate, easy air which I would have him possess, he will look on one side, then on the other, then down on the knees of his breeches, then dimple his visage with the most silly kind of half smile which I cannot well express in English.

The Scotch-Irish have a word that hits it exactly—*smudging.* God forgive me for the vile thought, but I cannot help thinking of a monkey just put into breeches when I saw him betray such evident marks of self-conceit.

May 14th

Now rose Mr. Lee to report on titles from the Joint Committee. He reported that the committee from the other House had adhered in the strictest manner to their former resolution. He moved that the report, which had been laid on the table, in favor of titles, should be entered on the files of the House, and that a motion which he had in his hand should be adopted.

The spirit of the motion was that, to keep up a proper respect for our Chief Magistrate, attention should be paid to the customs of civilized nations; that the appearance of the affectation of simplicity would be injurious; that the Senate had decided in favor of titles from these motives; but that, in conformity to the practice of the other House, for the present, they resolved to address the President without title.

Through the whole of this base business I have endeavored to mark the conduct of George Washington. I have no clew that will lead me fairly to any just conclusion as to his sentiments. I think it scarce possible, but he must have dropped something on a subject which has excited so much warmth. If he did, it was not on our side, or I would have heard it. But no matter. I have, by plowing with the heifer of the other House, completely defeated them.

1790-92: PA GETS A NEW COAT

IT WAS A LONG TIME in the making, and several dresses were cut from the cloth for Pa's coat before he finally got it. But the Fuller family were agreed that he needed it, especially 15-year-old Elizabeth, who began the project that Ma finished up about two years later. To the Reverend Timothy Fuller of Princeton, Massachusetts, his wife bore five sons and five daughters. When he died in 1805 all ten children were living, and long after the old house itself disappeared, the family circle held unbroken. Twenty-five years after Pa's death the ten held a reunion picnic at the site of the old home, sat in a circle around the cellar hole, and sang the hymns and sweet childhood songs that Pa had taught them.

"I did pretty well considering . . ."
ELIZABETH FULLER (1775-1856)

2 [December 1790]

Pa is very poorly having a very bad cough. I am a good deal afraid he will go into consumption.

Oh! if my soul was formed for woe
how would I vent my sighs
My grief it would like rivers flow
from both my streaming eyes.

I am disconsolate tonight.

9 [February 1791]

Storm weather. I am picking blue wool.

22

I began to break the blue wool for Pa's coat, broke a pound & three quarters in the P.M.

March 1

Pa went to Mr. Stephen Brighams to write his will. Ma began to spin the wool for Pa's coat. I card for her & do the household work.

3

Ma spun three skeins.

26

Ma went to Mrs. Miricks to get a slay Harness [movable frame for the loom].

28

I went to Mrs. Miricks & warped the Piece.

29

Mrs. Garfield came here to show me how to draw in the piece.

30

I tyed in the Piece and wove two yards.

April 1

I wove two yards and three quarters & three inches to-day & I think I did pretty well considering it was April Fool day.

6

I got out the White piece. Mrs. Garfield warped the blue, came here & began to draw in the Piece.

15

I began to spin Linnen, spun 21 knots.

18

I spun two double skeins of Linnen.

22

I spun two double skeins.

> *O dear Quadrille has murdered wit*
> *& work will do as bad,*
> *For wit is always merry*
> *but work does make me sad.*

29

I Pricked some Tunes out of Holyokes singing Book. I spun some.

20 [May]

Mrs. Garfield came here this Morning to show me how to make a Harness.

23

I got in my Piece to-day, wove a yard.

7 [June]

I made myself a blue worsted Coat.

9

Mrs. Brooks here a visiting. I helped Sally make me a blue worsted Gown.

12

Sally cut out a striped lutestring Gown for me.

15

I cut out a striped linnen Gown. Sally finished my lutestring.

16

Rainy weather. Ma cut out a Coattee for me.

20

Sabbath. I went to Church. Wore my lutestring. Sally wore hers.

23

Sally put in a Worsted Coat for herself and we quilted it out by the middle of the afternoon.

23 [January 1792]

I spun Swingling Tow [a coarse flax].

3 [February]

I spun to-day, very pleasant. I finished my thread Stocking.

8

I spun. I should think I might have spun up all the Swingling tow in America by this time.

14 [March]

I got out my Piece; there is fourteen yards & a half.

7 [April]

I finished weaving the linnen Piece; there is Thirty Yards of it.

3 [May]

I have woven a hundred and forty Yards since the ninth of March.

4

I sewed.

1 [June]

I wove five yards to-day.

> *Welcome sweet Liberty,*
> *Once more to me.*
> *How have I longed*
> *To meet again with thee.*

14

Ma cut out Pa's coat.

5 [July]

I am picking blue Wool for Pa's Surtout [overcoat].

12

Ma began to spin the blue Wool for Pa's Coat.

AT SUNRISE, July 11, 1804, under the heights of Weehawken, New Jersey, two duelists paced apart, stopped, turned, fired. Alexander Hamilton missed. Aaron Burr's shot struck home. For Burr, it was the evening of an old score.

Both men had served Washington. At war's end, each still in his twenties, they became rivals as the leading lawyers in New York. But there the similarities end. Men respected Hamilton; they loved—or hated—Burr.

In 1791 Burr ran for the Senate against Hamilton's father-in-law, General Philip John Schuyler, and defeated him. Hamilton never forgave him. In 1800, when Burr was a candidate for the Presidency against Jefferson, a tie in the electoral college vote threw the decision into the House of Representatives. There, largely through Hamilton's influence, the decision went to Jefferson, Burr becoming Vice-President.

Four years later Burr ran for Governor of New York. Again Hamilton, with unabating vindictiveness, threw his weight on the other side. Burr was licked. Smarting under the slurs Hamilton had cast on his character during that bitter campaign, Burr demanded an explanation, and when Hamilton quibbled, challenged. Hamilton accepted. On the day after the duel Hamilton died of his wound; and there was cut short a career of tremendous meaning to America— for better or worse.

On Gouverneur Morris devolved the rather delicate chore of delivering a proper funeral oration over a man whom, despite his great gifts, Morris found in few ways endearing. One of the nation's founding fathers, Morris had served as minister to France from 1792 to 1794, and as senator from 1800 to 1803.

"The scene is too powerful for me . . ."
GOUVERNEUR MORRIS (1752-1816)

[July 12, 1804]

I go to town but meet (opposite to the hospital) Martin Wilkins, who tells me General Hamilton is yet alive at Greenwich, and not, as I was told this morning, in Greenwich Street.

Go there. When I arrive he is speechless. The scene is too powerful for me so I am obliged to walk in the garden to take breath. After having composed myself, I return and sit by his side till he expires.

He is opened, and we find that the ball has broken one of his ribs, passed through the lower part of the liver, and lodged in the vertebrae of his back: A most melancholy scene—his wife almost frantic with grief, his children in tears, every person present deeply afflicted, the whole city agitated, every countenance dejected.

This evening I am asked to pronounce a funeral oration. I promise to do so if I can possibly command myself enough, but express my belief that it will be utterly impossible. I am wholly unmanned by this day's spectacle.

[July 13]

Take Mr. Harrison out to dine with me. Discuss the points which it may be safe to touch to-morrow, and those which it will be proper to avoid. To a man who could feebly command all his powers this subject is difficult. The first point of his biography is that he was a stranger [born in the Leeward Islands] of illegitimate birth; some mode must be contrived to pass over this handsomely. He was indiscreet, vain, and opinionated; these things must be told, or the character will be incomplete, and yet they must be told in such manner as not to destroy the interest.

He was in principle opposed to republican and attached to monarchical government, and then his opinions were generally known and have been long and loudly proclaimed. His share in forming our Constitution must be mentioned, and his unfavorable opinion cannot therefore be concealed.

The most important part of his life was his administration of the finances. The system he proposed was in one respect radically wrong; moreover, it has been the subject of some just and much unjust criticism. Many are still hostile to it, though on improper ground.

I can neither commit myself to a full and pointed approbation, nor is it prudent to censure others. All this must, somehow or other, be reconciled. He was in principle opposed to dueling, but he has fallen in a duel. I cannot thoroughly excuse him without criminating Colonel Burr, which would be wrong, and might lead to events which every good citizen would deprecate. Indeed, this morning, when I sent for Colonel Smith, who had asked an oration from me last night, to tell him I would endeavor to say some few words over the corpse, I told him—in answer to the hope he expressed, that in doing justice to the dead I would not injure the living—that Colonel Burr ought to be considered in the same light with any other man who had killed another in a duel; that I certainly should not excite to any outrage on him, but, as it seemed evident to me that legal steps would be taken against him, prudence would, I should suppose, direct him to keep out of the way.

In addition to all the difficulties of this subject is the impossibility of writing and committing anything to memory in the short time allowed. The corpse is already putrid, and the funeral procession must take place to-morrow morning.

July 14

A little before ten go to Mr. Church's house, from whence the corpse is to move. We are detained till twelve. While moving in the procession I meditate, as much as my feelings will permit, on what I am to say.

I can find no way to get over the difficulty which would attend the details of his death. It will be impossible to command either myself or my audience; their indignation amounts almost to frenzy already. Over this, then, a veil must be drawn. I must not, either, dwell on his domestic life; he has long since foolishly published the avowal of conjugal infidelity. Something, however, must be said to excite public pity for his family, which he has left in indigent circumstances.

I speak for the first time in the open air, and find that my voice is lost before it reaches one-tenth of the audience. Get through the difficulties tolerably well; am of necessity short, especially as I feel the impropriety of acting a dumb show, which is the case as to all those who see but cannot hear me.

I find that what I have said does not answer the general expectation. This I knew would be the case; it must ever happen to him whose duty it is to allay the sentiment which he is expected to arouse. How easy would it have been to make them, for a moment, absolutely mad!

This evening Mr. Coleman, editor of the *Evening Post*, calls. He requests me to give him what I have said. He took notes, but found his language so far inferior that he threw it in the fire. Promise, if he will write what he remembers, I will endeavor to put it into the terms which were used. He speaks very highly of the discourse; more so than it deserves.

Mr. Hammond, who dined with us, desired me to think of some means to provide for poor Hamilton's family. Mr. Gracie and Mr. Wolcott called for the same purpose. I had already mentioned the matter to Mr. Low, who seemed to think a subscription will not go down well, because the children have a rich grandfather. Be motives what they may, I will use the occasion and freely pay my quota. Clarkson [Matthew, an army officer] will unquestionably do as much. David Ogden says he, Clarkson, will do more than he ought. He is a worthy fellow, as, indeed, he always was, and is extremely wounded. He said to me on Thursday, just after our friend had expired, "If we were truly brave we should not accept a challenge; but we are all cowards." The tears rolling down his face gave strong effect to the voice and manner with which he pronounced this sentence. There is no braver man living, and yet I doubt whether he would so far brave the public opinion as to refuse a challenge.

Together with others of Hamilton's friends, Morris spent much time endeavoring to arrange his affairs, which were in sad disorder. He wrote to Robert Morris: "Our friend Hamilton has been suddenly cut off in the midst of embarrassments which would have required several years of professional industry to set straight: a debt of between fifty thousand and sixty thousand dollars hanging over him, a property which in time may sell for seventy thousand or eighty thousand, but which, if brought to the hammer, would not, in all probability, fetch forty; a family of seven young children. We have opened a subscription to provide for these orphans, and his warm-hearted friends, judging of others by themselves, expect more from it than I do."

1812:   EXPATRIATE BURR COMES HOME

As a POLITICAL LEADER and cosmopolite of rare charm, Aaron Burr drew his company from "the quality" on both sides of the Atlantic. Many were the brilliant gatherings in his home on Staten Island—until the duel with Hamilton put an abrupt finish to all this and to Burr's popularity in America. He went South, where a scattering of friends took him in until the storm should blow over.

But instead of returning, Burr found a new interest. He would set up a colony in Louisiana, and in the event of war with Spain, would extend his influence into Mexico and the American West—whether in the interest of his country or solely of himself as head of a new state, nobody knows. General James Wilkenson, an American who was himself a subversive in the pay of Spain, accused Burr of plotting a secession of the West.

There was no proof, but Jefferson chose to believe Wilkenson and had Burr arrested for treason. Two sensational trials blackened Burr's name, yet the best lawyers Jefferson could enlist were unable to make the charges stick.

Acquitted but very much an outcast, Burr went to Europe in 1808, presumably to see whether he could interest other powers in his scheme. If that was his purpose, he failed in it. He spent four years abroad—two of them in trying to get back. Blocked by American officials in his efforts to get a passport for his return, and out of money, he had to live for long stretches on his friends. His tremendous personal magnetism renewed the welcomes faster than his poverty could wear them out. He moved among high society with ease and among his creditors with agility.

He had heart, however, only for his daughter Theodosia and her little son. They were his world. His wish to come home centered solely on them. Burr's diary covering his wanderings in Europe, though not intended for Theodosia's eyes, is addressed to her. Through it there runs a current of affection, page to page, of a depth seldom equaled in the expression of a father's love for his child.

Scandal and prejudice have long blurred the picture of Aaron Burr. No historian has given us an adequate appraisal of this man's character; certainly no one could do so without attaching a great deal of weight to this neglected diary, of which only 200 copies were printed. From behind the dark stereotype that every school child gets of Aaron Burr the traitor, it brings the man to life. From the start, the two large volumes are full of pathos, delight, humor, and the wildest incongruity, down to the finish, where we witness the spectacle of a former Vice-President of the United States trying to decide whether to risk being arrested as a vagrant by spending the night on a doorstep in New York.

Like him or not, here is one of the most fascinating characters history has ever concealed.

"I saw the very lips I had kissed . . ."
AARON BURR (1756-1836)

London, August 21 [1808]
Received invitation from Jeremy Bentham to pass some days *chez lui.*

September 22
Lodged at Bentham's house at Queen's Square Place.

November 24
Rose at 9. Went to Turnevelli's [a sculptor]. He would have a mask. A

very unpleasant ceremony. To Sir Mark's; he was sitting down to breakfast. Sir Mark had engaged me to call on Signora B.

Just as we were going out, casting my eye in the mirror, I observed a great purple mark on my nose. Went up and washed it and rubbed it—all to no purpose. It was indelible. That cursed mask business has occasioned it. I believe the fellow used quicklime instead of plaster of Paris, for I felt a very unpleasant degree of heat during the operation. I sent Sir Mark off, resolved to see no Signora till the proboscis be in order.

November 25

At 11, went to Turnevelli's to sit. Relieved myself by cursing him for the nose disaster. He endeavored to console me by stating that the same thing happened to Lord Melville and to several others, and that the appearance passed off in a few days.

Took a hack, not liking to walk and exhibit my nose. Stayed two hours with Turnevelli. He will make a most hideous, frightful thing, but much like the original.

November 27

At 12 called at Reeves's. He showed me a letter from Colonel Jenkinson about my pretensions as a British subject. Dampier has given opinion that I may resume at pleasure, the Lord Chancellor, Eldon, that I cannot, and am forever an alien.

I am out of all patience at being detained in town, and am in danger of wearying my great and good friend Bentham.

From Reeves's walked on to visit the Donna; but, recollecting my nose, walked home.

Birmingham, December 24

I have taken passage for Liverpool, to set off at ½ p. 11, being advised that there is no other way to get on.

12 o'clock. Still at Birmingham. Full of contrition and remorse. Lost my passage. Lost or spent 28 shillings and a pair of gloves. Every bed in the house engaged. No hope of getting on but by the mail at 7 to-morrow morning. The office shut, and no passage to be taken to-night.

What business have I to go sauntering about the streets of a strange place, alone and unarmed, on a Christmas eve? Truly, I want a guardian more than at 15.

I have often heard that great sinners have relieved their consciences by a full confession. Let us try.

I sallied forth. There were hundreds of pretty dressed folks of all sexes and ages, in little groups and very gay. I joined one party, and then another, and another. At length I got so well suited with a couple that we agreed to walk and see the town.

I have always had a passion for certain branches of natural history. These, I thought, afforded me an opportunity of acquiring information; and even now, amid all my regrets, I must acknowledge that it was a most instructive and, abating one rencounter, which had very nearly ended in a riot, a most amusing lesson. Hence it would seem that all this penitence is for the money and not for the folly—on which a very good theological discourse might be written.

At this moment it comes into my head how to redeem this 28 shillings. It shall be done and then peace of conscience will be restored. I will take passage outside. Half price only. I am resolved, and you shall see how I execute.

August 29 [1809]

Got up [in a spell of insomnia] and attempted to light candle, but in vain; had flint and matches but only some shreds of punk which would not catch. Recollected a gun which I had on my late journey; filled the pan with powder and was just going to flash it when it occurred to me that though I had not loaded it someone else might; tried and found in it a very heavy charge! What a fine alarm it would have made if I had fired! Then poured out some powder on a piece of paper, put the shreds of punk with it, and after fifty essays succeeded in firing the powder; but it being dark, had put more powder than intended; my shirt caught fire, the papers on my table caught fire, burnt my fingers to a blister (the left hand, fortunately); it seemed like a general conflagration. Succeeded, however, in lighting my candle and passed the night till 5 this morning in smoking, reading, and writing this.

Hamburg, Germany, November 24

I find that, among the great number of Americans here and *there* all are hostile to A. B. [himself]—all. What a lot of rascals they must be to make war on one whom they do not know; on one who never did harm or wished harm to a human being. Yet they, perhaps, ought not to be blamed, for they are influenced by what they hear.

Cassel, Westphalia, December 28

Yesterday I must have been possessed by the devil. A pretty little girl about 15 years old came into my room with a little *guitarre* in her hand and muttering a few words in German began to sing and play. Could you imagine anything more calculated to fascinate me? I drove her rudely out! To be sure, I did give her a *gooden-groschen,* which was probably much more than she expected; but I was unkind. One minute after, I was sorry and sent for her, but she was not to be found; and I have been all day looking out for her in vain.

January 1, 1810, 7 A.M.

At Eisenach saw the first sleighs I have seen since leaving America. They were pretty little things; fine horses ornamented with cords and tassels and bells; gentlemen and ladies; saw a great number of pretty faces the hour I was there among the servants and *bourgeoise,* disfigured by a strange head-dress and all false hips, even girls of 5 years old. At the tavern I caught one to examine those hips; she screamed as if I was going to eat her, to the great amusement of twenty spectators.

4 P.M. *Gotha*

The Frankfort stage not arrived! Very pleasant, Madame, to be a whole day in a place where there is no being who can understand a sentence I say nor be understood by me. This is not the worst. I would amuse myself very well, could *go* (*have gone*) to church or to see some of the fine things, or could make acquaintances, but my great apprehension of losing the damned diligence [coach] keeps me from being abroad more than ½ hour at a time.

Nevertheless I have been all day roving; have made some acquaintances, some discoveries about those false hips, which, to be sure, cost me 1½ dollars. Several little adventures. Know the town. Every lady you look at sitting in her window nods to you. I drew strange conclusions at first; but how dangerous are rash inferences! Have seen only one beautiful woman. Lo, the diligence arrives, I saw it from my window!

Have been over to see the diligence. It goes at 7. There are two passengers, of whom one speaks French. A very forbidding phizz but not worse than my own.

Frankfort, January 18

To the *Comedie Alemande.* The opera of "Camilla." Left at the second act, being very cold and having an engagement proper to warm me. All this is written; no, not all, but this and the preceding page with the personage in the room. My tea is ready, and other matters claim my attention. *Bon soir.*

Paris, September 17

To the *marchand des varietes* to look again at the picture, and finally bought it, thinking it would please you; 48 francs! What extravagance!

Thence home, but alas! on my way a p. of *dem.* [pair of demoiselles] and so 8 francs. How many curses have I heaped on poor Gamp ["Gamp" was his nickname for himself] and yet he is rather to be pitied; only see how for the last fifteen days he has been so good considering his habits. And so we will try to forget it till next time.

October 4

Home, and ruminating on the blessings of life. At 3 set out to Vanderlyn's to dine. On my way home got entangled; 7 francs 10 sous. Thus you see I save in sous and waste in crowns. Got home extremely grave and full of devout reflections and sage resolutions.

October 29

Wrote Mr. McRae [the American consul] asking certificate of citizenship. Requested by the messenger verbally that he would send an answer. I expect some vulgar impertinence, coupled with a refusal. Have I told you that Duc d' A. [Alberg] says if I can get a certificate from the American consul, I shall have no further difficulty about a passport. Hence my application to McRae. If the latter answers insolently, the only revenge I will take, for revenge, you know, is not in my nature, will be to publish his letter. [Burr's request was formally denied by the consul.]

Took *bis.* and *cas.* [presumably for biscuit and cassonade, or brown sugar] in my room. My 25 sous wine is detestable, and has no sort of resemblance to the *vrai* Roussillon at 36 sous. Indeed, my dear little T., you must not scold so damd hard if I take pretty nearly a bottle a day of the *vrai* Roussillon. By way of compensation, will drink neither tea nor coffee in the evening, never dine at rest'rs, and eke out a pound *cassonade* a fortnight; and when I have no more money I will drink water.

Have removed my writing-table from my cabinet to my bedroom, where have a leetle fire, else you would not have had half so much journal.

October 31

At ½ p.4 took a long stroll along the Boulevard. On my way home met ——, who invited me to go home with him to communicate something.

It is that the Americans here have entered into a combination against A. B.; that every man who speaks to him shall be shunned as unworthy of society; that no master of vessel, or any other person, shall take any letter or parcel for him, and other like benevolent things; all which amused me but alarmed my friend.

Mr. —— of Boston, related in a large company that he, being on a jury at Boston last summer on an insurance case, Judge Chase presiding, and Luther Martin, one of the lawyers, on some dispute between them, the judge said to Martin, "I am surprised that you can so prostitute your talents." M. replied, "I never prostituted my talents except when I defended you and C. B. [Colonel Burr]"; and added, in the hearing of the jury, "a couple of the greatest rascals in the world."

A Mr. Thompson, of Charleston, S.C., a Scotchman, but naturalized in the United States, now settled here, being asked if he had called on Colonel Burr, said, No, and no good American would call on him. *Bon soir!*

November 2

We went to a *M'e de Vin* and took supper, 3 francs 10 sous; very cheap, costing 25 sous. (*La Cordonnierre* [shoemaker's wife]). *Voila, au folie,* 10 francs 10 sous and my glo.! [gloves]. Gamp, *quand deviendre tu suge?* [Gamp, when wilt thou get wise to thyself?] Engaged to dine at the same place on Monday with the last mentioned (*Lize la Cordonnierre*).

November 3

To my *mar'* [marchand] *vin*, to get him to take back his inferior 25-sous wine and give me the other, which he very cheerfully agreed to. To my new shoemaker's; not done. The mechanics here, I tell you, are far worse than in America. Home at 7.

I may as well tell you now of my economy in this wine affair. Eating my bread and cheese, and seeing half a bottle of the 25-sous wine left, I thought it would be too extravagant to open a bottle of the *bon;* so I tried my best to get down the *mauvaise,* constantly thinking of the other, which was in sight, and trying to persuade myself to give Gamp some of that. But no, I stuck to the bad, and got it all down. Then, to pay myself for this act of heroism, treated him to a large tumbler of the *vrai* Roussillon, and sallied forth to my *marchand de vin* to engage him to exchange the residue. You see I am of Lantara's opinion, that though a man may be a little the poorer for drinking good wine, yet he is, under its influence, much more able to bear poverty.

November 28

To Madame St. Claire's. Very civil; very prettily lodged. Engaged to eschort her Friday to the museum, to see the exhibition. On other days the doors are open to all. On fridays to those only who have tickets. Baron d'Alberg has lent me his, which admits three persons.

November 30

Home to dress for the Louvre. Took hack and called on Madame St. Claire. Found her dressed and ready. She is really ladylike and handsome; but of all the rest *ignoro*. She still more *ignor*. of me, not knowing even my name, having only learnt from her friend that I am a strange animal from the antipodes.

Vanderlyn met us at the Louvre, and we passed there three hours. An immense crowd. Several hundred carriages. This, I told you, is the ticket day.

Saw Madame *chez elle;* took a very modest leave.

December 1

To Madame F.'s, whom found alone. Staid an hour with her; am always amused and interested. She engaged me to take tea with her at 9 this afternoon. Thence to Duc d' Alberg's. The Duchess had promised me a ticket for the Louvre. As she had neglected it, the Duc gave me a note to Mons. Denon (author of the "Travels in Egypt"), who is director-general of the pictures and statues, and of all the arts of painting and sculpture. Before proceeding farther, however, I must tell you whence arose my solicitude to have a ticket, seeing that I have already the means of admittance. The case is this. The day I was with Madame St. Claire she expressed a very great desire to have a ticket for a friend, and I, having a very great desire to oblige Madame St. C. for reasons which may be already conjectured, took the measures aforesaid.

From the Duc's went immediately to Denon's; was admitted, and presented my credentials. Denon received me graciously, and I paid him a compliment on his book, and then he was more gracious. He gave me the ticket for "deux personnes."

Off set I for Madame St. Claire, assured of a very kind reception. On the way met Mr. G. "Sir," says he, "I am in the most distressing dilemma. A lady, whom I wish very much to oblige, asked me to procure her a ticket for the Louvre, and I promised to do it, but have been totally disappointed, and dare not see the lady's face; can you put me in the way to extricate myself?" "*Voila,*" said I, and gave him my ticket.

You may well presume that I altered my course, and did not go to Madame St. C.'s. We (G. and I) returned, and I came home to reflect on the state of things. Thence to Madame St. C.'s; out; of which I was very glad. Home.

December 2

To Madame St. Claire's. She was busy about her *menage;* had no fire, and was in bad humor, and very plainly told me she did not like to receive visits at that hour. Mine was very short; and, after getting rid of the affair of the ticket, think our acquaintance will cease.

To Mons. Denon's to get another ticket. Out. To Madame St. C.'s, having engaged to walk with her at 2. She was still in bad humor and declined to walk, of which I was very glad. Home again.

December 3

After great efforts, rose at 9. At ½ p. 10 to Mons. Denon's to get a ticket for St. Claire. There were at least a dozen persons in his hall of audience. Mr. Denon had not yet appeared. Sent in my name. Begged me to wait a few minutes. After a few minutes he came. I doubted whether he would recollect my name or person.

On entering he passed by the rest, sought me out, took me by the hand, and led me into his cabinet, and asked me to excuse him a few minutes till he should dismiss the persons waiting. On his return he took my hand again with both of his, assured me of the pleasure he had in meeting me, and his desire to be useful to me.

I took him at his word; told him that my wishes were now confined to a passport. He offered to speak of my memoir to Mr. Maret (Duc de Bassano) supposed to be the most intimate counselor of the Emperor, and begged me to permit him to peruse my *memoire.* Agreed; and to-morrow morning at 10 appointed for the purpose. Got my ticket and came off in triumph, that I could now fulfill my engagement to St. C.

December 4

To Madame St. Claire's and delivered the ticket.

December 10

Deliberating on the state of my finances, found that this *sans sou* state was not only inconvenient but dangerous; for instance, this morning I hit a glass window with my umbrella, and had nearly forced it through one of three large panes. In such a case you have only to pay, and there's an end of it; but had I broken the pane, and not being able to pay for it, I must infallibly have been taken before a *commissionaire de police* to abide his judgment.

Casting about for ways and means, not one occurred to me but that of robbing poor little Gampy [his grandson]. I opened his little treasure of coins and medals to see what could be spared, and finally seized one Danish dollar of Charles the VII, and two Swedish thalers of Gustave IV. With these I went off to a *changeur* who gave me 5 francs 5 sous each, making in the whole 15 francs 15 sous.

With this treasure my first resolution was to go and amuse myself with some folly. It then occurred to me that there were certain other wants which required consideration. I have been three days out of sugar, and more than ten out of coffee, having lately drank tea, and I had not a single segar.

After some debating and efforts and struggle I desperately sallied out once more in the rain, bought one pound of coffee, 5 francs 5 sous; one pound *cassonade*, 3 francs 16 sous, and seventy segars, 4 francs 15 sous. I had left of my robbery a balance of 4 francs 9 sous, of which about 3 francs must go to pay the washerwoman tomorrow. This act of desperation having put it out of my power to go a folly-hunting, I very gravely determined not to go abroad again.

December 23

I am about to undertake the translation from English into French of two octavo volumes for 100 louis. It will take me three months hard work. Better than to starve. But the most curious part of the story is that the book in question contains a quantity of abuse and libels on A. B. [himself!].

December 31

I deliberated whether I should do some, and what, folly for New Year's eve! A certain poet says, "He that deliberates is lost." It did not turn out so this time, for I resolved to go quietly on home.

Have great comfort in my little fireplace. Have been drinking cider and smoking segars, reading. Yesterday was cold, and to-day colder. Quite winter; the gutters all froze hard. Put on my flannel waistcoat this morning as I wear no *surtout* for a great many philosophic reasons; principally because I have not got one. Happy New Year! Mother and Gampy! Ah! I catched you both! The clock is now striking 12.

January 15 [1811]

Strolled gently homeward, contemplating the stars, which I had not seen for months, when I was stopped by a pretty, well-dressed woman. *"Quoi! Vous etes ici?"* It was that pretty Clotilde of whom something was said six months ago. All remonstrance was in vain. I have no money. "No matter, I have." Passed two hours very pleasantly and engaged to call sometimes and breakfast and play *aux dames* [checkers]. I had, indeed, a crown (5 francs) which on parting I offered; but it was refused as an indignity. *"Je ne suis pas parisienne, je suis picarde."* Home at ½ p. 9. This folly was certainly unnecessary. *Voila*, for three days past how much to repent, that is, the money. As follies give me a great appetite, having been eating an hour voraciously.

Amsterdam, June 12

At 9 came in Captain Combes, of the ship Vigilant, to say that he had got permission to sail [for America] and that if I chose to take passage, he would do all in his power to accommodate me.

June 14

Do you know, my T., that this overture of Captain Combes is a most interesting circumstance? A ship near 400 tons, in fine order, sails well, and the Captain, as he sais, anxious to serve me. Sais he has often kept awake whole nights about me, though he had never seen me. Will fit up a cabin to my own caprice, and appears to think he can never do enough. I hasten to Paris. What need I to go to Paris? Indeed, I can't exactly tell you; but a thousand nothings, of which, probably, the most important are to buy Gampy some beautiful marbles, and you some silk stockings. All these will cost perhaps 7 or 8 louis, and the journey will cost at least 12. But, then, there is your watch which I have ordered, and one for Gampy, if I can squeeze out the money; and some books, and some garden-seeds.

Paris, July 9

To the *Bureau des Passports Etrangeres, au Ministre des Relations Exterieurs* (Duc Bassano's). The *chef de cet department* told me he had mentioned my affair to the Duc, who said he would see me *"au premier jour,"* and would answer me personally. Don't at all like this. Why not grant my *passeport* and see me at his leisure, or not see me, as he pleased?

July 17

To Denon's at 10. He has seen the Duc, who replied that he found great embarrassment in *originating* a passport in his office for a foreigner to return to his country. It will be wholly without *"precedent"—est ce qui B. trouveroit de l'inconvenient que je commanderois moi un passeport pour lui de M. Russell.* [Would Mr. Burr have any objection to my asking Mr. Russell (of the American consulate) for a passport for him?] I replied at once that I would hazard all the inconveniences, and would be greatly obliged to his Excellency if he would forthwith make the application. Monsieur Denon, in my presence and under my dictation, wrote the Duc my assent to the measure. In fact, this mode is extremely disagreeable to me, for I perceive the use that will be made of it in the United States.

Home, very tired. On coming in, a letter from Captain Combes. A deadly blow. He will sail for the Texel [an island off the coast of Holland] on the 23d. No hope of getting my passport before that day, and to Amsterdam is five days' journey, going day and night. My dear T., I am afflicted, sadly afflicted, to lose his ship. The only American ship now in Europe which will go as a cartel [flying a flag of truce] and thus be secure from capture.

July 18

A letter was handed to me. A letter from Denon, enclosing one from Duke Bassano, saying that he would see about the thing instantly, and hoped I would have the passport to-morrow evening. This was to me matter of very great surprise, need I add, of pleasure.

Another note from Denon, enclosing another from the Duc Bassano. He has got the passport from Russell; has given his sanction, and has already passed it through the *bureau* of Rovigo. Now, indeed, I may hope. Now I feel as if I was embracing you and Gamp.

Have got my passport. Shall go to-morrow. Have your watch. Have bought you nothing, nor for my poor, dear little Gamp. Shall bring you nothing but myself.

Helder, Holland, September 14

I feel as if I were already on the way to you, and my heart beats with joy. Yet, alas! that country which I am so anxious to re-visit will perhaps reject me with horror.

London, February 22 [1812]

A bad, bad day. My hopes of being soon in New Orleans, or elsewhere in the United States, have vanished. A letter this day received from the Captain says that he has been warned *at his peril,* by the consul at Yarmouth, too, not to take me on board, and that he is afraid, and must refuse me a passage.

Friday, March 27

On board the ship Aurora, of Newburyport, Captain Potter, bound for Boston, now at anchor in the Thames, 26 miles below Gravesend.

April 5

The wind died away, and we lay quite becalmed part of the night. Towards morning a light breeze at S. E., which I hope my Gampies [Theodosia and her son] have, by their astronomical and geographical knowledge, discovered is a fair wind for us who are going West.

Boston, May 7

Sat up till 12 last night reading the newspapers, and have done nothing else all this day. Having heard no hints about A. Burr, nor seeing anything about him in the papers, conclude that he escaped notice. Besides being on the wharf yesterday more than five hours, I was obliged to walk no less than six times the whole length of State Street and the *long wharf,* the most public and crowded parts of the town. Thanks to Dr. Smith's wig and my huge whiskers if I have not been recognized.

May 19

I received *a letter;* yes, a letter from S. S., [a friend in New York] containing a pretty full answer to my queries, with assurance that I have very many and warm friends and no enemies. The letter is stamped with that enthusiasm which marks his character. As regards business, however, things are not propitious. The two creditors who have judgments against me are inexorable. Nothing will satisfy them but money or approved security, neither of which are in my power. The alternative is to be taken on execution and go to the limits [jail].

To this I should have no great repugnance in point of pride or feeling, but there are two objections pretty cogent; first and principally, *you.* I fear that your little heart would sink to hear that Gamp was on the limits. To be sure, if you could come here and see how gay he was, be supported by the light of his countenance, and catch inspiration from his lips, you would forget that he was not in paradise.

The second is, that I have a project of entering into the holy state of matrimony. The charming object is already designated, and love, almighty love! The fair object is a worthy lady some few years *older* than myself, with fortune enough, and, I think, good-nature enough to make the appropriation of it. Now, this fine sentimental project would be utterly defeated by the limits-establishment.

May 24

On Wednesday I embarked in one of those little sloops for New York, and shall there take my stand, constantly consoled and supported by your affection and your counsel.

May 25

"I can't get out." Mrs. G. [landlady] asked me this morning for $5, which having not, nor any part of it, sent to the goldsmith for change of the $10 bill I had given him to take out his $6; but he had supposed that I, meaning to pay *magnifiquement*, had given him the whole 10; and it was not till after a very unpleasant scene that I could get back 3, which appeased Mrs. G. for the day. It is not possible to leave the house till she is paid.

May 30, On board the sloop Rose, Captain Dimon, off Boston Harbor

At 12 last night I came on board, but the tide would not serve till 1. I agreed to keep watch till that hour, and then wake the captain. The sloop lay at the end of the long wharf, and I passed the hour walking on the wharf or sitting on the timber, ruminating on *things to come*, and talking with you and Gampillo.

June 5 [near New Haven, Conn.]

The Captain would go on shore and invited me to go and take breakfast with him, which I did. After breakfast the Captain rode out on horseback, and I strolled three or four hours round some miles in the neighborhood. Every object was as familiar to me as those about R. Hill [Richmond Hill, Staten Island], and the review brought up many pleasant and whimsical associations. At several doors I saw the very lips I had kissed and the very eyes which had ogled me in the persons of their grandmothers about six-and-thirty years ago. I did not venture into any of their houses, lest some of their grandmothers might recollect me.

June 8

When we were nearly opposite the Battery [Manhattan Island] I heard the sound of oars, and hailed; was answered; and I begged them to come alongside. It proved to be two vagabonds in a skiff, probably on some thieving voyage. They were very happy to set me on shore in the city for a dollar, and at ½ p. 11 I was landed; and S. S., having given me his address, 66 Water street, thither I went cheerfully, and rejoicing at my good fortune. I knocked and knocked, but no answer. I knocked still harder, supposing they were asleep, till one of the neighbors opened a window and told me that nobody lived there. I asked where lived Mr. S. Of that she knew nothing.

I was now to seek a lodging. But very few houses were open. Tried two or three taverns, all full; cruised along the wharf, but could find no place. It was now midnight, and nobody to be seen in the street. To walk about the whole night would be too fatiguing. To have sat and slept on any stoop would have been thought no hardship; but then, the danger that the first watchman who might pass would take me up as a vagrant and carry me to the watchhouse, was a *denouement* not at all to my mind.

I walked on, thinking that in the skirts of the town I might meet at that hour some charitable *et amiable personne,* who, for one or two dollars, and *l'amour de Dieu,* would give me at least half a bed; but seeing in an alley a light in the cellar of a small house, I called and asked for a lodging; was answered yes; shown into a small garret, where were five men already asleep; a cot and a sort of coverlid was given me. I threw open the window to have air, lay down, and slept profoundly till 6. Being already dressed, I rose, paid for my lodgings 12 cents, and sallied out to 66 Water Street, and there had the luck to find Sam alone.

He led me immediately to the house of his brother Robert, and here I am, in possession of Sam's room in Stone Street, in the city of New York, on this 8th day of June, *anno dom.* 1812, just four years since we parted at this very place.

1807: THE DEVIL IS GIVEN A HARD TIME
IN VIRGINIA

LONELINESS AND BOREDOM were chronic ailments of the early settlers. There were not many compensations for hardship on the American frontier, not many ways out of an engulfing drabness. When they turned to religion, they found it more interesting to think about sin than virtue; and the hunger of their very souls was for something of interest. As the eighteenth century drew to a close, preachers who shouted of guilt and of dread but fascinating punishment found wide followings. "I shall speak to you," promised one, "of the world, the flesh, and the devil. And when I get to the devil I shall serve it to you hot as you can sup it." They developed an idiom of their own. They held huge camp meetings, where they worked on the emotions of their followers until they literally had them rolling on the ground. In 1801, at a gathering of about 25,000 persons in Bourbon County, Kentucky, 3,000 fainted and 500 others "jerked" and "barked" in chorus.

Many of these preachers "rode circuit" from town to town over a repeated itinerary. The "Cumberland Circuit" of Virginia was the route of the diarist quoted here, whose title was Bishop of the Methodist Episcopal Church South.

"She wished I might go to hell."
JOHN EARLY (1786-1873)

[May 25, 1807]

Monday morning I left my father's to return to my circuit with much weeping around me. My father told some of the family he never expected to see me again in this world. It caused trouble on my mind as he was out of the ark of safety but I felt determined to serve God and call Sinners to repentence. I went on my way, crying, to Lynchburg, twelve miles.

Wednesday, 27th

Spoke to a wicked set of people and insulted a son of a Baptist preacher and the Baptist made a noise about it.

Friday, 29th

Had a powerful time. Spoke on the 42nd Psalm, 11th verse. That day two or three young women wanted to fight.

Wednesday, [June] 3rd

To Morris Langhorne, God bless the people. Five miles. Had a melting time.

6th

To Bold Springs, ten miles. Zion must travail before she can bring forth children.

8th

Four miles to Smith Chapel. All had a melting time. Some mourners. I hope for better times.

Tuesday, 9th

I gave a hint on Baptism because I knew sheep did not love water for we had just had a good many converted there and the Baptists was a'fishing after them.

Thursday, 11th

One shouter. Four mourners came to be prayed for.

Friday, 12th

Spoke to an attentive people; a melting time. Blessed be God. That night to Jesse Miller's. Spoke Glory to God in the highest. Happy Christians. Several mourners; two converted; two or three backsliding Baptists reclaimed. Meeting lasted all night. Glory to Jesus. Joy comes in the morning.

Tuesday, 16th

To Walker's Church, eight miles. Three or four professors preach there. Some preach Jesus and some preach for the devil or contention. A few Christians, many hypocrites.

Friday, 19th

Some got powerfully converted and cried for mercy aloud.

Friday [July 3]

To Cold Spring, twelve miles. A large number of professors there but they are degenerated too much and got too cold. God help the people. I love them much.

Saturday, July 4

The devil roared for prey. I went to Smith Chapel, eight miles. Sunday, to Charity Chapel, eighteen miles. That evening at Bold Spring, five miles. I told them who I thought would go to heaven. A powerful gracious time among Christians. Oh God, let Zion travel. Stayed at M. I. Hobson's. Oh, what chills of cold run over my body.

16th, to Ellot's

Spoke. A gracious time. Twelve miles at night to John Walker's. The devil was in camp and we did not get him out.

Saturday, 18th

Preaching, crying, shouting, and singing night and day.

19th

Sunday morning we had feast and many spoke feelingly. Some of the wicked cried and others were as mad as the devil could make them.

Wednesday, August 12th

I went to a house to see if God lived in the hearts of the people and it was a widow H. in Prince Edward. I found two young women living together. I asked if they feared God. Their answer was as though they never heard of God for the devil had a palace there and one of them asked me if I wanted a wife without a fortune to court her. I told her the devil would have her here and in hell hereafter.

15th

To Walker's, 5 miles, and spoke on the poverty of Christ and the riches of a Christian. The Lord remember Sister Walker for her charity and labor of love. She gave me a beautiful Virginia homespun coat which was more suitable for Virginians to wear than any other cloth and especially Methodist preachers. Gracious God, continue to make Methodists of the wicked. That night to Wood's S.H. six miles. I preached and almost killed myself. A gracious time. Brother W. and L. Isbell had the powerfullest time shouting and rolling on the floor.

Tuesday, September 6th

To Gray's, six miles. There came a man there, one of the neighbors. I prayed for him and he was afraid, he said, to go home by himself for fear the devil would get him alive. He started bellowing like a bull.

Monday 9th

To Prospect, nine miles. That night to Brother Venable's, a dear saint of God, and I hope all his family will get to heaven. There at that season of the year I ate as good a watermelon as ever I did in summer.

Wednesday, 18th

To Paterson's and back, six miles. There I saw a young woman who had had the jerks two years and was very wicked (her parents were Baptists). I told her I believed the jerks would never leave her until she prayed in earnest to God. She said it would be time enough for her several years hence and said the jerks came from the devil and would go back to him again. I told her to pray; or I did not know but what the jerks would kill her and she would go to hell. She said she wished I might go to hell.

22nd

At night we had a meeting at Mr. Thompson's. Christians shouted and jumped and jerked and rolled and for three or four hours my eyes or ears hardly ever saw or heard such a time among Christians. The Lord of all mercies came to the deliverance of the above young woman who only the week before wished I might go to hell. She had the most powerful manifestation I ever saw. She leaped from the floor and jumped and shouted and jerked all night and until I left the next day at ten o'clock. I hardly think, besides many others, I ever saw the like before.

★

1832: ANDREW JACKSON READS THE LAW
TO THE SOUTH

☆

OF ANDREW JACKSON, Franklin D. Roosevelt said, "An overwhelming proportion of the material power of the nation was against him. . . . It seemed sometimes that all were against him—all but the people of the United States."

This was true of the stormy Tennesseean in most of his undertakings, especially his long fight that put the Bank of the United States out of business— a business whereby the nation's credit could be manipulated to serve the uses of a minority of wealth. It was true of Jackson as the sign-giver and moving spirit of revolt against the neo-federalism of the 1820s and 30s, a revolt that proved to be one of the great countermovements of American democracy in transition.

Some thirty years earlier, in its popular support of Thomas Jefferson, the country had turned its back on the Hamiltonian concept of government of and by, if not for, a propertied class. In the years that followed, however, a series of inching economic surrenders to the persisting aim of an aristocracy of wealth had built up a heavy backlog of discontent among the working people, the farmers, the settlers of the West.

In the election of 1828, again the country was brought to the point of decision as between a government that would work to the advantage of the few and one pledged to serve the many, this time with the pressures from both sides vastly greater than they had been in 1800. Its choice was correspondingly emphatic.

The measure of that emphasis may best be judged from the character of the man the people chose to lead them. Jackson was described by his old friend Judge John Catron of Tennessee as a man of not only tremendous will but of power to inspire others not so endowed. "Timid men and feeble women have rushed to onslaught when he gave the command—fierce, fearless and unwavering for the first time."

From the day he took over, Jackson gave the people that kind of leadership. He found his strength in them. As his successor, Martin Van Buren explained, "They were his blood relations—the only blood relations he had . . . to labor for the good of the masses was a special mission assigned to him by his Creator and no man was ever better disposed." The result was a reawakening to the meaning of America as a nation governed for all, as well as may be through majority rule. There was to be no exception, economic or other.

But it was not true of Jackson that "all were against him" when he put down the Southern nullificationists in 1832 and in doing so welded into the American union of states the principle that it had the right to prevent, by force if necessary, the secession of any part of that union.

Far from opposing him, all but a handful of Americans stood ready to back him in this stand to the limit, and many Northern business leaders who had once cursed his "willful ignorance" now acknowledged him as a great statesman.

In July of that year Jackson had signed into law a new tariff, moderate but still protective. In November a South Carolina convention declared the tariff void. Thus came about the abortive but dangerous move to which was given the name "nullification"—the assumption by a state of power to set at nothing the weight of federal law.

Jackson countered at once with a resounding proclamation, intended to settle forever in the minds of the South Carolinians and anybody else who might be interested, just what the several states of America meant in calling themselves "united." At the same time he steered through Congress, as a compromise, a much lower tariff. South Carolina, given the face-saver, rescinded its nullification ordinance.

While the threat to defy the federal law-making power thus paid off in a sop to the South, the concept of an indivisible union of states emerged from the controversy, to be tested later in fire and bloodshed but never to be destroyed. A bloodless preliminary to the Civil War had been fought with words, and the South had lost.

Of Jackson's enemies none were as harsh and unforgiving as a little group of Southern leaders who, a few years before, had befriended and advanced him on his way to the White House. They had supposed that in this seemingly tired old war hero they had a puppet who would jump to every string they pulled. Instead, Jackson chose his own cabinet and made policy of his own will; and of course they were furious. They had learned that far from being the crude backwoods political hack they accused him of being, he was a great and skillful strategist, and this knowledge only heightened their hatred.

Bitterest of all was Governor John Floyd of Virginia. To his defiance of the federal power Floyd applied the euphemism "states' rights." When he discovered that Jackson did not propose to recognize a state's right to tell the union it could go climb a tree, he was filled with a fanatic fury. So extreme were his views that they gave pause to his own fellow-Southerners and eventually repelled them. When they refused to go along with him he turned on them too.

Floyd's ancestors were eminent Virginians. He was born in Kentucky but after getting a medical degree from the University of Pennsylvania he went to Christiansburg, Virginia, to practice. He served as an army doctor in the War of 1812, then was elected to the Virginia General Assembly. In 1817 he was sent to Congress.

There he proposed that the United States occupy the Columbia River Valley and establish an American territory of Oregon. Floyd was loud and long on this subject—so persistent, indeed, and his speeches such tremendous exercises in rolling oratory, that his colleagues nicknamed him Old Oregon. They never did anything about it while he was a member of Congress; but after he was out they voted to proceed with the colonization.

In January 1829, Floyd declined re-election. His reason was that he expected Jackson, then just elected to the Presidency, to give him a place in the cabinet. Jackson had no intention of doing anything of the sort. Floyd reacted with shock and pain, and from that time on was an unrelenting enemy.

Again in the election of 1832 it seemed that everybody was against Old Hickory except the people. Henry Clay, Jackson's major opponent, got only 49 electoral votes to Jackson's 219. Another of the four candidates in that election was John Floyd. He received 11 votes.

As revealing as any of the writings of Jackson's day in support of him are those against him—rich in unintended vindication of Old Hickory and even *richer in unwitting self-betrayal—which is the reason for this selection of ex-cerpts from John Floyd's diary.*

The diary begins in March 1831, and continues to February 1834. It was first published in 1918. The editor, Charles H. Ambler, takes occasion in a preface to make this interesting disclaimer:

"In bringing to light this Diary, neither the editor nor the publisher vouches for the truthfulness or justice of any of the references made by Mr. Floyd to Jackson and his friends."

"It is not the tyrant . . . it is the multitude."
JOHN FLOYD (1783-1837)

Eighth day [March 1831]

My resentment toward General Jackson, the President, I find has changed to pity and a total abstraction of feeling of interest in his future course.

It is possible that what I now write for amusement to gratify a momen-tary desire may some day become history and I will therefore take more care in writing the ideas and facts more distinctly. I have not nor do I in-tend to record anything but simple facts either known to me or my friends.

This President has disappointed friends and foes; all his enemies said of him before his election has been realized. The future historian will regret to record the error these States committed in raising a victorious general of their army to the first office in the States of a civil kind, merely because he had become popular for winning a great battle and closing a war with a splendid victory over the English armies at New Orleans.

I thought Jackson had mind, which by practice in the affairs of govern-ment, would soon be qualified to manage the machine and in a short space of time he would become a statesman. That all the talents of the Union were at his command, I know, and did believe in common with all other of his friends, that he would call around him the talented and dis-tinguished men throughout the confederacy and make as strong and splendid an administration as Jefferson's.

How sorrowfully all have been disappointed!

He has surrounded himself with men of narrow minds, some of them hardly gentlemen and none of them have much character and no prin-ciples, moral or political.

Twenty-ninth day [June]

The occurrences of the day fill me with disgust. The President has dismissed three of his cabinet officers because they would not permit their wives to associate with Mrs. Eaton, the wife of the Secretary of War. This Eaton and his wife daily become more and more his favorites. Jackson has had the folly to say "That no man should receive office or favor from him that would not receive Mrs. Eaton."

This Mrs. Eaton is, and has been, notoriously a woman destitute of virtue and of morals. She was pretty, the daughter of a tavern-keeper in the city where navy officers, army officers, and sometimes members of Congress lodged. Her father, William O'Neal, was a roguish, impudent Irishman, without any principles, but a good tavern-keeper, wherefore the officers lodged with him.

His daughter, Peggy, was pretty and found out means to make Timberlake, a purser in the navy, believe she was virtuous when he married her. He, Timberlake, was often at sea and at such times his wife indulged herself in many amours. Finally she got into an amour with John H. Eaton, a Senator from Tennessee, a man of as little morals as herself, but the favorite and pet of Jackson, the President.

Finally all this came to the ears of Timberlake, who cut his own throat. In eight months after this his widow married Eaton who was, in a few weeks after that, appointed Secretary of War by Jackson, and because she was not received into company, Jackson has dismissed and is dismissing all who will not receive her, the friend of his friend, as pure and spotless.

This amour is spoken of merely because she is the wife of Eaton and urges him and the President to these measures, for she has many, very many other paramours.

The President has had the meanness to ask and has obtained certificates to prove her pure, innocent and virtuous. Good God! What an office for the President! How debased. I know, myself, that all is true which has been said of her.

Sixteenth Day [June 1832]

Congress is still in session, the elements are more and more troubled. The Northern Members insist on keeping on the tariff and oppressing the South by its execution, as it operates as a monopoly to the northern states. The Southern members resist all this. My belief is that the great wealth which has flowed in upon the North under the operation of that law of Congress has given them so strong a predilection for that system which makes them rich by the labor of the South that they will never abandon it.

The South, on the other hand, will not bear it long and I do believe they could not bear it ten years if they were willing to pay the exaction.

First day [July]

Received to-day the news of the passage of the tariff bill by a majority in the House of Representatives of one hundred and twenty-one to sixty-five—a majority, too, of the Virginia delegation voting for it.

Ninth day

We got the news to-day of Jackson's having signed the bill for internal improvement which totally annihilates every position taken in his Maysville veto. Rumor says that he will veto the United States Bank Bill.

Eleventh day [November]

The elections for President of the United States are going through the confederacy, of course, all anxiously waiting what the result will be.

Seventeenth day

Yesterday afternoon I heard of the death of Charles Carroll of Maryland, the last signer of the Declaration of Independence. He was a Catholic by persuasion, a pious, good man. I am fearful the liberty of the country, the Declaration of whose Independence he signed, will not long outlive the last of its signers.

I have heretofore been as firm and dauntless a supporter of the rights of the people and the supremacy of the Constitution as any man now living. I declare before Heaven that I never had an object but to support the Constitution in its limited construction believing as I have, and as twenty years experience and observation in public life now fully prove to my mind, that this confederacy cannot long last unless the Federal Government is administered upon this principle, which I am now hopeless of.

Jackson is again elected to the office of the President of the United States. Should he still pursue his ignorant and violent course, which there is a strong probability he will do, we will never see another President of the United States elected.

Such has been the misrule of this man and so ignorant of the Constitution he has been called to administer the government under, that the States which feel their Sovereignty insulted, contemned and threatened, writhing under the oppressing exactions of the Tariff that they talk seriously of calling a Convention of the people of their States to decide upon the constitutionality of these acts and of arresting their operation in their States.

Such is the folly of Jackson that, dizzy with his power and maddened by his tyrannical disposition, he is ordering troops to South Carolina to threaten an attack should the convention now called nullify the Tariff.

This will, if an attack is made, destroy the confederacy. Such is the man who is President and the one in whom I had originally so large a share in putting into that place. My error was an honest one. I thought he was not so ignorant and would be assisted by the good, learned, and virtuous of his party, but he has quarreled with them and has chosen the mean, ignorant and unprincipled as his counsellors.

Twenty-second day

It is now ascertained beyond a doubt that Jackson is reelected President of the United States for four years from the fourth of March next.

Now comes the downfall of the liberties of my country, or at all events, the destruction of the Confederacy. I pray God that I may not be a true prophet, but I will with truth record the facts that future inspectors may know the truth and shun the danger.

Twenty-fifth day

I this day received a letter from South Carolina from a member of the Convention that they have in that body determined to nullify all the tariff laws of Congress and if force is used against them to enforce them, then, in that event, they declare South Carolina out of the Union.

I, as Governor of Virginia, will sustain South Carolina with all my power. Let others beware.

Twenty-seventh day

I have heard this day from South Carolina. Wm. C. Preston writes that the Committee have agreed to report a measure of unconditional nullification of all the laws on the subject of the tariff. So far it is well.

Second day [December]

South Carolina is much talked of and her nullification of the tariff laws of Congress. I will first learn the opinion of the members of the Assembly of this State, before I report anything as they will meet to-morrow.

I think the flatterers of Jackson are becoming alarmed at the course of South Carolina and begin to change their language and minds.

Thirteenth day

This day I received intelligence that something would transpire in Congress of deep import. At twelve o'clock I received from a Senator in Congress, the Honorable John Tyler, a copy of a "Proclamation by Andrew Jackson, President of the United States."

This is the most extraordinary document which has ever appeared in the United States. It concentrates all power in the President and denounces all meetings in any states, as treason if to call in question the constitutionality of any act passed by Congress, denies the States to be sovereign or this to be a confederacy, and acknowledges no authority but that vested in the President.

He has ordered his army to South Carolina and is making every preparation for war. I think I shall be able to check him.

Fourteenth day

I have this day laid before the General Assembly the ordinance adopted by the Convention of the People of South Carolina, with a message, which will call for their action whereby it will be seen whether the people of this State will submit tamely to be governed by a tyrant who acknowledges no law but his own will. A republic and constitutional liberty I will have or I will perish in the struggle.

Fifteenth day

There is some sensation created in the Assembly and among the people from my message and the President's Proclamation and the Ordinance of South Carolina.

Seventeenth day

The Committee to which my message conveying to the house the Ordinance of South Carolina has not yet reported. Strange to tell, some of them are for submission to the will of Jackson.

Nineteenth day

No report yet from the Committee. I understood this morning that when my message was received in the City of Washington the friends of the President were with him almost all night consulting upon the propriety of his retracing his steps but as yet his personal hate induces him to insist upon using the sword to inforce his doctrine of treason. If so, there is no government or Constitution but his will and that Proclamation. If he uses force, I will oppose him with a military force. I nor my country, will not be enslaved without a struggle.

Twenty-sixth day

I have this day received from the Governor of Pennsylvania sundry resolutions of the Assembly of that State, approved by the Governor, requesting them to be laid before the Commonwealth (Virginia), affirming all the power to belong to the Federal Government which is claimed for it by the President by his late Proclamation ordering the people of South Carolina to repeal their ordinance of nullification and offering the military aid of that State to subdue South Carolina.

If this should take place there is no limit to the Federal Government, and the United States becomes the most arbitrary government in the world and we have lost our liberty by the action of one section of the Union by force of arms appropriating the profits of the labor of the other for their own use.

I have often said and here state that Jackson is the worst man in the Union, a scoundrel in private life, devoid of patriotism and a tyrant withal, and is only capable of using power that he may have the gratification of seeing himself obeyed by every human being. He speaks the lan guage ungrammatically, writes it worse, and is exceedingly ignorant, but strange to tell, he is feared and most all seem disposed to give up their liberty rather than displease him, who is now so popular that many fear to encounter his frown and many, very many, seem willing to let him rule, the arbitrary despot, provided they can obtain office.

Thus office and a base love for gold and power have mainly contributed to enslave us by a brutal, ignorant soldier.

Notwithstanding all these things my countrymen are inert and many say, "Oh, I think Jackson does not mean to wage war, he is only getting his vast armies together, chartering steamboats, manning his ships, merely to scare South Carolina a little."

I, at this moment, feel assured we will soon be by that monster and villain, Jackson, involved deeply in a civil war. I deplore this the more as the Constitution of Virginia has so limited the power of the Governor and through jealousy of him, has made the most imbecile government that a free people ever lived under, and still more strange, they have had no fears in regard to the President, yet I will do the best I can to save the liberty of my country. I expect civil war and I expect to perish in it, but none shall say hereafter in the history of this coming conflict that I, as

Governor of Virginia, wanted either prudence, courage or patriotism. I will do my duty though I have no fondness for power of office.

Fifth day [January 1833]

The whole of this week the debate on our Federal Relations has continued and each day's debate convinces me that we hold our liberty by a very slender thread and a very uncertain tenure.

I have heard almost all the members of the Legislature speak who have delivered orations on this subject and am fully of the opinion that they are more afraid of offending the Tyrant, Jackson, than of preparing the minds of the people for resistance to encroachments upon their liberty.

Broadnax, Bruce, and Witcher feel like free men and assert like men of firmness the rights of the States, but all the others submit abjectly to the usurpations of Jackson. Mr. Brown, of Petersburgh, spoke yesterday and sustained the President's proclamation throughout. At last he said a "state had the right to judge the violations of the pact, treaty or constitution (call it what you will) and secede from the Union but that the remaining twenty-three had an equal right to judge whether they had or not so violated the Constitution and if they were of the opinion that they had not so violated the Constitution, or compact, that they had a right to compel the seceded State to submit to the law and return to the Union. That the President had not now power to wage war upon South Carolina, but that it was in the power of Congress to pass laws to enable him to subdue that State under the provisions of the Constitution!

This is the highest toned consolidation doctrine I have ever heard in my life, entertained by any man south of the Potomac, John Marshall, perhaps, excepted.

If the Legislature sustains that doctrine then the States cease to exist as Sovereignties, and the Union becomes one great consolidated despotism. This, by the by, seems the language of the whole Jackson party of this time, which is an immense majority and our liberty now depends entirely on our ability to prevent them from being carried into absolute execution until the people once more dispense with their fears so as to enable them to think.

If we fail, then we have lost our liberty forever! This results from the eclat which belongs to the drum and the sword. I know Jackson personally, he has not the capacity to govern the country, nor has he the information, but if he had the virtue to choose men of morals and character he would have acquitted himself to the country and to posterity. His vices and his violence have urged him onward and thousands sing praises to his progress because they have not the courage to say he is wrong or that they will not be his slaves.

Fifteenth day

This day the debate on Federal Relations came to a close so far as to take the vote between Brown of Petersburgh's substitute to the original resolution of the committee of twenty-one. These resolutions of Mr. Brown's are of a spirit so slavish and so submissive that I wonder men could be pleased to so easily surrender the liberty of the country to the caprice of a tyrant.

These resolutions were adopted by the House of Delegates by a majority of one vote. They were written to please General Jackson and adopted to please him. So ends the high character of the State of Virginia and such the end of liberty.

Though we have not chains upon our hands, still we have no guard for our liberty but hold it at the will of a tyrant, and all mouths exhaust all terms in his praises; and when they are told they have voted away their liberty they say no, "the General Assembly will meet as heretofore."

When they are told the General Assembly has voted away the power to protect them, they say, "O, we know General Jackson will not hurt us."

Poor, wretched men! I now perceive how all tyrants of the earth have overturned the liberties of their countries, and find the process clear, plain, and simple. It is not the tyrant who does this thing, it is the multitude.

1832:   LONDON'S DARLING IS VEXED

AMERICA was play-hungry enough in the 1830s to make the long Atlantic passage worth while to many a British stage star. Fanny Kemble, 23 years old, proved a sensation when she came to New York. Offstage, too, she was a prize package, with the town's best people vying for her like bidders at an auction. Though she kept her feelings to herself at the time, Fanny did not return their affection; and a few years later, when her diary was published, these same Americans were shocked to their marrow to learn what their imperious young visitor had really thought of them.

Fanny was of a long line of show people who were used to holding the limelight. She was a niece of the great Sarah Siddons; daughter of Shakespearean actor Charles Kemble, who accompanied her to America; and for three years prior to the incident here recounted in her far-famed diary, a leading lady in her own right.

While in America, despite her prejudices, she married Pierce Butler, a Southern planter, but later left him, and in 1847 went back to the stage and eventually to London.

"This worthless clapping of hands!"
FANNY KEMBLE (1809-1893)

11th [September 1832]

This day week we landed in New York.

At four o'clock sent for a hair-dresser, that I might in good time see that I am not made an object on my first night. He was a Frenchman, and after listening profoundly to my description of the head-dress I wanted, replied, as none but a Frenchman could, "*Madame, la difficulte n'est pas d'executer votre coiffure mais de la bien concevoir.*" However, he conceived and executed sundry very smooth-looking bows, and, upon the whole, dressed my hair very nicely, but charged a dollar for so doing; O nefarious.

14th

Drove all about New York, which more than ever reminded me of the towns in France; passed the Bowery theatre, which is a handsome, finely-proportioned building, with a large brazen eagle plastered on the pediment.

We passed a pretty house, which Col. —— called an old mansion; mercy on me, him, and it! Old! I thought of Warwick Castle, of Hatfield, of Checquers, of Hopwood—old, and there it stood, with its white pillars and Italian-looking portico, for all the world like one of our own city's yesterday-grown boxes. Old, quotha! the woods and waters, and hills and skies alone are old here; the works of men are in the very greenness and un-mellowed imperfection of youth; true, 'tis a youth full of vigorous sap and glorious promise; spring, laden with blossoms, foretelling abundant and rich produce, and so let them be proud of it.

But the worst of it is, the Americans are not satisfied with glorying in what they are—which, considering the time and opportunities they have had, is matter of glory quite sufficient,—they are never happy without comparing this their sapling to the giant oaks of the old world,—and what can one say to that? *Is* New York like London? No, by my two troths it is not; but the oak was an acorn once, and New York will surely, if the world holds together long enough, become a lordly city, such as we know of beyond the sea.

17th

At twelve, we went to rehearsal. That washed-out man who failed in London when he acted Romeo with me is to be my Fazio [in the tragedy of that name by Henry Hart Milman]; let us hope he will know some of his words tomorrow night, for he is at present most innocent of any such knowledge.

At seven, went to the theatre. It was my dear father's first appearance in this new world, and my heart ached with anxiety. The weather was intensely hot, yet the theatre was crowded: when he came on, they gave him what every body here calls an immense reception; but they should see our London audience get up and wave hats and handkerchiefs, and shout welcome as they do to us. The tears were in my eyes, and all I could say was, "They might as well get up, I think."

My father looked well, and acted beyond all praise; but oh, what a fine and delicate piece of work this is! There is not one sentence, line, or word of this part [Hamlet] which my father has not sifted grain by grain; there is not one scene or passage to which he does not give its fullest and most entire substance.

18th

Rose at eight. At eleven, went to rehearsal. Mr. Keppel is just as nervous and as imperfect as ever: what on earth will he, or shall I, do tonight!

Came home, got things out for the theatre, and set like any stroller stitching for dear life at my head-dress.

Mr. H—— and his nephew called: the latter asked me if I was at all apprehensive? No, by my troth, I am not; and that not because I feel sure of success, for I think it very probable the Yankees may like to show their critical judgment and independence by damning me; but because, thank God, I do not care whether they do or not.

At half-past six, went to the theatre. They acted the farce of Popping the Question first, in order, I suppose, to get the people to their places before the play began.

Poor Mr. Keppel was gasping for breath; he moved my compassion infinitely; I consoled and comforted him all I could, gave him some of my lemonade to swallow, for he was choking with fright; sat myself down with my back to the audience, and up went the curtain.

Owing to the position in which I was sitting, and my plain dress, most unheroine-like in its make and colour, the people did not know me, and would not have known me for some time, if that stupid man had done as I kept bidding him, gone on; but instead of doing so, he stood stock still, looked at me, and then at the audience, whereupon the latter caught an inkling of the truth, and gave me such a reception as I get in Covent Garden theatre every time I act a new part. The house was very full.

Mr. Keppel was frightened to death, and in the very second speech was quite out: it was in vain that I prompted him; he was too nervous to take the word, and made a complete mess of it. This happened more than once in the first scene; and at the end of the first act, as I left the stage, I said to D——, "It's all up with me, I can't do anything now;" for having to prompt my Fazio, frightened by his fright, annoyed by his forgetting his crossings, and positions, utterly unable to work myself into any thing like excitement, I thought the whole thing must necessarily go to pieces.

However, once rid of my encumbrance, which I am at the end of the second act, I began to move a little more freely, gathered up my strength, and set to work comfortably by myself; whereupon, the people applauded, I warmed (warmed, quotha? the air was steam) and got through very satisfactorily, at least so it seems.

She understates her success. Philip Hone, a leading citizen and theater-goer of the time, reported it as "such an exhibition of female powers as we have never before witnessed." See the account he gives in his own diary under the same date on page 200 of this volume.

My dresses are very beautiful; but oh, but oh, the musquitoes had made dreadful havoc with my arms, which were covered with hills as large and red as Vesuvius in eruption.

19th

Got up, breakfasted, and off to rehearsal; Romeo and Juliet.

Mr. Keppel has been dismissed, poor man! I'm sorry for him: my father is to play Romeo with me. I'm sorrier still for that.

20th

Rose at eight. After breakfast, went to rehearse Romeo and Juliet. Poor Mr. Keppel is fairly laid on the shelf. What a funny passion he had, by the by, for going down upon his knees. In Fazio, at the end of the judgment scene, when I was upon mine, down he went upon his, making the most absurd, devout looking *vis-a-vis* I ever beheld: in the last scene, too, when he ought to have been going off to execution, down he went again upon his knees, and no power on earth could get him up again, for Lord knows how long.

21st

They were talking of Mr. Keppel. By the by, of that gentleman: Mr. Simpson sent me this morning, for my decision, a letter from Mr. Keppel, soliciting another trial, and urging the hardness of his case, in being condemned upon a part which he had had no time to study.

My own opinion of poor Mr. Keppel is, that no power on earth or in heaven can make him act decently; however, of course, I did not object to his trying again; he did not swamp me the first night, so I don't suppose he will the fifth.

After dinner, Colonel   called, and began pulling out heaps of newspapers, and telling us a long story about Mr. Keppel, who, it seems, has been writing to the papers, to convince them and the public that he is a good actor, at the same time throwing out sundry hints, which seem aimed our way, of injustice, oppression, hard usage, and the rest on't.

When they were gone, went to the theatre; the house was very good, the play, the School for Scandal. I played pretty fairly, and looked very nice. The people were stupid to a degree, to be sure; poor things! it was very hot. Indeed, I scarce understand how they should be amused with the School for Scandal; for though the dramatic situations are so exquisite, yet the wit is far above the generality of even our own audiences, and the tone and manners altogether are so thoroughly English, that I should think it must be for the most part incomprehensible to the good people here.

22d

Went into a shop to order a pair of shoes. The shopkeepers in this place, with whom I have hitherto had to deal, are either condescendingly familiar, or insolently indifferent in their manner. Your washerwoman sits down before you, while you are *standing* speaking to her; and a shop-boy bringing things for your inspection, not only sits down, but keeps his hat on in your drawing-room.

The worthy man to whom I went for my shoes was so amazingly ungracious, that at first I thought I would go out of the shop; but recollecting that I should probably only go farther and fare worse, I gulped, sat down, and was measured.

24th

After breakfast, went to rehearsal: Venice Preserved, with Mr. Keppel, who did not appear to me to know the words even, and seemed perfectly bewildered at being asked to do the common business of the piece. "Mercy on me! what will he do tonight?" thought I.

The house was very full, and they received Mr. K—— with acclamations and shouts of applause.

In the senate scene, when I was entreating for mercy, and *struggling* for my life, he was prancing round the stage in every direction, flourishing his dagger in the air: I wish to Heaven I had got up and run away; it would but have been natural, and served him extremely right.

In the parting scene,—oh, what a scene it was!—instead of going away from me when he said, "Farewell forever," he stuck to my skirts, though in the same breath that I adjured him in the words of my part not to leave me, I added, aside, "Get away from me, oh, *do!*" When I exclaimed, "Not one kiss at parting," he kept embracing and kissing me like mad; and when I ought to have been pursuing him and calling after him, "Leave thy dagger with me," he hung himself up against the wing, and remained dangling there for five minutes. I was half crazy! and the good people sat and swallowed it all: they deserved it, by my troth, they did.

I prompted him constantly, and once, after struggling in vain to free myself from him, was obliged, in the middle of my part, to exclaim, "You hurt me dreadfully, Mr. Keppel!" He clung to me, cramped me, crumpled me,—dreadful! I never experienced anything like this before, and made up my mind that I never would again. I played of course like a wretch, finished my part as well as I could, and, as soon as the play was over, went to my father and Mr. Simpson, and declared to them both my determination not to go upon the stage again with that gentleman for a hero.

Three trials are as many as, in reason, anybody can demand, and come what may, *I* will not be subjected to this sort of experiment again. At the end of the play, the clever New Yorkians actually called for Mr. Keppel! and this most worthless clapping of hands, most worthlessly bestowed upon such a worthless object, is what, by the nature of my craft, I am bound to care for; I spit at it from the bottom of my soul!

1835: LIFE IN OLD NATCHEZ

THEY CALLED the early West wild and woolly, but the old South was, after its fashion, just as quick to violence. An outward serenity of colonnaded mansions and lazy, tree-lined streets was deceptive. For example, while the Mississippi community known as Natchez-under-the-hill had a well-earned reputation as a hangout of gamblers, whores, thieves and ruffians, any trigger-happy citizen was as readily accommodated in the Natchez above the hill, where there was actually more violence, blow for blow and brawl for brawl, than down on the busy, working riverfront.

In the diary of William Johnson old Natchez is brought to life as no later historian could possibly recreate it— life among rich planters, turfmen, young blades with hot blood or the dangerous pretense to it, tradesmen a step down from the plantation class, and slaves who were worth dollars without owning any.

William Johnson was a "free citizen of color." There were not many such in Mississippi; but this man was remarkable in many other respects too. As owner of the town's most fashionable barber shop he prospered, reached a fabulous estate for any Negro—estimated between $20,000 and $30,000—and owned slaves himself. He traded with white folks in many commodities, lent them money, counseled with them, accepted their gratitude and their condescension alike in good grace, and deftly tiptoed his way among the sinkholes of race rot in the land and time of his being.

For sixteen years he kept a diary. On his death the family put it away and succeeding generations guarded it jealously for a century. In 1938 Edwin Adams Davis and William Ransom Hogan, heads of the history departments of Louisiana State University and Tulane University respectively, were given permission by the widow of a grandson of Johnson to make a study of the scores of leather-bound volumes and smaller notebooks she kept in her attic. The result was publication of the diary in 1951 under the title William Johnson's Natchez. They had unearthed a historical treasure trove. "It is no understatement," commented the well-known Southern writer Hodding Carter, "to say that this is the most unusual personal record ever kept in the United States."

Interest in the diary was so widespread that Davis and Hogan published in 1954 a second book based on the diary, entitled The Barber of Natchez.

"If he bothers me I'll—never mind."
WILLIAM JOHNSON (1809-1851)

3 [November 1835]

Mr Bledsoe orders a wig to be made, very Light Hair—Finds William at Mr Parkers Kitchen with his Girls. Struck him with the whip 1st and then with the stick. He ran home and I followed him there and whiped him well for it, having often told him about going Down there—He then Comes Out on Bill Nix and Seys that he Bought five finger Rings &c.

4

I took Bill Nix and gave him a whiping. He then Confessed that he had taken the Key of Side Bourd which unlocked Mothers trunk and that he had got money frequently to the amount of Eight or ten Dollars. He had bought a finger Ring, cost $3.00, a whip from Mr Spielmans Zack, cost 1.00, a pair of Boots from Middleton, cost $2.50 He paid John for a pair of Pantaloons. His Mother was greatly hurt at the Conduct of Her Degraded Son.

5

Mr Duolon paid me for two months shaving $2.00. I paid Mr Mellen five Dollars for One years Subscription to the Weekly Courier & Journal for Mr Jas Miller [Johnson's brother-in-law, who had sold him the barber shop in 1830] Mr Smith paid me for One months Shaving 1.50. I paid Mr Bledsoes Boy $11 for 2 Gunea pigs

6

I paid $2.50 for a Bundle of Shingles. The Citizens went Out to the Race track in search of the Gamblers; they Brought in Elick Piper. Had a meeting at the Court House for the purpose of trying him—Gridley took him from them and put him to Jail—Twas their Intention to have whipd him.

The Adams County Anti-Gambling Society had elected a Vigilance Committee to order professional gamblers out of town.

8

The Fencibles [volunteer militia company] Left Here for Vicksburg on Bourd of the Steam Boat Ponchartrain—31 in Number.

12

Mc & myself went out to Parson Connelly Sale to look at his Cows. They were all Dry. I made Mag Dunbar a present of 2 guinea pigs.

13

Mother Buys Mary and her Child [slaves] from Mr Murcherson for $800.00.

24

A Bear belonging to Mr Phiffs Killed a Little Yellow Child Down at Mr Parkers Hotel. They had to shoot him Dead to Loose him—Mc takes his horse home to his own stable—Mr Pulling and Milne has a sort of a fight about the moving of some coal. Mr P. threw a Hatchet at Mr M. and it mist him. Mr M attempted to get a gun Down to shoot.

Juno 3, 1836

I Bot Moses from a man by the name of William Good, at Least I Bot him at auction under the Hammer for four Hundred Dollars cash—I Bot also 2 boxes of wine at 2.87½ per Box, 5 small Boxes of shaving soap, 43 cents per Box. I Bot of Mr Chew all the Birds that Mr Grayson Left here and their Cages also for ten Dollars Cash.

4

Old La Vine and a Little Frenchman by the name of Surie has a Street fight, the one with a shovell, the other with a stick. Surie made La Viene back clear Back from Mr Murchersons store to his own. It was very Laughable.

24

Roberson and Dr Hogg has a kind of a fight, old Dr Hogg made him Travell pretty fast. Particulars are those, Roberson Owed the Dr 12 dollars for Medical Services. The Dr gave his account to Whiting to Collect for him so he presented the Acct. to Roberson & R. said that he was not the man, so Dr suied on it, & Robs. Came to his office to abuse him about it, and the old Dr told him to Leave his office. The Dr and him came to Blowes, and the Dr struck him with a chair & R. ran in the Street and struck him in the Breast with a Brick, then ran up Street as Hard as he could split and the old Dr after him.

So Roberson run throuh Thistles Stable and came out at the Back side of the Stable and went Home. The Dr & Maj Miller went around to Robs House. Dr went in & struck him with his cane and R. caught the stick and the sword came out, and the Dr would have killed him if his arm had not been caught by Mr Ross—Roberson then Broke and run as hard as he could split to the Jail, and went in for Safe Keeping—In time of the fight Robs Brother Struck Maj Miller on the head with a Brick Bat and then Run and the old Maj after him as hard as he could split. The Maj stumbled and fell and as he fell he made a cut at Robison and Cut him in the Butt.

August 14

A pascel of young men very drunk at Mr West Tavern. They acted very much Like Fools.

November 28

To Day we had Bloody work for a while in the streets up at Throckmortons Corner. Last night up at Mrs Rowans Bourding House several gentlemen were in conversation about a Duel that was fought in South Carolina. When Mr Charles Stewart stated that those Gentlemen that fought actually fought with Bullits, Mr Dahlgreen Said they must have fought with paper Bullets—Mr C. Stewart then Said if any man would say that they fought with paper Bullits that he is a Damed Lyar and a Dd Scoundrel & a Dmd Coward—this was at the Supper Table

Mr Dalhgreen Jumped up and Slaped Mr C. Stewarts Cheek one very hard Slapp. They were then parted so young Stewart told him that they would settle it in the morning—So this morning young Stewart took a Stand up at Carpenters Drug Store for the purpose of making the attackt upon Dalhgreen as he would be going to the Bank—Dr Hubbard at the Request of his Brother went up to Carpenters with young Stewart to see him Out in the affair

Elick Stewart said that he would not take any part in the affair and he took a stand over on Sorias Corner—and as Dalhgreen past the Door Stewart steped up to him and told him that now was the time to Settle therr Dispute and at the Same time Struck Mr Dalhgreen with his stick; Mr D then Struck him Back with an umberralla—Stewart Struck him with the Stick again—Mr D. then steped Back and Drew a Pistol and Fired at Mr S. and missed him—Mr S. then Drew and Fired and the Ball Lodged under the arm in the Left Side of Mr Dalhgreen; Mr D. then steped in at Throckmortons Store.

S. steped in at the Door but finding that D. had another Pistol he steped Back and stood in the caseing of the Door.

D. then advanced on him, shot Him on Left Side of the face on the Temple or uper hinge of the Jaw Bone and the instant the Ball took Effect he Droped on his Knees and Fell over on the pavement as Dead, so Dead that he Barely Breathed.

At the instant he fell Mr Elick Stewart ran up and struck D. with his fist. D. then advanced on him with an Empty Pistol and in doing so Dr Hubbard shoved Him Back, E. S. Drew a Bouye Knife and commenced cuting at him—Mr D. had no weapon at this time and was fighting with his naked hands and Mr E. S. with the Knife—it was one of the gamest fights that we have ever had in Our City before— E. S. cut him twice over the Head and cut his Little finger nearly off and split his hand pretty Bad.

29

I went to day around to Dr Hubbards office to shave young Mr Stewarts head, he was quite ill—I then went on up to Mrs Rowans to Shave Dr Dalhgreens Beard off—he was very Comfortably Situated and in a thriving condition.

December 3

Poor young Stewart is worse to Day.

14

Business very Brisk and Simpson Sick—I took the measure of Mr Charles Stewarts Head to day for to have him a wig got.

February 1, 1837

Ganson Runaway from Natchez To Day. He sold Out his Liece & groceries the other day To Henderson the Carriage maker for $3500. He got the cash in hand for what He Sold & then Fled the City—Left his wife behind him in a particular situation.

14

I wrode out to Mr T. G. Elliss to Shave him and I did so. He had a Little Son there that was asking him all sorts of questions; then next came a Daughter of his, a very hansome Black Eyed Little Girl. She was older than the Boy. She stood there Looking on at me Shave her Father. All at Once she Broke wind—I was fit to Burst with Laughter.

27

Mr Quertomas came in this morning and paid me One Hundred Dollars, this being money that I Loaned Ever Since the 21st July, 1836 to Mr E Thomas. He gave me an Order on Mr Quertomas for the money which he excepted and paid. I call him a Gentleman, who Disputes it? Mr Ingraham sent me in a pair of Razors that I sold to him Some time ago. After he has had them set three or four times he concludes not to take them and sends for the money that he paid for them. I sent it out—It was $5 but I think if he comes a Bothering me any more I will be very apt to —Never mind.

On June 20, 1851, the Natchez Courier ran a story under the headline "SHOCKING MURDER" that began:

> Our city was very much excited on Tuesday morning by hearing that what could only be deemed a horrible and deliberate murder had been committed upon an excellent and most inoffensive man. It was ascertained that William Johnson, a free man of color, born and raised in Natchez, and holding a respected position on account of his character, intelligence and deportment, had been shot . . .

The murder was the culmination of a long quarrel with Baylor Winn, a neighbor, over the boundary between their lands in the swamp. Johnson, while riding home from downriver, was ambushed. Winn was arrested and there followed two years of sensational court action.

Mississippi law prohibited testimony by Negroes against whites. Winn declared himself a white man with a mixture of Indian blood. He was in fact married to a white woman, and this is what saved him; for when Johnson's family procured documents from Winn's native state of Virginia to show that he was a free Negro, the court, on a flimsy technicality, refused to admit these papers in evidence. Better to let the murder of a Negro go unpunished than involve a white woman in a race scandal! So ruled the court of justice in the state of Mississippi.

★

1836:   DAVY CROCKETT AT THE ALAMO

☆

WHEN RANGY, buckskin-clad frontiersman David Crockett came to Washington fresh from the Tennessee back country in 1827, he told the House of Representatives in his famous maiden speech that he'd "eat any man opposed to Jackson." Later he broke with Jackson, and when he came up for re-election in 1831, was licked. He mended his political fences in Weakley County, ran in

1833, and won. But again, embittered by Jackson's victory over the national bank, he joined the conservative opposition. Delighted Whigs paraded him around the country as a homespun exhibit of revolt against Jackson's "despotism." The folks back home, however, still liked Old Hickory. When election time came around again, Crockett lost by 255 votes. He declared himself through with politics: "They can go to hell and I'll go to Texas."

But Texas just then was not without its own brand of hell. On March 1, 1836, a handful of Texans declared independence of Mexico. Santa Anna immediately marched against them. Crockett arrived in San Antonio just in time to join 182 other Americans in defending the Alamo against 3,000 Mexican troops. Every man in the Alamo was killed.

Crockett's Exploits and Adventures in Texas, including an unfinished account of the Alamo fight, was published the following year in London. Its authenticity has been questioned, along with that of just about everything else Crockett "wrote." There is good reason to believe that his political crony, Augustin Smith Clayton, of Georgia, ghosted much of the writing that bears his name. In fact, at the conclusion of the Life of Martin Van Buren, which appeared under Crockett's by-line, the author brassily declares, "I wrote this just as truly as President Andrew Jackson wrote his state papers; which everybody knows, of course, he did not write at all."

What is obvious in this admission, however, may or may not apply to the Texas diary. Historians accept it as a truthful account of what happened at the Alamo. When it appeared as part of Crockett's Autobiography in 1860, the publisher, G. G. Evans, of Philadelphia, recalled that in 1833 Crockett had told newspapermen he was very angry about the way he had been made to appear ridiculous in the press, and that he was going to write the story of his life "to represent myself as I really am." The publisher insisted Crockett was in fact the author of every line of the work.

There is nothing to prove that he wasn't. And if it seems strange to us that he would find time in the midst of the siege to record it for posterity—well, taller tales than that were told by Davy Crockett.

"We did not escape unscathed . . ."
DAVID CROCKETT (1786-1836)

San Antonio, February 19, 1836

We are all in high spirits, though we are rather short of provisions for men who have appetites that could digest anything but oppression; but no matter, we have a prospect of soon getting our bellies full of fighting.

February 22

The Mexicans, about sixteen hundred strong, with their president, Santa Anna at their head, aided by Generals Almonte, Cos, Sesma, and Castrillon, are within two leagues of Bexar.

February 23

Early this morning the enemy came in sight, marching in regular order and displaying their strength to the greatest advantage in order to strike us with terror. But that was no go. We held a short council of war, and, finding that we should be completely surrounded and overwhelmed by numbers if we remained in the town, we concluded to withdraw to the fortress of Alamo and defend it to the last extremity.

We accordingly filed off in good order, having some days before placed all the surplus provisions, arms, and ammunition in the fortress. We have had a large national flag made; it is composed of thirteen stripes, red and white alternately, on a blue ground with a large white star of five points in the center, and between the points the letters *T-E-X-A-S.*

As soon as all our little band, about one hundred and fifty in number, had entered and secured the fortress in the best possible manner, we set about raising our flag on the battlements. The enemy marched into Bexar and took possession of the town, a blood-red flag flying at their head, to indicate that we need not expect quarters if we should fall into their clutches.

In the afternoon a messenger was sent from the enemy to Colonel Travis, demanding an unconditional and absolute surrender of the garrison, threatening to put every man to the sword in case of refusal. The only answer he received was a cannon shot; so the messenger left us with a flea in his ear, and the Mexicans commenced firing grenades at us, but without doing any mischief.

At night Colonel Travis sent an express to Colonel Fanning at Goliad, about three or four days' march from this place, to let him know that we are besieged. The old pirate volunteered to go on this expedition and accordingly left the fort after nightfall.

February 27

The cannonading began early this morning, and ten bombs were thrown into the fort, but fortunately exploded without doing any mischief. So far it has been a sort of tempest in a teapot, not unlike a pitched battle in the Hall of Congress.

February 28

Santa Anna appears determined to verify his threat and convert the blooming paradise into a howling wilderness. For just one fair crack at that rascal even at a hundred yards distance I would bargain to break my Betsey and never pull trigger again. My name's not Crockett if I wouldn't get glory enough to appease my stomach for the rest of my life.

February 29

I had a little sport this morning before breakfast. The enemy had planted a piece of ordnance within gunshot of the fort during the night, and the first thing in the morning they commenced a brisk cannonade point-blank against the spot where I was snoring.

I turned out pretty smart and mounted the rampart. The gun was charged again, a fellow stepped forth to touch her off, but before he could apply the match I let him have it and he keeled over.

A second stepped up, snatched the match from the hand of the dying man, but Thimblerig, who had followed me, handed me his rifle, and the next instant the Mexican was stretched on the earth beside the first.

A third came up to the cannon, my companion handed me another gun, and I fixed him off in like manner. A fourth, then a fifth, seized the match, who both met with the same fate, and then the whole party gave it up as a bad job and hurried off to the camp, leaving the cannon ready charged where they had planted it. I came down, took my bitters, and went to breakfast.

March 1

The enemy's forces have been increasing in numbers daily, notwithstanding they have already lost about three hundred men in the several assaults they have made upon us.

March 4

Shells have been falling into the fort like hail during the day, but without effect. About dusk in the evening, we observed a man running toward the fort, pursued by about half a dozen Mexican cavalry. The bee hunter immediately knew him to be the old pirate who had gone to Goliad, and calling to the two hunters, he sallied out of the fort to the relief of the old man, who was hard pressed. I followed close after.

Before we reached the spot the Mexicans were close on the heels of the old man, who stopped suddenly, turned short upon his pursuers, discharged his rifle, and one of the enemy fell from his horse. The chase was renewed, but finding that he would be overtaken and cut to pieces, he now turned again and, to the amazement of the enemy, became the assailant in his turn. He clubbed his gun and dashed among them like a wounded tiger, and they fled like sparrows.

By this time we reached the spot and in the ardor of the moment followed some distance before we saw that our retreat to the fort was cut off by another detachment of cavalry. Nothing was to be done but to fight our way through. We were all of the same mind. "Go ahead!" cried I, and they shouted, "Go ahead, Colonel!"

We dashed among them, and a bloody conflict ensued. They were about twenty in number, and they stood their ground. After the fight had continued about five minutes, a detachment was seen issuing from the fort to our relief; and the Mexicans scampered off, leaving eight of their comrades upon the field.

But we did not escape unscathed, for both the pirate and the bee hunter were mortally wounded, and I received a sabre cut across the forehead. The old man died, without speaking, as soon as we entered the fort.

March 5

Pop, pop, pop! Bom, bom, bom! throughout the day. No time for memorandums now. Go ahead! Liberty and independence forever!

1845:   FARMER BROWN KEEPS UP WITH HIS CHORES

IN THE STORY OF AMERICA, *such doings as making soap and going out after stray hogs cannot be passed over as negligible minutiae; too many people had to do them. William R. Brown was born in Urbana, Ohio. At 17 he apprenticed to a carpenter, but after the crash of 1837 found work scarce, and in 1841 went to Red Rock, Minnesota, to try farming. He took up a claim one mile square, but claim jumpers cut him down to 160 acres. In 1851, times having got better again, he sold the farm, crossed the river to West St. Paul, speculated in land, and became "worth" $50,000. Six years later there was another depression. William Brown went back to farming.*

"How time flies!"
WILLIAM R. BROWN (1816-1874)

Territory of Wiskonsan, Oct. 25 [1845]

Finished Harvesting & burying our Rutabagas and flat Turnips.

27

Warm & pleasant put up 2 barrels of ashes to leach. Hauled up sand and lime for Daubing purposes.

28

Martha made pot of soap; used 22 lbs Tallow in making it.

29

Commenced daubing the old Kitchen. Went just at night to burn around our hay stack but the grass would not burn.

Nov. 1

Castrated 4 Pigs.

7

We banked the dirt up around the Houses.

10

Sold 1 Barrel onions for $4.00, also 32 heads Cabbage at 2.00.

13

Steam Boat *Otter* arrived; did not stop. I walked up to Fork; intended bringing Flour, sugar, molases &c down but Capt. Mumford charged me so much I could not afford to pay Freight; received the Mail.

17

C. Cavileer & myself went to the Fork in a canoe. Brot home our canoe loaded with Leather & sadlery, sugar, molasses, &c.; got home late at Night.

19

Went to drive home our cattle; looked through the Bottom for them but found them not; went down below Brissettes House on the Slough, then found them; heard that Holtons cattle were destroying our hay.

24

Harrison & I choped & hauled 5 loads of fire wood.

25

After dinner H. & I Butchered a hog; at sunset Martha, Harrison & Charley & myself went over to Mr Holtons & helped to eat a fine fat roast goose.

27

H & I ground up our axes. At about one oclock today Harrison frosted the Tip of his nose.

4 [December]

Fine day. Harrison & I hauled 1 load of hay & loaded on another very large load, but crossing the Creek our sled upset & we left most of our hay.

13

Broke our sled. When we arrived at home found a party of our Neighbors there, a Weding party consisting James S. Norris & Sophia Haskell to be married, attended by Joseph Haskell, Mrs. Mary Davis & Clara Haskell. They arrived at 11 oclock, took dinner, tarried untill 8 in the evening, took supper. I married Norris & Sophia & they all went home.

14

This morning I discovered that 2 of my Turnip holes have commenced Roting & caved in; they had on them 3 inches of straw & 4 of Dirt and a small chimney fixed in the Top with a flue of 2 inches square; these had been stoped up when the weather set in very cold but still the Rutabagas were too warm. Last year I put on my Rutabagas about 8 or 10 inches of dirt & lost most of them in consequence of their being too warm; this year I only put on 4 inches & still they are Roting; this is astonishing to me.

16

E. Brissette & I went out on the hills to look for his hogs which have been lost for several weeks. I found them. Brissette & I followed them all day but could not get to them.

17

Brissette & I went out & built a pen over his hogs bed (we found where they slept) hoping at night we could slip up & shut the door.

23

Harrison & I went down to haul Brissettes hogs home; he had shut them all up but one little pig; it ran away.

29

I am assisting Ford to make a Train [*traineau de glace,* a long toboggan drawn by oxen, dogs or ponies].

January 1, 1846

This is the first day of the year 1846; how time flies.

★

1831-51: METROPOLIS IN THE MAKING

☆

IN 1825 a barrel of flour was shipped from the village of Cleveland to Buffalo, then sent through the just opened Erie Canal to Albany, down the Hudson River to a dock in New York City, and out again by sea to Charleston, South Carolina. Before the Canal was opened the freight on that barrel, to the same destination, would have been $30. Now it was $1.50. And New Yorkers knew their city was destined to become the metropolis.

Philip Hone watched it grow from 200,000 people to 500,000, and told the story in his diary. For this he was well qualified. To his mansion "uptown"— that is, across the street from City Hall Park—came the big men of trade, ton and politics.

Hone succeeded in business very early in life. Instead of going to college he was taken into partnership by his elder brother John. John Hone was running a highly profitable commission business and auctioning off cargoes that came into the city over the new trade routes.

At 25 Philip had an income of more than $50,000. Within a few years he was one of New York's richest men. Then, when he was not quite forty, he decided to quit business and catch up on his book-learning. "I would give half I possess in the world," he wrote, "to enjoy the advantages of a classical education." About this he was more sensitive than he need have been; for his diary makes it evident that he had managed a very serviceable self-education— good enough, indeed, to enable him to hold his own at the summit of society, as a power in politics, and as a patron of the arts.

Politically he was a conservative of the deepest dye. In 1825, through a lucky break which split the Democratic opposition, he was elected Mayor for a one-year term. But he lost the next year. Meanwhile in the national scene Andrew Jackson's star was in the ascendant, and Hone, who had always looked down his nose at "the mob," felt it was a pretty good time to stop running for office. He was content to work behind the political scene until 1839, when his Whig friends induced him to run for State Senator. He was badly beaten.

He was content too, and more in his element, when dickering with European agents for additions to his art collection, or playing host to Washington Irving or Fanny Kemble, or fishing with Daniel Webster, or hobnobbing with his fellow-founders of the Union Club. These were his walks of life until the financial panic of 1837 took away half his money or more and brought him to a decision to go back to work, first as postmaster, then as insurance executive, and finally as consultant to the collector of revenue. He left an estate of more than $100,000.

About his diary, he said in 1831, "It has become a habit with me to write in it and affords me pleasure. It is not like writing letters, which may be done or let alone, and becomes, therefore, a task, and as such is more or less irksome; but this is part of my daily occupation. If I should live some dozen or twenty years I shall enjoy the retrospection; or my children, if they revere the memory of their father, will in turning over the pages of this book have something to remind them of him—something that will 'prate of his whereabouts' and inform them how he thought and what he did 'about these times.'"

The twenty-eight blank books in which Hone kept his 23-year diary are now in the safekeeping of the New York Historical Society. A version was published by Bayard Tuckerman in 1889, and Allan Nevins brought out an excellent two-volume edition in 1927. For his selections Mr. Nevins had to sift through 2,000,000 handwritten words.

"Men have become immensely rich . . ."
PHILIP HONE (1780-1851)

May 5 [1831]

It is an interesting and gratifying subject of reflection that our country at large, and particularly this city, is at this time prosperous beyond all former example. Foreign commerce is in a thriving condition; vessels are worth fifty per cent more than they were two years since, and freights are nearly double; real estate, up and down town, equally high; houses in great demand, at advanced rents; the dealers in imported goods doing a safe and profitable business; the farmer selling his wool at seventy-five cents per pound, and availing himself of the increased price of bread-stuffs occasioned by the brisk foreign demand; the manufacturers, both of woollen and cotton goods, fully employed, and doing better than at any former period; and the lawyers doing nothing.

June 15 [1832]

The Albany steamboat which came down this afternoon brought the alarming news that the cholera, which has of late been the scourge of the eastern continent, has crossed the Atlantic and made its appearance first in Quebec and from thence traveled with its direful velocity to Montreal. It was brought to the former city in a vessel called the *Carricks,* with a cargo of Irish emigrants, of whom many died on the passage.

The alarm is great in Albany and Troy, and committees of the corporation of each of these cities have proceeded to the lines to ascertain and report the state of affairs and to adopt measures to prevent the passage of the emigrants by the Champlain Canal.

18

Prayers were offered up yesterday in all the churches to avert the threatened visit of the cholera and sermons preached to prepare the minds of the people for the affliction which now seems to be considered inevitable.

July 2

It is quite certain that the cholera now exists in our city. There have been nine cases, of which eight have died.

3

The devil is in the doctors again. Whenever cases occur in which the public safety requires union, confidence, and good temper, the members of that factious profession are sure to fall out among themselves and the public health is sacrificed to the support of theoretical opinions. The medical society has been at issue with the Board of Health, who presume to doubt if the cholera, such as prevailed in Asia and prevails now in Quebec, really exists in this city.

4

The Board of Health reports to-day twenty new cases and eleven deaths since noon yesterday. The disease is here in all its violence and

will increase. God grant that its ravages may be confined, and its visit
short!

16

The accounts of the cholera in New York have become dreadfully
alarming, and it is spreading rapidly over the whole country.

23

I hear many dreadful stories of cholera cases. The last of last week a
man was found in the road at Harlem, who had died of cholera. A
coroner's inquest was called, and of twenty persons, jury and witnesses,
who were present, nine are now dead.

Sept. 4

If the cholera is still amongst us, it proceeds quietly, uninterrupted by
municipal legislations and apparently unheeded by those who are exposed
to it.

18

Miss Fanny Kemble made her first appearance this evening in the
character of Bianca, in Milman's tragedy "Fazio." It is a fine part, well
calculated for a display of the strongest passions of the feminine heart—
love, hate, and jealousy. I predicted before we went that it would be no
half-way affair; she would make the most decided hit we have ever
witnessed, or would fail entirely; and so it proved. I have never witnessed
an audience so moved, astonished, and delighted. Her display of the
strong feelings which belong to the part was great beyond description,
and the expression of her wonderful face would have been a rich treat if
her tongue had uttered no sound. The fifth act was such an exhibition
of female powers as we have never before witnessed, and the curtain
fell amid the deafening shouts and plaudits of the astonished audience.

20

The distresses of the lower classes in England and Ireland have caused
emigration to America in numbers so great as to cause serious alarm. Besides the immense numbers which are daily arriving here and in other
parts of the United States, it is stated that 49,569 emigrants have arrived
at Quebec since the opening of the navigation of the St. Lawrence the
present year.

Of these a large proportion find their way into the United States,
destitute and friendless. They have brought the cholera this year and

they will always bring wretchedness and want. The boast that our country is the asylum for the oppressed in other parts of the world is very philanthropic and sentimental, but I fear that we shall before long derive little comfort from being made the almshouse and place of refuge for the poor of other countries.

Dec. 18

The Camden & Amboy Railroad was opened on Monday on the whole line, and passengers who left New York in the steamboat for Amboy at half past six were in Philadelphia about two. This is expected to be the best joint stock property in the United States.

June 13 [1833]

The President [Andrew Jackson] is certainly the most popular man we have ever known. Washington was not so much so. His acts were popular, because all descriptions of men were ready to acknowledge him the "Father of his Country." But he was superior to the homage of the populace, too dignified, too grave for their liking, and men could not approach him with familiarity.

Here is a man who suits them exactly. He has a kind expression for each—the same to all, no doubt, but each thinks it intended for himself. His manners are certainly good, and he makes the most of them. He is a *gourmand* of adulation, and by the assistance of the populace has persuaded himself that no man ever lived in the country to whom the country was so much indebted.

Talk of him as a second Washington! It won't do now; Washington was only the first Jackson.

Dec. 20

General Jackson's ill-advised measure of removing the public money from the Bank of the United States has occasioned great distress among those who unfortunately depend upon their credit to pay their debts. Stocks have fallen prodigiously, particularly railroad and canal company stock.

I hold $50,000 of stock in the Delaware & Hudson, the Camden & Amboy, and Boston & Providence companies which is not worth so much by ten or twelve thousand as it was three months since.

Jan. 31 [1834]

Wall Street was thrown into consternation this morning by the failure

of John G. Warren & Son, a house in good credit and one of the most
extensive in their line as brokers. This unexpected event is attributed to
the unprecedented fall in stocks occasioned by the derangement of the
money concerns of the city. If Gen. Jackson had visited Wall Street this
morning, he might have been regaled with a sight similar to that of the
field of battle at New Orleans. His killed and wounded were to be seen
in every direction.

Feb. 7

A public meeting having been called by a notice signed by 174 respectable names of "the citizens who are opposed to the removal of the
deposits from the Bank of the United States, and who are in favor of a
sound currency by means of a national bank," an immense concourse
assembled at twelve o'clock at the meeting place—the park.

The number is computed at from twelve to fifteen thousand. I was
waited upon by a committee and requested to officiate as chairman.
When I came on the ground precisely at twelve o'clock I found an immense crowd already assembled, consisting principally of the most respectable mechanics and others in the city—men of character, respectability, and personal worth, with a few miscreants who went, perhaps of
their own accord, but were more probably sent there to excite disturbance
and disturb the proceedings.

The rabble had gotten possession of the chair, and it required some
hard thumps to clear the way sufficiently for me to come forward. I attempted to address the meeting, but the yells of the mob, and the noise
of better disposed persons in attempting to command silence, rendered
all my efforts unavailing; so I put the question upon the resolutions,
which were carried by an immense majority, and then adjourned the
meeting; but the mob did not disperse for a considerable time afterwards.

May 2

Col. Crockett, the Tennessee member of Congress so celebrated for
eccentricity and strong natural talents, is in New York. He has been
feasted and carried about to places of public amusement. The Young
Whigs (for he is one of our party) gave him a supper this evening at the
American Hotel, at which there was speaking, singing, toasting, and
shouting until a late hour; very much to the annoyance of my household, for we are so near that the noise of the carouse disturbed such of
us as wished to sleep.

24

The mail stage was robbed on Saturday night near Stamford, Conn.

January 14 [1835]

The rage for speculating in lands on Long Island is one of the bubbles of the day. Men in moderate circumstances have become immensely rich merely by the good fortune of owning farms of a few acres of this chosen land. Abraham Schermerhorn has sold his farm of 170 acres at Gowanus, three miles from Brooklyn, at $600 per acre; four years ago, having got out of conceit of it as a residence, he offered it for sale at $20,000, and would have taken $18,000; to-day he pockets $102,-000 and regrets that he sold it so cheap.

April 14

I have passed a few hours delightfully in reading Washington Irving's "Tour of the Prairies." It is of the very best kind of light reading. Killing buffaloes, hunting wild horses, sleeping every night on the ground for a whole month, and depending from day to day for the means of existence upon the deer, wild turkey, and bears which the rifles of their own party can alone procure, are matters of thrilling interest to citizens who read of them in their green slippers seated before a shining grate, the neatly printed page illuminated by a bronze astral lamp.

August 2

A terrific system prevails in some of the Southern and Western States of late, which consists in the people taking the law in their own hands, and inflicting a summary punishment upon persons who have made themselves obnoxious to their high mightinesses; beating, tarring and feathering, and in some cases hanging the unhappy objects of their vengeance, and this is quaintly called Lynch's law.

At Vicksburg in the State of Mississippi from the 6th to the 10th of July scenes were enacted which are calculated to make humanity shudder, and to bring disgrace upon the country. A conspiracy among the negroes (real or pretended) was the avowed cause of the outrage, and the last accounts are filled with disgusting details of murder and violence committed without the least color of law upon the poor negroes and several whites who are accused of being their instigators.

Dec. 17

How shall I report the events of last night, or how attempt to describe the most awful calamity which has ever visited these United States? The greatest loss by fire that has ever been known, with the exception perhaps of the conflagration of Moscow, and that was an incidental concomitant of war.

I am fatigued in body, disturbed in mind, and my fancy filled with images of horror which my pen is inadequate to describe. Nearly one half of the first ward is in ashes; 500 to 700 stores,which with their contents are valued at $20,000,000 to $40,000,000 are now lying in an indistinguishable mass of ruins.

There is not perhaps in the world the same space of ground covered by so great an amount of real and personal property as the scene of this dreadful conflagration. The fire broke out at nine o'clock last evening. I was waiting in the library when the alarm was given and went immediately down. The night was intensely cold, which was one cause of the unprecedented progress of the flames, for the water froze in the hydrants, and the engines and their hose could not be worked without great difficulty.

The firemen, too, had been on duty all last night, and were almost incapable of performing their usual services.

The insurance offices are all, of course, bankrupt. Their collective capitals amount to $11,750,000; but those downtown have a large proportion of the risks, and will not be able to pay 50 per cent of the losses. The unfortunate stockholders lose all. In this way I suffer directly, and in others indirectly, to a large amount.

Feb. 23 [1836]

Twenty lots in the "burned district," the property of Joel Post, deceased, were sold at auction this day by James Bleecker & Son, at most enormous prices, greater than they would have brought before the fire, when covered with valuable buildings.

March 8

I have this day sold my house in which I live, No. 235 Broadway, to Elijah Boardman for $60,000. I bought this property on the 8th of March, 1821, after my return from Europe. I gave Jonathan Smith $25,000 for it.

24

I bought this day, from Samuel Ward, for $15,000, the lot corner of Broadway and Great Jones Street, 29 feet wide and 130 feet deep. It is my intention to build a house on this lot for my own residence.

June 2

There arrived at this port, during the month of May, 15,825 passengers. All Europe is coming across the ocean; all that part at least who cannot make a living at home; and what shall we do with them? They increase our taxes, eat our bread, and encumber our streets, and not one in twenty is competent to keep himself.

23 [Albany]

A party of gentlemen consisting of the managers of the Delaware & Hudson and others, went on board the *Novelty* this morning at 6 o'clock, at the foot of Chambers Street in New York, and came to Albany in twelve hours.

This was the first voyage ever made from New York to Albany by a steamboat propelled by anthracite coal.

Dec. 30

I went this evening to a party at Mrs. Charles H. Russell's, given in honor of the bride, Mrs. William H. Russell. The splendid apartments of this fine house are well adapted to an evening party, and everything was very handsome on this occasion. The home is lighted with gas, and the quantity consumed being greater than common, it gave out suddenly in the midst of a cotillion. "Darkness overspread the land." This accident occasioned great merriment to the company, and some embarrassment to the host and hostess, but a fresh supply of gas was obtained, and in a short time the fair dancers were again "tripping it on the light fantastic toe."

Gas is a handsome light, in a large room like Mr. Russell's, on an occasion of this kind, but liable (I should think) at any time to give the company the slip, and illy calculated for the ordinary uses of a family.

Feb. 13 [1837]

This city was disgraced this morning by a mob regularly convened by public notice in the park for the notable purpose of making bread cheaper by destroying the flour in the merchants' warehouses. The following notice was extensively published on Saturday by placards at the corners of the streets:

"Bread, Meat, Rent, Fuel—Their Prices Must Come Down.
"The Voice of the People Shall Be Heard, and Will Prevail.
"The People will meet in the Park, rain or shine, at four o'clock

on Monday afternoon to inquire into the cause of the present un-exampled distress, and devise a suitable remedy. All friends of humanity, determined to resist monopolists and extortioners, are invited to attend."

Many thousands assembled on this call. The day was bitter cold and the wind blew a hurricane, but there was fire enough in the speeches of Messrs. Windt and Ming to inflame the passions of the populace. These two men, disciples in the sect of the Loco-focos, did not tell them in so many words to attack the stores of the flour merchants, but stigmatized them as monopolists and extortioners, who enriched themselves at the expense of the laboring poor. They said that Eli Hart & Co. had 50,000 barrels of flour in their store, which they held at an exhorbitant price while the poor of the city were starving.

This was a firebrand suddenly thrown into the combustible mass which surrounded the speaker, and away went the mob to Hart's store in Washington near Cortlandt Street, which they forced open, threw 400 or 500 barrels of flour and large quantities of wheat into the street, and committed all the extravagant acts which usually flow from the unlicensed fury of a mob.

The mayor and other magistrates, with the police officers, repaired to the spot, and with the assistance of many well disposed citizens, succeeded after a time in clearing and getting possession of the store.

From thence the mob went to Herrick & co. in Water Street and destroyed about fifty barrels of flour.

The mayor ordered out a military force, which with the other measures adopted, kept the rioters in check.

March 4

This is a dark and melancholy day in the annals of my family. Brown & Hone stopped payment today and called a meeting of their creditors. My eldest son has lost the capital I gave him, and I am implicated as endorser for them to a fearful amount. The pressure of the times, the immense amount they have paid of extra interest, and the almost total failure of remittances have been the causes of their ruin. This is a heavy blow for me, and added to the difficulty I experience in raising money on my property to meet my own engagements almost breaks me down, but I have the consolation to know, and the public cannot fail to know it also, that the good name which it has been the object of my life to establish cannot be compromised in this matter.

14

This morning at a quarter past one o'clock the large unfinished granite building belonging to the Messrs. Josephs came down with a crash like that of an earthquake. It stood at the corner of Wall and Exchange Streets, was intended for insurance and brokers' offices, and rented at enormous rates.

17

The great crisis is near at hand, if it has not already arrived. The banking house of I. and L. Joseph, the people whose new edifice in Wall Street fell on Monday, stopped payment to-day, and occasioned great consternation in Wall Street, for their business has been enormous; and as it consisted principally of operations in internal exchanges, the merchants, jobbers, grocers, and other regular dealers are all implicated. The immediate cause of this disaster was the intelligence received from New Orleans by this day's mail of the stoppage of the House of Hermann & Co. and others connected with them, for whom the Josephs are under acceptances to the amount of two millions of dollars.

18

A number of failures have taken place to-day, only the forerunners of greater disaster.

20

The prospects in Wall Street are getting worse and worse. The Josephs do *not* go on. The accounts from England are very alarming; the panic prevails there as bad as here. Cotton has fallen. The loss of shipments will be very heavy, and American credits will be withdrawn. The paper of the southern and western merchants is coming back protested. Why should I be in such a scrape?

April 10

One of the signs of the times is to be seen in the sales of rich furniture, the property of men who a year ago thought themselves rich, and such expenditures justifiable, but are now bankrupt.

21

Lots at Bloomingdale somewhere about One Hundredth Street (for the whole island was laid out in town lots) which cost last September $480 a lot have been sold within a few days at $50. The immense fortunes which we heard so much about in the days of speculation have melted away like the snows before an April sun. No man can calculate to escape ruin but he owes no money; happy is he who has a little and is free from debt.

May 2

The number of failures is so great daily that I do not keep a record of them, even in my mind, but two very important ones have just occurred: Arthur Tappan & Company yesterday, who owed the enormous amount of $1,200,000, and this day P. & J. Crary & Company. The distress and ruin caused by these failures will be tremendous; general bankruptcy seems inevitable.

9

The Dry Dock Bank was laid under an injunction yesterday morning from the Chancellor. Its doors were not open. Crowds of exasperated creditors collected and great alarm prevailed. At about ten o'clock the Mayor (who is president of the Bank of the State of New York) addressed the people, and told them that an arrangement had been made by which the notes of the Dry Dock Bank would be redeemed by the other Wall Street Banks.

This allayed the tumult. But the crowd was great during the day, and a constant run was made for specie on all the other banks, which will inevitably drain them all in a week.

10

The *experiment* has succeeded. The volcano has burst and overwhelmed New York; the glory of her merchants is departed. After a day of unexampled excitement, and a ruthless run upon all the banks, which drew from their vaults $600,000 in specie yesterday, nearly as much having been drawn on Monday, the officers held a meeting last evening and resolved to *suspend specie payments*.

The Savings Bank also sustained a most grievous run yesterday. They paid to 375 depositors $81,000. The press was awful. The hour for closing the bank is six o'clock, but they did not get through the paying of those who were in at that time till nine. I was there with the other trustees and witnessed the madness of the people. Women were nearly pressed to death, and the stoutest men could scarcely sustain themselves, but they held on, as with a death's grip, upon the evidences of their claims, and exhausted as they were with the pressure, they had strength to cry "Pay! Pay!"

The trustees met in melancholy conclave and adopted an excellent statement, prepared by Mr. Peter A. Jay, first vice-president, which was published in all the papers this morning.

While we were in session intelligence was brought that the banks had suspended specie payments. Great fears were entertained that these measures would produce serious consequences when they became known, particularly those adopted by the Bank for Savings, where there are 25,-000 depositors, and those generally of the poorest and most ignorant classes.

The troops were out during the day, and Major General Hays and his regiment of clubadiers have shewn themselves at various points in strong force. Thus ends this most eventful day.

11

A dead calm has succeeded the stormy weather of Wall Street and the other places of active business. All is still as death. The fever is broken, but the patient lies in a sort of syncope, exhausted by the violence of the disease and the severity of the remedies.

The commercial distress and financial embarrassment pervade the whole nation. Posterity may get out of it, but the sun of the present generation will never again shine out.

October 26

Broadway in the neighborhood of the City Hotel has been crowded for the two last days by curious spectators, watching to obtain an occasional glimpse of a large party of Indians who, after having made a treaty at Washington by which their "broad lands" are diminished in quantity the trifling amount of a million and a quarter of acres, are now making a tour of the principal cities, receiving presents and being stared at for the benefit of theatres, fairs, and lectures.

There are two tribes, amounting in all to seventy individuals. The Sauks and Foxes, who constitute the most important part of the deputation, are at the City Hotel, and the Sioux at the National, opposite; for these two tribes are not on a friendly footing, and their white keepers do not think it expedient to get up a real war fight for the edification of the spectators.

I went to see the Sauks and Foxes this morning, and finding Mr. Daniel Jackson there, who is a sort of agent for the tribes, was introduced to the principal chiefs. The whole party, warriors, squaws, and papooses, were seated or lying on the ground; most of them employed in opening and dividing sundry pieces of colored cord, such as is used for hanging pictures, which had been presented to them at the fair of the American Institute and with which they appeared much pleased.

Keokuk, the chief of the confederated tribes of Sauks and Foxes, and his favorite squaw, were seated on a small carpet, separate from the rest. He is a fine-looking elderly man, of intelligent countenance and dignified deportment. I have heard Gen. Scott speak of him; he thinks him a great man.

In the expedition against the tribes, a few years since, Keokuk was friendly to the whites and opposed to Black Hawk, who was then the principal chief.

Black Hawk is with the party at present, but appears to have lost caste. He sits with his son in one corner of the square, enveloped in a bright scarlet blanket, silent, surly, and picturesque. The son is a majestic man, aged about 30, one of the noblest figures I ever saw—a perfect Ajax Telamon. I shook hands with these Hercules and Apollos of the woods. They are generally very stout and athletic, with immense lower limbs, but their arms and hands are delicate and small. The Indians went to Boston at four o'clock this afternoon.

April 21 [1838]

Gold has flowed into our city during the present week in streams more copious than has ever before been known. The influx of the tide is greater than was its reflux.

Sept. 14 [1842]

The amusement of prize fighting, the disgrace of which was formerly confined to England, to the grief and mortification of the moral and respectable part of her subjects and the disgust of travelers from other countries, has become one of the fashionable abominations of our loafer-ridden city. Several matches have been made lately. The parties, their backers, betters, and abettors, with thousands and tens of thousands of degraded amateurs of this noble science, have been following the champions to Staten Island, Westchester, and up the North River, out of the jurisdiction (as was supposed) of the authorities of New York; and the horrid details, with all their disgusting technicalities and vulgar slang, have been regularly presented in the New York *Herald* to gratify the vitiated palates of its readers, whilst the orderly citizens have wept for the shame which they could not prevent.

One of these infamous meetings took place yesterday on the bank of the North River in Westchester, the particulars of which are given at length in that precious sheet and others of a similar character. Two men, named Lilly and McCoy, thumped and battered each other for the gratification of a brutal gang of spectators, until the latter after 119 rounds fell dead in the ring, and the other ruffian was smuggled away and made his escape from the hands of insulted justice.

McCoy went into the battle, it is said, expressing a determination to conquer or to die. He was deficient in science, but a bulldog in courage. The fight lasted two hours and forty-three minutes. McCoy received one hundred square blows and was knocked down eighty-one times.

July 9 [1845] Marshfield, Massachusetts

After breakfast Mr. [Daniel] Webster drove Draper and me over his extensive grounds down to the beach, where his boats were ready for a fishing excursion, which is one of his greatest enjoyments.

Here was this wonderful man, on whose lips unsurpassed eloquence has so often hung, whose pen has directed the most important negotiations, and whose influence has governed Senates, in a loose coat and trousers, with a most picturesque slouch hat, which a Mexican bandit might have coveted, directing his people—whose obedience grows out of affection and who are governed by the force of kindness—regulating the apparatus, examining the bait, and helping to hoist the sails and "hold on the main sheet."

So off we went to sea in the good sloop *Comet;* and a tidier, more obedient, smarter little craft is not to be found in Massachusetts Bay. We had tolerably good sport for a couple of hours; but the sea was rough, and the vessel uneasy, the effect of which was that I became very sick; but it was some consolation to me that the Lord High Admiral was in the same condition.

"I don't wish it made too public, sir," said I; "nor would I have it put in a newspaper; but I am sick! sick!"

"My case exactly," said he; "and I have tried to keep this unusual circumstance a secret; but it won't do, and we must go ashore."

So we returned, and our health and cheerfulness returned with us also.

September 12 [1850]

The Jenny Lind excitement in New York seems to have increased to fever heat. Her second rehearsal was given with renewed spirit and effect, and received with new enthusiasm. Tickets have been sold to the amount of $55,000. The good people of New York are anxious to part with their money *for a song,* and the "nightingale" will make a profitable exchange of her *notes* for specie.

Jennie Lind's second concert took place on Tuesday, and was attended as numerously and enthusiastically as the first; crowds follow her wherever she goes. She has been compelled to leave the Irving House, in my neighborhood, to escape from the persecution.

This Siren, the tenth Muse; the *Angel* as Barnum calls her; the *nightingale,* by which she is designated by the would-be *dilettanti,*—has secured the affection as well as the admiration of the mass of the people by an act of munificence, as well as good policy. Her contract with Mr. Barnum has been changed. Instead of $1,000 a night, she gets one-half of the net profits; her share of which for the first night, after deducting the large expenses of a first performance, amounting to the enormous sum of $12,-600, all of which, with unprecedented liberality, she distributed among the charitable and benevolent institutions of the city. New York is conquered; a hostile army or fleet could not effect a conquest so complete.

April 30 [1851]

This volume of my journal, which has only four vacant leaves to be completed, has been suspended during nearly the whole month by continued unmitigated illness. Tomorrow will be the first of May. Volume 29 lies ready on my desk. Shall it go on?

Six days later Philip Hone died.

── ★

1849:   *LITTLE GIRL IN GLASS AND GOLD*

── ☆

CATHERINE HAVENS' FATHER was a shipowner. She lived in the same country where other children were at that time bumping in covered wagons over the plains and deserts, or working ten-hour days in New England textile mills, or being torn from their parents on the slaveblocks of the South, or living the hardening, healthy life of the farm. Born equals all, under the same broad sky, and so declared by the same government; nevertheless, the big house in New York's fashionable Ninth Street and the places where Catherine played and went to school were a different world.

"We had a picnic on Fifth Avenue . . ."
CATHERINE HAVENS (born 1839)

August 6 [1849]

I am ten years old today.

I am still living in our Ninth Street house [near University Place]. It is a beautiful house and has glass sliding doors with birds of Paradise sitting on palm trees painted on them. And back of our dining room is a piazza, and a grape vine, and we have lots of Isabella grapes every fall.

It has a parlor in front and the library in the middle and the dining room at the back. On the mantel piece in the library is a very old clock that my father brought from France in one of his ships. It has a gilt head of Virgil on top, and it is all gilt, and stands under a big glass case, and sometimes I watch my father when he takes off the case to wind the clock, and he has to lift it up so high and his hands tremble so, I am afraid he will break it.

I forgot to say I have a little niece, nearly as old as I am, and she lives in the country. Her mother is my sister, and her father a clergyman, and I go there in the summer, and she comes here in the winter, and we have things together, like whooping cough and scarlatina.

New York is getting very big and building up. I walk some mornings with my nurse before breakfast from our house in Ninth Street up Fifth Avenue to Twenty-third Street and down Broadway home. An officer stands in front of the House of Refuge on Madison Square, ready to arrest bad people, and he looks as if he would like to find some.

Fifth Avenue is very muddy above Eighteenth Street, and there are no blocks of houses as there are downtown, but only two or three on a block.

Last Saturday we had a picnic on the grounds of Mr. Waddell's country seat way up Fifth Avenue, [at 37th Street] and it was so muddy I spoiled my new light cloth gaiter boots.

August 15

My father is a very old gentleman. He was born before the Revolutionary War.

I love my music lessons. Last year my sister let me play at a big musical party she had, and I played a tune from "La Fille du Regiment," with variations. It took me a good while to learn it, and the people all liked it and said it must be very hard.

I love my music first, and then my arithmetic. Our teacher rattles off like this, as fast as ever she can, "Twice six, less one, multiply by two, add eight, divide by three. How much?" I love to do that.

I know a little girl who has a step-mother, and she has one own child, and this step-child, and she dresses her own child very prettily but she makes the step-child wear nankeen pantalettes, and when she plays in the Parade Ground, the boys tease her and call her ginger legs, and she is very unhappy. It is a very sad case.

Once in a while my sister takes me down to the Brick Church on Beekman Street where our family went before I was born. Mr. Hull is the Sexton, and he puts the coals in the foot-stoves in the pews. Sometimes the heat gives out and the lady gets up in her pew and waves her handkerchief and Mr. Hull comes and gets her stove and fills it again. When church begins he fastens a chain across the street to keep carriages away.

September 21

My parents went up to Saratoga in August for two weeks, to drink the water. They always stay at the Grand Union Hotel.

This summer I went up to my sister's, my own sister, at Old Church. Maggy, my nurse, took me in a carriage from Hathorn's Livery Stable on University Place, to Catherine Slip on the East River, where we get into a steamboat—sometimes it is the *Cricket*, and sometimes the *Cataline*—and we sail up the sound to the landing where we get off to go to Old Church, and then we get into the stage-coach to ride to my sister's parsonage. I was so wild to get there and to see Ella and the rest of them that I could hardly wait to have the driver let down the steps for me to get in, and put them up again.

October 1

I will now tell about the Ravels. They act in a theatre, called Niblo's Theatre, and it is corner of Broadway and Prince Street. My biggest own brother goes there with some of his friends to see the plays, and he said he would take me to see the Ravels. But when my father found out about it he would not let me go. He said he did not think it was right for Christians to go to the theatre. I went out on our front balcony and walked back and forth and cried so much I hurt my eyes.

November 8

We have been down to Staten Island to one of my sisters. She has ice cream on Thursdays, so we try to go then.

December 10

Ellen and I went out shopping alone. We went to Bond's dry-goods store on Sixth Avenue, just below Ninth Street to buy a yard of calico to make an apron for Maggy's birthday. We hope she will like it. It is a good quality, for we pulled the corner and twitched it as we had seen our mothers do, and it did not tear. Ellen and I call each other Sister Cynthia and Sister Juliana, and when we bought the calico, Ellen said, "Sister Cynthia, have you any change? I have only a fifty-dollar bill papa left me this morning," and the clerk laughed. I guess he knew Ellen was making it up!

Sometimes we play I am blind and Ellen leads me along on the street, and once a lady went by and said to her little girl, "See that poor child, she is blind," and perhaps when I get old I may be really blind as a punishment for pretending.

I hope Ellen will stay all winter. She is full of pranks, and smarter than I am if she is younger, and I hope we have lots of snow. When there is real good sleighing, my sister hires a stage sleigh and takes me and a lot of my schoolmates a sleigh ride down Broadway to the Battery and back. The sleigh is open and very long; and has long seats on each side, and straw on the floor to keep our feet warm, and the sleigh bells sound so cheerful.

Stages run through Bleecker Street and Eighth Street and Ninth Street right past our house, and it puts me right to sleep when I come home from the country to hear them rumble along over the cobble-stones.

There is a line on Fourteenth Street too, and that is the highest uptown.

Just opposite the Bowling Green on Whitehall Street, there is a sign over a store, "Lay and Hatch," but they don't sell eggs.

January 2, 1850

Next January we shall be half through the nineteenth century. I hope I shall live to see the next century, but I don't want to be alive when the year 2000 comes, for my Bible teacher says the world is coming to an end then, and perhaps sooner.

ALL THAT IS KNOWN about him today is that he was a student at Delaware College in Newark a century ago. His diary tells the rest—and suggests there are some things even a century doesn't change much.

"*A cold nest of doorhandles at my feet . . .*"
JOSEPH CLEAVER, JR. (1833-1909)

Aug. 31, 1853

Entering day at Delaware College. I set my room in order a little but found I was late for an assembly.

Sept. 1

Classes in the morning after prayers and breakfast which I did not like much and after dinner I had no classes so I set to housekeeping and felt more at home with my things about me but they look strange in a new place. We are talking of buying a shelf for our books. We look a lot better than most of the rooms where the boys have just opened their portmantos on a chair or on the floor and many have no books at all.

2

One of the boys came up before study hour and is sick for home and especially because the rain keeps us all in and it is cold and damp and dark in the College. I sounded very old and wise and made light of his feeling but it did not do him any good and when he was gone I had not been done any good either.

4

Morning prayers were very dull or over my head, and too long but I was . . . I was interrupted there and I cannot remember what I was going to say.

9

I put a great deal of time on my declamation which will be my first appearance before the Athenaean Literary Society and I want it to be good. They fired a canon of some sort in the hall tonight and it shook all the building so that it was a long time before anyone settled. The old boys say there was a lot of it last spring meant to call attention at one end of the College when hall police is not wanted at the other end. But some do it just for sport and everyone knows the five or six who are at the bottom of most of it. Apple pie. Progress in Algebra. Licorice...04.

10

I declaimed at Athenaean Literary Society and did better than I feared. I am up with Cacy, Chamberlin and Clymer to debate next week the affirmative of the question of abolishing the capital punishment.

15

There was a coffin with Professor Grover [in effigy] in it at prayers this morning. He turned the table by inviting those who thought it was funny to sit up on the mourning bench and nobody did and we all felt a little sheepy.

16

A bench gave way at prayers and made a great clatter while President Graham was speaking.

19

Slept through bells, prayers, breakfast and a part of class. Turner says I shall be called up to explain why I was out all night and though I know it is in jest I keep going over with my mind what I shall say and I almost begin to doubt my own story or my power to prove it to anybody.

20

Serenading which is against the rules but good sport or was until we got ourselves showered with cold water.

21

We learned today that we were misadvised about our serenades so that we would go to the dangerous places and it is the mystery that we have not been reported to the college. We went out again tonight but with more care and better success for we were asked in to milk and cookies.

Oct. 2

I called at Mr. Curtis's house in the afternoon and though I think I took them by surprise I was made welcome and they asked me to stay to supper and I wished I might but I did not and I wondered all the way back to College why I did not.

7

Out for a walk before bed time. I fell into an open ditch which I never saw before though it was heavily grass-grown. Wet myself through and for a minute I thought I had drowned myself.

10

Ashmead takes a bath every night and the boys on the hall burned paper in the hall and cried "Fire!" when he was covered with lather and carried his clothes away so that he ran almost to the front door that way and met Professor Boswell.

21

Set out my boots for cleaning last night and I have back a pair that are not mine and I do not think that any boy in the College ever war them.

22

I was called in Society to substitute in debate affirmative on the question "Would it be advantagious for a young man to acquire a classical education if he did not intend to pursue a profession?" My side always loses.

Nov. 5

I am with Cacy to debate the affirmative of "It is probable that the Federal Union will dissolve in 2000 years." It seemed a good question when we wrote it down but it seems silly now when I think of debating it.

10

I was unprepared in Mathematics and tried to pretend. He [the professor] let me hang myself and then laughed with the rest at my embarrassment.

15

We almost froze at the telescope where some of us had outs [permissions] until very late. I saw no more with the telescope than without it.

16

Butternutting.

19

Too many butternuts. I was elected Treasurer of the Athenaean Literary Society.

23

They say Thatcher has been excused prayers and that has started a lot of speculation on ways to be excused.

25

I gave a little girl a kiss who was crying in the street but she cried louder and put her arms around my neck and I had a chore drying her tears and finding her way home. Now I am the but of a lot of wit bearing on young ladies.

26

I still hear about kissing strange young ladies on the street.

29

I saw my little girl of the tearful kiss and waved to her and she waved to me.

Dec. 1

There was a Nigger boy at the College this morning making his way to Wilmington and the North and asking for shelter until night but Rev. Graham would not let him stay and said the college must not break the law even when the law seems wrong and after he had said that to the boys he went away and did not ask what was done with him. So we put him in the second floor lumber room until night and when he got cold Savin took him in and the boys in his room gave him a coat and went out collecting. I gave the boots that came to me for mine and Turner calls me "Nigger lover" but would have given too I think if he had had anything to give. He left during study hour. There is a strange suppressed excitement and it is a kind of sober quiet too.

3

I was called to debate the justice of taking America from the Indians but the Nigger boy has upset my thoughts about justice.

5

DuHamel heard in Wilmington of a niger boy being taken which sounds like our boy but not certain and did not dare ask details. Most of our boys are very sorry to hear of it and we hoped it is not the boy we helped which seems to me not to be the matter but that a black boy had been taken back from freedom to live all his life a slave. I am uncertain what I shall compose for Society. I may write about a black boy.

13

Roe walks in his sleep and he fell down the upper stairs. We were talking of the future and how God might have created a kind of man whose memory would work to the future and the past be un-knowable.

15

Playing pitch in the hall. We were reprimanded for the noise and explained that we did it to keep warm which I think did not convince him.

19

The hall is full of potato smoke which I left roasting and forgot.

21

The whole college has been in a whirl. A few have gone [home for vacation] and others are ready and waiting. I have been so anxious to go but I am a little surprised now not to be more excited than the others.

Feb. 1 [1854]

Roe went to sleep at study last night and overset his lamp which exploded and set him afire but Emanuel put it out with a blanket. Turner says Roe is the sort of a boy who would get drowned in a clearing up shower.

3

I lost this book yesterday which Biddle has just returned to me. I do not know whether I am more glad to have it again or more sorry to have it seen and recognized. Resolved to set down in future only those thoughts which do credit to someone and not idle gossip.

6

Today they got outs and put a bucket over the door and warned everybody on the hall. Roe was studying with Emanuel and needed a pencil pointed and went for his pocket knife and forgot the trap and was drowned. There was so much confusion and laughter that H. P. came up and we expected Katie [a local term denoting formal punishment] but he laughed too and sent Roe for a mop and gave him time to change his clothes.

10

We bought a lock for our coal box and put it on and when T. went out to it after supper he could not open it and we had to break it open. Lock ...70.

14

We made a Valentine for Ashmead as if it was from a young lady and he blushed and stammered and opened himself to a great deal of wit.

17

We have borrowed coal and when we broke open the lid this morning we found it all gone. There is much stealing on the second floor and some people who have lost nothing are suspected.

20

I traded my pocket compas for a blue leather writing case.

21

I bought ink and saw at Mr. Bunker's a gold pen with well attached.

24

Spring weather—it is very hard to stay in and study. I did not.

26

Reed showed me his likeness taken at the new shop and I mean to have one.

27

My cold is very bad. Some of the boys have been suspecting Cathcart of the stealing without any direct cause but last night his coat was taken and now he is going without one. Vindication may not be worth so much. But he has more friends than he had two days ago.

March 3

I have lost a day and I cannot remember anything about it. I am not even sure which day it was.

I have worked on my composition but I did not write what is on my mind and I cannot write what is not.

17

The men came to-day to mend the plaster in 20 but it all fell so the boys moved out and Bushnell came to sleep with us.

Turner says he understands the plaster trouble in 20 and that if Bushnell sleeps with us long we will need a new ceiling too.

18

Carlile and Row had a fire in their room this morning from starting their stove with fluid.

20

My mind must have been wandering. It wanders when I read and then I discover that I have only been reading words and have not understood it and when I read it over I do not remember even the words.

April 28

I dreamed my Mother came down a steep hill to me and had in a bucket two silver spoons and potato skins.

May 1

There were little children selling May-day baskets at the stile for a penny. I bought one for Miss M. but I did not have the courage to drop it in the daylight and now it has withered.

6

I slept badly and was waked by the night train up, wailing in the distance, and before I could go back to sleep by an even worse bawling of the down train.

8

At three hour after supper Baird who has been cultivating Churchman's friendship took him to see the creek road and when they were far out met a gang of unrecognized ruffians who admired C's clothes so much that they took them off one by one and when they had them all got him to say he was cold and built a fire for him and burned his clothes. Then they lost interest and wandered off with Baird whom they said they hated to leave alone in the woods with a wild man and he dared not follow naked but came into hall near morning by a low window which was left open red with mosquito bites and scratches, white with rage and blue with cold.

13

There has been a lot of stealing of door handles in our hall and when I went to bed I found a cold nest of them at my feet.

15

There has been much knotting of bed clothes in our hall.

17

There was a Gypsy in town telling fortunes who cursed me because I would not be told but told others so much that was true that if she had not cursed me I would have asked her who stole from our box.

21

Our Gypsy is back in town for stealing. The skeptical are asking why she did not foresee the result of her theft.

27

I am set to debate the affirmative of "Which affords the greater pleasure sight or hearing?" Even if it were not a silly and futile subject for discussion there is still a question as to which is the affirmative aspect.

June 3

The debate was as I expected and we lost.

14

I am pleased with a musical box that I saw at Mr. Evan's store but I have not money enough to buy it or anybody to give it to.

30

Mr. Hossinger's white bull is at the top of the college stairs and will not go down. Mr. Hossinger says whoever borrowed his bull must return him in as good condition as he took him and he will not come for him so the door has been locked and all passage is by the lower door.

July 1

The bull (and they say Mr. Hossinger) very troublesome in the night; he was still on those stairs this morning where they fed and watered him. He was taken away during Prayers so we did not see him go.

Sept. 4

Harlan reported a bee-tree south of town which we plan to raid on Saturday night.

10

There was a great ringing of the bell in the night but for no cause that we can learn unless it was that I. H. wagered G. B. P. yesterday that he could get into the belfry. He is wearing P.'s watch chain prominently today.

15

At night we went out but did not find the tree and I do not think anybody was sorry.

Nov. 20

Someone cut the bell rope during the night so everything went at odds until noon. The rope has turned up in everybody's room and is going to be found in the wrong one.

———————————————————————————————————★

1850-60: THOREAU DESCRIBES HIS
NEIGHBORS FOR POSTERITY

———————————————————————————————————☆

To THE THIRTY-NINE manuscript volumes of his journal Thoreau gave the title: Gleanings, or What Time Has Not Reaped of My Journal.

Today, a century later, time has reaped less of Thoreau than of contemporaries who were far more celebrated than he. The life he chose was dissident, isolate; but by the "oaken strength" of his writing, as Ralph Waldo Emerson described it, he has since reached the minds and lives of millions of his countrymen. In twentieth-century America he has proved one of the most quotable of all nineteenth-century authors.

Thoreau lived out most of his days in his native village of Concord, Massachusetts. After graduation from Harvard he worked for brief periods as teacher, surveyor, and pencil-maker in his family's shop. Sometimes he got along by doing odd jobs. But mostly he wrote, and as he wrote only what he wanted to write, this generally meant work without pay. It was a way of life that both insured and expedited his immortality.

For Thoreau, the little village of Concord consisted of three worlds—that of his friends in the circle of transcendentalists, mainly Emerson but including Nathaniel Hawthorne, Bronson Alcott, Theodore Parker, William Ellery Channing and Margaret Fuller; that of the farmers and working people who were his neighbors; and that of his beloved woods, earth and sky, plants and creatures, and of thoughts related to them.

Near the village, on the shore of Walden Pond, he built a hut in 1845. There he lived gloriously with his thoughts, and with not much more, for two years. From the notes in his diary for that period he wrote Walden; or, Life in the Woods, which was published nine years later and which stands today among the great masterpieces of American literature.

Thoreau's way of work in most of his output was the way of the diarist. He put down his observations day by day, then went back to the record to select, arrange, enlarge. From 1837, when he was 20, he kept a diary until November of 1861—a few months before his death. The whole runs to more than 2,000,-000 words. Of his craft he says:

"Surely the writer is to address a world of laborers and such therefore must be his own discipline. He will not idly dance at his work who has wood to cut and cord before nightfall in the short days of winter; but every stroke will be husbanded, and ring soberly through the wood; and so will the strokes of that scholar's pen, which at evening record the story of the day, ring soberly yet cheerily on the ear of the reader long after the echoes of his axe have died away. The scholar may be sure that he writes the tougher truth for the calluses on his palms."

Thoreau left the whole set of volumes of the handwritten diary in a stout wooden case which he had made himself especially to hold them. But in 1909, when J. Pierpont Morgan bought them for his library, one of them—Volume III, covering the period 1840-41—was missing.

In that volume Thoreau, who had never married, makes a few brief, oblique references to his love for Ellen Sewall, daughter of a minister in Scituate, Massachusetts. The romance, if such it may be called, died in the bud under the withering objections of Ellen's father. About this sad little episode Thoreau is very reticent; he refers to Ellen as "my friend," and to cover up further, pretends that the "friend" is masculine.

"My friend," he writes, "dwells on the eastern horizon as rich as an eastern city there. There he sails all lonely under the edge of the sky. But thoughts go out silently from me and belay him, till at length he rides in my roadstead. But never does he fairly come to anchor in my harbor. Perhaps I can afford no good anchorage."

Just when Volume III became separated from the set is not known. There are other, fragmentary bits of Thoreau's diary which overlap the material in the 39 main volumes and which have not been included. Thoreau bequeathed the whole diary to a sister. In 1876 it was acquired by Harrison Gray Otis Blake, who edited parts of it for publication in the 1880s and 90s. As Blake's edition included about two-thirds of the material in Volume III, presumably it was still in the set at that time. Thereafter the diary changed hands several times. One of its purchasers, George Hellman, sold it and eventually bought it back, then sold it again, the second time to the Morgan Library—without Volume III.

When, therefore, announcement was made in 1956 that the long lost Volume III had turned up and had been returned to its companions in the Morgan Library collection, the news made headlines across the country. The Morgan Library gave it the place of honor in a special exhibit and proudly invited the public to come and look. Arrangements were made at once for a new edition.

". . . the nobility of the land . . ."
HENRY DAVID THOREAU (1817-1862)

1850

Here and there still you will find a man with Indian blood in his veins, an eccentric farmer descended from an Indian chief; or you will see a solitary pure-blooded Indian, looking as wild as ever among the pines, one of the last of the Massachusetts tribes, stepping into a railroad car with a gun.

Still here and there an Indian squaw with her dog, her only companion, lives in some lone house, insulted by school children, making baskets and picking berries her employment.

You will meet her on the highway, with few children or none, with melancholy face, history, destiny; stepping after her race; who had stayed to tuck them up in their long sleep. For whom berries condescend to grow. A lone Indian woman without children, accompanied by her dog, wearing the shroud of her race, performing the last offices for her departed race. Not yet absorbed into the elements again; a daughter of the soil; one of the nobility of the land. The white man an imported weed,— burdock and mullein, which displace the ground-nut.

October 1, 1851. 5 P.M.

Just put a fugitive slave, who has taken the name of Henry Williams, into the cars for Canada. He escaped from Stafford County, Virginia, to Boston last October; has been in Shadrach's place at the Cornhill Coffee-House; had been corresponding through an agent with his master, who is his father, about buying himself, his master asking $600, but he having been able to raise only $500, heard that there were writs out for two Williamses, fugitives, and was informed by his fellow-servants and employer that Augerhole Burns and others of the police had called for him when he was out.

Accordingly fled to Concord last night on foot, bringing a letter to our family from Mr. Lovejoy of Cambridge and another which Garrison [William Lloyd, leading abolitionist] had formerly given him on another occasion.

He lodged with us, and waited in the house till funds were collected with which to forward him. Intended to dispatch him at noon through the Burlington, but when I went to buy his ticket, saw one at the depot who looked and behaved so much like a Boston policeman that I did not venture that time.

An intelligent and very well-behaved man, a mulatto.

The slave said he could guide himself by many other stars than the north star, whose rising and setting he knew. They steered for the north star even when it had got round and appeared to them to be in the south. They frequently followed the telegraph when there was no railroad. The slaves bring many superstitions from Africa. The fugitives sometimes superstitiously carry a turf in their hats, thinking that their success depends on it.

January 28, 1852

They showed me little Johnny Riordan the other day, as bright a boy of five years as ever trod our paths, whom you could not see for five minutes without loving and honoring him. He *lives* in what they call the *shanty* in the woods. He had on, in the middle of January, of the coldest winter we have had for twenty years, one thickness only of ragged cloth sewed on to his pantaloons over his little shirt, and shoes with large holes in the toes, into which the snow got, as he was obliged to confess, he who had trodden five winters under his feet!

Thus clad he walked a mile to school every day, over the bleakest of railroad causeways, where I know by experience the grown man would frequently freeze his ears or nose if they were not well protected,—for his parents have no thermometer,—all to get learning and warmth and there sit at the head of his bench.

These clothes with countless patches, which had for vehicle—O shame! shame!—pantaloons that had been mine, they whispered to me, set as if his mother had fitted them to a tea-kettle first.

I glimpsed him the other morning taking his last step from his last snow-drift onto the schoolhouse door-step, floundering still; saw not his face nor his profile, only his mien, but saw clearly in imagination his "old-worthy" face behind the sober visor of his cap, and he revived to my mind the grave nobility and magnanimity of ancient heroes.

He never was drawn in a willow wagon, but progresses by his own brave steps. Has not the world waited for such a generation? Here he condescends to his a-b-c without one smile, who has the lore of worlds un-counted in his brain. He speaks not of the adventures of the causeway. What was the bravery of Leonidas and his three hundred boys at the pass of Thermopylae to this infant's? They dared but to die; he dares to live, and takes his reward of merit, perchance, without relaxing his face into a smile, that does not reward a thousandth part of his merits, that over-looks his unseen and rewardable merit,—Little Johnny Riordan, who faces cold and routs it like a Persian army, who, yet innocent, carries in his knees the strength of a thousand Indras. Not to be so tenderly nurtured as you and I forsooth?

All day he plays with his coevals and equals, and then they go to their several homes.

Having carried off the palm in the intellectual contest with the children of luxury, how bravely he contemplates his destiny:

> *I shall grow up*
> *And be a great man,*
> *And shovel all day*
> *As hard as I can.*

This tender gobbet for the fates, cast into a cold world, with a torn lichen leaf wrapped about him! I would rather hear that America's first-born were all slain than that his little fingers and toes should feel cold while I am warm. Is man so cheap that he cannot be clothed but with a mat or a rag? That we should abandon to him our *wornout* clothes or our *cold* victuals?

Infancy pleads with equal eloquence from all platforms. Rather let the mature rich wear the rags and insufficient clothing, the infant poor and rich, if any, wear the costly furs, the purple and fine linen. Our charitable institutions are an insult to humanity,—a charity which dispenses the crumbs that fall from its overloaded tables! whose waste and whose ex-ample helped to produce that poverty!

While the charitable waddle about cased in furs and finery, this boy, lively as a cricket, passes them on his way to school. I see that, for the present, the child is happy, is not puny, and has all the wonders of nature for his toys. Have I not faith that his tenderness will in some way be cherished and protected, as the buds of spring in the remotest wintry dell no less than in the garden and summer-house?

February 9, 1852

Met Sudbury Haines on the river before the Cliffs, come a-fishing. Wearing an old coat, much patched, with many colors. He represents the Indians still. The very patches in his coat and his improvident life do so.

I feel that he is as essential a part, nevertheless, of our community as the lawyer in the village. He tells me that he caught three pickerel here the other day that weighed seven pounds all together. It is the old story. The fisherman is a natural story-teller. No man's imagination plays more pranks than his.

He has a ticket in the lottery of fate, and who knows what it may draw? He ever expects to catch a bigger fish yet. He is the most patient and believing of men.

January 27, 1854

Attended the auction of Deacon Brown's effects a little while to-day,— a great proportion of old traps, rubbish, or trumpery, which began to accumulate in his father's day, and now, after lying half a century in his garret and other dust-holes, is not burned, but surviving neighbors collect and view it, and buy it, and carefully transport it to their garrets and dust-holes, to lie there till their estates are settled, when it will start again.

Among his effects was a dried tapeworm and various articles too numerous and worthless to mention. A pair of old snow-shoes is almost regularly sold on these occasions, though none of this generation has seen them worn here.

July 25, 1856

The haymakers getting in the hay from Hubbard's meadow tell me the cock says we are going to have a long spell of dry weather or else very wet. "Well, there's some difference between them," I answer; "how do you know it?" "I just heard a cock crow at noon, and that's a sure sign it will either be very dry or very wet."

December 5, 1859

His [John Brown's] late career—these six weeks, I mean—has been meteor-like, flashing through the darkness in which we live. I know of nothing more miraculous in all history.

Nothing could his enemies do but it redounded to his infinite advantage, the advantage of his cause. They did not hang him at once; they reserved him to preach to them. No theatrical manager could have arranged things so wisely to give effect to his behavior and words. And who, think you, *was* the Manager?

The preachers, the Bible men, they who talk about principle and doing to others as you would that they should do unto you,—how could they fail to recognize him, by far the greatest preacher of them all, with the Bible on his lips, and in his act the embodiment of principle, who actually carried out the golden rule?

All whose moral sense is aroused, who have a calling from on high to preach, have sided with him.

On the day of his translation, I heard, to be sure, that he was hung, but I did not know what that meant,—and I felt no sorrow on his account; but not for a day or two did I even *hear* that he was dead, and not after any number of days shall I believe it. Of all the men who are said to be my contemporaries, it seems to me that John Brown is the only one who *has not* died.

January 9, 1860

I hear that R. M——, a rich old farmer who lives in a large house, with a male housekeeper and no other family, gets up at three or four o'clock these winter mornings and milks seventeen cows regularly.

When asked why he works so hard he answers that the poor are obliged to work hard. Only think, what a creature of fate he is, this old Jotun, milking his seventeen cows though the thermometer goes down to minus 25°, and not knowing why he does it,—draining sixty-eight cows' teats in the dark of the coldest morning!

Think how helpless a rich man who can only do as he has done!

———————————————————————————————★

1834-85: A TALE OF TWO AUTHORS

———————————————————————————————☆

PHILOSOPHER BRONSON ALCOTT was a wonderful talker. Prominent Bostonians came around quite often to hear him. His loyal, loving family, especially daughter Louisa May, thought his conversations were so brilliant that people ought to be willing to pay for them. Even the great Emerson was influenced by what he said about transcendentalism. And besides, if the landlord and the grocer wouldn't accept Bronson Alcott's talk, there was very little else he had to offer them.

But philosophy was something these people didn't want, and those who did want it expected to get it free. Now and then Emerson, out of the goodness of his heart, slipped Alcott a few dollars to help him out of a particularly desperate moment.

Above everything else, Alcott dreamed of selling his writings. But his ideas, the moment they hit paper, lost luster. Editors would not have them. There were those who called him impractical, a man of wild schemes—despite the fact that his suggestions for the reform of education were sound and came to be widely adopted generations later. Even Emerson, when he read Alcott's manuscripts, usually advised him to set them aside.

Alcott ran a not very successful school, experimented with a not at all successful model colony, and went on talking. The family situation—there were his wife Abigail and four daughters to be supported—went from bad to intolerable.

Then Louisa May got busy. She wrote to sell, and did. One of her stories, Little Women, proved the most popular girls' book ever published in America. Now all the bills were paid. The Alcotts began partaking of the good things of life. Bronson Alcott at last became famous—as Louisa May's father. His dream of presiding over a "Concord Summer School of Philosophy and Literature" was realized; there was even enough money for that.

For Louisa, life slipped by as she ground out book after book. She remained unmarried. There was no time for love, there was not enough of Louisa left over from what she put into the books—including her health. Two days after the death of her father, she died, her purpose accomplished.

Both father and daughter kept diaries. Between them sleeps a story as touching as anything created in Louisa May Alcott's imagination.

"I will not speak of family destitution."
AMOS BRONSON ALCOTT (1799-1888)

April 22 [1834]

My ideas, at present, are better than my style, and for many ideas, distinct and vivid in my own mind, I have no sign. This, more than anything else, is, I believe, the cause of my failure.

August 4 [1835]

I wish I could write as I feel and think—as I sometimes converse even. Not that I have ever, in any one instance, practically realized my conception of expression in any one of these forms, but approached more nearly in these than with my pen. I do not practice writing enough to give readiness, ease, grace, clearness, strength, to my style. I live too much in the ideal.

March 5 [1836]

Mr. Emerson returned my Ms. copy of the "Breath of Childhood" with suitable criticism on the style both of the thought and of expression. This I had asked him to do, and he has not disappointed me.

June, Week XXVI [1838]

Emerson returns my Ms., with his criticisms thereon. He points out the defect of the book, and seems disposed to have me withhold it from publication. I judge the counsel wise, and feel inclined at present to lay it aside.

January 13 [1839]

Last evening, just before going to bed, I happened to run over Emerson's critiques on my "Psyche"; and the effect was to make me despair, almost, of writing aught worthy of myself. It lamed me; it made me blind and dumb. I had music in my soul, but no voice.—Tonight, I feel quite encouraged. I shall sing one day.

May 27 [1850]

Mrs. A. quite dejected, feeble, weeps from anxiety, is disconsolate, and cannot be comforted. A crisis of some sort coming, and to be met. No income, no earnings, etc. etc.

Yet I will not permit myself to speak on this subject of family destitution, so complicate and intricate in its economics.

October 26-28 [1862]

Also examine myself and doings, to find how little I have to show for a life of near sixty-three years—a deplorable lack of early discipline in expression that leaves me lame at last.

March 6 [1869]

Louisa has had good success in her last book *Little Women*, part first, of which four editions have been sold, and her publishers today send her their check for $228.00, as their second payment, having paid her $300.00 last December. They have part second in press, and hope to find as ready a sale for it as for the first. The press generally commends it highly, and the young folks write expressing their admiration.

April 30

Louisa's *Little Women,* Part II, has been most favorably received and generally praised in the reviews. She has made friends of the New England girls, and is deluged with notes of thanks and admiration by almost every male. Her publishers are exulting in the pecuniary success, having sold thirteen thousand copies and are now putting a sixth edition to press, confident of selling twenty thousand before Christmas. This is most encouraging. She takes her growing repute modestly, being unwilling to believe her books have all the merit ascribed to them by the public. She is among the first to draw her characters from New England life and scenes.

May 9

After all I am here most at one with thought and myself, surrounded by my friendly books, and free to follow the mood of the moment,—read, write, meditate. Yet how little comes of it, after all! There are these voluminous diaries, and how little of life is transcribed upon their leaves!

August 24

Louisa is praised for her fine command of the English tongue, and May for the air and expression of her drawings. She is commended by the masters in art. They doubtless owe much to their mother's strength of mind and good spirits.

September 4

I read notices of Louisa's *Little Women* from all parts of the country, and, with one or two exceptions, all are not only highly commendatory but place her in the first rank of writers of fiction.

It is an honor not anticipated, for a daughter of mine to have won so wide a celebrity, and a great honor that she takes these so modestly. I indeed, have great reason to rejoice in my children, finding in them so many of their mother's excellencies.

December 1

I am introduced as the father of Little Women, and am riding in the chariot of glory wherever I go.

March 31 [1870]

To Boston with my wife.

Give Louisa a pocket book and May a mirror for their travels.

We bid them farewell and fear and hope. Deserving girls! They are now being rewarded for their toils and sacrifices in childhood and early womanhood. If Louisa can recover lost health and spirits and May gratify her thirst for art, then God be praised, and our cup will overflow.

April 1

The girls take their morning's train by Springfield for New York. John accompanies them to see them aboard the Steamer *Lafayette* which sails tomorrow for Havre, stopping at Brest, where they propose landing and travel leisurely through France, Switzerland, and thence into Italy to spend the coming winter. They take leave of Boston under fair omens. Louisa's *Old Fashioned Girl* is to be published tomorrow, the day of her leaving the country. Twelve thousand copies have been sold in advance of publication and four thousand are now in press. They are abundant in funds for their traveling expenses.

May 2

To Boston and see Niles concerning Louisa's books, which are having a large sale, the *Old Fashioned Girl* having reached 27,000 since the date of its publication, April 2nd, and *Little Women* is in the 48th edition, both books finding favor with the reviewers.

June 7

Inquire the price of a through ticket to San Francisco, and am told it is $130. One can see the Pacific in a week's time.

June 28

To Boston and home again, reading at the Athenaeum and seeing Niles. He shows me his accounts with Louisa for the year past.

There will be due on the first of July, for six months percentage on her books, $6,000.00. He has paid her, on these, Dolls. 12,292.50.

He thinks no American author has received so much during the current year, and says her works are selling better than others at present. It is unexpected success, and she deserves it and may well enjoy its fruits abroad. She seems to be finding favor also in England, where *Little Women* and *Old Fashioned Girl* have been printed.

July 3

Yet a diary is the most instructive of all writings, even though it records poorly the life of any man, however simple or wicked, revealing the story of the human heart without fear or equivocation.

". . . so cheer up, Louisa, and grind away!"
LOUISA MAY ALCOTT (1832-1888)

1853

Father to the West to try his luck,—so poor, so hopeful, so serene. God be with him!

1854

Father doing as well as a philosopher can in a money-loving world.

In February Father came home. Paid his way, but no more. A dramatic scene when he arrived in the night. We were awaked by hearing the bell. Mother flew down, crying, "My husband!" We rushed after, and five white figures embraced the half-frozen wanderer who came in hungry, tired, cold, and disappointed, but smiling bravely and as serene as ever.

We fed and warmed and brooded over him, longing to ask if he had made any money; but not one did till little Mary said, after he had told all the pleasant things, "Well, did people pay you?"

Then, with a queer look, he opened his pocketbook and showed one dollar, saying with a smile that made our eyes fill, "Only that! My overcoat was stolen and I had to buy a shawl. Many promises were not kept, and traveling is costly; but I have opened the way, and another year shall do better."

I shall never forget how beautifully mother answered him, though the dear, hopeful soul had built much on his success; but with a beaming face she kissed him, saying, "I call that doing *very well*. Since you are safely home, dear, we don't ask anything more."

Anna and I choked down our tears, and took a little lesson in real love which we never forgot, nor the look that the tired man and the tender woman gave one another. It was half tragic and comic, for father was very dirty and sleepy, and mother in a big nightcap and funny old jacket.

1854

To Father I shall send new neckties and some paper; then he will be happy, and can keep on with the beloved diaries though the heavens fall.

April, 1855

Summer plans are yet unsettled. Father wants to go to England: not a wise idea, I think. We shall probably stay here, and A. and I go into the country as governesses. It's a queer way to live, but dramatic, and I rather like it; for we never know what is to come next. We are real "Micawbers" and always "ready for a spring."

October [1856]

Pleasant letters from Father, who went on a tour to N. Y., Philadelphia, and Boston.

January, 1857

Father came to see me on his way home; little money; had had a good time, and was asked to come again. Why don't rich people who enjoy his talk pay for it? Philosophers are always poor, and too modest to pass around their own hats.

July [1857]

As we sat talking over Father's boyhood, I never realized so plainly before how much he has done for himself. His early life sounded like a pretty old romance, and Mother added the love passages.

August [1857]

A sad, anxious month. Betty worse; Mother takes her to the seashore. Father decides to go back to Concord; he is never happy far from Emerson, the one true friend who loves and understands and helps him.

[October, 1858]

Earned thirty dollars; sent twenty home.

December

Father started on his tour West full of hope. Dear man! How happy he will be if people will only listen to and *pay* for his wisdom.

November

Hurrah! My story was accepted; and Lowell asked if it was not a translation from the German, it was so unlike most tales. I felt much set up, and my fifty dollars will be very happy money. People seem to think it a great thing to get into the "Atlantic"; but I've not been pegging away all these years in vain, and may yet have books and publishers and a fortune of my own. Success has gone to my head, and I wander a little. Twenty-seven years old, and very happy.

February, 1860

Mr. ———— won't have "M.L." as it is anti-slavery, and the dear South must not be offended. Got a carpet with my $50, and wild Louisa's head kept the feet of the family warm.

November

Father sixty-one; L. aged twenty-eight. Our birthday. Gave Father a ream of paper, and he gave me Emerson's picture; so both were happy.

Wrote little, being busy with visitors. The John Brown Assn. asked me for a poem, which I wrote.

Kind Miss R. sent May $30 for lessons, so she went to B. to take some of Johnstone. She is one of the fortunate ones, and gets what she wants easily. I have to grub for my help, or go without it. Good for me, doubt-less, or it wouldn't be so; so cheer up, Louisa, and grind away!

December, 1861

A quiet Christmas; no presents but apples and flowers. No merrymak-ing; for Nan and Mary were gone and Betty under the snow. But we are used to hard times, and, as mother says, "While there is a famine in Kansas we mustn't ask for sugar-plums."

All the philosophy in our house is not in the study; a good deal is in the kitchen, where a fine old lady thinks high thoughts and does kind deeds while she cooks and scrubs.

January, 1861

Father had four talks at Emerson's; good people came, and he enjoyed them much; made $30. R. W. E. probably put in $20. He has a sweet way of bestowing gifts on the table under a book or behind a candlestick, when he thinks Father wants a little money, and no one will help him earn. A true friend is this tender and illustrious man.

Journal kept at hospital, Georgetown, D.C., 1862.

November

Thirty years old. Decided to go to Washington as nurse if I could find a place. Help needed, and I love nursing, and *must* let out my pent-up energy in some new way.

January, 1863

Union Hotel Hospital, Georgetown, D.C.

I never began the year in a stranger place than this; five hundred miles from home, alone, among strangers, doing painful duties all day long, and leading a life of constant excitement in this great house, surrounded by three or four hundred men in all stages of suffering, disease, and death.

January, 1864

On looking over my accounts, I find I have earned by my *writing* alone nearly *six hundred dollars* since last January, and spent less than a hundred for myself, which I am glad to know. May has had $70 for herself, and the rest has paid debts or bought necessary things for the family.

December [1864]

So my year closes with a novel *[Moods]* well launched and about $300 to pay debts and make the family happy and comfortable till spring. Thank God for the success of the old year, the promise of the new!

September, 1867

Niles, partner of Roberts, asked me to write a girls' book. Said I'd try.

January, 1868

Wednesday, 22nd—to the Club with Father. A good paper on the "Historical View of Jesus." Father spoke finely. It amuses me to see how people listen and applaud *now* what was hooted at twenty years ago.

The talk lasted until two, and then the hungry philosophers remembered they had bodies and rushed away, still talking.

May, 1868

Father saw Mr. Niles about a fairy book. Mr. N. wants a *girls' story,* and I begin "Little Women." Marmee, Anna, and May all approve my plan. So I plod away, though I don't enjoy this sort of thing. Never liked girls or knew many, except my sisters; but our queer plays and experiences may prove interesting though I doubt it.

June

Sent twelve chapters of "L.W." to Mr. N. He thought it *dull;* so do I.

January, 1869

Paid all the debts, thank the Lord!—every penny that money can pay— and now I feel as if I could die in peace. My dream is beginning to come true; and if my head holds out I'll do all I once hoped to do.

April

Very poorly. Feel quite used up. Don't care much for myself, as rest is heavenly even with pain; but the family seems so panic-stricken and helpless when I break down, that I try to keep the mill going.

August

Made up $1000 for S. E. S. to invest. Now I have $1,200 for a rainy day and no debts. With that thought I can bear neuralgia daily.

December [1871]

Mother is to be cosey if money can do it. She seems to be now, and my long-cherished dream has come true; for she sits in a pleasant room, with no work, no care, no poverty to worry, but peace and comfort all about her, and children glad and able to stand between trouble and her.

January, 1872

Roberts Brothers paid $4,400 as six months receipts for the book. A fine New Years gift. S. E. S. invested $3,000 and the rest I put in the bank for family needs.

June, 1872

Home, and begin a new task. Twenty years ago I resolved to make the family independent if I could. At forty that is done. Debts all paid, even the outlawed ones, and we have enough to be comfortable. It has cost me my health, perhaps; but as I still live, there is more for me to do, I suppose.

November, 1872

Forty on the twenty-ninth. Got Father off for the West, all neat and comfortable. I enjoyed every cent spent, and had a happy time packing his new trunk with warm flannels, neat shirts, gloves, etc., and seeing the dear man go off in a new suit, overcoat, hat, and all, like a gentleman. We both laughed over the pathetic old times with tears in our eyes, as I reminded him of the "poor as poverty, but serene as heaven" saying.

January, 1874

Father disappointed and rather sad, to be left out of so much that he would enjoy and should be asked to help and adorn. A little more money and a pleasant house and time to attend to it, and I'd bring all the best people to see and entertain *him*. When I see so much twaddle going on I

wonder those who can don't get up something better, and have really good
things.

When I had youth I had no money; now I have the money I have no
time; and when I get the time, if I ever do, I shall have no health to enjoy
life. I suppose it's the discipline I need; but it's rather hard to love the
things I do and see them go by because duty chains me to my galley. If I
come into port at last with all sail set that will be reward perhaps.

Life always was a puzzle to me, and gets more mysterious as I go on. I
shall find it out by and by and see that it's all right, if I can only keep
brave and patient to the end.

July, 1879

On the 15th the School of Philosophy began in the study at Orchard
House—thirty students; Father the dean. He has his dream realized at last,
and is in glory, with plenty of talk to swim in.

November 27th [1883]

Birthday—fifty-one. Home with gifts to poor Father—eighty-four.

July and August [1884]

Took care of father and house, and idled away the hot days with books
and letters. Drove with Father, as he enjoyed it very much.

August 8 [1885]

Lived in the past for days, and felt very old, recalling all I have been
through. Experiences go deep with me, and I begin to think it might be
well to keep some record of my life, if it will help others to read it when I
am gone.

1858: NEWCOMER TO THE LAND OF
PROMISE

UP TO NOW the United States has taken in more than forty million immigrants.
They began coming in large numbers shortly after the Napoleonic wars ended
in 1815. Over the Atlantic in wave after wave they poured for a century, the

bulk now from one country, now from another, until Congress choked the flow down to a trickle in the 1920s.

When it was heaviest, 1905-14, it was averaging more than a million a year. The Irish and English were earliest; biggest year for the Irish was 1851, for the English 1888. Germany, which sent over more than any other, reached a peak in 1882, Italy in 1907, Russia in 1913. In a typical New England mill town in the early 1900s forty-five languages could be heard on the streets between whistles of a working day. On greeting a visiting American official, a European mayor said, "I welcome you in the name of our city's four thousand people, three thousand of whom are now in your country."

They moved to America, these latecomers, to escape grinding poverty, military conscription, oppression, to look for a way beyond the blank walls of Old World hopelessness. And they were let come because America needed them. The nation's growth, its greatness, are today as much their story as that of Americans who can trace back a few generations beyond them.

The coming of Jacob Saul Lanzit was, in its essentials, like that of millions of others. At 28 or thereabouts, he left his home in the Austrian city of Czernowitz, made the rugged crossing—weeks in the airless but not odorless steerage of a sailing vessel, landed in New York with little money and less knowledge of where to go or what to do, was bewildered by "this noise, this tumult," soon learned that it was harder to get work than he had been led to believe by the tales of quick fortune he had heard back home, went through spells of despair, and finally began to claw a livelihood out of this indifferent but tremendously vital, busy new world.

Lanzit wrote his diary in German. Jacob R. Marcus, director of American Jewish Archives, translated it but left the place-names as Lanzit had spelled them.

"I have to take hold . . ."
JACOB SAUL LANZIT (about 1830-1912)

September 21, 1858

Nine-thirty o'clock. Rockets in the air. Gun fired. Ten-twenty-five o'clock: anchored in the channel. Passengers checked until Wed. 22 at 8 o'clock by customs inspectors. Not until eleven-thirty o'clock by steamboat to Castel Garden, entered my name; then to the Sackspear [Shakespeare] Hotel, 242-244 William Street, run by Joseph Fickler from Constance [Germany].

I paid particular attention to the Hirschberg family: father, mother, three daughters, and a brother-in-law, who were to go to Milwoke. They promised me every possible assistance, as they have very many friends in Milwoke and Chicago. But man proposes and God disposes, for I had hardly arrived in Castel Garden when I became separated from this family. In spite of my searching I could not find the family, for New York is altogether too big to find anyone.

This noise, this tumult, rattling traffic, drove me out of my mind. Without thinking it over too much, I bought a ticket on Septem. 24 in order to take the morning train on the Twenty-seventh to Chicago.

Monday, the twenty-seventh, at seven-forty-five o'clock

By steamer to [the Jersey City depot of] Philidelfia Railroad and left at 8 A.M. by train. Now it went fast as a cannon ball, without rest, except for ten minutes in the morning and evening, and at noon fifteen minutes; between stations one to two minutes each.

Wednesday, the twenty-ninth

I arrived in Chicago. I had myself taken to a German hotel, Hotel Meisner, [run by] a very decent man. Oh, how the blood stopped in my veins, not having spoken a word to anyone during the whole journey! I realized that I lack the English language. However, immediately upon my arrival I agreed with the hotelkeeper on $4 per week and ran to town to look for something.

I could not be very demanding. I am in Americka 3,200 miles from Europe, and in Chicago, too, which is 1,200 miles from New York.

September 30

I went, recommended by an offis to an innkeeper who needs a porter, who is supposed to pay board and $2 per week. I, for one, would be satisfied, but he believes that I am too good for this kind of work. He said, however, I should inquire tomorrow again.

October 1

No chance of getting a job with the innkeeper. I went to several tobacco dealers; perhaps they can use me in the factories. One of them proposed to hire me for three years: first year $25, second year $50, third year $100, plus board and laundry.

October 2

As I see, there is nothing to this either. I went from store to store and offered my services. No one would give me even an indefinite answer; they all said everything was taken.

Serious, bad, very bad. To be sure, I still have enough to live on for ten to twelve months, but the question is, what then, perhaps use my pistols? As I thus went in desperation once more to the cigar dealer, he offered me a small business, and if it should be the will of God, I can at least earn my board in it. May the Lord only give me success and health, and this little business that is to come to life on Tuesday, Octo. 5, will get started.

October 3

The biggest nuisance, that seems so troublesome for me here, are the so-called muskitos. That is a sort of fly, really gnats, that fly around buzzing at night and bite particularly the foreigner because he is new; he is more sensitive. My hands and face are full of bites; it is not a pain but itching and tickling which, however, is over soon.

October 5

Open the business at six in the evening. It consists of a cigar stand at the restaurant of August Redig. I have to pay him a monthly rent of $10 and have to help out a little at the bar and the tables, and for that I receive free board. I hope, if I cannot make any profit, at least to pass the winter without expenses.

October 12

Six o'clock. After closing the books of my business, had a profit of $3.05 after deducting rent of $2.50. Great God, I thank thee. Give me only health and success and life, for thou art the Almighty.

October 15

The little business is improving. I am working hard in the saloon and act as barkeeper; thereby I learn the business. Time passes; business gets worse.

November

Got a reduction of $2 on the business rent.

November 15

Uncommonly bad, the cold becomes considerable, though we are here on the forty-second parallel.

November 28

Only after my bar dismissed the other barkeepers and I did all the work did I realize how sour the bread is here. Shortly afterwards became acquainted with Nicklaus Bader, who recommended me to a business in Woodstock [Illinois]. That is about seventy miles from here.

December

Lost in the cigar business; lost in the beer business.

December 9

Bought in Chicago a ticket on the Central Railroad.

December 10

Departed at 8 P.M.

December 11

Boarded a wrong train in Dunkirk [New York], by mistake, 100 miles and back, then once more on the emigrant train. Stayed in Dunkirk until Monday.

December 13

To Boofalo. There was a pedlar, Adolf Mejer. He advised me to peddle in New York.

December 14

In Albany, and the same day, four o'clock, in New York. How I got here, I do not know myself. I managed to get into the Sackspare Hotel.

December 15

Lodging at Schamberg's Hotel for $1 a week.

December 16

Moved in. What will be from here on I don't know yet.

December 20

Days go by; still no work. Now I have to take hold of whatever there is, I decided to peddle stationery. I met a young man by the name of Bernhard Wasservogel who, like me, started the same business but soon gave it up. And now I have been going around for two weeks already, and there was no day when I made my expenses.

January 5 [1859]

I decided to learn a profession; that is, to learn either to make cigars or to sew on Singer's machine. I decided for the latter and began to learn in earnest. Tuition $3. I will probably have to learn for five or six weeks. However, I can make a living. It is hard work, to be sure, but I am now in America; that means working.

By chance I got into a factory after ten days' training, though for small wages.

January 29

But the way I manage, I still save money. The Enlisch tong is becoming easier and easier for me.

February 20

Still in the same factory with higher wages. By the end of February our factory closed down. I went around for three weeks without work. My money was partly used up. I bought a machine for $40 and went without eating. Finally I came to a Mr. Amer, where I received $7 a week and stayed one month. Now idle for a few days.

All at once I advertised in the paper and was hired by a lining maker for $9 a week. That was too hard. On May 18 a factory opened on William St. Many machines. I came there as an operator for $7 a week and with God's help I will be able to stay there for some time.

I met a Czernowitzer [a man from his home town] by the name of Hersh Feder who lives in Broocklin.

July 4

The most famous day in Americka. Love affairs upon love affairs. Patience.

July and August

I worked industriously all the time. Finally I saved something, and on August 1 I deposited $20 in the bank, and on the same day I met a girl named Miss Rachel Max. That was on Monday. The following Sunday I went out with her for the first time, to Central Parc. We love each other to a most extraordinary degree.

August 14

I bought a Singer's machine and traded in my machine, and Monday,

August 15, I entered into partnership with a certain Lewey and, God willing, we will do well.

My Roschen [Rachel] loves me; she now works for me.

On the sixteenth I spoke with her mother. Hardly had the business with Lewey begun when I learned the art of being involved with mean people. Whenever I want to visualize a mean character, I can only use the word tailor, and after six weeks of hard work I gave up my partner and remained without a cent. I even owed for board, and I still owed $17 on the machine. What could I do? I decided, therefore, to make linings on my own account.

September

My beloved Rosa [still Rachel] helped me with everything possible, not only with her hands but even with money, and within two weeks' time all my debts were paid. My former partner named Lewey, a red-haired creature (may God damn him in all eternity) insisted that I marry his cousin, who has a few hundred dollars, to be sure, but I love Rosa and therefore did not want the other girl. But he, the mean scoundrel, whose blood would not cool my anger, constantly stirred up quarrels and arguments between me and my Rosa, so that one day there almost was a knife battle between us and the redhead.

I moved out on October 4 and rented a small room on the same street, $4 rent. However, a terrible lack of work caused me at that time great financial embarrassment, and my Rosa gave me the ring off her finger to pawn.

Finally I got work. I was at odds with Rosa's father and made up, whereupon he bought me a stove [Stovepipe hat] and silk clothes.

I rented a larger apartment on Exex [Essex] Street (rent $6.50) and began to have a lot of work. I am doing good business.

Jacob married Rosa and they settled in New York's Lower East Side and there raised a family. In 1866 he quit his sewing machine to go into the fancy goods business. Later he tried millinery, then shirtmaking, but after a few more years he settled on printing as his life's work and went into business for himself. He was meticulous—too much so to equal the profits of competitors—but he managed to get along, and Rosa helped support the family by continuing to operate the millinery shop.

Jacob ruled his household in the patriarchal tradition of his forebears. In many ways he became "Americanized." But his children always greeted him by kissing his hand.

IN THE TOWN OF TOWANDA, northeast Pennsylvania, Lester Ward worked for his older brother Cyrenus. He made hubs for wagon wheels and cut hay on the mountain. At 19 Lester kept a diary. He wrote in French—for the exercise, he said, though our guess is that he had another reason. He probably hoped that way to protect his record from prying eyes. It was a candid one, and figuring prominently in it was his girl. Lizzie Vought, referred to in the diary only as "the girl," was one of the prettiest in the whole county. Life wasn't dull for Lester when "the girl" loved him; in fact, it got so interesting they decided they had better take it seriously. They did.

After service in the Union army, Lester went back to school at Columbian (now George Washington) University and finished with a law degree in 1871. He became a geologist for the government and then a professor of botany at Columbian University, but his most important work came later in life as a pioneer in the science of sociology. Holding a professorship at Brown University, he was the author of several important works on that subject, among them Dynamic Sociology, 1883; The Psychic Factors of Civilization, 1893; Outlines of Sociology, 1898; and Glimpses of the Cosmos, 1918.

"How sweet it is to sleep with her!"
LESTER FRANK WARD (1841-1913)

July 9 [1860]

I cultivated the corn this morning for the first time this year. I was a little annoyed with the horse's not keeping to the row. In the afternoon I gathered and bound the sheaves.

When the night came I had a fine time playing on the violin while Baxter played the tambourine. My heart was very light regarding the girl whom I loved, and whom I no longer esteem.

July 11

I went to the Post Office to look for the promised letter from the girl, but did not find it, so I came to the conclusion that I never wished to see her again. My heart is light. I was almost sick cutting the corn all this morning.

My girl, I am going to abandon you eternally, you whom I have loved so deeply! It will kill me, but let me perish.

August 19, Sunday morning

Hearing mention of an Episcopal meeting at six o'clock in the evening I decided to attend it. After having finished a letter I went to Sunday School and finally to the girl's, taking her a music book. I talked with her for an hour or two and she entertained me wonderfully—when I returned and got something to eat, I went to church.

Mr. Douglas, the minister, after having gone through all the ceremonies which belong to this church (which were, incidentally, very interesting to me) preached a very practical and profound sermon. The girl was there, and as I passed the stairs which lead to the gallery I saw her standing on the steps. It was a very awkward maneuver to approach her and ask for her company to another service.

But I accomplished it casually, and she could not refuse. We went at once to another church, chatting and enjoying ourselves marvelously. She fascinated me. I remembered my previous love. What a charming girl. If I could once more press my lips on hers and draw from them my soul's satisfaction!

We returned in the evening talking all the time but more gravely than before. We arrived at the door, I entered with her, she lit a lamp and we sat down together talking, but I could not keep myself from feasting my eyes ardently and with intensity on the object of beauty and attraction at my side.

Girl, I thought, if you were true to me, what a happy man I should be! I took the hand which I loved, and looked at it. We spoke little more from that moment, while I looked steadily at her face and was conquered.

I could no longer keep my place. Leaning forward I received her sweet and tender form in my arms and in an instant her face was covered with kisses. What a sublime scene! Who could have words to express my emotions?

And there we bathed ourselves in the passion of love until the crowing of cocks announced that it was day.

September 22

I could not sing long with her without feeling my trapped heart dart forth and come to rest in her loving breast. At half past three I parted from her

amid thousands of kisses. I have forgotten to remark that I collected forty
sets of hubs on Monday for myself. Tuesday and Wednesday I worked on
the fallow land, and Wednesday evening went to a meeting of the choir
in town.

I escorted the girl to her home which I did not leave until three. We had
considerable difficulty with the lamp, which finally went out at the critical
moment when it started to rain so that I could not go home.

Taking her by the hand, I attempted to find the door but in the shadows
we stumbled over a shoemaker's bench, and embracing her I sat down
with her on the bench, where we remained about an hour, embracing,
caressing, hugging and kissing. O bliss! O love! O passion pure, sweet and
profound! What more do I want than you?

Tuesday I finished 45 sets of hubs of which twenty are reserved for me.
Wednesday and Saturday I worked on the fallow land, which we have
finished.

(Evening)

It was with great difficulty that I finally succeeded in obtaining a team-
license to go and sell my hubs. I am going to leave tomorrow afternoon.
My route will be down the river to Standing Stone &c and I am determined not to sell a single hub without getting something useful to me
now.

Friday evening [February 15, 1861]

The girl and I had a very sweet time. I kissed her on her soft breasts,
and took too many liberties with her sweet person, and we are going to
stop. It is a very fascinating practice and fills us with very sweet, tender
and familiar sentiments, and consequently makes us happy. But the difficulty is that we might become so addicted in that direction that we might
go too deep and possibly confound ourselves by the standards of virtue.

July 16

I have just finished a day's work and am going up on the mountain. Yesterday afternoon I worked on the mountain cutting hay. Sunday evening
before I went to sleep I was summoned to watch beside the corpse of
Madame Partner. I found my darling there. We had a good time watching
until broad daylight.

I accompanied the girl home, and she insisted on my staying there and
getting a little sleep, but she came into my room to give me my socks and
to kiss me a little, and her mother found her there and she said several

things concerning us which made me angry and I got up and soon left the house. I shall never spend another night there.

August 14 [1862]

I shall resume with the narration of the events of this week. Sunday, being here, I was happy with my girl. We walked to May's and had a good time. On the way back we went to church to hear an Episcopal discourse by Mr. Brush. Not very good.

Monday morning I went to Towanda to buy some kerosine oil and do several other errands. I had been convinced by something I had read in the *Tribune* that I was exempt from military service, but I found that the *Tribune* was mistaken.

Immediately my intention was changed, and again I resolved to go to war. On my return I found Ed Owen who had already enrolled, and as I came here with him in his carriage, I found occasion to write my name among the brave men of Pennsylvania. I brought all my things from John's here this morning.

That same evening I joined the company, and Tuesday we all went to Towanda to elect officers. Every man who can is going to war, and everything is very exciting. But one more event is needed to crown the catalogue, and yesterday was the day.

Wednesday, August 13

I had to register my marriage! What? I, married? True enough. My heart's darling whom I have loved so long, so constantly, so frantically, is mine! We are keeping it a secret, but it has been guessed, but not yet discovered. How sweet it is to sleep with her!

III.

WESTWARD

THE

COURSE

1792: *SHIP* COLUMBIA *FINDS A NOBLE RIVER*

It was 17,000 miles from Boston around Cape Horn to the Pacific Northwest. But ever since Captain Cook explored Nootka Sound in 1778, Boston ship-owners knew there was a pot of gold waiting at the far end of the continent. One could pick up luxurious furs from the Indians there for the merest trinkets; cross the Pacific and get huge value for these pelts in trade with the Chinese; then bring home treasures of the Orient that would fetch enormous percentage profits. It was risky—"a venture into the unknown"—but so alluring that within a few years both British and New Englanders were sending ships on the great gamble.

Among these was the Columbia, out of Boston in 1790; and it was on this voyage that her skipper, Robert Gray, discovered a "noble river" falling into the Pacific. At that time, the finding of the Columbia River was incidental; note was made of it in the log, after which the ship went about her business, bought sea otter skins from the natives, departed for China, and eight months later made home port with a rich cargo and with an entry in her log that set Thomas Jefferson dreaming and eventually was to give a westward impetus to the settlement of America.

John Boit of Boston, fifth mate on the Columbia, was only sixteen years old. But his diary shows him to be a man of maturity and considerable Yankee acumen.

". . . a fine place for to sett up a Factory . . ."
JOHN BOIT (1774-1829)

The Ship Columbia was fited out for a four years cruize, on a trading voyage to the NW Coast of America, China etc.—about 250 tons burthen, mounted 12 Carriage Guns, and navigated with 50 men (including Officers)—own'd cheifly by Saml Brown, Joseph Barrell and Crowell Hatch Esqrs—and Commanded by Robert Gray. Cargo consisted of Blue Cloth, Copper and Iron.

October 8 [1790]

Ship sails dull, but is a fine seaboat, Crew appears to be a set of fine fellows.

November 25

54½ days from Boston. Keep all hands through the day in good weather employ'd in the various departments of the ship; it is best to keep them moving. They are allow'd tea or coffee each morning and in generall the ships fare is good, but proper attention to airing there beds and cloathing, and fumigating their berths is not paid.

January 17 [1791]

Saw the land to the Westward of Cape Blanco on the Coast of Patigonia. Very squally, haul'd our wind to the Eastward; find the ship embayed with the wind on shore. Stood on within 2 miles of the beach.

Our situation was very Critical, as we cannot weather the land on either tack; pass'd severall times over very shoal water but did not sound, for fear of intimidating the Crew.

February 27

Cape Horn is doubled.

March 21

Some of the Crew have the Scurvy in the Gums.

April 23

Between the hours of 3 and 4 PM departed this life our dear friend Nancy the Goat having been the Captain's companion on a former voyage round the Globe but her spirited disposition for adventure led her to undertake a 2d voyage of Circumnavigation; but the various changes of Climate and sudden transition from the Polar cold to the tropical heat of the Torrid Zone prov'd too much for a constitution naturally delicate; at 5 PM Committed her body to the deep.

29

Four seamen laid by with the Scurvey; their Mouths and Legs are very bad.

June 4

This day made the land, on the NW Coast of the American Continent

between Nootka (or King Georges sound) and Clioquot (or Coxes harbour).

5

This day anchor in Coxes harbour and found itt very commodious.
Above 300 of the Natives was along side in the Course of the day.

They all appear'd very freindly, brought us plenty of fish and Greens.
We landed the sick immediately on our arrivall and pitch'd a tent for their
reception, and although there was ten of them in the last stage of the
Scurvy, still they soon recover'd upon smelling the turf and eating Greens
of various kinds.

We buried severall of our sick up to the Hips in the earth, and let them
remain for hours in that situation; found this method of great service.

We purchas'd many of the Sea Otter skins in exchange for Copper and
blue Cloth. These Indians are of a large size, and somewhat corpulent.
The Women stand in great fear of the Males, but appear to be naturally
very modest; their garment is manufactor'd from the bark of a Tree, and
is well executed, being so constructed as to cover them complete from the
Neck to the Ancle; both Male and Female wear Hats of a conical form
made out of strong reeds, on them is painted, (in a rude manner) their
mode of Whale fishery. Attoo the Captain's servant (and a native of Sand-
wich Isle) ran away among the Indians. A cheif coming on board, placed
a guard over him, and sent his Canoe back to the village with the News;
they soon return'd with Mr Attoo, and ransom'd their Cheif.

20

At Meridian anchor'd in a small Cove (which we named Columbias). In
this situation we was completely land lock'd, vast many natives alongside.
These Natives was generally arm'd with Bows, arrows, and spears. They
wou'd pilfer whenever an opportunity offer'd; their Woman where more
chaste than those we had lately left. But still they where not all Dianas.
During our tarry here I visited one of the villages in the sound; found the
Natives busily employ'd building Canoes and packing provisions against
the ensuing Winter; they treated me quite friendly.

28

Enter'd the Straits of Juan de Fuca and Hove too. 'Twas evident that
these Natives had been visited by that scourge of mankind the Smallpox.
The Spaniards as the natives say brought it among them; these Indians
appear'd Freindly.

3d July, De fuca Straits

This Cheif at Tatooch's Isle offer'd to sell us some young Children they had taken in War.

8

This day anchor'd in Barrells sound on the SE part of the Queen Charlotte Isles. The Natives here are much stouter than any we had before seen, and appear to be very savage; the Women appear to carry full sway over the men and have an incision cut through the under lip, which they spread out with a peice of wood about the size and shape of a Goose egg (some much larger); itt's considered as an ornament, but in my opinion looks very gastly. Some of them booms out two inches from the chin. The women appear very fond of their ofspring, and the Men of both.

The Natives supplied us with plenty of Halibut and Rock Cod, for which we pd them in Nails.

The females are not very Chaste, but their lip peices was enough to disgust any Civilized being; however some of the Crew was quite partial.

23

Spoke the Brig Hope, Joseph Ingrahim master, from Boston, on the same business with ourselves; soon parted.

August 10

Mr. Caswell, this morning, took a Boatswain Mate and one Seamen with him in the Jolly Boat, by the permission of Capt. Gray, and went to the Cove a fishing. A breeze springing up soon after, and wishing to leave this place, a six pounder was fir'd, a Signal for the boat to return. She not appearing, soon after two more Cannon was fir'd. Got the Ship under way and stood off and on, and sent the pinnace under charge of the 4th officer in search of the small boat. Soon after, we see the Pinnace returning with Jolly Boat in tow, without any person in her and soon discover'd they had the Boat's Colours hoisted half mast; with this melancholy token they approach'd the Ship, when we soon discover'd our worthy freind and brother officer, Mr. Caswell lay dead in the bottom of the boat, stripp'd perfectly naked and stabb'd in upwards of twenty places. They saw nothing of John Folger (the boatswains mate) but Joseph Barnes (the Sailor) lay dead on the beach, and quite naked; fearing the Natives lay in ambush, they did not land to take off the corps. It is probable they where beset upon by a great superiority of natives, prompted by a desire to possess their cloaths and Arms.

13

We inter'd the remains of our departed, and much beloved, freind, with all the solemnity we was capable of.

The place was gloomy, and nothing was to be heard but the bustling of an aged oak whose lofty branches hung wavering o'er the grave, together with the meandering brook, the Cries of the Eagle, and the weeping of his freinds. So ends.

16

This day Spoke the Brig Hancock of Boston, Samuell Crowell, Master. They was on the same business as ourselves, and had been pretty successfull.

18

Came to Anchor, in a River which Capt. Crowell had named Hancocks, situated on the NW part of the Queen Charlotte Isles, in Company with the Brig, 6 fathom water, mud. The Brig's Longboat we found at this place, vast many of the Natives along side the Ship, and a few furs was purchased. Capt. Crowell had, upon some trifling offence, fir'd upon these Indians by which a number of them fell (such wanton cruelty throws him upon a levell with the savage), and perhaps this same fray was the means of our losing our worthy 2nd Officer as the places are not 20 leagues distant and mayhap they wreck'd their Vengeance upon us, thinking us all of one tribe. If it were so, bad luck to Crowell. Amen.

September 11

At Midnight saw Tatooch Isle, 3 miles. We thought ourselves further offshore. Almost calm, and an excessive strong tide sweeping us between some Ledges and the Isle. At daylight thick fog, saw the Rocks a head within pistol shot, with high breakers. Out all boats, and just towed the Ship clear; our situation was truly alarming, but we had no business so near the land in thick weather. However, Good Luck prevail'd.

12

Wind NE. Heard the roaring of Breakers, foggy; haul'd more ofshore. At 3 PM saw a rock about stone's throw distant, and narrowly escaped being dash'd upon itt; damn nonsense to keep beating about among rocks in foggy weather. At Midnight heard the surf roar again, sounded and found ground at 25 fathom. Rocks. The Captain at length was frighten'd, and proceeded with the Ship to a good offing (this ought to have been done long before).

20

On the 20th weigh'd, with light airs, and with the Boats ahead assisted by the Brig's Crew, we tow'd, and sail'd into winter quarters which we call'd Adventure Cove, and moor'd Ship for the winter. Vast many of the Natives along side, and appear'd to be highly pleas'd with the idea of our tarrying among them through the Cold Season.

October 13

Wickananish is the most powerfull cheif we have yet seen on this Coast. His tribe consists of upwards of 3000 souls; they allow polygamy, but the women are not prolific, as barrenness is very common among them. The Indians girls kept us well supplied with berries of different kinds, which was very grateful.

December 25

This day was kept in mirth and festivity by all the Columbia's Crew, and the principall Cheifs of the sound by invitation din'd on board ship. The Natives took a walk around the work shops on shore; they was suppriz'd at seeing 3 tier of wild fowl roasting at one of the houses—indeed, we was a little suppriz'd at the novelty of the sight ourselves, for at least there was 20 Geese roasting at one immense fire, and the Ships Crew appear'd very happy, most of them being on shore. The Indians cou'd not understand why the Ship and houses was decorated with spruce bows. At 12 Clock fir'd a federall Salute, and ended the day toasting our sweethearts and wifes.

April 28 [1792]

This day spoke his Britannic Majestey's Ships Discovery and Chatham, commanded by Capt. George Vancouver [noted English navigator] and Lietanent Wm. Broughton, from England, on a voyage of discovery.

May 7

Saw an inlett in the land, which had the appearance of an harbour; sent the Cutter under charge of 2d Officer to examine itt. Laying too; a strong Current with squally weather. The Boat returned, and the Officer reported that he cou'd find nothing but breakers at the entrance, but farther in itt had the appearance of a good harbour. This appearance being so flattering, Capt. Gray was determin'd not to give itt up. Therefore ordering the boat a head to sound, with nessescary signalls, the Ship stood in for the weather bar and we soon see from the Mast head a passage in between the breakers.

Bore off and run in NE b E, having from 4 to 9 fathom sand, an excellent strong tide setting out; the boat having made a signall for anchorage and a good harbour, we continued to stretch on till completely within the shoals where we anchor'd in 5 fathom. In an excellent harbour.

Vast many canoes came off, full of Indians; they appear'd to be a savage sett and was well arm'd, every man having his Quiver and Bow slung over his shoulder. Without doubt we are the first Civilized people that ever visited this port, and these poor fellows view'd us and the Ship with the greatest asstonishment. We purchas'd many furs and fish.

8

We was fearfull to send a Boat on discovery but I've no doubt we was at the Entrance of some great river, as the water was brackish and the tide set out half the time.

This evening heard the hooting of Indians; all hands was immediately under arms, sevrall canoes was seen passing near the Ship, but was dispers'd by firing a few Musketts over their heads. At Midnight we heard them again, and soon after 'twas bright Moon light, we see the Canoes approaching to the Ship. We fir'd sevrall cannon over them, but still persisted to advance with the war Hoop.

At length a large Canoe with at least 20 Men in her got within ½ pistol shot of the quarter, and with a Nine pounder and about 10 Musketts, loaded with Buck shot, we dash'd her all to peices, and no doubt kill'd every soul in her. The rest soon made a retreat. I do not think they had aney Conception of the power of Artillery. But they was too near us for to admit of any hesitation how to proceed.

9

Very plesent weather, many canoes came along side from down river, and brought plenty of Skins, likewise some canoes from the tribes that first visited us, and their countenances plainly show'd that those unlucky savages who last Night fell by the Ball was a part of the same tribe, for we cou'd plainly understand by their signs and gestures that they where telling the very circumstance to their Acquaintances from down River, and by Pointing to the Cannon, and endeavouring to explain the noise they made, made us still more certain that they had no Knowledge of fire arms previous to our Coming amongst them.

I am sorry we was oblidg'd to kill the poor Divells, but it cou'd not with safety be avoided. These Natives brought us some fine Salmon and plenty of Beaver Skins, with some Otters, and I believe had we staid longer among them we shou'd have done well.

12

This day saw an appearance of a spacious harbour abrest the Ship, haul'd our wind for itt, observ'd two sand bars making off, with a passage between them to a fine river. Out pinnace and sent her in ahead and followed with the Ship under short sail.

The [Columbia] River extended to the NE as far as eye cou'd reach, and water fit to drink as far down as the Bars at the entrance.

We directed our course up this noble river in search of a Village. The beach was lin'd with Natives, who ran along shore following the Ship. Soon after above 20 Canoes came off, and brought a good lot of Furs and Salmon, which last they sold two for a board Nail; the furs were likewise bought cheap, for Copper and Cloth.

At length we arriv'd opposite to a large village, situate on the North side of the river about 5 leagues from the entrance, came too in 10 fathom sand about ¼ mile from shore.

The river at this place was about 4 miles over. We purchas'd 4 Otter Skins for a Sheet of Copper, Beaver Skins, 2 Spikes each and other land furs, 1 Spike each.

We lay in this place till the 20th May, during which time we put the Ship in good order and fill'd up the water casks along side, itt being very good. The Indians inform'd us there was 50 Villages on the banks of this river.

18

Capt. Gray named this river Columbia's. This River in my opinion wou'd be a fine place for to sett up a Factory; the river abounds with excellent Salmon.

─── ★

1805: LEWIS AND CLARK GO WEST
TO THE SEA

─── ☆

GEOGRAPHY INTERESTED *Thomas Jefferson—especially when it held the key to one of the greatest dollars-and-cents business prospects in world history.*

The possibility that appealed to Jefferson was the same that may have led Columbus across the uncharted ocean, westbound for the Orient; the same that had sparked three centuries of search for a northwest passage—namely, a waterway of commerce to the east.

That was why, in 1803, Jefferson asked Congress to appropriate $2,500 for a certain "literary pursuit"—odd phrase for it!—which would take the form of an expedition "to explore the Missouri River & such principal stream of it as, by its course & communication with the waters of the Pacific Ocean, may offer the most direct & practicable water communication across this continent, for the purpose of commerce."

Jefferson had in mind that great river, the Columbia, which Captain Gray had discovered a decade before. Where it arose inland, no white man knew. Specifically, what Jefferson wanted to learn was this: Was there a way to reach the Columbia from the headwaters of the Missouri, across the Continental Divide? Was it true, as he had heard, that by a single portage of twenty miles, the one great river could be linked to the other?

While England, France and Spain were jockeying for the inside track to power over the fabulous American West, Jefferson bought Louisiana, a real estate deal that doubled the size of the United States, and dreamed on about the two rivers and the lay of the land between them.

He commissioned his secretary, 29-year-old army officer Meriwether Lewis, to go and see. Lewis divided his leadership of the forty-five man expedition with another army man, William Clark, four years his senior.

In fitness for high adventure these men far outshone their contemporary explorers of the New World. Both were engaging characters.

On May 14, 1804, the party, in three boats, crossed the Mississippi and "proceeded on under a Jentle brease up the Missourie." In their adventures of the next eighteen months, upriver, over the hump, and downriver to the sea, there was enough of suspense, of romance, for a dozen grade-A movies—all against the background of complex and momentous world politics.

At Fort Mandan, North Dakota, they hired a veteran trader, Touissant Charboneau, as guide. This was a happy stroke, because Charboneau took along his young Indian wife, Sacajawea. Born of the tribe of Shoshones, or Snake Indians, she had been captured as a child by enemies and made slave. Charboneau had bought her, brought her up, and married her. As it was in the country of the Snakes that Lewis and Clark had their greatest need of friendship and guidance, the Indian girl proved invaluable.

In Montana, west of what is now Yellowstone Park, Lewis and Clark traced the Missouri to its source, 2,700 miles from the mouth. As Lewis writes at this point, he hoped to find the Columbia just over the mountains "this evening." But from where he stood exulting on that morning of August 12, the Columbia, instead of 20 miles away, was 220! And instead of "this evening" it was nine weeks later when, having threaded their way through mountains and rugged waters, the party at last sailed down the Snake River into the Columbia. With those 220 miles, Jefferson's dream melted into the wild blue yonder.

But from Lewis and Clark the America of their time learned much. The people heard about the land beyond the horizon. It was more than a lesson in geography; more than all of Oregon and the "great Collumbia"; it was the beckoning to a venturesome people, the cry of the land to those who belonged to it and would go there—in time by the millions—to make it home.

"I did not dispair of taisting the Columbia."

MERIWETHER LEWIS (1774-1809)

WILLIAM CLARK (1770-1838)

[Lewis] August 8th 1805 [in southwestern Montana]

The Indian woman [Sacajawea] recognized the point of a high plain to our right which she informed us was not very distant from the summer retreat of her nation on a river beyond the mountains which runs to the west. This hill she says her nation calls the beaver's head from a conceived resemblance of its figure to the head of that animal. She assures us that we shall either find her people on this river or on the river immediately west of its source; which from its present size cannot be distant.

As it is now all important with us to meet these people as soon as possible I determined to proceed tomorrow with a small party to the source of the principal stream of this river and pass the mountains to the Columbia; and down that river untill I found the Indians; in short it is my resolution to find them or some others who have horses if it should cause me a trip of one month. For without horses we shall be obliged to leave a great part of our stores, of which it appears to me that we have a stock already sufficiently small for the length of the voyage before us.

August 10th

After passing a large creek at about 5 miles we fel in with the plain Indian road which led towards the point that the river entered the mountain. We therefore pursued the road. I sent Drewyer to the wright to kill a deer which we saw feeding and halted on the river under an immencely high perpendicular clift of rocks where it entered the mountain. Here we kindled a fire and waited for Drewyer.

He arrived in about an hour and a half or at noon with three deer skins and the flesh of one of the best of them; we cooked and eat a haisty meal and departed, returning a short distance to the Indian road which led us the best way over the mountains, which are not very high but are ruggid and approached the river closely on both sides. From the number of rattle snakes about the Clifts at which we halted we called them the rattle snake clifts.

The river below the mountains is rapid, rocky, very crooked, much divided by islands and withal shallow. After it enters the mountain it's bends are not so circuetous and it's general course more direct, but it is equally shallow, less divided, more rocky and rapid.

The mountains do not appear very high in any direction tho' the tops of some of them are partially covered with snow.

This convinces me that we have ascended to a great hight since we have entered the rocky mountains, yet the ascent has been so gradual along the vallies that it was scarcely perceptable by land. I do not beleive that the world can furnish an example of a river runing to the extent which the Missouri and Jefferson's rivers do through such a mountainous country and at the same time so navigable as they are.

If the Columbia furnishes us such another example, a communication across the continent by water will be practicable and safe. But this I can scarcely hope from a knowledge of its having in its comparatively short course to the ocean the same number of feet to decend which the Missouri and Mississippi have from this point to the Gulph of Mexico.

August 11th

The track which we had pursued last evening soon disappeared. I therefore resolved to proceed to the narrow pass on the creek about 10 miles West in hopes that I should again find the Indian road at the place; accordingly I proceeded through the level plain directly to the pass. I now sent Drewyer to keep near the creek to my right and Shields to my left, with orders to surch for the road which if they found they were to notify me by placing a hat on the muzzle of their gun.

I kept McNeal with me; after having marched in this order for about five miles I discovered an Indian on horse back about two miles distant coming down the plain towards us. With my glass I discovered from his dress that he was of a different nation from any that we had yet seen, and was satisfyed of his being a Sosone; his arms were a bow and quiver of arrows, and was mounted on an eligant horse without a saddle, and a small string which was attached to the under jaw of the horse which answered as a bridle.

I was overjoyed at the sight of this stranger and had no doubt of obtaining a friendly introduction to his nation provided I could get near enough to him to convince him of our being whitemen.

I therefore proceeded towards him at my usual pace. When I had arrived within about a mile he mad a halt which I did also and unloosing my blanket from my pack, I mad him the signal of friendship known to the Indians of the Rocky mountains and those of the Missouri, which is by holding the mantle or robe in your hands at two corners and then throwing it up in the air higher than the head bringing it to the earth as if in the act of spreading it, thus repeating three times. This signal of the robe has arrisen from a custom among all those nations of spreading a robe or skin for ther gests to set on when they are visited.

This signal had not the desired affect; he still kept his position and seemed to view Drewyer and Shields who were now comming in sight on either hand with an air of suspicion. I wold willingly have made them halt but they were too far distant to hear me and I feared to make any signal to them least it should increase the suspicion in the mind of the Indian of our having some unfriendly design upon him.

I therefore haistened to take out of my sack some beads, a looking glas and a few trinkets which I had brought with me for this purpose and leaving my gun and pouch with McNeal advanced unarmed towards him. He remained in the same stedfast posture untill I arrived in about 200 paces of him when he turned his horse about and began to move off slowly from me; I now called to him in as loud a voice as I could command repeating the word *tab-ba-bone* which in their language signifyes *white-man*.

But looking over his sholder he still kept his eye on Drewyer and Shields who wer still advancing neither of them haveing segacity enough to recollect the impropriety of advancing when they saw me thus in parley with the Indian.

I now made a signal to these men to halt. Drewyer obeyed but Shields who afterwards told me that he did not observe the signal still kept on.

The Indian halted again and turned his horse about as if to wait for me, and I believe he would have remained untill I came up with him had it not been for Shields who still pressed forward.

When I arrived within about 150 paces I again repeated the word *tab-ba-bone* and held up the trinkits in my hands and striped up my shirt sleve to give him an opportunity of seeing the colour of my skin and advanced leasurely towards him; but he did not remain untill I got nearer than about 100 paces when he suddonly turned his horse about, gave him the whip, leaped the creek and disapeared in the willow brush in an instant and with him vanished all my hopes of obtaining horses for the preasant.

I now felt quite as much mortification and disappoinment as I had pleasure and expectation at the first sight of this indian. I felt soarly chargrined at the conduct of the men, particularly Shields, to whom I principally attributed this failure in obtaining an introduction to the natives.

August 12th

We fell in with a large and plain Indian road along the foot of the mountains. At 5 miles we halted and breakfasted on the last of our venison, having yet a small peice of pork in reserve. After eating we continued our rout through the low bottom of the main stream 5 Mls. further in a S. W. direction.

The main stream now turns abruptly to the West through a narrow bottom between the mountains; the road was still plain; I therefore did not dispair of shortly finding a passage over the mountains and of taisting the waters of the great Columbia this evening.

At the distance of 4 miles further the road took us to the most distant fountain of the waters of the mighty Missouri, in surch of which we have spent so many toilsome days and wristless nights. Thus far I had accomplished one of those great objects on which my mind has been unalterably fixed for many years; judge then of the pleasure I felt in allaying my thirst with this pure and ice cold water which issues from the base of a low mountain or hill of a gentle ascent for ½ a mile.

August 17th

This portion of the journal was written by Nicholas Biddle, who used manuscripts furnished by Clark and a firsthand account given to him in conversations with George Shannon, a member of the expedition.

On setting out at seven o'clock, Captain Clarke with Charboneau and his wife walked on shore, but they had gone not more than a mile before Clarke saw Sacajawea, who was with her husband 100 yards ahead, began to dance and show every mark of the most extravagant joy, turning round him and pointing to several Indians, whom he saw advancing on horseback, sucking her fingers at the same time to indicate that they were of her native tribe.

We soon drew near to the camp, and just as we approached it a woman made her way through the croud towards Sacajawea, and recognising each other, they embraced with the most tender affection. The meeting of these two young women had in it something pecularly touching.

While Sacajawea was renewing among the women the friendships of former days, Captain Clarke went on, and was received by Captain Lewis and the chief, who after the first embraces and salutations were over, conducted him to a sort of circular tent or shade of willows.

Here he was seated on a white robe; and the chief immediately tied in his hair six small shells resembling pearls, an ornament highly valued by these people, who procure them in the course of trade from the sea-coast. The moccasins of the whole party were then taken off, and after much ceremony the smoking began.

After this the conference was to be opened, and glad of an opportunity to be able to converse more intelligibly, Sacajawea was sent for; she came into the tent, sat down, and was beginning to interpret, when she recognized her brother: She instantly jumped up, and ran and embraced him; throwing over him her blanket and weeping profusely: The chief was himself moved, though not in the same degree.

After some conversation between them she resumed her seat, and attempted to interpret for us, but her new situation seemed to overpower her, and she was frequently interrupted by her tears. After the council was finished the unfortunate woman learnt that all her family were dead except two brothers, one of whom was absent, and a son of her eldest sister, a small boy, who was immediately adopted by her.

[Clark]

October 16th [on the Snake River]

A cool morning. Determined to run the rapids. Put our Indian guide in front of our Small Canoe next and the other four following each other.

The canoes all passed over Safe except the rear Canoe which run fast on a rock at the lower part of the Rapids. With the early assistance of the other Canoes & the Indians, who was extreamly ellert, every thing was taken out and the Canoe got off without any enjorie further than the articles which it was loaded all wet.

At 14 miles passed a bad rapid at which place we unloaded and made a portage of ¾ of a mile haveing passd 4 Smaller rapids, three Islands and the parts of a house above. I saw Indians & Horses on the South Side below. Five Indians came up the river in great haste. We Smoked with them and gave them a piece of tobacco to Smoke with their people and sent them back. They Set out in a run & continued to go as fast as they could run as far as we could see them.

After getting Safely over the rapid and haveing taken Diner, Set out and proceeded on Seven miles to the junction of this river and the Columbia which joins from the N.W. In every direction from the junction of those rivers the countrey is one continued plain, low, and rises from the water gradually, except a range of high Countrey on the opposit Side about 2 miles distant from the Collumbia.

October 18th

The fish being very bad, those which was offerd to us we had every reason to believe was taken up on the shore dead, we thought proper not to purchase any. We purchased forty dogs for which we gave articles of little value, such as beeds, bells & thimbles, of which they appeared verry fond.

At 4 oClock we set out down the Great Columbia accompanied by our two old Chiefs.

November 7th

A cloudy foggey morning, Some rain. We Set out early, proceeded under high rugid hills with Steep assent, the Shore boald and rockey, the fog so thick we could not See across the river. Two canoes of Indians met and returned with us to their village. They gave us to eate Some fish, and Sold us fish, *wap pa to* roots, three dogs and 2 otter skins for which we gave fish hooks principally of which they were verry fond.

About 14 miles below the last village we landed at a village of the same nation. It contains 7 indifferent houses. Here we purchased a Dog, some fish, *wap pa to* roots, and I purchased 2 beaver skins for the purpose of makeing me a roab, as the robe I have is rotten and good for nothing.

Opposit to this village the high mountaneous countrey leaves the river on the Larboard Side below which the river widens into a kind of Bay & is crouded with low Islands Subject to be covered by the tides.

We proceeded on about 12 miles below the Village under a high mountaneous Countrey on the Starboard Side, Shore boald and rockey, and Encamped under a high hill opposit to a rock Situated have a mile from the shore, about 50 feet high and 20 Deamieter. We with dificuelty found

a place clear of the tide and Sufficiently large to lie on and the only place
we could get was on round stones on which we lay our mats.

Rain continud moderately all day & Two Indians accompanied us from
the last village. They we detected in Stealing a knife and returned.

Great joy in camp. We are in *view* of the *Ocian*, this great Pacific Ocean
which we been so long anxious to See. And the roreing or noise made by
the waves brakeing on the rockey Shores (as I suppose) may be heard
distinctly.

*Clark was mistaken. It was not until eleven days later, on November 18, after
a march of 19 miles, that he and ten of his men got their first view of the
Pacific. His entry on that day ends with: "Men appear much Satisfied with
their trip beholding with estonishment the high waves dashing against the
rocks & this emence Ocian."*

1828:   ON THE SANTA FE TRAIL

LIKE THE ROAD to almost anywhere in America, the Santa Fe Trail is older than
the oldest recorded traveler. When a company of adventurers in Boonlick,
Missouri, went into the business of trading in New Mexico in 1821, the trail
from Independence, Missouri, southwest across the country of the Cimarron
had already been thirty years wearing. Because profits ran in the neighborhood of
2,000 per cent, the Boonlick company in the next ten years increased its annual shipments of westbound merchandise from $3,000 to $270,000.

In 1828 Lawyer Wetmore, one of the Boonlick company, made the trip.
Three years later, when the United States government asked him for information about New Mexico, he incorporated into a letter to the Secretary of War
the diary he had kept.

"*. . . the foibles of mule teams . . .*"
ALPHONSO WETMORE (1793-1849)

May 28 [1828]

Reached the Blue Spring, the rendezvous of the Mexican traders, in
season to attend to the election of officers; ourself elected captain of the

host. "There may be some honor in it," as the deacon remarked on his own promotion, "but not much profit."

June 1

Tempest just as we were ready to set forward, the mules disengaged from the wagons in haste and double reefs taken in the wagon covers. All hands employed in detaining the mules, who are disposed to take leave of nos amigos. At 9 o'clock under way, reached the "Big Blue" [ten miles southwest of Independence, Mo.], all our spades in requisition to make the descent into the river practicable; the wagons eased down the bank by 20 men at a trail rope; encamped in the prairie beyond the river; met here two bee hunters; one of our hunters brought in a deer in the red, and lean, of course; my Mexican servant furnished with a gun, proud as Franklin was with his whistle.

6th

At 5 miles reached Elk Creek, where we discovered the corpse of a wagon which had been left by the preceding caravan. O Temperance! O Ditch Water! Made 16 miles.

9th

Ate this morning bacon and goose eggs, and at noon turtle soup. Not an alderman present!

12th

Detained by high water; one mess breakfasting on ham and eggs, another dining on alderman soup; met here a return caravan.

14th

Made only six miles, and encamped in time to reef wagon cover before a Noah-like tempest descended.

15th

Under way at 8 o'clock; made eight grievous miles and encamped early at Diamond spring; a mutinous disposition repressed by bandit logic.

21st

A little before daylight the mules made an abortive attempt to raise a stampido; half an hour later an alarm was created by a shot from one of the sentinels, and the cry of Indians, aroused the whole camp. Killed and wounded, blank; alarmed, none.

22d

At 5 o'clock A.M., after moving quietly forward three hours and a half, a team in rear of the caravan took fright, and, in an instant, more than twenty were coursing over the prairie with Olympic speed. An Irish Senti- nel of the horse guard, about 10 o'clock, mistook one of the co. for an Indian; he fired, and then challenged.

24th

Dined at a different crossing of another branch of Cow creek, which we passed after an interesting entertainment of a wagon race. It is one of the foibles of mule teams that, after they have traveled four or five hundred miles and when it is supposed they are about to tire, to take fright from a profile view of their shadows, and run like the antelope of these plains.

25th

Reached the Arkansas [Great Bend, Kansas] at 4 o'clock, encamped and replenished our shot pouches. "Keep your eyes skinned now," said the old trapper. "We are entering upon the most dangerous section of the trace, the war ground of the Panis [Pawnees] Osages, and Kansas." This is likewise a fine buffalo country, but we have no hump! no marrow bones! and no tongues, except our own parts of speech. Our hunters have brought in an antelope.

29th

Fine short grass prairie; buffalo in immense herds on all sides; selected several fat ones, and encamped, after a march of 19 miles.

July 1st

During this day's march, the caravan *bachi* shot his own mule through the head in a buffalo chase. Stearne's lament over the dead ass repeated.

3d

Our march to-day is through a plane and rolling prairie, surrounded with buffalo. A herd of these attempted to break through our column of teams. "It will take a smart scrimmage and sprinkle of shots," said the old trapper, "to turn them aside," and the leader fell at the flash of his rifle. Marched 20 miles, and encamped without timber—our supper dressed as usual, over buffalo fuel.

11th

Our course to-day was parallel with the Semiron [Cimarron]. Crossed Sandy creek, and, at 14 miles, halted. The Semiron here presents a fine view of water, and 8 miles further up, at our camp, not a drop of water appears in the channel. Our course from the Arkansas to the Semiron is generally south-west.

13th

At 8 miles reached the Semiron, the earth whitened with salt and salt-petre; thunder and wind; the earth thirsting, but not a drink obtained from the clouds. This day's march 18 miles.

15th

At 12 o'clock, encountered an Indian and squaw of the Kiawa nation. Several teams tired; the road good, but the saltpetre along the river bottom weakens our animals. This might be avoided by keeping out on the plains. Only 17 miles today.

16th

Crossed and filed off from the Semiron, and at 10 miles reached the upper Semiron spring, at the base of a very abrupt rocky hill, on the summit of which is a cross standing over the bones of two white men, who were slain while asleep by the gallant, high-minded, persecuted, gentlemen Indians. Saw here the first timber in nine days' march.

18th

In the evening, our road lies up an inclined plane, towards the Rocky mountains; seven miles to our camp, on the bank of a muddy pool around which one hundred and sixty mules are pressing; a puddle is reserved for ourselves, which is deemed a luxury, after having drank unto pickling the salt waters of the Semiron, our long eared stoics opened their konks half an hour before we halted, inviting this humane measure.

19th

In the evening discovered three Kiawa Indians, who were at war with a buffalo bull; they hid themselves in clift of a rock; when they came forth, they uttered all the Spanish they were masters of, bellowing lustily amigo! amigo! friend! friend! This day's march estimated at 15 miles.

20th

The road to-day hilly until noon. Yesterday morning after we encamped, a small party of red gentlemen called on us; smoked, ate, drank, and slept with us; one of them, at the first setting, drank nine pints of water; he was probably a secretary of some cold water conventicle. The chief of this little band claimed the honor for them of being Kiawas. Through the medium of the Pani [Pawnee] language, we learned that they had been on a gentleman-like horse stealing expedition against the Chians [Cheyennes], in which they were at first successful, but when they believed they had escaped with their booty, the Chians were down upon them, and retook the cavalry and a few scalps. They had walked at double quick step for the last two or three days; finding themselves at ease and secure in our camp, they "slept fast." Our march of the day was 15 miles.

21st

This morning, we parted with our guests, with mutual expressions of esteem and good will; our old trapper told them that when he returned their visit, he would leave his card, meaning a ball cartridge. The soil to-day is improving as we advance. Saw wild horses, deer, and antelope.

22d

Sent a party of 8 men ahead to-day to make arrangements for payment of duties; the supposed distance from Taos, the nearest settlement, is one hundred miles. This evening our road is fine, and lies over a plane, on all sides of which, detached mountains render the scenery extremely pic-turesque; a few wild horses in view; the buffalo have been banished their usual range in these plains, by the drought of the seasons. Recent rains have afforded us a supply; and in the deep rocky branch near where we are to-night encamped, there is really a deficiency.

23d

Reached this morning the summit of the ridge which divides the waters of the Semiron and Canadian branch of the Arkansas. From this point, we have a view of a spar of the Rocky mountains; we observe, likewise, Cievas las Gallinas, which are situated not far from St. Magill [San Miguel]. The atmosphere on this mountain region is so clear that we can, with the naked eye, take in incalculable distances; a hill that may seem within an hour's ride, proves to be ten leagues from us.

24th

After four hours' march, we find ourselves at the Point of Rocks. We were to-day gratified with a full view of the Rocky mountains ranging along to the right. When our Mexican, from a hill top, caught a distant view of the mountain, he lept for joy, discharged his carabine, and exclaimed, "Las luz de mis ojos, mi casa, mi alma;" Light of my eyes, my house, my love.

25th

In the morning entertained with mule races by several teams; crossed the Canadian branch of the Arkansas [Taylor's Springs, New Mexico].

26th

This evening when threatened with a famine, or a mule feast, two black specks appeared far off, up the ravine leading to the mountains: they were buffalo, and they cost us only two ball cartridges.

27th

Marched to-day twenty-five miles, and encamped at the Pilot Knobs. The only occurrence worthy of note is a sample of sharp shooting by Maj. Nimrod; he attempted to crease a wild mule, and shot him somewhere about the hips.

August 1st

The caravan in motion at the usual time; at one mile from camp, "a horse loose in cane brake," said the old trapper; turned around and saw twenty teams in full career; the mules had rested one day, and grateful for the indulgence, volunteered this entertainment. About noon saw a party of horsemen on the trace ahead; they were our advance party, with several Mexicans. Continued our march, and encamped at Rio las Gallinas.

2d

Left the caravan, which was within a day's march of San Magill, the first Mexican settlement through which the wagon road passes. A guide proposed to lead the light party which I have joined, by a direct route, in one day to Santa-Fe; he did so, but over Alps and Appenines. Before we reached the summit of the mountain, in mercy to our mules, we were constrained to dismount. All marvelous, and some scientific, travelers write "that, on ascending the summit of cloud-ridden mountains, they feel great difficulty in respiration, on account of a change in the atmosphere"; never bearing in mind that their impatience to reach the end of the journey imposes on their lungs the double duty of a blacksmith's bellows.

Wetmore's letter to Secretary of War Lewis Cass, dated October 11, 1831, reports that "the Blackfeet Indians have this year, for the first time, made their appearance in great force on the trace," and adds:

"In expressing an opinion that the caravans are competent to self-defence, I have perhaps adopted the impression that prevails among men with arms in their hands and impelled by that fearless spirit which animates the people of this country.

"But the loss of several valuable lives in this trade has occurred; and this evil may be extended if the Blackfeet Indians and the Chians continue to infest the route of the traders. These tribes are numerous, warlike, and extremely hostile."

The wagon trail traversed by Wetmore, now part of the route of the 3,000-mile National Old Trails Highway, lost its commercial importance temporarily when the railroad came. Even then, the Atchison, Topeka & Santa Fe Railroad didn't go to Santa Fe. Because of the high cost of putting a roadway through the nearby hills, the management announced it would have to bypass the town some seventeen miles away.

The citizens were dismayed—in particular the good father, Archbishop Juan Bautista Lamy, who had given nearly thirty arduous years of his life to the physical as well as spiritual improvement of his beloved City of the Holy Faith. The archbishop forthwith petitioned the Territorial Government to spend $150,000 on a spur. In 1880, while a brass band played, Governor Lew Wallace drove the last spike in the branch that kept the Santa Fe Railroad honest.

1829:   THE BUFFALO HUNTERS

HERDS OF BUFFALO that roamed the American West only one lifetime ago were estimated by eyewitnesses to number in the millions. Single mass formations covered areas of fifty to eighty square miles. In 1869 one of these herds, crossing the track of the Kansas Pacific Railroad, held up a train nine hours.

Before the white man came the Indian killed only for his needs. The early plainsman killed for meat, for sport, and for a dollar a robe in the Eastern market. The herds still spread out as far as the eye could see when, in the early 1870s, a new white man's market developed—for hides—and buffalo hunters swarmed over the plains, literally hell-bent for leather.

After that it took only a little more than a decade to clear the plains of buffalo, almost to the point of extermination. Bones whitened the prairies for miles, so many that ranchers found a profit in gathering them for the makers of carbon and fertilizer. There were those who deplored the wanton slaughter and there were those who saw in it the solution of the "Indian problem"; but arguments changed nothing, and suddenly the herds were gone and there was room for the farmer and the cowboy and the builder.

Earlier in the century, the great shaggy beast that would one day have to go was a favorite subject of artist George Catlin, who went west from Wilkes-Barre, Pennsylvania, to live eight years among the Indians and to draw them and write about them. Authentic on-the-spot pictures of the American West were greatly in demand at that time, not only in this country but throughout Europe and especially in England. Catlin became internationally known for an illustrated diary he kept in the West. The book was a best seller for years in London.

The scene of the buffalo hunt he describes here is on the present border of North Dakota and Montana, near Williston, North Dakota.

". . . *sublime for a picture* . . ."
GEORGE CATLIN (1796-1872)

Mouth of the Yellowstone, undated

I will give a little sketch of a bit of fun I joined in yesterday with Mr. M'Kenzie and a number of his men.

We all crossed the river and galloped away a couple of miles or so, when we mounted the bluff; and there was in full view of us a fine herd of some four or five hundred buffaloes, perfectly at rest, and in their own estimation, probably, perfectly secure. Some were grazing, and others were lying down and sleeping; we advanced within a mile or so of them in full view, and came to a halt.

Mons. Chardon "tossed the feather" (a custom always observed, to try the course of the wind) and we commenced "stripping" as it is termed (every man strips himself and his horse of every extraneous and unnecessary appendage of dress &c. that might be an incumbrance): hats are laid off, and coats—and bullet pouches; sleeves are rolled up, a handkerchief tied tightly around the head, and another around the waist—cartridges are prepared and placed in the waistcoat pocket, or a half dozen bullets "throwed into the mouth," all of which takes up some ten or fifteen minutes.

Our leader lays the whole plan of the chase; and preliminaries all fixed, guns charged and ramrods in our hands, we mount and start for the onset. The horses are all trained for this business, and seem to enter into it with as much enthusiasm, and with as restless a spirit, as the riders themselves.

In this way we carefully and silently marched until within some forty or fifty rods; when the herd discovering us, wheeled and laid their course in a mass.

At this instant we started! (and all *must* start, for no one could check the fury of those steeds at that moment of excitement) and away all sailed, and over the prairie flew in a cloud of dust which was raised by their trampling hoofs.

I dashed along through the thundering mass as they swept away over the plain, scarcely able to tell whether I was on a buffalo's back or my horse—hit, and hooked, and jostled about, until at length I found myself alongside of my game, when I gave him a shot as I passed him.

I saw guns flash in several directions about me but I heard them not. Amidst the trampling throng Mons. Chardon had wounded a stately bull, and at this moment was passing him again with his piece leveled for another shot; they were both at full speed and I also, within the reach of the muzzle of my gun, when the bull instantly turned, receiving the horse upon his horns, and the ground received poor Chardon, who made a frog's leap of some twenty feet or more over the bull's back, and almost under my horse's heels.

I wheeled my horse as soon as possible and rode back, where lay poor Chardon, gasping to start his breath again; and within a few paces of him his huge victim, with his heels high in the air, and the horse lying across him.

I dismounted instantly, but Chardon was raising himself on his hands, with his eyes and mouth full of dirt, and feeling for his gun, which lay about thirty feet in advance of him.

"Are you hurt, Chardon?"

"Hic—hic—hic—no, no, I believe not. Oh! This is not much, Mons. Cataline —this is nothing new—but this is a d———d hard piece of ground here —hic—oh!—hic!"

At this the poor fellow fainted, but in a few moments arose, picked up his gun, took his horse by the bit; which then opened *its* eyes, and with a *hic* and an *ugh—Ughk!* sprang upon its feet, shook off the dirt, and here we were, all upon our legs again, save the bull, whose fate had been more sad than that of either.

At a little distance at the right I beheld my huge victim endeavoring to make as much headway as he possibly could, from this dangerous ground, upon three legs.

I galloped off to him, and at my approach he wheeled around and bristled up for battle; he seemed to know perfectly well that he could not escape from me, and resolved to meet his enemy and death as bravely as possible.

I found that my shot had entered him a little too far forward, breaking one of his shoulders and lodging in his breast, and from his very great weight it was impossible for him to make much advance upon me.

As I rode up within a few paces of him, he would bristle up with fury enough in his looks alone almost to annihilate me; and making one lunge at me, would fall upon his neck and nose, so that I found the sagacity of my horse alone enough to keep me out of reach of danger; and I drew from my pocket my sketch-book, laid my gun across my lap, and commenced taking his likeness.

He stood stiffened up, and swelling with awful vengeance, which was sublime for a picture, but which he could not vent upon me. I rode around him and sketched him in numerous attitudes.

I defy the world to produce another animal that can look so frightful as a huge buffalo bull, when wounded, turned around for battle, and swelling with rage; his eyes bloodshot, and his long shaggy mane hanging to the ground; his mouth open, and his horrid rage hissing in streams of blood from his mouth and through his nostrils, as he is bending forward to spring upon his assailant.

After I had had the requisite time for using my pencil, Mr. M'Kenzie and his companions came walking their exhausted horses back from the chase, and in our rear came four or five carts to carry home the meat. The party met from all quarters around me and my buffalo bull, whom I then shot in the head and finished.

I rode back with Mr. M'Kenzie, who pointed out five cows which he had killed, and all of them selected as the fattest and slickest of the herd. This astonishing feat was all performed within the distance of one mile— all were killed at full speed, and every one shot through the heart. In the short space of time required for a horse under "full whip," to run the distance of one mile, he had discharged his gun five, and loaded it four times—selected his animals, and killed at every shot!

There were six or eight others killed at the same time, which altogether furnished abundance of freight for the carts; which returned, as well as several packhorses, loaded with the choicest parts which were cut from the animals, and the remainder of the carcasses left a prey for the wolves. Such is the mode by which white men live in this country.

★
1837: SMALLPOX IN DAKOTA

☆

ON A BLUFF 55 miles above Bismarck, North Dakota, Francis Auguste Chardon held down Fort Clark and did business for a fur-trading combination of Eastern capital known as the Upper Missouri Outfit. He was the same "Mons. Chardon" who had figured rather spectacularly a few years earlier in George Catlin's buffalo hunt.

Born in Philadelphia, Chardon went west early in life. When he took charge at Fort Clark in 1834 he was known as one of the West's most successful fur traders. He understood the Indians. He had married three of them. But when disease struck fiercely among them and their leaders blamed the whites, the job suddenly brought to Chardon new problems, new perils, and no little heartbreak.

In the early 1920s an old-fashioned chest was dug out of a heap of long-forgotten office keepsakes of the Topographical Bureau of the War Department in Washington. The chest bore the name of J. N. Nicollet. Nicollet was a French expatriate, a noted mathematician and explorer, who had intended to write a book about America. When he died in 1843 the book was still unwritten. But inside the chest, in a cloth bag where it had lain for nearly a hundred years, was Chardon's diary.

"But to die with my face rotten . . ."
FRANCIS AUGUSTE CHARDON
(died 1848)

14 [July 1837]

A young Mandan died to day of the Small Pox—several others has caught it—the Indians all being out Makeing dried Meat has saved several of them.

19

We are in a fair way of starveing, but few provissions on hand, and thirty Mouths to feed.

25

Several Young Men arrived from the dried Meat Camp, bringing With them each, one piece of Meat for those who remained at the Village. They will all be in tomorrow—they say that the small pox has broke out at the Camp.

26

The Rees [Arickarees] and Mandans all arrived to day well loaded with Meat. The 4 Bears [a Mandan chief] has caught the small pox, and got crazy and has disappeared from camp—he arrived here in the afternoon—The Indians of the Little Village all arrived in the evening well loaded with dried Meat—the small pox has broke out among them, several has died.

27

Indians all out after berrics. No News from any quarter. The small pox is killing them up at the Village. Four died to day.

28

Rain in the morning—This day was very Near being my last—a young Mandan came to the Fort with his gun cocked, and secreted under his robe, with the intention of Killing me. After hunting me in 3 or 4 of the houses he at last found me. The door being shut, he waited some time for me to come out. Just as I was in the act of going out, Mitchel caught him, and gave him in the hands of two Indians who conducted him to the Village. Had not Mitchel perceived him the instant he did, I would not be at the trouble of Makeing this statement—I am upon my guard.

The Rees are outrageous against the Mandans. They say that the first Mandan that kills a white, they will exterminate the whole race. I have got 100 Guns ready and 1,000 lb Powder, ready to hand out to them when the fun commences.

The Mandans & Rees gave us two splendid dances. They say dance, on account of their Not haveing a long time to live, as they expect to all die of the small pox—and as long as they are alive, they will take it out in dancing.

29

Several more Mandans died last night. Two Gros Ventres arrived from their dried Meat Camp. It appears that it has not broke among them as yet.

30

Another report from the Gros Ventres to day say that they are arrived at their Village, and that 10 or 15 of them have died, two big fish among them. They threaten Death and Distruction to us all at this place, saying that I was the cause of the small pox Makeing its appearance in this country. One of our best friends of the Village (The Four Bears) died to day, regretted by all who Knew him.

31

Mandans are getting worse, Nothing will do them except revenge. Three of the war party that left here on the 26th of last Month arrived to day, with each of them one horse that they stole from the Yanctons on White river.

Speech of the 4 Bears a Mandan Warrior to the Arricarees and Mandans, 30th July 1837—

> My Friends one and all, Listen to what I have to say. Ever since I can remember, I have loved the Whites. I have lived With them ever since I was a Boy, and to the best of my Knowledge I have never Wronged a White Man; on the Contrary, I have always protected them from the insults of Others, Which they cannot deny.
>
> The 4 Bears never saw a White Man hungry, but what he gave him to eat, Drink, and a buffaloe skin to sleep on, in time of Need. I was always ready to die for them, which they cannot deny. I have done every thing that a red Skin could do for them, and how have they repaid it!
>
> Wth ingratitude! I have Never Called a White Man a Dog, but to day I do Pronounce them to be a set of Black harted Dogs. They have deceivd me, them that I always considered as Brothers has turned out to be My Worst Enemies.
>
> I have been in Many Battles, and often Wounded, but the Wounds of My enemies I exhalt in. But to day I am Wounded, and by Whom, by those same White Dogs that I have always Considered and treated as Brothers. I do not fear *Death*, my friends. You know it. But to die with my face rotten, that even the Wolves will shrink with horror at seeing Me, and say to themselves, that is the 4 Bears the Friend of the Whites—

Listen well what I have to say, as it will be the last time you will hear Me. Think of your Wives, Children, Brothers, Sisters, Friends, and in fact all that you hold dear, are all Dead, or Dying, with their faces all rotten, caused by those dogs the whites. Think of all that, My friends, and rise all together and Not leave one of them alive.

The 4 Bears will act his Part.

[August] 1st

The Mandans are Makeing their Medicine for rain, as their Corn is all drying up. To day we had several light showers.

2nd

Yesterday an Indian that was out after berries discovered a band of [buffalo] Cows—all hands out to run them. They all arrived in the afternoon well laden with fresh meat—haveing run three Bands.

4

Only two deaths to day.

5

Indians out after berries, others out after Meat. News from the Gros Ventres, they say that they are encamped this side of Turtle Mountain, and that a great many of them have died of the small pox—several cheifs among them. They swear vengence against all the Whites, as they say the small pox was brought here by the Steamboat.

7

Six More died to day. Several Rees left the Mandan Village, and pitched their Lodges Out in the Prairie.

8

Four More died to day—the two thirds of the Village are sick. To day I gave six pounds of Epsom salt in doses to Men, Women, and Children. The small pox has broke out at the Little Mandan Village—three died yesterday, two cheifs.

9

Seven More died to day.

10

All the Ree's that were encamped in the Mandan lodges, except a few that are sick, Moved down to the Island hopeing to get rid of the small pox. The Mandans talk of Moveing to the other side of the river. 12 or 15 died to day.

11

Sent old Charboneau up to the Gros-Ventres with some tobacco, and a bag full of good talk, as yesterday they sent a very severe threat to me. Mandans all crossed to the other side of the river to encamp—leaveing all that were sick in the Village. I Keep no account of the dead, as they die so fast that it is impossible.

12

Cool and pleasant weather. One of my best friends of the Little Village died to day. News of a war party of Gros Ventres and Rees (70) being used up by the Saons [Cheyennes], quicker work than the small pox.

13

Several reports from the Gros Ventres that they are bent on the distruction of us all. As yet I do not place Much confidence in what report says. Charboneau will bring us the strait news. The Mandans are dying 8 and 10 every day. An Old fellow who has lost the whole of his family to the Number of 14 harrangued to day, that it was time to begin to Kill the Whites, as it was them that brought the small pox in the Country.

14

Charboneau arrived late last night. All the reports from the Gros Ventres, it appears to be without foundation, as they say they never had any thoughts of Killing the Whites, but that the Rees have made several threats. Which of the two to believe I Know not; however, I will still be on my guard. (The White Cow) a Mandan cheif came early this morning and appeared to be very angry—telling me that I had better clear out, with all the Whites, that if we did not, they would exterminate us all. I told him that we would not leave the place, and that if they were disposed to Kill us to Come on quick, that we were ready for them at all times.

The Rees are Makeing medicine for their sickness. Some of them have made dreams, that they talked to the Sun, others to the Moon. Several articles has been sacrifised to them both. The Principal Cheif of the Mandans died to day—The Wolf Cheif. An other dog, from the Little Village came to the Fort naked with his gun cocked, to Kill one of us. We stopped him.

15

Gardepie with an other half breed arrived last evening from the North bringing with them 200 Muskrats and 50 lb Beaver. Sold him two horses. They left here early this Morning. The small pox scared them off. J. Be Jonca a half breed Kanza who has been liveing with the Gros Ventres several years, came on horse back at full speed to inform us that the Mandans went up to the Gros Ventres with a pipe, to Make them smoke, to try to get them to help them to Murder us. The Gros Ventres refused to smoke with them, saying that they were friendly to the Whites and that they would not take part with them. Jonca started back immediately.

The War Party of Rees and Mandans that left here the 26th of June, all came back to day, haveing Killed seven Sioux, men, women and children. It appears that the small pox has broke out amongst the Sioux, as some of the Party, on their way back, was taken sick at Grand River, haveing caught the disease from those that they butchered.

16

Several Men, Women, and Children that has been abandoned in the Village, are laying dead in the lodges, some out side of the Village, others in the little river not entered [interred] which creates a very bad smell all around us. A Ree that has lost his wife and child threatened us to day. We are beset by enemies on all sides—expecting to be shot every Minute.

17

The Rees started out after buffaloe, the Indians dying off every day. Were the disease will stop, I know not. We are badly situated, as we are threatened to be Murdered by the Indians every instant; however we are all determined, and prepared for the worst.

A Young Ree for several days has been lurking around the Fort, watching a good opportunity to Kill me, but not finding a good chance, this Morning he came, full intent to sit himself down in front of the Fort gate, and waited a few Minutes for me to go out.

In the Mean time one of my Men a Dutchman, John Cliver—stepped out and sat himself down a long side of the Indian. After setting a few Minutes, he got up to come in the Fort. He only Made five paces, when the Indian shot him in the back bone and Killed him instantaneously. He made off immediately. We pursued after him shooting at him, but without effect. He got as far as the little river, where one of his Brothers is entered. On arriving there he made a stop, and hollowed to us that that was the place he wanted to die.

Garreau approached in 15 paces of him and shot. The contents knocked him over. He then rushed on him with his large Knife and ripped his body open. They were both entered at 2 P.M. I hoisted the Black flag.

An Indian (The two Bulls) showed himself to day, with several others. How it will turn Out I know not, but thus far—Man for Man. The Rees appear to not say much about it. Garreau deserves the highest praise from us all. He acted manfully although against his own nation—he always told me that he would always act as he has done. The Mother of the fellow we Killed came to the Fort crying, saying that she wanted to die also, and wished for us to Kill her.

Garreau stepped up, and with his tommahawk would of Made short work of the Old Woman, but was prevented.

18

Nothing but an occasional glass of grog Keeps me alive as I am worried almost to death by the Indians and Whites. The latter (the men) threaten to leave me. Put up some tobacco to send to the Gros Ventres.

19

Charboneau and his family started for the Gros Ventres last night, being afraid to trust himself in the day time. A Mandan and his Wife Killed themselves yesterday, to not Out live their relations that are dead.

Sent ten pounds of tobacco to the Soldiers of the Gros Ventres, begging them to Not come to their summer Village, as the disease has not yet broke out amongst them. If it does I am afraid that they will put their threat in execution.

I was in hopes that the disease was almost at an end, but they are dying off 8 and 10 every day—and new cases of it daily. Were it will stop, God only Knows.

An Old Mandan harrangued from the opposite side, to the few that are remaining in the Village, to Prepare themselves, but for what I could not find out. Wether it is to come in a body to attack us, or some other reason, time will only tell. I prefer them to come all in one body and then we will Know what we have to do, but they are so treatcherous that it is impossible to Know Friend or Enemie. However I consider them all the latter, as an Indian is soon turned, like the wind, from one side to the other.

As I was sitting out side of the Fort, an Indian came to me, and told me that I had better go in the Fort as it was dangerous for me to go out. I took his advice and went in, although ashamed to say so.

In the hurry and confusion on the 17th some dog made way with one of my guns. The disease broke out in the Fort six days ago.

20

Three more died in the Village last night. The Wife of a young Mandan that caught the disease was suffering from the pain. Her husband looked at her, and held down his head. He jumped up and said to his wife, When you was young, you were hansome, you are now ugly and going to leave me, but no, I will go with you. He took up his gun and shot her dead, and with his Knife ripped open his own belly. Two young men (Rees) Killed themselves to day, one of them stabbed himself with a Knife and the other with an arrow.

Visited by four young men of the Little Village. There has been but eight deaths at their Village. Gave them a pipe of tobacco, and they went off.

A young Ree that has been sick for some time with the small pox, and being alone in his lodge, thought that it was better to die than to be in so much pain. He began to rub the scabs untill blood was running all over his body. He rolled himself in the ashes, which almost burnt his soul out of his body. Two days after he was perfectly well. It is a severe operation, but few are disposed to try it—however, it proved beneficial to him.

22

The disease still Keeps ahead, 8 and 10 die off daily. Thirty five Mandans have died. The Women and Children I Keep no account of. Several Mandans have came back to remain in the Village. One of my Soldiers—(Ree) died to day. Two young Mandans shot themselves this morning.

News from the Little Village that the disease is getting worse and worse every day. It is now two months that it broke out. A Ree that has the small pox, and thinking that he was going to die, approached near his wife, a young woman of 19—and struck her in the head with his tommahawk, with the intent to Kill her, that she might go with him in the Other World. She is badly wounded. A few Minutes after he cut his throat. A report is in circulation that they intend to fire the Fort. Stationed guard in the Bastion.

25

An other Mandan cheif died to day—(The long fingers). Total Number of Men that has died—50.

I have turned out to be a first rate doctor. St. Grado, An Indian that has been bleeding at the Nose all day, I gave him a decoction of all sorts of ingredients Mixed together, enough to Kill a Buffaloe Bull of the largest size, and stopped the effusion of Blood. The decoction of Medicine was, a little Magnisia, peppermint, sugar lead, all Mixed together in a phial, filled with Indian grog—and the Patient snuffing up his nose three or four times. I done it out of experiment, and am content to say that it proved effectual. The Confidence that an Indian has in the Medicine of the whites is half the cure.

26

The Indians all started Out on the North side in the quest of Buffaloe, as they had Nothing to eat. A young Ree, the nephew of Garreau, died at the Village last night.

A young Ree that has the small pox, told his Mother to go and dig his grave. She accordingly did so. After the grave was dug, he walked with the help of his Father to the grave. I Went Out with the Interpreter to try to pursuade him to return back to the Village—but he would not, saying for the reason that all his young friends were gone, and that he wished to follow them. Towards evening he died.

27

Strong east wind, rain in the Morning. The Indians came back from the Cerne [roundup] well loaded with Meat. Report Cattle [buffalo] in abundance 20 Miles off—News from the Gros Ventres of the disease breaking out amongst them.

28

Several more Indians arrived with fresh Meat. Gave us a small quantity which we found very good. Three more fell sick in the Fort to day—My Interpreter for one. If I lose him I shall be badly off.

29

Last Night I was taken very sick with the Fever. There is six of us in the Fort that has the Fever, and one the small pox.

An Indian Vaccinated his child by cutting two small pieces of flesh out of his arms, and two on the belly—and then takeing a Scab from one that was getting well of the disease, and rubbing it on the wounded part. Three days after, it took effect, and the child is perfectly well.

30

All those that I thought had the small pox turned out to be true. The fever left them yesterday, and the disease showed itself. I am perfectly well, as last night, I took a hot whiskey punch, which made me sweat all last night. This Morning I took my daily Bitters as usual. Indians arrived with fresh Meat, report cattle in abundance opposite the Little Lake below.

31

A young Mandan that died 4 days ago, his wife haveing the disease also —Killed her two children, one a fine Boy of eight years, and the other six. To complete the affair she hung herself.

The Number of Deaths up to the Present is very near five hundred— the Mandans are all cut off, except 23 young and Old Men.

Killed 89 Rats this month—Total 1867.

[September] 1

This Morning two dead bodies, wrapped in a White skin, and laid on a raft passed by the Fort, on their way to the regions below. May success attend them.

2

Being out of wood, risqued the Men—to the Point of Woods below, hauled eight loads. Several Indians arrived with fresh Meat, out 2 days. But one death to day. Although several are sick, those that catch the disease at Present seldom die. One Fellow that I had numbered with the dead, I saw on horseback to day—he looked more like a gohst than a being.

3

A young Mandan came to pay us a visit from the Little Village. He informes us, that they are all Most all used up, and that it is his opinion that before the disease stops, that there will not one be left, except 8 or 10 that has weathered Out the sickness.

4

A young Mandan that was given over for dead, and abandoned by his Father, and left alone in the bushes to die, came to life again, and is now doing well. He is hunting his Father, with the intent to Kill him, for leaveing him alone.

19

I was visited by a young fellow from the Little Village. He assures me that there is but 14 of them liveing, the Number of deaths Cannot be less than 800.

21

The Mandans fearing their Allies, the Rees, should unite with the Sioux, have all fled to the opposite side of the river. What their intention is, I Know not, but the few that are left (41) are Miserable, surrounded on all sides.

22

My youngest son died to day.

1846:   PARKMAN HITS THE OREGON TRAIL

THE YEAR 1846 was one of momentous stirrings over the broad land beyond the Missouri. America was trying on a continent for size. Great slices of it were still claimed by other nations, but that did not stop the people. From Independence, Missouri, to Fort Hall, Idaho, and then to the northwest on one fork, the Oregon Trail; to the coast on the other fork, the California Trail; and from Independence southwest on the Santa Fe Trail—these were the routes to destiny, that "manifest destiny" which was a handy way to settle geopolitical questions.

Francis Parkman was only 23 when he went west. He was not a frontiersman or an emigrant, but neither was he going just for the ride. His purpose was to study the Indians.

He saw much else besides—the many kinds of people it took to turn a land into a nation—and what he saw fascinated him. He ran into Price's army of Missouri volunteers, Andrew Jackson Smith's Mormons, the ill-fated Donner Party, a great human prism of adventure, greed, faith, hope, and need.

From the notes in his diary, he wrote his classic The Oregon Trail. Between the trip and the book there was many a slip. Ill when he returned east and unable to use his eyes, he listened while others read his diary back to him; from it he dictated the book. The process, he said, was "as easy as lying." Nevertheless, the truth comes through in The Oregon Trail. What he may have meant was that the rewritten version lacked some of the earthiness and virility of the diary. This was partly because he himself was striving for literary polish and partly because his editor, Charles Eliot Norton, a very proper Bostonian, took out or toned down passages he considered indelicate. Here are some notes from Parkman's diary.

"How infinite the diversity of character!"
FRANCIS PARKMAN (1832-1895)

Carlisle, Pennsylvania, April 2nd [1846]

Crossed the Susquehanna in a flat boat filled with quiet, stupid, stout Dutch—men, women, and pretty girls. Some octogenarian veterans, and two young, fat dandies with checked breeches and frogged wrappers. The whole was a striking contrast to a corresponding group of Yankees.

In the wretched cars, too, the same phlegm and stolidity were apparent—their minds were gone to sleep.

9th

My careless, frank, lighthearted New York acquaintance, P.M.

The man who, on some delay occurring, saluted me with: "I shan't see my wife tonight," this being our first acquaintance. Poor fellow—he was neglected in his youth, and though of a susceptible turn of mind, had—according to his own account—plunged into every kind of excess. About six years ago, he "got religion"—and he lately married. His constitution is injured by hardships when an engineer on a railroad, and he seems of a melancholy temperament; but is most frank and unreserved in his disclosures. He is on his way to see his new wife in Cincinnati.

A precious set of gamblers and ragamuffins on board.

Passed the rapids at Louisville in the steamboat.

The English reserve or "offishness" seems to be no part of the western character—though I have had no opportunity of observing a gentleman of high standing. I observe this trait in myself—today, for instance, when a young fellow expressed satisfaction that he should accompany me to St. Louis, I felt inclined to shake him off, though he had made himself agreeable enough.

11

Passed the site of Fort Massiac, situated on low, wet land. The banks of the Ohio grow more low as we descend, and now the forests rise from the very margin of the water—it is a wide expanse, with here and there an island.

At night, at Paduca three flat boats of West Virginian emigrants came on board—they had built their flat boats on the Holston River, near which they lived, and had been from the first of March descending to the mouth of the Tennessee. The boats were like floating houses—the same, probably, with those originally used in navigating the Ohio.

The men were good-looking and hearty, though not so large as the West Pennsylvanians. Some were dressed in red rifle-frocks, and they tell me that Indian leggings are still occasionally used in the Valley. All their domestic implements had an old-fashioned air: chairs with bottoms of ash-slivers—gourd dippers—kettles—anvil—bellows—old bureaus—clothing—bedding—frying pan, etc. etc. were rapidly passed into the stream. Several old long-barrelled, flint-locked rifles followed. Conversing with the men, I found them intelligent and open, though apparently not much educated. They were going to Iowa.

We are on the Mississippi, with its rapid muddy current, and low, forest-covered banks.

The men of the migrant party are manly, open, and agreeable in their manners—with none of the contracted, reserved manner that is common in New Englanders. Neither have the women, who are remarkably good-looking, any of that detestable, starched, lackadaisical expression common in vulgar Yankee women.

The true philosophy of life is to seize with a ready and strong hand upon all the good in it, and to bear its inevitable evils as calmly and carelessly as may be.

St. Louis, April 15

A crowd was gathered round the door of the Planters' Hotel, and in the midst stood Henry Clay, talking and shaking hands with any who chose. As he walked away, he asked an old man for a pinch of snuff, at which the mob was gratified, and the old man, striking his cane on the bricks, declared emphatically that Clay was the greatest man in the Union, and that it was a burning shame he was not in the presidential chair. So much for the arts by which politicians—even the best of them—thrive.

19th

How infinite is the diversity of human character! Old M. Cerré of nearly eighty—lively, bright, and active—the old man goes about rejoicing in his own superiority to age—wrapped up in himself, unobservant, impenetrable, impassive.

27 On board Steamer Radnor

All our equipments embarked. A number of Kanzas or Caw Indians on board. Their gravity seems to me rather *vacant* than *dignified*. When they speak, their gestures are lively and natural.

29th

On board the boat are a party of Baltimoreans—flash genteel—very showily attired in "genteel undress," though bound for California. They make a great noise at table, and are waited on by the Negroes with great attention and admiration. Also a vulgar New Yorker, with the mustache and air of a Frenchman, bound for Santa Fe.

A young man on board from St. Louis, bound for Santa Fe, has one brother on the Atlantic, another on the Pacific, and a third on the Mississippi, while he is going to the Rio Grande del Norte. So much for American wandering.

May 1

The Indians are playing cards about the deck. They have a paper for begging, and one of them sat on the deck collecting contributions yesterday.

2

The landing at Independence [Missouri] the storehouses—the Santa Fe waggons—the groups of piratical-looking Mexicans, employees of the Santa Fe traders, with their broad, peaked hats—the men with their rifles seated on a log, ready for Oregon. Among the waggons behind, some of the Mexicans were encamped. The Baltimoreans got shamefully drunk, and one of them, an exquisite in full dress, tumbled into the water.

Speyer, the Santa Fe trader, has an immense number of goods on board.

C. W. of St. Louis, who harnessed his mule into his waggon and drove off for Santa Fe, bent on seeing. He seemed about eighteen years old, open, enterprising, and thoughtless. He will come back a full-grown man.

7

Rode by vile roads, through the woods, to Independence. The clouds in this region are afflicted with an incontinence of water—constant alternations of showers and sunshine—everything wet, bright, and fresh. Plenty of small game and gorgeous birds.

At Independence, every store is adapted to furnish outfits—the public houses were full of Santa Fe men and emigrants. Mules, horses, and waggons at every corner. Groups of hardy-looking men about the stores, and Santa Fe and emigrant waggons standing in the fields around.

While I was at the Noland House, the last arrival of emigrants [the ill-fated Donner Party] came down the street with about twenty waggons, having just broken up their camp near Independence and set out for the great rendezvous about 15 miles beyond Westport.

What is remarkable, this body, as well as a very large portion of the emigrants, were from the extreme western states—N. England sends but a small proportion, but they are better furnished than the rest. Some of these ox-wagons contained large families of children, peeping from under the covering. One remarkably pretty little girl was seated on horseback, holding a parasol over her head to keep off the rain. All looked well—but what a journey before them!

The men were hardy and good-looking. As I passed the waggons, I observed three old men, with their whips in their hands, discussing some point of theology—though this is hardly the disposition of the mass of the emigrants.

I rode to Westport with that singular character, Lieut. Woodworth. He is a great busybody, and ambitious of taking a command among the emigrants. He tells me that great dissensions prevail in their [the Donner Party's] camp—that no organization had taken place, no regular meetings being held—though this is to be done on Saturday and Sunday, and the column to get under weigh on Monday.

Woodworth parades a revolver in his belt, which he insists is necessary —and it may be a prudent precaution, for this place seems full of desperadoes—all arms are loaded, as I have had occasion to observe. Life is held in little esteem.

This place, Westport, is the extreme frontier, and bears all its characteristics.

As we rode home, we met a man itching for Oregon, but restrained by his wife—at McGee's at Westport, there was a restless fellow who had wandered westwards from N.Y. in search of work, which he had not found; and now he was for Oregon, working his passage as he could not supply himself with provisions.

Plenty of vagabond Inds. are about here, trading at the different stores, and getting drunk.

I saw many at the store of Mr. Boone, a grandson of Daniel.

9th

An old Caw Ind. in full paint came riding up, gave his hand, and sat down to smoke.

Presently the whole tribe passed along on their way to Westport, on miserable little horses. Some were in full costume, but the greater part were ragged vagabonds, with bad or vacant faces, and a very mean appearance. They crowded around, men, women and children, the first offering their hands as they came up. Many had bows and arrows—all were adorned with wampum or beads, and often a snake skin. In the beautiful country we had passed, Shawnees were constantly riding by on a canter, upon little stubborn ponies, and with their calico shirts fluttering in the wind.

Not far from where we met the Caws, there was a religious meeting of the Shawnees. Most of those present were good-looking—much more robust than the Caws, and well-dressed in the English fashion. The place was the Methodist meeting house.

12

Returning, we stopped at the trader's. We were hot and tired; and the trader showed us into a neat, dark, and cool parlor, where he gave us iced claret and an excellent lunch—a most welcome refreshment. His mistress, a yellow woman, brimful of merriment, entertained us with her conversation.

24

We have struck upon the old Oregon Trail, just beyond the Big Blue, about seven days from the Platte. The waggons we saw were part of the emigrant party, under a man named Keatley. They encamped about a mile from us, behind a swell in the prairie. The Capt. paid them a visit, and reported that the women were damned ugly.

June 4

11 boats were coming down the river from Laramie.

The crews were a wild-looking set—the oarsmen were Spaniards—with them were traders, French and American, some attired in buckskin, fancifully slashed and garnished, and with hair glued up in Ind. fashion.

11

Set out early, and dragged some ten miles through an abominably sandy

trail along the Platte. Scenery monotonous to the last degree. Very hot—
the sand flies outrageous. Nooned on a pleasant spot and lay sleeping
some three or four hours, when Henry awakened us with the announcement that people were coming.

They were the van of the emigrants—first came a girl and a young man,
on horseback, the former holding a parasol—then appeared the line of
wagons, coming over the sand hills. We saddled in a trice, pushed ahead,
and kept on. The girl and her beau apparently found something very
agreeable in each other's company, for they kept more than a mile in advance of their party, which H. considered very imprudent, as the Sioux
might be about.

12

The Oregon men returning to the settlements—the vulgar-looking fellow in the white shirt and broad-cloth pants, who gave us the acct. of the
Oregon settlements and govnt. His companions around their campfire.
What a character of independence and self-reliance such a life gives a
man!

14

A fellow who had been back to look for stray cattle, remained and
camped with us—a true specimen of the raw, noisy, western way. "Hullo,
boys, where do you water your horses?"—this was his style of address.

15

Laramie appeared, as the prospect opened among the hills. Rode past
the fort, reconnoitered from the walls, and passing the highest ford of
Laramie Fork River, were received at the gate by Boudeau, the *bourgeois*.
Leading our horses into the area, we found Inds.—men, women, and children—standing around, voyageurs and trappers—the surrounding apartments occupied by the squaws and children of the traders.

Fort divided into two areas—one used as a *corale*—two bastions or *clay
blockhouses*—another blockhouse over main entrance. They gave us a large
apartment, where we spread our blankets on the floor. From a sort of
balcony we saw our horses and carts brought in, and witnessed a picturesque frontier scene. Conversed and smoked in the windy court. Horses
made a great row in the *corale*. At night the Inds. set up their songs. At
the burial place are several Inds. laid on scaffolds, and a circle of buffalo
skulls below.

Fort Laramie, June 16

This morning, Smoke's village appeared on the opposite bank, and crossed on their wild, thin little horses. Men and boys, naked and dashing eagerly through the water, horses with lodge poles dragging through squaws and children, and sometimes a litter of puppies—gaily attired squaws, leading the horses of their lords—dogs with their burdens attached swimming among the horses and mules—dogs barking, horses breaking loose, children laughing and shouting—squaws thrusting into the ground the lance and shield of the master of the lodge—naked and splendidly formed men passing and repassing through the swift water.

They held a kind of council in the fort. Smoke presided, but he had another man to speak for him, and ask for presents, and when they were placed on the floor before him, they were distributed under his eye, by one of the "soldiers." Several of the warriors had their faces blackened, in token of having killed Pawnees, or at least of having been on the war-party when they were killed.

Some who visited us kept looking, with great curiosity, at the circus pictures that Finch has nailed up in the room.

At their camp in the even'g, the girls and children, with a couple of young men, amused themselves with a dance, where there was as much merriment and fooling as could be desired.

19

The begging dance in the area of the fort. Led by three dandies, the young squaws moved round singing in a circle. Montalon brought out the presents and placed them in the middle—and here the characteristic self-restraint of the Inds. was apparent. The squaws did not rush forwards to look, but stood quite quietly, and looked on with apparent indifference and without showing any jealousy while one of the young men distributed them.

21

That species of desperation in which an Ind. upon whom fortune frowns resolves to throw away his body, rushing desperately upon any danger that offers. If he comes off successful, he gains great honor.

To show his bravery, an Ind. rushed up to a grizzly bear and struck him three times on the head with his bow. Such acts are common.

The terrible penance to gain success in war, etc.—remaining for days, starving, with buffalo skulls fastened to cords run through the sinews of the back. The animal that is dreamed of when in this state is the guardian spirit.

28

Yesterday rode down to swap a wild horse, to Richard's fort. Found there comp'y engaged in drinking and refitting, and a host of Canadians besides. Russel drunk as a pigeon—some fine-looking Kentucky men—some of D. Boone's grandchildren—altogether more educated men than any I have seen. A motley crew assembled in Richard's rooms—squaws, children, Spaniards, French, and emigrants. Emigrants mean to sell liquor to the Miniconques, who will be up here tomorrow, and after having come all the way from the Missouri to go to the war, will no doubt break up if this is done.

July 3rd

An Ind. gift is like a Turkish—it is revoked unless an equivalent is given.

4

The squaws are constantly laughing. It is astonishing, what abominable indecencies the best of the Inds. will utter in presence of the women, who laugh heartily.

5

Saw a domestic quarrel, where the rebellious squaw pulled down the lodge, packed her horse, and rode off, while her husband looked quietly on.

6

An Ind.'s meanest trait is his unsatiable appetite for food and presents. They are irrepressible beggars, and at meals, no matter how slender the repast may be, chiefs and warriors surround us with eager eyes to wait for a portion, and this although their bellies may be full to bursting. If one wishes to see an Ind. village, send a notice that you will feast, and they will come a two days' journey for the sake of your cup of coffee. What a life! where the excitement of an enjoyment so trifling can tempt them to such pains-taking. In fact, the greater part of a trapper's or an Ind's life is mere vacancy—lying about, as I am now, with nothing to do or think of.

1846: "FIRST WOMAN TO CROSS THE PLAINS"

In ANSWER to a hurry call from Senator Thomas Hart Benton in the summer of 1846, Santa Fe trader James W. Magoffin rushed to Washington. On the evening of June 15 he went into an important huddle with President Polk. Just what the President wanted of him was kept secret at the time, and so it remains today.

The Magoffin brothers, James and Samuel, had made large fortunes in the Santa Fe trade. They knew everybody there, including Mexican Governor Manuel Armijo, Lieutenant-Governor Diego Archuleta, and their underlings.

When James Magoffin got the summons to Washington, war with Mexico had already started. President Polk was hoping Stephen Watts Kearny could take over New Mexico without a fight, though Kearny would march in with only 1,700 men as against some 3,000 troops, of a sort, that Armijo could muster on the spot.

In advance of Kearny, Magoffin rode hard for Santa Fe. There he had talks with Armijo and Archuleta. These, too, were secret. Magoffin carried a letter from Kearny that warned Armijo not to resist the Americans; but he may have conveyed other ideas to Armijo too—not on paper, and perhaps among them a substantial bribe.

In any case, when Kearny came marching through Apache Canyon on the approach to Santa Fe, Armijo gave up without firing a shot—this despite the fact that his own men wanted to fight, and that a mere handful of them, in that narrow defile, could have held off a large attacking force. Though fierce and bloody engagements took place in the war that followed, Santa Fe was like candy taken from a child.

The busy James Magoffin went on to Chihuahua, Mexico, and tried to accomplish something along the same order in advance of American General John E. Wool's intended march on that city. When Wool failed to show on schedule, the Mexicans accused Magoffin of spying and jailed him. He avoided a date with the firing squad by fast talk and by passing out gifts of champagne among his captors.

When it was all over and the United States had relieved Mexico of the onus of holding an enormous expanse of territory in defiance of manifest destiny, James Magoffin went back to Washington and put in a bill for $50,000—the amount, he said, that he was actually out of pocket on the mission.

The Senate authorized the War Department to pay up. But meanwhile Taylor had replaced Polk in the White House, and Taylor's Secretary of War, George Washington Crawford, balked. He said the Department had made no contract with Magoffin. True, Magoffin may have had to pass around the champagne to save his skin at Chihuahua. But not, said Crawford, $50,000 worth! Ultimately Crawford offered a settlement of $30,000. Magoffin settled.

A century later Pulitzer Prize historian Bernard DeVoto, in his The Year of Decision: 1846, wrote that the view that Magoffin had bought Armijo was "almost certainly untrue." Pulitzer Prize historian Paul Horgan, through one of the principals in his The Centuries of Santa Fe, stated flatly that "the governor [Armijo] sold himself and his state—yes, really."

The truth may lie somewhere between zero and $50,000, with the guess of the United States government about halfway, and with the stakes a crucial advance toward victory in the war to acquire all of New Mexico, Nevada, Utah, Arizona, California, and great expanses of Texas and Colorado.

So much for background. When James Magoffin hustled off from Washington, brother Samuel, in command of the firm's regular spring caravan, had left Independence, Missouri, on June 11, also bound for Santa Fe. In the train were fourteen huge wagons of goods, a baggage cart, a carriage, a dearborn, 20 men, and 200 animals.

With Samuel, too, was his eighteen-year-old bride Susan. They had been married just a few months.

Brother James overtook the caravan at Bent's Fort, the trading post on the Arkansas River. He told Samuel of his mission for the government, outlined what Samuel's own part in it should be—to build up in New Mexico what we call today a fifth column—and raced ahead. Samuel was to follow as fast as he could.

Susan, who had been brought up on a big, luxurious estate in Kentucky, could pretty well guess the trip was not going to be a lark. War, Indians, the wild prairie, the desert. And she had another reason for doubting whether she should go. She was pregnant. But Samuel wanted her along. She kept her fears to herself. The long trek would be an adventure. And she would be the first woman, so they said, to cross the plains. And most important of all, Susan was very much in love.

"A new world has been shown to me."
SUSAN MAGOFFIN (1827-1855)

June [1846]

From the city of New York to the Plains of Mexico is a stride that I myself can scarcely realize. Tuesday evening we went into Independence; there we stayed one night only at Mr. Noland's Hotel.

11th

Now the Prairie life begins! We left "the settlements" this morning. Our mules travel well and we joged on at a rapid pace till 10 o'clock when we came up with the waggons.

We crossed the branch and stretched our tent. It is a grand affair indeed. 'Twas made in Philadelphia by a regular tent-maker of the army, and every thing is complete. Our bed is as good as many houses have; sheets, blankets, counterpanes, pillows &c. We have a carpet made of sail duck, have portable stools.

Well after a supper at *my own table* and in *my own house* I can say what few women in civilized life ever could, that the first house of his own to which my husband took me to after our marriage was a *tent;* and the first table of my own at which I ever sat was a cedar one, made with only *one leg* and that was a tent pole.

12th

At night we struck camp at "Black Jack," fourteen miles from the last, & 49 from Independence. Being tired of the carriage I got out and took a ramble.

I picked numberless flowers with which the plains are covered, and as *mi alma* [her term for her husband] told me before we started, I threw them away to gather more. I wearied myself out at this, and as the tent was now up, I returned *"home."*

There before supper I had a little piece of work to attend to, I mean the feeding of my chickens. It is quite a farm house this; poultry, dogs, cattle, mules, horses &c. Altogether my home is one not to be objected to.

13th

This A.M. about 10 o'clock we met an Indian trader returning from "Bent's Fort" up the big Arkansas River. He is returning with his cargo of skins; we stoped and had half hour's conversation with him respecting the road, war news &c. It is all pretty good. Says the Indians are pretty bad about Pawnee Fork, which is 298 miles from Independence. His wagons we met about half a mile back; they are loaded with skins.

14th

This is my first sabbath on the plains!

A very quiet one it has been too, something I had not looked for. But all the men seem to recollect it and hitch in their teams with half the trouble, and I have scarcely heard an oath the whole day.

Camp No. 7. Wednesday, 17th

Last night I had a wolfish kind of a serenade!

Ring, my dear, good dog! was lying under my side of the bed, which was next to wolves, the instant they came up, he had been listening, he flew out with a firce bark, and drove them away. I felt like caressing him for his kindness.

It was solitude indeed. The howling of ravinus beasts, and the screech of not less ravinous birds. I lay perfectly still with *mi alma* breathing a sweet sleep by my side. I could not waken him, just to keep me company, when he was so well engaged. So I remained quiet occasionally knocking off a musquito and listening to the confused sounds without and wishing that my faithful Ring would not sleep so soundly.

Just then, he gave one spring from his hiding place, and in a twinkling had driven them off entirely.

Council Grove, 145 miles from Independence. Friday, 19th. Camp No. 9

In our travels today we stoped two miles the other side of Council Grove at what is called Big John's Spring.

The scenery around is very wild and rather awing. While I stood apparently very calm and bold as *mi alma* bent down to fix a little *toddy* with water from the clear flowing stream, I could not suppress the fear, or rather the thought of some wily savage or hungry wolf lurking in the thick grape vines, ready the first advantageous moment to bounce upon my shoulders. I would not tell *mi alma* these foolish fears, for I knew he would ridicule them, and this was torture to me, but Ring, my faithful Ring, came by me just then and I commenced patting his head which made him lie at my feet and I felt *safe* with this trusty soldier near me.

Thursday, 25th. Camp 15. Cotton wood creek. 12 miles.

While Jane [her maid] and I were on a little stroll after dinner, I carelessly walking along steped almost onto a large snake; it moved and frightened me very much. Of course I screamed and ran off.

Noon. No. 20. Little Arkansas River. June 30th

Now, about dark, we came into the musquito regions, and I found to my great *horror* that I have been complaining all this time for nothing, yes absolutely for *nothing;* for some two or hundred or even thousands are nothing compared with what we now encountered. The carriage mules became so restless that they passed all the wagons and swishing their tails from side to side, as fast as they could, and slaping their ears, required some strength of our Mexican driver to hold them in.

About 10 o'clock the mules became perfectly frantic, and nothing could make them stand. They were turned out to shift for themselves, and Magoffin seeing no other alternative than to remain there all night, tied his head and neck up with pocket handkerchiefs and set about having the tent stretched.

I drew my feet up under me, wraped my shawl over my head, till I almost smothered with heat, and listened to the din without. And such a noise as it was, I shall pray ever to be preserved. Millions upon millions were swarming around me, and their knocking against the carriage *reminded me of a hard rain.* It was equal to any of the plagues of Egypt.

I lay almost in a perfect stupor, the heat and stings made me perfectly sick, till Magoffin came to the carriage and told me *to run if I could,* with my shawl, bonnet and shoes on (and without opening my mouth Jane said, for they would *choke* me) straight to bed.

When I got there they pushed me straight in under the musquito bar, which had been tied up in some kind of a fashion, and oh, dear, what a relief it was to breathe again. There I sat in my cage, like an imprisoned creature frightened half to death.

Magoffin now rolled himself up some how with all his clothes on, and lay down at my side, he dare not raise the bar to get in. I tried to sleep and towards daylight succeeded. On awakening this morning I found my forehead, arms and feet covered with knots as large as a pea.

Camp No. 23

A thunder storm at sunset on the Prairie is a sublime and awing scene indeed. The vivid and forked lightning quickly succeeded by the hoarse growling thunder impresses one most deeply of his own weakness and the magnanimity of his God.

July 4 Pawnee Fort.

What a disasterous *celebration* I have today. It is certainly the greatest miracle that I have my head on my shoulders. I think I can never forget it if I live to be as old as my grandmother.

The wagons left Pawnee Rock some time before us—for I was anxious to see this wonderful curiosity. We went up, and while *mi alma* with his gun and pistol kept watch, for the wily Indian may always be apprehended here; it is a good lurking place and they are ever ready to fall upon any unfortunate trader behind his company—and it is necessary to be careful, so while *mi alma* watched on the rock above, and Jane stood by to watch if any should come up on the front side of me, I cut my name, among the many hundreds inscribed on the rock and many of whom I knew. It was not done well, for fear of Indians made me tremble all over and I hurried it over in any way.

The wagons being some distance ahead we rode on quite briskly to overtake them. In an hour's time we had driven some six miles, and at *Ash creek* we came up with them. No water in the creek and the crossing pretty good only a tolerably steep bank on the first side of it; all but two had passed over, and as these were not up we drove on ahead of them to cross first.

The bank though a little steep was smooth and there could be no difficulty in riding down it. However, we had made up our minds always to walk down such places in case of accident, and before we got to it *mi alma* hallowed "Woe" as he always does when he wishes to stop, but as there was no motion made by the driver to that effect, he repeated it several times and with much vehemence.

We had now reached the very verge of the cliff and seeing it a good way and apparently less dangerous than jumping out as we were, he said, "Go on." The word was scarcely from his lips, ere we were whirled completely over with a perfect crash. One to see the wreck of that carriage now with the top and sides entirely broken to pieces, could never believe that people had come out of it alive. But strange, wonderful to say, we are almost entirely unhurt!

I was considerably stunned at first and could not stand on my feet. *Mi alma* forgetting himself and entirely enlisted for my safety carried me in his arms to a shade tree, almost entirely without my knowledge, and rubing my face and hands with whiskey soon brought me entire to myself. My back and side are a little hurt, but is very small compared with what it might have been.

Mi alma has his left hip and arm on which he fell both bruised and strained, but not seriously. Dear creature, 'twas for me he received this, for had he not caught me in his arms as we fell he could have saved himself entirely. And then I should perhaps have been killed or much crushed for the top fell over me, and it was only his hands that kept it off of me. It is better as it is, for we can sympathise more fully with each other.

[July] 6th. Camp No. 26

It is a rich sight indeed to look at the fine fat [buffalo] meat stretched out on ropes to dry for our sustinence when we are no longer in the regions of the living animal. Such soup as we have made of the hump ribs, one of the most choice parts of the buffalo. I never eat its equal in the best hotels of N. Y. and Philada. And the sweetest butter and most delicate oil I ever tasted, 'tis not surpassed by the marrow taken from the thigh bones.

Mi alma was out this morning on a hunt, but I sincerely hope he will never go again. I am so uneasy from the start till he returns. There is danger attached to it that the excited hunter seldom thinks of till it overtake him. His horse may fall and kill him; the buffalo is apt too, to whirl suddenly on his persuer, and often serious if not fatal accidents occur. It is a painful situation to be placed in, to know that the being dearest to you on earth is in momentary danger of losing his life, or receiving for the remainder of his days, whether long or short, a tormenting wound.

11th. Camp 31st.

I am sick, rather sad feelings and everything around corresponds with them.

We have never had such a perfectly dead level before us as now. The little hillocks which formerly broke the perfectly even view have entirely disappeared. The grass is perfectly short, a real buffalo and Prairie dog and rattle snake region.

Road to Bent's Fort. Saturday, 18th. Camp 38, Bank of the Arkansas

The idea of being sick on the Plains is not at all pleasant to me; it is rather terrifying than otherwise, although I have a good nurse in my servant woman Jane, and one of the kindest husbands in the world, all gentleness and affection.

Bent's Fort, July 28th

Dctr. Mesure brought me medicine, and advises *mi alma* to travel me through Europ. The advice is rather better to take than the medicine, anything though to restore my health. I never should have consented to take the trip on the plains had it not been with that view and a hope that it would prove beneficial; but so far my hopes have been blasted, for I am rather going down hill than up, and it is so bad to be sick and under a physician all the time.

July 30th

Well this is my nineteenth birthday! And what? Why I feel rather strange, not surprised at its coming, nor to think that I am growing rather older, for that is the way of the human family, but this is it, I am sick! strange sensations in my head, my back and hips. I am obliged to lie down most of the time, and when I get up to hold my hand over my eyes.

There is the greatest possible noise in the *patio* [of Bent's Fort]. The shoeing of horses, neighing, and braying of mules, the crying of children, the scolding and fighting of men, are all enough to turn my head. And to add to the scene, like some of our neighbours we have our own private troubles. The servants are all quarreling and fighting among themselves, running to us to settle their difficulties; they are gambling off their cloths till some of them are next to nudity, and though each of them are in debt to *mi alma* for advancement of their wages, they are coming to him to get them out of their scrapes.

August, 1846. Thursday 6th

The mysteries of a new world have been shown to me since last Thursday. In a few short months I should have been a happy mother and made the heart of a father glad, but the ruling hand of a mighty Providence has interposed and by an abortion deprived us of the hope.

My pains commenced and continued until 12 o'c. at night, when after much agony and severest of pains, which were relieved a little at times by medicine given by Dctr. Mesure, *all was over.* I sunk off into a kind of lethargy, in *mi alma's* arms. Since that time I have been in my bed till yesterday a little while, and a part of today.

My situation was very different from that of an Indian woman in the room below me. She gave birth to a fine healthy baby, about the same time, *and in half an hour after she went to the River and bathed herself and it,* and this she has continued every day since. Never could I have believed such a thing, if I had not been here, and *mi alma's* own eyes had not seen her coming from the River. And some gentlemen here tells him, he has often seen them immediately after the birth of a child go to the water and *break the ice* to bathe themselves!

It is truly astonishing to see what customs will do. No doubt many ladies in civilized life are ruined by too careful treatments during child-birth.

The Fort is quite desolate. Most who are here now of the soldiers are sick. Two have died, and have been buried in the sand hills, the common fate of man.

Camp No. 1. Saturday, 8th. Second start.

The crossing of the Arkansas was an event in my life, I have never met with before; the separating me from my own dear native land. Perhaps I have left it for not only the first, but the last time.

Saturday, 15. Camp No. 9

We have an abundance of game, fine turkies, one of which we had roasted for dinner today, prairie chickens, hares, and they say we are to have bear meat soon. Three were seen this morning by the teamsters, and we passed in the road the carcass of one seeming to have been killed yes-terday. I must look sharp when I ramble about through these woods, or I will get myself into a nice hugging scrape.

24th. Camp No. 18. Olla de Galinas

Traveled late tonight and it has been so dark too, it was almost neces-sary to feel our way—with *mi alma's* careful driving though, I felt little fear.

How cheering it is to one when groping their way in the dark, over roads and through country he knew nothing about, all bewildered, and not knowing whether he is about pitching over a precipice, or driving into some deep ravine, whole, &c., to have the light of the camp fires of those ahead of them, to break suddenly before the eye. It is like drink to a thirsty traveler, or a straw to a drowning man.

27. Near San Miguel

We have passed through some two or three little settlements today and I am glad to think that much is accomplished of my task. It is truly shock-ing to my modesty to pass such places with gentlemen.

The women slap about with their arms and necks bare, perhaps their bosoms exposed (and they are none of the prettiest or whitest). If they are about to cross the little creek that is near all the villages, regardless of those about them, they pull their dresses, which in the first place but little more than cover their calves—up about their knees and paddle through the water like ducks, sloshing and spattering every thing about them.

Some of them wear leather shoes, from the States, but most have buck-skin mockersins, Indian style.

And it is repulsive to see the children running about perfectly naked, or if they have on a chimese it is in such ribbands it had better be off at once. I am constrained to keep my veil drawn closely over my face all the time to protect my blushes.

Santa Fe. August 31st, 1846

It is really hard to realize it, that I am here in my own house, in a place too where I once would have thought it folly to think of visiting. I have entered the city in a year that will always be remembered by my country-men; and under the "Star-spangled banner" too, the first American lady, who has come under such auspices, and some of our company seem dis-posed to make me the first under any circumstances that ever crossed the Plains.

Susan Magoffin eventually had two daughters, but died when she was 28.

★

1846:   THE DONNER TRAIN IS TRAPPED
IN THE HIGH SIERRA

☆

FIRST THE PROFESSIONAL, *hard-bitten and knowing—explorer, soldier, trader, trapper, plainsman, mountain man. Later, over the trails they had blazed, the amateur adventurer—speculator, fortune-seeker, settler, with hands that liked the axe handle and the hoe better than gun barrel and trigger. And finally, in great following waves, the tenderfoot—the "emigrant," soft, undisciplined, blundering, his only target the coming-true of blue-hazed dreams, his urgency the escape from the humdrum. As America rolled out her frontier, this was the succession, the order of appearance.*

One of the biggest emigrant trains to go through Independence in the busy summer of 1846 was that of the Donner Party, so called after one of the fami-lies that made it up. The people were from Illinois, Missouri, Iowa, Tennessee; their leaders well-to-do men—but not one of them wise in the ways of the wil-derness.

Their destination was California. What happened to them is one of the great horror stories of America's peacetime past, a tale of death, both sudden and gradual; of starvation, freezing, the last extremes in love and self-sacrifice; and of murder and cannibalism.

For a generation afterward it was told mainly in scattered bits and pieces and lived mainly in the diaries and minds of those who would rather have forgotten it. But in 1880 a badly written book appeared under the title History of the Donner Party by C. F. McGlashan. It oozed the cheap sentimentality, the diarrhetic elegance of nineteenth-century journalism at its worst. But it did pull the story together. In less than two weeks the first printing was sold out. The book went through eleven more editions. It was published again in 1947. And there followed such an avalanche of wordage from other writers as few episodes in our history have loosed.

The Donner Party bickered, botched and bungled its way from Independence to Fort Bridger in southwest Wyoming. Much of the summer was gone. Days were precious. Instead of taking the well-known trail from Fort Bridger northwest to Fort Hall, Idaho, the leaders decided to strike out due west over the Wasatch Mountains on the then little-known Hastings Cut-off in a direct line to Salt Lake. The distance—not counting vertically—would be reduced by 300 miles.

It was a fatal mistake. Whereas they had hoped to reach Salt Lake in a week, a desperate struggle over the mountains cost them more than a month. Because of this and other delays along the Humboldt and Truckee rivers, it was November when they reached the Sierra Nevada Mountains. There, high in the wilderness—as jagged and grim a piece of America as they could have found anywhere between two oceans—they were stopped by the onset of winter. And such a winter they had never known.

At scattered camps and cabins in the vicinity of Truckee (now called Donner) Lake, they holed in. But their provisions were soon gone, their animals lost in the snow. Groups of desperate parents tried to take their children over the mountains. Anyone who sees today the terrifying terrain of what is still called Donner Pass knows why they couldn't make it. And the alternative was to starve.

News of their plight traveled farther than they could. Money was raised by public appeal in what is now San Francisco. Rescue parties went out from Sutter's Fort, near Sacramento, and from Bear Valley. But horses couldn't make their way through soft snow that had drifted to depths of thirty feet. Forced to drop the burden of supplies along the way and go it afoot, many of the would-be rescuers, when they reached the Donner Party, were themselves starving and dependent on rescue.

Of the eighty-two emigrants trapped in the Sierra, forty-seven came through alive. For most of these, survival had been possible only by eating the bodies of the dead. After the event, recriminations among them brought out many grisly details which have not been overlooked by the retailers of the tragedy.

The two diaries excerpted here are the hurried jottings of men in desperate extremities, set down in the very hour of crisis, unadorned by ghost writers, unedited to conform to second thoughts. They do not tell the whole story of the Donner tragedy. For that, one must wade through a complex of comings and goings, of groupings and regroupings, which to the casual reader may or may not be worth the tracing. The diaries are but half-told tales. Bernard DeVoto, in his book, The Year of Decision: 1846, calls the diary of Patrick Breen "one of the most soul-shocking documents in our literature."

Breen and James F. Reed and their families got through. Breen, an Irish immigrant, had become a successful farmer in Iowa. He had with him his wife Peggy, six sons, the eldest fourteen, and a baby daughter.

"The soft white snow was a dreadful sight."
PATRICK BREEN (1805-1868)

Nov. 20 [1846]

Came to this place [now called Donner Lake] on the 31st of last month. It snowed. We went on to the pass. The snow so deep we were unable to find the road, when within 3 miles of the summit. Then turned back to this shanty on the Lake. We again took our teams & waggons & made another unsuccessful attempt to cross. We returned to the shanty, it continueing to snow all the time we were here. We now have killed most part of our cattle having to stay here untill next spring & live on poor beef without bread or salt. It snowed during the space of eight days with little intermission, after our arrival here.

21st

22 of our company are about starting across the mountain this morning.

23rd

The expedition across the mountains returned after an unsuccessful attempt.

29th

Still snowing. Now about 3 feet.

Killed my last oxen to day. Will skin them to-morrow. Hard to get wood.

30th

Snowing fast. About 4 or 5 feet deep. Looks as likely to continue as when it commenced. No liveing thing without wings can get about.

December 1st

Still snowing. Snow about 5½ feet or 6 deep. Difficult to get wood. No going from the house. Completely housed up. Our cattle all killed but three or four of them, the horses & Stantons mules gone & cattle suppose lost in the Snow. No hopes of finding them alive.

8th

Deep snow. The people not stirring round much. Hard work to get wood sufficient to keep us warm & cook our beef.

9th

Took in Spitzer yesterday so weak that he cannot rise without help. Caused by starvation. All in good health. Some have scant supply of beef.

15th

Fair & pleasant. Froezen hard last night & the company started on snow shoes to cross the mountains.

17th

Bill Murphy returned from the mountain party last evening.
Bealis Williams died night before last.

20

Tough times but not discouraged. Our hopes are in God. Amen.

21

Milt. got back last night from Donos [Donner's] camp. Sad news. Jake Donno, Sam Shoemaker, Rinehart, & Smith are dead. The rest of them in a low situation.

23rd

Began this day to read the Thirty days prayer. May Almighty God grant the request of an unworthy sinner that I am. Amen.

24th

Poor prospect of any kind of Comfort spiritual or temporal. May God help us to spend the Christmas as we ought, considering circumstances.

25th

Snowed all night & snows yet rapidly. Great difficulty in geting wood. John & Edwd. has to get it. I am not able. Offered our prayers to God this Cherimass morning. The prospect is apalling but hope in God. *Amen.*

27

Scarce of wood to day. Chopt a tree down. It sink in the snow & is hard to be got.

30th

Charley dies last night about 10 o clock. Had with him in money $1.50, two good loking silver watches, one razor, 3 boxes caps. Keysburg took them into his possessions. Spitzer took his coat & waistcoat, Keysburg all his other little effects, gold pin, one shirt & tools for shaveing.

31st

Last of the year. May we with God's help spend the comeing year better than the past which we purpose to do if Almighty God will deliver us from our present dredful situation which is our prayer if the will of God sees it fiting for us. Amen. Looks like another snow storm. Snow Storms are dredful to us. Snow very deep. Crust on the snow.

Jany. 1st 1847

We pray the God of mercy to deliver us from our present Calamity if it be his Holy will. Amen. Commenced snowing last night. Provissions geting scant. Dug up a hide from under the snow yesterday for Milt. Did not take it yet.

3rd

Mrs. Reid talks of crossing the mountains with her children.

4th

Fine morning. Looks like spring. Thawing. Now about 12 o clock. Mrs. Reid, Milt., Virginia Reed & Eliza Williams started about ½ hour ago with prospect of Crossing the Mountain. May God of Mercy help them. Left ther Children here. It was difficult for Mrs. Reid to get away from the Children.

6th

Eliza came back from the mountain yesterday evening. Not able to proceed. The others kept ahead.

8th

Very cold this morning. Mrs. Reid & company came back this morning. Could not find their way on the other side of the Mountain. They have nothing but hides to live on.

13th

Snow higher than the shanty. Must be 13 feet deep. Dont know how to get wood this morning. It is dredful to look at.

14th

Very pleasant to day. Sun shineing brilliantly renovates our spirit. Prais be to God. *Amen.*

15th

Mrs. Murphy blind. Lanth Murphy not able to get wood. Has but one axe betwixt him & Keysburg.

17th

Lanthrom crazy last night so Bill says. Keysburg sent Bill to get hides off his shanty & carry thim home this morning. Provisions scarce. Hides are the only article we depend on. We have a little meat yet. May God send us help.

19th

Lanthrom very low. In danger if relief dont come. Hides are all the go, not much of any other in camp.

21

John Battice & Denton came this morning with Eliza. She wont eat hides. Mrs. Reid sent her back to live or die on them.

23

Blew hard & snowed all night. The most severe storm we experienced this winter.

26

People geting weak liveing on short allowance of hides.

27th

Mrs. Keyberg here this morning. Lewis Suitor she says died three days ago. Keysburg sick & Lanthrom lying in bed the whole of his time. Don't have fire enough to cook their hides.

31st

Lantron Murphy died last night about 1 Oclock.

[February] 5th

Snowed hard all yesterday untill 12 O'clock at night. Peggy very uneasy for fear we shall all perish with hunger. We have but a little meat left & only part of 3 hides has to support Mrs. Reid. She has nothing left but one hide & it is on Graves shanty. Milt is living there & likely will keep that hide. Eddys child died last night.

6th

It snowed faster last night & to day than it has done this winter & still continues without intermission. Murphys folks or Keysburgs say they cannot eat hides. I wish we had enough of them.

7th

McCutchins child died second of this month.

8th

Spitzer died last night about 3 o clock. Today we will bury him in the snow. Mrs. Eddy died on the night of the 7th.

9th

Pikes child all but dead. Milt at Murphys not able to get out of bed. Keyburg never gets up. Says he is not able. John went down to day to bury Mrs Eddy & child.

10th

To day thawing in the Sun. Milt Elliot died last night at Murphys Shanty about 9 Oclock P.M. All are entirely out of meat, but a little we have. Our hides are nearly all eat up, but with Gods help spring will soon smile upon us.

12th

We hope with the assistance of Almighty God to be able to live to see the bare surface of the earth once more. O God of Mercy grant it if it be thy holy will. *Amen.*

15

Mrs. Graves refused to give Mrs. Reid any hides. Put Suitors pack hides on her shanty. Would not let her have them. Says if I say it will thaw it then will not. She is a case.

16th

We all feel very weakly to day. Snow not geting much less in quantity.

19th

7 men arrived from California yesterday evening with som provisions but left the greater part on the way. Some of the men are gone to day to Donnos Camp. Will start back on monday.

22nd

The Californians started this morning, 24 in number. Some in a very weak state. Mrs. Keysburg started & left Keysburg here unable to go. I burried Pikes Child this morning in the snow. It died 2 days ago.

23

Shot Touser [dog] to day & dressed his flesh. Mrs Graves came there this morning to borrow meat. Dog or ox. They think I have meat to spare but I know to the Contrary. They have plenty hides. I live principally on the same.

25th

Mrs Murphy says the wolves are about to dig up the dead bodies at her shanty. The nights are too cold to watch them, we hear them howl.

26th

Hungry times in camp, plenty hides but the folks will not eat them. We eat them with a tolerable good apetite. Thanks be to Almighty God. *Amen.* Mrs Murphy said here yesterday that she thought she would Commence on Milt. & eat him. I dont believe that she has done so as yet, it is distressing. The Donnas told the California folks that they would commence to eat the dead people 4 days ago, if they did not succeed that day or next in finding their cattle then under ten or twelve feet of snow & did not know the spot or near it. I suppose they have done so ere this time.

March the 1st

There was 10 men arrived this morning from bear valley with provisions. We are to start in two or three days & Cash [cache] our goods here. There is amongst them some old [mountaineers] they say the snow will be here untill June.

JAMES FRAZIER REED (born 1800)

All knew him to be of stout heart and open hand, this big fellow from Springfield, Illinois. But as the Donner Party was making its way along the Humboldt River in Nevada, Reed got into a quarrel with John Snyder over the handling of an ox team. Snyder inflicted a great gash in Reed's head with a crack of his bullwhip, and also bruised Mrs. Reed's face. Reed killed Snyder with a stab of his knife. One group wanted to hang Reed. Another defended him. Before they came to gunfire, they held a court. The decision was to banish this man, one of their bravest and ablest, from the train. The others promised to take care of his wife and four children.

Reed went on to California. There he joined William McCutchen, who had also ridden ahead of the Donner Party to get supplies. The depths of snow blocked their first attempts to get back to their families. But in February they tried it again, and this time succeeded.

We pick up Reed's diary after he reaches William Johnson's ranch on Bear Creek, a way point en route eastward to the winter camp in the Sierra.

[February 12, 1847]

I was at Mr. Johnsons today preparing Beef by drying, and keeping his Indians at work night & day in a small hand mill.

14

I kept fire under the Beef all night which I had on the scafold and next morning by sun rise I had about 200 lbs dryed and baged. We packed our horses and started with the addition of men and one Indian, our supplies 700 lbs flour, 4½ Beeves, 25 horses. In all 17 men in my party and Mr Greenwood had 2 men. 3 men including himself—& 2 boys traveled this day about 10 miles.

16

Left camp early this morning and encamped early on acct grass. Tomorrow we will reach the snow.

17

Encamped at the Mule Spring this evening. Made preparations to take to the snow in the morning. Here we left at camp our saddles, Bridles, etc.

18

Started with 11 horses & mules lightly packed about 80 lbs. Traveled about 2 miles and left one mule, and pack. Made this day with hard labour for the horses in the snow about 6 miles. Our start was late.

19

Left our encampment early thinking the snow would bare the horses. Proceeded 200 yard with difficulty when we were compelled to unpack the horses and take the provision on our backs. Here for a few minutes silence with the men. When the packs were ready to sling on the back the hilarity commenced as usual.

Made the head of Bare Valley, a distance of 15 miles. We met in the valley about 3 miles below the camp Messrs Glover & Road, belonging to the party that went to the lake for the people, who informed me they had started with 21 persons 2 of whom had died, John Denton of Spring-field & a child of Keesberger. Mr. Glover sent 2 men back to the party with fresh provisions.

I here lightened our packs with a suficiency of provisions to do the people when arrive, and I sent back to our camp of the 26, 2 men to bring provision. They will return tomorrow. And left one man to prepare for the people which were expected today.

I left camp early on a fine hard snow and proceeded about 4 miles when we met the poor unfortunate starved people. As I met them scattered along the snow trail I distributed bread that I had baked the 2 nights previous in small quantities. Here I met Mrs. Reed and two children. Two still in the mountains. I cannot describe the death like look they all had. Bread Bread Bread Bread was the beging of every child and grown person except my wife.

I gave to all what I dared and left for the scene of desolation and now I am camped within 25 miles which I hope to mak this night and tomorrow. We had to camp soon on account of the softness of the snow, the men falling in to their middles.

One of the party that passed us today, a little boy, Mrs. Murphy's son, was nearly blind when we met them. They were overjoyed when we told them there was plenty of provision at camp. I made a cach 12 miles and encamped 3 m eastward on Juba. Snow about 15 feet.

21

Left camp about 12 o'clock at night and was compl to camp about 2 o'clock, the snow still being soft. Left again about 4. All hands. And made this day 14 miles. In camp early. Snow soft. Snow here 30 feet. 3 of my men, Cady, Clark & Stone, I told if they wished they might keep on during the night which they intended but halted within 2 miles of the cabins and remained without fire during the night on acct of 10 Indians which they saw. The boys not having arms and supposed they had taken the cabins and destroyed the people. In the morning they started and arrived all alive in the houses. Give provision to Keesbergrs, Brinn [Breen] and two. Then left for Donners. A distance of ten miles which they made. By the middle of the day I come up with the main body of my party.

March 1st

The people, that is all who ware able, should have to start day after tomorrow. Made soup for the infirm. Washed and clothed afresh Mrs. Eddy & Fosters children and rendered every assistance in our power. I left Keesbergs people Mr. Stone to cook and watch the eating of Mrs. Keesberg & 3 children.

Left early this morning with 3 of the men and went to Donners where Cady & Clark had arrived on yesty. Found all alive and sent Cady back for more provisions. At Gorge Donner tent there was 3 stout hearty children. His wife was able to travel but preferred to stay with her husband until provision should arrive.

Here I left two of my men, Cady & Clark, one with each tent, to cook and as fast as possible resusitate the enfeebled so that they might in a few days start. Took 3 children of J. Donner and the men and returned the same day making this 20 miles carrying 2 of the child. Got back to the other cabins about 8 o'ck, much worn down. As I passed Mrs. Graves told them I would be off in the morning. The men that remained with her today cached the pricipal of her effects and got for her out of one of the waggons about 800 in gold & silver which was concealed in a slat or bracket that was nailed in the middle of the bed, the money being placed in grooves made for the purpose.

2d

After leaving with Keesburgh I [instructed] Mr. Stone to get wood, cook and take care of the helpless. I left with the following persons, P Brin, Mrs. Brin, John Brin, young man & 4 other smaller children, 2 of which had to be carried. In all of Brins 7. Mrs. Graves—& 4 children 2 of which had to be carried. In all of her family 5. Solomon Hook, young man and May & Issac Donner, in all 3—with two children of my own, one a girl of 9 years, the other a little boy 4, in all 2—making in all 17 souls— proceeded about 2 miles and encamped on the edge of the lake on a bare spot of ground.

3

Left camp early. Traveled on the lake 2 miles and encamped under the mountain. Made this day about 4 miles.

4

This morning after breakfast I had 2 scanty meals left for all hands, which would do to the night following. I sent ahead 3 of my best men to push to our first cach and if not disturbed to bring it up, while the other two proceed on and bring up our second. And if they should meet our supplies which we all had a right expected close at hand to hurry them on. But to our misfortune there was none nigher than 65 miles and at this juncture no prospect of starting, which I learned afterwards to be the fact.

I moved camp and after a great fatiguing day arrived at the praire, now Starved Camp at the head of Juba. It was made by the other Compy. who had passed in but a few days previous.

Here the men began to fail being for several days on half allowance, or 1½ pints of gruel or sizing per day. The sky look like snow and everything indicates a storm. God forbid.

Wood being got for the night & Bows for the beds of all, and night closing fast, the clouds still thicking. Terror. Dare not communicate my mind to any. Death to all if our provisions do not come, in a day or two and a storm should fall on us. Very cold. A great lamentation about the cold.

5

Still in camp. The last of our provisions gone. Looking anxiously for our supplies. None. My dreaded Storm is now on us. Commcd a perfect hurricane in the night. A great crying with the children and with the parents praying, crying and lamentations on acct of the cold and the dread of death from the Howling storm. The men up nearly all night making fires. Some of the men began to pray. Several became blind. I could not see even the light of the fire when it was blazing before me. I continued so to the next day when my sight returned.

Young Brinn fell of his feet into the pit the heat of the fire had made in the snow to the depth of 15 feet.

It has snowed already 12 inches, still the storm continues. The light of Heaven is as it ware shut in from us. The snow blows so thick that we cannot see 20 feet looking against the wind. I dread the coming night. 3 of my men only able to get wood. The rest give out for the present.

After some time, wood being secured, we had a great dificulty in fixing a foundation for our fire. The snow having melted to a great depth, I think now 15 feet—and no earth in sight. It must be from 6 to 10 feet snow before the earth is seen in the fire pit. The manner of making our fires on the snow are as follows, we lay 2 pcs of timber or saplin about 10 feet apart— then Roll close together large green logs on the two pcs in a transverse position. These form a bed for the dry logs to lie on so as to prevent the coals of the dry wood which we lay on from falling through into this deep Pit which has melted below.

Still storming verry cold. So much so that the few now employed in cutting the dry trees down have to come and warm about every 10 minutes. Hunger, hunger is the cry with the children and nothing to give them. Freezing was the cry of the mothers with [illegible] to their little starving freezing children. Night closing fast and with it the Hurricane increases—not quite so much snow falling as before night.

6th

Thank God day has once more appeared, although darkened by the storm. Snowing as fast as ever and the Hurricane has never ceased for ten minutes at a time during one of the most dismal nights I ever witnessed, and I hope I never shall witness such in a similar situation. Of all the praying and crying I ever heard nothing ever equaled it. Several times I expected to see the people perish by the extreme cold.

At one time our fire was nearly gone and had it not been for Mr Mc-Cutchen's exertions it would have entirely disapeared. Had the fire been lost two thirds of the camp would have been out of their misery before morning, but as God would have it we soon got it blazing in comfortable order and the sufferings of the people became less.

At this time hope began to animate the bosoms of many young and old when the cheering blaze rose through the dry pine logs we had piled together. One would say thank god for this fire. Another how good it is. The little half starved half frozen poor children would say I'm glad. I'm glad. We have got some fire. Oh, how good it feels, it is good our fire didn't go out.

At day light I discovered the storm to slack by hushing as it were entirely for a few minutes, and then it would burst forth with such fury that

I felt often alarmed for the safety of the people on acct of the tall timber that surrounded us. The storm continues to lull. Snow now nearly ceased. The location of our camp a bleak point under the summit of the great California Range, about 1000 feet. Consequently our altitude about 8300 above the sea with a small Prairie on our south and west, about 3 miles in length & one in breadth. Here the snow and wind had full sweep.

This camp was used by the other party that had passed out of the mountain. The under or bed logs for the fire having remained, it saved the men from considerable labor in cutting and rolling green logs together. I estimate the snow in this valley about 20 feet deep.

The Breen and Reed families came through the ordeal intact. All were brought down the west slope of the Sierra to the end of the California Trail at Sutter's Fort, near Sacramento.

A final relief expedition, mainly for the recovery of belongings of the emigrants, on reaching the camp at Donner Lake on April 17, was confronted with a shocking scene—"sights from which we would have fain turned away." Thomas Fallon, a mountain man who headed this group, reported that he had found the body of Mrs. Eddy, "the limbs sawed off and a frightful gash in the skull." In a hut at nearby Alder Creek he saw a kettle full of pieces of the body of George Donner, whom he judged to have been dead only about four days. A macabre note came into Fallon's report when he added pointedly that he had also found legs of oxen in the hut, recently recovered from the snowdrifts, and that although these had been kept from spoiling by the cold, they were not eaten.

Reed's 13-year-old stepdaughter Virginia wrote from California to a cousin back home in Illinois, "It is a beautiful country. It ought to be a beautiful country to pay us for our troubles in getting to it."

-- ★

1848: *GOLD IN CALIFORNIA!*

-- ☆

ON A MORNING IN JANUARY 1848, Wheelwright James W. Marshall was standing beside a ditch at the sawmill he was building at Sutter's Fort, California, 36 miles from Sacramento. His eye caught a glint of reflected sunlight from something in the water, something half the size of a pea. He picked it up. "It made my heart thump," he said. "I was certain it was gold."

It was indeed. The story "spread like wildfire," and next year the wagons of the Forty-niners were deepening the ruts on the California Trail in the wildest gold rush of all time.

Two years before Marshall's discovery, war was on with Mexico, and American forces had marched into Monterey, capital of Spanish California. The American warship Congress was anchored in Monterey Bay. Walter Colton, a Vermont preacher who was serving as ship's chaplain, was set ashore and appointed alcalde—mayor and chief magistrate. He takes inventory of the community in his diary:

> My jurisdiction extends over an immense extent of territory and over a most heterogeneous population. Almost every nation has, in some emigrant, a representative here. Here is the reckless Californian, the half-wild Indian, the roving trapper of the West, the lawless Mexican, the licentious Spaniard, the scolding Englishman, the absconding Frenchman, the luckless Irishman, the plodding German, the adventurous Russian, and the discontented Mormon. All have come here with the expectation of finding but little work and less law.

When the gold fever hit Monterey, this, as Alcalde Colton witnessed it, was what happened:

"The blacksmith dropped his hammer . . ."
WALTER COLTON (1797-1851)

May 29 [1848]

Our town was startled out of its quiet dreams today by the announcement that gold had been discovered on the American Fork.

June 12

A straggler came in today from the American Fork, bringing a piece of yellow ore weighing an ounce.

June 20

My messenger, sent to the mines, has returned with specimens of the gold; he dismounted in a sea of upturned faces. As he drew forth the yellow lumps from his pockets and passed them around among the eager crowd, the doubts, which had lingered till now, fled. The blacksmith dropped his hammer, the carpenter his plane, the mason his trowel, the farmer his sickle, the baker his loaf, and the tapster his bottle. All were off for the mines, some on horses, some on carts, and some on crutches; and one went in a litter.

An American woman who had recently established a boardinghouse here pulled up stakes and was off before her lodgers had even time to pay their bills.

July 18

Another bag of gold from the mines and another spasm in the community. It was brought down by a sailor from Yuba River and contains a hundred and thirty-six ounces. My carpenters, at work on the schoolhouse, on seeing it, threw down their saws and planes, shouldered their picks, and are off for the Yuba. Three seamen ran from the [ship] *Warren*, forfeiting their four years' pay; and a whole platoon of soldiers from the fort left only their colors behind. One old woman declared she would never again break an egg or kill a chicken without examining yolk and gizzard.

August 16

Four citizens of Monterey are just in from the gold mines on Feather River, where they worked in company with three others. They employed about thirty wild Indians who are attached to the ranch owned by one of the party. They worked precisely seven weeks and three days and have divided seventy-six thousand eight hundred and forty-four dollars, nearly eleven thousand dollars to each.

Make a dot there, and let me introduce a man, well known to me, who has worked on the Yuba River sixty-four days and brought back as the result of his individual labor five thousand three hundred and fifty-six dollars.

Make a dot there, and let me introduce another townsman who has worked on the North Fork fifty-seven days and brought back four thousand five hundred and thirty-four dollars.

Make a dot there, and let me introduce a boy, fourteen years of age, who has worked on the Mokelumne fifty-four days and brought back three thousand four hundred and sixty-seven dollars.

Make another dot there and let me introduce a woman, of Sonorarian birth, who has worked in the dry diggings forty-six days and brought back two thousand one hundred and twenty-five dollars. Is not this enough to make a man throw down his ledger and shoulder a pick?

Colton did not shoulder a pick himself. He founded the first newspaper in California, kept a diary which later became one of the most popular books about the Coast, and in 1849 went east.

1849: A MISSOURIAN IN THE GOLD RUSH

> My little girls can make from 5 to 25 dollars per day washing gold in pans.
>
> —Report from California in
> the Daily Missouri Republican,
> April 16, 1849

The stories were coming back thick and fast. They were fantastic. So everybody believed them and picked up and went. From store and office, mill and field, they came elbowing through Missouri with the self-same dream that had flitted before the eyes of swashbuckling hidalgos three hundred years before. A man at Fort Kearny counted 2,577 wagons westbound on the California Trail.

It wasn't so rough at the start—not until the dry air of western Nebraska began shrinking the spokes out of your wheels and the road got so bad you had to build "dug-outs" over pieces of it and you ran into long lines waiting at the ferries.

The road across America lay along the North Platte to Fort Laramie, then across Wyoming over South Pass, where the Continental Divide was no more than a long thank-you-ma'am, to Fort Bridger, northwest to Fort Hall, Idaho, then sharply southwest across Nevada, over the Sierra and on to San Francisco.

You learned how important grass was. Without grass for your animals, you would never make it; and if you couldn't make it there, you couldn't make it back. The most grueling stretch was the eighty miles (some said eighty, some said infinity) of Nevada desert between the sink of the Humboldt and the Truckee River. That was where your mules started chewing on dust and where the downbeat spirit of the wasteland tightened on you step by step, mile by mile.

It was natural that many of these adventurers should keep diaries—as one of them explained, "so my grandchildren will know how the family fortune was made."

Bennett C. Clark quit his job as clerk of the court of Cooper County, Missouri, to set out with 23 other young men on the "long and toilsome journey."

Despite a similarity in names, a search of records to discover a relationship, if any, of the diarist to the family of Bennett Champ Clark, prominent Senator from Missouri in 1933-39 and son of James Beauchamp (Champ) Clark, who was the Democratic presidential candidate in 1912, proved unfruitful.

322

"Wagons as far as the eye can reach . . ."
BENNETT C. CLARK (1819-1890)

[May 3, 1849]

Finally we broke up our camp [at Westport, Missouri, now a part of Kansas City] and started on our long and toilsome journey.

6th

Came up with a train of about forty wagons under the guidance of Capt. Hedgepeth, numbering in all about six hundred head of stock.

7th

The camp was roused at 4 oclock in the morning and all hands went briskly to work getting ready to take the road early in order to keep ahead of Capt. Hedgepeth's company—but to our surprise a short time after sunrise one of our men sung out "there they come." Our men exerted themselves to the utmost to get into the road before this mammoth train came up, but to no purpose.

Before we were ready to take the road about 20 of Capt. H.'s wagons had passed & being mule teams were a little ahead of their friends who had ox teams, thereby leaving a vacancy between, which our company took advantage of, and drove in, making a continuous line of wagons for nearly a ¼ of a mile.

One of our wagons driven by Andrew B. Cole struck out on the grass for the purpose of passing the wagons in front and was followed by our whole train. After driving in this manner about 3 miles our train got ahead.

24th

While lying by this morning trains have been constantly passing. Today a train of government wagons 47 in number passed us and one Company of mounted men destined for the California service.

26th

Commenced our march at 6 oclock. Our course continuing up the Platt River the road in maney places being very heavy and trains dotting the road as far as the eye could reach, presenting a cheerful picture in this wild and barren country. I found on today's march several friends.

27th

On the roadside today I saw a human scull with several names written upon it with pencil.

28

We passed the forks of Platte this morning. In consequence of the scarcity of grass we travelled quite late.

June 2nd

We passed today a hunting party of the Sioux some 30 in number which we were not at all afraid of as their wives and children were along. About night we got down among the hollows & there not being grass enough in any one hollow for our stock we travelled on until 10 oclk at night when we reached the Platte bottom, but here the bottom was so narrow & so crowded with wagons as far as the eye could reach that we almost dispaired of finding camping place at all.

4

On a review of our stock today we think they begin to fail considerably and in consequence there is considerable alarm manifested & long faces are very common. The 3 year old mules are considerably cut down.

8

Passed over some rough road in the neighborhood of Scotts Bluffs [western Nebraska], passing the Black smiths shop about 35 miles below or east of Fort Laramie [in what is now Goshen County, Wyoming, on the left bank of the Laramie River, a short distance above its junction with the North Platte]. Here is some of the most beautiful scenery we have yet seen. Some of our party ascended the Bluff the next morning to get a view of the rockey mountains. When we arrived at the summit they were enveloped in dense fog and could see nothing.

13

This evening we travelled some 2 miles & stopped at the first tolerable grass. Capt Clark [the diarist] resigned in order to effect a devision in the Company which all considered as politic on account of the scarcity of grass. One of the teams struck out to itself & 3 others did likewise.

16

Reached the lower platte Ferry about 10 oclk A. M. where we found some 2 or 300 wagons awaiting their turns to ferry. We understood that as many were assembled at the upper ferry [west of Casper, Wyoming].

18

Left the Platte for the last time and struck out across the most barren country we had ever yet seen. In addition to having little or no grass our stock did not this day have a drop of water until sunset—all the water in this region being strongly impregnated with alkali and very poisonous. Passed a mineral spring but were afraid to use the water. We were overtaken this evening by the mormon mail & some of their party told us that by driving on to Willow Spring we would find excellent water & grass. We did so, making our drive some 32 miles & camping sometime after night. Find grass all eaten out. Stock fared badly.

20

Reached Independence Rock [central Wyoming] about 8 oclk this morning, a vast mass of bold barren rocks rising some hundred feet perpendicularly from the roads. Names innumerable we found here inscribed by travellers who had preceded us on this long tedious toilsome journey.

24

Reached the South Pass [Fremont County, Wyoming] & camped for the night, on the summit, where we found the grass superb. The assent to the summit of the Pass has been so gradual that we can scarcely realize that we have accomplished it.

July 2d

Reached Smith's fork of Bear River [near the western boundary of Wyoming] after a rough day's travel—where we found a large number of Snake Indians encamped. Here on account of the increased illness of Alfred Corum who had been sick a week or ten days we laid by a day.

3d

Whilst lying by some 200 wagons passed us & Alfred continued to grow worse & as there was no prospect of his living it was deemed prudent for the wagons to start the next morning. Accordingly they left on the 4th leaving behind the Dearbourn [a four-wheeled carriage] & a party of 6 men to render every service to our dying friend. As there was no wood nor water near us we concluded to move him about 1½ miles where we found both. About 1 o'clock he died without a struggle and in full possession of all his faculties to the last.

20

Two spectacles (their affinity would perhaps warrant us in calling them a pair) of rather uncommon interest presented themselves to us today— the first a beautiful cluster of delicate roses on the wayside looking delightfully fresh amid all the dust that surrounded them—the second a female dressed in the extreme of fashion in a green habit exactly personifying the roses or green spot of the desert. Looked in her face as we passed & was quite horrified to find her homely.

23d [At the Humboldt River, Nevada]

Drove 6 or 8 miles this morning & camped for the day as it was important to rest and graze our stock. Every other train is reduced to the same necessity. We learn that Capt. McCullocks ox train & Finley's banded together and destroyed the boat in which they ferried this stream in order to prevent the emigrants from following them.

24

No vegitation to be seen on the hills and mountains except the wild sage a growth which has become most sickening to us.

25

A dusty barren bottom covered with the eternol dust from 6 to 8 inches deep.

Passed another grave today. These are melancholy sights to the travellor as they serve to remind him that he too may die far away from home & kindred, "a stranger in a strange land."

During the night the wolves were quite noisy & alarmed our mules.

26 [crossing the Humboldt Desert, Nevada]

Nothing but the sterile lands and dust immediately around us & naught in the distance to releave the eye, but bare rugged hills of basalt. Our feelings just now is that if we once get safely out of this great Basin we will not be cought here in a hurry.

27th

We are beginning to feel alarmed lest our stock will not take us through.

29

A continuance of yesterday's hard work & poor fare for our stock. We were struck with the contrast between our appearance now & when we left home. Then we had gay outriders prancing along proudly on their fiery steeds & our teams pressing forward with fierce resolution. Now what a scene—the teams crossing along slowly their gaunt sides marked with many a whip cut & their rigging defaced with dust—a sorry show. And where are all these gay outriders? Look before the train & you see them strung along the road for a mile on foot their faces and clothes covered with dust and looking worn & livid. What a picture.

30

We hear many reports hereabouts of the state of things in California. An express is said to have gone back to meet the troops destined for Oragon & turned them to California to repress the disorders of that Country.

Guerilla bands are said to be very troublesome—stopping wagons & pressing provisions as there is an absolute famine there at present. Gold they say is very abundant. We regret to hear these reports but if we knew them to be true & a return was practicable (which is not) we would still go on.

Men who have risked their lives by sickness, casualties, hardships of every kind and the remote prospect of starvation continually present to their minds are not to be detered from endeavoring to obtain some reward by the uncertain reports that float along this great highway.

They are now traversing the most difficult part of the route to California— the desert between the sink of the Humboldt River and the Truckee River, most of which lies within the present limits of Churchill County, Nevada, near Reno.

August 1

The mules were by this time so hungry that they greedily devoured the leaves of the willow. Fortunately we here found some grass—although of an inferior quality. This is a more trying time than any we have yet encountered & as we have yet some 71 miles to go over of the same kind of fare, we feel altogether uncertain about the result. We think, however, that at the worst we can walk the balance of the way.

2

Started early and drove 10 miles to the slough without water. The stock look very badly.

4

A general panic now seezed upon all & doubt & fear prevailed every where. There is yet a stretch of 45 miles ahead of us without grass or water except at the boiling spring 25 miles from this point.

We left here at 4 oclk this evening & taking the right hand or old route travelled all night & reached the Hot Spring at daylight.

This is the most dreary desolate looking place we ever saw. It is on the top of a mountain & the water bubbles & boils up from the fissures in the rocks & forms into a small lake quite clear but so hot that it scalds. We dipped up the water & pourd it into some holes in the earth & cooled it & then watered our animals, mixed flour with it. The mules were so hungry that they ate dust & gravel & chewed up whatever came in their way—gearing, wagon covers or any thing they could reach.

5

We had 20 miles to accomplish & the heat of the day to make it. About 2 oclk we struck the heavy sand 10 miles from Truckey river & had the utmost difficulty in getting our stock thro—stopping every few yards to rest. A little before night we reached the [Truckee] river. We all felt greatly releaved. We found grass very abundant and the water very fine.

All along the desert road from the very start even the way side was strewed with the dead bodies of oxen, mules & horses & the stench was horrible. All our traveling experience furnishes no parallel for all this. Many persons suffered greatly for water during the last 8 or 10 miles, and many instances of noble generosity were developed on these occasions. Some trains that got over before us sent water back in kegs & left them on the road marked for the benefit of the feeble. We slept here for the first time for four nights.

The diary ends with the dateline August 11 but no entry. Clark had reached a point near the present western boundary of Nevada. There he fell ill and had to be carried to San Francisco. He left that city for home by boat, around the Horn—without ever reaching the gold fields!

1853: CORONADO'S SUCCESSORS

HALF A CENTURY AFTER COLUMBUS, men from Spain were still listening to and passing along tales of gold in North America. The Indians obliged white travelers with what they wanted to hear—except for one thing: Always the gold was in some other part of that vast country.

When word came to Mexico of great cities and rich hoards to the north, General Francisco Vasquez de Coronado, governor at Guadalajara, organized in the year 1540 an expedition of 300 Spaniards and 1,000 Indians. The objective was the fabulous country of Quivira where, so he was told, even the bathroom facilities were of gold.

Coronado's story from beginning to end suggests that he had a knack for surrounding himself with liars. The result was one of the longest marches of all time, deep into what is now the United States—for nothing. "After traveling

77 days," he writes, "I arrived, by God's will, in Quivira. By the way I came it is 950 leagues [3,500 to 4,000 miles] from Mexico."

But what a contrast between the country of the fables and the terrible emptiness of those plains that stretched endlessly before him! Bare earth, miserable little knots of half-starved natives, houses of mud or straw or the hides of the buffalo.

From Quivira, for 25 more days he hunted the dream. "They [his guides] had pictured it as having stone houses many stories high. Not only is there none of stone, but they are of straw, and the people are savage, like all I passed up to this place. There is no gold in all that country."

Where Coronado's Quivira really was, no one can be certain. Historians have differed. One of his men, Pedro de Castaneda, wrote up the adventure in detail, but from memory twenty years afterward. From Castaneda's narrative, most historians bring Coronado all the way to the Missouri River, somewhere between Kansas City and Council Bluffs. A few have confused Quivira with a place in New Mexico that was called Gran Quivira, a hundred miles south of Santa Fe, although Castaneda's descriptions do not fit this locality.

Wherever Coronado may have gone, his destination was still a moving flicker on an undrawn map—just over the next horizon, beyond the Seven Cities of Cibola, across the River (Colorado) That Hangs in the Sky.

But the narrative of Castaneda comes to a curiously prophetic conclusion. "Granted," he writes, "that they did not find the gold of which they had heard, they did find a place in which to search for it."

Their successors have been searching ever since. Rumors of gold, of lost mines and hidden hoards, still buzz through the American Southwest. Of these stories J. Frank Dobie says in his book Coronado's Children, published in 1930: "An amazing thing is that they seem to be increasing rather than diminishing in number; they are incredibly, astoundingly numerous—as are the people who tell them and halfway, at least, believe them."

In the following diary a U.S. Army officer tells how his expedition found and authenticated the site of Gran Quivira a century ago. Major Carleton was among those who were misled by the similarity of place names. Hazy as the route of Coronado may have been, the scene of these crumbling towns in Gran Quivira, New Mexico—the land, the people, the way they lived—did not at all fit the picture that Castaneda left of Coronado's Quivira. Hence the somewhat puzzled observations of contrast made by the army officer as he read his history and then looked about him.

But perhaps the expeditions themselves, though three centuries apart, were not so disparate. Except to say that the Army wanted to learn certain things about the Apache Indians, Major Carleton is not very communicative about his venture. Could it have been that the U.S. Army was officially titillated, touched with gold fever by old tales that had drawn the great processions of hidalgos and caballeros over the American wilderness 300 years before? Major Carleton's diary suggests that he himself was not immune.

"It will be worth the trouble to explore . . ."
JAMES HENRY CARLETON (1814-1873)

December 14, 1853

A squadron of cavalry, formed of company "H," first dragoons, commanded by First Lieutenant Samuel D. Sturgis, and company "K," first dragoons, commanded by Brevet Major James Henry Carleton, in all one hundred strong, with one 12-pounder mountain howitzer, left Albuquerque, at eleven o'clock this morning, as an expedition to explore the country around the ruins of Gran Quivira, New Mexico, and for other objects connected with the bands of Apache Indians who often infest that portion of the territory.

December 15

Three Mexican citizens of respectability, a Mr. Chavis and two of his sons-in-law, came to our camp this evening, and informed Major Carleton that it was their intention to establish a colony of settlers at a point east of a range of mountains known as the Sierra Blanca, and along some streams affluent to the Pecos, called the Seven Rivers; that they proposed going with this command as far as Gran Quivira; and that from that point to the Seven Rivers they desired to be furnished with an escort of dragoons.

They were told that they could accompany the expedition as far as Gran Quivira, but that no escort would be given beyond that point.

Mr. Chavis concluded to go by the way of Gran Quivira, at all hazards; and to proceed across the country, from that point, even without an escort. The truth doubtless is, the old gentleman fancies that the purpose for which this squadron is going into that country is to search for a great amount of treasures which are said to be buried beneath the ruins there, and he hopes he may be able to obtain a share of them.

December 17

The long Sierras towards which we were now moving were clothed in a winter robe of white. They bounded the whole eastern horizon. Their tall summits and jagged outline, like a fringed edge, standing sharp and clearly defined against the morning sky, glowed in the light as if burnished with silver. While towards us, along their whole western slope—which descended toward the plain as a coast towards the ocean—the valleys and precipices repose in cold blue shadows, chilly enough to make the beholder shudder in looking upon them.

The Ruins of Abo consist of a large church, and the vestiges of many other buildings, which are now but little else than long heaps of stone, with here and there portions of walls projecting above the surrounding rubbish.

A large population must have occupied this town and its neighborhood, if one were to judge of the number of people by the size of the church to accommodate them at their devotions.

It was nearly night when we reached Abo. The whole appearance of the country was cheerless, wintry, and desolate. The tall ruins, standing there in solitude, had an aspect of sadness and gloom. They did not seem to be the remains of an edifice dedicated to peaceful religious purposes, a place for prayer, but rather as a monument of crime, and ruthlessness, and violence.

The cold wind when at its height appeared to roar and howl through the roofless pile like an angry demon. But when at times it died away, a low sigh seemed to breathe along the crumbling battlements.

In the mystery that envelopes everything connected with these ruins—as to when, and why, and by whom, they were erected; and how, and when, and why, abandoned—there is much food for very interesting speculation.

Dec. 18

We then came to the Ruins of Quarra.

The church of Quarra is not so long by thirty feet as that at Abo. When the first settlers came here they found two groves of apple trees, one just above the site now occupied by the town [of Manzana, N. M.] and one just below.

Tradition says these trees were planted at the time Abo and Quarra were inhabited; and yet tradition has lost all traces of when that time was. Two of the largest trees in the lower grove were found to be respectively eight feet and six feet in circumference. Apple trees are not indigenous to New Mexico. Assuming it to be true, however, that the largest of these trees were planted at the period referred to, then the ruins of Abo and Quarra are more than two centuries old.

December 19

We retraced our steps to a point on the road known as Arroyo de la

Cienega—a dry bed of a wet-weather stream. Here we left the beaten
track and took a course across the country. After traveling some six miles
we struck an Indian trail which leads from Manzana to the country of
the Mescalero Apaches.

December 20

After we had filled our kegs and tanks at the laguna, we ascended a
high ridge for a mile or more, when our guide pointed out to us what he
said was the great church or cathedral at Gran Quivira. It was in an
air line all of thirteen miles distant, and yet we could see it distinctly
with the naked eye. We could have seen it easily when five or six miles
further off, had there been no obstruction to the view; a proof of the remarkable clearness of the atmosphere in this elevated region.

So still another day has passed away, and the ruins are not yet reached.
Quivira would seem always to have been a difficult place to arrive at.
We find in Castaneda's history of the expedition into this country made
by Francisco Vasquez de Coronado, in 1540, '41, and '42, that that general
was forty-eight days in hunting for it, starting from some point between
the Rio Grande and the Gila River.

All the way from Albuquerque we have asked the people of the country where the ruins were situated? How they looked? Who built them?
&c., &c. To all these questions we could seldom get a more definite reply
than *Quien sabe?* It seemed as if the genii who, in the Eastern tale at
least, are said to guard the depositories of great treasures, were determined to make the existence of such a place as Gran Quivira as much
of a problem to us as to the Mexicans themselves.

We had seen, before the fog set in, an edifice in the distance, which
had seemed to move away as we approached it, like the weird lakes of
water in a mirage. But to-morrow, at all events, will decide for us whether
that edifice be a Fata Morgana or not.

December 21

Soon after we left camp we again saw the cathedral of Gran Quivira;
but in surmounting one eminence after another as we moved along over
a rolling country, the ruins, phantom like, seemed to recede before us
the same as yesterday. When we first saw them this morning they appeared to be about a mile and a half distant, when in reality they were
more than five miles off.

The horses sank more than fetlock-deep into the soft yielding sand;
while it was with great difficulty that the mules, at a snail's pace, drew
the wagons along.

At eleven o'clock in the forenoon we came to the last high ridge on the point of which the ruins are situated.

We all felt rejoiced that finally we had reached a place about which so much had been written, and yet so little had really been known.

We found the ruins of Gran Quivira to consist of the remains of a large church, or cathedral, with a monastery attached to it; a smaller church or chapel; and the ruins of a town.

The remains of the town are but heaps of stones, where here and there are some evidences of narrow streets. Through these stones, pieces of beams and sticks of wood are seen to project; these indicate, by moss and otherwise, that they are of very great antiquity; they are bleached white by the weather, and are deeply gnawed by the tooth of time.

We saw some deep pits, which were circular, and walled around like wells; we believe them to be the remains of cisterns—they were not deep enough for wells; some have concluded that they were *estufas* [stoves]. Two hundred and ninety feet north of the cathedral there are evident traces of an *estanque* to collect the rain-water which ran from the different buildings.

Toward the east we saw a well defined road, which kept the ridge for a few hundred yards, and then turned off toward the southeast, where all further vestiges of it are lost in the sand.

In every direction about the ruins we found great quantities of broken pottery, many specimens of which we have collected to take to Albuquerque. Some of it is handsomely marked and well glazed. We also found several stones which were evidently once used as *matates*. These *matates* are in use to this day, to rub boiled corn upon until it becomes a kind of dough, suitable to be kneaded into cakes called *tortillas*.

We have selected two which we shall take home with us. These prove to us that the ancient inhabitants of Gran Quivira knew the use of corn as an article of food.

There is no sign that the ground in the vicinity has ever been cultivated, and no mark whatever of irrigating ditches. Indeed, an *acequia*, or open aqueduct could not, it is believed, have brought water to the Gran Quivira, for the point occupied by the town appears to be considerably higher than the surrounding country.

Mr. Gregg [Josiah Gregg, historian of the West] in speaking of the ancient ruins of New Mexico, says:

"The most remarkable of these are *La Gran Quivira*. This appears to have been a considerable city, larger and richer by far than the capital of New Mexico has ever been. Many walls, particularly those of churches, still stand erect amid the desolation that surrounds them, as if their sacredness had been a shield against which time dealt his blows in vain.

"The style of architecture is altogether superior to any thing at present to be found in New Mexico. What is more extraordinary still is, that there is no water within less than ten miles of the ruins; yet we find several stone cisterns, and remains of aqueducts, eight or ten miles in length, leading from the neighboring mountains, from whence water was no doubt conveyed. And as there seem to be no indications whatever of the inhabitants having ever been engaged in agricultural pursuits, what could have induced the rearing of a city in such an arid woodless plain as this, except the proximity of some valuable mine, it is difficult to imagine.

"From the peculiar character of the place, and the remains of cisterns still existing, the object of pursuit, in this case, would seem to have been a *placer*—a name applied to mines of gold dust intermingled with the earth. Other mines have, no doubt, been worked in the adjacent mountains, as many spacious pits are found, such as are usually dug in pursuit of ores of silver; and it is stated that in several places heaps of scoriae are found.

"By some persons these ruins have been supposed to be the remains of an ancient pueblo, or aboriginal city. This is not probable; for though the relics of aboriginal temples might possibly be mistaken for those of Catholic churches, yet it is not presumed that the Spanish coat of arms would be found sculptured and painted upon their facades, as is the case in more than one instance. The most rational accounts represent this to have been a wealthy Spanish city, before the general massacre of 1680, in which calamity the inhabitants perished,—all except one, as the story goes,—and that their immense treasures were buried in the ruins.

"Some credulous adventurers have lately visited the spot in search of these long-lost coffers, but as yet (1845) none have been found."

There is no indication that the escutcheon of Spain was ever sculptured or painted on any facade about the ruins; and the facts, as regards the style of architecture and the remains of an aqueduct, do not agree with his statement.

Mr. Gregg must have described the appearance of this place from what he heard about it; for on all those subjects of which he wrote from personal observation he is most excellent authority.

General Vasquez de Coronado arrived in a country which was called *Quivira,* in the month of June, 1542. If the present ruins of the Gran

Quivira are in a region identical with the Quivira then visited, it may be
of interest to state what Castaneda says of its inhabitants:

> "Up to that point the whole country is only one plain; at
> Quivira, mountains begin to be perceived. From what was seen, it
> appears to be a well peopled country. The plants and fruits greatly
> resemble those of Spain: plums, grapes, nuts, mulberries, rye, grass,
> oats, pennyroyal, origanum, and flax, which the natives do not culti-
> vate, because they do not understand the use of it. Their manners
> and customs are those of the Teyas: and the villages resemble those
> of New Spain. The houses are round, and have no walls; the stories
> are like lofts; the roofs are of straw.
> "The inhabitants sleep under the roofs; and there they keep what
> they possess."

The manners and customs of the Teyas, to which he likens those of the
people of Quivira, are described as follows:

> "These natives are called Querechos and Teyas. They live under
> tents of buffalo skins tanned, and subsist by the chase of these ani-
> mals. These nomadic Indians are braver than those of the villages;
> they are taller, and more inured to war.
> "These Indians live on raw meat, and drink blood; but they do
> not eat human flesh. Far from being evil, they are very gentle, and
> very faithful in their friendships. They can make themselves very
> well understood by signs."

The present ruins are not the remains of the round houses with roofs
of straw, which Castaneda describes as the dwellings of the inhabitants
of Quivira, three hundred and twelve years ago.

Besides, the *matates* we have found are almost positive proof that the
people who once resided here ate as food tortillas made of corn; while,
from Castaneda's account, one is obliged to believe that the inhabitants
of the country which he calls Quivira lived entirely upon the flesh of the
buffalo, as the Comanches do at the present day.

Many have supposed that the ancient Aztecs built the edifices at Gran
Quivira, Abo and Quarra, during their migration from Aztlan toward Ana-
huac; and that the ruins now found in the Navajo country, and the *Casas
Grandes* which are still to be seen along the Gila river, were built by the
same people and at about the same period of time.

It has been shown that in 1542 there were no buildings of the size and
character of Casas Grandes, or such as are found here now, in all the
country called Quivira, which Castaneda visited and described. So one
must conclude that, so far as the Aztecs are concerned, whatever they

may have had to do with the building of the edifices either in the Navajo
country, or on the Gila, or those 250 miles northwest of Chihuahua, they
never planned or constructed those of Gran Quivira.

History represents that Vasquez de Coronado, finding no gold during
his great expedition, returned to Mexico, where he fell into disgrace and
died in obscurity.

The Spaniards did not return to colonize the province of N. M. until
the year 1581; and the country could not be considered as conquered
until 1595. For eighty-five years after this the colony seems to have prospered and to have grown in power. Towns and villages were built, and
valuable mines of gold and silver were found and worked with success.

It was during this time, doubtless, that the large edifices at Abo, Quarra,
and Gran Quivira were erected. It is more than probable that valuable
mines of the precious metals were found in their vicinity, and worked
under the direction of the Spaniards by the Indians who had been sub-
jugated; for there is every reason to believe that the mountains east of the
Rio Grande are at this day rich in gold and silver.

It appears that during these eighty-five years the Spaniards treated the
Indians with the most cruel oppression, until finally the latter revolted
against them. The night of the 13th of August, 1680, was the time set
throughout all New Mexico, when the Indians should rise and make an
indiscriminate massacre of all the Spaniards in the country. This plot was
made known to Don Antonio de Otermin, then the governor and military
commandant of the province, by two Indian chiefs. Every effort was made
for defence and to avert the coming storm, but without success. The Indians rose as agreed upon: after various conflicts, they destroyed great
numbers of the inhabitants; and finally, by the latter end of September of
that year, succeeded in driving all the rest, with Governor Otermin included, to El Paso del Norte, entirely beyond the confines of the territory.

We have been informed that there is now a tradition amongst the Indians, that as soon as their forefathers had become successful in expelling
the Spaniards, they filled up and concealed all traces of the mines where
they had toiled and suffered for so many years; declaring the penalty to
be torture and death to any one who should again make known their
locality.

Old Mr. Chavis who overtook us soon after our arrival at Gran Quivira, informed Major Carleton that he had been told, when in his youth,
by very old people, that a tribe of Indians once lived here called the
Pueblas of Quivira; that the Spanish priests came and lived amongst
them, in peace and security, for twenty years; that during this period
these large churches were erected; and that at the time of the great mas-

sacre there were seventy priests and monks residing here—all of whom were butchered excepting two, who contrived to make their escape; that, previous to their massacre, the priests had intimation of the approaching danger, and had not only buried the immense treasures which had been collected, but had concealed likewise the bells of the churches; that many years afterwards the people of Quivira died off until few remained; that one of these, a descendant of the chief, knew where the treasures were buried; that the remnant of the tribe afterwards emigrated and joined other Pueblas below El Paso; and that many years ago an old man, one of the last of the tribe, had told in what direction from the church these great treasures had been concealed.

So far as the building of the churches and the massacre of the monks and priests are concerned in this account, as well as the final decrease and removal of the people who once lived here, there is no doubt but the story told by Mr. Chavis is, in the main, correct.

The account of the depositories of the bells and the treasure is said to have been written down as given from the lips of the last cacique [chieftain] of Quivira, who, at the time he made the disclosure, was living away below Mesilla, on the Mexican side of the river.

A copy of this paper has been secured, and is here inserted in the original language, for the benefit of those who may take an interest in such matters.

The insertion referred to: "In the cemetery of the great parish church, in the centre of the right side, there is a pit, and by digging will be found two bells. By taking the line of the opening left by the two bells, there will be seen to the east, along the lane left by the old church and the town, a hill, at the distance of three hundred yards, more or less, which forms precisely a line with the bells. At the foot of said hill is a cellar of ten yards or more, covered with stones, which contains the great treasure. Mentioned by Charles Fifth of Gran Quivira."

The grammar of this document is preserved as in the original. There can be no doubt but the belief that a large amount of gold and silver has been buried here, has for a great number of years been seriously entertained.

We find in the cathedral and in the chapel, in every room in the monastery, in every mound of stones in the neighborhood, and in every direction about the ruins, large holes dug, in many places to the depth of ten feet, by those who have come from time to time to seek for these hidden treasures.

Some of these holes look as if they were made more than a century ago, while others appear to be quite recent. Even the ashes of the dead have not been left undisturbed during these explorations. Near the east end of the chapel we saw where the people who had been digging had thrown up a great many human bones, which now lie scattered about.

From there we have selected six skulls to send to some one who is skilled in the science of craniology, that he may determine, if possible, to what race of people they once belonged. These skulls are thought to be unusually large.

The ruins of Gran Quivira have hitherto occupied the same position with respect to the boundless prairies which the fabulous island of Atlantis did to the ocean in days of antiquity. No one seemed to know exactly where this city was situated.

Men of genius and distinction have taken great pains in following up mazes in the labyrinth of reports concerning it, whether oral or written, and in their glowing descriptions it has appeared almost like a city of enchantment.

Historical societies had taken up these descriptions, and filed them away among their transactions as documents of deep interest. Venerable and learned ethnologists searched in dusty manuscripts and black-letter volumes of antiquity for some authentic account of that race of men who reared and then abandoned such a city.

But to this moment their researches have proved fruitless.

December 24

This morning, before we left camp, an old Mexican brought us some ore, which he said is to be found in great abundance near the Tetilla Peaks, but that is now covered so deeply in the snow as to be difficult to be procured.

We believe the specimen he gave us contains silver. When the snow has melted, it will be worth the trouble, perhaps, to explore these mountains thoroughly, with a view to the discovery of precious metals.

1853: A PIONEER WOMAN'S BUSY TRIP
TO THE NORTHWEST

FIVE YEARS AFTER *Lewis and Clark had found their way overland to Oregon, John Jacob Astor was in on the ground floor of the northwest fur business with a trading post which he called Astoria at the mouth of the Columbia River. He sold out in 1813 to the British.*

The Hudson's Bay Company wanted no American settlers coming in to civilize its enormously profitable game preserve in Oregon, but it soon learned that Methodist missionaries would go where Wall Street tycoons feared to tread. In the 1830s Jason and Daniel Lee established missions in the Willamette Valley; and in 1838, when Jason came east to raise money for the good work, his talk of the lush, untapped valley found eager listeners wherever he went.

In 1842, Elijah White, a missionary who had turned real estate operator, led the first immigrant train over the Oregon Trail. The next year the "Great Migration" brought 900 persons to the way point on the Columbia River known as The Dalles. The land route from there to the destination at the mouth of the Willamette led over the Cascade Mountains, and this was the roughest stretch of the whole 2,000 miles from Independence. The Great Migration went to pieces in that ordeal, some of its members losing their lives in an effort to make the river passage on rafts, others in trying to build a wagon road over the mountains. Many were rescued by the Hudson's Bay Company.

But none of this could stop the talk of Oregon back in the States, nor the stream of humanity that had been set in motion over that incredibly difficult route through the northwest wilds. Three thousand persons hit the trail in 1845. Seeking an easier way by crossing central Oregon, one large group fell into panic and starvation. There were 75 deaths. But the people kept coming.

In 1850, with the signing of the Webster-Ashburton Treaty, America and England ended their long dispute over boundary lines, which had made "Fifty-four forty or fight" a campaign slogan in the election of Polk. At the same time Congress passed the "Donation Land Act" which held out the bait of free acreage to settlers in the Territory. Eight thousand claims were registered. Traffic on the Oregon Trail steadily increased.

But free land at the end of that long road did not make the getting there any less rugged. Who were these people with the courage—or was it foolhardiness—to make such a grueling trek?

One of them was Amelia Knight, and her diary preserves to us a sample of the pioneer character at its best. Joel Knight came over from England in 1825 at the age of 17, went to Boston to study medicine in 1834, and married Amelia Stewart. Three years later the Knights went with a five-month-old child to live in Iowa. They remained there sixteen years, brought six more little ones into Knighthood, then hit the Oregon Trail with the whole lot of them. Amelia tells the story of her trip—with an ending worthy of O. Henry.

"Oh, Oregon, you must be wonderful!"
AMELIA STEWART KNIGHT

April 9th [1853]

Started from home about 11 o'clock and traveled 8 miles and camped in an old house; night cold and frosty.

11th

Rains all the afternoon and all night, very unpleasant. Jefferson and Lucy have the mumps. Poor cattle bawled all night.

14th

Sixteen wagons all getting ready to cross the creek. Hurrah and bustle to get breakfast over. Feed the cattle. Harrah boys, all ready, we will be the first to cross the creek this morning. Gee up, Tip and Tyler, and away we go, the sun just rising.

Evening—We have traveled 24 miles today altogether and are about to camp in a large prairie without wood. Cool and chilly; east wind. The men have pitched the tent and are hunting something to make a fire to get supper. I have the sick headache and must leave to boys to get it themselves the best they can.

16th

Camped last night three miles east of Chariton Point in the prairie. Made our beds down in the tent in the wet and mud. Bed clothes nearly spoiled. Cold and cloudy this morning, and every body out of humor. Seneca [a son, 15] is half sick. Plutarch [another son, 17] has broke his saddle girth. Husband is scolding and hurrying all hands (and the cook), and Almira [daughter, 5] says she wished she was home, and I say ditto. "Home, sweet Home."

18th

Evening—Have crossed several bad streams today, and more than once have been stuck in the mud.

20th

Cloudy. We are creeping along slowly, one wagon after another, the same old gait; and the same thing over, out of one mudhole into another all day.

22nd

Still bad weather; no sun; traveling on, mile after mile, in the mud, mud.

23rd

All the tents were blown down, and some wagons capsized.

Evening—It has been raining hard all day; everything is wet and muddy. One of the oxen missing; the boys have been hunting him all day. Dreary times, wet and muddy, and crowded in the tent, cold and wet and uncomfortable in the wagon. No place for the poor children.

24th

Found the ox, and lost our muley cow.

25th

On our way again, at last, found our cow with a young calf; had to leave the calf behind.

27th

Paid two dollars 40 cts. for crossing a bridge.

29th

Cool and pleasant; saw the first Indians today. Lucy [daughter, 8] and Almira afraid and run into the wagon to hide.

May 2nd

Indians came to our camp every day, begging money and something to eat. Children are getting used to them.

5th

We crossed the river this morning on a large steam boat called the *Hindoo,* after a great deal of hurrahing and trouble to get the cattle all aboard. One ox jumped overboard and swam across the river, and came out like a drowned rat. The river is even with its banks, timber on it, which is mostly cottonwood, is quite green. Costs us 15 dollars to cross.

We here join another company, which will make in all 24 men, 10 wagons, and a large drove of cattle. Four men watch 2 hours and then call up four more to take their places, so by that means no person can sleep about the camp.

Such a wild, noisy set was never heard.

11th

The men all have their false eyes on to keep the dust out.

13th

Got breakfast over after a fashion. Sand all around ankle deep; wind blowing; no matter, hurry it over. Them that eat the most breakfast eat the most sand.

14th

Wind so high that we dare not make a fire, impossible to pitch the tent, the wagons could hardly stand the wind. All that find room are crowded into the wagons; those that can't, have to stay out in the storm. Some of the boys have lost their hats.

16th

Hard times, but they say misery loves company. We are not alone on these bare plains, it is covered with cattle and wagons.

17th

We had a dreadful storm of rain and hail last night and very sharp lightning. It killed two oxen for one man. We have just encamped on a large flat prairie, when the storm commenced in all its fury and in two minutes after the cattle were taken from the wagons every brute was gone out of sight, cows, calves, horses, all gone before the storm like so many wild beasts. I never saw such a storm.

19th

Crossed Dry Creek this morning and have traveled 10 miles and came to Wood Creek, and are up a stump again; it is also very high and we will have to cross it as we did Elkhorn, in a wagon bed, and swim the stock. Just got things packed away nicely this morning, now they must all be tumbled out again.

24th

Stay in camp today, to wash and cook, as we have a good camping ground, plenty of wood and water, and good grass. Weather pleasant. I had the sick headache all night, some better this morning; must do a day's work. Husband went back a piece this morning in search of our dog, which he found with some rascals who were trying to keep him.

May 31st

Evening—Traveled 25 miles today. When we started this morning there were two large droves of cattle and about 50 wagons ahead of us, and we either had to stay poking behind them in the dust or hurry up and drive past them. It was no fool of a job to be mixed up with several hundred head of cattle, and only one road to travel in, and the drovers threatening to drive their cattle over you if you attempted to pass them.

They even took out their pistols. Husband came up just as one man held his pistol at Wilson Carl and saw what the fuss was and said, "Boys, follow me," and he drove our team out of the road entirely, and the cattle seemed to understand it all, for they went into the trot most of the way. The rest of the boys followed with their teams and the rest of the stock. I had rather a rough ride, to be sure, but was glad to get away from such a lawless set.

June 1st

The men and boys are all soaking wet and look sad and comfortless. The little ones and myself are shut up in the wagons from the rain. Still it will find its way in and many things are wet; and take us all together we are a poor looking set, and all this for Oregon. I am thinking while I write, "Oh, Oregon, you must be a wonderful country." Came 18 miles today.

7th

Just passed Fort Laramie, situated on the opposite side of the river. This afternoon we passed a large village of Sioux Indians. Numbers of them came around our wagons. Some of the women had moccasins and beads, which they wanted to trade for bread.

I gave the women and children all the cakes I had baked. Husband traded a big Indian a lot of hard crackers for a pair of moccasins and after we had started on he came up with us again, making a great fuss, and wanted them back (they had eaten part of the crackers). He did not seem to be satisfied, or else he wished to cause us some trouble, or perhaps get into a fight. However, we handed the moccasins to him in a hurry and drove away from them as soon as possible. Several lingered along, watching our horses that were tied behind the wagons, no doubt with the view of stealing them, but our folks kept a sharp lookout till they left.

8th

We are traveling through the Black Hills, over rocks and stones. There is some splendid scenery here. Beautiful valleys and dark, green clad hills with their ledges of rock.

11th

Not a drop of water, nor a spear of grass to be seen, nothing but barren hills, bare broken rock, sand and dust.

16th

We are now traveling up Sweetwater Valley between two mountains, one of them being covered with snow.

21st

Husband brought me a large bucket of snow and one of our hands brought me a beautiful bunch of flowers.

24th

Henry Miller left us this morning. We started with 5 hands and have only two left.

26th

We are on our way again traveling in the dust, dust. We must go 17 miles or more without water or grass.

Evening—All hands come into camp tired and out of heart. Husband and myself sick. No feed for the stock. One ox lame. Camp on the bank of Big Sandy.

27th

It is all hurry and bustle to get things in order. It's children milk the cows, all hands help yoke these cattle, the d———l's in them. Plutarch answers, "I can't, I must hold the tent up, it is blowing away." Hurrah, boys. Who tied these horses? "Seneca, don't stand there with your hands in your pockets. Get your saddles and be ready."

Evening—Traveled 18 miles today and have camped on the bank of Green River and must wait our turn to cross on a ferry boat. No grass for the poor cattle. All hands discouraged. We have taken in two new hands today, which will make us full handed again.

28th

As far as the eye can reach it is nothing but a sandy desert and the road is strewn with dead cattle, and the stench is awful. All along this road we see white men living with Indians; many of them have trading posts; they are mostly French and have squaw wives.

July 3rd

Bad luck this morning. Soon after starting one of our best oxen took sick, and in less than an hour he was dead. Suppose he was poisoned with alkali water or weeds.

4th

Chat [her two-year-old son] has been sick all day with fever, partly caused by mosquito bites.

6th

Traded a cow and a calf today for a steer to yoke up with the odd one.

And find after using him half a day that we have been cheated as he can't stand it to travel.

7th

Our poor dog gave out with the heat and sand so that he could not travel. The boys have gone back after him.

9th

We passed the forks of the emigrants' road yesterday noon, after leaving the California road [at Fort Hall, Idaho]. We find the grass much better, as most of the large trains are bound for California.

13th

We have just been spending an hour at the American Falls on Snake River. There are several falls on this river. The river is wide and deep, and very swift in places. We should cross it, and keep down on the other side, but there is no ferry boat, and we have no way to cross it, therefore we must keep down on this (south) side, with very little grass, while on the other there is plenty. Travel 22 miles and camp.

14th

As far as the eye can reach it is nothing but a sandy desert, covered with wild sage brush, dried up with heat; however, it makes good firewood.

15th

Last night I helped get supper and went to bed too sick to eat any myself. Had fever all night and all day. It is sundown and the fever has left me. I am able to creep around and look at things and brighten up a little.

17th

We crossed Swamp Creek this morning, and Goose Creek this afternoon. Goose Creek is almost straight down, and then straight up again. Several things pitched out of the wagons into the Creek. Travel over some very rocky ground. Here Chat fell out of the wagon, but did not get hurt much.

18th

Rock Creek. It is here the Indians are so troublesome. I was very much frightened while at this camp. I lay awake all night. I expected every minute we would be killed. However, we all found our scalps on in the morning.

22nd

Here Chat had a very narrow escape from being run over. Just as we were all getting ready to start, Chatfield, the rascal, came around the forward wheel to get into the wagon, and at that moment the cattle started and he fell under the wagon. Somehow, he kept from under the wheels, and escaped with only a good, or I should say, a bad scare. I never was so much frightened in my life.

23rd

Travel about 5 miles and here we are, up a stump again, with a worse place than we ever had before us to be crossed, called Bridge Creek. I presume it takes its name from a natural bridge which crosses it. This bridge is only wide enough to admit one person at a time. A frightful place, with the water roaring and tumbling ten or fifteen feet below it.

Here we have to unload all the wagons and pack everything across by hand, and then we are only on an island. There is a worse place to cross yet, a branch of the same. Have to stay on the island all night, and wait our turn to cross. There are a good many camped on the island.

25th

We have got on to a place that is full of rattlesnakes.

27th

Came 15 miles today, and have camped at the boiling springs, a great curiosity. I felt as if I was in the bad place. I still believe it was not very far off.

28th

Chat is quite sick with scarlet fever.

29th

Came 18 miles over some very rocky road and camped by a spring. Chat is some better.

August 1st

This evening another of our best milk cows died. Cattle are dying off very fast all along this road. We are hardly ever out of sight of dead cattle on this side of Snake River. This cow was well and fat an hour before she died.

5th

Fort Boise is nothing more than three new buildings, its inhabitants, the Hudson's Bay Company officials, a few Frenchmen, some half-naked Indians.

8th

Here we left, unknowingly, our Lucy behind, not a soul had missed her until we had gone some miles, when we stopped a while to rest the cattle; just then another train drove up behind us, with Lucy. She was terribly frightened and so were some more of us when we found out what a narrow escape she had run.

11th

Frost this morning. Three of our hands got discontented and left this morning, to pack through. I am pleased, as we shall get along just as well without them and I shall have three less to wait on.

12th

Lost one of our oxen. We were traveling slowly along, when he dropped dead in the yoke. I could hardly help shedding tears, when we drove round this poor ox who had helped us along thus far, and had given us his very last step.

We have camped on a branch of Burnt River.

14th

After traveling 10 miles we have camped on the bank of Powder River.

17th

Lucy and Myra have their feet and legs poisoned, which gives me a good deal of trouble. Bought some fresh salmon of the Indians this evening, which is quite a treat to us.

18th

Commenced the ascent of the Blue Mountains. It is a lovely morning and all hands seem to be delighted with the prospect of being so near the timber again, after the weary months of travel on the dry, dusty sage plains. Just now the men are hallooing to their echo through the woods.

22nd

We are now traveling on the Nez Perce plains. Warm weather and very dusty. Grass all dead, but the stock eat it greedily. For fuel, willows and some little sage brush.

26th

Came 6 miles tonight and 12 today, and have just reached a small spring, where we can only water one ox at a time, by dipping up buckets full.

31st

Split up some of the deck boards of our wagons to make fire.

September 1st

After traveling 11 miles and descending a long hill, we have encamped not far from the Columbia River.

3rd

Here husband (being run out of money) sold his sorrel mare (Fan) for a hundred and twenty-five dollars.

4th

Had a fine view of Mount Hood.

5th

Ascended a long steep hill this morning, which was very hard on the cattle, and also on myself, as I thought I never should get to the top, although I rested two or three times.

6th

Camped near the gate or foot of the Cascade Mountains (here I was sick all night, caused by my washing and working too hard).

8th

Traveled 14 miles over the worst road that was ever made, up and down, very steep, rough and rocky hills, through mud holes, twisting and winding round stumps, logs and fallen trees. Now we are on the end of a log, now over a big root of a tree; now bounced down in a mud hole, then bang goes the other side of the wagon, and woe be to whatever is inside.

9th

We hear the road is still worse ahead. There is no end to the wagons, buggies, yokes, chains, etc., that are lying all along this road. Some splendid good wagons just left standing, perhaps with the owners names on them.

10th

It would be useless for me with my pencil to describe the awful road we have just passed over. We kept as near the road as we could, winding round the fallen timber and brush, climbing over logs, creeping under fallen timber, sometimes lifting and carrying Chat. To keep from smelling the carrion, I, as others, holding my nose.

13th

We are in Oregon, making our camp in an ugly bottom, with no home except our wagons and tent.

15th

I was sick all night.

[No date]

A few days later my eighth child was born.

1854: RIDING HERD ON THE TEXAS LONGHORNS

CALIFORNIA GOLD pushed America around and jogged up the economy in strange ways and far corners. One of the ways was to set a 1500-mile cattle drive going from Texas to the Pacific. None but the tough, stringy, free-stepping longhorns of Texas could have made it over that trail from San Antonio with its wide, thirsty deserts, its alkali holes, its stony ridges. For twenty years it was thought worth while to gamble on the longhorns getting there and fetching a good price. Then, suddenly, it wasn't; and a colorful page of trail history was turned and the story ended forever.

If the critters were tough, so were the men who rode herd on them. One of the very few records of this unique traffic is the diary kept by 22-year-old James G. Bell, who, like many others, hit the trail with the longhorns in order to earn his way west.

Tracking down a stray manuscript sometimes takes an editor on a longer trail than the one James Bell hit. Knowing of the existence of this diary, Editor J. Evetts Haley finally traced it in 1930 to a nephew of the diarist, Ned C. Bell —on the little island of Aruba in the Dutch East Indies.

"It will be a loosing business . . ."
JAMES G. BELL (born 1832)

June 3 [1854]

Left San Antonio at 9 o'clock P.M. Rode 10 miles, encamped near some Mexican carts, in company with Mr. John James on our route to California. Lost my mule by carelessness, let every pararie traveler make the safety of his mule of the first importance.

6

Travelled about 9 miles, came up in front and found an hombre skinning 3 rattlesnakes. When I enquired the use he would put the skins to, he told me that by stretching the skin on the cantle of the saddle no harm would come to my posteriors I.E. no Gall or sore.

Evening, killed a beef being in want of fresh meat,—it would astonish a regular bred butcher to see with what dispatch 3 Mexicans can rope, kill, and have a beef cut into *ropes*. The beef is first thrown down by means of rope then stuck, not struck on the head. The head is turned to one side which holds the beef in the proper position, one side is skined, the skined side is allowed to turn up—half of the beef is dissected, the entrails then taken out, the ribs are left whole and roasted before the fire, the other half and head is made into ropes and exposed on a line in the sun until jerked.

11

We have been on the road one week; riding on a mule, with her easy swinging gait make me verry drowsey.

12

There were some Lipan Indians in camp begging for *carna*. They are miserably poor and only the shadow of their former greatness, but still endeavor to keep up appearances by painting their faces various colours.

14

An order has just been isued in camp that a gunshot is an alarm for Indians.

16

One of the men disobeyed orders in leaving the Train to shoot at some game. Mr. James ordered his horse on and the poor fellow had to run a mile to catch up.

17

Fine weather for travelling, found wild sage growing about 3 to 4 feet high. Passed 2 heaps of stones. 4 men were burried under one.

18

There are three men in camp 1 Mexican 1 American and 1 German who are perfectly worthless and it would be a God send if the indians would kill them.

We have crossed Rio Diablo seven times this morning, twice where it was dry, the water sinking, and when up running over the dry beds. The ground is entirely covered with cobble stones and is hard on cattle's feet.

There is a fine spring in the neighborhood, plenty of fish, but the worst of it is that I never catch anything.

19

Come to a Government post, do not know the name.

The whole party are in doubt as to whether to-day is Sunday or Monday. Went to the spring for water passed the post and inquired the day of the week. Found it is Monday.

The men are busily engaged loafing about the camp.

21

Having been in camp about two days, resting the cattle for a forty mile travel without water, we left camp about four o'clock. Travelled 12 miles to camp, found no water.

22

Found about 10 barrels water scattered around in pockets. This gave the cattle a mouth washing each. Made 30 miles.

24

In Rio Diablo cannon for 10 days, got out this evening. Mountain scenery the same—entirely surrounded with broken mountains where if a man should get lost he should at once come to the conclusion to die with thirst or be killed by the Indians.

25

After about ten miles we entered the cannon again—passed thro' a large [prairie] dog town, about four miles in circumference. The grass is croped close around the town; a number of the inhabitants poped their heads just above the edge of the holes, bark a few times and disappear. Several were killed. When cooked their meat resembles squirrel meat; the claws are sharp, and always uncovered for the purpose of digging; the tail like a dog, hair between a Gray and Fox squirrel; the head resembles the Chewawah dog with his ears cropped, are about the size of a grown fox squirrel.

There is a fall of six feet in Live Oak Creek, several of us are going bathing now—returning I found an oblong pile of stones. At one end found the inscription Amanda Lewis, 1852. I read it aloud when one of the young men present spoke with astonishment. He was acquainted with the persons in Mississippi. She was a mother of a large family; how desolate must have been the husband and children when they performed the last sad rights over their loved mother.

In this vast expanse of hill and plane when by mere chance I came upon this grave, a feeling of desolation and insignificance came over me.

26

The sun is rising clear and grateful.

Come seven miles to the crossing of the Pecos Rio [near what is now Sheffield, Texas]. Our cook got sick and I helped get supper, we live verry poor, cooking bad and very little to cook. Some men who, when living in town appear to have a good deal of nobleness, are entirely different under different circumstances.

30

Have just washed my face—the first time in two days, forget when I combed my head last, about once a week is quite a luxury.

I intend to school myself to bear the yoke of patience and meekness, for when I arrive in California it will be a Herculanean task for me to attempt to fight every one who will call me *Boy!*

Seen more Horned Frogs today than before; I had a verry pretty little fellow to send Peg, but had no convenience of carrying, and lost it.

I feel very well this evening, about as well as could be expected of a man who is on this trip for it is rough and no mistake.

July 2

The bones of a man was found, the guide was acquainted with the man; on the knee cap & foot the muscels still remain, although it has been three years since he was killed, some of the clothing is laying about. The man was a notorious horse thief.

There is a cattle train about five miles in advance of us. The only sign we had of their presence was the clouds of dust.

3

Probably you would like to have some idea of my manner of sleeping, personal appearance &c.—ants in my boots, both boots and pants begin to have rather a shocking bad appearance for after eating (having left my handercheifs at home)—I use the pants for wiping my knife & hands on; in riding the bosom of my check shirt works open, and along down the center of my breast is a brown stripe. My nose and ears and neck are undergoing the scaling prosses untill I look as scaly about the face and gills as a buffalow fish. My riding outfit consists of—on either side of the horn is a rope and canteen, behind the cantle is my tin cup and iron spoon, while occasionally there is to be found a dead rabbit hung by the neck waiting to be devoured. And when we expect to travel over dinner time, a slab of jerked beef finds itself flaping against the side of the mule.

My bed is made with the Indian rubber coat next the ground, saddle at the head, horse blanket on the saddle to make it soft, bed blanket over all, and myself on top of that; sometimes to luxuriate a little I pull off my boots and hat.

5

By the by, on the fourth I eat a peice of prairie dog. They are better than the Jackass Rabbitt, the name might not suit some, but I don't mind such little things.

There are more than 1,000 head of cattle and horses in the cannon and I cannot see over ½ a dozen. Such is the deceptiveness of these pockets.

7

None but a poet could appreciate this evening; the rising moon, the setting sun, the calm sensation, the clear sky and smooth verdant prairie. Makes any one who has "music in the soul" wish to be a Painter.

8

Mr. James and myself went to a point on the mountain to watch for a signal within one hour to sun set. About the time stated a light smoke assended from a mountain twenty miles distant. This was the signal for water. We answered by a similar smoke, so the men could tell at what time we would start and arrive.

10

I must here say that most of this journal was written in the hury and bustle of arrival or departure in or from camp, and must nessesarily be imperfect.

We will probably commence our 80 mile trip [without water] tonight, have indifferent water here. We may get through in 3 days.

11

Found water earlier than we expected. Were from 10 o'clock untill dark watering the cattle. It was tiresome business indeed; but sound sleep and good appetite came from it. In the evening had a prospect of a rain. The smell of the air combined with thunder, while we were up in the mountains, made every one hope that the rain was not far distant, but we were doomed to disappointment; these mountain signs all fail as far as rain is concerned.

12

Today opens fairly, we commenced watering the cattle directly, left camp. 16 men were sent forward, myself among the rest. We took about 550 head of cattle, designing to go immediately on to the Rio Grande; water being scarce trains are obliged to push forward.

13

12 o'clock. We had first meal, being without food,—except dry bread— some 18 hours; when we examined the provisions, found everything contrary to what was ordered. The cook previous to leaving our carts behind did not prepare any coffee, bread, salt, pepper; you may guess the cooks would have been in a bad way had they been with us.

Mother look at these leaves how dirty, and you can imagine how *dirty* my hands are. I expect to get on some clean clothes in a few days.

Traveled all night, lost some stock, one ox fought the drivers; although he was not able to travel it was truly dangerous to urge him forward; driving cattle when they are almost perishing for water looks like punishing the animals for amusement, but they are compelled to go forward or die.

14

The mail from San Antonio came in. I expected to receive some way mail, but was disappointed. I certainly shall not be so again, cause why, I will not expect anything.

Mr. James arrived in camp—3 hours ahead of the carts—he seemed verry cool when informed of the loss of 75 head of cattle the night before; the cause was the guard went to sleep, and the cattle broke for the nearest water; instinct learns them where it is, and when verry thirsty they can smell water 5 miles.

Left camp at 4 o'clock, traveled all night, had a verry hard time; being divided, all the men had to drive, and driving is something more than merely urging the animals forward.

Arrived in camp, or rather, near the Rio Grande at day break. The last part of the train came in 3 hours after; lost some animals during the night, some dying and some straying off for water. The majority of dead cattle are nearest the river.

16

Discharged 3 Mexicans this morning, 2 that slept on guard a few nights since and lost seventy-five head of cattle. The other came in, complained of guard duty, and was impudent, and was starving without anything to eat. The other two were furnished with enough to last to El Paso, 80 miles distant.

Have been reviewing this diary, and am almost induced to destroy it. From El Paso to California I will write a better one or none at all.

Franklin and Dean are here without anything to eat; we divided what little we had. The remainder will be used up by tomorrow noon. Then if our waggons do not arrive, we shall be in a bad way.

Two of the best venison were brought into camp this evening I have ever eaten of. I laid hold of one tender loin, spitted it and had the supper of all suppers.

17

This morning our carts, some of the men and 50 head of cattle arrived from Eagle Springs. They came in verry opportunly, for we were entirely out of every thing to eat except venison; the men report the probable loss of several men who went out in search of cattle. Mr. James with about 15 men still remain behind, hunting for cattle.

18

One of the Mexicans whom we discharged two days ago,—came into camp this morning, beging for something to eat. The poor devil was out all night in the storm. We gave him something to eat with a warning to not return or loaf about camp, on the penalty of being whipped out.

The Mexicans, at breakfast were discussing whether they would be considered white people or not in California. One settled the discussion by saying they would be considered negroes.

24

Made ten miles to camp. My canteen is worth five dollars to me, the only thing to regret is that it keeps the water so cool, that everyone runs to me for a drink, consequently when I want a drink my canteen is out.

I did not inquire to what Saint this town is dedicated to but, I imagine it out to be to St. Diablo; for I honestly beleve his Majesty had a hand in laying it out, it was with difficulty we could get through, owing to the crookedness of the streets, the mud puddles and hills. I suppose not one of our men but what left with a curse and blessing on his lips; a curse because we got into it, and a blessing because we got out.

I will continue my Journal when we leave this place.

Closed at Smith rancho, opposite El Paso, July 31, 1854.

August 17 [1854]

Yesterday we crossed the line which divides the U.S. into east and

West; we have rounded cape Horn, over land, or in other words are now in the great dish which slopes to the Pacific; up to this time we have been coming up hill; henceforth will be going down, untill we reach the shore of the Pacific Ocean.

September 23

Our train is very fortunate. We have not seen more than three or four Indians on the whole trip, while almost every other train has been attacked.

24

Still in camp near Teuson, preparing the cattle for the road to Fort Yuma.

28

Went to bed supperless, being unwell, from drinking so much mud and water.

October 2

We are now encamped off the [Gila] river and at the commencement of a *jornado* [a stretch of trail without water] of forty miles.

The Pemos villages extend along the banks of this stream for twelve or fifteen miles.

The women are a beautifully formed race with the exception of the face which is tolerably ugly.

Some few make desperate attempts to improve their facial features by painting and tattooing with various colors.

It is impossible to trade with them to advantage, or even as an accommodation; for instance, two bits is asked for all size melons, and a good cotton shirt will not buy more than one. They seem to have no idea of the value of anything we Americans possess; we bought some Corn and Melans as matter of necessity.

Ever since we struck their town, their presence has been a great annoyance to us, for, beside their begging, they will steal anything that can be carried off, even to scraps of rawhide.

This morning I missed my canteen.

3

Sitting quietly down after supper, a few nights ago, several of us made a calculation of the amount of property lost during the present year, on this route. At reasonable calculations we make out that, three thousand head of cattle at $25 each, $75,000, and enough mules, horses, and other property destroyed to make $25,000 more, making in all $100,000, not very far from the true amount.

The Indians are in possession of ¾ of it.

12

On the road, saw a Cactus twenty feet high, with a hub band around it, one foot from the top, this must have been put on several years ago.

16

Remained in camp all day, while James has gone to the Colorado to make arrangements for crossing his cattle. Erskine's camp is about four miles below; he is in a quandry, whether to swim his cattle or ferry; the price of ferrying is—for cattle—$1.50 per head; Man $2.00, Waggon $8. The ferryman offered that he would deliver him over entire for $1500.

21 [At Fort Yuma, near the junction of the Gila and Colorado rivers]

About fifteen miles brought us to the ferry or within a few miles where we encamped until next morning.

For crossing the entire train it cost about $850.00, one day's work; we made an effort to swim about one hundred head by using a decoy ox, but did not succeed.

The men of the Yuma tribe are remarkable for stature. I have not seen one who was less than six feet high.

The clothing they manage to get hold of is almost indescribable and runs from a common cotton long shirt to a military coat. I noticed one Indian, who seemed particularly proud of his coat, and had endeavored to make an improvement by sewing brass buttons along the seams of the back.

These Yuma women seem conscious of their handsom forms, and when walking give a pecular grace and beauty to their locomotion; the bark hanging down to the knees like fringe, swinging from side to side exposing from the knees down the well-turned leg and ankle and small foot; from the waist upward the fine bust, breasts, indicating their age, the beautiful tapering arms having strength as well as beauty. In fact, their appearance when in motion reminded me very much of the Peacock strutting with his tail spread.

After crossing we encamped and herded on the Western bank; had much difficulty for the cattle were hungry.

After feeding for one or two hours they were driven back to water, preparatory for starting; in half an hour Mr. James came to camp, *ordered all* to make ready for an immediate start, that the cattle were dying, and about forty then dead; in an hour one hundred were dead, others were tumbling about ready to fall and die; such havoc among cattle was never seen; it looked like taking a man's property away at one sweep; James was cool about it, believing in the old saying, "that it was no use to cry."

29

It will be a loosing business for all who have brought cattle this year; at Los Angeles fat beef cattle are worth only from twenty-five to thirty dollars per head.

November 28

While in the Rancheria the other evening, an aged Indian came up and requested something. The interpreter explained what he wanted—Tobacco—and I gave him a small piece; he received it thankfully, invoked a blessing on my head, and informed me that "God would pay for it."

Started early next morning; by 8 o'clock we had made forty miles; very tired, stopped at a Mexican house—a cup of coffee with some bread and beef we brought along, made our supper; slept in the kitchen—after some breakfast next morning early, started for Los Angeles—about forty-five miles. Great many Cattle, horses, & sheep in this valley; the hills look as if vegitation never would spring up again, they are kept so clean by the animals grazing on them.

Arrived in Los Angeles de Pueblo at nine o'clock—found several acquaintances and others from San Antonio.

★

1857: "THE BLACKEST CRIME ON AMERICAN SOIL"

☆

LONG GRASS SWAYED PEACEFULLY, invitingly, in a lonely valley in Utah just east of what is now the Nevada line, a spot called Mountain Meadows by the dwellers of the surrounding Mormon "Kingdom." It was a favorite stopping place for the wagon trains bound for California. But in September 1857, an emigrant party of about 140 persons was betrayed and murdered there, all except a few little children, in what historians of the West have called "the blackest crime ever committed on American soil."

About fifty miles to the eastward was the town of Harmony. Here lived—when he was not with the families of his eighteen other wives in settlements scattered over the southern part of the territory—a powerful leader of the Mormons named John D. Lee. Lee, and Lee alone, was accused, convicted and

executed for the Mountain Meadows Massacre. Ever since then, deeper op-
probrium has been heaped on his name than on that of any other man in the
history of the West.

It is a tale of murder committed in the name of religion, of a travesty on
justice in the name of the law. The Mormons, because they held beliefs that
were strange and extreme in the eyes of other Americans, especially their sanction of polygamy, had been driven out of one community after another—from
New York, from Ohio, Missouri, Illinois. At their city of Nauvoo, which they
built on the east bank of the Mississippi, some 20,000 were settled in 1844
when the founder of the sect, Joseph Smith, and his brother Hyrum were arrested, jailed at Carthage, and lynched. Two years later Brigham Young, Smith's
brilliant successor, decided to lead the whole community on a tremendous
undertaking into the wilderness of the Far West, outside the United States,
there to establish the "Kingdom of Zion."

Early in 1848 thousands gave up their homes in Nauvoo and crossed Iowa to
the Missouri River. Where Omaha is now they stopped for more than a year
to make ready for the long hard trek along the Platte River, through South Pass,
down the Green River and over the Wasatch Mountains to the basin of the
Great Salt Lake.

Lee, who with his wife Agatha Ann had joined the church in Missouri in
1838, was now Brigham Young's "adopted son" and confidant. He took a leading part in the great migration of 1848, helped build the city at Salt Lake, then
went on to colonize southern Utah.

Short but powerfully built, an expert with axe and rifle, and a shrewd and
commanding administrator, he was just the man to serve Young in the enormous enterprise, especially as he hung on every word of his leader as if it were
relayed straight from the Almighty. Lee was a mystic, ever on two-way speaking
terms with God and given to interpretation of his own dreams and visions as
supernatural messages.

He shared with other Mormons a consciousness of martyrdom and an abid-
ing bitterness toward the "Gentiles"—that is, all other Americans—who were
regarded as persecutors of the only true faithful. This resentment rose to fury
when the autonomy and "freedom from persecution" which the Mormons had
struggled so mightily to find in the desert waste proved a vain hope, foredoomed
by the decision of the United States to take over the country from Mexico and
also by the discovery of gold in California.

Congress refused to recognize the "provisional state of Deseret" which a
Mormon convention decreed in 1849. Instead it created the American Territory of Utah the following year, to be governed by American law and if necessary policed by American military force. At the same time, although Salt Lake
was not on the California Trail proper, both the Hastings Cut-off and the Virgin

River Route to San Bernardino led thousands of gold-seeking emigrants straight through the Kingdom. This, as the Mormons saw it, was trespass, and many an ugly clash arose from it.

It was in this atmosphere, charged with defiance of the United States and resentment against the intruding emigrants, that the mass slaughter took place at Mountain Meadows. Charles Kelly, one of the editors of Lee's diary, writes:

> "It had originally been planned to incite the Indians to wipe out the emigrant train, and Lee was ordered by church authorities to assemble the natives from surrounding territory and direct their attack. When the Indians met stubborn resistance and fled, the Mormon militia completed the bloody business, after disarming the emigrants under promises of protection."

In the area the news was suppressed. The dead were left in shallow graves, the wolves and the buzzards quickly did their part, and nobody, to all intents, knew anything.

Two years later the federal authorities issued 36 writs for arrest and sent out a judge and a detail of troops, but not one of the accused men could be found. The Mormons, from the top down, were protecting their own.

Lee admitted having been at the scene of the crime but denied that he had committed any part of it. And through the years he refused to say anything that would implicate Young or the Mormon priesthood. Meanwhile many Mormons were turning against him. The story of treachery and brutality at Mountain Meadows would not die. Young advised him to leave Harmony. Lee moved into the wilds near the Arizona border. Almost immediately afterward he was notified that the Mormon Church had excommunicated him.

This was a crushing blow. Still he refused to turn on Young, or to inform on him. In 1872, to escape arrest, he went further into the wilderness, holing in beside the Colorado River in northern Arizona at a spot which he described as "the loneliest on earth."

Nevertheless, in 1875, eighteen years after the crime, he was arrested on an indictment for murder. A jury of eight Mormons and four others voted eight for acquittal, four against. A second trial was held in September 1876. This time there was an all-Mormon jury, and Lee was sure he would be freed.

His confidence was sadly misplaced. The jury brought in a unanimous verdict of guilty. The only plausible explanation for this was that a deal had been made between the prosecution and the Mormons. Prior to the trial the government had arrested Young. Charles Kelly writes:

> "Knowing it would be impossible to convict Lee with a Mormon jury, the prosecution made an agreement whereby charges against Brigham

Young would be dropped if he [Young] instructed the jury to bring in a verdict of guilty [against Lee]. Lee was promptly convicted."

Lee was an untiring diarist. In 1938 two parts of his diary, edited by Kelly, were printed in a limited edition. In 1955 a two-volume edition of five other parts was published by the Henry E. Huntington Library of San Marino, California. Robert Glass Cleland and Juanita Brooks were the editors. From the manuscript of one of these parts twelve pages—presumably Lee's own account of the Mountain Meadows Massacre—had been torn out and were never found.

After his second trial Lee was freed on bail and allowed to go to his home on the bank of the Colorado River to arrange his affairs. There he wrote a story of the massacre and of how the Mormon priesthood had made him the scapegoat. This paper was given to his daughter, Mrs. Amanda Smithson. Later one of her daughters destroyed it.

The part of Lee's diary that follows was written in 1859, two years after the massacre. The beginning is missing. Where we pick it up—in the midst of a quotation of uncertain origin—Judge John Cradlebaugh and a detail of troops have come into Utah Territory to prosecute Lee, Philip K. Smith, and others.

"I done nothing designedly wrong . . ."
JOHN DOYLE LEE (1812-1877)

[Page 17]

". . . not as easy to scare as you are, and besides I was not in the country when it happened you g———d liars. Dam you, you are all engaged in it." Seeing that they refused to hear reason, he went on his course and told them to kiss his ass; with that the sergeant ordered one of the Indians to shoot him. No sooner said than done, the ball whistling under his ears as he rode off.

After their excitement was over a little they removed their quarters to the foot of the Santa Clara where they are waiting the arrival of Maj. Prince with 200 cavalry, escort and guard to the paymaster who has about one million dollars from California.

Prince's division will then return and guard the 150 teamsters through to Cal. while Judge Cradlebaugh will return to Camp Floyd with the remainder of the troop; but before they return, my scalp they want, let it cost what it may. They say that they would rather arrest me than to have all the Piedes [an Indian tribe], Haight, Bishop Smith and all other criminals, but catching is before hanging and my trust is in God.

May 11

About 10 the Bishop, P.K.S. [Philip Klingen Smith, bishop of Cedar City and one of the church authorities suspected in the massacre] and I concluded to change our quarters. Went into the settlement and got breakfast. I eat at Bro. Barney's. We then got up our animals and bent our course across the mountains up the Leverkins about 12 miles distant from this place and camped by a precipice of limestone rock.

12

We bent our course north up the Leverkin and a distance of 5 mi. we ascended the mountain on the west side. Mountain is rough, rugged and steep, limestone. After I had ascended I found that I had lost two of my revolvers.

About 1 hour after dark I reached the summit almost tired out and famished for water and faint for the want of food. The wind blew like a torrent. I was in my shirt sleeves and my clothes wet with sweat. The change of atmosphere chilled me instantly.

13

By day I was up, found my horse near camp, went to the brow of the mountain, asked the Lord to direct me to the spot where my revolvers were. I saw the spot and went to it, and there they laid about 100 yds. from where I stood. I returned thanks to God and mounted my steed and started in pursuit of my partner, P.K. Smith. Followed his tracks from range to kanyon over the roughest country that I ever traveled over before, and came up with him on Dry Kanyon some 6 mi. east of Harmony. Was much fatigued and worn, done a distance 20 mi. about 4 p.m. Here we encamped for the night.

14

I stood on the summit of the mountain east of Harmony about 12 noon and with my spy-glass looked over the whole valley. Saw some of my family; from this point I could overlook the whole country, from the tops of the mountains down to the base, and a more lovely and beautiful landscape I never saw before; the snow caped mountain on the south with the lofty pines on its summit clothed in their green foliage, gently sloping to the North and North East, tinged with red and blue down to the slopes of the mountain; the vale covered with green vegetation intermingled with shady groves of cedar, presented a romantic though majestic scenery.

My residence and farm appeared more dear and lovely to me than ever;

and above all, that of my family from whose society I was deprived by wicked and corrupt men, for the gospel's sake.

I saw the brethern and my family plowing, planting, hauling pickets, making fence, irrigating, etc., after which I descended into the field un- observed to a brother-in-law, Samuel E. Groves [brother to wife number 15] and sent him to Rachel, my second wife, to bring me some provisions, pen and ink and a pint of spirits; to meet me at the east end of my pasture fence, and let no person know my request save it would be his father, E. H. Groves and Rachel.

In a short time the old man came. Appeared glad to see me, offered his services in anything that he could. He then said that intelligence had lately reached here from G. S. L. C. [Great Salt Lake City] that Gov. Cummings notified Pres. Young to prepare to defend himself against the troops; that the Judge was determined to hold court in S. L. City, and arrest him and his council the 12, and every other man that they wished, and that Gov. Cummings could not control them. That all his efforts thus far in a measure was spurned at and had proved abortive and in vain.

Pres. Young replied that the troops and officials were all in his hands and had been all the while and he by the help of the Lord could have wiped them out of existence long ago, but that he did not wish to shed blood if it could be avoided; but if it must come we can control them and will do it, let them commence, and the first drop of blood or attack they make on any of the settlements or person belonging to this people their blood shall flow to atone for it.

If this report is true it accounts for a dream that I had on the night of the 12th. I saw many of the cities of the Saints as though they were painted red as blood. Houses, roofs and all, even the fencing, railing, and everything was red. Again I saw as it were a river of blood. The blood appeared to be a little above the earth. I marveled at the strange sight, yet I knew not the meaning thereof.

My wife having arrived with the articles that I sent for, father E. H. Groves returned. From her I learned that Jos. Johnson, a man that I hired for 8 months, became alarmed when the soldiers came, and left for some more congenial clime, which to me was a great disappointment, as my crop was, and spring work was behind.

Rachel and I returned to camp, told Bishop P. K. Smith the news. The Bishop then packed up, blessed each other and parted; he bent his way northward. I remained with my wife at the old camp ground.

15

I arrose troubled in spirit, the cogitations of my mind through the night plainly indicated that I in connection with others were threatened with trouble, and that my eyes were not open to it, and that I must change my position, which I did after paying my morning's devotions to Him who rules all things, and asked Him to guide me through the day.

Left my horse at the same place, hid my saddle, etc., took my position on an high eminence where I could overlook the country for the day, and to change my quarters when night would come.

Rachel returned. In the evening I returned to my old camp ground, saw the tracks of my horse where he had been around camp, but finding that I was gone, together with the camp equipage, he started out too, took my trail and followed it as far as he could track me for rocks. He then went to the field. I took my saddle and rigging to the field, turned my horse on the range, and concluded to take the mountains on foot.

About 8 at night Aggathean [Agatha Ann], Rachel and Caroline, my 1st three wives, met near my pasture fence. They embraced me in their arms and wept with joy and sorrow. Brought with them excellent supper consisting of roast beef, short cake, pies, eggs, pancakes, butter and molasses. We sat down and eat together though my health was very poor.

I then blessed Rachel and Caroline and they returned home. Aggathean accompanied me to my retreat which was between two pinion pines and a cedar on a high eminence where we laid without fire to prevent discovery.

16

After sunrise Aggathean returned, took home my horse that was near the field.

Aggathean, Terressa and Jos. my son 13 yrs. old, was shearing my sheep. Have sheared 90 head in three days. Maryleah will help today. My pasture fence will also be finished today. The cost of my portion of it is about $3000.

I sent word to Bro. Tenny, my foreman, to start 4 plows and put in the remainder of the oats, corn, peas, beans, squashes, melons, potatoes, etc., forthwith.

Today I put on a pair of moccasins in order that my tracks might be taken for an Indian. This evening I took a shower bath for my health at the falls of Dry Creek. About 8 o'clock P.M., Rachel, Maryleah, Terressa, my wives, met me with hot coffee, beef steak, crab, custard, etc. From then I learned that I. Riddle and Wm. Slade from Pine Valley, had arrived. Reported the judge and troops at the foot of the Clara waiting the arrival of Maj. Prince from Cal. Had sent out a detachment to meet him. They are getting verry uneasy, and afraid too, for fear that the Mormons and Indians will cut them off. The fact is the fear of the Lord is fallen upon them in answer to the prayers of His people.

23

Today I planted potatoes. Shell Stoddard took dinner with me, it being the first meal that I have eat in my house in 4 weeks.

25

Bishop Smith returned from the mountains; happy reception. Spent the night with me.

28

About sunrise Moquetas, (one of the Piede chiefs in command of the Indians at the massacre) and a number of Indians came in search of me at dawn, 5 mi. from home. They felt warm and greeted me with a cordial welcome. Related the bribes that had been offered them by Cradlebaugh for my head. $5,000.00 reward, a considerable reward for a man that is endeavoring to obey the gospel requirements.

They also had a little squaw to trade me for a horse and wanted me to give them beef and ammunition, flour, etc.

29

This morning I gave the different chieves presents to the amount of some $20.00 in ammunition, shirts and provisions. I also gave Moquetas a young horse for an Indian girl some 8 years of age, also traded for a buckskin.

They having no regard for the Sabbath I was obliged to trade with them.

June 4

Reported that I. C. Haight had returned; and that Judge Cradlebaugh was called, or rather removed from this Territory and that an express had arrived from the States. Two men supposed to be peace commissioners had come in, but their business was not yet known. Troops rather uneasy for fear of the Mormons, etc.

12

This evening Pres. Haight and Hopkins returned and came and lodged with me. Elder Hopkins said there were feelings now between me and Elder Haight that ought to be settled. I replied that if Elder Haight wished to be friendly and drop the past, he must not turn a cold shoulder nor wear an air of scorn thinking that I would bow to him for I never would with my present feelings. I am the injured person.

15

By mail intelligence reached us of the removal of Judge Cradlebaugh and other officials for their injudicious course pursued against the Mormons. Also the protest of all the public papers against them for violating the treaty of pardon [extended in 1858 to Mormons who were in rebellion against the United States] of the chief executive of the nation, and governor of this territory.

Thus for once the public print has taken up our rights and defended them. The storm that so recently threatened us with destruction has again been dispelled by the hand of Almighty God and the prospects of peace is again restored. I feel like exclaiming in the language of one of the old prophets who is like unto our God, "He heareth our prayers and revealeth His secrets to His servants, the prophets. He confoundeth the wicked in their secret devices and bringeth righteousness to pass to those who put their trust in Him."

Fifteen years later a federal grand jury sitting at Beaver City, Utah, indicted Lee, and in November 1874 he was arrested. After the first trial, in July 1875, which resulted in a hung jury, he was released on bail. The following excerpts from his diary begin with his arrest and imprisonment to await his second trial.

Beaver Prison, U. T. August 9, 1875

At 9 o'clock & 30 M. Evening, I was hurried away in an open carriage, with a guard on Each side of Me, leaving My loved Family weeping in the bitter anguish of their souls.

The cries & importunities of My wives & dear little children were treated with contempt, with the officeals in general.

12

About 7 morn we arrived at Nephi & fed, then drove to the Terminus of the Rail Road. We took Dinner & started on the carrs.

Every station was crouwded with spectators, anxious to see that wonderful Man, John D. Lee, of whom so Much is said. 4 hours ride brought us to Salt Lake City. Before landing Gen. Maxwell [George R., United States Marshal] sat doun by me & talked verry kindly, & said that when the train stoped he wantd Me to step off quietly with him to avoid any Demenstration.

We were at the stepts when the Train stoped. Gen. Max took me by the arm and fourced his way through the crowd to a fine carriage & Matched Sorrel Horses worth $1000 at least. My luggage & the guard got in with Me & drove to the Marshal's office. 1000s of spectators were at the depo

waiting the arrival of the Train. I was received at the Marshal's office by
some of his Dupts. The crowd became so large that a Demonstration was
feared, & I was taken in the same carriage to the penitentiary for protection.

September 6

Sixty-four years ago to day I came strugling into existence & have been
strugling & batling with the Tide and Element of opposition ever since.
My path, for causes unknown to Me, has been a thorny one. A great portion of the Human race, even many thousands whoes Faces I have never
beheld, have taken a lively interest in my welfare here upon this Earth.

All the powers of Earth & Hell seemingly have been brought into requisition & arrayed ready to call to account every act of My life, & to expose
every weakness of my Nature, & not being content with that, I have been
Made to attone for the wrongs & follies that My accusers even supposed
that I probably may have done, & some have gone Still further & have
thought it necessary to hold me responsible for something that they
supose that I Might possibly have thought of Saying or doeing that was
Evil.

I am a prisoner for Gospel sake. I here honestly & sacredly declare that
I done nothing designedly wrong that caused My imprisonment, suffering
& bondage.

18

This Morning the Marshal Burgher alowed Me on the outside of the
walls as a change. I enjoyed the surrounding scenery with pleasure &
delight, as the Penetentiary is located on a high Eminence, overlooking
the valey & surrounding city & country until the Eye is lost in distance.

A carriage drove up with Col. Chas. W. Gilberson.

He was acquainted with 2 of my sons, J. David & James Y., a couple
of Nice Young Men, both of which had expressed a desire to have their
father come out & expose the Guilty Party, & no longer suffer for the
wrongs of others. To Make a statement now was not turning state's evidence, but as an honest Man Making a statement of fact, which is the duty
of an honest Man to do.

Our interview upon the whole was quite pleasant.

23

I had a long talk with Dupt. M. Stokes. He advised Me to avail myself
of the offer of the court & become a Witness [that is, to implicate Young
and the priesthood]. I replied that I could not in truth testify to what
they wanted & to purjure myself to save myself by testifying to things

I do not know to be so, or true, I would rather take chances then to do so. I am honest in what I say, & I lie not.

He replied that that would not sattisfy the court, that they could prove more than that by others, and that it would be no advantage to them to let me go, unless I would give more information than they already had. You Must take your own course, then, said I.

With heavy heart I fell into a deep train of reflection. The scenes of the past from My boyhood up to the present roled vividly before Me; then passed on into the dark future & despair almost overwhelmd Me into a sad Melancholly grief, when hope was made menifest & rebuked my erring thoughts, & pointed Me to that life to come & to do what is right, let the consiquence follow, & I became perfectly resigned that if it was My Blood that they thursted for, let them have it.

24

About noon Dupt. Marshal W. M. Stokes called according to promise & wished to know what conclusion I had come. My reply was that I stood firm in the conviction that duty demanded of me a plain Statement of Facts relative to that unfortunate affair (that Mountain Meadow Massacre). As the whole church are acused of it, the Truth I have proposed to tell (and nothing more) that the blame Might rest where it Justly belongs & not upon the innocent.

You can inform Judge Cary Baskin & Gen. Maxwell that if the Truth will satisfy them they can have it, on the condition mention & nothing more; that I have weighed the Matter over carefully & with resignation to My fate in future, I have concluded to prefer to take up winter Quarters in this Prison & there remain till I rot & be Eat up with the Bedbugs before I will dishonor myself by bearing fals witness against any Man, much less an innocent Man.

October 16

Not only Feeble in Body, but low spirited also. Each day seem a week long. The thoughts of whiling off 6 or 8 months in this way is like an Eternity of ages.

Gen. Maxwell was quite gruff & gave me but litle satisfaction. Said that he had never tried to befriend a Man more than he had Me with as litle Sucess, that I did not nor would not apreciate their kindness, but would stick to the g. d. Mormon instead of My Friends, until it will be too late for Me, that they intended to have let Me go if I would only tell what I knew, but no, I must hold out.

I replied that I understood My own business, and was a better Judge of what I knew than any other Person was, that I chose to die like a man then to live a villian, that the Truth they did not want, and as for lies, they Must call on Some other Person to tell them besides Me & from this time fourth, I would Paddle my own canoe & all I asked of him to treat Me as an american should be, that I wanted nothing else of him.

I asked the liberty of sending for & bringing one of My wives here Nearby. Said that I must Get permission from Capt. D. Burgher. I am satisfied that they are intending to run a bluf on Me & coherce Me into Measures.

After our interview, My Mind became more composed & reconciled, & rested well through the Night.

November 3

Mr. Calkins [a Chicago newspaperman] said that So Much had been circulated about Me that I was Stiled by Some, The Terror of the West, that he had a diser to interview me in person, for his own private benefit, & would report the interview. Said that I was altogeather a different man from what I was represented to be bye the public in general, that I was the last man that he would pick for a murderer; that kindness, Philanthropy & Benevolence was imprinted in My countenance.

7

Mr. Goodwin, Reporter for the Tribune, called no doubt to interview Me. Said to me that I would have the Prophet [Brigham Young] in here before long, and what would I think of that. I replied that that would be nothing Strange. I would not like to see him here on account of his age & infirmitys, yet as good men as either he or I have been in Prison before.

Asked if I had got tired of a Prison life. Ans., No, if would alow one of My wives to come & stay with Me, I would try & be as hapey as a king.

Wouldn't like liberty? Ans., No. It is a fool that longs for that he can't get, so I make the best of it I can, especially when I can do no better. Mormonism says hold on to the wheel & you will be up half the Time. I am at the bottom now.

Yes, says reporter & you are like to be there, unless you climb with us. I admit, said I, that the gentiles are trying to clog the wheel, is about dead set between the Mormons & gentiles. It seems to be at a dead stand Just now, but every dog will have his day, & a bitch will have two after noon.

19

To day's paper showed that Judge White Set Prest. B. Young at liberty. This Evening I had interview with the warden with refference to my situation, my health being delicate & the Prison thronged with all kinds influence & Foul air from chambers, having to ease & urinate in the

Same Room Night, is rather more then My constitution can Endure long; that I am willing to pay for the prevelege of having a Bunk in the guard room or outside of the inner yard & alow my wife Rachel to stop with me while here, that I would either pay for the Room or would help do the work, & that I would pledge him My word & honor that I would not to attempt to leve without permission.

He replied that he would lay my situation before Gen. Maxwell & on Sunday he would give Me answer, to defer writing till then, but presumed all would be right.

22

To day after Brakefast, each man was called one by one into the guard Room & a discription taken & entered in a Book. My height is 5 foot 7 in., Floral complection, auburn Hair, light Blue Eyes, stout built. The tribune is full of epithets against Judge White for releasing B. Y.

30

Through the Night, when I was wreathing with Pain, some would laugh and others Mock, saying that My God did not pay Much attention to My cries, & thus the unfeeling wretches would continue to tantalize & torment me in the hour of affliction. O God, my Father in Heaven, how long will this scene of treatment continue?

December 20

About 10 morning it was anounced that My Wife Rachel A. had arrived by the Guard at the Door. I droped My Pen, left My Paper, ink & all & Made for the Door, where we greeted each other through Iron Grates. She had a pass from Gen. Maxwell to allow her to remain with Me till he could come & see me.

After Some 15 Minets delay the Iron Door was unlocked & I was let out in the guard Room to talk with my wife alone.

We were finally conducted on the out side in the Warden's quarters where we were alowed to remain through the Night to geather.

21

The warden asked my wife when she was going away. She replied that Gen. Max instructed her to come here & stop with me, till he, Maxwell, would come up, then he would Make arrangements. He replied that he runs that establishment & not Maxwell, & when he got through with it then Maxwell could run it, that he could not & would not alow that house to be made a tavern of, that other Men had wives, & that he had informed them that if their wives came here, that they must see them on the outside, that they would not be alowed inside.

I replied that I never sponged on anny one, when I could help myself, & that I was ready to pay for each Meal that My wife had eat, which was 3, & those Meals were the scraps that were lef from the 2nd table. I considered it an insult, & belive it was intended as such, yet My wife would put up with almost any treatment sooner then be seperated from Me.

23

The Dupt. Warden called me into a room & said that he would furnish Me a room in the oficers' department for Myself & wife, provided I would furnish My own stove, My wife take charge of the cooking &c. & I pay him $12 a Month for extra grub & the liberty of being on the out side &c. I replied that I wished to see Gen. Maxwell & if possible I wanted to return South to the Destrict where I properly belong.

He said that he did not want Me to Mention to Maxwell the offer that he had Made. I told him that I would talk to My wife about it & then give him an answer.

24

I have spent the forenoon in reading & writing, waiting with Much anxiety My wife Rachel's return that I May come to some understanding about what I am to depend upon in future, whether I am to be locked up again in Prison or have more liberty granted Me to be on the outside, have exercise &c. The Idea of going back into that Prison is like death to me, yet I hardly can stand the pressure of $12 a Month & the labour of My wife as chief cook besides, for that little liberty is at a verry dear price.

April 7 [1876]

I am loath to accept liberty & favours at the hands of those who are not of my religious Faith. But what can I do? I am here in their hands & am powerless. Near 18 months have past since my arrest & confinement. A good portion of the time in Irons. I have suffered a thousand deaths through Pain, anguish, & affliction durring my bondage & confinement, as well as privation, when a few dollars would have obtained a temporal release from the Prison gloom, where my life was endangered and I be alowed on the outside where I could be cared for & nursed by my wife Rachel A. who had come over 400 Miles to nurse and take care of me in my sickness.

It was denied & withheld from me, although my wife waded through the Mudd & Snow on foot from house to house, day after day, and night after night, to raise the pitiful sum of $12.00, only to keep me from being put back into Prison, & I confined to my sick bed not even able to sit up at the time.

She even offered to sell or pawn her shawl at ½ its value to raise the money, but failed. While lying on My back in my sick Bunk, I wrote an Epistle using pathetic language that would touch the heart & call forth the sympathies of almost any human Being on Earth, reminding them that I was no begar, that I always was an independent man & would rather give then to receve.

I only asked the loan of $30.00 which would relieve my presant wants, that I would pay back with good interest Just as soon as I could get the money. Bishop W. A. C. Smoot promised to lay my situation before them & I believ he did so, but no hand was lifted to help me in My hour of distress except Bp. Smoot. He has a large Family & is poor. He loaned my wife $3.00. He said it was all he had and I have no right to doubt his word. He also got me a botle of Bitters & I think that he has done all he could for me & I will reward him and ask heaven to do likewise.

I have tried with all the energy of my soul & body to call fourth aid from those who should stand by me, but as yet I have failed to elicit their sympathy. Their hearts seem to be closed against my importunities & I am fourced to accept assistance from the hands of strangers.

11th

Attorney Brailey sent me word that I would soon be a free man, that this thing of Judges holding prisoners in duress from year to year without a trial was played out, that he had authority to act & would show them that they could not have it all their own way.

The second trial, with its surprise conviction, took place in September 1876. Old, sick, betrayed by his own, Lee no longer wanted to live. On March 23, 1877, he was taken out to Mountain Meadows and there executed by a firing squad.

───★

1860-64: CALIFORNIA'S GOLD FEVER
DIES HARD

───☆

TEN YEARS AFTER THE GREAT GOLD RUSH, *thousands of hungry prospectors were still scrabbling through the hills of California in the hope of a "strike." To restore sanity and encourage development of the state's mining industry on a* sound basis, the legislature voted a geological survey in 1860, and scientist Josiah Dwight Whitney was named to head it.

The survey was not a complete success, but the diary of one of its staff members was. Whitney engaged as his specialist on plants William Henry Brewer, who afterward joined the faculty of Yale, established the first agricultural experiment station in the country, and organized the Yale Forestry School. Brewer had a curiosity about gold mines as well as plants, and about people as well as gold. Through the four years he served on the survey, he wrote his observations into his diary.

"Here men come to strike it quick . . ."
WILLIAM HENRY BREWER
(1828-1910)

North Fork of Cottonwood Creek August 24 [1862]

All the way from Shasta here is a placer region—a high table-land, furrowed into innumerable canyons and gulches. The soil is often a hundred feet thick—a very compact, red, cement gravel. In this is the gold, especially in the gulches or ravines. Here in an early day miners "pitched in"—many made their "pile" and left, others died.

Little mining towns sprang up, but as the richest places were worked out they became deserted and now look delapidated enough.

Many are mining here still, and many years will elapse before all the placers here will be exhausted. Water is supplied during the summer by ditches, dug for miles in length, by which the mountain streams are carried over the lower hills and the water used for washing the dirt.

Visalia, April 12 [1863]

Tuesday we came on to Firebaugh's Ferry—I ought to have mentioned that near our Sunday's stopping-place a murderer had just been arrested, and that at Hill's four horses had just been stolen.

When we got to Firebaugh's we found more excitement. A band of desperadoes were just below—we had passed them in the morning but luckily did not see them. Only a few days before they had attempted to rob some men, and in the scrimmage one man was shot dead and one of the desperadoes was so badly cut that he died on Monday. Another had just been caught. Some men took him into the bushes, some pistol shots were heard, they came back and said he had escaped. A newly made grave on the bank suggested another disposal of him, but all were content not to inquire further.

This semi-desert plain and the inhospitable mountains on its west side are the grand retreats of the desperadoes of the state. It is needless to say that knife (newly ground) and six-shooter are carried "so as to be handy," but I trust that I will ever be spared any actual use for them.

Murphy's, Calaveras County, June 7

A view, comprising a field as large, or nearly as large, as the state of Connecticut, *has not a single tree in sight*. Such are the Californian deserts.

Wednesday, May 20, the rain stopped and we rode from Greenhorn to Tailholt (a good sample of Californian names).

On the Stanislaus River July 20

You doubtless have heard of the mining district of Esmeralda. Well, Aurora is the head of this—is a city, in fact, and the second in importance on the east side of the mountains. It has grown up entirely within two years, numbers now probably five thousand inhabitants, and is like California in '49.

With so large a population there are not accommodations for a fourth of the people. Thousands of "prospectors" come there poor as rats and expect to grow immensely rich in a few months—but, alas! most of them will either die here or leave still poorer.

They live in hundreds of huts made of stones or dug in the earth with a canvas roof—such are the houses of the outskirts.

The center of the town, however, is better—whole streets of wooden buildings, erected in the most cheap and expeditious manner, a few of brick.

Aurora of a Sunday night—how shall I describe it? It is so unlike anything East that I can compare it with nothing you have ever seen. One sees a hundred men to one woman or child. Saloons—saloons—saloons— liquor everywhere. And here the men are—where else *can* they be? At home in their cheerless, lonesome hovels or huts? No, in the saloons, where lights are bright, amid the hum of many voices and the excitement of gambling.

Here men come to make money—make it *quick*—not by slow, honest industry, but by quick strokes—no matter *how*, so long as the law doesn't call it *robbery*. Here, where twenty quartz mills are stamping the rock and kneading its powder into bullion—here, where one never sees a bank bill, nor "rag money," but where hard silver and shining gold are the currency —where men are congregated and living uncomfortably, where there are no home ties or social checks, no churches, no religions—here one sees gambling and vice in all its horrible realities.

Here are tables, with gold and silver piled upon them by hundreds (or even thousands) with men (or women) behind, who deal *faro*, or *monte*, or *vingt-et-un*, or *rouge-et-noir*, or to turn *roulette*—in short, any way in which they may win and you may lose. Here, too, are women—for nowhere else does one see prostitutes as he sees them in a new mining town. All combine to excite and *ruin*.

July 13 we visited one of the mines. Immense sums of money have been spent here in this region. I hear that *five thousand claims* have been recorded, and I question if ten have as yet paid the money expended on them; in fact, only a very small part of this immense number have ever been worked at all, only taken to speculate on. One or two mines *may* pay, the majority never will.

Volcano, Cal., August 13

Silver Mountain is a good illustration of a *new* mining town. We arrived by trail, for the wagon road is left many miles back. As we descended the canyon from the summit, suddenly a bright new town bursts into view. There are perhaps forty houses, all new (but a few weeks old) and as bright as new, fresh lumber, which but a month or two ago was in the trees, can make them.

This log shanty has a sign up, "Variety Store"; the next, a board shanty the size of a hogpen, is "Wholesale & Retail Grocery"; that shanty without a window, with a canvas door, has a large sign of "Law Office"; and so on to the end.

The best hotel has not yet got up its sign, and the "Restaurant and Lodgings" are without a roof as yet, but shingles are fast being made.

On the south of the town rises the bold, rugged Silver Mountain, over eleven thousand feet altitude; on the north a rugged mountain over ten thousand feet. Over three hundred claims are being "prospected." "Tunnels" and "drifts" are being run, shafts being sunk, and every few minutes the booming sound of a blast comes on the ear like a distant leisurely bombardment.

Perhaps half a dozen women and children complete that article of population, but there are hundreds of men, all active, busy, scampering like a nest of disturbed ants, as if they must get rich today for tomorrow they might die. One hears nothing but "feet," "lode," "indications," "rich rock," and similar mining terms. Nearly everyone is, in his belief, in the incipient stages of immense wealth.

One excited man says to me, "If we strike it, as in Washoe, what a town you soon will see here!" "Yes—*if*," I reply. He looks at me in disgust. "Don't you think it will be?" he asks, as if it were already a sure thing. He is already the proprietor of many "town lots," now worth nothing except to speculate on, but when the town shall rival San Francisco or Virginia City, will *then* be unusually valuable. There are town lots and streets, although as yet no wagons. I may say here that it is probably all a "bubble"—but little silver ore has been found at all—in nine-tenths of the "mines" not a particle has been seen.

"Mining fever" is a terrible epidemic; when it is really in a community, lucky is the man who is not affected by it. Yet a *few* become immensely rich.

I got back to Hermit Valley that night, and stopped at a house there. The house is a mere cabin, although now a "hotel." Twelve men slept in a little garret, where there were ten bunks, called "beds."

In winter the only way of getting about is on snowshoes, not the great broad Canadian ones that we see sometimes at home, but the Norwegian ones—a strip of light elastic wood, three or four inches wide and seven to ten feet long, slightly turned up at the front end, with an arrangement near the center to fasten it to the foot. With these they go everywhere, no matter how deep the snow is, and downhill they go with frightful velocity. At a race on snowshoes at an upper town last winter the papers announced that the time made by the winner was half a mile in thirty-seven seconds! and many men tell of going a mile in less than two minutes.

Lake Tahoe, August 23

We struck the Placerville road, the grand artery of travel to Washoe. Over it pass the Overland telegraph and the Overland mail.

It is stated that five thousand teams are steadily employed in the Washoe trade and other commerce east of the Sierra—not little teams of two horses, but generally of six horses or mules, often as many as eight or ten, carrying loads of three to eight tons, on huge cumbrous wagons.

Clouds of dust arose, filling the air, as we met long trains of ponderous wagons, loaded with merchandise, hay, grain—in fact everything that man or beast uses. We stopped at the Slippery Ford House. Twenty wagons stopped there, driving over a hundred horses or mules—heavy wagons, enormous loads, scarcely any less than three tons. The harness is heavy, often with a steel bow over the hames, in the form of an arch over each horse, and supporting four or five bells, whose chimes can be heard at all hours of the day.

On the Truckee River, August 27

We passed through the town of Centerville, its streets all staked off among the trees, notices of claims of town lots on trees and stumps and stakes, but as yet the *town* is not built. Six weeks ago, I hear, there were but two miners here; now there are six hundred in this district.

The crowd are all working or speculating in "feet."

Let me explain the term "feet" as used here. Suppose a hill has a vein of metal in it; this is called a "lead." A company "takes up" a claim, of a definite number of "feet" along this vein, and the land 150 to 200 feet each side. The length varies in different districts—the miners decide that themselves—sometimes 1,000 feet, sometimes 1,500, at others 2,000 feet are allowed.

In a mine that claims 1,000 feet, a foot sold or bought does not mean any particular foot of that mine, but one one-thousandth of the whole. Thus, the Ophir Mine has 1,500 feet, now worth over $4,000 per foot. One never sees shares quoted in the market, but feet; and feet may be bought at all prices, from a few cents in some to over $5,000 in the Gould & Curry Mine in Washoe. A man speculating in mines is said to be speculating in feet.

There is great excitement here—many think it a second Washoe. I have but little faith in it myself. I surely would not invest money in any mine I have seen today, and I have visited eight or nine of the best.

Crescent City, November 15

From Scott's Bar we followed down the river three miles to the Klamath River, and then followed down that.

We passed what was once the town of Hamburg, two years ago a bustling village—a large cluster of miners' cabins, three hotels, three stores, two billiard saloons, and all the other accompaniments of a mining town—now all is gone. A camp of Klamath Indians on the river bank is the only population at present! Their faces were daubed with paint, their huts were squalid. Just below were some Indian graves.

In contrast with this was a sadder sight—a cluster of graves of the miners who had died while the town remained. Boards had once been set up at their graves, but most had rotted off and fallen—the rest will soon follow. Bushes have grown over the graves, and soon they, as well as the old town, will be forgotten.

Friends in distant lands, mothers in far off homes, may still be wondering, often with a sigh, what has become of loved sons who years ago sought their fortunes in the land of gold, but who laid their bones on the banks of the Klamath and left no tidings behind. Alas, how many a sad history is hidden in the neglected and forgotten graves that are scattered among the wild mountains that face the Pacific!

Virginia City, Nevada, November 4, 1864

November 1, I took the steamer for Sacramento, took the cars at midnight and passed over the hot plains in the cool night; then the stage. Daylight found us at Placerville. The old name of Hangtown, so well bestowed in early days, is about forgotten.

Here we took the Overland stage across the Sierra. This has been the great road to Washoe—sometimes three thousand teams with twenty-five thousand animals at work at one time. We passed hundreds of freight wagons, with from six to ten horses or mules each. Three or four rival roads now divide the patronage—all, like this, toll roads and built at an enormous expense.

Hotels and stables abound, even on the very summit, where the snow falls to an immense depth every winter. An aggregate of *fifty feet* fell there the "wet winter."

We had all the features of this grand Sierra scenery—high, barren peaks streaked with snow, rising above the dense, dark forests of the lower slopes, and deep canyons and steep precipices, around which at times the road passes at such a dizzy height that an upset would send the persons of the passengers several hundreds of feet below and their souls to the other world. But such *drivers* as there are! They manage the big coaches and their six-horse teams as if it were but play, and go dashing along steep grades and around short curves at a rate to make the hair stand on end.

We passed through Silver City and Gold Hill, lively mining towns, where the clatter of nearly a thousand stamps greets the ear for miles.

It is a popular idea on this coast that a country utterly barren, uncomfortable, with bad climate, worse water, nothing inviting about it, must of necessity contain the precious metals. "What else is it good for?" is their triumphant shout if you dispute it.

Following this idea, this region was "prospected" by various parties and at various times from 1850 on. Gold was found quite early, and at last, about 1858 or 1859, silver ore. It attracted no attention, however, until 1860, when suddenly the tide set in here—such an immigration as only gold and silver can cause. Thousands poured in from California, Oregon, the Colorado, the States—adventurers, gamblers, speculators, miners, prospectors, lawyers—in short, all of that numerous class that "makes haste to get rich" who could get here.

Some of the mines proved immensely rich, and as a consequence "wild-cats" flourished in all their glory. A few mines turned out bullion at such a rate that statesmen and financiers feared that silver must fall in value. Last year it culminated—when nearly a *ton a day* of gold and silver bullion was shipped from here; when more than five thousand teams were employed in bringing freight in; when stock in the paying mines was held at perfectly wild rates and values, even to *over twenty thousand dollars per foot;* when probably a dozen mines were paying high dividends, and millions of dollars were being expended in working the thousand "wildcat" mines whose stock was in the market; when a population variously estimated from sixteen thousand to twenty-four thousand was congregated here within a few miles, all drawing their "supplies and forage" from over the mountains; when speculation ruled the day and in the streets were met men poor three years ago, now worth their hundreds of thousands—then, I say, the excitement raised and culminated—and this summer the vast bubble broke.

All at once the stocks of the gold mines went down from far above their real value to as much below, and "wildcat" collapsed. Ophir stock, once held at over $4,000 per foot, is now a drug at as many hundreds. Gould & Curry, once over $6,000 per foot, now sells for less than $1,500, and everything in the same way.

As a consequence, thousands have been ruined, work has stopped on much "wildcat," and good mines must in future be worked in a more healthy manner. Of course, a portion of the floating population has left, but still perhaps sixteen thousand are in Virginia City, Gold Hill, Silver City, and the environs.

This is the center of a region on which many hundreds of gold and silver mines have been located, but only a few of these have ever paid expenses, certainly less than twenty of them. All of these (unless it be one or two) are located on one line or vein—the famous Comstock Lead as it is called—all within a distance of 1½ miles.

The yield of the mines of this vicinity last year was about nineteen or twenty million dollars—nearly a ton a day of bullion went to San Francisco. Such are the resources of this new state.

Gold Hill lies 1½ miles south on the same "lead." Its mines are even richer, but are smaller, so make less noise.

The Bowers Mine is only twenty feet. Sandy Bowers, the lucky owner, four years ago drove an ox team in the territory, his wife an industrious, hard-working Irishwoman. He located a claim and held onto it, letting the other men work it. It rose in value enormously. In three years it netted him an income of some *ten thousand dollars per month,* and he refused $400,000 for it, or at the enormous rate of $20,000 per foot. Last year he built a house costing him $240,000, adorned with $3,000 mirrors and all the window curtains cost $1,200 each. The wife, who three years before thought $3 per day good wages for her man, told a friend of mine that she "didn't see how one can get along on this coast with less than $100,000 per year." Poor Sandy—he lived too fast—his $10,000 per month was too little, and he ran into debt $100,000, on which he pays Nevada interest, so I suppose he is a poor man again—if not, he soon will be.

One more—the Plato Mine is only ten feet. Five years ago, in San Francisco, an Irishwoman sold apples by day, and by night "received calls" for compensation. The latter business proved the more profitable and required the less capital, so she gave up her apple stand and came up here to the new mines, when they first began to attract attention, to ply her trade. She was successful, as is usually the case in the new mining towns, and an admiring lover gave her ten feet of his claim—either as a token of esteem, as he says—or, "for value received" in her line, as she says. No matter which, she got the feet, which rose to be worth some $150,000 to $200,000. He finally married her to get his "feet" back, but died soon after, and she owns the mine yet, which, of course, yields her a handsome income.

IV.

DEDICATION

TO

A

PROPOSITION

1836-45: J. Q. ADAMS WINS A FIGHT
FOR FREEDOM

No PUBLIC SERVANT has ever done his job with greater integrity than did dour, grumpy, censorious John Quincy Adams. In a country that was groping restively, needful of a reawakening to its democratic destiny, Adams the aristocrat was miscast as President. His administration could not give the nation the direction which it lacked, and which it had to wait for Jackson to give. But what Adams achieved in lesser rank—as diplomat, shaper of foreign policy, lawmaker—far outweighed that failure in the balance of a long life.

The historical span of his career is impressive. He was keeping his diary when Cornwallis surrendered to Washington. Sixty-five years later he was still keeping it; and America, now with a population of 20,000,000, with burgeoning cities, factories, railroads, was well on the way to becoming an industrial giant and world power.

On graduation from Harvard he went into law. But his father, John Adams, who wanted and expected him to be the second President Adams, saw to it that John Quincy should enter the foreign service at an early age. He was sent to Holland, Portugal and Prussia, later to Russia and England. In 1803 he was elected to the Senate. He was one of the negotiators at Ghent of the treaty which ended the War of 1812. He formulated the Monroe Doctrine.

In the 1824 Presidential election, although Jackson had 99 electoral votes against Adams' 84, the House of Representatives chose Adams. Four years later Jackson came in with a thumping victory, 178 to 83 for Adams. From that time until his death Adams served as a member of the House of Representatives, and it was here that, as an old man, singlehanded, he carried to a finish his gallant nine-year fight for the right to present petitions against slavery. On hearing the vote that ended the gag rule, he wrote in shaky letters in his diary, "Blessed, forever blessed, be the name of God!"

But it was not for a personal triumph that John Quincy Adams was grateful to God on that day; it was for America. He had struck a telling blow for freedom.

In the Massachusetts Historical Society in Boston there is a bookcase, seven shelves tall, containing the papers of the Adams family. So voluminously articulate have been its several eminent members—John, John Quincy, Charles Francis, and their relatives and descendants, including Brooks Adams and Henry Adams—that even today, editors and printing presses have not caught up with manuscript. They wrote down everything and with one exception—the younger Charles Francis, who burned his diary—they never threw away anything. And fortunate it is for us that they were like that, for in this collection is recorded a big sector of the story of America.

Ownership of the whole collection of Adams papers was transferred by the family to the Historical Society a few years ago, and the latter is now engaged in a major re-editing and publishing project which will comprise about a hundred volumes.

The fifth shelf of the bookcase is filled with the original of John Quincy Adams' diary. In 1874-77 portions of it were published in twelve large volumes edited by his son Charles Francis. In 1954 the Historical Society began work on a new edition.

The scope of this vast diary, the range of its myriad interests, cannot be represented in a few pages of excerpts. We pick out here a single thread of the fabric—the fight on the gag rule as Adams tells of it.

"My conscience presses me on . . ."
JOHN QUINCY ADAMS (1767-1848)

Aug. 11 [1835]

There is a great fermentation upon this subject of slavery at this time in all parts of the Union. The emancipation of the slaves in the British West India Colonies; the Colonization Society here; the current of public opinion running everywhere stronger and stronger into democracy and popular supremacy contribute all to shake the fetters of servitude.

There has been recently an alarm of slave insurrection in the State of Mississippi, and several persons have been hung by a summary process of what they call Lynch's law.

Aug. 14

We are in a state of profound peace and over-pampered with prosperity; yet the elements of exterminating war seem to be in vehement fermentation, and one can scarcely foresee to what it will lead.

Jan. 18 [1836]

Petition day at the House.

Adams presented several petitions for the abolition of slavery. As a maneuver to clap a gag on all such petitions, a committee was set up with H. L. Pinckney as chairman, and the question of whether a vote was required on petitions was referred to it. Five months later this committee made its report, declaring that Congress had no right to interfere with slavery in the states, and that any petition on slavery should be tabled, without printing, and no further action should be taken on it—in other words, a gag rule protecting slavery from the demands of the people.

May 18

Immediately after the reading of the journal, H. L. Pinckney presented the report of the select committee. He moved that five thousand copies of the report should be printed for the use of the House. It was immediately attacked with extreme violence, and a fiery debate arose, which continued until one o'clock, and then, by a suspension of the rules, for another half-hour.

July 11

With praise and prayer to God, and a solemn sense of my earthly condition, and hopes of a better world, I enter upon the seventieth year of my pilgrimage.

Dec. 26

I presented the petition of Joseph Page and twenty-six citizens of the town of Silverlake, Susquehanna County, Commonwealth of Pennsylvania, praying for the abolition of slavery and the slave-trade in the District of Columbia.

In the next nine years Adams presents hundreds of these petitions from citizens throughout the United States as part of his long fight to break the gag rule.

April 19 [1837]

The most insignificant error of conduct in me at this time would be my irredeemable ruin in this world, and both the ruling parties are watching with intense anxiety for some overt act by me to set the whole pack of their hireling presses upon me.

The exposure through which I passed at the late session of Congress was greater than I could have imagined possible; and having escaped from that fiery furnace, it behooves me well to consider my ways before I put myself in the way of being cast into it again.

Philadelphia, Sept. 1

The abolitionists are constantly urging me to indiscreet movements, which would ruin me and weaken and not strengthen their cause. My own

family, on the other hand—that is, my wife and son and Mary—exercise all
the influence they possess to restrain and divert me from all connection
with the abolitionists and their cause. Between these adverse impulses my
mind is agitated almost to distraction.

Dec. 5

Van Buren's message gave me a fit of melancholy for the future fortunes
of the republic. Cunning and duplicity pervade every line of it. The sacrifice of the rights of Northern freedom to slavery and the South, and the
purchase of the West by the plunder of the public lands, is the combined
system which it discloses.

Dec. 21

Patton had a resolution ready drawn, agreed upon at the slavery meeting of yesterday—a resolution like that of the 16th of January last—that
no petitions relating to slavery or the trade in slaves in any State, district
or Territory of the United States shall be read, printed, committed, or in
any manner acted upon by the House.

I objected to the reception of the resolution, and Patton moved to sus-
pend the rules; which was carried—136 to 65; and after a speech, he
moved the previous question; which was carried, as was the resolution.

When my name was called, I answered, "I hold the resolution to be a
violation of the Constitution, of the right of petition of my constituents,
and of the people of the United States, and of my right to freedom of
speech as a member of this House."

Jan. 28 [1838]

My duty to defend the free principles and institutions is clear; but the
measures by which they are to be defended are involved in thick darkness. The path of right is narrow, and I have need of a perpetual control
over passion.

Feb. 14

Henry, of Pennsylvania, moved and carried a suspension of the rules,
that the States might be called for the presentation of petitions. The call
commenced with me, and I presented three hundred and fifty petitions; of
which one hundred and fifty-eight were for the rescinding of the Patton
gag, or resolution of 21st December; sixty-five for the abolition of slavery
and the slave trade in the District of Columbia; four in the Territories;
seventeen for the prohibition of the internal slave trade; two against the
admission of any new State whose constitution tolerates slavery; and fifty-
four against the annexation of Texas to the Union.

There was one, praying that Congress would take measures to protect citizens of the North going to the South from danger to their lives. When the motion to lay that on the table was made, I said that "in another part of the Capitol it had been threatened that if a Northern abolitionist should go to North Carolina and utter a principle of the Declaration of Independence—" here a loud cry of "Order! Order!" burst forth, in which the Speaker yelled among the loudest. I waited till it subsided, and then resumed, "that if they could catch him they would hang him." I said this so as to be distinctly heard throughout the hall; the renewed deafening shout of "Order! Order!" notwithstanding.

The Speaker then said, "The gentleman from Massachusetts will take his seat"; which I did, and immediately rose again, and presented another petition.

Dec. 14

W. B. Calhoun presented several slavery abolition petitions, all at once; upon which Mr. Wise [Henry A., of Virginia] objected to their being received. The Speaker said that, under the resolutions which had been adopted by the House, the question of reception could not be made. From this decision Wise took an appeal. At last Taylor of New York called for the previous question; which was carried—the main question being, whether the decision of the Speaker should stand.

When my name was called by the clerk, I rose and said, "Mr. Speaker, considering all the resolutions introduced by the gentleman from New Hampshire as—" The Speaker roared out, "The gentleman from Massachusetts must answer aye or no, and nothing else. Order!"

With a reinforced voice—"I refuse to answer because I consider all the proceedings of the House as unconstitutional." While in a firm and swelling voice I pronounced distinctly these words, the Speaker and about two-thirds of the House cried, "Order! Order!" till it became a perfect yell.

I paused a moment for it to cease, and then said, "A direct violation of the Constitution of the United States."

While speaking these words with loud, distinct and slow articulation, the bawl of "Order! Order!" resounded again from two-thirds of the House. The Speaker, with agonizing lungs, screamed, "I call upon the House to support me in the execution of my duty!"

I then coolly resumed my seat.

Jan. 28 [1840]

Going to the House, I met in the Capitol yard Daniel Webster, and greeted him upon his recent return from his visit to England. I found the

House in session, and W. Cost Johnson upon the floor, concluding his anti-abolition speech, which took him between two and three hours. He was about half-tipsy, and in his merriest and wittiest mood. In undertaking to answer my last speech, he took the course, under the form of nauseous and fetid flattery, to make me as ridiculous before the House and the country as he possibly could.

Jan. 29

Morning visits from John G. Whittier, Isaac Winslow, and Samuel Mifflin, all of the Society of Friends, and all abolitionists. Whittier said that he thought this last outrage upon the right of petition, the establishment of a rule refusing to receive or entertain any abolition petition, might perhaps be the best thing that could have been done to promote the cause of abolition. It was, at least, casting off all disguise.

I said it would depend on the impression which it would make on the people; and I have little expectation from that. They had been familiarized to the privation of the right, and could not be roused to take an interest in it. The difference between the resolution of the four preceding sessions of Congress and the new rule of the House is the difference between petty larceny and highway robbery.

Feb. 16

Mr. Meehan, the Librarian of Congress, yesterday told me that in the violent storm of the night before last one arm of the emblematical statue of America in the pediment over the entrance-door of the hall of the House of Representatives—my design, so beautifully executed by Persico —had been blown away, and came down with a tremendous crash. He said the group was of freestone. I said it was ominous. He said he hoped not. But he was mistaken as to the statue mutilated. It is not the figure of America, but that of Justice, which has lost her right arm nearly to the elbow—still more ominous, and painfully significant of the condition of the Hall within, where Justice has emphatically lost her right arm.

March 29 [1841]

The world, the flesh, and all the devils in hell are arrayed against any man who now in this North American Union shall dare to join the standard of Almighty God to put down the African slave trade; and what can I, upon the verge of my seventy-fourth birthday, with a shaking hand, a darkening eye, a drowsy brain, and with all my faculties dropping from

me one by one, as the teeth are dropping from my head—what can I do?
Yet my conscience presses me on; let me but die upon the breach.

June 11

Wise began in a tone which I saw would break him down—loud, vocif-
erous, declamatory, furibund; he raved about the hell-hounds of abolition, and at me, as the leader of the abolitionists throughout the Union,
for a full hour—till his voice had broken into a childish treble two or three
times. Arnold, of Tennessee, came to my seat and with deep earnestness
entreated me not to reply to him; and I promised that I would not.

Without abatement of his vehemence, Wise came to speak of the controversy between the States of Virginia and New York; and then his tone
suddenly fell, he became bewildered in his argument, his voice failed him,
he became ghastly pale, said he felt himself unwell, sank into his chair,
and fainted.

Jan. 24 [1842]

I presented sundry petitions. One from Benjamin Emerson and 45
others of Haverhill, Mass., praying Congress to take measures for peace-
ably dissolving the Union, with an assignment of three reasons. I moved
its reference to a select committee, with instructions to report an answer
assigning the reason why the prayer of the petition ought not to be
granted. Then came another explosion, and after a snarling debate, a
resolution offered by Thomas W. Gilmer, that I deserved the censure of
the House for presenting a petition praying for the dissolution of the
Union.

Jan. 31

My occupations during the month have been confined entirely to the
business of the House, and for the last ten days to the defense of myself
against an extensive combination and conspiracy, in and out of Congress,
to crush the liberties of the free people of this union by disgracing me
with a brand of censure and displacing me from the chair of the Committee on Foreign Affairs for my perseverance in presenting abolition
petitions.

I am in the midst of that fiery ordeal, and day and night are absorbed
in the struggle to avert my ruin. God send me a good deliverance!

Feb. 6

One hundred members of the House represent slaves; four-fifths of whom would crucify me if their votes could erect a cross; forty members, representatives of the free, in the league of slavery and mock Democracy, would break me on the wheel, if their votes or wishes could turn it round; and four-fifths of the other hundred and twenty are either so cold or so lukewarm that they are ready to desert me at the very first scintillation of indiscretion on my part. The only formidable danger with which I am beset is that of my own temper.

Feb. 7

I was belated, and the House had been about ten minutes in session when I entered and took my seat. Other business was under consideration, but the question of privilege, or my trial [censure], was called up. I observed that, having perceived on Saturday some impatience on the part of the House to get rid of this subject, and persevering in the determination not to be responsible for one hour of time unnecessarily consumed on this subject, if the House was ready to lay it on the table forever, I would acquiesce in that decision without requiring further time for my defense; of which I should need much if required to proceed.

Botts then moved to lay the whole subject on the table forever; carried, by yeas and nays—106 to 93.

June 17 [1843]

This was the day of the great celebration of the completion of the monument on Bunker Hill; and never since the existence of the three hills was there such a concourse of strangers upon their sides as has been assembled on the banks of "majestic Charles" this day. What a name in the annals of mankind is Bunker Hill! what a day was the 17th of June, 1775! and what a burlesque upon them both is an oration upon them by Daniel Webster, and a pilgrimage of John Tyler and his Cabinet of slave-drivers, to desecrate the solemnity of their presence!

Daniel Webster is a heartless traitor to the cause of human freedom; John Tyler is a slave-monger. What have these to do with the Quincy granite pyramid on the brow of Bunker Hill? What have these to do with a dinner in Faneuil Hall, but to swill like swine, and grunt about the rights of man?

Dec. 21

In the House, the life-and-death struggle for the right of petition was resumed. The question of reception of the petition from Illinois was laid on the table—98 to 80—after a long and memorable debate. I then presented the resolves of the Massachusetts legislature of the 23rd of March, 1843, proposing an amendment to the Constitution of the United States, making the representation of the people in the House proportioned to the numbers of free persons, and moved it should be read, printed, and referred to a select committee of nine.

And now sprung up the most memorable debate ever entertained in the House, in the midst of which the House, at half-past three, adjourned.

The crisis now requires of me coolness, firmness, prudence, moderation, and fortitude beyond all former example. I came home in such a state of agitation that I could do nothing but pace my chamber.

Jan. 31 [1844]

I hurried up to the Capitol, to be there at the meeting of the House. The report on the rules was immediately taken up, and Andrew Johnson, a new member from Tennessee, made an hour's speech in support of the gag rule, and especially abusive upon me.

So they all are. I am compelled not only to endure it with seeming insensibility, but to forbear, so far as I can restrain myself, from all reply.

Dec. 3 [1845]

I moved the following resolution:

"Resolved, that the twenty-fifth standing rule for conducting business in this House, in the following words, 'No petition, memorial, resolution, or other paper praying the abolition of slavery in the District of Columbia or any State or Territory, or the slave trade between the States or Territories in which it now exists, shall be received by this House, or entertained in any way whatever,' be, and the same is, hereby rescinded."

I called for the yeas and nays. Jacob Thompson of Mississippi moved to lay the resolution on the table.

I called for the yeas and nays on that motion.

As the clerk was about to begin the call, the President's message was announced and received. A member called for the reading of the message. I said I hoped the question upon my resolution would be taken. The clerk called the roll, and the motion to lay on the table was rejected—81 to 104. The question was then put on the resolution; and it was carried—108 to 80.

Blessed, forever blessed, be the name of God!

1844:   A VISITOR TO AMERICA WITNESSES
A SALE

EXCEPTING EDMUND KEAN, William Charles Macready was rated by London critics the greatest actor of his time; and Macready himself disputed the exception. Vain, sensitive, tempestuous, he managed to get into his full share of the squabbles that attend show business. But he was also widely loved.

In 1843, on a visit to America, he met Edwin Forrest, New York's leading tragedian. A warm friendship ensued. But American newspapers, with odious insistence, kept comparing the two and declaring Forrest the better artist.

The controversy rose to a bitter pitch. Worse, it affected Forrest. He grew envious of Macready. Three years later, at a performance by Macready in Edinburgh, Forrest, from a box close to the stage, hissed. The feud deepened. On both shores of the Atlantic, people took sides furiously. On May 10, 1849, during another of Macready's visits to America, it culminated in a tragic brawl at the Astor Place Opera House in New York.

Just before the British actor's scheduled appearance as Macbeth, Forrest's friends had organized a gang of hoodlums to drive him off the stage. From outside the crowd bombarded the theater with stones. Inside it tried to howl him down. Macready went on with the play. "I flung my whole soul into every word I uttered," he wrote, "acting my very best and exciting the audience to sympathy even with the glowing words of fiction, whilst these dreadful deeds of real crime and outrage were roaring at intervals in our ears and rising to madness all round us."

At the finish Macready's friends made him change into the costume of Malcolm and whisked him out of his dressing room to safety. Meanwhile the mob at Astor Place ran riot. Soldiers were rushed to the scene. They fired into the crowd and killed twenty-two persons.

While Macready's name is forever associated with the much publicized but utterly senseless riot, we find more interesting his reactions to many other scenes he witnessed in America and recorded in his diary. He wrote fully—an edition of the diary by William Toynbee, covering the years 1833-51, with much omitted, runs to more than a thousand closely printed pages—and flamboyantly, explosively, often calling on God to witness the truth of his remarks and to perform other little chores for him.

He had much to say about the South. His horror at the spectacle of slavery he expressed—as did many another visiting Englishman during those years—

with a peculiar gusto, as if he might have been thinking, "Well, America, land of the free, what about it? We of your mother country, whom you once accused of oppression, have nothing to match this!" Here are a few of his impressions.

"Do the Negroes—oh God!—forget?"
WILLIAM CHARLES MACREADY
(1793-1873)

January 3 [1844] Charleston, South Carolina

Was delighted with the warm sunshiny day, the fresh air, the foliage of the wild orange, the palmetto, the roses in bloom, the violets, the geraniums, etc., but was pained to see the coloured people go out of the way and show a deference to us as to superior beings.

January 7th

Dined with Judge King; was amused at dinner with a negro boy whose sole business was with a long feather brush to beat away the flies from the viands at table. After the ladies had retired, I introduced again the subject of the General who had shot deliberately a young man, said to have seduced his daughter, and whom an editor of this city had justified, saying that no judge or jury would find him guilty, and in fact extolling, not lamenting and palliating by circumstances the murder.

The two judges, King and Chivers, both seemed to admit that of right it was a case beyond the law, and in short virtually *justified the act against the law.*

Now this I cannot understand. Either the law is undisputed sovereign— it is supreme—or it is worse than nothing: when the sentence of the law is pronounced the arm of power may be extended in mercy to prevent its execution on account of extenuating circumstances; but if such deeds as these and *practicing for duels* are to be admitted as usage by the law, give me bondage before *such freedom.*

January 12th

Dr. Irving called for me. We went to the gaol—it is a very small building—for both debtors and felons, who are, however, apart. It was very clean. I saw the negro crew of a ship locked up together until the sailing of the vessel, the law of the State not allowing them to be at liberty. I saw some prisoners for minor offenses; one had been whipped for petty lareeny; some negroes below who were kept in the premises of the gaol till they could be sold! Good God! Is this right? They are an inferior class of men, but still they are *man*.

They showed me the condemned cells; one in which a murderer had spent his last night last summer. The world is a riddle to me; I am not satisfied with this country as it at present is. I think it will, it must, work out its own purification.

January 13th

Ogilby called, and confidentially related circumstances of great atrocity occurring in this State. An overseer, against his master's orders, flogging a runaway negro, tying him up all night, getting up in the night to repeat the torture, and repeating it till the wretched creature died under the lash. The felon was acquitted. A person supposed by another to trench upon ground which he claimed, was, in the midst of his own labourers, shot dead by the villain in open day; the felon was acquitted!

These are heart-sickening narratives. Judge King called for me and took me to Chancellor Dunkin's, where the judges of the State met to dine. I was introduced to all. About eighteen or twenty dined; here was no want of character or manner, nor of any needful gravity or grace befitting a meeting of republican judges. I could not help feeling that these judges of a country asserting itself free were waited on by slaves!

January 25 [Savannah, Georgia]

Was accosted by a rough person, who gave his name Nichols, whom I heard say—to the observation that "crowds were hurrying down below"— "they need not be in such a hurry; the duel is not to be till twelve." I turned round and looked with amazement in his face. "How do you do, sir?" he answered to my surprised and shocked gaze.

"Did you say a duel was to be fought?"

"Oh, yes; just over the water, but not before twelve."

"And can such a thing be publicly known, and no attempt on the part of the legal authorities to interfere?"

"Oh, Lord, no, they dursn't; they've too many friends about them for any number of officers that could be got together to have any chance with them."

"And are the crowds going down to see them fight?"

"No; they go to wait for the news—it's across the river they fight."

"Do they fight with pistols?"

"I don't know; either pistols or rifles—but they generally fight with rifles in this part of the country. They are two gentlemen of the Bar here. It was a quarrel in Court: One said, 'the lie was stamped in the other's face,' so there was a challenge. I suppose you don't do such a thing as take a glass of wine in the morning? Ah, well, it's our way; just come in and see the reading-room; it's the best room in all the South; come, it's just here."

I complied with the importunity of my new acquaintance, who informed me all about himself, but my stomach felt sick with horror at the coldblooded preparation for murder.

Mobile, February 2nd

Went on to the Exchange; a sale of men and women. Mr. Cole an acquaintance of Ryder's, told him they "had no feeling; they did not mind being parted from wife and children; they forgot it in a week. You see a cat when one drowns her kittens, she soon forgets it—it's just the same with the coloured people."

Is it—oh, God!—the same? But time will tell.

One man, about forty, a blacksmith, had his merits expatiated on. "This hale man going for $550, it's throwing him away—no more bid? It's a sacrifice! Going, going, etc."

Another mulatto, a field servant—the same language, the same odious blasphemy against nature and the God of nature.

1854: A SLAVE IS DRAGGED BACK
TO THE SOUTH

A CASE OF MEASLES *left Richard Henry Dana with eye trouble so acute that he had to drop out of Harvard in his junior year. In 1834 he said good-by to his family in Cambridge, Massachusetts, and went to sea as a foremast hand in the brig Pilgrim. Two years later he returned, his trouble cured. He took his law degree, taught a little while, and then went into practice.*

While at sea he had kept a diary. Six years later—he was 25 then—he wrote up the diary into a book-length narrative. He sent the manuscript to his father's friend in New York, William Cullen Bryant, the poet. Bryant took it to a publisher. The editors refused to offer a royalty but said they would buy it for a small sum, outright. Bryant tried to get more, was denied, and finally gave in. A hundred years later, after selling millions of copies, the book was still going strong. So was the publishing house, which had paid Dana, in all, $250. The title of the book was Two Years Before the Mast.

Fortunately, writing was a sideline. Dana was a brilliant lawyer. In 1848 he allied himself with the Free Soilers, a political party that fought extension of slavery into the Territories.

In 1850 Congress passed the new Fugitive Slave Law which made it possible for Southern masters to have their runaway slaves arrested in free states and brought back. The law was boldly tested by the South and bitterly contested by the North. Dana took up the cause of the runaways, volunteered his legal services, and became widely known in connection with these cases.

On May 24, 1854, a Negro named Anthony Burns was arrested in Boston. He was dragged before Colonel Charles T. Suttle, son of a Virginia slaveholder, who claimed ownership of him. Two years before, Burns had been put to work on a ship at one of the wharves in Richmond. When she sailed he stowed away, and so escaped. At the time of his arrest he was earning his living in a Boston clothing store.

The people of Massachusetts were shocked. Although a commissioner of the United States Court had issued a warrant for the arrest, they showed strong sympathy for the Negro. A similar incident three years before had worked them into a fighting mood against what they considered to be the arrogance and aggression of the Southerners. Now a fugitive was "kidnaped" within sight of Faneuil Hall. A rumble of anger arose in Boston and reverberated through all New England. Nevertheless, the slave lost his case and was returned to the South.

"Anthony Burns was the last fugitive slave ever seized on the soil of Massachusetts," wrote Charles Francis Adams, Dana's biographer, "and every incident connected with his trial and condition has a lasting historical interest."

In the account which is given in Dana's diary there is a note of deep concern over the illegal use of military power to suppress the will of the people.

"A perfect howl of 'Shame!'"
RICHARD HENRY DANA (1815-1882)

May 25 [1854]

This morning, at a little before nine o'clock, as I was going past the court-house, a gentleman told me that there was a fugitive slave in custody in the United States court-room. I went up immediately, and saw a negro, sitting in the usual place for prisoners, guarded by a large corps of officers. He is a piteous object, rather weak in mind and body, with a large scar on his cheek, which looks much like a brand, a broken hand from which a large piece of bone projects, and another scar on his other hand. He seemed completely cowed and dispirited.

I offered to act as his counsel. He said, "It is of no use. They will get me back; and if they do, I shall fare worse if I resist." I told him there might be some flaw in the papers, or some mistake, and that he might get off. The officers told him he had better have counsel, as it would cost him nothing and could do him no harm. He seemed entirely helpless, and could not say what he wished to do; but the great thing on his mind seemed to be the fear that any delay and expense he caused his master would be visited upon him when he got back, and that the best policy was to conciliate his master as best he could.

I would not press a defense upon him under these circumstances, but felt it my duty to address the court and ask for a delay. I did this upon the ground that from all I could observe myself and from what I had heard from others, it was plain that he was in no condition to determine whether he would have counsel or not, and that no court would proceed to a trial and condemnation under such circumstances.

The counsel for the claimant, a Mr. Edward Griffin Parker, objected to the delay in bad taste and bad judgment. The commissioner, Edward G. Loring, at my private suggestion, called the prisoner to him and told him what his rights were, and asked him if he wished for time to consider what he would do. The man made no reply and looked round bewildered, like a child. Judge Loring again put the question to him in a kind manner, and asked him if he would like to have a day or two and then see him there again. To this he replied faintly, "I would." The judge then ordered a delay until Saturday.

The claimant, Colonel Suttle of Virginia was present, and sat in full sight of the poor negro all the time. I could not get over a feeling that he had seen cruel usage. His scars, his timid and cowed look, his running away, all seemed to indicate it.

May 26

At my suggestion Rev. Mr. Grimes and Deacon Pitts (the clergyman and deacon of the congregation of colored people) and Wendell Phillips [prominent Boston abolitionist] asked leave of the marshal to see him. Phillips reported to me that he was a much more intelligent and resolute man than they supposed him to be, that he could read and write, and only needed a little encouragement to be brought out. He denied entirely having said he was willing to go back. He gave them a power of attorney to act for him, and desired counsel and defense.

They, as his attorneys, engaged me, and I engaged Mr. Ellis to aid me.

At about six o'clock P.M. I went up to see the fugitive. He was confined in a small room, in the third story, west end of the court-house, with some six or eight men in the room with him. The men were of the rough, thief-catching order and were smoking and playing cards. I withdrew to a window and talked quietly with the man.

He appeared a very different man from what he was the day before. He seemed self-possessed, intelligent, and with considerable force of mind and body. His hand had been broken in a saw-mill, he told me, and his face was scarred by a burn. He said that he had not lived with his master since he was seven years old, but had always been hired out by him. That his master had offered him for sale, and he knew very well that if he was delivered up he would never see Alexandria again, but would be taken to the first block and sold for the New Orleans market. He said that there he might be put to some new work he was not accustomed to, and be badly treated for not doing it well. He was in fear of his master, who, he said, was a malicious man if he was crossed.

To-night a great meeting is to be held at Faneuil Hall. There is a strong feeling in favor of a rescue, and some of the abolitionists talk quite freely about it. But the most remarkable exhibition is from the Whigs, the Hunker Whigs, the Compromise men of 1850. Men who would not speak to me in 1850 and 1851 stop me in the street and talk treason.

Amos A. Lawrence [a leading Boston merchant] called to offer any amount of retainer to enable me to employ some eminent Whig counsel. He said he was authorized to do this by a number of active 1850 men, who were determined it should be known that it was not the Free Soilers only who were in favor of the liberation of the slaves, but the conservative, compromise men.

May 27

Last night an attempt was made to rescue the slave. It was conducted by a few and failed for want of numbers, the greater part being opposed to an action then. They broke in a door of the court-house and a few of them entered, but they were not supported. They killed one man, a truck-man named Batchelder, who has volunteered three times to assist in catching and keeping slaves, and the officers retreated. But the men who entered were at first driven back, and the crowd thought themselves re-pulsed and retreated also. The men who went in first were wounded, and on being driven out, they found that the crowd outside had deserted them. The leader of this mob, I am surprised to hear, in secrecy, was Rev. T. W. Higginson of Worcester. I knew his ardor and courage, but I hardly expected a married man, a clergyman, and a man of education to lead the mob.

Robert Carter tells me that Dr. Samuel G. Howe offered to lead a mob of two hundred to storm the court-house, and that it would probably have been done had not Higginson's attempt led the marshal to call out the military.

Immediately after this mob, the marshal sent for a company of United States Marines from Charlestown, and a company of artillery from Fort Independence. The mayor, too, ordered out two or three companies of volunteer militia to keep the peace, but not to aid in the return of the slave.

The hearings began at ten o'clock. The court-house was filled with hire-ling soldiers of the standing army of the United States, nearly all of whom are foreigners. The lazy hounds were lounging all day out of the windows, and hanging over the stairs, but ready to shoot down good men at a word of command. Some difficulties occurred between them and the citizens, but nothing very serious.

This evening I met Rev. Mr. Grimes and Mr. Williams collecting a sub-scription to buy a man's freedom. They had then obtained a subscription to the amount of $700. The price asked was $1,200.

The slave told me that his life had been insured at $1,800 when he was in Richmond, from which he supposed he was valued at about $1,000. It was a new language to hear a man estimating his own value by the rate at which his owners insured him.

The trial of the Burns case occupied all day of Monday, Tuesday and Wednesday, 29th, 30th and 31st of May. Each day the court-room was filled with the United States marshal's "guard" as he called them, a gang of about one hundred and twenty men, the lowest villains in the com-munity, keepers of brothels, bullies, blacklegs, convicts, prize-fighters, etc.

Mr. Andrews, the ex-jailer, says that he finds forty-five men among them who have been under his charge at various times.

To reach the court-room one has to pass two or three cordons of police and two of soldiers. Personally I have been well treated, and all whom I desire to have admitted have been admitted; but there has been a great deal of rudeness and violence to others. In one instance a sergeant or corporal in command of a guard at the foot of the stairs ordered his men to charge. They did so in good earnest and drove the people down the entry and it seemed to me, who had just passed them, a wonder that some were not run through.

There were frequent instances of men prohibited from going into the courts of the state, and no one was permitted to enter the court-house— Judges, jurors, witnesses or litigants—without satisfying the hirelings of the United States marshal that they had a right to be there.

Beside the general "guard" which the marshal had to keep his prisoner, there was a special guard of Southern men, some of them law students from Cambridge, who sat round Colonel Suttle and went in and out with him.

My argument was on Wednesday and lasted four hours. I spoke entirely to my own satisfaction. My friends say it is the best speech I ever made. Even the "guard" were somewhat affected by it, and many of them said they wished the man would get off.

Judge Loring paid great attention to all that related to the identity, but took no notes of my points as to the record, the escape and the title. This puzzled me a good deal.

June 1

I spent all day at home writing out my argument for the newspapers. My whole brief was on the sides of a piece of small note paper, and consequently I was obliged to write from recollection.

June 2

This was a day of intense excitement and deep feeling in the city, in the State and throughout New England, and indeed a great part of the Union. The hearts of millions of persons were beating high with hope, or indignation, or doubt. The mayor of Boston, who is a poor shoat, a physician of a timid, conceited, scatter-brain character, raised by accident to a mayoralty, has vacillated about for several days, and at last has done what a weak man always does, he has gone too far. He has ordered out the entire military force of the city, from 1,500 to 1,800 men, and undertaken to place full discretionary power in the hands of General Edmunds. These troops and the three companies of regulars fill the streets and squares from the court-house to the end of the wharf where the revenue cutter lies, in which it is understood that Burns, if remanded, will be taken to Virginia.

The decision was short. Convicted on an *ex parte* record, against the actual evidence, and on his own admissions made at the moment of arrest to his alleged master! A tyrannical statute and a weak judge!

The decision was a grievous disappointment to us all, and chiefly to the poor prisoner. He looked the image of despair.

The court-room was ordered to be cleared at once of all but the prisoner and the "guard." I remained with the prisoner, and so did Mr. Grimes, the preacher. We remained in the court-room a full hour, in company with the prisoner, and this horrible pack, the "guard." Mr. Grimes talked constantly with the prisoner and kept up his spirits as he best could. He told him he thought that it was only a point of honor with the Government and the slaveholders to take him to Virginia, and that he would be bought as soon as he arrived there. This cheered him.

Mr. Grimes and I walked to and fro in front of the court-house for an hour or so, the entire square being cleared of the people, and filled with troops. Every window was filled, and beyond the lines drawn by the police was an immense crowd. Whenever a body of troops passed to or fro, they were hissed and hooted by the people, with some attempts at applause from their favorers.

Nearly all the shops in Court and State streets were closed and hung in black, and a huge coffin was suspended across State Street and flags [hung] union down. A brass field-piece, belonging to the Fourth Artillery, was ostentatiously loaded in sight of all the people and carried by the men of that corps in rear of the hollow square in which Burns was placed. Some 1,500 or 1,800 men of the volunteer militia were under arms, all with their guns loaded and capped, and the officers with revolvers. These men were stationed at different posts in all the streets and lanes that led into Court or State streets, from the court-house to Long Wharf.

The police forced the people back to a certain line, generally at the foot or middle of the lanes and streets leading into the main streets, and whenever there was a passage, there, a few paces behind the police, was a body of troops, from twenty or thirty to fifty or one hundred, according to the size and importance of the passage.

The mayor having given General Edmunds discretionary orders to preserve peace and enforce the laws, General Edmunds gave orders to each commander of a post to fire on the people whenever they passed the line marked by the police in a manner he should consider turbulent and disorderly.

So, from nine o'clock in the morning until towards night, the city was really under martial law. The entire proceeding was illegal. The people were not treated as rioters or ordered to disperse. No civil officers were on the spot to direct the military or to give orders when and how to act. But the people were given their line, as on a parade day, and the troops were ordered, by a military commander, to fire upon them, at the discretion of the various commanders of posts. An accident would have cost lives, and it was with great reluctance, and only after repeated orders, that these men would uncock their guns and bring them to order. It has been the greatest good fortune in the world that not a gun was fired by accident or design. No one could limit the consequences; and all concerned would have been in the eye of the law murderers.

Mr. Grimes and I remained in the court-house until the vile procession moved. Notwithstanding their numbers and the enormous military protection, the marshal's company were very much disturbed and excited. They were exceedingly apprehensive of some unknown and unforeseen violence.

The "guard" at length filed out and formed a hollow square. Each man was armed with a short Roman sword and one revolver hanging in his belt. In this square marched Burns with the marshal. The United States troops and the squadron of Boston light horse preceded and followed the square, with the field-piece.

As the procession moved down, it was met with a perfect howl of Shame! Shame!

Anthony Burns was bought out of slavery after his return to Virginia. He studied theology at Oberlin College and became pastor of a Baptist church in St. Catherine's, Ontario. He died in 1862, in his thirty-second year.

1854: CRY FROM THE HEART OF A
BLACK GIRL

A SIXTEEN-YEAR-OLD Negro girl was in the crowd that milled angrily through the streets of Boston while troops guarded the courthouse where the arrested runaway slave, Anthony Burns, awaited his fate. Had she been a man, Charlotte Forten might have led an attack on the soldiers, guns or no guns. Such was the girl's spirit.

Charlotte was of the fifth generation in America of a family with a proud tradition. Her grandfather had served the cause of freedom as a drummer boy in the Revolutionary War. Later in life, in the business of making sails, he became one of the richest men in Philadelphia. But always in James Forten's eyes, ahead of business, ahead of money, came freedom. He was one of the first leaders of the abolitionist movement. Charlotte's father, Robert Bridges Forten, carried on the fight. He refused to let the child attend the segregated schools of Philadelphia. Instead he sent her to live with the family of Negro abolitionist Charles Lenox Remond in Salem, Massachusetts, and go to school there.

Charlotte studied hard. She wrote well. At the graduation exercises in Higginson Grammar School "A Parting Hymn," written especially for the occasion, was sung. Afterward the principal announced that the "beautiful hymn" was written by a student, but she didn't know which one. "Will the author step forward?" Nobody moved. She repeated her request. And as the hall rang with applause from Salem's leading citizens, Charlotte timidly went to the platform. Later she wrote for the Atlantic Monthly and many other publications.

She became a teacher in Salem—a teacher of white children—but in 1862 she was sent to Port Royal, one of the Sea Islands off the coast of South Carolina, which had been wrested from the Confederacy early in the war.

The North was embarked on an interesting social experiment there. Some 10,000 slaves in the vicinity had been abandoned by their fleeing masters. As liberated people they were gathered at Port Royal. General Sherman, commanding 12,000 soldiers at the island, saw the need for demonstrating to the world that these untaught slaves could learn to live in peace with each other and with the whites and to become useful free citizens. It was Charlotte Forten's job to help in their education.

The new community proved a success. Charlotte then returned North to go on with her writing. In 1878 she married Francis J. Grimke, a student at Princeton Theological Seminary whose father was a white man, a South Carolina planter, and whose mother had been a slave. He became a Presbyterian minister in Washington and an untiring fighter for Negro rights.

Charlotte Forten's journal was published in 1953. In his introduction editor Ray Allen Billington gives the whole of the unique and fascinating story of the Forten family. Of Charlotte and her diary he says:

> "This racial consciousness endows Miss Forten's Journal with an importance in the twentieth century that it scarcely enjoyed in the nineteenth. Enlightened individuals today have dedicated themselves to a crusade for equality and human decency. Yet how few among them— how few among the nonpersecuted, that is—can know the effect of prejudice on its victims. Miss Forten's Journal makes this effect terrifyingly clear."

"We endeavor vainly not to hate."
CHARLOTTE L. FORTEN (1838-1914)

May 26, 1854

Had a conversation with Miss Shepard [principal of the Higginson Grammar School in Salem] about slavery; she is, as I thought, thoroughly opposed to it, but does not agree with me in thinking that the churches and ministers are generally supporters of the infamous system; I believe it firmly.

Mr. Barnes, one of the most prominent of the Philadelphia clergy, who does not profess to be an abolitionist, has declared his belief that "the American church is a bulwark of slavery."

Words cannot express all that I feel; all that is felt by the friends of Freedom, when thinking of this great obstacle to the removal of slavery from our land. Alas! that it should be so.

June 2

Our worst fears are realized. The decision was against poor Burns [Anthony Burns, arrested in Boston under the Fugitive Slave Act], and he has been sent back to a bondage worse, a thousand times worse than death.

With what scorn must that government be regarded, which cowardly assembles thousands of soldiers to satisfy the demands of slave holders; to deprive of his freedom a man, created in God's own image, whose sole offense is the color of his skin! And if resistance is offered to this outrage, these soldiers are to shoot down American citizens without mercy; and this by the express orders of a government which proudly boasts of being the freest in the world; this on the very soil where the Revolution of 1776 began.

I can write no more. A cloud seems hanging over me, over all our persecuted race, which nothing can dispel.

June 4

To-morrow school commences, and although the pleasure I shall feel in again seeing my beloved teacher, and in resuming my studies will be much saddened by recent events, yet they shall be a fresh incentive to more earnest study, to aid me in fitting myself for laboring in a holy cause, for enabling me to do much towards changing the condition of my oppressed and suffering people.

Would that those with whom I shall recite to-morrow could sympathize with me in this; would that they could look upon all God's creatures without respect to color, feeling that it is character alone which makes the true man or woman!

June 5

Miss Church [Elizabeth, a student from Bridgetown, Nova Scotia, who became a close friend] and I counted the merits of the first and second classes for Miss Shepard; after school, had an hour's conversation with her about slavery and prejudice.

I fully appreciate her kindness and sympathy with me; she wishes me to cultivate a Christian spirit in thinking of my enemies; I know it is right, and will endeavor to do so, but it does seem very difficult.

June 16

As I sit by the window, studying, a robin redbreast perched on the large apple tree in the garden, warbles his morning salutation in my ears; music far sweeter to me than the clearer tones of the Canary birds in their cages, for they are captives, while he is free.

June 25

This afternoon went to an anti-slavery meeting in Danvers, from which I have just returned. Mr. Foss [Rev. Andrew D., an agent of the Massachusetts Anti-Slavery Society] spoke eloquently, and with that warmth and sincerity which evidently comes from the heart.

He said he was rejoiced that the people at the North were beginning to feel that slavery is no longer confined to the black man alone, but that they too must wear the yoke; and they are becoming roused on the subject at last.

He spoke of the objections made by many to the Abolitionists, on the plea of their using too violent language; they say that the slaveholders are driven by it to worse measures; what they need is mild entreaty, etc. But the petition against the Nebraska Bill, couched in the very mildest terms by the clergymen of the North, was received even less favorably by the South than the hardest sayings of the Abolitionists; and they were abused and denounced more severely than the latter have ever been.

July 17

I have seen to-day a picture of a dear old English church. Oh, England, my heart yearns towards thee as to a loved and loving friend! I long to behold thee, to dwell in one of thy quiet homes, far from the scenes of my early childhood; far from the land, my native land, where I am hated and oppressed because God has given me a dark skin. How did this cruel, this absurd prejudice ever exist? How can it exist?

August 11

I have been thinking lately very much about death, that strange, mysterious, awful reality that is constantly around and among us, that power which takes away from us so many of those whom we love and honor, or those who have persecuted and oppressed us, our bitter enemies whom we vainly endeavor not to hate.

Oh! I long to be good, to be able to meet death calmly and fearlessly, strong in faith and holiness. But this I know can only be through One who died for us, through the pure and perfect love of Him who was all holiness and love.

But how can I hope to be worthy of His love while I still cherish this feeling towards my enemies, this unforgiving spirit? This is a question which I ask myself very often. Other things in comparison with this seem easy to overcome. But hatred of oppression seems to me so blended with hatred of the oppressor I cannot separate them. I feel that no other injury could be so hard to bear, so very hard to forgive, as that inflicted by cruel prejudice. How can I be a Christian when so many in common with myself, for no crime, suffer so cruelly, so unjustly?

September 5

I have suffered much to-day. My friends Mrs. Putnam [an educated Negro woman, wife of a Salem grocer] and her daughters were refused admission to the Museum, after having tickets given them, solely on account of their complexion. Insulting language was used to them. Of course they felt and exhibited deep, bitter indignation; but of what avail was it? None, but to excite the ridicule of those contemptible creatures, miserable doughfaces who do not deserve the name of men. I will not attempt to write more. No words can express my feelings. But these cruel wrongs cannot be much longer endured. A day of retribution must come. God grant that it may come very soon!

September 12

I wonder that every colored person is not a misanthrope. Surely we have everything to make us hate mankind. I have met girls in the school-room—they have been thoroughly kind and cordial to me, perhaps the next day met them in the street—they feared to recognize me; these I can but regard now with scorn and contempt; once I liked them, believing them incapable of such meanness. Others gave the most distant recognition possible. I, of course, acknowledge no such recognitions, and they soon cease entirely.

These are but trifles, certainly, to the great public wrongs which we as a people are obliged to endure. But to those who experience them, these apparent trifles are most wearing and discouraging; even to the child's mind they reveal volumes of deceit and heartlessness, and early teach a lesson of suspicion and distrust.

O! it is hard to go through life meeting contempt with contempt, hatred with hatred, fearing, with too good reason, to love and trust hardly any one whose skin is white,—however lovable, attractive and congenial in seeming.

In the bitter, passionate feelings of my soul again and again there rises the questions "When, oh! when shall this cease?" "Is there no help?" "How long oh! how long must we continue to suffer—to endure?" Conscience answers it is wrong, it is ignoble to despair; let us labor earnestly and faithfully to acquire knowledge, to break down the barriers of prejudice and oppression. Let us take courage; never ceasing to work,—hoping and believing that if not for us, for another generation there is a better, brighter day in store,—when slavery and prejudice shall vanish before the glorious light of Liberty and Truth; when the rights of every colored man shall everywhere be acknowledged and respected, and he shall be treated as a *man* and a *brother!*

1856:   DEATH RACES THE GOVERNOR
OF KANSAS

SENATOR STEPHEN A. DOUGLAS of Illinois wanted a transcontinental railroad. He wanted it so badly that to get the necessary support of the South he was willing to trade away the solemn pledge of the federal government to hold the soil of Kansas forever free. The result was the Kansas-Nebraska Act of 1854 which provided for a territorial government and substituted the euphemism "popular sovereignty" for the guarantee against slavery given in the Missouri Compromise of 1821.

Thus were sown the winds of strife in the West, and Kansas reaped the whirlwind—a stream of resolute emigrants from New England to settle and vote against slavery; vote-and-run raids from slave-holding Missouri, crossing over to stuff the ballot boxes and then go home; hired ruffians from Alabama with rifles slung over their shoulders; and the inevitable outbreak of bloody clashes that helped speed the nation into civil war.

Such backbone as President Franklin Pierce possessed he wore thin bowing to the will of the South. As the first governor of Kansas Territory he named a man of known pro-slavery leanings, a Pennsylvania lawyer named Andrew H. Reeder. When Reeder went to Leavenworth to take over, he didn't know the character of the Missouri raiders. He expected Kansas to legalize slavery forthwith by popular vote, and if he had any troubles they would come from the New England infiltration.

He learned better soon enough. When an election took place in November of a delegate to Congress, 1,700 gun-toting Missourians crossed over, cast their votes, threatened the lives of antislavery emigrants if they came near the ballot box, and went home the same day. By the same process a pro-slavery legislature was voted in for the Territory the following March.

Reeder, a man of integrity, was shocked and angered. His viewpoint toward slavery in Kansas, moreover, was completely changed. He refused to grant election certificates to the members of the legislature and called for new elections in several districts.

This threw the pro-slavers into a frenzy. To them, Reeder was a traitor. In Washington Jefferson Davis, the Confederate President-to-be, demanded his removal. A charge was trumped up against him of land speculation. The Territorial Legislature met without benefit of certificates. It voted extreme slave laws —jail for uttering a word against slavery, the death penalty for helping a slave to escape. Reeder vetoed its every act. In July he was notified from Washington of his removal from the office of Governor.

Now he was in the fight all the way. He attended a convention of the Free State Party, was elected its delegate to Congress, went to Washington on the futile mission of claiming his seat, and then returned to Kansas. In the spring of 1856, while he was in Lawrence, groups of armed men from South Carolina, Alabama and Georgia began quietly entering the area. They camped around Lecompton and Lawrence. A grand jury was called. It charged Reeder with treason and served a subpoena on him, which he ignored.

But with the forces now brought in against him, Reeder knew he was helpless, and he had good reason to believe they were after his life—with a pretense of legality if possible; if not, then with gun or rope.

In his diary he tells what happened then.

". . . this drunken, crazy mob . . ."
ANDREW H. REEDER (1807-1864)

Lawrence, Kansas, May 8 [1856]

I had learned from good authority that my life was not safe from private assassination at Lecompton and I had made up my mind that I would not go there to be kept for six months, in danger of nightly assassination. Same night a discussion was had whether I should wait and fight the posse that would come after me. Decided to wait till next day, and I stayed at my quarters at the hotel.

May 9

Considered best that I should disappear for the present, and about 10 A.M. I left in a buggy with Lyman Allen, and with a borrowed overcoat and cap, drove to the ravine and walked down its bed to E. W. Clark's, where I remained secreted all day.

Evening. First night's travel will be dangerous, as we must pass through the enemy's scouts. I decided to hide till the next evening and then start for Kansas City; Jenkins to make the arrangements.

Left at once with Jenkins and rode to the house of —— Morgan and G. W. Goss, who roused up and gave me a bed; (about a mile south of town).

May 10

Remained shut up in bedroom all day. Concluded to avoid the main road on account of a company at Franklin and the height of the Wakarusa [River]. Went by Blanton's—missed the road, and did not reach Fish's till near 1 o'clock at night, too late to pass Westport till long after daylight.

Stayed at Fish's concealed; put horses and carriage out of sight.

May 11

Kept concealed upstairs. Many persons passed, through the day, and stopped; among them Milt. M'Gee, who would have given his whole team to know who was up stairs. Left at 7:30 P.M. Road clear. Arrived at Kansas City about 2 o'clock in the morning; found Col. Eldridge; room ready for us; dangerous neighbors across the passage.

May 12

Remained concealed. Boat came up, and among passengers was G. W. Brown, of Lawrence. Rumors of a mob to take him, and I was removed to [Room] No. 25 for greater safety.

Brown shut himself up in No. 28.

A mob of 30 or 40 assembled, headed by Milt. M'Gee, who came into the hotel, and going by mistake to O. C. Brown's room, they dragged him out and took him down town—discovered their error and let him go.

Looking out of my front windows, I saw and heard M'Gee, H. C. Pate, and another, in conversation, and Pate was instructing a man to go in and look for some one and described me so that from what I heard I recognized the description.

In the evening it was found that men were posted all around the house to prevent any escapes—all over the hill back of the house and in the hacks and wagons in front, besides those walking up and down the street. No light kept in my room, which Mrs. Arms had kindly abandoned to me.

May 13

I remained a prisoner in my room, but was most kindly waited on by the ladies, who took a lively interest in my safety, and whose kindness I cannot soon forget.

Evening. Colonel Eldridge came to my room, much excited, to say that the deputy marshal, with two of the same posses that had come to arrest

me at Lawrence, had just arrived and were in the house. We concluded
of course that they were after me, and I supposed they had heard of my
leaving Lawrence on Saturday evening. Expecting them to come, I concealed this diary, and made preparations. I remained up, till midnight,
and there was a constant running up and down from the street to their
room.

May 14

After dinner it was thought best to remove me to [Room] 25, as the
disturbance of orderly arrangements consequent on Mr. and Mrs. Arms
being out of their room, and the door being locked all day, might excite
suspicion; and it was accordingly done.

May 15

About 100 young men said to be from South Carolina and Georgia,
arrived, as I am told, last evening, all armed and have evidently come, not
as emigrants, but only to fight. This looks as though the crisis was to
come sooner than we expected. God grant it may not be till we get more
men, more arms, and more powder.

May 17

Boat after boat passes down before my window, and my confinement
begins to be more and more galling and chafing. I must leave here soon,
at all risks. The nights have been very unfavorable, and are so still. It
has been bright moonlight for a week past.

May 18

I must be off before the assailants of Lawrence come here, for they
will swarm down here like a pack of wolves, and will probably search the
house. Coates says the *Amazon* will be down to-night, and he can, he
thinks, get me on board, as he is well acquainted with Captain Choteau.
   Midnight. Amazon has not arrived as expected.

May 19

The *Amazon* still not here, and this almost the last chance to get off. If
she should be delayed till to-night it might yet answer.
   12 o'clock. Amazon arrives and goes down the river without me.

May 22

This morning the *Star of the West*. A note from Coates is thrown over
my door, saying that Lawrence is taken. Hotel destroyed. The mob will
probably be here to-night or to-day, and will be very likely to attack or
search the house. What will become of me? My poor, dear wife! She is
uppermost in my thoughts. And should I be murdered by this crazy,

drunken mob, as is probable if they should discover me, she will probably first learn it from a newspaper. God have mercy on her and my dear,
dear Ida, my own fond Emma, and my three loved and precious boys.
How these ties drag me down! If not for them, how boldly and proudly
could I not denounce and defy my pursuers, and die in conflict with a
thousand of them. But God's will be done. If I am taken from the dear
ones He has given me it will be for the best, and He will care for them.

Mr. Leonard Arms comes in to say that it is beyond all question the intention to destroy this house, as soon as they get back from Lawrence;
but he thinks that if I can get out by 8 or 9 o'clock, I can get away. Sad
Chance! I can perhaps find a place to stay for a few days, but how am
I to get away? What will twenty-four or even twelve hours produce? If I
can refrain from speaking or thinking of my wife and children, I think I
can show them how a brave and honest man can die. But when I recur
to them, my throat chokes and my eyes fill.

Mrs. Coates reports that I can go to Brown's, but that I must not come
till after dark. It is now 5 o'clock P.M., and I have put on such disguise as
I can get, the dress of an Irish laborer. Have cut off my whole beard and
soiled my face with cork—burnt.

As I write, a party of the invaders come down and cross the ferry on
their way home, shouting threats against the American Hotel, and whooping and yelling like Indians, and, as soon as they reach the opposite shore,
firing off their arms. Give me four hours more and will leave the house. I
have written a hasty last will, which I leave in this book, care of Mr.
Coates.

6 o'clock. News is received of the attack on Lawrence and the destruction of the hotel. A few men killed.

8:30 o'clock. Mr. Hubbard and Mr. Eldridge came up to say that all
is ready, and that Brown is waiting to go with me. I declined to leave the
house with Brown, preferring to walk out alone and join Brown on the
road.

After they left, I lit my pipe and walked boldly down the front stairs,
through the office, which was crowded with people. Elbowing through
them, I passed into the bar-room and out on the steps. Dozens of people
were sitting and standing about the door and on the sidewalk, many of
them the most obnoxious men, who were well acquainted with me.

I stood quite unconcerned on the steps until I saw a vacant chair, and
went to it and sat down. My friends were about, and by my previous directions engaged those in conversation who were nearest and most dangerous. After sitting some minutes, I walked deliberately up the road,
unmolested and unrecognized, with a sense of great relief; found Brown

on the way, and went on to his house in the edge of the timber, and quite out of town; found there Mr. Davis and wife, who have a room rented— D. E. Adams, and J. McIntyre.

Sat out of doors and enjoyed the freedom and fresh air.

May 23

Obliged to keep close house during the day, in a stifling room. Determined I could not stay here; consulted with Adams as to taking a small skiff and running down the river at night so as to be taken on board the *Converse* as she passed.

Agreed on the plan. Sent Adams to buy a skiff and tell Eldridge to send some provisions and have him or Coates make the arrangements with Capt. G. W. Bowman as he shall come down to-morrow.

Adams returns and reports; and the plan during the day is fully matured by help of Hubbard and McIntyre. In the evening Adams leaves to get the skiff and scull it out of the Kansas river to a place about a mile below town.

About 9 o'clock McIntyre and I start, each with an axe, and, skirting the town for a while, then passed along the main road to the river.

Hunted along the shore; could not find Adams or the boat. I went into a ravine and McIntyre continued his lookout. Adams made his appearance. He and I took the road to the skiff unperceived. We floated quietly down the river to Randolph landing. The moon was then fully risen, and bright. Got safely into the woods above the road, where we slept till morning.

May 24

About 7½ o'clock we shouldered our axes and bundle and sack, and trudged up the road past the few houses that constitute Randolph. Encountered five or six persons on the road, but no one paid much attention to us.

At 12 o'clock heard the whistle of the boat for Kansas City, five miles above. Waited one-half hour by the watch, and then left the ravine. Saw the boat coming, but could not make out her name till she was so near that we had to run down the road. She hauled up to the landing full of passengers, and as the plank was run out I went on board panting with heat, fatigue and thirst.

Passed back among the deck passengers, where, according to my dress, I belonged. The deck clerk soon called for my fare, and I took a ticket to Waverly. I turned into one of the hot and stifling berths.

Toward evening I got up, and walked about, got some water, and to my consternation I learned from their talk that some of my fellow-passengers were a part of the invading force returning from the sacking of Lawrence. Among them I saw Henry L. Rout, a lawyer of Liberty, Mo., who picked up my pipe which I had dropped in the berth, and made some jocular remark to me. I was confident he knew me, and was very uneasy, especially as we were to lay that night at Lexington.

Arrived at Lexington about 8 o'clock; divested myself of all that would lead to my identification or that was inconsistent with my dress. Sat about on the boat till about 11 o'clock, and then went to bed.

May 25

Laid in my bunk till near 9 o'clock. As we passed Waverly the clerk came and notified me. I told him that a gentleman on board had informed me that my friends did not live there any more, and that I would go on to Booneville.

My bedfellow was a pro-slavery man by the name of Ross, very genteelly dressed, of whom I had become very suspicious and who seemed to watch me very closely.

This evening was laid up at Booneville, and there I quietly paid on to St. Louis.

May 26

When we stopped at Jefferson City I watched, as I did at all the landings, the persons who passed on and off the boat, and to my surprise I saw Mr. Ross, my bedfellow, going ashore with his carpet-sack, although he had paid to St. Louis. Watching, I observed that he went direct to the railroad depot. This being about 11 A.M., it was plain that he could get to St. Louis before evening and have a warrant for me so as to arrest me at once. Sent for captain, proposed that he should see the man at the woodyard where we were lying and get me a guide across the country to Alton, so that I could arrive before the boat from St. Louis, and take a conveyance to the next railroad station above.

Captain could get no guide, but had the route described. The steward got my bundle upstairs for me, into the room of Bassett and Brackett. My valise was taken there.

Passed quickly into the room of Bassett and Brackett. I changed my clothes and then learned from my friends that two of the deck passengers were out on the guards evidently on the watch.

Determined, however, to go, and if followed to fight it out. Bassett and Brackett had no weapons. I had two revolvers and a knife, and supplied them. A violent thunder storm came up, and in it, toward the close, we put out the lights and started.

The woods being close to the shore we stopped in them to see if we were followed. Waited a short time; no one came off the boat, and we struck through the woods; lost the road twice; traveled on, and finally, at 8 o'clock A.M., struck the Mississippi River fifteen miles above Alton.

Got a man to take us across in a skiff.

May 27

In Illinois. Bassett and Brackett found a boat going down to Alton, and I hired a team to take me to Jerseyville, fourteen miles.

At Jerseyville found a good hotel and livery stable, and hired a man to take me to Brighton, where I got on the evening train for Chicago.

I learned the night before, as we traveled through the woods, that the ruffians had broken open my trunk at Lawrence, stolen and put on my clothes, and chased Chapin, of Ohio, as he came out of the hotel, calling out that it was me, firing at him, and threatening to kill him; and that there was a universal determination expressed among them to kill me.

Arrived at Chicago.

1851-66: LINCOLN'S UNFADING OLD SOLDIER

FEW AMERICANS have ever heard of Ethan Allen Hitchcock. In many a history he is not even mentioned. Yet this soldier from Vermont, grandson of Ethan Allen, was one of the most brilliant and—behind the scenes—influential men in Lincoln's war councils.

Years before, in the Mexican War, he had proved himself an able strategist. Bernard DeVoto in his history The Year of Decision: 1846 describes Hitchcock as "the most intelligent officer in the highest ranks of the army." In 1847 he was one of the chief planners of the sensational capture of Mexico City for which Congress voted a medal to General Winfield Scott.

But Hitchcock was chronically ill and continually wanting to get out of the service to give himself over wholly to the study of classical literature, in which he was advanced. Reluctantly he agreed to go to California in 1851 to "explore" —actually to see if he could help consolidate the newly won American position there and gain the support and loyalty of disgruntled Indians and Mexicans.

In 1862 he was even more hesitant to answer a call from Washington. There he was told he would be placed in command over Grant in the operations against Fort Henry, Tennessee. He refused, saying Grant was "doing all he could." Then he was told he could have any command he wanted. He chose to remain in Washington as military adviser to Lincoln, which may account for the fact that Lincoln's military decisions were pretty consistently sounder than those of his field generals. If Hitchcock's role was a quiet one, it was also unique. So was the man, and so was his story as he himself tells it.

"I am heartsick."
ETHAN ALLEN HITCHCOCK
(1798-1870)

New Y., April 27 [1851]

Here's a change! but it was not unexpected. Yesterday orders reached this city announcing my promotion to be Colonel of the 2d Infantry, and directing me to join my regiment in California. Am getting ready for a start.

28th April

On board steamer for Troy. Must go to Burlington [Vermont] once more and look upon the gravestones of my father's family. Went to church twice yesterday. In the morning Rev. Mr. S. preached from Revelations, a sermon as dark as the Apocalypse; in the afternoon a jackanapes preached on the resurrection, and assured us that we should know our friends hereafter—I thought 'twas more than most of us do here.

Burlington, Vt. April 29

Most of those I knew are in the graveyard, where, last evening, I wandered for an hour reading the inscriptions commemorating the death of great numbers whose names were once so familiar to me and whose appearance my memory recalls as if I were looking at them.

But there they are—or their bodies are—in repose—eternal repose. And once or twice it crossed my mind that perhaps 'tis just as well to be there as to be living the feverish life of most of us which, be the life what it may, is always "rounded with a sleep."

It amazes me to think that people should look with terror at what is beyond the grave. That we should shrink from the pain which sometimes accompanies dying is natural enough, and that those who have friends should regret to part with them is equally natural; but that anyone should fear what is beyond the tomb is mere wide-awake madness and folly.

Portland, Oregon, August 15

Arrived last evening. The town is new, only three or four years old, hastily built up of timber.

August 25

I must establish a post in Rogue River Valley. I can find nobody who has been over the country from Fort Oxford to the East; I must therefore send out an exploring expedition. This is one of the official results of my coming here; one of the unofficial results is that I paid seventy-five cents to have my hair cut.

August 29

Saw some emigrants, just arrived. Four months coming from Lexington, Ky. A party of about a dozen men with wives and children—two children born on the way and doing well—one three and the other four weeks old. Mothers proud of the feat. The party stopped only an hour for one of them and but a short time for the other. Indians gave them no trouble, but other parties recently have had trouble. One of them stole an Indian horse and was followed and had a woman and child killed. This, of course, will be reported as an Indian outrage.

December 21

What do writers mean by talking about the primitive condition of life and "primitive times," when close by me here are natives who go naked throughout the year, winter and summer, the men not wearing moccasins or even a breach cloth and the women using only the fig leaf or its substitute.

San Francisco, Apr. 18 [1852]

My books have arrived—30 boxes in all—cost of carriage $200. Am waiting to get them. Have driven out to the Presidio, and listened with delight to the surf breaking on the rocks below—relief from the everlasting talk about "property," "water lots" etc. Great God! What an affliction, to hear this eternal chatter about this man and that who has made so much money in such a time!

July 31

I called to see the Methodist minister to-day. Found there a man dressed like a gentleman, who would be doubtless offended to be told he was none, who had the audacity to say that Providence designed the extermination of the Indians and that it would be a good thing to introduce the small-pox among them! He soon found himself alone in that savage sentiment, but it is the opinion of most white people living in the interior of the country.

Dec. 6

At breakfast this morning, having thought much of resigning from the army, I tried to realize how I should feel as a private man. Certainly no one can value the externals of a position less than I do. I am so far from priding myself upon place that to get rid of the feeling of it is one of the objects I hope to accomplish by resigning. How many thousands of my fellow-men look with envy upon my power and privileges—as if I had no sense of my higher obligation to duty or Nature!

Feb. 16 [1854]

Just after I had retired last evening, Capt. Tecumseh Sherman called and told me of the sad calamity of the loss of the *San Francisco* with Colonel Washington and 150 of our troops and the arrival here of General Wool to supersede me.

Feb. 17

General Wool has issued this day his first order as in command of the Department of the Pacific. I may tarry here some weeks to settle my private business. I am now not in command, and not on duty—and I really feel relieved, in an agreeable sense. Have been employed in burning old letters and memoranda—an exceedingly unpleasant task. Is it I myself? Am I the same person I was in 1844? Or in 1824? It seems very strange.

New York, May 9

Arrived at the dock at midnight, twenty-three days from San Francisco—a remarkably short passage. Have been received in the most cordial manner by Gen. Scott. After asking my preferences he has given me an order putting me on duty in the city in command of my regiment. I am to superintend recruiting.

[May 28]

I have been seriously thinking of resigning from the army. I consider the slavery in our country an element guided by passion rather than by reason; its existence among us is shaking the whole fabric of our government.

As to leaving the army: I may do so if I choose at this time and no one notice me, for I am unknown except to a few friends. If I wait and a war with Spain be forced on us, such a war would be a downward instead of an upward step for our republican institutions, and might easily justify my own conscience in refusing to be an instrument in the unjust campaign.

I might draw a line between my duty to remain in the army to repulse any attempt made from abroad upon us, and the questionable duty of going beyond our borders to inflict a direct wrong upon another people.

May 31

I consider war an evil, whether necessary or not.

Carlisle, Pa., July 13

An order here by the Secretary of War to assume command of the barracks, where my regiment (six companies of it) is to be assembled.

St. Louis, May 6 [1861]

I am packing up for New York, my object being to get out of the secession fever which now agitates the city and State. There are 27 boxes of books.

Many friends urge my return to the army. But I have no heart for engaging in a civil war. I cannot think of it. If fighting could preserve the Union (or restore it) I might consider what I could do to take part—but when did fighting make friends? To my vision—and I note it with a feeling of dread—the great American Republic is broken up. What is to come out of it can hardly be imagined just now.

Saratoga Springs, New York, July 6 [1861]

The President asks for unlimited men and money to put down the great Rebellion in the South. It may be done if the war is understood to be against the rebellious party as a party, and not against the South as a people. If its effect should be to divide the North on questions connected with it—then farewell to the Republic!

Feb. 2 [1862]

General Halleck told me this morning that he had received a letter from General McClellan and that I would "certainly" be appointed a major general of volunteers. This news does not please me.

St. Louis, Feb. 20

Have been appointed major general of volunteers and the appointment has been unanimously confirmed by the Senate. And before it reaches me I have written to the Secretary of War declining it. My health will not allow me to accept it, if there were no other reason.

Washington, March 15

On the 7th I received a telegraph dispatch from the Secretary of War [Stanton] saying that he would like a "personal conference" with me. I jumped into the next departing train, had a serious and violent hemorrhage at Pittsburgh, arrived here on Monday the 10th, and weak and covered with dust as I was, went directly to the War Department.

Secretary Stanton was with the President and the Assistant Secretary said he would send me word. I returned to my hotel, and there was seized with a profuse bleeding at the nose—the sixth or seventh time in three weeks. Two physicians stopped the bleeding and I was sent to bed, very much exhausted.

In the morning the Secretary himself came to see me. He told me that he wanted me in the service. I replied that I was not fit for service, and appealed to his own eyes. He remarked, "You must leave that to us," and went on to say that he and President Lincoln wanted me here, close by, where they could have the opportunity of consulting me. I said I must go to New York to consult physicians.

I got up and started at 11 A.M. for New York. At New York I finally determined to say by note to the Secretary that if, with his knowledge of my broken health, I could be useful in the way he had pointed out, he might announce my acceptance of the commission and order me to report to him. That was done and I reached here this morning.

On reporting to the Secretary he asked me if I would take McClellan's place in command of the army of the Potomac! I was amazed and told him at once I could not.

He then took me to President Lincoln, and introduced me. The President took a letter from his pocket and read it as a sample, he said, of what he was exposed to. It was anonymous, marked "urgent," and called on him to "remove the traitor McClellan"—using the most extravagant language of condemnation.

He then expressed the wish to have the benefit of my experience: said he was the depository of the power of the government, and had no military knowledge. I shortly left him. Now, what is to come of this?

Monday evening, March 17

Towards evening he [Stanton] came in, and shutting the door behind him, stated to me the most astounding facts, all going to show the astonishing incompetency of General McClellan. I cannot recite them: but the Secretary stated fact after fact, until I felt positively *sick*—that falling of the heart that excludes hope.

I do not wonder, now, that the Secretary offered even me the command of the army of the Potomac, which, he says, is 230,000 strong. The Secretary is dreadfully apprehensive of a great disaster, which is not improbable. I am heartsick.

New York, May 21

Again sent in my resignation as Major General on the 15th inst. I could not persuade the Sec. to accept it, and could not require it against his wishes.

By this time I have discovered that the whole country has begun to look upon me as the "Military Adviser" of the Secretary of War. This is very distasteful to me because it seems to make me responsible for those very movements of which I have disapproved.

Washington, Sept. 24 [1863]

I make very few notes—have made few since the war began. I go to my duties in the War office at 9 or 10 in the morning and remain usually till 4 or 5 o'clock.

May 18 [1864]

Grant fought a battle every day for a week—a great series of encounters. I could not endure the exposure of a campaign for a month. I rejoice now that I had the strength to resist the instigations of pride [in 1862 when he was offered command over Grant] and leave Grant to continue uninterruptedly in his path of glory. His name is now the most honored of any in the nation. I thank God I do not envy him but rejoice that the country finds in him an able commander.

July 6

The enemy (Jubal Early) appeared at Harper's Ferry last Saturday ('tis now Wednesday). I went to the President. I said that although Early was on the Potomac near this city, General Halleck seemed very apathetic.

"That's his way," said Mr. Lincoln; "he is always apathetic."

I looked him in the eye, leaning forward on the table, and said:

"If Stonewall Jackson were living and in command of Early's troops, in my opinion, sir, he would be in Washington in three days."

Mr. Lincoln was very much struck with the expression of such an opinion, and said he guessed something ought to be done. "I'll speak to the Secretary of War about it."

July 28

Halleck told me, some days after Early had been driven away from the front of the capital that the President had, after my call, telegraphed a "request" to General Grant to send some troops for the defence of the capital, and that General Grant sent hurriedly part of the 6th and part of the 19th corps. The force reached here just in time. I consider that my earnest intervention with the President saved this city from capture by Early's army.

June 4 [1866]

I called this morning to see Secretary Seward. I was very cordially greeted. After some general conversation he remarked, "We have lost General [Winfield] Scott. He was the first man I ever heard speak of you at the beginning of the war. He presented a list of names for generals and among them was yours—the first on the list."

I had heard as much from others. I have reason to be thankful that I was not tempted to allow the Secretary to give me precedence over officers who have been effective in putting down the rebellion. I am content.

1861:   THE FEDERALS ARE ROUTED AT
BULL RUN

FROM THE CONFEDERATE ATTACK *on Fort Sumter which began the Civil War on April 12, 1861, the North believed it was going to be a short war. But with the disastrous defeat at Bull Run three months later, all complacency vanished. Enlistment was changed forthwith from three months to three years. More upsetting than the tactical loss was the lack of morale it revealed. And just how serious this was the North learned mainly from one man.*

William Howard Russell (Sir William after 1895) had been a war correspondent for twenty years when the London Times sent him to America in 1861. He had a wide reputation, not only for unbending honesty but also as an influential interpreter. So devastating had been his exposé of British bumbling in the Crimean War that it had helped bring about the fall of the ministry in London.

With the same candor Russell reported what he saw at Bull Run. The North was scandalized. At the capital he was accused of depicting it as worse than it really was. Later when he wanted a pass to go with McClellan he was turned down. Years afterward, however, students of the Civil War agreed that he had not exaggerated.

If Russell was in his element when describing what went on before his eyes, he was less so when gazing into the crystal ball. He expected two nations to emerge from the Civil War. Back home, in 1862, he wrote:

> Although I have never for one moment seen reason to change the opinion I expressed in the first letter I wrote from the States, that the Union as it was could never be restored, I am satisfied the Free States of the North will retain and gain great advantages by the struggle, if they will only set themselves at work to accomplish their destiny, nor lose their time in sighing over vanished empire or indulging in abortive dreams of conquest and schemes of vengeance.

Here, from Russell's diary, is the battle story that shook the North to its vitals.

"They have cut us all to pieces."
WILLIAM HOWARD RUSSELL
(1821-1907)

July 20 [1861]

The great battle which is to arrest rebellion or to make it a power in the land is no longer distant or doubtful. McDowell has completed his reconnaissance of the country in front of the enemy, and General Scott anticipates that he will be in possession of Manassas tomorrow night. All the statements of officers concur in describing the Confederates as strongly entrenched along the line of Bull's Run covering the railroad.

July 21

It was a strange scene before us; the landscape, inclosed in a framework of blue and purple hills, softened into violet in the extreme distance, one of the most agreeable displays of simple pastoral scenery that could be conceived.

But the sounds which came upon the breeze and the sights which met our eyes were in terrible variance with the tranquil character of the landscape. The woods far and near echoed to the roar of cannon, and thin, frayed lines of blue smoke marked the spots whence came the muttering sound of rolling musketry; the white puffs of smoke burst high above the treetops, and the gunners' rings from shell and howitzer marked the fire of the artillery.

The road was cut up by gun-wheels, ammunition and commissariat wagons that our horses made but slow way against the continual draft upon the collar; but at last the driver, who had known the country in happier times, announced that we had entered the high road for Fairfax Courthouse.

I perceived several wagons coming from the direction of the battlefield, the drivers of which were endeavoring to force their horses past the ammunition carts going in the contrary direction near the bridge; a thick cloud of dust rose behind them, and running by the side of the wagons were a number of men in uniform, whom I supposed to be the guard. My first impression was that the wagons were returning for fresh supplies of ammunition. But every moment the crowd increased; drivers and men cried out with the most vehement gestures, "Turn back! Turn back! We are whipped."

A few shells could be heard bursting not very far off, but there was nothing to account for such an extraordinary scene. A third officer, however, confirmed the report that the whole army was in retreat, and that the Federals were beaten on all points, but there was nothing in this disorder to indicate a general rout.

All these things took place in a few seconds. I got up out of the road into a cornfield, through which men were hastily walking or running, their faces streaming with perspiration, and generally without arms, and worked my way for about half a mile or so, as well as I could judge, against an increasing stream of fugitives, the ground being strewed with coats, blankets, firelocks, cooking tins, caps, belts, bayonets—asking in vain where General McDowell was.

Two fieldpieces unlimbering near the house, with panting horses in the rear, were pointed toward the front, and along the road beside them there swept a tolerably steady column of men mingled with field ambulances and light baggage cars, back to Centreville.

I had just stretched out my hand to get a cigar-light from a German gunner, when the dropping shots which had been sounding through the woods in front of us suddenly swelled into an animated fire. In a few seconds a crowd of men rushed out of the wood down towards the guns, and the artillery men near me seized the trail of a piece and were wheeling it round to fire, when an officer or sergeant called out, "Stop! Stop! They are our own men;" and in two or three minutes the whole battalion came sweeping past the guns at the double, and in the utmost disorder.

Some of the artillery men dragged the horses out of the tumbrils; and for a moment the confusion was so great I could not understand what had taken place; but a soldier whom I stopped, said, "We are pursued by their cavalry; they have cut us all to pieces."

It could not be doubted that something serious was taking place; and at that moment a shell burst, scattering the soldiers near it, which was followed by another that bounded along the road; and in a few minutes more out came another regiment from the wood, almost as broken as the first.

The scene on the road had now assumed an aspect which has not a parallel in any description I have ever read. Infantry soldiers on mules and draft horses with the harness clinging to their heels, as much frightened as their riders; Negro servants on their masters' chargers; ambulances crowded with unwounded soldiers; wagons swarming with men who threw out the contents in the road to make room, grinding through a shouting, screaming mass of men on foot, who were literally yelling with rage at every halt and shrieking out: "Here are the cavalry! Will you get on?"

This portion of the force was evidently in discord.

There was nothing left for it but to go with the current one could not stem. I turned round my horse from the deserted guns, and endeavored to find out what had occurred as I rode quietly back on the skirts of the crowd.

I talked with those on all sides of me. Some uttered prodigious nonsense, describing batteries tier over tier, and ambuscades and blood running knee deep. Others described how their boys carried whole lines of entrenchments, but were beaten back for want of reinforcements. The names of many regiments were mentioned as being utterly destroyed. Cavalry and bayonet charges and massed batteries played prominent parts in all the narrations.

Some of the officers seemed to feel the disgrace of defeat; but the strangest thing was the general indifference with which the event seemed to be regarded by those who collected their senses as soon as they got out of fire, and who said they were just going as far as Centreville, and would have a big fight tomorrow.

I was trotting quietly down the hill road beyond Centreville, when suddenly the guns on the other side, or from a battery very near, opened fire, and a fresh outburst of artillery sounded through the woods. In an instant the mass of vehicles and retreating soldiers, teamsters, and civilians, as if agonized by an electric shock, quivered throughout the tortuous line.

With dreadful shouts and cursings, the drivers lashed their maddened horses, and leaping from the carts, left them to their fate, and ran on foot. Artillery men and foot soldiers, and Negroes mounted on gun horses, with the chain traces and loose trappings trailing in the dust, spurred and flogged their steeds down the road or by the side paths. The firing continued and seemed to approach the hill, and at every report the agitated body of horsemen and wagons was seized, as it were, with a fresh convulsion.

Once more the dreaded cry, "The cavalry! cavalry are coming!" rang through the crowd, and looking back to Centreville, I perceived coming down the hill, between me and the sky, a number of mounted men, who might, at a hasty glance, be taken for horsemen in the act of sabreing the fugitives. In reality they were soldiers and civilians, with, I regret to say, some officers among them, who were whipping and striking their horses with sticks or whatever else they could lay hands on.

I called out to the men who were frantic with terror beside me, "They are not cavalry at all; they're your own men"—but they did not heed me. A fellow who was shouting out, "Run! run!" as loud as he could beside me, seemed to take delight in creating alarm.

July 22 [Washington]

I awoke from a deep sleep this morning about six o'clock. The rain was falling in torrents and beat with a dull, thudding sound on the leads outside my window; but louder than all came a strange sound as if of the tread of men, a confused tramp and splashing and a murmuring of voices.

I got up and ran to the front room, the windows of which looked on the street, and there, to my intense surprise, I saw a steady stream of men covered with mud, soaked through with rain, who were pouring irregularly, without any semblance of order, up Pennsylvania Avenue toward the Capitol.

A dense stream of vapor rose from the multitude, but looking closely at the men, I perceived they belonged to different regiments, New Yorkers, Michiganders, Rhode Islanders, Massachusetters, Minnesotans, mingled pellmell together. Many of them were without knapsacks, crossbelts, and firelocks. Some had neither greatcoats nor shoes; others were covered with blankets.

Hastily putting on my clothes, I ran downstairs and asked an officer who was passing by, a pale young man who looked exhausted to death and who had lost his sword, for the empty sheath dangled at his side, where the men were coming from.

"Where from? Well, sir, I guess we're all coming out of Virginny as far as we can, and pretty well whipped, too."

"What! The whole army, sir?"

"That's more than I know. They may stay that like. I know I'm going home. I've had enough of fighting to last my lifetime."

The news seemed incredible. But there before my eyes were the jaded, dispirited, broken remnants of regiments passing onward, where and for what I knew not, and it was evident enough that the mass of the grand

army of the Potomac was placing that river between it and the enemy
as rapidly as possible.

1862:   THE LADY SPY OF CAPITOL HILL

SHE EARNED A NICHE among the greatest of her calling. She might have been
even greater if she had loved it a little less. But that was the nature of Rose
Greenhow—beautiful, clever, "the most persuasive woman in Washington,"
articulate, and histrionic. As a spy for the Confederacy she claimed credit for
the defeat of the North at Bull Run. Certainly she was entitled to some part of
it, for she had managed to learn in advance the Northern strategy and then get
three messages to General Beauregard which gave him his chance to redeploy
the Southern forces and crush McDowell's attack.

They knew in Washington that she was spying. They couldn't discover how.
Even if they had, she was too well connected to hang or shoot. They settled it
by jailing her. But she went on spying from the jail! In their bumbling man's
world, there was only one way to cope with a woman as clever as Rose—get
rid of her. So they sent her to the South.

Rose went to England. In 1864, coming back loaded with gold for the South
—the coins were even sewn into her clothes—and planning to run the blockade,
she was shipwrecked off the Carolina coast. She might still have made it. The
ship had run onto a bar, and the captain told her she was still safe. But Rose
insisted on being rowed ashore. A boat was put over. It capsized. The two men
who were in the boat with her were saved. Next morning the gold coins in her
overweighted clothes jingled to the rolling of the surf as the body of Rose
Greenhow was washed ashore.

"You are charged, Madam, with treason."
ROSE O'NEAL GREENHOW (died 1864)

March 25 [1862. Washington, D.C.]

This day I received a summons to appear before United States Commissioners for the trial of State prisoners. I decided to obey the summons,
as I felt some curiosity to know in what manner the trial would be conducted, what was the nature of the charges against me, and to what
results it would be likely to lead.

It was one of those raw uncomfortable days in which the cold penetrated to the marrow. The sun was obscured by clouds as dark as Yankee deeds, and heavy flakes of snow were falling thick and fast. As I drove through the avenue from the prison to the Provost-Marshal's Office, which was at the other end of the city, the filth and desolation were appalling, for even in those first days of the occupation the effects had not been so visible. However, I had no time for reflection upon the contrast which the present and the past presented, as by this time the carriage drew near the Provost-Marshal's. But here truly was there room for comparison.

This had been the house of Mrs. Gwin, one of the most elegant and agreeable in the city; and, as I passed up through the filthy halls and stairs, and the filthy crowd of soldiers and civilians who lined the way, my mind instinctively reverted to the gay and brilliant scenes in which I had mingled in that house, and the goodly company who had enjoyed its hospitality.

I was conducted to the third story, and put in a room without fire, and kept there until my hands and feet were completely benumbed with cold. A guard was stationed at the door, who rattled his musket in order that I should have a comfortable sense of his proximity. Numbers of officers in gay uniforms came in, upon one pretext or another, in order to stare at me. I was detained in this manner for nearly an hour, when the super-intendent of the Old Capitol Prison, Mr. Wood, in whose custody I was still regarded as being, came to conduct me before the commissioners, whose presence I reached with difficulty—a passage being forced for me to pass through the soldiers who filled the ante-chamber.

Arriving before the door of the room in which the commissioners held their *seance*, it was thrown open, my name announced, and the commis-sioners advanced to receive me, with ill-concealed embarrassment. I bowed to them saying, "Gentlemen, resume your seats" (for they were still stand-ing). "I recognize the embarrassment of your positions; it was a mistake in your Government to have selected gentlemen for this mission. You have, however, shown me but scant courtesy in having kept me waiting your pleasure for nearly an hour in the cold."

They apologised, protesting their ignorance of my arrival, &c. Some few complimentary remarks followed, and I now took a survey of the scene.

A large table was placed in the middle of the room, at the upper end of which sat General Dix, and at the other extremity Governor Fairfield. Mr. Webster, private secretary of Mr. Seward—as secretary of the com-mission—sat at a small table a little to the left of General Dix; and two other persons at a similar table to the rear of Governor Fairfield. My own seat was midway between the commissioners, in full view of the whole party.

Large piles of papers lay before General Dix, which he fingered un-
easily, and seemed uncertain what to do. Governor Fairfield made some
unimportant remark; to which I replied, "I suppose this is a mimic court,
and I can answer or not, according to my own discretion."

One of the reporters now said, "If you please to speak louder, madam."
I rose from my seat, and said to General Dix, "If it is your object to make
a *spectacle* of me, and furnish reports for the newspapers, I shall have
the honour to withdraw from this presence."

Hereupon both of the commissioners arose, and protested that they had
no such intention; but that it was necessary to take notes, in order to lay
before the President and Congress. I then resumed my seat; and Governor
Fairfield continued in a strain in no respects different from that of an
ordinary conversation held in a drawing-room; and to which I replied
sarcastically, or caustically, as suited my purpose; and a careless listener
would have imagined that the commissioner was endeavouring with plausible argument to defend the Government, rather than criminate me.

Finally, and after it had continued some time, I said, "But when is this
dreadful ordeal—this trial for treason, which has been heralded to the
world with so much circumstance—to commence? For I can scarcely believe that I have been brought from my prison on this inclement day for
the purpose of this very facetious and irrelevant conversation, or be induced to regard it in the light of a formal trial for life, liberty, and estate,
attainder of blood, and all the other ills of feudal times."

At this the subordinates laughed outright. Governor Fairfield coloured,
attempted to speak several times, and changed his mind; and finally said,
"General Dix, you are so much better acquainted with Mrs. Greenhow,
suppose you continue the examination?"

I laughingly said, "Commence it, for I hold that it has not begun."

General Dix turned over and over again the papers before him, which
were my letters seized by the detective police, and which, though relevant
to the subject-matter, had no legal importance or bearing at this time. He
selected one, laying his hand upon it, but still hesitated. I watched him
keenly.

At last he said, "You are charged with treason."

"I deny it, sir. During the eight months of my imprisonment I have had
ample time to study the Constitution of the United States, and there is
no act or provision in it which will justify a charge of that nature against
me."

"And so you deny the charge of treason?"

"I do, sir, most emphatically; and, moreover, report the charge against
yourself as being the minister of a President who has violated the Consti-

tution, destroyed the personal rights of the citizen, and inaugurated revolution. At this moment, sir, you are presiding at, and conducting, a trial
unlawful in every sense, and without even a pretence of the legal form
prescribed; for the Constitution of the United States is very precise and
specific as to the mode in which a trial for treason shall be conducted.
It requires that the charge for treason shall be sustained by two respectable witnesses, which you could not find in all Yankeedom."

He then held up the letter which he had selected. I immediately recognized it as the one I had caused to be mailed in Baltimore, and to which
I have before alluded. I held out my hand, saying, "Let me see it." After
a moment of indecision he gave it to me. I glanced my eye over its contents and returned it to him, saying, "It is rather a clever letter, is it not?"

General Dix replied, "Mrs. Greenhow requires no new testimony in
favour of her ability in the use of her pen."

I bowed my head, "Well, General, what next have you to say?"

"You are charged, madam, with having caused a letter which you wrote
to the Secretary of State to be published in Richmond."

"That can scarcely be brought forward as one of the causes for my
arrest, as I was some three months a prisoner when that letter was written;
and I myself regarded its undue publicity (prior to its publication at Richmond) as a grave cause of complaint against the Secretary of State."

"You are charged, madam, with holding communication with the enemy
in the South."

"If this were an established fact, you could not be surprised at it. I
am a Southern woman, and I thank God that no drop of Yankee blood
ever polluted my veins; and as all that I have ever honoured or respected
have been driven by ruthless despotism to seek shelter there, it would
seem the most natural thing in life that I should have done so."

"How is it, madam, that you have managed to communicate, in spite
of the vigilance exercised over you?"

"That is my secret, sir; and, if it be any satisfaction to you to know it,
I shall, in the next forty-eight hours, make a report to my Government at
Richmond of this rather farcical trial for treason."

"General M'Clellan, madam, charges you with having obtained a thorough knowledge of his plans, and of forcing him consequently four times
to change them."

At this I smilingly shrugged my shoulders, without reply, saying, "Well,
what else?"

After a few moments General Dix said, "Governor, I think we have
nothing else to say to Mrs. Greenhow?" To which Governor Fairfield
replied, "No, sir, I think not."

Of course I do not pretend to relate the entire conversation—for it could not be called an examination—but have gleaned the most important points. I now said, "It seems to me a little extraordinary that, after such grave charges as that of penetrating Cabinet secrets and fathoming and thwarting the plans of commanding generals, no curiosity should have been felt to arrive at the source of my so-called treason, if only as a measure of prevention for the future—as it is but reasonable to suppose I must have had able coadjutors high in the national councils, and that this information must have sought me at my own house—as it can be clearly established that I have never crossed the threshold of a Lincoln-ite."

"Oh, that reminds me," resumed General Dix. "Did Lieutenant Sheldon ever take out communications for you?"

"Oh, certainly, by authority of the Provost-Marshal. But if you wish to criminate Lieutenant Sheldon, you had better send for him and question him on that subject, as I certainly should not betray him or anyone else who might have rendered me a service."

General Dix asked, "Where is Lieutenant Sheldon?"

Mr. Webster replied, "With his regiment in Virginia."

General Dix then said, "I shall be very glad to serve you, madam, and shall certainly advise the Government to allow you to go South, or consult your wishes in any other respects;" that he regretted deeply my extreme bitterness, for which he could see no reason, &c.

I replied, "That is the difference between *meum* and *tuum*. I have been now eight months a prisoner, subject during that period to every insult and outrage which capricious tyranny could invent; my property stolen and destroyed; shut up in close imprisonment, and actually suffering the torments of hunger.

"To this treatment has my child of eight years been also exposed, thereby seriously impairing her health. Not content with this, I have been daily assailed in the journals of the Administration and sought to be dragged down to the level of the inmates of your White House. Knowing me then as you do, it will not seem strange that, instead of crushing, this system should have excited my contemptuous defiance and undying hatred.

"On examining this evidence, you can but smile at the absurdity of the charges, and the extreme care not to extract any information from me. I have, however, sir, to return my most sincere thanks to you and your colleague for the delicacy and kind feeling which has characterized your bearing towards me, and to congratulate you upon the conclusion of a task which can be but little in unison with the feelings of gentlemen."

Thereupon both commissioners advanced and shook hands, and expressed an earnest hope that I would very soon be sent South.

THE WORLD would never forget, Lincoln said, what 23,000 Union soldiers had done at Gettysburg. As he spoke November was silvering the new grass over their graves. A few months before, they had fought in the battle that proved the turning point of America's most terrible conflict. In those graves lay more than a fourth of the North's original battle force.

The South had paid even more heavily. In the grim march of Pickett's division against the crucial salient on Cemetery Hill three out of four Confederate soldiers were mowed down. Lee's total losses in the three-day engagement were 30,000 men; and the South had been dealt a strategic blow from which it never recovered.

From what Lieutenant-Colonel Arthur James Lyan Fremantle of His Majesty's Coldstream Guards could read of the war in America he had developed "a sentiment of great admiration for the gallantry and determination of the Southerners"—so much so, he explained, that "I was unable to repress a strong wish to go to America and see something of this wonderful struggle."

On leave from the British army, and going as a tourist, spyglass slung over his shoulder, diary in his pocket, he arrived at Brownsville, Texas, in April 1863. Never was tourist more out of place, never sight-seeing more hazardous. Yet three months later Fremantle had talked his way into the company of Lee's forces at Gettysburg. On the second day of the battle Southern officers, as they went into a huddle to discuss their next moves, were astonished to see an oddly dressed Englishman, sitting in the fork of a tree, calmly peering down at them.

Fremantle witnessed the fateful battle. Then, "Having successfully accomplished my design, I returned to England and found amongst all my friends an extreme desire to know the truth of what was going on in the South; for in consequence of the blockade, the truth can with difficulty be arrived at, as intelligence coming mainly through Northern sources is not believed; and, in fact, nowhere is the ignorance of what is passing in the South more profound than it is in the Northern States."

The diary was published in 1863 in London and the following year was reprinted in New York and Mobile, Alabama. Because there was nothing else on hand to use as a cover, the Mobile edition was bound in flowered wallpaper.

Fremantle had not underestimated the hunger for news. On both sides of the Atlantic there was an enormous demand for the book. Ninety years later, in America, it was printed again.

"Lee was sublime."

ARTHUR JAMES LYON FREMANTLE
(1835-1901)

1st July [1863]

At 4:30 P.M. we came in sight of Gettysburg, and joined General Lee
and General Hill, who were on the top of one of the ridges which form the
peculiar feature of the country round Gettysburg. We could see the enemy
retreating up one of the opposite ridges, pursued by the Confederates
with loud yells.

2nd July

At 7 A.M. I rode over part of the ground with General Longstreet, and saw
him disposing of M'Laws's division for today's fight. The enemy occupied
a series of high ridges, the tops of which were covered with trees, but the
intervening valleys between their ridges and ours were mostly open, and
partly under cultivation. The cemetery was on their right, and their left
appeared to rest upon a high rocky hill. The enemy's forces, which were
now supposed to comprise nearly the whole Potomac army, were concen-
trated into a space apparently not more than a couple of miles in length.

The Confederates enclosed them in a sort of semicircle, and the extreme
extent of our position must have been from five to six miles at least.

Until 4:45 P.M. all was profoundly still, and we began to doubt whether
a fight was coming off today at all.

At that time, however, Longstreet suddenly commenced a heavy cannonade on the right. Ewell immediately took it up on the left. The enemy
replied with at least equal fury, and in a few moments the firing along
the whole line was as heavy as it is possible to conceive. A dense smoke
arose for six miles. There was little wind to drive it away, and the air
seemed full of shells.

The Southern troops, when charging, or to express their delight, always
yell in a manner peculiar to themselves.

When the cannonade was at its height, a Confederate band of music,
between the cemetery and ourselves, began to play polkas and waltzes,
which sounded very curious, accompanied by the hissing and the bursting of the shells.

Major Fairfax arrived at about 10 P.M. in a very bad humor. He had
under his charge about 1,000 to 1,500 Yankee prisoners who had been
taken today; among them a general, whom I heard one of his men ac-

cusing of having been "so G———d d———d drunk that he had turned his guns upon his own men."

3d July

At 6 A.M. I rode to the field with Colonel Manning, and went over that portion of the ground which, after a fierce contest, had been won from the enemy yesterday evening. The dead were being buried, but great numbers were still lying about; also many mortally wounded, for whom nothing could be done. Amongst the latter were a number of Yankees dressed in bad imitations of the Zouave costume. They opened their glazed eyes as I rode past, in a painfully imploring manner.

The distance between the Confederate guns and the Yankee position—that is, between the woods crowning the opposite ridges—was at least a mile, quite open, gently undulating, and exposed to artillery the whole distance. This was the ground which had to be crossed in today's attack.

Pickett's division, which had just come up, was to bear the brunt in Longstreet's attack. Pickett's division was a weak one (under 5,000) owing to the absence of two brigades.

At noon all Longstreet's dispositions were made; his troops for attack were deployed into line and lying down in the woods; his batteries were ready to open. The General then dismounted and went to sleep for a short time.

A small boy of twelve years was riding with us at the time. This urchin took a diabolic interest in the bursting of the shells, and screamed with delight when he saw them take effect. I never saw this boy again, or found out who he was.

Finding that to see the actual fighting it was absolutely necessary to go into the thick of the thing, I determined to make my way to General Longstreet. It was then about two-thirty. After passing General Lee and his staff, I rode on through the woods in the direction in which I had left Longstreet.

I soon began to meet many wounded men returning from the front. Many of them asked in piteous tones the way to a doctor or an ambulance. The further I got, the greater became the number of the wounded. At last I came to a perfect stream of them flocking through the woods as great as the crowd in Oxford Street in the middle of the day.

Some were walking alone on crutches composed of two rifles, others supported by men less badly wounded than themselves, and others were carried on stretchers by the ambulance corps; but in no case did I see a sound man helping the wounded to the rear unless he carried the red badge of the ambulance corps.

They were still under a heavy fire; the shells were continually bringing down great limbs of trees and carrying further destruction amongst this melancholy procession. I saw all this in much less time than it takes to write it, and although astonished to meet such vast numbers of wounded, I had not seen enough to give me any idea of the real extent of the mischief.

When I got close up to General Longstreet I saw one of his regiments advancing through the woods in good order; so, thinking I was just in time to see the attack, I remarked to the General that "I wouldn't have missed this for anything." Longstreet was seated at the top of a snake fence at the edge of the wood and looking perfectly calm and unperturbed. He replied, laughing, "The devil you wouldn't! I would like to have missed it very much; we've attacked and been repulsed; look there!"

For the first time I then had a view of the open space between the two positions and saw it covered with Confederates, slowly and sulkily returning toward us in small broken parties, under a heavy fire of artillery. But the fire where we were was not so bad as further to the rear, for although the air seemed alive with shell, yet the greater number burst behind us.

The General told me that Pickett's division had succeeded in carrying the enemy's position and capturing his guns, but after remaining there twenty minutes, it had been forced to retire.

Soon afterward I joined General Lee, who had in the meanwhile come to the front on becoming aware of the disaster. If Longstreet's conduct was admirable, that of Lee was perfectly sublime. He was engaged in rallying and in encouraging the broken troops and was riding about a little in front of the wood, quite alone, the whole of his staff being engaged in a similar manner to the rear.

His face, which is always placid and cheerful, did not show any signs of the slightest disappointment, care or annoyance; and he was addressing to every soldier he met a few words of encouragement, such as: "All this will come right in the end; we'll talk it over afterwards; but in the meantime all good men must rally. We want all good men and true just now."

He spoke to all the wounded men that passed him, and the slightly wounded he exhorted to "bind up their hurts and take up a musket" in this emergency. Very few failed to answer his appeal, and I saw many badly wounded men take off their hats and cheer him.

He said to me, "This has been a sad day for us, Colonel—a sad day. But we can't expect always to gain victories."

I saw General Willcox (an officer who wears a short round jacket and a battered straw hat) come up to him and explain, almost crying, the state of his brigade. General Lee immediately shook hands with him and said cheerfully, "Never mind, General, all this has been *my* fault—it is I that have lost this fight, and you must help me out of it in the best way you can."

1864:   HORROR AT ANDERSONVILLE

STARVING, drinking polluted water, and breathing air that was heavy with the smell of death, the 28,000 Union soldiers in the big prison camp at Andersonville, Georgia, didn't know from day to day how much more frightful their ordeal would become. In those fifteen crowded acres, scurvy, dropsy, dysentery and wound infections were making life steadily less bearable, but there was no way of measuring, of forecasting. Nothing like it had ever happened in America.

When Dr. Joseph Jones, a medical authority and himself a Southerner, appeared as a witness against prison commandant Henry Wirtz after the war, he couldn't find words to fit the horror. He did say:

> The haggard, distressed countenances of these miserable, complaining, dejected living skeletons, crying for medical aid and food, and the ghastly corpses with their glazed eyeballs staring up into vacant space, with the flies swarming down their open and grinning mouths and over their ragged clothes, infested with lice as they lay amongst the sick and the dying, formed a picture of helpless, hopeless misery which it would be impossible to portray.

In all, from November 1863, to the end of the war, nearly 50,000 men were brought into Andersonville. Thirteen thousand died. In October of 1864 death was taking every other one.

Twenty-year-old John L. Ransom, of Jackson, Michigan, brigade quartermaster sergeant of the Ninth Michigan Cavalry, was captured on November 6, 1863, in east Tennessee. He was taken to the Confederate prison at Belle Island, near Richmond, Virginia, kept there until early in March, then sent by rail to Georgia.

Andersonville looked bad enough when Ransom arrived—no permanent shelter, no sanitation, and a death rate of eighteen or twenty a day—but there were only 1,800 men inside the stockade then. Things rapidly got worse as each day brought in about 600 more.

The terror of gangsterism was added to the suffering of these men when a fellow-prisoner, Willie Collins, alias Moseby, attracted to himself a following of raiders and proceeded to victimize the whole camp. For months they carried on their gruesome business of robbing the starving, denuding the sick, and beating, sometimes killing, the defiant, until the whole camp, united in wrath, demanded of Captain Wirtz the right to move against them and punish them. Wirtz consented. While he and his hundreds of guards looked on, Collins and five of his henchmen were hanged.

An Indian prisoner from Minnesota, known only as Battese, befriended Ransom. Together they set up a business of washing clothes and cutting hair for other prisoners. At heavy sacrifice to himself, Battese saved the life of his friend by scrounging an onion or other fresh vegetable whenever he could. Finally, risking his life in defiance of a prison inspector, Battese managed to smuggle Ransom out of Andersonville as narrated in the part of Ransom's diary given here.

MacKinlay Kantor's popular novel Andersonville, published in 1955, draws frequently on the Ransom diary for background and in some places quotes directly.

The blankbooks and ledgers in which Ransom kept the diary were destroyed by fire a few years after the war. The text was saved, however, as he had previously published it serially in his home-town newspaper, the Jackson, Michigan, Citizen.

"No escape except by death . . ."
JOHN L. RANSOM (1843-1919)

July 3 [1864]

Three hundred and fifty new men from West Virginia were turned into this summer resort this morning. They brought good news as to successful termination of the war, and they also caused war after coming among us. As usual, the raiders proceeded to rob them of their valuables and a fight occurred, in which hundreds engaged.

The cut-throats came out ahead. Complaints were made to Captain Wirtz that this thing would be tolerated no longer, that these raiders must be put down, or the men would rise in their might and break away if assistance was not given with which to preserve order.

Wirtz flew around as if he had never thought of it before, issued an order to the effect that no more food would be given us until the leaders were arrested and taken outside for trial. The greatest possible excitement. Hundreds that have before been neutral and non-committal are now joining a police force. Captains are appointed to take charge of the squads, which have been furnished with clubs by Wirtz.

As I write, this middle of the afternoon, the battle rages. The police go right to raider headquarters, knock right and left, and make their arrests. Sometimes the police are whipped, and have to retreat, but they rally their forces and again make a charge, in which they are successful.

Can lay in our shade and see the trouble go on. Must be killing some by the shouting. The raiders fight for their very life, and are only taken after being thoroughly whipped. The stockade is loaded with guards who are fearful of a break. I wish I could describe the scene today. A number killed. After each arrest a great cheering takes place.

Night

Thirty or forty have been taken outside of the worst characters in camp, and still the good work goes on. No food to-day, and don't want any. A big strapping fellow, called Limber Jim, heads the police. Grand old Michael Hoare is at the front, and goes for a raider as quick as he would a Rebel.

Patrol the camp all the time, and gradually quieting down. The orderly prisoners are feeling jolly.

July 4

The men taken outside yesterday are under Rebel guard and will be punished. The men are thoroughly aroused and now that the matter has been taken in hand it will be followed up to the letter. Other arrests are being made today, and occasionally a big fight. Little Terry, whom they could not find yesterday, was today taken. Had been hiding in an old well, or hole in the ground. Fought like a little tiger, but had to go. "Limber Jim" is a brick, and should be made a Major General, if ever he reaches our lines.

Mike Hoare is right up in rank, and true blue. Wm. B. Rowe also makes a good policeman, as does "Dad" Sanders. Battese says, "He no time to fight, must wash."

Jimmy Devers regrets that he cannot take a hand in, as he likes to fight, and especially with a club. The writer hereof does no fighting, being on the sick list. The excitement of looking on is most too much for me. Can hardly arrest the big graybacks [insects] crawling around. Captain Moseby is one of the arrested ones. His right name is Collins, and he has been in our hundred all the time since leaving Richmond. Has got a good long neck to stretch.

It is said that a court will be formed of our own men to try the raiders. Any way, so they are punished. All have killed men, and they themselves should be killed. When arrested, the police had hard work to prevent their being lynched. Police more thoroughly organized all the time. An extra amount of food, this P.M., and police get extra rations, and three out of our mess are doing pretty well. They are all willing to divide. They tell us all the encounters they have, and much interesting talk.

Mike has some queer experiences. Rebel flags at half mast for some of their dead men. Just heard that the trial of raiders will begin tomorrow.

July 5

Court is in session outside, and raiders being tried by our own men. Wirtz has done one good thing, but it's a question whether he is entitled to any credit, as he had to be threatened with a break before he would assist us. Rations again to-day. I am quite bad off with my diseases, but still there are so many thousands so much worse off that I do not complain much, or try not to.

July 6

Boiling hot, camp reeking with filth, and no sanitary privileges; men dying off over a hundred and forty per day. Stockade enlarged, taking in eight or ten more acres, giving us more room and stumps to dig up for wood to cook with.

Mike Hoare is in good health; not so Jimmy Devers. Jimmy has now been a prisoner over a year, and poor boy, will probably die soon.

Have more mementoes than I can carry, from those who have died, to be given to their friends at home. At least a dozen have given me letters, pictures, &c. to take North. Hope I shan't have to turn them over to someone else.

July 7

The court was gotten up by our men and from our own men; judge, jury, council. Had a fair trial, and were even defended, but to no purpose. It is reported that six have been sentenced to be hung, while a good many others are condemned to lighter punishment, such as setting in the stocks, strung up by the thumbs, thumbscrews, head hanging.

The court has been severe but just.

Mike goes out tomorrow to take some part in the court proceeding.

The prison seems a different place altogether; still, dread disease is here, and mowing down good and true men. Would seem to me that three or four hundred died each day, though officially but one hundred and forty odd is told. About twenty-seven thousand, I believe, are here now in all. No new ones for a few days.

Rebel visitors, who look at us from a distance. It is said the stench keeps all away who have no business here and can keep away. Washing business good. Am negotiating for a pair of pants. Dislike fearfully to wear dead men's clothes, and haven't, to any great extent.

July 8

O, how hot, and O how miserable. The news that six have been sentenced to be hanged is true, and one of them is Moseby.

The camp is thoroughly under control of the police now, and it is a heavenly boon. Of course, there is some robbery, but not as before. Swan, of our mess, is sick with scurvy. I am gradually swelling up and growing weaker.

Guards shoot now very often. Boys, as guards, are the most cruel. It is said that if they kill a Yankee they are given a thirty days' furlough. Guess they need them as soldiers too much to allow of this.

The swamp now is fearful. Water perfectly reeking with prison offal and poison. Still men drink it and die. Rumors that the six will be hung inside. Bread today, and it is so coarse as to do more hurt than good to a majority of the prisoners.

The place still gets worse. Tunneling is over with; no one engages in it now that I know of. The prison is a success as regards safety; no escape except by death, and very many take advantage of that way.

A man who has preached to us (or tried to) is dead. Was a good man, I verily believe, and from Pennsylvania.

Our quartette of singers a few rods away is disbanded. One died, one nearly dead, one a policeman and the other cannot sing alone, and so, where we used to hear and enjoy good music evenings, there is nothing to attract us from the groans of the dying.

Having formed a habit of going to sleep as soon as the air got cooled off and before fairly dark, I wake up at two or three o'clock and stay awake. I then take in all the horrors of the situation. Thousands are groaning, moaning and crying, with no bustle of the daytime to drown it. Guards every half hour call out the time and post, and there is often a shot to make one shiver as if with the ague. Must arrange my sleeping hours to miss getting up early in the morning.

Have taken to building air castles of late on being exchanged. Getting loony, I guess, same as all the rest.

July 9

Battese brought me some onions, and if they ain't good, then no matter; also a sweet potato. One-half the men here would get well if they only had something in the vegetable line to eat, or acids. Scurvy is about the most loathsome disease, and when dropsy takes hold with the scurvy, it is terrible. I have both diseases, but keep them in check, and it only grows worse slowly. My legs are swollen, but the cords are not contracted much, and I can still walk very well.

Our mess all keep clean, in fact are obliged to, or else turned adrift. We want none of the dirty sort in our mess. Sanders and Rowe enforce the rules, which is not much work, as all hands are men who prefer to keep clean.

I still do a little washing, but more particularly hair cutting, which is easier work. You should see one of my hair cuts. Knobby! Old prisoners have hair a foot long or more, and my business is to cut it off, which I do without regard to anything except to get it off.

I should judge there are one thousand rebel soldiers guarding us and perhaps a few more, with the usual number of officers.

A guard told me today that the Yanks were "gittin' licked," and they didn't want us exchanged, just as soon we should die here as not. A Yank asked him if he knew what exchange meant; said he knew what shootin' meant, and as he began to swing around his old shooting iron, we retreated in among the crowd.

Someone stole Battese's wash board, and he is mad; is looking for it. May bust up the business. Think Hub Dakin will give me a board to make another one. Sanders owns the jack-knife of this mess, and he don't like to lend it either; borrow it to carve on roots for pipes.

Actually take solid comfort "building castles in the air," a thing I have never been addicted to before. Better than getting blue and worrying myself to death. After all, we may get out of this dodrotted hole. Always an end of some sort to such things.

July 10

Have bought of a new prisoner quite a large (thick, I mean) blank book, so as to continue my diary. Although it's a tedious and tiresome task, am determined to keep it up. Don't know of another man in prison who is doing likewise. Wish I had the gift of description, that I might describe this place. Know that I am not good at such things.

Nothing can be worse or nastier than the stream drizzling its way through this camp. On all four sides of us are high walls and tall trees, and there is apparently no wind or breeze to blow away the stench, and we are obliged to breathe and live in it. Dead bodies lay around all day in the broiling sun, by the dozen and even hundreds. It's too horrible for me to describe in fitting language.

Only those who are here will ever know what Andersonville is.

July 11

This morning lumber was brought into the prison by the Rebels, and near the gate a *gallows* erected, for the purpose of executing the six condemned Yankees. At about ten o'clock they were brought inside by Captain Wirtz and some guards, and delivered over to the police force.

Captain Wirtz then said a few words about their having been tried by our own men, and for us to do as we choose with them; that he washed his hands of the whole matter.

After Wirtz made his speech, he withdrew his guards, leaving the condemned at the mercy of 28,000 enraged prisoners, who had all been more
or less wronged by these men.

Their hands were tied behind them, and one by one they mounted the
scaffold. Curtiss, who was last, a big stout fellow, managed to get his
hands loose and broke away and ran through the crowd and down towards
the swamp. It was yelled out that he had a knife in his hand, and so a
path was made for him. He reached the swamp and plunged in, trying to
get over on the other side, presumably among his friends.

It being very warm, he over-exerted himself, and when in the middle
or thereabouts, collapsed and could go no farther. The police started
after him, waded in and helped him out. He pleaded for water and it
was given him. Then led back to the scaffold and helped to mount up.

All were given a chance to talk. Munn, a good looking fellow in marine
dress, said he came into the prison four months before, perfectly honest,
and as innocent of crime as any fellow in it. Starvation, with evil companions, had made him what he was. He spoke of his mother and sisters in
New York, that he cared nothing as far as he himself was concerned, but
the news that would be carried home to his people made him want to
curse God he had ever been born.

Delaney said he would rather be hung than live here as the most of
them lived, on their allowance of rations. If allowed to steal, could get
enough to eat, but as that was stopped had rather hang. Bid all good bye.
Said his name was not Delaney, and that no one knew who he really was,
therefore his friends would never know his fate, his Andersonville history
dying with him.

Curtiss said he didn't care a ———, only hurry up, and not be talking
about it all day; making too much fuss over a very small matter.

William Collins, alias Moseby, said he was innocent of murder and
ought not to be hung; he had stolen blankets and rations to preserve his
own life and begged the crowd not to see him hung as he had a wife and
child at home, and for their sake to let him live.

The excited crowd began to be impatient for the "show" to commence,
as they termed it.

Sarsfield made quite a speech. He had studied for a lawyer; at the outbreak of the rebellion he had enlisted and served three years in the army,
been wounded in battle, furloughed home, wound healed up, promoted
to First Sergeant, and also commissioned; his commission as a Lieutenant
had arrived but had not been mustered in when he was taken prisoner;
began by stealing parts of rations, gradually becoming hardened as he be-

came familiar with the crimes practiced; evil associates had helped him to go down hill, and here he was.

The others did not care to say anything. While the men were talking they were interrupted by all kinds of questions and charges made by the crowd, such as "don't lay it on too thick, you villain," "get ready to jump off," "cut it short," "you was the cause of so and so's death," "less talk and more hanging."

At about eleven o'clock they were all blindfolded, hands and feet tied, told to get ready, nooses adjusted, and the plank knocked from under. Moseby's rope broke and he fell to the ground with blood spurting from his ears, mouth and nose. As they were lifting him back to the swinging-off place he revived and begged for his life, but no use, was soon dangling with the rest, and died very hard.

Munn died easily, as did also Delaney, all the rest died very hard, and particularly Sarsfield, who drew his knees nearly to his chin and then straightened them out with a jerk, the veins in his neck swelling out as if they would burst.

It was an awful sight to see, still a necessity. Moseby, although he said he had never killed anyone, and I don't believe he ever did deliberately kill a man, such as stabbing or pounding a victim to death, yet he has walked up to a poor sick prisoner on a cold night and robbed him of his blanket or perhaps his rations, and using all the force necessary to do it. These things were the same as life and death to the sick man, for he would invariably die. The result has been that many have died from his robbing propensities.

It was right that he should hang, and he did hang most beautifully, and Andersonville is the better off for it.

None of the rest denied that they had killed men, and probably some had murdered dozens. It has been a good lesson; there are still bad ones in camp, but we have the strong arm of the law to keep them in check.

All during the hanging scene, the stockade was covered with Rebels, who were fearful a break would be made if the raiders should try and rescue them. Many citizens, too, were congregated on the outside in favorable positions for seeing.

Artillery was pointed at us from all directions, ready to blow us all into eternity in short order; Wirtz stood on a high platform, in plain sight of the execution, and says we are a hard crowd to kill our own men.

After hanging for half an hour or so, the six bodies were taken down and carried outside.

I occupied a near position to the hanging, and saw it all from first to last, and stood there until they were taken down and carried away. Was a strange sight to see, and the first hanging I ever witnessed. The raiders had many friends, who crowded around and denounced the whole affair, and but for the police, there would have been a riot; many both for and against the execution were knocked down.

Have got back to my quarters, fairly prostrated. Battese suspended washing long enough to look on and see them hang, and grunted his approval.

Rebel negroes came inside and began to take down the scaffold; prisoners took hold to help them, and resulted in its all being carried off to different parts of the prison to be used for kindling wood, and the Rebels got none of it back, and are mad.

The ropes even have been gobbled up, and I suppose sometime may be exhibited at the North as mementoes of today's proceedings.

Mike Hoare assisted at the hanging. Some fears are entertained that those who officiated will get killed by the friends of those hanged. The person who manipulated the "drop" has been taken outside on parole of honor, as his life would be in danger in here.

Jimmy thanks God that he has lived to see justice done the raiders; he is about gone nothing but skin and bones, and can hardly move hand or foot; rest of the mess moderately well. The extra rations derived from our three messmates as policemen helps wonderfully to prolong life.

Once in a while some of them gets a chance to go outside on some duty, and buy onions and sweet potatoes, which are a great luxury.

July 12

Good order has prevailed since the hanging. The men have settled right down to the business of dying with no interruption. I keep thinking our situation can get no worse, but it does get worse every day, and not less than one hundred and sixty die each twenty-four hours. Probably one-fourth of these die inside the stockade, the balance in the hospital outside.

All day up to four o'clock P.M., the dead are being gathered up and carried to the south gate and placed in a row inside the dead line. As the bodies are stripped of their clothing, in most cases as soon as the breath leaves, and in some cases before, the row of dead presents a sickening appearance. Legs drawn up in all shapes. They are black from pitch pine smoke and laying in the sun. Some of them lay there for twenty hours or more, and by that time are in a horrible condition.

At four o'clock a four or six-mule wagon comes up to the gate, and bodies are loaded on to the wagon and they are carted off to be put in trenches, one hundred in each trench, in the cemetery, which is eighty or a hundred rods away.

I was invited today to dig a tunnel, but had to decline. My digging days are over. It is with difficulty now that I can walk, and only with the help of two canes.

July 13

Can see in the distance the cars go poking along by this station, with wheezing old engines snorting along. As soon as night comes a great many are blind, caused by sleeping in the open air, with moon shining in the face.

Many holes are dug and excavations made in camp. Near our quarters is a well, about five or six feet deep, and the poor blind fellows fall into this pit-hole. None seriously hurt, but must be shaken up. Half of the prisoners have no settled place for sleeping, wander and lay down wherever they can find room.

Have two small gold rings on my finger, worn ever since I left home. Have also a small photograph album with eight photographs in. Relics of civilization.

Should I get these things through to our lines they will have quite a history. When I am among the Rebels I wind a rag around my finger to cover up the rings, or else take them and put them in my pocket. Bad off as I have been, have never seen the time yet that I would part with them. Were presents to me, and the photographs had looked at about one-fourth of the time since imprisonment.

One prisoner made some buttons here for his little boy at home, and gave them to me to deliver, as he was about to die. Have them sewed on to my pants for safe keeping.

July 14

We have been too busy with the raiders of late to manufacture any exchange news, and now all hands are at work trying to see who can tell the biggest yarn. The weak are feeling well tonight over the story that we are all to be sent North this month, before the 20th. Have not learned that the news came from any reliable source.

Rumors of midsummer battles, with Union troops victorious. It's "bite dog, bite bear" with most of us prisoners; we don't care which licks, what we want is to get out of this pen. Of course, we all care, and want our side to win, but it's tough on patriotism.

A court is now being held every day, and offenders punished for misdemeanors. The hanging has done worlds of good, still there is much stealing going on yet, but in a sly way, not openly.

July 15

Blank cartridges were this morning fired over the camp by the artillery, and immediately the greatest commotion outside. It seems that the signal in case a break is made is cannon firing. And this was to show us how quick they could really get into shape. In less time than it takes for me to write it all were at their posts and in condition to open up and kill nine-tenths of all here.

Sweltering hot.

July 16

Well, who ever supposed it could be any hotter; but today is more so than yesterday, and yesterday more than the day before. My coverlid has been rained on so much and burned in the sun, first one and then the other, that it is getting the worse for wear. It was originally a very nice one, and home made. Sun and rain goes right through it now, and reaches down for us. Just like a bake oven.

July 17

Cords contracting in my legs, and very difficult for me to walk—after going a little way have to stop and rest, and am faint. Am urged by some to go to the hospital, but don't like to do it; mess say had better stay where I am, and Battese says shall not go, and that settles it.

Jimmy Devers anxious to be taken to the hospital but is persuaded to give it up. Tom McGill, another Irish friend, is past all recovery; is in another part of the prison. Many old prisoners are dropping off now, this fearful hot weather; knew that July and August would thin us out, cannot keep track of them in my disabled condition.

A fellow named Hubbard, with whom I have conversed a good deal, is dead; a few days ago was in very good health, and it's only a question of a few days now with any of us.

Succeeded in getting four small onions about as large as hickory nuts, tops and all, for two dollars, Confederate money. Battese furnished the money but won't eat an onion; ask him if he is afraid it will make his breath smell. It is said that two or three onions or a sweet potato eaten raw daily will cure the scurvy. What a shame that such things are denied us, being so plenty the world over. Never appreciated such things before, but shall hereafter. Am talking as if I expected to get home again. I do.

July 18

Time slowly dragging along. Cut some wretch's hair almost every day. Have a sign out, "Hair Cutting," as well as "Washing," and by the way, Battese has a new washboard, made from a piece of the scaffold lumber.

About half the time do the work for nothing; in fact, not more than one in three or four pays anything—expenses not much though, don't have to pay any rent.

All the mess keep their hair cut short, which is a very good advertisement. My eyes getting weak, with other troubles. Can just hobble around. Death rate more than ever, reported one hundred and sixty-five per day.

Jimmy Devers most dead, and begs us to take him to the hospital, and guess will have to. Every morning the sick are carried to the gate in blankets and on stretchers, and the worst cases admitted to the hospital. Probably out of five or six hundred, half are admitted. Do not think any live after being taken there; are past all human aid. Four out of every five prefer to stay inside and die with their friends rather than go to the hospital.

Hard stories reach us of the sick out there, and I am sorry to say, the cruelty emanates from our own men, who act as nurses. These dead beats and bummer nurses are the same bounty jumpers the United States authorities have had so much trouble with.

July 19

There is no such thing as delicacy here. Nine out of ten would as soon eat with a corpse for a table as any other way. In the middle of last night I was awakened by being kicked by a dying man. He was soon dead. In his struggles he had floundered clear into our bed. Got up and moved the body off a few feet, and again went to sleep.

July 20

My teeth are all loose, and it is with difficulty I can eat. Jimmy Devers was taken out to die today. I hear that McGill is also dead. John McGuire died last night. Both were Jackson men and old acquaintances.

Mike Hoare is still policeman and is sorry for me. Does what he can. And so we have seen the last of Jimmy. A prisoner of war one year and eighteen days. Struggled hard to live through it, if ever anyone did. Ever since I can remember, have known him. John McGuire also, I have always known. Everybody in Jackson, Michigan, will remember him as living on the east side of the river near the wintergreen patch, and his father before him. They were one of the first families to settle that country. His people are well to do, with much property. Leaves a wife and one boy. Tom McGill is also a Jackson boy, and a member of my own company. Thus you will see that three of my acquaintances died the same day, for Jimmy cannot live until night, I don't think. Not a person in the world but would have thought either one of them would kill me a dozen times enduring hardships. Pretty hard to tell about such things.

Small squad of poor deluded Yanks turned inside with us, captured at Petersburg. It is said they talk of winning recent battles.

Battese has traded for an old watch and Mike will try to procure vegetables for it from the guard. That is what will save us, if anything.

July 21

And Rebels are still fortifying.

Battese has his hands full. Takes care of me like a father. Hear that Kilpatrick is making a raid for this place. Troops (Rebel) are arriving here by every train to defend it.

Nothing but corn bread issued now, and I cannot eat it any more.

July 22

A petition is gotten up, signed by all the Sergeants in the prison, to be sent to Washington, D. C., *begging* to be released. Captain Wirtz has consented to let three representatives go for that purpose. Rough that it should be necessary for us to *beg* to be protected by our Government.

July 23

Reports of an exchange in August. Can't stand it till that time. Will soon go up the spout.

July 24

Have been trying to get into the hospital, but Battese won't let me go. Geo. W. Hutchins, of Jackson, Michigan, died today—from our mess. Jimmy Devers is dead.

July 25

Rowe getting very bad. Sanders ditto. Am myself much worse, and cannot walk. And with difficulty stand up. Legs drawn up like a triangle, mouth in terrible shape, and dropsy worse than all. A few more days.

At my earnest solicitation was carried to the gate this morning, to be admitted to the hospital. Lay in the sun some hours to be examined, and finally my turn came and I tried to stand up, but was so excited I fainted away. When I came to myself I lay along with a row of dead on the outside. Raised up and asked a Rebel for a drink of water, and he said, "Here, you Yank, if you ain't dead yet, get inside there!" And with his help was put inside again.

Told a man to go to our mess, and tell them to come to the gate, and pretty soon Battese and Sanders came and carried me back to our quarters; and here I am, completely played out. Battese flying around to buy me something good to eat. Can't write much more. Exchange rumors.

July 26

Ain't dead yet. Actually laugh when I think of the Rebel who thought if I wasn't dead I had better get inside. Can't walk a step now. Shall try for the hospital no more. Had an onion.

July 27

Sweltering hot. No worse than yesterday. Said that two hundred die now each day. Rowe very bad and Sanders getting so. Swan dead, Gordon dead, Jack Withers dead, Scotty dead, a large Irishman who has been near us a long time, is dead.

These and scores of others died yesterday and day before.

Hub Dakin came to see me, and brought an onion. He is just able to crawl around himself.

July 28

Taken a step forward toward the [burial] trenches since yesterday, and am worse. Had a wash all over this morning. Battese took me to the creek; carried me without any trouble.

July 29

Alive and kicking. Drink some soured water made from meal and water.

July 30

Hang on well, and no worse.

Marine Hospital, Savannah, Ga., September 15

A great change has taken place since I last wrote in my diary. Am in heaven now, compared with the past. At about midnight, September 7th, our detachment was ordered outside at Andersonville, and Battese picked me up and carried me to the gate.

The men were being let outside in ranks of four, and counted as they went out. They were very strict about letting none go but the well ones, or those who could walk. The Rebel Adjutant stood upon a box by the gate, watching very close. Pitch-pine knots were burning in the near vicinity to give light.

As it came our turn to go, Battese got me in the middle of the rank, stood me up as well as I could stand, and with himself on one side and Sergeant Rowe on the other, began pushing our way through the gate. Could not help myself a particle, and was so faint that I hardly knew what was going on.

As we were going through the gate the Adjutant yelled out: "Here, here! Hold on there, that man can't go, hold on there!"

And Battese crowding right along outside. The Adjutant struck over the heads of the men and tried to stop us, but my noble Indian friend kept straight ahead, hallooing: "He all right, he well, he go!"

And so I got outside, the Adjutant having too much to look after to follow me. After we were outside, I was carried to the railroad in the same coverlid which I fooled the Rebel out of when captured, and which I presume has saved my life a dozen times.

At Savannah Ransom recovered and was able to walk with the help of a cane. After two months of improvement he weighed 117 pounds. When he went into Andersonville he weighed more than 170. In November he was transferred to a camp at Millen, Georgia—"not bad and food fair." A few weeks later, carrying the four volumes of his diary with him, he entrained for Blackshear, near the Florida line. His next entry:

In the Woods Near Doctortown, Station No. 5, Georgia, November 23

During the night the cars ran very slow, and sometimes stopped for hours on side tracks. Two guards at each side door, which was open about a foot. Manage to get near the door, and during the night talked considerable with the two guards on the south side of the car.

At about 3 o'clock this A.M., and after going over a long bridge which spanned the Altamaha River and in sight of Doctortown, I went through the open door like a flash and rolled down a high embankment. Almost broke my neck, but not quite. Guard fired a shot at me but did not hit me.

Am happy and hungry and considerably bruised and scratched up from my escape.

For the next six days he was fed and sheltered by Negroes in the vicinity—at great risk to themselves—then captured again and sent to the prison camp at Blackshear. On December 11 he was put on another train with about sixty prisoners. They traveled on open flatcars. On the night of December 13, while the train was going through a woods, Ransom and two others jumped off, with bullets whizzing by their ears.

Again the Negroes gave assistance. On December 19 the three arrived at the house of an old man who had been imprisoned himself for a time because of his sympathy for the Union. He gave them a good dinner, told them Sherman was only fifty miles away, supplied them with an axe, a knife, and provisions, and took them off three miles to a hiding place, where they built themselves a hut.

On December 22 the sound of heavy gunfire signaled the presence of the Union army nearby. Next day the three left their hiding place and joined troops of the 80th Ohio Regiment.

Seventeen years afterward, when Ransom's diary came out in book form, he wrote:

"My good friend Battese, I regret to say, I have never seen or heard of since he last visited me in the Marine Hospital at Savannah. Have written many letters and made many inquiries, but to no effect. He was so reticent while with us in prison that we did not learn enough of him to make inquiries since then effective. Although for many months I was in his immediate presence, he said nothing of where he lived, his circumstances, or anything else. I only know that his name was Battese, that he belonged to a Minnesota regiment, and was a noble fellow.

"I don't know of a man in the world I would rather see today than him, and I hope some day when I have got rich out of this book (if that time should ever come) to go to Minnesota and look him up. There are many Andersonville survivors who must remember the tall Indian, and certainly I shall, as long as life shall last."

The written record ends there. Ransom never got rich from the sale of his book. From his descendants we learn that he went to Chicago and later to Long Beach, California, and that he died September 13, 1919, in Pasadena.

Captain Henry Wirtz, the prison commandant at Andersonville, who was described by Ransom and many others as a brute, was tried in Washington, in a court presided over by General Lew Wallace, and was found guilty on charges of mistreatment, cruelty and murder. On November 10, 1865, he was hanged.

1865: THE DEATH OF ABRAHAM LINCOLN

SHOES OF THE FALLEN GIANT are not easily filled by men, even those of a mighty nation. This the people of America have learned more than once. And this they knew on a dreary morning in April of the year 1865. The night before, at Ford's Theatre in Washington, Abraham Lincoln had been shot. An account of his last hours is given in the diary of his Secretary of the Navy, Gideon Welles.

Welles was only 24 when he became editor of the Hartford, Connecticut, Times. He was a strong believer in Jacksonian democracy, but later when the Democratic party was pressing for slavery in the Territories and particularly with the repeal of the Missouri Compromise in 1854, he parted company with it and helped found the Republican party. On that ticket he ran for governor of Connecticut in 1856—with defeat a foregone conclusion.

Lincoln gave him the navy cabinet post despite the fact that he knew nothing of ships and seafaring. But Welles "stuck close to his desk and never went to sea" and proved himself a shrewd and able administrator in meeting the tough problems of the war. He was held on in the cabinet of Andrew Johnson.

Welles's diary, spanning the years from 1862 to 1869, and filling nearly 2,000 printed pages, reveals the man as vain, censorious, often venomous in his many squabbles with fellow cabinet members. As it turns out, he is almost always right; but in this respect the diary, for many years regarded as one of the most valuable records of the Civil War, has a curious history.

In a preface to the three-volume edition published in 1911, Edgar T. Welles, the diarist's son, says, "It had seemed to me that the free criticism and personal allusions should have been in some degree eliminated, but the advice of the most eminent authorities has been adverse to any omission. I should have much preferred it otherwise, but have yielded to those to whose judgment I should defer . . . and the reader may have full confidence that the text of the diary has been in no way mutilated or revised."

Not, that is, by anyone except Gideon Welles himself. Unfortunately, this is just what the diarist had done. Edgar Welles may have been naïve. He may not have realized that a rewrite years later by the diarist himself may do more to destroy the value of such a "contemporaneous" record than would editing by others.

In any event, there appeared in the American Historical Review for April 1925, an article by Howard K. Beale showing conclusively that in his old age Gideon Welles had gone over his own diary and revised it to give himself the benefit of hindsight. Beale had examined the manuscript, which is kept at the Library of Congress in Washington, and had found that it had been gone through for important changes, not once but twice—once in blue ink and once in pencil. Where later event proved him wrong, Welles simply took out the passage or changed it to put himself on the side of the angels.

Because of this, the Welles diary is no longer relied on by Civil War students to resolve important doubts or controversies like the many that arose between the diarist and Seward, Stanton, Grant, and other contemporaries. No important afterthoughts intrude, however, in the account of Lincoln's death.

"They wept—especially the Negroes . . ."
GIDEON WELLES (1802-1878)

April 14 [1865]

General Grant was present at the meeting of the Cabinet to-day and remained during the session.

Inquiry had been made as to army news and especially if any information had been received from Sherman. None of the members had heard anything, and Stanton, who makes it a point to be late, and who has the telegraph in his department, had not arrived.

General Grant said he was hourly expecting word. The President remarked, it would, he had no doubt, come soon, and come favorable, for he had last night the usual dream which he had preceding nearly every great and important event of the War. Generally the news had been favorable which succeeded this dream, and the dream itself was always the same.

I inquired what this remarkable dream could be. He said it related to your (my) element, the water; that he seemed to be in some singular, indescribable vessel, and that he was moving with great rapidity towards an indefinite shore; that he had this dream preceding Sumter, Bull Run, Antietam, Gettysburg, Stone River, Vicksburg, Wilmington, etc.

"I had," the President remarked, "this strange dream again last night, and we shall, judging from the past, have great news very soon."

I write this conversation three days after it occurred, in consequence of what took place Friday night, and but for which the mention of this dream would probably have never been noted. Great events did, indeed, follow, for within a few hours the good and gentle, as well as truly great, man who narrated his dream closed forever his earthly career.

I had retired to bed about half past ten on the evening of the 14th of April, and was just getting asleep when Mrs. Welles, my wife, said some one was at our door. Sitting up in bed, I heard a voice twice call to John, my son, whose sleeping-room was on the second floor directly over the front entrance.

I arose at once and raised a window, when my messenger, James Smith, called to me that Mr. Lincoln, the President, had been shot, and said Secretary Seward and his son, Assistant Secretary Frederick Seward, were assassinated.

James was much alarmed and excited. I told him his story was very incoherent and improbable, that he was associating men who were not together and liable to attack at the same time. "Where," I inquired, "was the President when shot?" James said he was at Ford's Theatre on 10th Street. "Well," said I, "Secretary Seward is an invalid in bed in his house yonder on 15th Street."

James said he had been there, stopped in at the house to make inquiry before alarming me.

I immediately dressed myself, and, against the earnest remonstrance and appeals of my wife, went directly to Mr. Seward's, whose residence was on the east side of the square, mine being on the north. James accompanied me.

As we were crossing 15th Street I saw four or five men in earnest consultation, standing under the lamp on the corner by St. John's Church. Before I had got half across the street, the lamp was suddenly extinguished and the knot of persons rapidly dispersed. For a moment, and but a moment, I was disconcerted to find myself in darkness, but, recollecting that it was late and about time for the moon to rise, I proceeded. Hurrying forward into 15th Street, I found it pretty full of people, especially near the residence of Secretary Seward.

Entering the house, I found the lower hall and office full of persons, and among them most of the foreign legations, all anxiously inquiring what truth there was in the horrible rumors afloat.

Proceeding through the hall to the stairs, I found one and I think two of the servants there holding the crowd in check. The servants were frightened and appeared relieved to see me.

I asked for the Secretary's room and proceeded to the foot of the bed. Dr. Verdi and, I think, two others vere there. The bed was saturated with blood. The Secretary was lying o: his back, the upper part of his head covered by a cloth, which extend(l down over his eyes. His mouth was open, the lower jaw dropping down

I exchanged a few whispered wo ds with Dr. V. Secretary Stanton, who came after but almost simultaneousiy with me, made inquiries in a louder tone till admonished by a word from one of the physicians. We almost immediately withdrew and went into the adjoining front room, where lay Frederick Seward. His eyes were open but he did not move them, nor a limb, nor did he speak. Doctor White, who was in attendance, told me he was unconscious and more dangerously injured than his father.

As we descended the stairs, I asked Stanton what he had heard in regard to the President that was reliable. He said the President was shot at Ford's Theatre, that he had seen a man who was present and witnessed the occurrence.

The streets were full of people. Not only the sidewalk but the carriageway was to some extent occupied, all or nearly all hurrying towards 10th Street. When we entered that street we found it pretty closely packed.

The President had been carried across the street from the theatre to the house of a Mr. Peterson. We entered by ascending a flight of steps above the basement and passing through a long hall to the rear, where the President lay, extended on a bed, breathing heavily.

Several surgeons were present, at least six, I should think more. Among them I was glad to observe Dr. Hall, who, however, soon left. I inquired of Dr. H. as I entered the true condition of the President. He replied the President was dead to all intents, although he might live three hours or perhaps longer.

The giant sufferer lay extended diagonally across the bed, which was not long enough for him. He had been stripped of his clothes. His large arms, which were occasionally exposed, were of a size which one would scarce have expected from his spare appearance. His slow, full respiration lifted the clothes with each breath that he took. His features were calm and striking. I had never seen them appear to better advantage than for the first hour, perhaps, that I was there. After that, his right eye began to swell and that part of his face became discolored.

Senator Sumner was there, I think, when I entered. If not he came in soon after, as did Speaker Colfax, Mr. Secretary McCulloch, and the other members of the Cabinet, with the exception of Mr. Seward.

A double guard was stationed at the door and on the sidewalk, to repress the crowd, which was of course highly excited and anxious.

The room was small and overcrowded. The surgeons and members of the Cabinet were as many as should have been in the room, but there were many more, and the hall and other rooms in the front or main house were full. One of these rooms was occupied by Mrs. Lincoln and her attendants, with Miss Harris. About once an hour Mrs. Lincoln would repair to the bedside of her dying husband and with lamentation and tears remain until overcome by emotion.

April 15

A door which opened upon a porch or gallery, and also the windows, were kept open for fresh air. The night was dark, cloudy and damp, and about six it began to rain. I remained in the room until then without sitting or leaving it, when, there being a vacant chair which some one left at the foot of the bed, I occupied it for nearly two hours, listening to the heavy groans, and witnessing the wasting life of the good and great man who was expiring before me.

About 6 A.M. I experienced a feeling of faintness and for the first time after entering the room, a little past eleven, I left it and the house and took a short walk in the open air. It was a dark and gloomy morning, and rain set in before I returned to the house, some fifteen minutes later.

Large groups of people were gathered every few rods, all anxious and solicitous. Some one or more from each group stepped forward as I passed, to inquire into the condition of the President, and to ask if there was no hope. Intense grief was on every countenance when I replied that the President could survive but a short time. The colored people especaily—and there were at this time more of them, perhaps, than of whites— were overwhelmed with grief.

Returning to the house, I seated myself in the back parlor, where the Attorney General and others had been engaged in taking evidence concerning the assassination.

A little before seven, I went into the room where the dying President was rapidly drawing near the closing moments. His wife soon after made her last visit to him. The death-struggle had begun. Robert, his son, stood with several others at the head of the bed. He bore himself well, but on two occasions gave way to overpowering grief and sobbed aloud, turning his head and leaning on the shoulder of Senator Sumner.

The respiration of the President became suspended at intervals, and at last entirely ceased at twenty-two minutes past seven.

A prayer followed from Dr. Gurley, and the Cabinet, with the exception of Mr. Seward and Mr. McCulloch, immediately thereafter assembled in the back parlor, from which all other persons were excluded, and there signed a letter which was prepared by Attorney General Speed to the Vice-President, informing him of the event, and that the government devolved upon him.

I went after breakfast to the Executive Mansion. There was a cheerless cold rain and everything seemed gloomy. On the Avenue in front of the White House were several hundred colored people, mostly women and children, weeping and wailing their loss. This crowd did not appear to diminish through the whole of that cold wet day. They seemed not to know what was to be their fate since their great benefactor was dead, and their hopeless grief affected me more than almost anything else, though strong and brave men wept when I met them.

At the White House all was silent and sad. As we were descending the stairs, "Tad," who was looking from the window at the foot, turned and, seeing us, cried aloud in his tears, "Oh, Mr. Welles, who killed my father?"

Neither Speed nor myself could restrain our tears nor give the poor boy any satisfactory answer.

April 18

From every part of the country came lamentation. Every house, almost, has some drapery, especially the homes of the poor. Profuse exhibition is displayed on the public buildings and the dwellings of the wealthy, but the little black ribbon or strip of black cloth from the hovel of the poor negro or the impoverished white is more touching.

BETWEEN THE NIGHT OF April 14, when he shot Abraham Lincoln, and April 26, when a bullet ended his own life in a barn near Port Royal, Virginia, John Wilkes Booth set down some of his thoughts in a diary.

Through these wild pencilings come the delusion of grandeur that had built up in Booth's mind: his hope that the South, and perhaps in time the whole country, would hail him as a hero; his subsequent shock at learning that he was condemned for his act in North and South alike; his self-pity and feeling of betrayal; and finally the growing doubt that God would forgive him.

The diary stirred much curiosity and indecisive detective work among researchers, mainly because of Booth's cryptically stated hope, while he is toying with the idea of going back to Washington, that he might "clear his name" there. How accomplish that, after his crime had been publicly witnessed? By implicating others? Perhaps men in high places? That was the idea behind the research; but it unearthed nothing more than the outpouring of a twisted mind that here meets the eye.

"See the cold hands they extend to me!"
JOHN WILKES BOOTH (1838-1865)

April 13, 14, Friday the Ides [1865]

Until today nothing was ever thought of sacrificing to our country's wrongs. For six months we had worked to capture. But our cause being almost lost, something decisive and great must be done. But its failure was owing to others, who did not strike for their country with a heart.

I struck boldly and not as the papers say. I walked with a firm step through a thousand of his friends, was stopped, but pushed on. A colonel was at his side. I shouted *Sic semper* before I fired. In jumping broke my leg. I passed all his pickets. Rode sixty miles that night, with the bone of my leg tearing the flesh at every jump.

I can never repent it, though we hated to kill. Our country owed all her troubles to him, and God simply made me the instrument of his punishment. The country is not what it was. This forced Union is not what I have loved. I care not what becomes of me. I have no desire to outlive my country. This night (before the deed) I wrote a long article and left it for one of the editors of the *National Intelligencer* in which I fully set forth our reasons for our proceeding.

The article never reached the editors of the National Intelligencer. *Before the murder Booth sealed it in an envelope, gave it to a friend, John Matthews, and asked him to deliver it the following morning. When the news came out of the assassination, Matthews opened and read it, and in terror of being implicated, burned it.*

Friday, 21

After being hunted like a dog through swamps and woods, and last night being chased by gunboats till I was forced to return, wet, cold and starving with every man's hand against me, I am here in despair.

And why? For doing what Brutus was honored for—what made William Tell a hero; and yet I, for striking down an even greater tyrant than they ever knew, am looked upon as a common cutthroat.

My act was purer than either of theirs. One hoped to be great himself; the other had not only his country's but his own wrongs to avenge. I hoped for no gain; I knew no private wrong. I struck for my country, and her alone.

A people ground beneath this tyranny prayed for this end, and yet now see the cold hands they extend to me! God cannot pardon me if I have done wrong; yet I cannot see any wrong, except in serving a degenerate people. The little, the very little, I left behind to clear my name, the Government will not allow to be printed.

So ends all! For my country I have given up all that makes life sweet and holy—tonight misfortune upon my family, and am sure that there is no pardon for me in the heavens, since man condemns me so. I have only heard of what has been done (except what I did myself) and it fills me with horror.

God, try and forgive me and bless my mother. Tonight I will once more try the river, with the intention to cross; though I have a greater desire and almost a mind to return to Washington, and in a measure clear my name, which I feel I can do.

I do not repent the blow I struck. I may before my God, but not to man. I think I have done well, though I am abandoned, with the curse of Cain upon me, when, if the world knew my heart, that one blow would have made me great, though I did desire no greatness.

Tonight I try once more to escape these bloodhounds. Who, who, can read his fate? God's will be done. I have too great a soul to die like a criminal. Oh! may He spare me that, and let me die bravely.

I bless the entire world. I have never hated nor wronged anyone. This last was not a wrong, unless God deems it so, and it is with Him to damn or bless me.

I do not wish to shed a drop of blood, but I must fight the course. 'Tis all that's left me.

1865:   BAD NEWS AT THE OLD PLANTATION

"COLONEL CHESNUT, now ninety-three, blind and deaf, is apparently as strong as ever, and certainly as resolute of will. Partly patriarch, partly grand seigneur, this old man is of a species that we shall see no more—the last of a race of lordly planters who ruled this Southern world, but now a splendid wreck. His manners are unequaled still, but underneath this smooth exterior lies the grip of a tyrant whose will has never been crossed."

So Mary Boykin Chesnut, in 1865, sketches in her diary the character of her father-in-law. And so, through the five-year chronicle, a world symbolized by this old man and his family crumbles and is never more to be.

Mary was the daughter of Stephen Decatur Miller, South Carolina cotton planter and onetime governor and senator. At 17 she married James Chesnut, Jr., whose father, the Colonel, was one of South Carolina's wealthiest citizens. The young couple lived mostly in a massive brick home on one of the Colonel's several plantations called Mulberry, near Camden. James Junior went into politics but resigned a seat in the United States Senate to become aide to General Beauregard, later to President Davis. In 1864 he was given the rank of brigadier general and placed in command of reserve troops.

Mary began her diary in Charleston when the Convention was passing the Ordinance of Secession. From a housetop she watched the bombardment of Fort Sumter. Throughout the war her husband's connections kept her moving among the top leadership of the Confederacy.

Though she had never written for publication, her diary is the work of a skilled hand and a great heart. As one of the outstanding social records of the Civil War it has outlived many a professional attempt at the same thing.

On November 25, 1864, at Columbia she writes: "My journal, a quire of Confederate paper, lies wide open on my desk in the corner of my drawing room. Everybody reads it who chooses. Isabella [Martin, a friend] still calls me Cassandra [Greek prophetess whom nobody would believe] and puts her hands to her ears when I begin to wail. Well, Cassandra only records what she hears; she does not vouch for it."

Five months later, at Chester, South Carolina, as a refugee, she had to hide the diary for fear it would fall into the hands of the enemy. "April 22—This yellow Confederate quire of paper, my journal, blotted by entries, has been buried three days with the silver sugar-dish, teapot, milk-jug, and a few spoons and forks that follow my fortunes as I wander."

The diary was not published in Mary's lifetime, and it was only by a happy chance that it ever was. On her death in 1886 she had bequeathed the forty-eight slender volumes to Isabella Martin. In 1904 Myrta Lockett Avery, a writer and student of the Civil War, went to Columbia, South Carolina, to dig up material for a new book she had in mind. She met Miss Martin and learned of the existence of Mary Chesnut's diary. On reading it, she was entranced, knew she had made a great find, put off her original project, and edited the document for publication.

Among the most poignant entries are those of the closing year of the war.

"Nothing is left but the bare land and the debts . . ."

MARY BOYKIN CHESNUT

(1823-1886)

Lincolnton, North Carolina, February 16, 1865

A Miss Patterson called—a refugee from Tennessee. She had been in a country overrun by Yankee invaders, and she described so graphically all the horrors to be endured by those subjected to fire and sword, rapine and plunder, that I was fairly scared, and determined to come here. This is a thoroughly out-of-all-routes place.

We thought that if the negroes were ever so loyal to us, they could not protect me from an army bent upon sweeping us from the face of the earth, and if they tried to do so, so much worse would it be for the poor things with their Yankee friends. I then left them to shift for themselves, as they are accustomed to do, and I took the same liberty.

My husband does not care a fig for the property question, and never did. Perhaps, if he had ever known poverty, it would be different. He talked beautifully about it, as he always does about everything. I have told him often that, if at heaven's gate St. Peter would listen to him a while, and let him tell his own story, he would get in, and the angels might give him a crown extra.

Now he says he has only one care—that I should be safe, and not so harassed with dread.

Here I am, broken-hearted and in exile. And in such a place! We have bare floors, and for a feather-bed, pine table, and two chairs I pay $30 a day. Such sheets! But fortunately I have some of my own. At the door, be-fore I was well out of the hack, the woman of the house packed Lawrence back, neck and heels: she would not have him at any price. She treated him as Mr. F.'s aunt did Clenman in *Little Dorrit*. She said his clothes were too fine for a nigger.

"His airs" indeed! Poor Lawrence was humble and silent. He said at last, "Miss Mary, send me back to Mars Jeems." I began to look for a pencil to write a note to my husband, but in the flurry could not find one. "Here is one," said Lawrence, producing one with a gold case. "Go away," she shouted, "I want no niggers here with gold pencils and airs." So Lawrence fled before the storm but not before he had begged me to go back. He said, "If Mars Jeems knew how you was treated he'd never be willing for you to stay here."

February 18

Here I am, thank God, settled at the McLeans', in a clean, comfortable room, airy and cozy. With a grateful heart I stir up my own bright wood fire. My bill for four days at this splendid hotel here was $240, with $25 additional for fire.

February 19

The Fants say all the trouble at the hotel came from our servants' bragging. They represented us as millionaires, and the Middleton men servants smoked cigars. Mrs. Reed's averred that he had never done anything in his life but stand behind his master at table with a silver waiter in his hand. We were charged accordingly, but perhaps the landlady did not get the best of us after all, for we paid her in Confederate money.

Now that they won't take Confederate money in the shops here, how are we to live? Miss Middleton says quartermasters' families are all clad in good gray cloth, but the soldiers go naked. Well, we are like the families of whom the novels always say they are poor but honest. Poor? Well-nigh beggars are we, for I do not know where my next meal is to come from.

February 22

A letter from my husband who is at Charlotte. He came near being taken a prisoner in Columbia, for he was asleep the morning of the 17th, when the Yankees blew up the railroad depot. That woke him, of course, and he found everybody had left Columbia, and the town was surrendered by the mayor, Colonel Goodwin. Hampton and his command had been gone several hours. Isaac Hayne came away with General Chesnut. There was no fire in the town when they left. They overtook Hampton's command at Meek's Mill. That night, from the hills where they encamped, they saw the fire, and knew the Yankees were burning the town, as we had every reason to expect they would.

Charleston and Wilmington have surrendered. I have no further use for a newspaper. I never want to see another one for as long as I live. Shame, disgrace, beggary, all have come at once, and are hard to bear—the grand smash!

February 25

The McLeans are kind people. They ask no rent for their rooms—only $20 a week for firewood. Twenty dollars! And such dollars—mere waste paper.

Mrs. Munroe took up my photograph book, in which I have a picture of all the Yankee generals. "I want to see the men who are to be our masters," said she. "Not mine," I answered, "thank God, come what may. This was a free fight. We had as much right to fight to get out as they had to fight to keep us in. If they try to play the masters, anywhere upon the habitable globe will I go, never to see a Yankee, and if I die on the way so much the better." Then I sat down and wrote to my husband in language much worse than anything I can put in this book. As I wrote I was blinded by tears of rage. Indeed, I nearly wept myself away.

February 29

Trying to brave it out. They have plenty, yet let our men freeze and starve in their prisons. Would you be willing to be as wicked as they are? A thousand times, no! But we must feed our army first—if we can do so much as that. Our captives need not starve if Lincoln would consent to exchange prisoners; but men are nothing to the United States—things to throw away. If they send our men back they strengthen our army, and so again their policy is to keep everybody and everything here in order to help starve us out. That, too, is what Sherman's destruction means—to starve us out.

March 5

My letter from my husband was so—well, what in a woman you would call heart-broken, that I began to get ready for a run up to Charlotte. My hat was on my head, my traveling bag in my hand, and Ellen was saying, "Which umbrella, ma'am?" "Stop, Ellen," said I, "someone is speaking out there." A tap came at the door, and Miss McLean threw the door wide open as she said in a triumphant voice: "Permit me to announce General Chesnut."

We went after luncheon to see Mrs. Munroe. My husband wanted to thank her for all her kindness to me. I was awfully proud of him. I used to think that everybody had the air and manners of a gentleman. I know now that these accomplishments are things to thank God for.

How kind my friends were on this, my fete day! Mrs. Rutledge sent me a plate of biscuits; Mrs. Munroe nearly enough food supplies for an entire dinner; Mrs. McLean a cake for dessert. Ellen cooked and served up the material happily at hand very nicely indeed. There never was a more successful dinner. My heart was too full to eat, but I was quiet and calm; at least I spared my husband the trial of a broken voice and tears.

March 6

To-day came a godsend. Even a small piece of bread and the molasses had become things of the past. My larder was empty, when a tall mulatto woman brought a tray covered by a huge white serviette. Ellen ushered her in with a flourish, saying, "Mrs. McDaniel's maid." The maid set down the tray upon my bare table, and uncovered it with conscious pride. There were fowls ready for roasting, sausages, butter, bread, eggs, and preserves. I was dumb with delight. After silent thanks to heaven my powers of speech returned, and I exhausted myself in messages of gratitude to Mrs. McDaniel.

"Missus, you oughtn't to let her see how glad you was," said Ellen. "It was a lettin' of yose'f down."

March 10

Colonel Childs has been here bringing rice and potatoes and promising flour. He is a trump. He pulled out his pocketbook and offered to be my banker. He stood there on the street, Miss Middleton and Isabella witnessing the generous action, and straight out offered me money. "No, put up that," said I. "I am not a beggar, and I never will be; to die is so much easier."

Alas, after that flourish of trumpets, when he came with a sack of flour I accepted it gratefully.

March 13

We are surprised to see by the papers that we behaved heroically in leaving everything we had to be destroyed, without one thought of surrender. We had not thought of ourselves from the heroic point of view. Isaac McLaughlin hid and saved everything we trusted with him. A grateful negro is Isaac.

Chester, South Carolina, March 27

In this high and airy retreat, as in Richmond, then in Columbia, and then in Lincolnton, my cry is still: If they would only leave me here in peace and if I were sure things never could be worse with me. Again am I surrounded by old friends. People seem to vie with each other to show how good they can be to me.

To-day Stephen D. Lee's corps marched through—only to surrender.

The camp songs of these men were a heartbreak; so sad, yet so stirring. They would have warmed the blood of an Icelander. The leading voice was powerful, mellow, clear, distinct, pathetic, sweet. So, I sat down, as women have done before, when they hung up their harps by strange streams, and I wept the bitterness of such weeping. There they go, the gay and gallant few, doomed; the last gathering of the flower of Southern pride, to be killed, or worse, to a prison. They continue to tramp by, light and jaunty. They march with as airy a tread as if they still believed the world was all on their side, and that there were no Yankee bullets for the unwary.

March 29

I was awakened with a bunch of violets from Mrs. Pride. Violets always remind me of the sweet South wind that blew in the garden of paradise part of my life. Then, it all came back: the dread unspeakable that lies behind every thought now.

March 30

General Lee says to the men who shirk duty, "This is the people's war; when they tire, I stop." Wigfall says, "It is all over; the game is up." He is on his way to Texas, and when the hanging begins he can step over into Mexico.

I am plucking up heart, such troops do I see go by every day. They must turn the tide, and surely they are going for something more than surrender. It is very late, and the wind flaps my curtain, which seems to moan, "Too late." All this will end by making me a nervous lunatic.

April 19

Just now, when Mr. Clay dashed up-stairs, pale as a sheet, saying, "General Lee has capitulated," I saw it reflected in Mary Darby's face before I heard him speak. She staggered to the table, sat down, and wept aloud. Mr. Clay's eyes were not dry. Quite beside herself Mary shrieked, "Now we belong to negroes and Yankees!" Buck [Sally Buchanan Preston, Mrs. Chesnut's close friend] said, "I do not believe it."

How different from ours of them is their estimate of us. How contradictory is their attitude toward us. To keep the despised and iniquitous South within their borders, as part of their country, they are willing to enlist millions of men at home and abroad, and to spend billions, and we know they do not love fighting *per se* nor spending money. They are perfectly willing to have three killed for our one.

While the Preston girls are here, my dining-room is given up to them, and we camp on the landing, with our one table and six chairs. Beds are made on the dining-room floor. Otherwise there is no furniture except buckets of water and bath-tubs in their improvised chamber. Night and day this landing and these steps are crowded with the *elite* of the Confederacy, going and coming, and when night comes, or rather, bedtime, more beds are made on the floor of the landing-place for the war-worn soldiers to rest upon.

My husband is rarely at home. I sleep with the girls, and my room is given up to soldiers. General Lee's few, but undismayed, his remnant of an army, or the part from the South and West, sad and crestfallen, pass through Chester. Many discomfited heroes find their way up these stairs.

We are to stay here. Running is useless now; so we mean to bide a Yankee raid, which they say is imminent. Why fly? They are everywhere, these Yankees, like red ants, like the locusts and frogs which were the plagues of Egypt.

The plucky way in which our men keep up is beyond praise. There is no howling, and our poverty is made a matter of laughing. We deride our own penury. Of the country we try not to speak at all.

April 22

It has been a wild three days, with aides galloping around with messages, Yankees hanging over us like a sword of Damocles. We have been in queer straits. We sat up at Mrs. Bedon's dressed, without once going to bed for forty-eight hours, and we were aweary.

Colonel Cadwallader Jones came with a despatch, a sealed secret despatch. It was for General Chesnut. I opened it. Lincoln, old Abe Lincoln, has been killed, murdered, and Seward wounded! Why? By Whom? It is simply maddening, all this.

I sent off messenger after messenger for General Chesnut. I have not the faintest idea where he is, but I know this foul murder will bring upon us worse miseries. Mary Darby says, "But they murdered him themselves. No Confederates are in Washington." "But if they see fit to accuse us of instigating it?" "Who murdered him? Who knows?" "See if they don't take revenge on us, now that we are ruined and cannot repel them any longer."

The death of Lincoln I call a warning to tyrants. He will not be the last President put to death in the capital, though he is the first.

April 23

My silver wedding day, and I am sure the unhappiest day of my life.

They say Mulberry has been destroyed by a corps commanded by General Logan. Someone asked coolly, "Will General Chesnut be shot as a soldier or hung as a Senator?" "I am not of sufficient consequence," answered he. "They will stop short of brigadiers. I resigned my seat in the

United States Senate weeks before there was a secession. So I can not be hung as a Senator. But after all it is only a choice between drumhead court martial, short shrift, and a lingering death at home from starvation."

These negroes are unchanged. The shining black mask they wear does not show a ripple of change; they are sphinxes. Ellen has had my diamonds to keep for a week or so. When the danger was over she handed them back to me with as little apparent interest in the matter as if they had been garden peas.

One year ago we left Richmond. Now we have burned towns, deserted plantations, sacked villages. "You seem resolute to look the worst in the face," said General Chesnut wearily. "Yes, poverty, with no future and no hope." "But no slaves, thank God!" cried Buck. "How does our famous captain, the great Lee, bear the Yankees' galling chain?" I asked. "He knows how to possess his soul in patience," answered my husband.

May 1

General Preston came to say good-by. He will take his family abroad at once. "There will be no more confiscation, my dear madam," said he; "they must see that we have been punished enough." "They do not think so, my dear general. This very day a party of Federals passed here in hot pursuit of our President."

A terrible fire-eater, one of the few men left in the world who believe we have a right divine, being white, to hold Africans, who are black, in bonds forever; he is six feet two; an athlete; a spendid specimen of the animal man; but he has never been under fire; his place in the service was a bomb-proof office, so-called.

Camden, South Carolina, May 2

Since we left Chester nothing but solitude, nothing but tall blackened chimneys to show that any man has ever trod this road before. This is Sherman's track. It is hard not to curse him. I wept incessantly at first. The roses of the gardens are already hiding the ruins. My husband said Nature is a wonderful renovator. He tried to say something else and then I shut my eyes and made a vow that if we were a crushed people, crushed by weight, I would never be a whimpering, pining slave.

May 4

The fidelity of the negroes is the principal topic. There seems to be not a single case of a negro who betrayed his master, and yet they showed a natural and exultant joy at being free.

Mrs. Bartow drove with me to Mulberry. On one side of the house we found every window had been broken, every bell torn down, every piece of furniture destroyed, and every door smashed in. But the other side was intact.

Maria Whitaker and her mother, who had been left in charge, explained this odd state of things. The Yankees were busy as beavers, working like regular carpenters, destroying everything, when their general came in and stopped them. He told them it was a sin to destroy a fine old house like that, whose owner was over ninety years old. He would not have had it done for the world. It was wanton mischief. He explained to Maria that soldiers at such times were excited, wild, and unruly.

They carried off sacks full of our books, since unfortunately they found a pile of empty sacks in the garret. Our books, our letters, our papers were afterward strewn along the Charleston road. Somebody found things of ours as far away as Vance's Ferry.

Indeed, nothing is left to us now but the bare land, and the debts contracted for the support of hundreds of negroes during the war.

The negroes would be a good riddance. A hired man would be a good deal cheaper than a man whose father and mother, wife and twelve children have to be fed, clothed, housed and nursed, their taxes paid, and their doctor's bills, all for his half-done, slovenly, lazy work. For years we have thought negroes a nuisance that did not pay. They pretend exuberant loyalty to us now. Only one man of Mr. Chesnut's left the plantation with the Yankees.

With our cotton saved, and cotton at a dollar a pound, we might be in comparatively easy circumstances. But now it is the devil to pay and no pitch hot. Well, all this was to be.

When we crossed the river coming home, the ferry man at Chesnut's Ferry asked for his fee. Among us all we could not muster the small silver coin he demanded. There was poverty for you.

Old Cuffey, head gardener at Mulberry, and Yellow Abram, his assistant, have gone on in the even tenor of their way. Men may come and men may go, but they dig on forever. And they say they mean to "as long as old master is alive." We have green peas, asparagus, lettuce, spinach, new potatoes, and strawberries in abundance—enough for ourselves and plenty to give away to refugees.

Floride Cantey heard an old negro say to his master: "When you all had de power you was good to me, and I'll protect you now. No niggers nor Yankees shall tech you. If you want anything call for Sambo. I mean, call for Mr. Samuel: dat my name now."

May 21

Went to our plantation, the Hermitage, yesterday. Saw no change; not a soul was absent from his or her post. I said, "Good colored folks, when are you going to kick off the traces and be free?" In their furious, emotional way, they swore devotion to us all to their dying day. Just the same, the minute they see an opening to better themselves they will move on. William, my husband's foster-brother, came up. "Well, William, what do you want?" asked my husband. "Only to look at you, marster; it does me good."

June 12

We are shut in here, turned with our faces to a dead wall. No mails. A letter is sometimes brought in by a man on horseback, traveling through the wilderness made by Sherman. All railroads have been destroyed and the bridges are gone. We are cut off from the world, here to eat out our hearts. Yet from my window I look out on many a gallant youth and maiden fair. The street is crowded and it is a gay sight. Camden is thronged with refugees from the low country and here they disport themselves.

June 27

My sister-in-law is in tears of rage and despair, her servants all gone to "a big meeting at Mulberry," though she had made every appeal against their going. "Send them adrift," someone said, "they do not obey you, or serve you; they only live on you." It would break her heart to part with one of them. But that sort of thing will soon right itself. They will go off *to better themselves*—we have only to cease paying wages—and that is easy, for we have no money.

July 4

There was talk of the negroes where the Yankees had been—negroes who flocked to them and showed them where silver and valuables had been hid by the white people. Ladies' maids dressed themselves in their mistresses' gowns before the owners' faces and walked off.

Now, before this every one had told me how kind, faithful, and considerate the negroes had proven. I am sure, after hearing these tales, the fidelity of my own servants shines out brilliantly. I had taken their conduct too much as a matter of course.

In the afternoon I had some business on our place, the Hermitage. John drove me down. Our people were all at home, quiet, orderly, respectful, and at their usual work. In point of fact things looked unchanged. There was nothing to show that any one of them had ever seen the Yankees, or knew that there was one in existence.

August 2

Dr. Boykin and John Witherspoon were talking of a nation in mourning, of blood poured out like rain on the battle-fields—for what? Never let me hear that the blood of the brave has been shed in vain! No; it sends a cry down through all time.

1865: *WALT WHITMAN SUMS UP*
FOR THE DEAD

SIX-HUNDRED-AND-TEN THOUSAND KILLED. But that was only a statistic. "Future years," wrote Walt Whitman, "will never know the seething hell of countless minor scenes, and it is best they should not—the real war will never get in the books."

In some of the most heartbreaking of these scenes he had taken part himself, not as a soldier but as a volunteer ministering to the wounded in Washington and in the battle camps. In his diary called Specimen Days he violates his own suggestion that they are best left undepicted.

Years before his war work Whitman had come into his own as a poet, if of disputed artistry nevertheless of admittedly broad horizons and a breath-taking newness. He had steeped himself in the faith of Emerson and the transcendentalists, especially hope for democracy and trust in the common man. In 1848, for his blasts at slavery, he was fired from the Brooklyn Daily Eagle, where he had worked as editor two years. Seven years later he published his book Leaves of Grass—poetry in form and content unlike any other the country had ever known.

He sent a copy to Emerson. Though almost alone in his opinion, Emerson saw at once that here were both the promise and the beginning of true greatness. He called it "the most extraordinary piece of wit and wisdom America has yet contributed."

But behind the book was a baffling character—a broad streak of bravado, more than a dash of homosexuality, a cast of fakiness over the "good gray poet"—all to be taken along with the pure gold and the dross in his work. Malcolm Cowley, in his introduction to a 1948 edition of Whitman, writes, "In no other book of great poems does one find so much trash that the poet should have recognized as trash before he set the first line of it on paper." But of the best of the poems Cowley exults: "Reading them almost a century after their publication, one feels the same shock and wonder and delight that Emerson felt.

. . . They carry us into a new world that Whitman discovered as if this very morning, after it had been created overnight."

The Civil War did not leave Whitman physically unscathed. In 1873, probably as the result of former hardship and exposure, he suffered a stroke, and from that time to the end of his life the old fire was missing from his poetry.

"There they lie, strewing the fields . . ."
WALT WHITMAN (1819-1892)

Falmouth, Virginia, opposite Fredericksburg, December 21, 1862

Begin my visits among the camp hospitals in the army of the Potomac. Spend a good part of the day in a large brick mansion on the banks of the Rappahannock, used as a hospital since the battle—seems to have receiv'd only the worst cases.

Outdoors, at the foot of a tree, within ten yards of the front of the house, I notice a heap of amputated feet, legs, arms, hands, &c., a full load for a one-horse cart. Several dead bodies lie near, each cover'd with its brown woollen blanket. In the door-yard towards the river, are fresh graves, mostly of the officers, their names on pieces of barrel-staves or broken boards, stuck in the dirt.

The large mansion is quite crowded upstairs and down, everything impromptu, no system, all bad enough, but I have no doubt the best that can be done; all the wounds pretty bad, some frightful, the men in their old clothes, unclean and bloody.

After first Fredericksburg, December 23 to 31

The results of the late battle are exhibited everywhere about here in thousands of cases (hundreds die every day), in the camp, brigade, and division hospitals. These are merely tents, and sometimes very poor ones, the wounded lying on the ground, lucky if their blankets are spread on layers of pine or hemlock twigs, or small leaves. No cots; seldom even a mattress.

It is pretty cold. The ground is frozen hard, and there is occasional snow. I go around from one case to another. I do not see that I do much good to these wounded and dying; but I cannot leave them. Once in a while some youngster holds on to me convulsively, and I do what I can for him; at any rate, stop with him and sit near him for hours, if he wishes it.

Thursday, Jan. 21, 1863

Interesting cases in ward One; Charles Miller, bed 19, company D, 53d Pennsylvania, is only 16 years of age, very bright, courageous boy, left leg amputated below the knee; next bed to him, another lad very sick; gave each appropriate gifts.

In the bed above, also, amputation of the left leg; gave him a little jar of raspberries; bed one, this ward, gave a small sum; also to a soldier on crutches, sitting on his bed near. (I am more and more surprised at the very great proportion of youngsters from 15 to 21 in the army. I afterwards found a still greater proportion among the southerners.)

May '63

As I write this, the wounded have begun to arrive from Hooker's command from bloody Chancellorsville. I was down among the first arrivals. The men in charge told me the bad cases were yet to come. If that is so, I pity them, for these are bad enough.

You ought to see the scene of the wounded arriving at the landing here at the foot of Sixth Street, at night. Two boat loads came about half-past seven last night. A little after eight it rain'd a long and violent shower. The pale, helpless soldiers had been debark'd, and lay around on the wharf and neighborhood anywhere. The rain was, probably, grateful to them; at any rate they were exposed to it.

The few torches light up the spectacle. All around—on the wharf, on the ground, out on side places—the men are lying on blankets, old quilts, &c., with bloody rags bound round head, arms, and legs. The attendants are few, and at night few outsiders also—only a few hard-work'd transportation men and drivers. (The wounded are getting to be common, and people grow callous.)

The men, whatever their condition, lie there, and patiently wait till their turn comes to be taken up. Nearby, the ambulances are now arriving in clusters, and one after another is call'd to back up and take its load. Extreme cases are sent off on stretchers. The men generally make little or no ado, whatever their sufferings. A few groans that cannot be suppress'd, and occasionally a scream of pain as they lift a man into the ambulance.

To-day, as I write, hundreds more are expected, and to-morrow and the next day more, and so on for many days. Quite often they arrive at the rate of 1,000 a day.

Wednesday, February 4th, 1864

Visited Armory-square hospital, went pretty thoroughly through the wards E and D. Supplied paper and envelopes to all who wish'd—as usual found plenty of men who needed those articles. Wrote letters. Saw and talk'd with two or three members of the Brooklyn 14th regt. A poor fellow in Ward D with a fearful wound in a fearful condition, was having some loose splinters of bone taken from the neighborhood of the wound.

The operation was long, and one of great pain—yet, after it was well commenced, the soldier bore it in silence. He sat up, propp'd—was much wasted—had lain a long time quiet in one position (not for days only but weeks), a bloodless, brown-skinn'd face, with eyes full of determination—belong'd to a New York regiment. There was an unusual cluster of surgeons, medical cadets, nurses, &c., around his bed—I thought the whole thing was done with tenderness and done well.

In one case, the wife sat by the side of her husband, his sickness typhoid fever, pretty bad. In another, by the side of her son, a mother—she told me she had seven children, and this was the youngest. (A fine, healthy, gentle mother, good-looking, not very old, with a cap on her head, and dress'd like home—what a charm it gave to the whole ward.)

One young New York man, with a bright, handsome face, had been lying several months from a most disagreeable wound, receiv'd at Bull Run. A bullet had shot him right through the bladder, hitting him front, low in the belly, and coming out back. He had suffer'd much—the water came out of the wound, by slow but steady quantities, for many weeks—so that he lay almost constantly in a sort of puddle—and there were other disagreeable circumstances. He was of good heart, however. At present comparatively comfortable, had a bad throat, was delighted with a stick of horehound candy I gave him, with one or two other trifles.

February 24th [1864]

A spell of fine soft weather. Tonight took a long look at the President's house. The white portico—the palace-like, tall, round columns, spotless as snow—the walls also—the tender and soft moonlight, flooding the pale marble, and making peculiar faint languishing shades, not shadows—everywhere a soft transparent hazy, thin, blue moon-lace hanging in the air—the brilliant and extra-plentiful clusters of gas, on and around the facade, columns, portico, &c.—everything so white, so marbly pure and dazzling, yet soft—the White House of future poems, and of dreams and dramas.

May 28-9, 1865

I staid to-night a long time by the bedside of a new patient, a young Baltimorean, aged about 19 years, (2d Maryland, southern) very feeble, right leg amputated, can't sleep hardly at all—has taken a great deal of morphine, which, as usual, is costing more than it comes to. Evidently very intelligent and well bred—very affectionate—held on to my hand, and put it by his face, not willing to let me leave.

As I was lingering, soothing him in his pain, he says to me suddenly, "I hardly think you know who I am—I don't wish to impose upon you—I am a rebel soldier." I said I did not know that, but it made no difference.

In an adjoining ward I found his brother, an officer of rank, a Union soldier, a brave and religious man (Col. Clifton K. Prentiss, sixth Maryland infantry, Sixth Corps, wounded in one of the engagements at Petersburg, April 2—linger'd, suffer'd much, died in Brooklyn, Aug. 20, '65).

It was in the same battle both were hit.

[Undated]

The dead in this war—there they lie, strewing the fields and woods and valleys and battle-fields of the south—Virginia, the Peninsula—Malvern Hill and Fair Oaks—the banks of the Chickahominy—the terraces of Fredericksburg—Antietam bridge—the grisly ravines of Manassas—the bloody promenade of the Wilderness—the varieties of the strayed dead (the estimate of the War Department is 25,000 national soldiers kill'd in battle and never buried at all, 5,000 drown'd—15,000 inhumed by strangers, or on the march in haste, in hitherto unfound localities—2,000 graves cover'd by sand and mud by Mississippi freshets, 3,000 carried away by caving-in of banks, &c.,), Gettysburg, the West, Southwest—Vicksburg—Chattanooga —the trenches of Petersburg—the numberless battles, camps, hospitals everywhere—the crop reap'd by the mighty reapers, typhoid, dysentery, inflammations—and blackest and loathesomest of all, the dead and living burial-pits, the prison-pens of Andersonville, Salisbury, Belle-Isle, &c., (not Dante's pictured hell and all its woes, its degradations, filthy torments, excell'd those prisons)—the dead, the dead, the dead—*our* dead—or South or North, ours all (all, all, finally dear to me)—or East or West—Atlantic coast or Mississippi valley—somewhere they crawl'd to die, alone, in bushes, low gullies, or on the sides of hills—(there, in secluded spots, their skeletons, bleach'd bones, tufts of hair, buttons, fragments of clothing, are occasionally found yet)—our young men once so handsome and so joyous, taken from us—the son from the mother, the husband from the wife, the dear friend from the dear friend—the clusters of camp graves, in Georgia, the Carolinas, and in Tennessee—the single graves left in the woods or by the roadside, (hundreds, thousands, obliterated)—the corpses floated down the rivers, and caught and lodged (dozens, scores, floated down the upper Potomac, after the cavalry engagements, the pursuit of Lee, following Gettysburg)—some lie at the bottom of the sea—the general million, and the special cemeteries in almost all the States—the infinite dead—not only Northern dead leavening Southern soil—thousands, aye tens of thousands, of Southerners, crumble today in Northern earth.

And everywhere among these countless graves—we see and ages yet may see on monuments and gravestones, singly or in masses, to thousands or tens of thousands, the significant word *Unknown*.

V.

NEW

FRONTIERS

FOR

OLD

At MID-CENTURY there were no important railroads in the West. The great gold rushes, first to California and shortly afterward to Colorado, heightened the need of a transcontinental line and dangled the carrot before Eastern capital.

A leading advocate was the New York Tribune. Its editor, that far-famed eccentric Horace Greeley was focusing his bespectacled gaze on the "news" of America's future more than on events of the day. Perhaps that was why he plumped for occasional cultish notions like spirit-rapping and the planning of socialistic colonies in far-off places; but it was also why the younger generation liked his paper while their elders largely preferred James Gordon Bennett's stuffy, cynical Herald.

Greeley kept up the refrain, "Go west, young man," because to him the West was America's great adventure, not only in material fortune but in moral renascence as well. He looked toward it with stars in his eyes. If, as his critics suspected, there were also rocks in his head, they were glittering ones, gold that would combine with the waiting wealth in Western soil to make utopia, a country where there would be so much of everything good that it would be a waste of time to carry on the old social injustices. Poverty, crime, corruption, class struggle, sectional hate—all would be taken care of by wealth, sheer superabundance. Men would forget the very evil that was in them.

Publicly Greeley talked convincingly of the need for moving labor out of overcrowded eastern cities and of expanding the market for capital. It was economically sound; it was morally essential.

There were only two flaws in the dream. For one thing, it presupposed a limit to the greed of which human beings were capable. Confronted with the unlovely spectacle of promoters and politicos scurrying to cash in on the coming western boom, Greeley asked naïvely, "Can't we have a Pacific railroad bill that don't stink of land-jobbing? I have got to go for any Pacific bill but I hate to go for one that smells of corruption."

Second, slavery had no place in the dream. Neither did war clouds gathering over this issue in the eastern states nor extension of the struggle to the states-to-be beyond the Missouri. But the minority that would hold out for human enslavement in the face of such a magnificent prospect, Greeley believed, would be small, would be overwhelmed. Why, the South itself would put down any such nonsense!

In 1859 he went west himself. In rumpled white duster, and armed with his umbrella, he traveled by rail, by stagecoach, on horseback, wondering at all he saw and stopping to tell the people who lived with it every day how wonderful

475

it was. Many a conversation piece rippled out of that journey to the far corners of the country. Mark Twain told how Greeley begged stagecoach driver Hank Monk to hurry it up from Carson City to Placerville because he was due to give a lecture, and how Hank cracked the whip, shook all the buttons off Greeley's coat and finally "shot his head clean through the roof of the stage," and how Greeley yelled to Hank to go easier—"he warn't in as much of a hurry as he was awhile ago." Six years afterward, Mark said, they were still telling that story on the route across the Sierras, and Mark himself had heard it "481 or 482 times."

But Greeley's purpose was not to get people telling funny stories about himself. They did that anywhere. He was deeply in earnest, and as his diary shows, he came back bringing the dream with him, bigger and more enticing than ever.

"Let us have a railroad to the Pacific!"
HORACE GREELEY (1811-1872)

Atchison, Kansas, May 15, 1859

I left New York by Erie Railroad on Monday evening. I tried a "sleeping car" for the third time, and not very successfully. We all "retired" at ten o'clock, with a fair allowance of open windows and virtuous resolutions; but the rain poured, the night was chill and damp; and soon every orifice for the admission of external air, save the two or three humbug ventilators overhead, was shut, and a mephitic atmosphere produced.

The builders of cars have no right to be ignorant of the laws of life with which they tamper; and two or three presentments by Grand Juries of the makers of unventilated cars, especially sleeping-cars, as guilty of manslaughter, would exert a most salutary influence. I commend this public duty to the immediate consideration of prosecutors.

We took our course westward to St. Joseph on the Missouri, two hundred and six miles distant, which we reached in a little more than twelve hours. The road was completed in hot haste last winter, in order to profit by the "Pike's Peak" migration this spring; no gravel is found on its line, unless in the immediate vicinity of the Mississippi; and it was raining pitilessly for the second day nearly throughout, so that the roadbed was a causeway of mortar or ooze, into which the passing trains pressed the ties, first on one side, then on the other, making the track as bad as track could well be.

A year hence, it must be better; after a dry week, it will probably be quite fair; but yesterday it afforded more exercise to the mile than any other railroad I ever traveled.

St. Joseph is a busy, growing town of some ten thousand inhabitants.

I believe this is further west than any other point reached by a railroad connecting eastward with the Atlantic ports.

I took passage from St. Joseph for this place at eight this morning on the good steamer Platte Valley.

Atchison gives me my first foothold on Kansas. The Salt Lake mail, though made up at St. Joseph, is brought hither by steamboat and starts overland from this place; hence many [wagon] trains are made up here for Laramie, Green River, Fort Hall, Utah, and I hear even for Santa Fe.

I have seen several twelve-ox teams, drawing heavily-loaded wagons, start for Salt Lake. A little further away, the tents and wagons of parties of gold-seekers, with faces set for Pike's Peak, dot the prairie; one of them in charge of a gray-head who is surely old enough to know better.

Lawrence, Kansas, May 20

Twelve or fifteen miles south of Atchison we struck the great California trail from Leavenworth. The great California trail, like the Santa Fe and all other primitive roads through this prairie country, keeps along the highest "divides" or prairie swells, avoiding the miry bottoms of the streams and (so far as possible) the ravines which the water falling on the high prairie has cut down to them, of course winding considerably, but making the best and most serviceable natural road that can be.

But each settler along this trail, in the absence of any legal establishment of the trail as a highway, is at liberty to run his fences right across it as the line of his land runs, and so crowd it off the high "divides" into all manner of angles and zigzags, across this ravine and into that slough, until the trail is fast becoming the very worst road in all Kansas.

No stage made its way out of Leavenworth in any direction which was not forced to return, baffled by the high water. So at 3 P.M. we shipped our horse and wagons on board the steamboat *D. A. January,* and dropped down the Missouri some fifty miles, past the bleaching bones of several dead cities to Wyandot, in the lower corner of Kansas, with Kansas City, Missouri, three miles off, in plain sight across the mouth of the Kansas or Kaw River.

Leavenworth, May 23

Whenever our people shall have grown wise enough to maintain no standing army whatever but the barest skeleton of one, to be clothed with flesh whenever needed by calling out volunteers, the annual expenditures may be reduced at least one-fourth, and we may build a railroad to the Pacific with the savings of three or four years.

But Russel, Majors & Waddell's transportation establishment, between

the fort and the city of Leavenworth. Such acres of wagons! such pyra-
mids of extra axletrees! such herds of oxen! such regiments of drivers and
other employees! No one who does not see can realize how vast a business this is, nor how immense are its outlays as well as its income. I
presume this great firm has at this hour two millions invested in stock,
mainly oxen, mules and wagons. (They last year employed six thousand
teamsters, and worked forty-five thousand oxen.)

Whether the three great cities of America are to be New York, St.
Louis, and Leavenworth, as one set of friends seem to think, or New York,
St. Louis and Atchison, as another set assure me, I do not pretend to decide. If Atchison had the start that Leavenworth now has, I think she
would probably keep it.

I turn my face westward tomorrow.

Manhattan [Kansas] May 26

Land speculation here is about the only business in which a man can
embark with no other capital than an easy conscience. For example: I
rode up the bluffs back of Atchison, and out three or four miles on the
rolling prairies, so as to have some fifteen to twenty square miles in view
at one glance. On all this inviting area, there were perhaps half a dozen
poor or middling habitations, while not one acre in each hundred was
fenced or broken.

My friend informed me that every road I saw was "preempted," and
held at thirty up to a hundred dollars or more per acre. "Preempted!" I
exclaimed. "By living or lying?" "Well," he responded, "they live a little
and lie a little."

To obtain a preemption, the squatter must swear that he actually re-
sides on the quarter-section he applies for, has built a habitation and
made other improvements there, and wants the land for his own use and
that of his family.

The squatters who took possession of these lands must every one have
committed gross perjury in obtaining preemption.

May 12, Chicago

Chocolate and morning newspapers last seen on the breakfast-table.

23d—Leavenworth

Room-bells and baths make their final appearance.

24th—Topeka

Beef-steak and wash-bowls (other than tin) last visible. Barber ditto.

26th—Manhattan

Potatoes and eggs last recognized among the blessings that brighten as they take their flight. Chairs ditto.

27th—Junction City

Last visitation of a boot-black, with dissolving views of a board bed-room. Beds bid us good-by.

28th—Pipe Creek

Benches for seats at meals have disappeared, giving place to bags and boxes.

Denver, June 6

The "foot hills" of the Rocky Mountains seemed but a few miles west of us during our rapid ride down the smooth valley of the Cherry Creek. If the adjacent gold mines realize the sanguine expectations now entertained here, this region will require millions on millions worth of food from the rich prairies and bottoms of Kansas proper, Nebraska and Missouri, and we shall need but the Pacific railroad to open up a most beneficent home trade, and give the rich valley of the Missouri and its immediate tributaries better markets than those of the east.

For the sake of the weary, dusty, footsore thousands I have passed on my rapid journey from civilized Kansas to this point, I pray that gold may be found here in boundless extent, and reasonable abundance. Throughout the next six weeks, they will be dropping in here, a hundred or more per day; and I trust that they are not to be sent home disappointed, spirit-broken, penniless.

June 21

The rival cities of Denver and Auraria front on each other from either bank of Cherry Creek, just before it is lost in the South Platte. Of these rival cities, Auraria is by far the most venerable—some of its structures being, I think, fully a year old, if not more. Denver, on the other hand, can boast of no antiquity beyond September or October last.

South Pass, Rocky Mountains [Wyoming] July 5

Hitherto, since I left civilized Kansas, I had traversed routes either newly opened, or scarcely known to the mass of readers; but from Laramie I have followed the regular California and Oregon Overland Trail.

New York, October 20

There are thousands of usually intelligent citizens, who have decided that a Pacific railroad is a humbug—the fantasy of demagogues and visionaries—without ever having given an hour's earnest consideration to the facts in the case.

I know I am within bounds in estimating the number who have passed from the Atlantic slope to California and Oregon or Washington at an average of fifty thousand, while the average number who have annually returned thence cannot have fallen below thirty thousand.

Can there be any doubt that nine-tenths of these would have traveled by railroad, had such a road stretched from the Missouri or the Mississippi to the Pacific, the fare being moderate, and the passage made within ten days?

I estimate that twice to thrice the number who actually did go to California would have gone, had there been such a means of conveyance. I estimate that a railroad from the Missouri at Kansas City, Wyandot, Leavenworth, Atchison, or St. Joseph, to San Francisco, must be nearly or quite two thousand miles long, and that it would cost, with a double track and fully equipped, seventy-five thousand dollars per mile, or one hundred and fifty millions of dollars.

Men and brethren! Let us resolve to have a railroad to the Pacific—to have it soon. It will add more to the strength and wealth of our country than would the acquisition of a dozen Cubas. It will prove a bond of union not easily broken, and a new spring to our national industry, prosperity and wealth. It will call new manufactures into existence, and increase the demand for the products of those already existing. It will open new vistas to national and individual aspiration, and crush out filibustering by giving a new and wholesome direction to the public mind.

My long, fatiguing journey was undertaken in the hope that I might do something toward the early construction of the Pacific railroad; and I trust that it has not been made wholly in vain.

Greeley lived to see the railroad link East and West. But the hopes he had pinned on it were far from realized. It did expand the markets for products of the Missouri valley farms and the Eastern mills, but not to any great benefit of the people whose hands produced them. The Midwestern farmer was paying 52 cents to ship a 76-cent bushel of wheat and the Eastern millhand was getting five dollars for a seventy-two hour week.

These were symptoms of something that ailed postwar America, a sickness that went deep and wide throughout the land. There were other signs—a doubled cost of living; huge tariff-protected profits for textile and other manufacturers; enormous government handouts to the big timber interests and the mining combines; high rents from spreading slums; and most flagrant of all, outright giveaways of millions of acres of the public lands to the Union Pacific and Northern Pacific railroads.

The Republican party that Greeley had helped found as a force against racial slavery in the South was now accused as the abettor of economic enslavement in the North. With honest but inept Ulysses S. Grant as a figurehead, it was lending itself to a design for living in which Greeley saw evil and ruin.

"I should despise myself," he said, "if I pretended to acquiesce in his [Grant's] re-election." There were those who thought they knew whose election Greeley had in the back of his mind, among them Thomas Nast, the cartoonist of Harper's Weekly. Nast began a devastating attack on Greeley with a cartoon showing unkempt old "Uncle Horace" standing at the White House door and gazing enviously at Grant in the presidential seat.

Greeley broke with the Republican party and joined a motley revolt of old Jacksonians, young Western radicals and disgusted Eastern conservatives. In May 1872, he went to the convention of this insurgent group in Cincinnati. He came out of it—to the surprise of practically everybody but himself—with the nomination for President. When the Democratic party convened in July it was faced with the choice of giving him its nomination too or hopelessly splitting the opposition to Grant. Gingerly it kicked the honor to Greeley.

While millions of Americans loved the character of Uncle Horace, the fact remained that he was just that—a "character," and politically a disconcerting one. To realistic men of state, among them many of Greeley's own friends, his candidacy was fantastic. Democratic leader John Bigelow summed it up: "Greeley is an interesting curiosity . . . in whom we all feel a certain amount of pride, but I do not think anyone can seriously believe in his fitness for any administrative position whatever. If they do, they know as little of him as he knows of himself."

Greeley realized, after the first flush of excitement, that the tide was against him. He foresaw his own defeat more clearly as the weeks passed. Then toward the end of the campaign his wife Mary succumbed to a long illness. Greeley rushed home and stayed there. "I am not dead," he wrote, "but wish I were. My house is desolate, my future dark, my heart a stone."

The election went even worse than he expected—3,600,000 for Grant against his own 2,800,000. He tried going back to work at the Tribune but found his orders no longer obeyed and guessed, correctly, that other men, backed by substantial shareholdings, were wresting control of the paper away from him. He stumbled out in a daze.

On November 12 he went to the home of his friend Alvin Johnson, fell into bed, and within a few hours had sunk into delirium. He spent much of his time wildly rewriting his will, then tearing it up. Twenty-three days after the election he was dead.

1860:   CAPTAIN JOSHUA QUITS THE SEA

TO THE YANKEE SEA CAPTAIN of a century ago a fair wind was money in the bank. Speedy voyages meant more freights and profitable trades in more foreign ports, hence more of the good things of life back home—the burning of the mortgage, retirement at fifty, pipe and slippers, and a seat on the Yarner's Bench.

Until the 1840s all of America's ships at sea—the "line," the coasters, Liverpool packets, East Indiamen—were stubby, bluff-bowed, square-sterned craft that "picked up a few knots when the breeze blowed and a few barnacles when it didn't." Then came the clippers—sharp, hollow-cheeked, graceful, the fastest sailing craft ever built.

The new design appeared just in time for owners to compete for the lush freights on the run from Boston and New York to San Francisco during the gold rush. The long voyage around Cape Horn was grueling enough without crank ships and reckless skippers, but it was a time of "gold fever" at sea as well as ashore. The clippers made it more exciting, more profitable, and more dangerous. After dropping cargo at San Francisco many a skipper had orders to proceed around the world, via Hongkong, Calcutta, around the Cape of Good Hope to European ports, and home across the Atlantic.

Captain Joshua Sears of East Dennis, Cape Cod, was notorious for cracking on more sail than was safe for ship or crew. He hailed from a town where, so they said, as soon as a lad let go his mother's apron-string he grabbed a halyard. At one time, in the tiny village, there were twelve Captain Searses living on the same street!

On March 7, 1857, Captain Joshua sailed from Boston in the beautiful clipper ship Wild Hunter, bound for San Francisco and the Orient. What with side trips, doublings back, and layovers in port, it turned out to be a voyage of three and a half years. There was many a stiff breeze in which the skipper was caught with too much sail, many a narrow escape from Davy Jones's locker. But his only lament, repeated time and again in his log, was that it took so long to go anywhere. Once, when the first mate begged him to show a little discretion, he wrote in his log, "Had a quarrel with the mate, he finding fault with me for interfering with his work. Who ever heard of such a thing!"

His entry for July 8, 1860, when he was homeward bound, reads, "Shipped a sea over the starboard quarter and broke off six stanchions of the hand rail—washed away the binnacle—stove in two windows of the cabin and filled it with water, wetting charts, books and nautical instruments. Latter part more pleasant." And on July 19, "O for a cot in some vast wilderness where I shall never see a ship again. If ever one poor fellow was tired of anything, it is I, Josh Sears, that is sick and tired of going to sea."

Though he received several offers from shipowners after that voyage, he never went to sea again. Here are a few other excerpts from his log.

"O for a Cot in some wilderness."
JOSHUA SEARS (born 1817)

April 6 [1857, San Francisco for Singapore]

At 8 P.M. took in Top Gallant sails and outer jib. Midnight split the upper main Topsail, unbent it and bent another. Ship going like a mad horse.

September 5

That heavy swell keeps running from the West. Patience, patience—put your trust in God. Distance run 66 miles.

September 6

Slow getting along—Thy ways O Lord, are inscrutable.

September 9

The Lord is my Shepherd; He'll guide me safe through. I wish there was someone else to share this weather with me; Misery loves company.

September 13

O for a Cot in some wilderness.

September 20

This is certainly very tedious, but I trust it is all for the best—J. Sears. Thy ways, O Lord, are past finding out.

September 25

Dead calm all this day; Current set the ship 20 miles due East. I have never had such hard luck before. I feel almost discouraged. Think some of going down the China Sea if I ever get out of this calm place.

September 26

Commences calm, dead calm, latter part moderate and ends dead calm.

Oh how disconsolate I do feel. Next voyage I will go down the China Sea and face all the Typhoons that blows.

March 9, 1858 [Akyab to Falmouth]

The whole Ocean as far as the eye can see is one complete mirror; not one breath of air the blue waves do curl—nor make the ship go either.

March 10

Oh for a home in some vast wilderness, where the waves of the Ocean will trouble me no more.

March 16

Ship going 8 knots; the fullest ship that ever was built will go as fast as that.

April 14

We have got a staggering breeze from the North East. The old ship is going twelve knots and tearing the water up some, I tell you. The ship is so crank that I never think of taking in skysails until the lee plankshear goes under water.

April 25

Last Tuesday I commenced, with the assistance of one of the sailors that is a bit of a Jack Knife Carpenter to make a turning lathe, and it is a capital one. One of the boys turns a crank, and it goes like lightning. Yesterday I turned some belaying pins and a lot of door knobs. I expect I could turn a little baby all but the legs and some other little fixings that it would want to make it perfect.

May 23 [1858]

We had four or five vessels in company last week, and they all sail as fast as we do, and some of them outsail us. I don't know what is the matter with the old ship. I have been almost angry enough to sink the old ship sometimes.

May 30

I am lonely, lonesome, disconsolate and low-spirited and have got the blues the worst kind—Oh for a cot in some vast wilderness, but on Cape Cod will do. I shall be forty-one years old, time to hang up my harp.

September [Cardiff to Ceylon]

She ran for four days, 268, 265, 280, 272 miles, which I call pretty good going, drawing 21 feet, 3 inches of water. Ask Levi Howes [a rival Cape

Cod skipper] if he has got a ship that will beat that and carry 1500 tons of coal too. Oh for a cot down by the sea-side where we could dig clams.

December 19

I hope and pray night and day that I shall have orders in Galle [Ceylon] to go to Calcutta and load for home. If I have to go to China, I really believe that I should lay right down in the furrow and let them plow me under.

December 16, 1859 [Hong Kong]

I have never seen the need of a wife before so much as I have this voyage. But it will certainly take six months to get me tame enough to live with one.

1860:   MAD PACE ON THE MISSISSIPPI

To THE TRAVELER in the West of a century ago it was always a relief and a joy to make the change from stagecoach to river steamboat. He did it wherever he could, and he could—so the daring pilots of these shallow-draft vessels boasted —just about anywhere there was "enough river to make mud."

Around the middle of the century a thousand steamboats were carrying passengers and freight on the Mississippi. Hundreds more were plying the Missouri, some of them going the whole 2,000 miles and more between St. Louis and destinations in Dakota and Montana.

In 1862 James Harkness, one of the owners of the steamer Emilie, recorded in his diary a trip from St. Louis to Fort Benton, Montana, 34 days port to port, "and the passengers are well pleased and give great credit for success." As the Emilie steamed through the Dakota badlands a rival, the Spread Eagle, overtook her. "The Spread Eagle is just alongside, and we are having a race, probably the first ever run on the upper Missouri. . . . She passed us and then we passed her, when she ran into us, breaking our guards and doing some other damage. There was a good deal of angry talk."

Even after laws were passed limiting the head of steam a boat could carry, racing on the rivers caused many an accident. It wasn't so risky in the best boats, with alert pilots who obeyed the rules. Mark Twain, one of the few great writers to give us the story of this colorful traffic, said, "The dangerous place was on slow, plodding boats, where the engineers drowsed around and allowed chips to get into the 'doctor' and shut off the water supply from the boilers."

Perhaps, then, Charles Francis Adams, Jr. underestimated the adventure he was having when the old Alhambra raced the Winona as recorded below.

Young Adams and his father were accompanying William H. Seward on a tour of campaigning for the election of Abraham Lincoln to the Presidency. The following year Charles Francis, Jr. went to war. Later in life he took up railroading and was president of the Union Pacific until Jay Gould forced him out.

Only a few pages remain of the diary he kept as a young man. Before he joined the Union army he wrapped all the volumes he had filled into a package and sealed it. He didn't open it until years later. "It was with great difficulty I forced myself to read through that dreadful record; and as I finished each volume, it went into the fire; and I stayed over it until the last leaf was ashes."

At the request of a friend he had copied the few pages covering the journey beyond Madison, Wisconsin, from which this excerpt is taken.

"The competition was bitter."

CHARLES FRANCIS ADAMS, JR.

(1835-1915)

Wednesday, September 19 [1860]

At 8 o'clock we bade farewell to St. Paul.

During the 18th and 19th we steamed down the river in the *Alhambra*. The boat was in every respect a wretched one—old, dirty, and full of vermin. All day we glided down the river, sometimes grounding on a sand bank, and then again fouling a raft. The day was glorious, and the river not less so. The air was damp and chill; but, in a heavy overcoat I kept the deck till 3 A.M. briskly walking in the bright starlight.

Finally we had a performance worth seeing, a boat-race on the Mississippi. We had left St. Paul that morning about ten minutes before the *Winona* of the opposition line—and the competition was then bitter. Neither our boat nor the *Winona*—both old stern-wheelers—could boast of much speed, and the only question between them was as to which was the worst.

They were, nevertheless, good for a scrub race and that we soon found. It was quite exciting. A little after 2 o'clock A.M. we heard strange noises behind us, and looking over the stern of our boat, we made out the *Winona*, close behind us and in full chase. There were her colored lanterns, her three tiers of light, and from time to time when her furnace doors were opened to replenish her fires, lurid flashes lit up the river.

The stream was so low and the channel so narrow, that it was largely a question of pilotage; and, for some time, the two boats sped along in line. Then, as the channel widened somewhat, the *Winona* tried to pass us. She did not succeed this time; for she only lapped the *Alhambra,* and was again pushed, cut, and forced to fall behind. Again the channel widened, and now the *Winona* got half way by; and the two boats, both running at the top of their speed, moved along side by side, at times close together, at times thirty or forty feet apart—sometimes one apparently gaining and sometimes the other. At last, as the channel broadened, the two got fairly alongside of each other, neck and neck, and so kept it up, slowly converging until separated by only some twelve or fifteen feet; and then they would again separate.

Finally the channel apparently narrowed, and the interval was closed rapidly up, until, with a bump, the two boats collided heavily, almost throwing me from my feet. The guards seemed to groan and tremble, but neither boat gave; and so the two rushed along with rubbing sides. I suddenly found myself standing face to face with a passenger on the other boat, and somewhat apparently to his surprise, extended my hand, and wished him good morning.

He shook my hand, remarking that he proposed to leave us; and so on the two boats went.

I think we must have rushed along in this way for several minutes; but, finally, they shouldered us out of the channel, and, giving a triumphant whistle, shot ahead and down the river, leaving us to follow.

1868:   SAD PLIGHT OF THE WHALESHIP

MINNESOTA

A CENTURY AGO some 22,000 men were chasing whales in American ships. It was the most adventuresome, most far-flung, most colorful, and most soul-trying of all great American industries. It was also the most persistent in the face of doom. For more than fifty years after Pennsylvania began producing oil from the ground in 1859, New England blubber-boilers continued to ply their hazardous business in great waters.

The life of the whaleman was hard. Harpoons failed to hold, boats were stove, men paid with their lives. But no disaster weighed on the spirit so heavily as the long emptiness, the days at sea that stretched into weeks with never a spout, never a cry from aloft of "Thar she blows!" Many a skipper was moved to put his lament to paper, but there is nothing to match the tearful entries of Captain Clothier Peirce of the whaleship Minnesota.

The "unfortunate bark," as her skipper liked to describe her, sailed from New Bedford, June 25, 1868, on a voyage to the Pacific and Indian oceans. It wasn't Captain Peirce's first whaling venture, and in an earlier logbook he had shown a marked talent in the art of mourning his fate. But the log of the Minnesota was his masterpiece.

The voyage lasted nearly four years. Before he was one week at sea the captain was referring to his ship as the "poor old Minnesota."

"Will the Lord send us just one whale?"
CLOTHIER PEIRCE

Remarks on Board the Unfortunate Minnesota

Wednesday, July 1 [1868]

Morderate Breeze from Eastward Heading N. E. by the Wind. Variously Employed. No signs of LIFE here. Nothing for us. June has passed & we get Now-wheir. No chanc for us this season I fear. Three seasons in the North Atlantic to get One Whale in this Unfortunate Vessel. A.M. Very light Breeze. Heading about N.E. on Barren Water. Nothing to be seen.

July 2d

Will the Lord ever favour us to get One Whale. I fear not very soon: A.M. Fresh Breeze from East wheir it will continue for all future time.

July 4th

This is the Fourth of July. A Day of rejoicing with People at Home: But a Sad Day with us. No Whales in the Ocean that we can find. (A Head Wind.) No chanc to do any thing or to ever get One Whale. The LORDS Hand appears to be against the Poor Old *Minnesota* and all concerned in her. Will the Lord in his infinite Mercy ever suffer us to get One Whale: A.M. Calm Employed sheathing the Deck; many are rejoicing to day but our hearts are filled with sadness that this Poor Vessel cannot get A Whale.

July 13th

Morderate Breeze from the W.S.W. and fine Weather; three or four Finbacks in sight. No Whale this season for the Poor Old *Minnesota*: The LORD will Not suffer us to get One (I am so wicked). A.M. Strong Breeze from SW. Stearing East over the Desert. Nothing to be seen. Oh if the

LORD would but favour us to get something—all in vain I fear. Nothing for us.

14

Comes in ruged. Strong.

The Ocean is Barren wheir we go. Not a Whale can this Poor vessel get. The last Whale has been Caught here; None now live here—the *Commodore Morris* or som Lucky Ship Has Boiled the Last One. Never did I feel more cast down; this a dark period in my Live; why did I come Whaling but for my own Distruction; I think my damnation is fixed now.

Remarks on board this Unfortunate Vessel

July 22d

Saw quite a Number of Ships bound to the Eastward; all are doing something but this Unfortunate Vessel. I believe the Hand of Providence is against me for beeing so Uncharitable to my Brother in his *day of misfortune and trial.* Heavenly Parent, in mercy I pray that I may be forgiven Uncharitable feelings toward him in his Day of *Calamity and Trouble.*

Aug. 1

I am ruined. No Oil in the Ocean for the Poor Old *Minnesota*. My destiny is sealed to destruction. I am a Ruined Man in consequence of ingratitude to my Brother and Parents.

Remarks on Board the Poorest Vessel That Is in the Whaling Business

Aug. 18, 1868

It is no use for the *Minnesota* to try to get anything. The LORDS Power is against the *PEIRCE Family* & the *Name of Peirce.*

Wednesday 28

Barren Water. Only One Finback has been seen all this Long Day: Pleanty of Birds; but No Whales. I am about discouraged.

Remarks on Board the Most Unfortunate Vessel in the Whaling Business

5th [December]

Strong Breeze from E to E by North; Dead against us & allways will be; Here it will continue this Year: Never, Never again shall We be Favoured to Ever get another Gallon of Oil this Voyage. I have given up all Hopes: My Ruin is fixed, is Certain (I know). The LORDS Power or

Vengeance is against the PEIRCE Family; they shall Not succede in Whaling; NO WHALES at Chatham This Season; No Chance to Ever Go Their; all, all in vain. Will the Allmighty Ever suffer the Wind to Change from E.N.E. or will the East Wind always Continue Here. (Dead ahead) Their is No account in all the Old Journals I have got of any Wind being so Fixed at E.N.E. As this has been.

At long last, in March 1869, the Minnesota got a whale! But alas, when she has hauled the prize alongside and chained it to her, suddenly the breezes blow. The log continues.

Wednesday 24

Unfortunately Blowing A Severe Gale from W.S.W. Tore out the Fluke Chain Pipe; tearing out the Fluke Chain Bitt from the Deck. *Impossible to Save the Whale.* It Blows so Hard. The Boats Hoisted to davy Heads; the Vessel under Bare Spars; Barometer down; The Whale surging very Hard. Impossible to Hold the Whale. A.M. Strong Gale still Blowing Hard. The Elements is bound to distroy our Whale & ruin all concerned; No prospect of Morderating; Halled the Whale alongside this Morning to Hook on. Could not; impossible to save the Body. The Sea Breaking over the Rails in this dreadful Storm.

Thursday

Still Blowing a Severe Gale from S.W. wheir it will Continue Untill I am a ruined Man. Not the least Chance to save any Portion of this Whale; at Meredian discovered that the Whale was tearing off all our Nette on the Starbourd Side; and also the Sheathing. Cut off the Hawser from the Whales Flukes & Shackeled it on to Fluke-Chain & Slacked off the Whale; wheir we shall loose it; something will part soon; We cannot Hold him long; in this dreadful Weather Impossible. No Human Power can save this Whale. The Whale Caved in last Night, is Now Lying allmost Flat on the Sea, is fast rotting away.

Friday

Blowing a Sever Gale, if Possible worse than Yesterday; our Whale rotting in the Sea. No Vessel so Unfortunate as this. Shall Not Only Loose the Whale But the Cable & Hawser attached to it. A.M. Still ruged. Halled the Poor Old Whale alongside, tryed to get off some of what was once Bluber: it was all rotten & Spoiled. Such is my Hard Fortune. Lost Eighty Barrels of Sperm Oil. Had to Cut off the Head and let it go before we could rool the Whale over. The Head was the Best part.

And so, back to the long search. Nine months later:

Wednesday 21st [December, 1870]

Saw the Fortunate Bark *James Maury* Stowing Down [oil]. All the Ships Have taken Whales Now but the Unfortunate *Minnesota* & We cannot See One; nor do I Expect to Ever Boil again. All the other Ships will Get Full before We can Get One: No Other Ship But has Got Whales. Oh, Could We Get One Whale; How Greatful I should be: I, Favoured again, I will devote my Share to Charatable Purposes.

1868: LITTLE LAURA GOES A-WHALING

MANY A YANKEE WHALEMAN took his wife to sea with him. If she liked it, all well and good; if she didn't, he took her anyway. An exception was Captain Jared Jernegan of Martha's Vineyard, in command of the whaleship Oriole. From many a neighbor on the island, Rebecca Jernegan had heard of those long, lonely voyages, the hardships when the weather was rough, the monotony when it wasn't. None of that for her. She stayed home. In 1858, while the skipper was at sea, she died.

Captain Jernegan married again. He was 37, pretty Helen Clark 22. Again he went a-whaling. But this time, after a cruise in the Arctic, three years and 17,000 miles away from Helen and their little daughter Laura, he sent for them, and thereafter kept them with him except for the Arctic whaling season, when he left them at Honolulu. Helen Jernegan liked the sea—or said she did. On a single voyage the captain's share was $16,000.

Once they went home. But in 1868 they sailed again on the bark Roman, out of New Bedford. In the five-month trip around Cape Horn, Helen made a log-cabin quilt of 2,310 pieces. By this time there was another member of the family, Prescott, aged two and a half. When they reached Honolulu, Prescott had been so long at sea he was afraid of the land. When he was told to step out of the boat to the dock, he cried!

The captain didn't make his family go on all his sixteen voyages, which totaled up 33 years of cruising and $100,000 of earnings. He died in 1899. Helen Jernegan lived on in the home on Martha's Vineyard until she was 94. Laura grew up to be a beautiful woman and married an officer of a revenue cutter.

Of her adventures in the Pacific, little Laura left a record, beginning when she was six years old. Here is part of it.

"We got six whales."

LAURA JERNEGAN (born 1862)

December 1st [1868]

It is Sunday and a very pleasant day. I have read two story books. This is my journal. Good Bye For To Day.

Tuesday 14

To day Papa is making a mark to show the men where the whales arer. Good Bye For To Day.

Saturday 12th

We had a tempest last night and a squall this morning. Papa spoke the ship *Chnticleer* and reported our oil. We have 60 barrels of sperm oil. Good Bye For To Day.

Sunday 13

It is quite rough today. There is a ship in sight. We have put on our flannels. Good Bye For To Day.

Thursday 17

There is no wind today. The men are stowing the oil down. We have four ducks on board our ship. Good Bye For To Day.

Friday 18

The wind blows very hard. We had ducks for dinner. I study my lessons every day. Mama has given me some wosted and I am making a toilet cushion. Good Bye For To Day.

Monday 4th [January 1869]

We past by Cape Horn to day. It is a large black rock. Some of the rocks look like a steeple of a church. Good Bye For To Day.

Friday 12

They have taken forty teeth out of the largest sperm whale. The deck is very clean and white. Good Bye For To Day.

Honolulu, September, 1870 Monday 26

It has blown real hard for two days. I am in Honolulu. It is a real pretty place. Good Bye For To Day.

Bark Roman *February 10th [1871]*

It is quit rough to Day. But is a fair wind. We have 135 barrels of oil,

60 of humpback and 75 of sperm. We had two birds, there is one now. One died. There names were Dick and Lulu. Dick died. Lulu is going to. Good Bye For To Day.

Saturday 11th

Lulu died last night. It is quite smooth to day. It does not blow very hard to day. Papa is fixing the sink. Good Bye For To Day.

Thursday 16th

It is quite pleasant to day, the hens have laied 50 eggs. Papa is fixing the water closet. Good Bye For To Day.

Sunday 19th

It is quite pleasant today. I have not been on deck to day. The Longitude was 117-23. I dont know what the Latitude was. Good Bye For To Day.

Monday 20th

It is quite pleasant to day. We saw whales this morning, we lowered the boats and we got six, the men are cutting them in now. Papa said the men would get 2 cut in to night but I think we shall only get one cut in. Good Bye For To Day.

Tuesday 21th

Papa said that he would put some whales down in my journal but I don't think so. Good Bye For To Day.

Wednesday 22th

It is a pleasant day, it is quite smooth to day. The men are boiling out the blubber in the try pots. The pots are real large. When the men are going to boil out the blubber, too men get in the pots and squis out the blubber and are way up to there knees of oil. Would you like to hear some news well I don't know any. Good Bye For To Day.

————————————————————————————————★

1869: EAST AND WEST ARE LINKED BY RAIL

————————————————————————————————☆

WHILE THE CIVIL WAR was still being fought, work on the first rail route to span America got under way. The Union Pacific was building westward from Omaha, while eastward the Central Pacific extended from Sacramento. On May

10, 1869, at Promontory, Utah, 55 miles west of Ogden, the spike was driven
that completed the connection.

Silas Seymour, an engineer, was sent west in 1866 to help determine the
route over the Rockies.

"One year ago it was a myth . . ."

SILAS SEYMOUR (1811-1872)

Denver City, Colorado, Monday, Sept. 17, 1866

It is now about two weeks since I left New York, in company with the
Government Directors of the Union Pacific Railroad, for the purpose of
inspecting the rapid construction of that greatest of modern enterprises;
and also examining the different routes which have been proposed for the
road through the passes of the Rocky Mountains; and it seems to me
that during that time I have learned more of the vast extent and resources
of our continent than I had ever known before.

On Friday evening the 7th, we continued our journey from Chicago
westward over the Iowa division of the Chicago and Northwestern Railroad in the magnificent Directors' car, which conveyed us to the end of
the track, a distance of about four hundred miles west of Chicago.

From this point we were compelled to make the balance of the distance to Omaha, about ninety miles, by stage. The rails are to be laid,
however, upon this portion of the route by the 1st of April next.

We arrived at Omaha, the eastern terminus of the Union Pacific Railroad, on the morning of the 10th, and spent the day in examining the
extensive shops of the Company, which have all been constructed within
the past year.

On the morning of the 11th, the Directors accompanied by Gen. G. M.
Dodge, Chief Engineer, Major Bent, Major Chesbrough and myself, took
a special train for the end of the track, which was then laid two hundred
and seventeen miles westward, in the Great Platte Valley.

We arrived opposite Fort Kearny at four P.M., having passed over two
hundred miles of road in eight hours or at the rate of twenty-five miles
an hour.

We left Fort Kearny at 1 P.M., on Wednesday, the 12th inst., and arrived at Denver at 10 A.M., on the following Saturday, making the entire
distance of four hundred miles in less than three days and nights. The
speed, comfort, and regularity of these Ben Holladay Overland stages is

certainly astonishing, when we consider the fact that they pass through hundreds and thousands of miles of almost uninhabited country; and that it is only five years since the experiment was first attempted.

Denver boasts of four or five thousand inhabitants. The streets are regularly laid out; and there are many fine brick blocks, either constructed or in course of construction. You can purchase almost anything here that can be purchased in New York, but at prices from fifty to one hundred per cent. higher.

Empire City, Colorado, September 19

Hon. Jesse L. Williams, one of the Government Directors of the Union Pacific Railroad, and myself, accompanied on horseback by Mr. P. T. Brown, the Assistant Engineer, who had been making the surveys for the road through this wild and forbidding portion of the route, started out from Denver on the morning of the 17th, in a comfortable covered carriage, drawn by a pair of lazy, broken down mules, these being considered the most safe and reliable for the rough mountain roads we were to traverse.

The *outfit,* as all conveyances are designated in this country, was under the special charge of Mr. Brooks, a most venerable and experienced mountaineer and driver. Our objective point was Berthoud Pass, and our route lay up the Valley of Clear Creek, or as near it as the road would allow us to travel.

Mr. Brown had informed us that we could not travel with our carriage nearer than a point about two miles from the pass; and that it would therefore be necessary for Mr. Williams and myself to procure saddle horses at Empire for the balance of our journey.

We reached Berthoud Pass at two P.M. on Tuesday, September 18; and were, for the first time in our lives, greeted with a most extended and magnificent view of the Pacific slope of the Western Continent. The summit of the Pass is but a few hundred feet below the timber, or arborescent line; and is about 6,100 feet above Denver City, and 11,200 feet above the level of the sea.

The main range, or divide of the continent, was visible to the north and west for a distance of 100 miles at least, far beyond Long's Peak, which reared its bald head, spotted with eternal snow, high above the average level of the range.

The exhilarating effect of the high mountain air and sublime scenery inspired Mr. Williams with a desire for a patriotic song. After some urging from Mr. Brown and myself, he led off with "Sherman's March to the

Sea." Mr. Brown followed with the "Star Spangled Banner," and I closed the exercises with Moore's serenade, "Come o'er the Sea," etc. The entire range, from Long's to Pike's Peak, seemed to catch the inspiration, and join in the chorus.

Denver City, Colorado, Thursday, Sept. 20

On our way down the valley of North Clear Creek, we passed through the town of Black Hawk, about two miles below Central City, where we stopped an hour to examine two of the largest quartz mills now in operation in this valley. One, the Black-Hawk mill, which adheres to the old method of stamping and washing the ores from the quartz; and the other, the Lyons mill, in which the new process of decomposing the quartz and separating the ores by the action of heat, is being carried on.

This matter of separating the precious metals from the quartz is one of vast importance to the mining interests of Colorado; and he who shall first succeed in economically and successfully accomplishing the object will be entitled to the lasting gratitude of "all the world and the rest of mankind." The exact and proper process seems yet to be hidden in the womb of the future; and many an alchemist is now racking his brain, and experimenting in his crucible over his midnight lamp, in the hope of first discovering this great secret in chemical science, which the Almighty has, for some great and wise purpose, thus far withheld from us.

Mr. Williams had intimated that he would like to approach, and enter the city [Denver] by another road from that by which we had departed, so that he might obtain a different view of its present extent and future resources.

This induced the driver to take a road which, unfortunately, led past his stable, on the way to the Planter's House, where we were to stop.

On passing the stable, the contest between the driver and the mules was most spirited and exciting; business in town for the moment seemed to be suspended; and every one was anxiously awaiting the result of the driver's efforts to reach the hotel on the next block. It was in vain that I suggested that we had plenty of time to stop at the stable, and exchange our outfit before proceeding to the hotel—the driver swore that he would drive the g——n mules to the hotel or h—ll, and he did not much care which. And he came near succeeding in both; for, on finally reaching the hotel, and just as our venerable friend had taken the last article of baggage from the carriage, the pesky animals started off suddenly on their own hook for a run-away.

The driver was knocked down while closing the carriage door, but fortunately the wheels did not pass over him. And the outfit went sailing and crashing down the street, among the carriages, and herds of mules and cattle, towards the river.

I assisted our venerable friend to his feet. He was covered with mud, his countenance was pale with rage and fright, and his lips and clenched teeth muttered curses low but deep against the whole family of mules and their offspring now, henceforth and forever.

Omaha, Nebraska, Oct. 8.

We took a special train for Omaha, over the Union Pacific Railroad, at ten A.M. Here we learned that during our absence, the Government Commissioners had been out and accepted thirty-five additional miles of track, making in all two hundred and forty miles of road, from the initial point at Omaha.

The scene along the road was both interesting and exciting. Here was a fine passenger station in course of construction; there, a freight or water station was being put up, as if by magic. Now, we were halted upon a sidetrack to allow a train of thirty or forty cars laden with ties, rails, chairs, and spikes for the track, to pass. And then, we would meet a train laden with stone or other material for the foundations or superstructure of a distant bridge. Everything, and everybody, seemed full of life and energy; and all working to the same great end, and being directed by the same master mind.

One year ago, not a mile of road had been accepted by the Government; only twelve or fifteen miles had been laid west of Omaha; and it was struggling along at the rate of from one-quarter to a half mile per day. To-day, two hundred and forty miles of track have been accepted by the Government. Some twelve or fifteen miles additional have been completed, and it is steadily progressing at the rate of from one and a half to two miles per day. Fourteen thousand and two hundred feet, or *two and seven-tenths miles,* have been laid in a single day.

One year ago, passengers for Denver, Salt Lake and San Francisco were obliged to ride the whole distance from the Missouri River in old-fashioned stagecoaches, hacks, or mud-wagons. To-day, there are no stages running east of Fort Kearny; and nearly one-half the distance to Denver may be traveled in ten hours, and in the most luxurious passenger cars.

One year ago, every pound of freight, owned either by the Government or individuals, had to be transported west of the Missouri by means of ox or mule teams, at the slow rate of fifteen or twenty miles per day. To-day, cars heavily laden with Government stores and private freight, destined for the western slope of the continent, are attached to the construction trains, and find their way in twenty-four hours to the end of the track, many miles west of the one-hundredth meridian.

One year ago the great Union Pacific Railroad was regarded as a myth, and the men controlling it, as a set of stock-jobbing Wall Street speculators. To-day, it is known and felt to be a power and a reality.

Oct. 23

A pleasant incident was the advent of Messrs. Tappen, Patrick and Brown, heads of the freight and passenger departments of that "*Great connecting link,*" the Chicago and Northwestern Railroad, who tarried a few days at Council Bluffs and Omaha, as they were passing on their way to Denver, for the purpose of establishing offices, and making other business arrangements in connection with their road, and its farreaching Western tributaries.

As they started westward, on the morning of the 17th October, in a special train laden with demijohns, cases, canned meats, fruits and pickles, rolls of buffalo robes and blankets; together with almost any number of breach-loading carbines and revolvers, one would think that they expected to spend at least six months among savage beasts and Indians, before returning to the land of civilization.

When the train was about starting from the depot at Omaha, Mr. Tappen was loudly called upon by his friends who remained behind, for a few parting words. Upon which he promptly made his appearance upon the rear platform, raised his hat, bowed gracefully to the audience, steadied himself by a firm hold upon the railing, and spoke substantially as follows:

"Fellow Citizens: But a few short years ago, the spot on which my foot now rests was part and parcel of a *howling* wilderness—" Just here, the sudden starting of the train so disturbed the spot on which the distinguished speaker's foot was resting that he came near being thrown overboard; but, on recovering himself instantly, he proceeded with great composure to say:

"During a somewhat short but eventful life, I have held every position from—" At this point, the train being fairly under way, it became quite difficult to hear distinctly, except the closing sentence, which was as follows:

"I leave the *Great connecting link* in your hands, while I proceed to swing around the—" the remainder of this happy speech was lost; but the speaker evidently alluded to a curve in advance of the train.

The train disappeared.

PHILIP HONE saw the city more than double its size to become half a million people. George Templeton Strong saw it more than double again. He also saw, pouring into it and through it to the country across the Hudson River, the great human tide that eventually was to add 32,000,000 foreign-born to America's population.

Eminent lawyer, trustee of Columbia College, churchman, music lover, and civic leader, Strong moved in a stratum of money and power, of social elegance and culture. He was not a rich man but it was to the great well-washed that he gave first loyalty. He found there many a stain that would not out—indeed to the end of his life he despised, deplored and was constantly shocked by corruption in high places—and his proper anger is one of the many revelations of a complex, engaging personality whom the editors of his diary describe as "most cultivated, sincere, intelligent, high-minded and delightful."

When editors Allan Nevins and Milton Halsey Thomas started working on Strong's diary for publication, some seventy-five years after his death, they were confronted with 2,500 pages filled with a fine hand—over 4,000,000 words. With skillful bluepenciling they managed to get it down to five printed volumes.

"Whom can we trust?"
GEORGE TEMPLETON STRONG
(1820-1875)

September 16 [1865]

Old John Austin Stevens tells me that the prospects of Southern trade are brilliant, that far more specie has been hoarded at the South than we suppose, and that Southern merchants are ordering largely and (wonderful to relate) paying off their old debts.

As president of the Bank of Commerce, Stevens ought to know.

November 17

General Grant is to dine here tomorrow with his staff, and I feel quite nervous about so august a transaction.

November 18

Grant appeared at last, with Mrs. Grant. I made it a point to have Johnny, Temple and Louis [his children] present, and to bring them severally up to shake hands with the General. They will remember it fifty years hence if they live so long, and tell their children of it, if they ever have any.

It was a brilliant, distinguished, or "nobby" assemblage, and they all seemed to have a pleasant time, as people always do at any party organized by Mistress Ellen [his wife]. I must say that I think it a great honor and privilege to have received Grant here, and there is no element of snobbishness in my feeling about it.

Mrs. Grant is the plainest of country women, but a lady, inasmuch as she shews no trace of affectation or assumption, and frankly admits herself wholly ignorant of the social usages of New York.

Miss Fanny allowed me to take her to the piano and sang Mrs. Julia Ward Howe's version of the John Brown song with immense spirit and effect.

August 29

Sultry and lowering. The city upside down, looking for the advent of A. [Andrew] Johnson, who is making a progress to Chicago. All vehicles ordered out of Broadway. My omnibus broke down in Center Street, and I had to walk home through ill-flavored side streets. Turned into Broadway at Bleecker Street. Broadway full of people, sidewalks lined by a continuous crowd. Windows and housetops fully occupied.

Johnson came along at last, preceded and followed by large militia-escort. With him were Seward and Welles, Grant and Meade and Farragut, and a lot of notables besides. There was much cheering and waving of hats and handkerchiefs.

I did not quite like the President's bearing as he stood in his barouche. His bows were a little assiduous and too lowly, like those of a basso called before the curtain, not such as to become the Chief Magistrate of a great nation. But that may be hyper-criticism.

November 24

General Vinton dined here and we went to Theodore Thomas's second concert at Steinway's new music hall. William Schermerhorn sat with us. We had the pretty *Nozze di Figaro* overture, an inane piano concerto by Schumann, and then Beethoven's Ninth Symphony, for which precious gift to mankind let all who love music thank God.

January 16 [1867]

Am just from a dinner at John Astor's. There were President Barnard, Dr. Vinton, William J. Hoppin, Schroeder of the Astor Library, Charles H. Russell, Tuckerman, Mayor Hoffman, Bishop Potter, Hamilton Fish, Henry Brevoort, Dr. Markoe, Henry Day, old James Gallatin, and myself.

The dinner was sumptuous and splendid, of course, but apart from the viands and the marvelous wines, Astor's dinner parties are always pleasant. He receives his guests with perfect cordiality and simplicity, and his wife's graceful manner is worthy of a duchess. Neither of them seems conscious of the splendor of their drawing-rooms and their dinner-table.

September 13

Andrew Johnson is certainly the best-hated man this side of the Atlantic. Even the Democrats repudiate him, and he has no supporters outside his office-holding gang. One might be pardoned for hoping he would undertake some great crime and outrage, if one were sure he would be hanged for it.

Congress had just passed the Reconstruction Act which split up the South into five districts, each to be governed temporarily by a general of the Federal Army. The act also provided for local elections, in which ex-slaves would have the vote, of delegates to state conventions, and the adoption of constitutions providing for Negro suffrage. Johnson vetoed the act, but Congress, led by the vindictive Thaddeus Stevens in the House and Charles Sumner in the Senate, passed it over the veto. For his inept efforts to carry out Lincoln's postwar aims of moderation and fairness "with malice toward none"—a policy that required a man of Lincoln's stature to carry over the bitterness of the times—Johnson was cordially hated and subjected to impeachment proceedings.

September 17

I don't want A. Johnson to be encouraged in his execrable courses by anything he can construe into a popular endorsement. I fear he is among the worst men we have ever had in high place. Will he be impeached next November? Probably, and his impeachment will breed no end of agitation and mischief. Far better to let him go on eating dirt till his term ends, and then set up a tailor's shop in Tennessee, conducted strictly on constitutional principles.

October 9

Was buried today old Peter Lorillard, tobacconist and millionaire. How many cubic miles of smoke and gallons of colored saliva are embodied in the immense fortune that was *his* last week! Stupendous thought!

October 22

To Fifty-ninth Street this afternoon, traversing for the first time the newly opened section of Madison Avenue between Fortieth Street and the College, a rough and ragged track, as yet, and hardly a thoroughfare, rich in mudholes, goats, pigs, geese, and stramonium.

Here and there shanties "come out" (like smallpox pustules) each composed of a dozen rotten boards and a piece of stove-pipe for a chimney.

November 6

Badeau told me, of his own knowledge, and on the authority of his own eyes and ears, certain queer stories about Mrs. Lincoln. I always heard she was underbred, but I never supposed it possible she could be the "stuck-up" vulgar vixen he says she was. I listened with interest, because I signed a paper only this morning, and at the request of young Ingersoll, recommending or endorsing a proposed movement to raise $100,000 for her benefit.

The incidents Badeau mentions were in 1864 and 1865. He says he knows that Grant and Stanton with their respective wives were invited to be of the theatre party on the fatal night of April 14, and that the ladies demurred and declined because of Mrs. Lincoln's uncertain temper and manners, and kept their husbands away.

November 11

Home by Sixth Avenue railroad, and then General Sheridan dined here.

The general is a stumpy, quadrangular little man, with a forehead of no promise and hair so short that it looks like a coat of black paint. But his eye and his mouth shew force, and of all our chieftains he alone has displayed the capacity of handling men in actual shock of battle, turning defeat into victory, rallying a broken fugitive mob and hurling them back upon the enemy. His talk is pleasant.

December 5

Yesterday Mrs. Albert Gallatin, Blake, and Jem Ruggles dined here, and went to the opera to hear *Trovatore*, poor souls!

There was a great meeting at Cooper Institute last night to nominate Grant and to formulate a Grant Party. I expect to vote for him next fall. We know next to nothing of his political notions, to be sure, so choosing him is a little like buying a pig in a poke, but then, his integrity has never been questioned, and a man who can conduct great campaigns success-fully and without being ever accused of flagrant blunders must possess a talent for affairs that fits him for any administrative office. Therefore, hurrah for Grant!

December 10

Charles Dickens's first Reading last night at Steinway Hall is said to have been admirable. It doubtless was so, but I am in no fever to hear him. I remember the *American Notes* and the American chapter in *Martin Chuzzlewit*, which were his return for the extravagant honors paid him on his first avatar twenty-five years ago. I also remember that both books, especially the former, were filled with abuse and sarcasm against the slaveholding republic, and that during our four years of death-struggle with slavery, Mr. Dickens never uttered one word of sympathy with us or our national cause, though one such word from the most popular living writer of prose fiction would have been so welcome, and though it would have come so fitly from a professional "humanitarian."

February 25 [1868]

The [Andrew Johnson] Impeachment Resolution was carried yesterday (126 to 47, I think), and a Committee of the House duly appeared at the bar of the Senate today and announced the fact. Clamor of newsboys to-day recalled the most exciting period of the war. " 'Ere's the extry *Tele-gram*—got the great excitement at Washington!"

April 16

Another railroad accident (so-called) on the Erie Road. Scores of people smashed, burned to death, or maimed for life. We shall never travel safely till some pious, wealthy, and much beloved railroad director has been hanged for murder, with a "gentlemanly conductor" on each side of him. Drew or Vanderbilt would do to begin with.

April 27

Johnny and Temple heard *Richard III* read by Mrs. [Fanny] Kemble this evening. They enjoyed and appreciated it, though Temple "does not see why Mrs. K. should holler so."

April 29

Last night with Ellie to the theatre appurtenant to the Union League Clubhouse, whilom "Jerome's Theatre," and heard Mrs. Fanny Kemble read *Cymbeline*. It was an admirable reading, but perhaps a little stagey and overdone, here and there.

Pity Mrs. Kemble is such a tartar. The ladies (Mrs. Cooper, Mrs. Barlow, and others) at whose request she read last night, for the benefit of some charity which they administer, addressed her a very civil note, proposing to send a carriage for her, and to meet her at the door, and introduce her into the house. Mr. Tighe tells me he saw her answer. "She would be happy to read for the benefit of the (whatever it was); she needed no introduction, and she could pay her own hack-hire. Yours resp'y."

May 16

Another day of dull uncertain weather. Before two o'clock it was generally known that H. E. the President was acquitted, and the streets were full of newsboys, whose extras confirmed the report. It was close work— 19 to 35.

May 10 [1869]

Fine weather. The Pacific Railroad was (or was to have been) formally completed today by the laying of its last rail. So there was a *Te Deum* at Trinity Church at twelve, by request of Chamber of Commerce. This seems to have been the only public notice in New York of a most important event—national and international.

May 26

Otis Swan, who has taken the late Washington Irving's place for the summer, tells me of the vexations to which he and his wife are subjected by intrusive and pertinacious tourists. "I have come all the way from St. Louis, sir, and I cannot go back without looking through the immortal Irving's house and grounds." So they force themselves in, roam about, poke their noses into everything, and make audible comparisons between Irving and the present tenant of his classical country seat to the disadvantage of the latter.

September 30

James Fisk, Jr., keeps in some shady place, and is commonly said to have become a *non-est* man at last. He cannot shew his ugly face in Wall Street without bodily peril. Old Vanderbilt is no less dearly hated. These great operators and Railroad Kings (or other Vikings of the stock market) will discover some day that ruining their weaker neighbors by a piratical combination of capital, though good for the assets, is bad for the bones, perhaps even for the vertebrae of the neck.

October 9

Applications from three infatuated young women for admission to Law School. No woman shall degrade herself by practicing law, in New York especially, if I can save her. "Women's-Rights Women" are uncommonly loud and offensive of late. I loathe the lot. The first effect of their success would be the introduction into society of a third sex, without the grace of woman or the vigor of man.

October 12

I fear Grant does not stand quite as well with the swinish multitude as he did a year ago. So much dirt has been thrown at him that some of it must stick.

November 11

The grand *Vanderbilt* Bronze on the Hudson River Railroad Depot "unveiled" yesterday with much solemnity. There was a prayer and there were speeches. Vanderbilt began life penniless. He acquired a competence —honestly, I assume—by energy, economy, and business tact, and then increased his store to a colossal fortune of sixty millions (as they say) by questionable operations in railroad stocks. Anyhow, he is a millionaire of millionaires. And, therefore, we bow down before him, and worship him, with a hideous group of molten images, with himself for a central figure, at a cost of $800,000.

January 25 [1870]

At half-past ten last evening, Delano, wending his way home from a dinner at John Astor's, was set upon and robbed by three men on the corner of Fifth Avenue and Eleventh Street. Of course there was no arrest. Crime was never so bold, so frequent, and so safe as it is this winter. We breathe an atmosphere of highway robbery, burglary, and murder.

March 18

At the Trust Company I heard of G. C. Verplanck's death, at nine-fifteen this morning, at the Everett House.

I met him last with the Life and Trust Company on March 1, and we had some little talk. He did not appear more infirm than he has at any time these two years. Verplanck will be missed, especially in art circles. He was the founder of the Century Club.

March 20

The *World's* eulogistic obituary says: "It will hardly be credited that he [Verplanck] was turned out of the presidency of the Century Club during the war for his political opinions." Such was the bitterness and fanaticism of those days. I, for one, voted (with great regret) to turn him out; and I remember my vote, even at this time, with no shade of remorse. He was a Copperhead of the worst type—hotel-burners, draft-rioters, and

consignors of small-pox clothing and bedding excepted. All his social influence and weight of character were thrown into the scale of rebellion.
He did all he could to discourage and depreciate our endeavor to suppress
it.

November 10

The "Ballad of the Heathen Chinee," by some Californian [Bret Harte]
is in everybody's mouth, and very funny.

January 10 [1871]

Jim Fisk's last recorded antic was on New Year's Day. He made calls
in a gorgeous chariot drawn by four high-stepping horses, with four smart
footmen in flamboyant liveries. When he stopped before any favored
house, his mamelukes descended, unrolled a carpet, laid it from the carriage steps to the door, and stood on either side in attitude of military
salute, while their august master passed by.

April 21

The state legislature is about to become inodorous and adjourn. The
[Tweed] Ring has carried all its measures with the help of a Republican
member, O. Winans of Chautauqua, who ratted opportunely (I hope he
had self-respect enough to insist on a good price) and the city of New
York is now at its mercy—autonomy, self-government, rights of suffrage,
and "democratic principles" being ignored. "Boss" Tweed and his tail are
sovereigns of this city and county.

William Marcy Tweed's political power as state senator, Grand Sachem of
Tammany and boss of New York was excceded only by his rapacity at the public trough. For more than two years he held dictatorial control over government,
the courts, and the political leadership of both parties, and he made full use of
all three to plunder the people. In thirty months of the Ring's operations the
loot was estimated at $70,000,000.

Many of New York's wealthiest men—its "best people"—became involved
in Tweed's network of bribery and graft. This gave the corruption a protective
coating that was hard to crack. But two years of devastating cartoons by Thomas
Nast in Harper's Weekly and a dogged crusade by The New York Times slowly
built up public sentiment for an inquiry. Then the thieves fell out, ratted on
each other, and laid open the greatest scandal in New York's history. Tweed
was brought to trial. The jury disagreed, but in a second trial he was convicted
and sentenced to twelve years. He escaped, went to Spain, was brought back,
and died in jail in the spring of 1878. Of the Tweed Ring's loot, New York
City recovered $1,121,000.

September 4

We the people are a low set, without moral virility. Our rulers, Tweed and Company, are about good enough for us. The Alcibiades of New York is Mr. James Fisk. Mr. J. G. Bennett, Jr., who makes money by printing the advertisements of abortionists is elected "commodore"—or some such thing—by the aristocratic Yacht Club of New York, and is a leader of fashion in the Belmont clique. John Astor, Willy Duncan, William T. Blodgett, and others sit in the same railroad direction with vermin like Bill Tweed.

December 16

Indictment for felony against Tweed, and he was lodged in the Tombs but was bailed out by Mr. Justice Barnard. He has a great array of counsel.

General Frank Barlow, who has recently had occasion to call on Tweed, says he finds that chieftain in a broken and demoralized condition, confessing that he has lost heart and quails under concentric fire now playing on him.

December 30

The Tammany Society itself repudiates Tweed and degrades him from his place as chief Sachem. It throws him over reluctantly, no doubt, and from an instinct of self-preservation; but that makes the blow more severe. Even Tammany cannot stand Tweed.

January 7 [1872]

The great Fisk died this morning. No loss to the community—quite the reverse—but it's a pity he should have escaped the state prison in this way.

January 8

Much talk about Fisk. The remains were conveyed to the railroad depot in great state for interment at poor little Brattleboro. What a scamp he was, but what a curious and scientifically interesting scamp! When he "took to the road" a very few years ago and opened his campaign against society he was penniless.

By talent and audacity he raised himself to the first rank among business scoundrels, and (I suppose) to great wealth—certainly to opportunities of great wealth—but then he was reckless in spending. He was opera impresario, "commodore," financier, roue, mountebank, corrupt to the core, with great faculty of corrupting others, judges included, colonel of a regiment of militia, which he uniformed at his own cost and the splendid band of which he supported. He paid its first cornet-player $10,000 a year, it is said.

Illiterate, vulgar, unprincipled, profligate, always making himself conspicuously ridiculous by some piece of flagrant ostentation, he was, nevertheless, freehanded with his stolen money, and possessed, moreover, a certain magnetism of geniality that attracted to him people who were not particular about the decency of their associates. He was liberal to distressed ballet dancers and munificent to unfortunate females under difficulties.

March 11

It would seem that the Erie Ring has come to grief. There has been a conspiracy and a *coup d' état*. The company is rid of the scoundrelly cabals that have ruled and swindled it so long. But Jay Gould (the dethroned president) and D. D. Field will doubtless fight hard to recover their opportunities of peculation, and they will be backed by judges they own.

March 12

Jay Gould resigned at two-thirty this afternoon and the Erie Ring has finally collapsed, after doing the country infinite disgrace and mischief throughout Christendom. Fisk's sudden death seems to have destroyed it.

March 27

Erie stock has gone up like a balloon, and great fortunes have been made by people whom *I* think quite rich enough already.

September 13

Last night the Philharmonicals serenaded the illustrious [Anton] Rubinstein, who arrived by the *Cuba* on Wednesday. We met at eleven at a very beery and smoky lager shop in East Fourteenth Street, and proceeded thence to the Clarendon. Was introduced to the great man, a longhaired Kalmuck, who looks as if he belonged to the conservatoire of Pobolsk or Nizhni-Novgorod. But his expression and manner are kindly.

January 8 [1873]

Johnny witnessed the majestic spectacle of impaneling a jury in the case of Boss Tweed this morning and saw how careful the law is to admit as jurors in an important criminal case only those who are willing to swear that they are devoid of common sense and incapable of forming an opinion as to the truth or falsehood of notorious facts.

June 30

Received a nice note from nice Mrs. William Astor enclosing a check for $300 with which she requests me to give the poor children of Trinity Church a picnic or rural holiday of some kind. Good for Mrs. William Astor! I must go to work straightway and write the lady the prettiest note I can devise.

July 15

Ethelbert S. Mills of Brooklyn drowned at Coney Island, whither he used to drive every morning before breakfast for a sun bath. He was a prominent and public-spirited Brooklynite, a respectable lawyer, and a very specially favorite law student of my father's.

July 19

Poor Ethelbert Mills's trust company, the Brooklyn Trust Company, of which he was president, with a most respectable board that left him to run the machine in his own way, has come to grief and closed its doors. An investigating committee finds overdrafts by the president and investments on queer security that have sunk half its capital. Mills had been operating in real estate, not very successfully, and building fine houses near Prospect Park that would neither sell nor rent. It is suggested that he was tempted to these alleged overdrafts so that he might be saved the necessity of sacrificing this property. But I suppose the state of the case is not yet accurately understood. Of course the Mungo Malagrowthers will whisper that his accidental drowning is stuff and nonsense. All this is unfortunate. His reputation was unblemished. I never heard him spoken of but with praise.

July 21

There can be little doubt of Mills's suicide.

July 22

Great wealth, unless inherited, or acquired by professional energy and industry, is now, as a general rule, presumptive evidence against the character of its owner. Most of the dodges, devices, and complots which Wall Street considers legitimate and in which millions are lost and won (on paper) every day, are, of course, plainly guileful, dishonest, and wicked. But how many of our nice, fresh, ingenious boys are plunged into this filthy pool every year at eighteen or even younger.

November 19

Everyone expected Boss Tweed's jury to disagree—they were out so long

—but they brought that scoundrel in guilty this morning; thank Heaven. Sentence is postponed till Friday. Pity he can't be hanged. But he'll get a new trial, I suppose, and probably get off altogether, the rank, old felonious dog-fox!

November 22

Boss Tweed sentenced to twelve years and a moderate fine. Good as far as it goes.

January 7 [1875]

I have stood up for Grant through evil report and good report for ten years, but he is "coming it rather too strong" now. There are reasonable people who think it Grant's deliberate purpose to stay in the White House after his term expires.

January 23

Whom can we trust, and who can feel sure of even his own honesty? Henry Nicoll, after forty years of honorable practice, after having won the unquestioning confidence of every businessman in New York, after coming to be universally regarded as the embodiment of oldfashioned integrity, caution, and conservatism—Henry Nicoll is in every man's mouth today and in the newspapers, besides, as having used, or embezzled, several hundred thousand dollars of the trust funds in his keeping!

1871:   A CHICAGO GIRL'S HOME BURNS

THE TOLL OF THE CHICAGO FIRE was 250 lives, 17,000 commercial buildings, 100,000 homes. Eighteen-year-old Julia Newberry was in Paris when it happened. Because of the girl's failing health, her mother, widow of multimillionaire Walter L. Newberry, kept her abroad much of the time. Yet dearer to Julia than all the travels and luxuries the family millions could buy for her was home. This pathetic little diary is one of the few written by Chicagoans to survive the fire. Although there had been a village and a fort on the portage connecting the Great Lakes with the Mississippi River since 1795, Chicago as a city was only 34 years old at the time of the fire. Among the buildings that were destroyed was the library of the Chicago Historical Society, a storehouse of treasures that no money could replace.

"I saw my Chicago for the last time."
JULIA NEWBERRY (1853-1876)

Home, June 6, 1869. Chicago, U.S.A. In the Library

Europe is a dream, while hotels, bad eating, & sea-sickness, are things of the past. I know that it won't last but a few months, nevertheless I am home, yes, actually at home.

Here I am in the old house, where I was born, & where I wish I could always live; it is the dearest place on earth to me, & worth all London, Paris & New York put together; Sister & Mother may talk, & say what they like, still I shall persist in my opinion, that there is no place equal to Chicago, & no place like home.

Breevort House [New York], Saturday, Dec. 26, 1869

The Low-Pierrepont wedding came off Thursday, December 9th, & was supremely gorgeous! Mama & I arrived early at the church, three interesting "ushers" in white satin favours assigned us front seats. No one but invited guests were admitted, & the seats were soon filled with what the "papers" would have called the "elite" of Brooklyn & New York.

Everyone was very "swell," & the scene was very animated. The organ played a variety of lively tunes, & finally at one o'clock swelled into a wedding march, & the bridal procession entered.

First came two "ushers," Gussie Jay & Mr. Brevoort, followed by six groom's men two-by-two, & then Harry with his Father. Then the six bride's maids in pairs, dressed in alternate pink & white dresses, with overskirts of "crepe de chine," looped up "en panier" & trimmed with morning-glories.

Then Mrs. Low in yellow satin & white lace, leaning on her son Seth's arm, who just at that moment looked as handsome as a picture; & then came the bride with her Father. The great Paris "Worth" made her dress, & consequently nothing could be handsomer; white satin with a long train, & sprays of white orange blossoms falling all over it, & to crown all a beautiful real lace veil made expressly for her.

The chancel was strewed with flowers, & the altar decorated. Coming back each groom's-man took his bride's-maid as follows:

> Hattie Low—Jay Pierrepont
> Miss Jay—Willie Low
> Miss Vinton—Mr. Constable
> Mary Newberry—Gussie Low

Alice Osborne—Jay Dubois
Miss Lyman—Mr. Ogden

Home in Chicago, May 9th, 1870

We arrived here Friday the 28th of April, & I stayed the first night at the Sherman House, & then came directly over here. I was amazed & delighted with the house, which has been almost entirely rebuilt since last summer at the gentle cost of $60,000.

Everyone says it is the handsomest house in Chicago & everyone in town, including many strangers, have been to see it.

I am writing in what (to me) is the most perfect room I ever was in, my studio. It fronts South & East, with the most beautiful view of the lake, & the most delicious window, so wide & deep. It is irregular in shape also, & just the right size, with a genuine skylight, & private stair-case leading into my dressing-room.

There are two book-cases, & the loveliest closet; indeed it is just perfection. My real room down stairs is splendid, but I like the Studio best; down stairs I shall have to keep it in order, but here the door can be eternally locked if I choose, and no one can enter without permission. I dont believe there is another girl in the United States, or even in the world that has a real studio room built for *her;* it nearly breaks my heart to think of leaving at all & going to Europe again, & I am so afraid I shall get to be like every-one else, and not want to come home, getting so accustomed to the life over there, that I shall care for nothing else. I like Chicago so much, so much better than any other place, & we have such a beautiful home, & it is all associated with Papa, & now to go and leave it all!

If I only keep on liking it just as well, why then when I am an old maid I can always live here, & even if I *should* marry, my husband will have to live here, and there is one comfort in that, for then my children would live here too, and it would all go down in the family; it is too dreadful to think of strangers ever living here.

The handsomest thing in the house is the hall, wainscoated & finished beautifully in hard wood, & a clear sweep through the house, with a vestibule at either end. The library & dining-room are very large, & beautiful rooms, while the "Butler's Pantry" is too charming. And as regards bathrooms, light, heat, there is nothing to desire. The window glass is splendid and cost alone $3,000. And still though the house has been so very much improved, there is enough of the old building left to make us feel that it is always our old home.

Paris, October 13th, 1871

I am perfectly bewildered with the rush of events, I dont know what to write or what to think. Half of Chicago is in ashes, it is too awful to believe, too dreadful to think about. And the suspense is so fearful, the reports so vague & no one can get direct information. Mr McCagg & seven or eight other Chicago men are here; the fire began Sunday night; here it is Friday & we know nothing.

I haven't a doubt the stores on Kinzie Street are gone, but I cant and wont imagine our house is burnt. But oh the misery of the people, & the destitution of the poor, the sick people & the little babies. And all the people who are just comfortably off, & have lost their all. The immediate destitution is bad enough but the wearing, saving, pinching years that will come to so many are worse.

We may lose a very great deal, but Papa once said that if the entire city were to burn down, we should still have enough to live on. I am so thankful that he was saved the knowledge of this awful fire, & the destruction of the city he was so proud of. It would have embittered all the last days of his life.

This state of suspense is perfectly dreadful; and I have begun to run down again, as fast as possible. My head is as heavy as lead, & I am so nervous & wretched that I dont know what to do.

Tuesday, Oct 17

The fire began at twelveth street on Sunday night. It swept the two magnificent avenues, & every building on the South side from twelveth street to the river. The Court House, with the original copy of Father's will & no one knows how many invaluable papers, legal documents, records, the beautiful Crosbie Opera house, a perfect bijoux of a theatre, all the banks, insurance offices, railway depots, churches & block after block of stores, unequalled any where.

And then, oh misery, the fire, the red, angry, unrelenting fire, lept across the river, & burnt & burnt, till Mr. Mahlon Ogden's house was the only one left standing up to Lincoln Park. Yes the whole North Side is in ashes, literally in ashes, & every memory connected with my home is gone. Every association, every link; never never to be again, irreparably & irrevocably gone. No one ever loved their home more than I did mine; I loved every angle in the house, every carpet, every table, every picture on the walls, every book in the library, the stairs, the basement, the garret.

When the house was rebuilt Papa's room was left untouched, & it was so exactly as it has always been, that his presence seemed to be there; it was sacred, & that is gone! And then my studio, my beautiful studio, & the private staircase, & my room that I have looked forward to furnishing myself in pink & gray.

Thursday, October 19th

I shall go crazy if I write any more about the fire—I have felt so bad that I have been in bed for several days, & yesterday afternoon when Mama & Sister came in, I was lying on the sofa & feeling as bad as I have ever done since I was first taken sick.

Not a thing was saved from our house, not a thing; Mama's picture, Sister's, my dear little brother Jimmy's, Jamie Clapp's & my own painted when I was twelve years old, which Papa was so proud of that he declared there was nothing in the world he would take for it, all were burned to ashes.

Then we have lost all our letters; those of my grandfather, great-grandfather, and even further back, besides those of all my friends, & Sister has lost all of hers; but worse far worse than all, I have not a morsel left of any of the letters Papa wrote to me; no not one; they were so precious that I did not dare to carry even a few around with me; I had them back-to when I was a wee little girl six years old, & I used to write to him, & he to me. I remember one,

> *My dear Papa*
> There was an old man named Grundy, who whipped all his boys every Monday, so all through the week, unable to speak, they only had rest on a Sunday. Your loving little July.
> Nice, 1861

He took the most extraordinary pains during his long illness to write me the kindest & best letters that ever a Father wrote to his daughter & he kept mine as carefully as I did his; I had them all, every one; & now? If I had put them in the safe it would have done no good either for it was burned with the Newberry block; the silver met the same fate in a bank on the South side, & some of it was very pretty. The tea-pot from which Mama poured the tea, & the china-service beautifully painted which we used on Christmas, the spoons we ate with & the silver mugs we drank from all are gone.

The library too with all Papa's favorite books, that beautiful library in which I expected to spend so many cozy evenings; all my drawings from the beginning at my first water-colors, my monogramme book, & oh misery all my journals that I have taken such pains to write & keep, a record of all my ideas since I first began to have any! My twenty-five dollies, poor wretches, each roasted in turn, & all my innumberable presents & keepsakes, my beautiful pink bonboniere with the rest!

Mama lost all her jewelry except her diamond earrings, her cachemere shawls, laces, dresses, &etc. Papa's letters to her; letters from Fenimore Cooper, President Van Buren, Washington Irving, Aaron Burr (written to Grandfather Clapp) & quantities of others besides.

But what is the use of trying to write about it, I have begun this over & over again & I never can go on beyond the first few lines. Who could have dreamed that when I drove away from the house on that beautiful June morning 1870, that I saw it, & all my Chicago for the last time; if but one or two houses were burned, but they are all gone, all!

—— ★

1872: A BRITISH LAD SEES THE WILD WEST
—— ☆

WHEN A U.S. GOVERNMENT EXPEDITION was organized in 1871 "to explore the Yellowstone," the territory had been pretty well traveled. There really wasn't much left there for exploration. But Ferdinand V. Hayden, noted geologist, knew what he was doing. Today it would be called "promotion." He knew how to make newspaper headlines; and what he wanted was to publicize the wonders of that northwestern corner of Wyoming and convince America it ought to be made a national park. His expedition succeeded in doing just that.

William Blackmore, one of the founders of the town of Colorado Springs, Colorado, was a friend of Dr. Hayden. While the expedition was being formed he told the scientist he had a nephew in England who was coming with his mother, sister and two brothers for a visit to this country. Would Dr. Hayden take along 17-year-old Sidford Hamp, of Bedfordshire, on this "rock-hunting trip"? No people, not even the Americans themselves, showed as much enthusiasm for the American Wild West, as much curiosity about it, as the British. Books about it went like hotcakes there. What a wonderful adventure, then, for an English lad! Many an American boy would have given his all for a chance to go with the Hayden expedition; but Blackmore was a man of affluence and influence, and long, gangly Sidford Hamp was added to the staff. And as it turned out, the trip was all that Sidford could have hoped for—and a bit more.

In later years, back home in England, Sidford went into the tea business and made good. Then in 1877 his brother Frank began to fail in health, and the doctor advised a change of climate. Uncle William Blackmore wanted the whole family to come to Colorado Springs. They did, and in 1880 Sidford got a job on the Colorado Springs Gazette. As a journalist, he made good again and became well known as a writer of stories for boys.

Here is part of the diary he kept on that wonderful trip to the Yellowstone.

"It was a lark to see the Injuns . . ."
SIDFORD HAMP (1855-1919)

May 23 [1872], Washington, D. C.

We went to the Capitol, which is a Magnificent building, even better than our houses of Parliament. It is entirely built of white marble, except some parts inside and it is also painted inside in a most beautiful stile.

There are too a good many pictures, mostly upon the war of Independence which are anything but pleasant to an Englishman's feelings.

May 25

When I came down this morning I found Mr. Moran and Professor Hayden in the room, and having breakfasted with them, we all went to see some Indians. The first we saw was a chief named "Red Cloud" to whom Uncle gave a knife, and the chief shook hands and said How! How! which is the utmost extent of their English.

Sunday 26

We went to the church of the Epiphany, they have the service rather different here, for they pray for President Grant instead of for the Queen, and for the Senate.

29

We went down to dinner. It was such a lark to see the Injuns eat. One mixed strawberries and olives to-gether, another plumbcake and pickled oisters. Some ate holding the things in their hands, and some ate ice cream, pineapple, and fowl all at once, with a knife and fork. Altogether, they manage very well.

I forgot one anecdote of the Indians; one of the ladies had some gold in her teeth, and one Indian put his finger right into her mouth to point it out to his companions.

1st of June [at the canal in Georgetown]

We heard lots of tree frogs, and one bull-frog, which makes an awfull row just like a bull.

June 4

Aunt and I went today to New York. They have a splendid dodge for taking care of your luggage. When you go to the station you get some brass checks for it and when you give it up you have no more trouble with it, for they send it anywhere you like when the train stops. I don't suppose it could be done in England where there is so much traveling, and the towns are so large.

12

5 weeks [from home].

We started for the west, and slept on the car for the first time. There was plenty of room, and you could lie in bed and see out of the window, if you had the lower berth.

13

We arrived at Chicago, and saw some of the ruins [left by the great fire of October, 1871] but they have built up a great many fine houses again; we slept on the car again that night. When I woke up that same morning I found that we were on the prairies, and the first thing I saw was 2 imigrant waggons crossing the praries all alone.

July 1st

I started today, as it began to clear up a bit, on the Hayden Surveying Expedition, under Captain Stevenson, to the Source of the Snake River, and the Lake of the Yellowstone, where no white man but solitary hunters have ever been before, and which is a very fine thing to be able to do, for Capt. Stevenson says he has received 500 applications for the place from young men of the best American families, General Grant's nephew for one.

3

We got up at 5 o'c. and started at 6/15 for Fort Hall [Idaho]. We stoped at Ross Fork and had some biscuits, and saw 5 Indians. They were small, but better looking than the Sioux. The squaws there were quite nice looking. We saw a mountain 110 miles off, and it looked as plain as you could see a thing in England at 20 miles. We got to the top of what they call the divide, which is a mountain separating two valeys, and there we saw some mountains 180 or 170 miles off.

4th

Glorious.

This day is what the Americans call "the Glorious Fourth," dash 'em! because they got their liberty on that day, a short time ago (I don't know when). How jolly it must be for the Americans to have no history to learn. I suppose that is why they push ahead so, because they want a little. When I woke up, I found something warm at my feet, and saw a—(not a grizzle bear—) but a cat.

They had horse, & foot races, and climbing a greasy pole to celebrate the fourth and a game of base ball, which is very much like rounders, in the evening. We had a jolly good dinner, & a great big English plum pudding.

Expedition Starts for the Yellowstone Region

12

We got up at 4 o'c. before sun-up, and packed our beds, clothes, and mules, saddled our horses, and started at 9/30 oc. for the region of bears, Indians, and worst of *all* the region of *Musquitoes*. I am much more afraid of musquitoes than of Indians or snakes, or anything else, and so is every-one else.

How astonished any Bedfordite would be to see me, riding a grey horse with two coats rolled up in a "gunny-sack" (which is a sort of sack, made very coarse) tied behind me, without a coat, with a pistol on one side, and a great knife on the other, chaceing mules, with great packs on their backs, to make them keep to-gether, or to see me writing this in a tent on the bank of a stream, in the midst of the Rocky Mts. with out a coat, my book on my knee, my ink on a sack of clothes, a dog close to me asleep, the therm'r. at 95° in the tent, and myself sitting on a keg of whiskey. *GUM!*

16

There was an awful joke played on two of the boys today, it was a very old joke called Snipe driving. They were told "that if they went out into the marsh, and held a sack open, with a lighted candle in front, whilst the others drove the snipes toward them, they would jump into the sack, and stay there"; so these two fellows went out and sat in the marsh, in the manner I have shown, surrounded by musquitoes, while the others all ran back to camp and left them. Then one of the packers went near them and yelled like an Indian, and fired his pistol three times. We didn't know if they were frightened, for of course they wouldn't acknowledge it, if they were, anyhow they came to camp directly afterwards, and got most awfully laughed at.

Oct. 15

Logan and I walked into Virginia City [Montana] and left all our baggage to be sent after us. We started on and changed coaches at about 1 oc.

Wednesday, 16 (23 weeks from home)

There were 6 inside [the coach] and 8 out, so we were pretty tightly fixed. We changed again during the day, and had more room. About 8 oc. P.M. we were stoped by highwaymen, and completely cleaned out.

In a letter to his mother, written at Corinne, Utah, October 27, he elaborates on this incident, as follows:

I was asleep when suddenly the coach stopped which woke me up.

I was going to look out (for the blinds were down) when I heard some-one out side say, "Put in your head there!" & in a little while the voice said again, "Get out one at a time & throw up your hands." Then I knew in an instant that the coach was stopped by *highwaymen.*

One of the passengers got out & then I did and all the others followed & stood in a row with their hands over their heads. There were seven of us besides one on the box with the driver & a lady and child inside.

When we were outside, I had time to look about & the first thing I saw was a man with a double-barrelled shotgun full cocked pointed at the driver & another behind the coach with 2 six barrelled pistols in his hands, casting sheepseyes at the passengers (I think the eyes were rather wolf-in-sheep's-clothing sort of eyes).

I took the end nearest the shotgun man so that I could see what he was up to. When we were all out the man with the pistols told the coachman to throw out the treasure boxes which he did (the treasure boxes contain money or gold dust generally).

He then took a small hatchet he had with him and split them open but there was nothing in them. Then he came to us & searched us. He began with me, he first took out my watch but he only looked at it & put it back & said he didn't want it. Then he felt in my other pockets & found a leather case in which I had $8 & all my letters. I told him there was only $8. in it & he said if he thought so he would give it me back. I asked him to look inside but he wouldn't. He asked me what I had been doing as I only had $8 so I told him I was traveling with another fellow. I had 2 £5 notes in my pocket which he didn't find.

Then he searched the others & got from the 1st $300, 2nd $2400, 3rd $4000, 4th $150, 5th $0, from the man on the box they got $150. The man who lost none had handed his purse to the lady as he got out & as she wasn't searched he saved it.

They then took the candle out of the coach lamp & searched inside the coach. The man on the box had a bottle of whiskey, which the robbers took from him & handed round for the passengers to drink. I took some just for the joke of it & because I was cold with standing out with my hands up.

Fancy such a thing as a highway-robbery in England.

THOMAS ALVA EDISON'S BRIEF DIARY covers only a few delicious days which he took out of a mercilessly self-disciplined life one summer to have fun with his family and friends, especially his little daughter Dot. He had already invented the phonograph and the incandescent lamp, but here there is no mention of these nor of the 1,032 other patents by which he helped shape the course of the world during his lifetime and for all time to come. This, in fact, is a diary of no importance whatever except to those who take an interest in such impractical and unmattering creatures as baby angels, the souls of great men riding butterflies, and flirtations with flowers. But it does give us a glimpse at an Edison whom neither the industrial giants nor the American public ever knew.

"A ray of sunshine got stuck."
THOMAS ALVA EDISON (1847-1931)

Menlo Park, N. J., Sunday, July 12 [1885]

This is by far the nicest day of this season, neither too hot nor too cold. It blooms on the apex of perfection—an Edensday. Good day for an angels' picnic. They could lunch on the smell of flowers and new mown hay, drink the moisture of the air, and dance to the hum of bees. Fancy the soul of Plato astride of a butterfly riding around Menlo Park with a lunch basket.

At 4 o'clock Dot [his 12-year-old daughter] came around with her horse "Colonel" and took me out riding—beautiful roads—saw 10 acre lot full of cultivated red raspberries. "A burying ground, so to speak." Got this execrable pun off on Dot.

Dot laughed heartily when I told her about a church being a heavenly fire-escape.

Holzer is going to use the old laboratory for the purpose of hatching chickens artificially by an electric incubator. Just think, electricity employed to cheat a poor hen out of the pleasures of maternity. Machine-born chickens! What is home without a mother?

I suggested to H that he vaccinate his hens with chicken-pox virus. Then the eggs would have their embryo hereditarily inoculated and none of the chickens would have the disease. For economy's sake he could start with one hen and rooster. He being a scientific man with no farm experience, I explained the necessity of having a rooster. He saw the force of this suggestion at once.

July 13

Went to New York via Desbrosses Street ferry. Took cars across town. Saw a woman get into car that was so tall and frightfully thin as well as dried up that my mechanical mind at once conceived the idea that it would be the proper thing to run a lancet into her arms and knee joints and insert automatic self-feeding oil cups to diminish the creaking when she walked.

Woodside Villa [Nantucket], July 14

Arrived at Woodside Villa and was greeted by Mama with a smile as sweet as a cherub that buzzed around the bedside of Raphael. A fresh invoice of innocence and beauty had arrived in my absence in the persons of Miss Louise Igoe and her aunt, from Indianapolis, that producer of Hoosier Venuses. Miss Igoe is a pronounced blonde, blue eyes, with a complexion as clear as the conscience of a baby angel, with hair like Andromache. Miss Igoe's aunt is a bright elderly lady who beat me so bad at checkers that my bump of "strategic combination" has shrunk in about two inches.

July 17

We are going out with the ladies in yacht to sail, perchance to fish. The lines will be baited at both ends.

Hottest day of season. Hell must have sprung a leak.

Fish seem to be rather conservative around this bay. One seldom catches enough to form the fundamental basis for a lie.

July 18

Went out yachting, all the ladies in attendance. I was delightfully un-hot. Ladies played game called memory-scheme. No. 1 calls out name of prominent author, No. 2 repeats this name and adds another and so on. Soon one has to remember a dozen names, all of which must be repeated in the order given. Result, Miss Daisy had the best and I the poorest memory.

Miss Daisy smiled so sweetly all the evening that I imagined a ray of sunshine tried to pass her and got stuck.

July 19

Moon was shining brightly. Girls called my attention several times to beauty of the light from said moon shining upon the waters. Couldn't appreciate it, was so busy taking a mental triangulation of the moon, the two sides of said triangle meeting the base line of the earth at Woodside and Akron, Ohio.

July 20

Satan is the scarecrow in the religious cornfield.

July 21

Arose early, went out to flirt with the flowers.

Then my dream changed. Thought I was looking out upon the sea. Suddenly the air was filled with millions of little cherubs as one sees in Raphael's pictures. Each, I thought, was about the size of a fly. They were perfectly formed and seemed semi-transparent. Each swept down to the surface of the sea, reached out both their tiny hands, and grabbed a very small drop of water, and flew upward, where they assembled and appeared to form a cloud.

This method of forming clouds was so different from the method described in Ganot's Physics that I congratulated myself on having learned the true method and was thinking how I would gloat over the chagrin of those cold-blooded savants who would dissect an angel or boil a live baby to study the perturbations of the human larynx. Then this scheme was wrecked by my awakening.

VI.

OF

RECENT

MEMORY

The Dow-Jones stock market service and the Wall Street Journal were good business. At his death their owner, Clarence Barron, left an estate of a million dollars. But the men who were Barron's friends were the owners not of businesses but of empires. What qualified Barron for their society and their confidence was his deserved reputation as Wall Street's ace reporter. Sometimes it was better to be friends with Barron and tell him what you knew than to risk letting him tell what he knew.

A sharp memory, plus a knowledge of shorthand, enabled Barron to record many of these conversations practically word for word immediately they were over. After his death, Editors Arthur Pound and Samuel Taylor Moore got some of them together and published them under the title They Told Barron. So lively was the public interest that they made another book out of what was left and called that More They Told Barron.

"They have all been unhappy."
CLARENCE W. BARRON (1855-1928)

May 1892

Notes of interview with Mr. George Westinghouse, Jr., at his factory.

"Mr. Coffin [Charles A. Coffin, president of General Electric Company] has a very swelled head. He talks about making the General Electric Company bigger than the Standard Oil Company.

"At one of our interviews, I think it was in New York, he asked me if I would be willing to go into any electrical combination of which I was not the head. I said most emphatically that I would not go into any electrical combination of which I was to *be* the head. I had done work enough in this life to have earned some rest, and furthermore, I told him that I would not go into an electrical combination of which *he* was to be the head.

"At another time Pevear [Henry A. Pevear, director of the Excelsior Electric Co.], Insull [Samuel Insull, gas and electric magnate who was later sent to prison] were at a hotel in New York and Coffin proposed, I forget the exact details of the arrangement, that we should form a combination, so that whatever occurred, whether the companies were successful or unsuccessful, we should make money under any circumstances.

"I said to Coffin in Pevear's presence that I was not in the habit of robbing my stockholders. There was no reply."

Boston, May 4, 1892

Called upon Mr. Charles Francis Adams at his office in the Adams Building, Court Street, and talked about Union Pacific affairs from 1:30 to 2:30 P.M.

Mr. Adams said: "I was receiving assault from all quarters of the West, from a hand which I could not see and could not understand. There would be something published in Chicago and then copied in the East, attacking our credit, and then there would be an attack upon us in some Salt Lake City paper, or at Portland, Oregon, and the ball would move around the country to hit us in the back.

"I thought it was some attack from our rivals in the railroad business. I even suspected the Vanderbilts, and the lines to Chicago that were opposing the Northwest Alliance. Or that it might be something connected with the Interstate Commerce Commission.

"It was none other than the hand of Jay Gould.

"Finally Mr. Gould threw off the mask and came out openly in an interview in the *New York Evening Post*, in which he attacked me, and the credit of the company, and said that as a large stockholder—I think his interest had reached about 35,000 shares besides a considerable interest in the bonds—he was going to turn me out of office, and take the management of the company himself.

"I immediately wrote Mr. Gould, saying that I should not carry the burden of the Union Pacific, with a division within the line, and that he must take the responsibility, that I would resign, and that he could take the management of the company."

On the Pennsylvania Limited, May 14, 1892

Enroute westward yesterday, I met Edwin E. Jackson, Jr. Jackson is somewhat familiar with the copper combination in a general way, as he is the representative of the wire pools. He says the copper manufacturers are nearly all in a pool—wire pool, sheet brass pool, and other pools—and they will welcome any copper combine that advances the price of copper.

The copper combination would have put the price to thirteen cents per pound but for arrangements pending with Chile and France, which he does not look for to hold very long. It is bad enough to attempt to hold a pool of American manufacturers, but with foreign lying and deception it would be almost impossible to hold together an international pool. His firm was approached to form and manage it, but they declined on account of its international character. He does not expect copper to go above twelve cents, for above this price Chile bars would take the market.

Jackson believes that the doctrine, "competition is the life of trade," is a great fallacy.

May 21, 1892

Told Mr. Coffin that I have been to see Mr. Westinghouse and proposed to give him a little show, as he felt he had been abused from Boston. He said, "Mr. Westinghouse will hear a great many things soon that will surprise him. We are sweeping right through the country and are cleaning the Westinghouse Company right out.

"If Westinghouse thinks he can make money by selling a double motor equipment for street cars for $1,200 I say he will be bankrupt by it. He has not figured in his whole cost. He makes good apparatus; he always did. The trouble with him is he sells it too cheap.

"If he should combine with us he would be a great deal better off, but still it is a good thing for us to have him outside. He fights off and kills all the little fellows with his low prices."

New York, February 9, 1900

Mr. Veiller introduced me to Frank Savin [spectacular broker in many Standard Oil transactions] who said:

"A few years ago John D. Rockefeller owned one-half of the Standard Oil and I think he owns it today. I think he alone is worth $400,000,000 to $500,000,000, but he is unhappy, never going on the street without a detective behind him and has two detectives guarding his house day and night."

Boston, December 26, 1900

F. H. Prince [banker and railroad executive] tells me that when Moore & Schley formed the Whiskey pool, it was given to James R. Keene to operate. The question came up as to whether individual members of the pool could also operate on their own account. Mr. Keene said, "Certainly. Operate all you want to; buy it and sell it; go long and go short, and you will please me, but just understand that I will get the best of you all."

Then Mr. Keene began. Ten thousand shares went out one day and were bought back the next day. He began moving it so many shares a day up and down, and kept swinging it back and forth—some days it was 20,000 shares a day, again it was 50,000 shares a day. Then when the whole public was trading in whiskey with a great big swing to the market Keene gave them the whole business, possibly went short 50,000 shares himself, and landed the entire stock of the pool on the public.

June 1903

I learned from people identified with the American Sugar Refining Company that H. H. Rogers [oil, copper and railroad man], Stillman [James Stillman, president of National City Bank], and William Rockefeller were given 180,000 shares in the Beet Sugar Company at the original issue price, when it was worth double that price in the market, as a matter of compromise because Havemeyer would not have Rogers on the board.

In other words, this stock was taken out of the treasury of the company and given to these interests to keep them out of the company.

August 11, 1903

W. H. Coolidge [Boston corporation lawyer] tells me:

"The Standard Oil people have set out to break William C. Whitney [Secretary of the Navy under President Cleveland, father of Payne Whitney and Harry Payne Whitney] and this may shed some light upon Whitney's recent stock market transactions.

"You probably know that I have very close business connections in Cleveland, the home of the Standard Oil Company. My information, and I consider it A-1, is that Oliver Payne [one of the original Standard Oil partners] has solemnly sworn to take William C. Whitney's wealth away from him. You probably remember that Whitney married Oliver Payne's only sister and that marriage was the foundation of his wealth as when Whitney married Miss Payne, Oliver H. Payne gave her $3,500,000 in cash and securities and a $500,000 residence in New York.

"He then became a member of the Standard Oil family and was at one time a large owner of Standard Oil shares and other Standard Oil investments.

"After his wife died Whitney married again. This angered Oliver H. Payne, who swore that he would take away every cent from Whitney that he secured by reason of his former marriage. He got his Standard Oil stock away from him and has been pursuing him relentlessly ever since."

January 28, 1904

With my wife dined in the Astoria Garden with Mr. and Mrs. Herman Sielcken [coffee king]. It had been the largest day on the Coffee Exchange, some 600,000 to 800,000 bags changing hands, with Sully [Daniel J. Sully, speculator] a large buyer. Mr. Sielcken said to me:

"I can put coffee down again just as easily as I put it down once before. There was some years ago a tremendously short crop of coffee. In anticipation of small receipts, coffee rose in fright to above twenty cents per pound, but when it was determined that the crop was only 3,000,000 bags, almost the shortest on record, coffee fell back to around ten cents per pound. The coffee business is largely a matter of sentiment. There is just as much coffee drunk one year as another."

November 14, 1904

On train to New York, my friend Webster [Frank G. Webster, member of Kidder, Peabody & Company, brokers] tells me that the biggest deal he has ever heard of was that of the Tobacco people. Ryan [Thomas Fortune Ryan] and Whitney were given the opportunity to go in on the tobacco deal and were allowed to make the Continental Tobacco Company. They subscribed $50,000 of which only $12,500 was used and they came out with $50,000,000 of bonds for their $12,500.

New York, March 27, 1911

Engineer Hoadley tells me that Consolidated Gas Company [New York] sells $22,000,000 worth of gas at eighty cents, which it costs them forty cents to make and distribute, leaving them $11,000,000 profit.

He also said that the Edison Company which they control gets six cents per kilowatt hour for electricity and it costs them a cent to manufacture and a cent to distribute, a total expense of one-third of what they get.

May 12, 1913

F. H. Prince said: "Frick [Henry C. Frick, president, H. C. Frick Coke Company; president of board of managers, Carnegie Steel Company] is worth $100,000,000. He keeps turning his investments and sold out his Chicago & Northwestern some time ago. Frick's estimate of Morgan is that he may leave from $50,000,000 to $55,000,000.

"The Pujo Committee Investigation [a Congressional investigation of money trusts in 1912] killed Morgan. Morgan was a very sensitive, shrinking man and all his exterior bluff was simply a protecting coating."

New York, December 4, 1915

Dined with Percy N. Furber [president, Trans-Lux Company] and eight others at the Metropolitan Club. Among them James N. Hill, with whom I talked most of the evening. He is the oldest son of Jim Hill of the Great Northern road.

Hill said: "My father is one of the most interesting men I have known and he is the strongest man in the northwest and he could lick any man in the whole country. My father knew everybody in the country and knew everybody that worked for him.

"When I was a kid at school and came home on a vacation, father confided to me that there was trouble in England and that some big banking house would have to fail. This was in the spring and the Baring failure did not come till June. He said he thought he ought to sell some Great Northern stock because it would have a big drop and he should be in position to buy it back.

"My father's wrist was one-half inch wider than mine. When I was nineteen we had a bout upstairs and I gave him a punch that should have knocked him out. The most marvelous thing in the world was that he took it unflinchingly and gave me a crack that laid me unconscious for six hours."

Enroute to Boston, March 4, 1916

Had a half-hour's talk with James Phillips, Jr. [Boston industrialist]. He says H. H. Rogers and William Rockefeller always divided equally on their enterprises. Rockefeller furnished the money on Rogers's Amalgamated Copper. Lawson [Thomas W. Lawson], A. C. Burrage [organizer of Anaconda Copper and others], and Rogers did the work. They took in Burrage on the copper business and Burrage attended to that part and they gave him one-third. Rogers got the evidence that Burrage was selling Butte & Boston against them and telegraphed him to come on from Southern California. Burrage had to admit that he had been selling some stock. Thereupon Rogers closed his interest and gave him $10,000,000 and never had any more transactions with him. Burrage could come and go in the office as he knew too much to be turned out, but he was never in with them again.

Chicago, June 6, 1920

Luther Holden [Utah copper man] told me: "Once when [H. H.] Rogers had A. C. Burrage at the foot of the table with four other guests, one of the guests said to Mr. Rogers: 'How can you tolerate that Mr. Burrage opposite you at the table?' Rogers said: 'I am enjoying it immensely. I was thinking all the time how he would look after I had plucked him.'"

New York, December 6, 1917

Called at the office of J. P. Morgan & Company 2:45 P.M. and discussed with Lewis Cass Ledyard the Interstate Commerce Commission decision as it was running on the Dow-Jones ticker, recommending government control of the railroads instead of advancing rates, then dropped in for a twenty-minute chat with Morgan, who said:

"This country is approaching the condition of Russia, where no leaders are wanted and the moment one appears, the Bolsheviki throw him down.

"Legislation is aimed and boastfully aimed against business and the destruction of values. But nobody can say anything or do anything at the present time. Sentiment has got to run its course.

"I would not do a thing to interrupt, and I would certainly put no sand in the gear boxes or attempt to stay the machinery. This war has got to be fought out and won and Mr. Wilson has got to win it in his own way, with his own party, his own men, his own machinery, and his own methods, and it is our duty to support him."

Washington, D. C., February 12, 1918

Breakfasted with B. M. Baruch at 8 A.M. at his residence. Baruch said:

"I suppose I am closer to McAdoo than anybody else except the President, for I have known him for many years and believed in him. You remember perhaps a remark of McAdoo's that a friend walked into his office at the time of the First Liberty Loan and wrote on a piece of paper a subscription for $5,000,000 bonds. That happened to be I. I had more money on hand than usual and my affairs were very liquid, and although I wanted more than $5,000,000 of those bonds I put down for that amount and I have got them all now. Three and one-half per cent tax free is good enough for me."

New York, November 2, 1921

Mr. Ernest R. Graham said: "When I was in New York over Sundays I used to call on Carnegie and walk around the reservoir with him. He had the smallest feet, and was one of the vainest of men. At one time I said to him: 'You have got to look out for the other side. They are grafters.' This was a South American contract. He replied: 'Oh, that is all right. I have bought that side, so we have both of them.'"

January 16, 1922, on Knickerbocker train to New York

Ex-Governor McCall of Massachusetts said: "Thomas W. Lawson told me once he was worth $30,000,000, of which $17,000,000 was in government and municipal securities and I think he was telling me the truth. He had made millions in his manipulation of copper stocks.

"His father was an old soldier and in his youth Tom said to his mother they must all now turn in and help support the family as his father could no longer work. So Tom went over to Boston, saw a sign 'State Street Boy Wanted,' and hurried in to Mr. Amory who said: 'Do you know anything about the stock market?' Tom said he did not but would learn. Amory took a fancy to him because he was a good-looking boy and set him to counting gold which was then a speculative commodity. But Tom learned about the stock market and soon had $50,000.

"He had his own coterie or pool. They bought a gas stock which had a contract with the city which was very lucrative. Somebody would introduce a motion in City Hall to break the contract and down would go the price of this stock. Then at the next meeting in City Hall the motion to cancel the contract would be defeated and up would go the gas stock. This made them lots of money.

"One day the usual bill or motion was presented and down went the stock and they all loaded up for the usual rise. But that night the motion went through instead of being defeated and all that was left of Tom's $50,000 was $157."

New York, October 30, 1922

Sargent, the portrait painter, said John D. Rockefeller was the most interesting sitter he ever had. His brother, William Rockefeller, said the portrait was good, but he didn't like the look of John D.'s hand—it was still reaching.

En route from Florida, November 29, 1922

Samuel Spring said: "I am now with the Associated First National Pictures. We have three contracts for eight pictures from Charlie Chaplin and he is holding back the eighth.

"*The Kid* was the fifth picture of the series. He has received already for it $850,000 profits before taxes and his taxes trouble him very much, for he is as close as Harry Lauder. When we were paying him $100,000 a month he was riding around in an old Buick. We have actually paid him $1,000,000.

"Chaplin is probably worth about $3,000,000. He puts his money into municipal bonds, which is the favorite investment of the moving picture people.

"It is probable that the United States including Canada has paid more than $6,000,000 to see *The Kid*. England has paid about $1,000,000.

"Griffith is always broke because he puts too much into his pictures. Chaplin puts only $150,000 and his brain into a picture like *The Kid*."

Aboard S.S. Olympic, eastbound, Feb. 10-14, 1923

Charles M. Schwab said: "At 17 I lived at Loretto and had never worn a suit of clothes that was not made by my mother. As I swung around on the railroad curve I saw the great Edgar Thomson Steel Works for the first time in my life.

"It was the biggest thing I had ever seen, employing 10,000 men. Yet in seven years, or at the age of 24, I was president of the Edgar Thomson Steel Works and a few years later had built the Homestead plant.

"When Carnegie put me in charge he said, 'You can make as many mistakes as you like, but don't make the same one twice.' Carnegie never wanted to know the profits. He always wanted to know the cost.

"One day Morgan asked me to dine with him and I excused myself by saying that it was Carnegie's birthday and I must dine with him. He said, 'How old?' I said, 'Mr. Carnegie is sixty-two today.' Morgan said, 'I am sixty-one and he must be much older.' I said, 'Mr. Morgan, I have been trying to find out for some time how to get together two important men and now that you are the younger, suppose you call on Mr. Carnegie.' I took him up there to call. Out of that contact came United States Steel."

New York, March 13, 1924

Eugene Meyer, Jr., called me on the telephone at Dow, Jones & Company about ten-thirty and suggested I go up to see him. He said there was a great fallacy about short sales.

"The short sellers do not support the market as a rule; nor do they stop high prices," said he. "The bears are always the sellers at the lowest and buyers at the highest price."

At eleven-fifteen called upon Winthrop Burr, chairman of the Committee on Business Conduct at the Stock Exchange by appointment.

He said he thought it a gross error to report American Woolen as earning $18 a share, as such reports are blamed on the Stock Exchange, as is 'most everything else. He said he thought more damage was done by buying stocks at high prices than by selling them at low prices. The Stock Exchange had studied this matter of short sales more than people knew. For two years during the war they kept record of all short sales, and the confidential reports made by the brokers showed that their sales were made on advancing prices and that stocks were bought back on receding prices. This was the absolute record which had convinced the Stock Exchange Committee of the usefulness of short selling. Indeed, at one time the only support to the market appeared to be the covering of shorts by [Jesse] Livermore, who bought back all the 60,000 shares which he was short.

May 8, 1924

Knudsen of the Chevrolet Company says:

"Ford has the best organization in the world without the appearance of organization. He himself never discharges a man. He is too tenderhearted; other people always do his 'firing.' "

Palm Beach, April 1, 1928

Spent the forenoon with Mr. and Mrs. John Shepard, Jr. Dr. Billings of

Chicago called when I was there. He told Shepard that he had never seen a very rich man who died happy. He named five big men, including George M. Pullman, whom he had attended to their deathbeds, and they have all been unhappy, notwithstanding their millions. There was always family trouble, or woman trouble, or some other trouble.

1918: A YANK AT ST. MIHIEL

ONLY THE DWINDLING RANKS of Memorial Day paraders knew at first hand what Sherman had meant, could remember from Gettysburg or San Juan Hill the real hellishness of war; and even among these, there were no memories of Big Berthas, tanks, shellshock, mustard burns, the "rotten pear" gas that made you vomit in your gasmask and tear it off, the searing tentacles of the flame-thrower, the rain of death from the air.

A new generation plunged into war confidently, eagerly, and went "over there" singing. Then came Lorraine, Belleau Wood, Chateau-Thierry, St. Mihiel, the Argonne. And they learned, as Sherman's men had learned before them, what war was.

At the time, anyone could explain how America happened to get into it— the whole devious coil of "what-where-when" from Sarajevo to the Lusitania, the two years more of U-boat attacks, and finally the declaration on April 6, 1917, of war with Germany. There were some who could also tell, in a vague sort of way, the "why"—that is, until the smoke had cleared and one could see it from the vantage of hindsight; then the "why" seemed to get vaguer and fuzzier than ever.

Twenty-one-year-old Corporal Elmer Sherwood, of Linton, Indiana, a soldier of the Rainbow Division assigned to scout and observation detail, was one of 2,000,000 men America put into the field. He was not one of the 126,000 who never came back. With the gallantry of youth, hour by hour he played the great game with fate, tempting it with the one blue chip that was his life. But he was not even one of the many thousands, uncounted, on whom the shock of modern warfare had left deeper marks than met the eye. Healthy, extrovert Elmer, like the majority, took the horrors in stride, wept when he saw his buddies die, left it to the "poets and thinkers" to reason why, waited for the German shell that "had his number on it," and when it didn't come, went home. After faithfully carrying out each day's round of assignments, on finding himself alive, he set down in his diary an explanation of the phenomenon. He wrote in good humor and in the serenity of unshakable loyalties.

For himself, Elmer makes no literary claims. "In reading these pages," he says, "it should be constantly borne in mind that they were written at the front, when cooties were biting and bullets were sizzling, with no thought of future publication."

He need not have apologized. His were the feelings and thoughts of the Yank, of millions in the same bewildering horror with himself, and for this reason his record has values that were missing from many a paid writer's account of the same events.

Back home after the war, his qualities took him far and fast in the business world. He formed a public relations firm in Indianapolis and later founded the American Travelers Life Insurance Company. Still in his forties when America went into World War II, he served in the army again—this time as a brigadier general.

Here we pick him up in midsummer, 1918, on the Champagne front; and after the leaves have fallen, go with him into the battle of St. Mihiel, in which the American forces were, for the first time, on their own; and finally to victory in the Meuse-Argonne.

"It is too gigantic and awesome . . ."
ELMER W. SHERWOOD (born 1897)

July 21 [1918]

"Black Jack" [Pershing] has given us training in open warfare because he thinks a victory can be obtained only by attack, not merely by defensive tactics.

July 25

The odor of dead things permeates the atmosphere everywhere, but we have become used to the stench—used to almost everything sickening.

July 28

Airplanes have many battles above us. An enemy plane came over today and swooped down upon Battery E. The pilot turned his machine gun loose on the battery and bumped off two more of our men. An American plane evened up the score today by bringing down a German from over our heads. It was a pretty battle.

30

One company captured eight German nests today and turning the machine guns the other way gave the Germans a dose of their own medicine. The war cry is "guts and bayonets" and believe me, they are using both. Sergeant Joyce Kilmer, the poet, was one of the Rainbows who fell today with a bullet through his brain.

August 3

Hundreds of bodies of our brave boys lie on Hill 212, captured with such a great loss of blood. We will never be able to explain war to our loved ones back home even if we are permitted to live and return. It is too gigantic and awesome for expression through words.

September 3

We agreed upon one thing—that a great majority of the men in the Rainbow Division are fatalists. As they express it, "There is a shell in Germany that has my number on it, and when it comes over I will be pushing up daisies."

4

Some cynic pacifists say, "They do not know what they are fighting for." Perhaps our fellows could not tell you in concise terms just what the reasons are. After all, it is left to a few poets and thinkers to express the innermost thoughts and hopes of nations and peoples.

Many of us will not live to know the results, but those who do will see America enshrined as the first power of the world.

8

We hiked all last night, pulling into our present position on this (St. Mihiel) front at 2:30 A.M.

We worked like blazes camouflaging our position and placing our guns until 5 A.M.

After this we turned into blankets and slept until 8:30.

Three and a half hours after an all-night hike isn't much, but perhaps tonight I can get more; at any rate, we have the satisfaction of knowing that all communications are in good order, and that is the main job I have to perform in this man's army.

I have just come back from the front-line trenches where we located an O.P. (Observation Post) for our battery. The first soldier I ran across in the trenches was just over from the U. S. and didn't know "what it is all about." I asked where the enemy was located, and he didn't know. Then I asked him if there had been much excitement up here. He said, "Lord, yes! A fellow out of G Company was killed by a shell last night." He seems to think this bloody warfare. I just wonder what he would say if he could see the fields before Chateau-Thierry as they were when we were up there, literally covered with corpses. Well, all hell will soon break loose here too.

9

This will be the first battle of the war in which the participating troops of our side are to be commanded by Pershing personally, according to the snow [rumor] and it will be the first big all-American drive.

The command may be endeavoring to keep the plans secret. If so, it has not altogether succeeded, because it seems to me everybody in France surmises that we are going to fight to flatten the St. Mihiel salient. Even the French peasants spoke of it as we came up to the front.

This projection of the battlefront is popularly known as the "hernia of St. Mihiel," and it has existed for almost four years. In 1914 the German horde forced its way to this point, which has been held by the enemy ever since.

The salient has an area of some 150 square miles, almost the size of the former Chateau-Thierry salient, and among other things, it contains a very important railway junction. It is a grand and glorious feeling to know that it is the American army which will carry on this operation.

These fellows have so much confidence that they swear they will capture Metz if ordered to, or die in the attempt. I actually believe it is possible for us to deliver the knock-out punch to the enemy within three months, though, of course, that isn't probable.

Signal detail has been running new lines and repairing old ones today, and communications are in shipshape. The guards make every one wear gas masks at alert; can you beat that? I suppose the order was designed primarily to protect the green troops who are in battle for the first time, and who might forget in the confusion that they have gas masks.

I asked one of these birds if any one had been gassed on this front, and he said, "No," but added that a soldier had been hit by a shell yesterday. He seemed to think it a terrible calamity, and I told him the fellow might have been hit by a street car if he had stayed in the States.

11

Beaucoup ammunition has been placed at our gun positions and we are all set for the party. Unlike the Champagne front, we do not have any reserve positions picked out in case of retreat on this front. Evidently Pershing feels that there is no doubt but that this battle will go our way.

12

The zero hour was 1:05 A.M., the heavy artillery starting it off. The earth seemed to give way when the rest of our guns joined in the stupendous and fierce barrage. The roar was so loud that we could scarcely distinguish the deep intonation of our own howitzers from the reports of the 75s.

For four hours the deafening roar continued as our messengers of death were hurled into enemy territory. Then at 5:00 our infantry preceded by tanks went over the top, making a picture of dash and activity.

Not content with ordinary progress the boys of our division leaped ahead of the clumsy tanks and pressed forward in irresistible waves to the German trenches.

The enemy artillery reply was feeble, though the infantry machine-gun and rifle fire was more menacing.

Our artillery fire in the first place demoralized enemy resistance, and the Boche are surrendering in droves. Surely they must regret giving up these luxurious dugouts and trenches which they have lived in for four years. Many of them even have electric lights and good furniture "requisitioned" from nearby French villages.

We must have slipped up on the enemy because they left a great deal of equipment, ammunition and food. Before we left the battery on detail work, two or three hundred prisoners passed our position. Up here in the advance we pass prisoners in droves of from ten to a hundred with a doughboy in the rear prodding the laggards with a bayonet whenever necessary.

A good many of the Germans are being utilized to carry back wounded. A sedate-looking officer wearing white gloves had to bow his back in the work just as his men did. It seemed to do these enemy enlisted men good to see their officers thus reduced to their own plane. Most of them became quite cheerful after they found that they weren't going to be scalped as they had been led to believe these aboriginal Americans were wont to do.

The condition of the roads is very bad and No Man's Land is a mess of shellholes and mud. A good many enemy dead are lying about and a few of our own men are lying where they were struck down by enemy fire this morning.

The doughboys are still advancing swiftly. In the air we are supreme. We are not in the position of the rat in the cage, as we were at Chateau-Thierry when enemy planes swooped down upon us and threw streams of machine-gun bullets into our ranks. This time the tables are turned. We see our aviators flying over the retreating enemy, dropping bombs and creating havoc.

13

No rest for the weary last night. We were on the go, or rather on the march, but the battery did not make much headway because of the bad condition under foot and the congestion of what roads are left since our bombardment of yesterday.

By inches we progressed to Seicheprey, the town which saw such terrific fighting between the 26th division and the Germans late last winter.

At daybreak we pulled into a wood and made camp for a short rest.

Everything is going along swimmingly, as all objectives were taken yesterday and things are moving along even better today, so reports say.

One thing is sure, our bull (prison) pens are becoming glutted with captured Boches. Some of them have lived in the United States and want to fraternize, but our fellows aren't much in the mood. These Germans are under real Yankee authority now. Some of them are used in constructing roads and others in carrying litters.

Several majors and colonels, one general, a couple of counts, and a prince were among the captives.

It seems as if America is coming across with what it takes to win the war. The Allies could not have done it without us. Of course, the war isn't over, by any means, but this battle is a darn good omen of ultimate victory for the Allies.

20

Campbell spied a garden just beyond town which had been planted for German consumption and he remarked, "Guys, what do you say we light out for the patch and get some fresh vegetables from under Heinie's nose?"

"The slope is in plain view of the enemy," I said, "but I'll take a chance on anything once."

Well, this garden was a paradise for hungry soldiers, and we had dug three sacks of potatoes, a sack of cabbages, and a basket of beans, when Shriek! Bang! came a Hun shell right into the patch.

"Goodby, boys," shouted Campbell as he started to make himself scarce.

"Grab a sack," I yelled at him, and he threw one over his shoulder and made for a little wagon we had found.

Another one exploded so close to us that it scattered dirt over us, but believe me, Grim and I were not going to throw up the job and leave the fruits of our labor. No, Sir! We piled the cabbage, beans and potatoes into the little wagon and then made tracks.

I was never so glad to get out of a place in my life. By the time we got fifty yards away that garden was being plowed up right by German bombardment of shells.

October 3

We are now hiking up to the line over newly captured territory. For four years this land had been in German hands.

A doughboy who was under fire for the first time Thursday was on the way back today on some detail. He told me that half of his company was wiped out by gas attack. These fellows, without actual battle experience, didn't detect gas in time, and the officers gave no command to put on masks. By the time they did get their masks on, if indeed they got them on at all, half of them were casualties; many of them died.

I feel sure that we are going to suffer heavy casualties in this drive, due to the nature of the German defense—enemy machine guns scattered through the forests in front of us like snakes in the grass.

4

At midnight we were awakened and prepared to move up to the front. We had breakfast and pulled out at 4:30.

They must be having hell up there, judging from the noise of the fierce cannonading which comes to our ears. From down the column comes the shout, "Is everybody happy?" And the chorus from every throat rings out, "Hell, yes!"

8 [Northeast of Montfaucon]

This morning Cliff Schwartz awakened us and I rolled out of my blankets hungry and thirsty. Our little signal detail is located in a trench to the left of the battery, just at the bottom of the hill on which the village of Montfaucon stands.

Cliff had obtained a paper from a passing Red Cross worker, and I read the German peace appeal which the enemy had made to President Wilson.

Art Long interrupted me with, "These whizz-bangs Fritz is putting over don't sound like peace to me, any more than the steel we are dousing him with."

"Well, any way you take it, boys, we've got him licked, and I believe that all of us who are lucky enough to live through this battle will get back home," replied Danny Slentz.

I stopped the discussion by announcing that I was going to get some mess.

"You're crazy, Doc," Cliff remarked. "A big H. E. [High Explosive] will pounce on you and leave nothing but a grease spot. Better wait for a while right here in the trench until things clear up a bit."

Two of our fellows had already been wounded by an explosion near our kitchen this morning, but I was determined to go back for some mess because I was so confounded hungry. Besides, shells seemed to be landing everywhere and one place seemed about as safe as another (or as dangerous), so I climbed out of the trench and made my way carefully back to the clump of bushes where our kitchen was concealed.

I had just got a panful of slum and started eating when I saw part of the temporary trench which I had left screened by an exploding shell. I thought it had come over the trench, but no—just then Smithy and Netterfield jumped out calling for stretchers.

I dropped my mess and ran to the trench and looked in. Poor Art was dead, one arm completely severed from his body. Danny had a hole in his stomach and we placed him on a stretcher and sent him back to the first aid station.

Dan Slentz looked at me with a smile on his face as we loaded him into the ambulance. I gave him a word of cheer and he said, "I don't know, Doc old boy. I've got a pretty bad wound in my stomach. You boys give 'em hell for me." [He died the same day.]

I have seen many die, but none have been so close to me as these fellows. I have worked with them and fought beside them every day since I joined the outfit, and they have been my best pals. But we must carry on, whatever happens.

11 [Exermont]

Paul and I went in search of a little warmth at midnight as we were chilled through. We found it in a first aid station where many wounded were being given treatment before being sent to hospitals by ambulance. It was a horrible scene, some of the fellows groaning, some with limbs shot off, others blinded.

17

I talked to a sergeant whom I had known back in Lorraine. He told me that replacements had filled the great gaps in the lines of the old regiments until only non-coms and a few officers remained of those who had come across with the Division.

He said the new men were filling the places well and got right into the spirit of the Division. Of course some of them can't survive the strain. The history books won't tell, for example, of the green private who blew off his trigger finger with his rifle yesterday because he couldn't stand the gaff up here.

30

Last night Fritz put on a whale of a bombardment, and I don't see how any of us escaped to tell the story. In the thick of it our communications were knocked out and I was detailed to repair the telephone line. How kind they are to me! Well, I thought of all the mean things I'd done in my life, breathed a little prayer, climbed out of my foxhole, and darted out into the inferno.

Flashes of exploding artillery at intervals lighted up the blackness of the night. Explosions of enemy shells on every hand and the scream of big ones going overhead to back areas added to the thunderous uproar so that I could not have heard my own voice had I dared to speak. Boy! I was glad when I came to that break in the line. I was splicing the wire when —Shriek! Bang! A ton of steel came over me. Just as I finished the job— hell's bells!—another hit knocked the line out in another place.

For once I lost my cocky self-assurance, and I wasn't so certain that I would ever see home and Mother again. But finally, after stumbling over the body of a dead German, I came upon the next break and spliced it in a hurry. Then I raced back to my hole after reporting communications in order.

Jack Skull has just been sent back to the hospital suffering from shell-shock. No wonder nerves give way and normal men go crazy.

November 1

Sommerance is filled with wounded and dying. I saw many die, but heard no complaint, no bitterness. Those who are not too badly maimed were enjoying smoking; others did nothing but sit or lie still.

4

German bombers visited us again last night. They must have dropped a hundred bombs or more on this town (Buzancy) during the raid.

It is difficult to describe our feelings during an air raid. We hear the hum of motors over our heads. Our anti-aircraft guns and machine guns fire into the darkness hoping against hope that they may be lucky enough to hit an enemy plane. Then a series of explosions shake the earth and throw up debris like a volcano in eruption. All we can do is to lie still while the cold sweat pops out on our foreheads, and wait for fortune's decision—life or death.

8 [driving on Sedan]

The battle has changed from a slow, bloody, inch-by-inch fight to a mad chase. The enemy is in full retreat.

11 [Harricourt]

Just before eleven, Lieutenant Bennett, looking at his watch, said to me, "In four minutes the war will be over."

At eleven the great rumble of artillery and small arms was stilled.

Eleven o'clock!

How strangely solemn, almost painful to ears long accustomed to the din and tumult of the front!

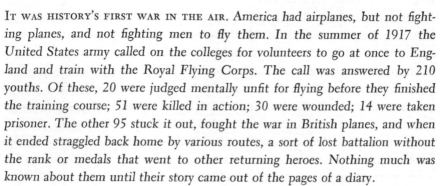

1918:   WAR IN THE AIR

It was history's first war in the air. *America had airplanes, but not fighting planes, and not fighting men to fly them. In the summer of 1917 the United States army called on the colleges for volunteers to go at once to England and train with the Royal Flying Corps. The call was answered by 210 youths. Of these, 20 were judged mentally unfit for flying before they finished the training course; 51 were killed in action; 30 were wounded; 14 were taken prisoner. The other 95 stuck it out, fought the war in British planes, and when it ended straggled back home by various routes, a sort of lost battalion without the rank or medals that went to other returning heroes. Nothing much was known about them until their story came out of the pages of a diary.*

The diarist lost his life in battle; but before that he had given instructions to one of his buddies, Elliott White Springs, to take the diary home with him "just in case." Mr. Springs, now a textile manufacturer, carried out the dead man's wishes. He published the diary in an edition of just 210 copies. But one of these got into the hands of an editor of Liberty, *then a popular magazine, and the piece was published serially under the title* War Birds. *Later a book publisher brought it out and it went into many printings.*

"We pilots were modest."

AN UNKNOWN AVIATOR

June 22 [1918]

I was some distance back of the patrol and saw a Hun two-seater about three miles across the lines so went for him. I expected about thirty seconds at close quarters under his tail and then to watch him go down in flames. It looked like cold meat.

I started my final dive about one thousand feet above him and opened fire at one hundred yards.

Then I got a surprise. I picked the wrong Hun. Just as I opened fire, he turned sharply to the left and I was doing about two hundred so couldn't turn but had to overshoot and half-roll back. As I half-rolled on top of him, he half-rolled too and when I did an Immelman, he turned to the right and forced me on the outside arc and gave his observer a good shot at me as I turned back the other way to cut him off from the other side.

I fired a burst from my turn but my shots went wild so pulled up and half-rolled on top of him again and opened fire from immediately above and behind. He stalled before I could get a burst in and side-slipped away from me but gave me a no-deflection shot at him when he straightened out.

I didn't have to make any allowance for his speed or direction and his observer was shooting at me. The observer dropped down in his cockpit so I suppose I killed him. But I couldn't get the pilot.

He put the plane in a tight spiral and I couldn't seem to get in position properly. Cal and Tiny Dixon came in about that time and everybody was shooting at him from all angles. I know he didn't have any motor because he came down very slowly and didn't attempt to maneuver.

We were firing from every conceivable angle but we couldn't seem to hit the tank or the pilot and every now and then he'd take a crack at me with his front gun when I'd try him head on.

He was a stout fellow. A good fighter and I hope he is still alive. If his observer had been any good I wouldn't be writing this now. He hit one of my front spars and that was all. I left him at one hundred feet as my engine was overheating and sputtering.

June 24

My motor got to acting funny and the water began to boil. It cut out a few times and I just did get back. I am going to ask for a new one. These Hispano Vipers are fine when they are all right but the slightest trouble bawls them all up.

June 25

Springs and I flew up to Dunkirk to get some champagne yesterday.

There was a brand new American major up there in a new Cadillac named Fowler. We turned our nose up at him but he insisted on being nice. He was so new the tags were still on his gold leaves and he didn't know how to salute—saluted like an Englishman.

When he heard why we'd come up he insisted on driving us into Dunkirk in his Cadillac. We got the champagne and he insisted on taking us into the Chapeau Rouge for a drink. We shot down a couple of bottles of champagne, and he was all right, we thought, even for a new Kiwi.

He kept on asking such simple questions. He wanted to know all about how our patrols were led and if we led any ourselves, and how we got along with the British. He acted awfully simple, just like an ordinary U. S. major, and we did the best we could to enlighten him as to the proper method of picking cold meat and bringing most of our men back.

His ideas were all wrong and we concluded that he must have been reading some of the books by the boys at home. We got a snoutful and he brought us back to the field and we invited him down to dinner at 85 and then he left.

We asked Sam what Fowler had done to get a gold leaf and he told us that Fowler had been out with the British since 1914 and had the Military Cross and had done about five hundred hours flying over the lines. The joke is certainly on us. But he ought to know better than to fill a pilot full of champagne and then ask him how good he is. To tell the truth I think we were very modest.

★

1919:   WILSON SIGNS THE TREATY OF VERSAILLES

☆

"I AM AS SURE of the ultimate triumph of our cause as I am that God reigns," said Woodrow Wilson. The cause was world peace. "Ultimate," perhaps. But even as he said it, he knew the peace he had made in his six grueling months in Paris to June of 1919 was a failure.

Other nations, each looking to its own interests in an atmosphere of realpolitik, had torpedoed his hope of a fair and democratic settlement. He had succeeded in embodying the League of Nations covenant in the treaty, but immediately this met with formidable opposition at home. His presentation of the treaty to the Republican-controlled Senate for ratification was followed by weeks of debate and watering down. Reservations were proposed to Article X, key to the great project of collective security, which Wilson would not accept.

In the autumn he tried to take his cause to the people over the head of the Senate. The effort was too much for his already overtaxed strength. On September 26, in Wichita, Kansas, he suffered a stroke. Six months later the Senate finally rejected the treaty.

Shortly before the trip to Paris the President engaged Edith Benham as White House social secretary. When Warren G. Harding was elected in 1920 Edith, now Mrs. James Helm, resigned. But in 1933, when the Franklin D. Roosevelts moved into the White House, she was called back to work. She served until Roosevelt's death in his fourth term and then worked on for President and Mrs. Harry S. Truman.

Early in 1952 Mrs. Helm announced her retirement, and in the fall of that year said good-by to the White House, after twenty-five years with three Presidential families. After such a long time, she says, the atmosphere of the White House envelops one. "The spirit of Abraham Lincoln most pervades the place, because he suffered so much personally . . . but there was tragedy in my time as well. I saw a great man stricken before his life work was finished. Not like Franklin Roosevelt, of whom one can write 'Well done,' Woodrow Wilson was cut off before his purpose was achieved."

From the social secretary's diary, here is a series of close-ups of Woodrow Wilson during the fateful mission to Paris.

"The people are behind him . . ."
EDITH BENHAM HELM

December 11 [1918, en route to Paris]

I have taken in a detective story for the President to read. He is very fond of them. He likes to play solitaire and plays nearly every night before going to bed. At the White House he is very apt to come in at noon when he has no appointments, and play for an hour before luncheon. I think Mrs. Wilson taught him to play, and that he never did it much until lately.

December 13—Plount, Brittany

As we neared the harbor [at Brest] a squadron of French ships came out from the land on our left, made a fine sweep and came into the harbor behind us.

Brest is a socialistic port, very turbulent at best I believe, and the Mayor is very Bolshevik. Jusserand had cautioned Mr. Wilson about him. Having arrived at a standstill on this raft, more black-coated gentlemen, some with broad sashes of tricolor, stepped up to Mr. Wilson and one ponderous person who turned out to be the Mayor started an eloquent address to which Mr. Wilson listened with polite attention and made a reply, neither one understanding the other.

We made two stops before dinner and at each one deputations of the military and civil authorities came aboard with wonderful bunches of flowers. They look upon the President as almost divine.

At the station in Paris, Mrs. Wilson and the President were met by the President of France and Mme. Poincaré. He is a small, rather insignificant-looking man and she is rather handsome in a kind of way, with very painted lips.

We had scarcely arrived in the house when we had to get ready for the grand luncheon at the Elysée, the French President's palace.

I was glad to see dear old Joffre, to whom I spoke after luncheon. I also saw the famous Clemenceau, who is very little, very old, and no hair. Colonel House says Clemenceau has quite a keen sense of humor, speaking English perfectly, and said in discussing the Armistice terms, "Well, we have taken everything away from the Kaiser but his breeches."

December 26, London

We walked along a beautifully decorated covered way and little girls strewed flowers in our paths, and then reached the station platform where the Mayor of Dover received us, and dressy-looking gentry in gray jute wigs were also there. One of the gray wigs read a speech for the Mayor, who had an imposing person with a mace beside him. The President replied very happily and then we got on the train and pulled out.

The train—a Pullman—was one of the royal coaches and very handsome. The President had a conference going up with Lord Reading.

Arrived at Charing Cross station. The King and Queen and Princess Mary were there to welcome our royalty, and the Queen is surely a much-maligned woman by her photographs, for she is very handsome, very tall, and has a superb carriage, but I noticed both she and her Lady-in-waiting had the busty, small-waist figure of 1890.

Mr. Wilson came in [at Buckingham Palace] looking tired. He has had a hard day and has dreaded the trip. He is shy and has to be met more than half-way, and the English are shy too, but there is no doubt but that the English people met him more than half-way. He sat by the fire and laughed at our chatter, always a little alarmed someone would hear us.

Tonight was the great event of my life over here, the state banquet. It is the first time in four years and the first one, of course, that a President of the United States had ever attended, and the English seemed to feel the historic importance as much as we did.

The King and Queen and President and Mrs. Wilson appeared in the next room. The Queen is surely a royal figure and wears her crown or diadem or whatever it is called, her orders and ribbons, splendidly. They walked around and spoke to us and all the women had to curtsey. Then they all went to the center of the room and the men all filed in and were presented.

I asked Lord Curzon to tell me who they were and he did as they went along. Every one looked like his picture save Winston Churchill, who is blond and quite insignificant-looking.

Mrs. Wilson was much amused last night. Some woman came up to her and asked if she was a Quakeress. Mrs. Wilson, surprised, said, "No," and the woman said, "Oh, I thought you were because you wore no tiara."

Mrs. Wilson said, "I would wear one, but, you see, my husband can't afford to give me one."

Jan. 3, 1919—Rome

At one place the King, Queen, President and Mrs. Wilson went on a balcony and showed themselves to the immense crowd below.

Mrs. Wilson has a high priest in black with a chain and two acolytes in red guarding the entrance to her door and living anteroom. The President has the same, and he is always so funny about his royal state. He waves his hand comprehensively toward them and says, "Will you be so kind as to indicate to one of these gentlemen that I should like a glass of water?"

January 8

At Modane, the border town in the Alps, a cable was brought in announcing [Theodore] Roosevelt's death. The President sat quiet for a moment then asked Close to take his dictation and sent the message, which was this: "May I offer my deep sympathy in the loss of your distinguished husband, the news of whose death has just reached and deeply grieved me." He thought for a moment and changed it to "shocked." Speaking later of Colonel Roosevelt and his life, he said he had no constructive policy to his record. He saw the evils of the trusts and enacted certain laws, but he left the constructive part to later legislation.

January 10

It seemed too good to be true to get back to Paris again and have a little rest.

Mrs. Wilson and I had to go out the afternoon of our arrival to hunt up presents. These dear people are suffering for the gifts royalty makes and this traveling like a king is a very expensive business. Doctor Grayson inquired and found at Buckingham that Poincaré, who had been there with the same number of people the Wilsons had, gave $800 in tips. That was the usual amount.

Yesterday at luncheon the President spoke of the delays the English are putting in the way of the conference and trying to discredit it in the eyes of everyone by making it appear that it is not of much importance. I judge Clemenceau is being annoying for siding with the English, but the President said he could put the screws on in the matter of the loan. He also dropped a fearful bombshell to the effect of a surprise he intended springing on them by coming back. So far as I can judge they hope to delay things as long as possible for him, and as soon as he gets away make combines and arrange things as they choose. That is, Lloyd George and

Clemenceau and I imagine Orlando. That he hoped to defeat by coming back.

January 14

This evening is one of the first times I have had a really long talk with the President about really vital things, for conversation is usually more or less general. Tonight Dr. Grayson was out, and Mrs. Wilson, the President and I were alone.

The Conference is very much wrought up over the leakage of news to the press. They have tried to give it out through a central news bureau or committee, but very important things are constantly filtering, with constant bad feeling with the reporters. The leakage is entirely with the French, the President feels.

Mrs. Wilson spoke of what Mr. Henry White has said to her this afternoon with regard to the inadvisability of the President's returning to America. He thought from what people told him that it would be in the nature of an anticlimax if the President came back again and that it would be better if he could settle most of the great questions before he left.

The President said he agreed with the anticlimax part and he could see much against it, but he felt Mr. White took the viewpoint of the newspapers and he could not consider them representative of the American feeling as they were controlled by large moneyed interests and not in touch with the people. The President said that he always found out if you told the people the truth and pointed out the ideals to be followed, they invariably backed you up.

January 18

At dinner the President asked Dr. Grayson to carry down to General Smuts a copy of his draft of the constitution of the League of Nations. It was, of course, such an important document and still so secret that Grayson had to deliver it into the hands of Smuts himself. Smuts had written what the President considered one of the best expositions of the aims of the League of Nations and its practical application and constitution. Someone asked the President if he hadn't written most of this present draft himself, and he said no, that the original was made by an English society. He had made certain additions and changes to that, then Smuts had presented certain other features and a very statesmanlike addition and he (the President) had made another draft of his own which he had sent down to Smuts for criticism and change.

January 22

Mrs. Wilson is unusually self-contained, admits scarcely anyone to her friendship, though always wonderfully gracious. Her smile and charm are proverbial. I do not believe there has been any other woman who has occupied the position she has who has her beauty and charm and is so good. She is very quiet about her dislikes, but a very intense and very loyal friend. There never was anyone with a keener sense of humor. He has the same, but she is a born mimic. I have never seen anyone enjoy anything more than he does one of her stories or experiences after she has been somewhere without him, for she always sees something funny.

The Serbian Minister told Mrs. Wilson at dinner at the Lansings last night that a Princess de Rohan had said she had heard Mrs. Wilson was quite democratic—meaning, she supposed, common—but he said he had heard Mrs. Wilson was descended from one of the first princesses of the original natives of America, the Princess Pocahontas, and now she would come to call. Mrs. Wilson said that when I met her I must tell her that Mrs. Bolling lives at the Castle of Powhatan (Hotel Powhatan in Washington).

January 29

The long-expected clouds are growing around the Conference, for the President had a very bad day today. These smaller meetings are called conversations and are necessarily behind closed doors. I think the press criticism of closed sessions is not well founded, for the President said he never believed in all public meetings, for every premier of the big and particularly little countries would be talking for the benefit of their people at home and much time would be wasted in fruitless orating. He believes the results of all discussions—I mean resolutions adopted and all treaties made—should be absolutely public and that there should be no more secret treaties or understandings such as the Bolsheviks discovered in Russian archives.

The "conversation" today was a most exhausting one. I think this has been one of the hardest he has had, and I fear there will be many more. There is no doubt the people of every country are solidly behind him. The politicians know this and are afraid, and I imagine the governments, knowing this, while outwardly friendly are putting every spoke they can in the wheels.

He said this is the test of the League of Nations, and if the majority of the nations of the world didn't want it he might just as well give up and go home.

The longer I am over here, the more I hear, the more I am convinced that the old order of things has gone and the masses will have a change. It was Bolshevism in Russia and we can't have that at home, and the only way seems making changes in our social and economic fabric. I don't advocate this as a disciple of socialism. It is to apply remedies before the Bolshevist plague spreads around the world.

February 1

Mr. George Creel came to luncheon and gave an account of a trip he has just completed through Poland, Czechoslovakia, and those other mysterious old-new countries. He brought back some posters and the inscriptions translated read, "We want a Wilson Peace." He went among the poor people, who regard the President as a new popular Saint. His pictures hung in many windows and the people told Mr. Creel that they wanted Wilson to reign over them. The President says that such expressions make him very nervous, for he fears the revulsion which is bound to come when they find he can't do all they hope.

April 11

I am rather putting the cart before the horse, for I didn't write yesterday and while today's memories are fresh I thought I would put them down. The great event, of course, was the Queen of Roumania's coming for luncheon.

She was invited at one and the President arranged to meet her upstairs. Harts and Grayson met her at the door and conducted her and her party upstairs. Of course, the President and Mrs. Wilson were ready promptly, and we all went upstairs to wait, looking out of the windows of the drawing room so the President and Mrs. Wilson would have time to go out to the head of the stairs to meet her.

Nothing infuriates the President like waiting or being late. The Queen had come to establish a propaganda for Roumania, a greater Roumania, and she did the worst thing she could in being nearly twenty-five minutes late. Every moment we waited I could see from the cut of the President's jaw that a slice of the Dobruja, or Roumania, was being lopped off.

April 21

These are very trying days for the President with the continual wrangling over the Italian question. Lloyd George and Clemenceau had agreed day before yesterday to stand by him and refuse Fiume to the Italians. This morning—no, yesterday morning—they came and said they had been considering it over night and had decided they must stand by the pact of London. Today the President said that Orlando, for whom he says he has not only a liking but a real affection—and I haven't often heard him say that—made a very moving speech at the Big Four Conference. He read this speech, which was really Italy's ultimatum of what she must have or withdraw, and then when the end came he gave a little gulp, went to the window and sobbed piteously.

April 24

The house is just as tense today as it was the day before war was declared at home. At luncheon Ike Hoover came in to say Mr. Kerr, Mr. Balfour's secretary, was there and he wanted to know if the President would come to Mr. Lloyd George's apartment, as they looked on that as neutral territory and would prefer going there to coming here. The President said, "What children!"

May 7

At luncheon the President said how he hates to meet any of the Germans. He wouldn't mind the old crew so much, but not these nondescripts. A *New York Times* correspondent asked him what he thought about the peace, if he felt it was all right, and he said, "Yes, as far as it was possible and the Germans would be the only ones to object," but he didn't feel it was unduly severe for them.

May 22

Yesterday the President had a sick headache and he really does look very thin and bad. Mrs. Wilson hoped he would go for a game of golf, but he had an appointment at four.

June 24

The great excitement of the day was the Treaty signing. About six Mrs. Wilson saw a French officer jump out of the motor before it came to a stop, and dash up the street pavement into the house. Then the President came down a few minutes after, from the Conference, to tell her the Germans had agreed to sign. After a little while pandemonium broke loose, sirens moaning and guns being fired and the church bells ringing.

The road to Versailles was spaced at intervals by policemen, and there seemed an endless procession of cars. Arrived at Versailles we turned into the broad Avenue de Paris, a splendid wide avenue, imposing always, and doubly so then, with a double line of cavalry, each blue-coated poilu with a banner on his lance. The effect was a lovely one of misty horizon blue and the colors of the banners.

In the courtyard was a company of the Garde Républicaine, stunning figures in white trousers, cuirasses, and helmets with a long horse tail. They lined the staircase we went up. The setting was certainly all that could be desired for impressiveness. The demand for seats was so great that a number of people had to be put in a room adjoining the long Galerie des Glaces, and consequently saw none of the signing.

The Galerie des Glaces is a long room running along the front of the Palace.

A ripple of suppressed interest passed over the place, for we knew the Germans were near, and, attended by an officer from each of the Allied nations, they came in. They were certainly a contrast to the men of blood and iron who had signed in '71 in that room, or stood around when the Empire of Germany was made there, and very different from the Hindenburgs and Von Tirpitzes who succeeded them.

There were two miserable-looking, ill, shaking men. They looked like druggists—second-rate ones—tall and thin, not even scholarly-looking. They did carry themselves with a certain dignity and, because they were so wretched physically, I couldn't hate them.

They were taken to their seats directly in front of us, with their backs to us, and their legs shook when they sat down, though when they came to sign they walked with perfect composure, and seemed quite at ease later, and when they went out.

When the President went to sign with the Americans we stood to see, but I could only see the top of his head. He said he realized he was very excited, because after signing "Woodrow" with perfect ease he had difficulty signing "Wilson."

As the delegates walked to their seats he looked at Mrs. Wilson and smiled.

1921:   A VISITING VIP IS MISUNDERSTOOD

CLARE SHERIDAN, British sculptor and writer, widow of a World War hero, was a celebrity when she came to America in 1921. She was known the world over for her portrait busts of famous people—Princess Patricia, Margot Asquith, Guglielmo Marconi, Mohandas Gandhi. But her diary of the visit to America is dedicated "To those I have met in this country who have not misunderstood me." Those who did misunderstand were puzzled because she had recently been to Russia and had portrayed in her sculpture both Nikolai Lenin and Leon Trotsky. What business, they asked, had a woman of top-drawer social connections in London doing that? Their questions in turn puzzled Clare Sheridan. But if America was sometimes incomprehensible to her, she adds emphatically, "Never was it dull!"

"*I have been slapped and kissed . . .*"
CLARE CONSUELO SHERIDAN
(born 1885)

February 2 [1921], The Biltmore, New York

What a funny life! I do not know myself, nor what I have become, and yet when I look in the glass I am the same.

I seem to be a machine—I have no soul; rapidly I am losing all mind.

From morning till night newspaper reporters ask me questions, I am told I have to submit—if I were impatient or cross they would write something nasty. So I am amiable! I go on talking the same stuff about Lenin and Trotsky! How they would laugh if they could hear me!

I've been photographed in this room over and over; by flashlight, by electric light, by daylight. In day dress, in evening dress, in Russian head dress, in work dress, with child, with roses, and so on!

I go out to lunch with a reporter in the taxi—and what luncheons: hen luncheons in Fifth Avenue! Lovely women with bare white chests, pearls, and tulle sleeves—never saw such clothes—and apparently all for themselves. There is never a man. They even pay one another compliments. I wonder if they can be contented.

Today I lunched with Rose Post, who is a great kind dear. I had a very pleasant woman on my right, but on my left was a Mrs. Butler, whose husband is president of Columbia University. She wouldn't speak to me— she couldn't bear even to look at me. I expect she thought I was a Bolshevik.

I went from there to see Mrs. Otto Kahn. She received me among Botticellis and tapestries. It was a beautiful room, and one had a feeling of repose. Money can buy beautiful things, but it cannot buy atmosphere, and that was of her own creating.

She dropped me at the *Vanity Fair* office, and I went up to the fifteenth floor and saw Mr. Crowninshield and Mr. Conde Nast, editors respectively of *Vanity Fair* and *Vogue.* I knew them in London.

They were all very humorous, and there is a good deal to be humorous about at this moment, where I am concerned!

"Crownie" was an angel; he and Mr. Nast decided to give a dinner for me. A "fun" dinner, all of people who "do" things, what he called "tightrope dancers" and "high divers"—not social swells! He offers me a peace room to write in—a lawyer to protect me, and advances of money! Truly I have good friends!

At six when I got back to the Biltmore, Colin Agnew, whose firm gave me an exhibition in London last year, rushed in—he goes to England on the *Aquitania* tomorrow; he says I may have the firm's flat on East 55th St. till April! What a godsend: a private place in which to lay my weary head, and a home for Dick [her small son]. How happy I shall be! Colin says the only trouble is that the heating apparatus occasionally breaks down. This is good news, for central heating is asphyxiating. If I open the windows I freeze, and if I shut them I suffocate. Dick drinks ice water all day and says he likes America!

February 6

I dined with Maxine Elliot, and had on one side of me Mr. George Creel, and on the other Mr. Swope. The latter is the editor of the *World*.

In England one hesitates to accept to dine out unless one is very sure who is going to be there. Here one can go at random, it may be strange, it may be incomprehensible, but never is it dull!

February 7, 13 East 55th Street

Mr. Wiley sent his secretary and his car to convey me to the *Times* office. There in the building we lunched, and I was the only woman with seven men, all of them interesting. Mr. Miller, Mr. Ochs, Mr. Ogden, and so on, it was rather alarming, but they gave me orchids.

February 9

Mr. Liveright, my publisher, fetched me and took me to the Ritz, where we dined with Mr. Pulitzer, Mr. and Mrs. Swope, and Mr. B. M. Baruch. Mr. Baruch (whose name I mistook for Brooke) has white hair, fine features and stands 6 ft. 4. I gathered from the general conversation that I was talking to someone whom I should have heard of, and as I could think of no distinguished Brooke but Rupert Brooke the poet, I asked if he was related. And then Mr. Baruch rather reprovingly spelt his name for me. Instantly by a faint glimmer of memory "Wall Street" came to my mind, and I seemed to have heard in London that he was a friend of Winston. He was interesting and unprejudiced.

February 13

I lunched with "The Kingfisher" as we call Mrs. Cornelius Vanderbilt in London! I was rather disappointed with her Fifth Avenue palazzo, it does not compare with the Otto Kahns and has not the atmosphere. There was a beautiful Turner in one of the drawing rooms and a gallery full of Corots and Millets, but they were not very interesting or decorative, or else there were too many of them.

After lunch when the women left the dining room someone hazarded a remark to the effect that the big rooms were pleasant with nobody in them. Our hostess said that was not an idea with which she was in sympathy, that she thought a big house should be full of people and as many enjoy it as possible, "whatever I have I want to share," she said, and then turning to me, "Please tell that to the Bolsheviks—". Then suddenly, conversation drifted onto me and my plans.

I was asked if when I returned I was going to live in Ireland, hadn't my father got a place there? I answered that I lived where there was work, and, therefore, I might remain where I was, or go to Russia.

Mrs. Vanderbilt looked rather surprised, and asked whether Russia paid better than any other country. That I did not know, but certain it is that any country pays more than England!

Altogether, it was rather unpleasant, and I left as soon as I could, and wondering, as I walked home, why she had asked me to her house.

February 14, The William Penn Hotel, Pittsburgh

At 6:50, on my arrival, I was received by Mr. and Mrs. Robinson and their son, who are managers in the firm of Heinz Pickles, 57 varieties! Emil Fuchs, who is doing a Heinz memorial, told them I was coming. They had a car and drove me to the William Penn Hotel. I refused their invitation to dinner as I felt rather tired. After dinner some reporters came to see me in my room.

February 15

Mrs. Robinson fetched me at ten A.M. and took me first for a drive in the town and then to the Heinz factory. The sun was struggling to break through the mist of grime caused by the factory smoke. Mrs. Robinson apologised for the lack of beauty of the town. She was wrong, it was terribly beautiful. Everything looked like a Whistler picture, but of course there is no color, no nature, and one longs for these things after a time.

When we drove to the Heinz factory we went in first to the Administration Building; the hall of which is lined with marble, has marble columns, a fountain in the middle, marble busts on pedestals all around, and a frieze by an English artist, representing the various Heinz processes. Mr. Robinson came and appointed a guide to show us all over. It is the first factory I have ever seen that was interesting. It really is wonderful to see the flat piece of tin go into the machine, become round and soldered, move along to have its bottom put on, and without stopping, go careering along overhead and down to the next floor to be mechanically filled with baked beans, and have its lid put on.

From the moment the flat piece of tin gets into the machine to the moment when it is sealed up full is four and a quarter minutes. The tin manufacturing room was delightful, little bright, glistening, shining tins, ran, rolled and leapt, as it seemed overhead and all round, dancing fairy-like to the music and hum of the machinery. The space over one's head was full of them, impelled in different directions at different speeds on different levels, on little iron ways. The process itself interested me, but when I had grasped the process, I just stood in the middle of the hall and gave way to the impression of the whole, and it had the effect of making me laugh outright, it was so ridiculously joyous.

February 21, New York

As for America! Since I landed I have been metaphorically slapped and kissed alternately until I'm so bewildered I have almost lost judgment. Yet I claim nothing for myself but the right, as a citizen of the world to be free, to think as I like, and to speak as I think.

March 11

Mr. Pulitzer dropped me at the Pierpont Morgans for tea. Florrie Grenfell and her husband are staying there, and have been yachting with them in the Indies. Mrs. Morgan and her daughter and son were there, and mother looked like their sister. The atmosphere of restraint and politeness among themselves gave one the impression of being with Austrian Royalties.

Florrie Grenfell took me over to the library. It is a wonderful place, and inconceivable that it is a private possession. Everything is arranged and labeled as though it were a public museum. Even the bibelots have their labels, and the smallest thing on a shelf is a priceless work of art. There was a little bronze Benvenuto Cellini, a Michelangelo baby head, a Botticelli on an easel. I asked if the place were open certain days of the week to the public, but was told *no*.

When we came out, I saw two men leaning against the lamp post. Florrie Grenfell said they were detectives. I asked her how she knew—she said she had been there long enough to know them by sight! Round the angle of the block, opposite the front door was another. I observed that this was rather fantastic; but the answer is that the police say they will not be responsible for Mr. Morgan's life, and he has already been shot at! It seems to me that if he metaphorically shook hands with the world, he'd be as safe as, for instance, our Prince of Wales. The world reacts to one's own attitude.

March 19

I dined with Mrs. Willard Straight, almost the nicest woman I've met since I arrived here. She gives one a feeling of sincerity and absence of pose. She is real. It was a delightful party, the Walter Lippmanns and

Bullitts and B. Berenson, all people I like, were there. Her house has the right atmosphere.

March 26

We have been here nearly two months, and in those two months we have learnt that American ideas are on the whole, good ideas.

April 3

Dined with the Swopes, it being Mrs. Swope's birthday party.

I had a long talk with Barney Baruch who came in afterwards. I had not seen him since that bewildering night when I first arrived, and thought he was Mr. Brooke!

I've never forgotten him, he has a dominating personality, and a nose and a brow that I keep modelling in my mind while I am talking to him. But he is "the king with two faces," he can look hard and Satanic one minute, kind and gentle the next. He has a great love of Winston, and a loyalty to Wilson. His ideas about life and the world in general are fine. He has the dynamic force of a Revolutionary, but his idealism is to get the world straight sanely, calmly and constructively, not violently, bitterly and destructively.

He believes in an ideal League of Nations, and in reasoning rather than arming. The answer to all that is, that nothing gets done at all except by force, bitterness and violence, and so Russia is the only one among us who has gotten something done! Perhaps if there were more Barney Baruchs in the world something might evolve, who knows? I don't really know enough about him and his life, and to what purpose he puts his activities.

He talked to me a good deal about his father and mother, especially his mother. He has that Jewish love of family.

It always amuses me in this country when people ask me if Russia is entirely run by Jews. I didn't meet half as many there as I have met here!

April 5

Dined with Mr. Otto Kahn at his house, a small party, and went on afterwards to Carnegie Hall to hear the Philadelphia Orchestra which was heavenly.

At dinner we discussed the psychology of men and women here. He has a fine analytical mind. We talked of the American woman being starved emotionally. He said about the position of women in different countries, "Here they are an ornament, in England they are an object, in France they are a passion." It is a good summing up.

We talked about Bolshevism. He had an amusing point of view, so different from the usual "foaming-at-the-mouth" reactionary. He said that the Russians are naturally an anarchistic and rebellious people incapable of self-government. That Bolshevism was a form of self-expression that would pass, as everything would pass—but why, he said, take it so tragically? It was none of our business! The world had lost its sense of humor. Our attitude toward the Russian experiment should be that of interested spectators. But the idea of getting cross about it, of exchanging furious notes, of sending soldiers to "walk up the hill and down again." It was ridiculous! He talked of Bolshevism as a great play, and the Bolsheviks as being living actors, fulfilling their part dramatically, but that the play, acted in French, or English, or Italian, was another thing. What would succeed in Russia would fail in translation.

April 6

I dined with Kenneth Durant and Ernestine Evans, Crystal Eastman and a young Art critic from Boston. We went afterwards to see *Emperor Jones*. This is practically a one man play, and its success is due to the genius of Gilpin, the colored actor. It is a grim and powerful representation, that the "grand Guignol" might well produce.

The only thing is, that it deals so entirely with the psychology of the colored race that no European would quite understand it. I would have lost a lot of it if Kenneth hadn't explained here and there. I see the Negro in a new light. He used to be rather repulsive to me, but obviously he is human, has been very badly treated, and suffers probably a good deal from the terrific race prejudice that prevails here.

April 16

Colonel William Boyce Thompson sent his car for me at twelve, and I drove out to his place in Yonkers. It interested me to hear that Wilson is the author of a work entitled *The New Freedom* which was discovered at the headquarters of the I.W.W. and declared to be seditious literature!

I got home at six o'clock and an hour later dined with a compatriot, Frank McDermott, and having nothing planned we drove to Broadway. This is a marvelous place at night. The whole locality is illuminated with electric advertisements. They baffle description. The American advertiser, not content with lighting up his advertisement, must needs have movement in those lights. All of them dance, twinkle, rain, run, sparkle, circulate. It is metaphorically a shrieking competition. There are even a pair of dogs pulling a sleigh, the man in the sleigh flicks his electric whip in the air, and the dogs just gallop! Far fewer lights on a Coronation or a Peace night in London, bring forth crowds into the street, walking arm in arm "to see the illuminations." In Broadway it seems to be a perpetual Coronation Night!

We went into the "Capitol" film palace. The first time I had been to one. It is gigantic, and the house was packed. An opera sized orchestra started off by playing Wagner to us. The house listened intently. The American public is very musical, even if it has gone expecting to see a film, it will listen to Wagner without whispering.

Finally we sat through a rather dull film play.

Washington, April 22

I went to tea with Mrs. William Hard where a great many people drifted in and out. Among them Alice Longworth, with whom I made a date, and Mrs. Brandeis and her daughter, who invited me to go to tea on the morrow to meet Mr. Justice Brandeis. I have a great curiosity to see him, I have heard his name over and over again. Everyone says to me, "You should do a head of Brandeis." I am told he looks like Lincoln.

I met "Mr. Baker of the Mint" as he was described to me when I asked who he was. A man with a very fine, characteristically American face, and a charming personality. Later, when everyone else went on to a ball, Mr. Baker took me for a drive in his car before dropping me at the Shoreham. I like him, I like his face, and I like his talk, although he is "the man of the mint" who refuses to buy Soviet gold. I asked him why, "Is it because you are a very high principled man and you feel the gold belongs to someone else?"

"I am a high principled man but it is not for any principle that I will not buy Soviet gold."

"So much the better," I said, "there will be more for England and we want it—and it will come to you just the same I suppose in the end, only it will come through us!"

April 23

Lunched with Sinclair Lewis at the Shoreham. He is full of imagination. One of the few Americans I have met who is not submerged by domesticity, although he is married.

He tells me he wrote four or five novels before he wrote *Main Street,* but they were not successes. I asked him why that had not discouraged him. He laughed, he said it was no use being discouraged, that writing novels was all he could do, he might starve at it, but he was incapable of any other form of work. (Truly an artist!)

He had expected some people would like *Main Street,* but he had not expected it to sell. It was a great joke being famous, though sometimes a great bore. He was extremely funny about it.

I went to tea with Mrs. McCormick, then on to see Mr. Justice Brandeis, who expected me at his chambers. He was very nice, though rather shy.

He certainly is extremely like Lincoln, but a Lincoln who has not suffered. Certainly a fine head to do. I am told he is one of the big brains of the United States.

April 24

I lunched with Senator Henry Cabot Lodge and his daughter-in-law, Mrs. Lodge, and a beautiful girl, his granddaughter. Although I hardly knew the Senator I feel as if he were a relation. He was, until recently, a trustee for the children under my mother-in-law's will.

I dined at Medill McCormick's. A big party at small tables in several rooms. I sat next to Mr. Richard Washburn Child on one side. He looks very young. He asked me why I was "here," which I took to mean America, not Washington, and I found myself telling him everything that I haven't told even some of my best friends. He seemed to understand my feeling about the adventure of life. Some people never awaken, others start with their eyes wide open.

I wish I could decide whether I want to live in America, France or Russia, and whether I should like my immediate headquarters to be in New York or Washington.

I wish I knew how much the people who are nice to me really like me, or how much I am a curiosity.

I wish I knew whether I am happier than anyone else or happy at all.

May 16, Philadelphia

Going through people's private grounds seems to be no offense in this country. Some time ago—at Bernardsville, New Jersey, I walked for miles unmolested through people's woods and gardens, enjoyed their fountains and their flowers and their lawns. Yesterday was much the same. We rode peacefully, not "across country," but across property. Honorably sticking to the paths, of course.

People don't surround their grounds with walls and hedges and ditches here as in England. There appear to be no lodges and gates and furious people. A gateless entrance is a great temptation, it looks to me like an invitation. No Communist could war against these conditions.

[Los Angeles] October 31

Charlie Chaplin arrived in Los Angeles today at noon, on his return from Europe. I met him at dinner. We were just a party of four at the Lehrs'. It has been a wonderful evening—I seem to have been talking heart to heart with one who understands, who is full of deep thought and deep feeling. He is full of ideals and has a passion for all that is beautiful. A real artist. He talked a great deal about his trip to England. It had been, I gathered, one of the big emotions of his life. He left, as he said, "poor and unknown" to return ten years later famous.

A good country to belong to, we agreed, but not a country "for a creative artist," he advised me to remain where I am. And then, in spite of his emotional, enthusiastic temperament, with a soundness of judgment that surprised me, he said: "Don't get lost on the path of propaganda. Live your life of an artist; the other goes on—always."

January 9, 1922

I have wondered a good deal about America and Americans during the year I have spent here. They have amused, surprised and bewildered me, but it was not until I came to Boston that I felt I was at home. Even the town is English. There was Beacon Street, with its long row of individual small houses just as in London, and every one had a street door. I never went into an apartment. People's rooms seemed to be full of books instead of American beauty roses.

I am glad I have been to Boston, it seems to complete one's great perplexity concerning the United States. Here is a country that is composed of such widely different towns as Washington, Philadelphia, San Francisco, Los Angeles, all as different from one another as they are different from New York, and as different as New York is from Boston.

I wonder there is any co-ordination of movement or feeling at all in such a country. I wonder there is any political unity, any fraternity, and yet there is more than all that; there exists a national patriotic spirit.

1927: A JOURNALIST FIGHTS FOR SACCO AND VANZETTI

WHEN ORGANIZED LABOR *began the long struggle to broaden its influence after the Civil War, the weapons used against it were many and varied. In addition to the more obvious ones—the company union, labor espionage, provocation, lockouts, strikebreaking, the resort to head-on violence—there was misuse of the courts to condemn the leaders.*

The pattern was set in 1877 when nineteen Pennsylvania coal miners, allegedly members of a secret conspiratorial society called the Molly Maguires, were tried for murder, convicted on the flimsiest of evidence, and hanged. Other cases followed over the years, among them the Chicago Haymarket trial and the conviction in San Francisco of Tom Mooney and Warren Billings.

Nobody can assess the guilt of these men now and nobody could prove it then. But on one point the record permits of no question—the conduct of many such trials was shamefully unjust.

Popular outrage at this kind of judicial misconduct reached its peak in the case of Nicola Sacco and Bartolomeo Vanzetti. These men were Italian immigrants. Both had taken part in strikes. Both were anarchists. On May 5, 1920, they were arrested as suspects in an attempted holdup in Bridgewater, Massachusetts, but shortly afterward a more serious charge was brought against them, namely the murder of a paymaster and his helper in a $16,000 holdup at South Braintree, Massachusetts.

A hint of the kind of justice they were to get came in Judge Webster Thayer's instructions to the jury during the trial of Vanzetti on the earlier charge: "This man, although he may not have actually committed the crime attributed to him, is nevertheless morally culpable because he is the enemy of our existing institutions."

In the murder trial, a verdict of guilty was brought in on July 14, 1921. But to many Americans it had become all too clear that these men were being tried for one thing and punished for another. Of the trial Felix Frankfurter, later to become a justice of the U.S. Supreme Court, wrote:

> By systematic exploitation of the defendants' alien blood, their imperfect knowledge of English, their unpopular social views and their opposition to the war, the district attorney invoked against them a riot of political passion and patriotic sentiment; and the trial judge connived at—one had almost written co-operated in—the process.

There followed a six-year battle to save the condemned men. In the course of it Lawrence Letherman, Boston agent of the Department of Justice, admitted in an affidavit that government agents were of the general opinion "that Sacco and Vanzetti had nothing to do with the South Braintree crime." And in 1925 another convict, Celestino F. Madeiros, confessed the crime.

Nevertheless, Judge Thayer denied a motion for retrial, and in 1927 the Massachusetts Supreme Court rejected an appeal. As thousands gathered around the statehouse in Boston Governor Alvan T. Fuller appointed three men, President A. Lawrence Lowell of Harvard, President Samuel W. Stratton of Massachusetts Institute of Technology, and Robert Grant, a retired judge, to decide whether Sacco and Vanzetti should live or die. They ruled for death. On August 23, 1927, the execution was carried out.

As the legal struggle neared its end protest was heard across the land and around the world. Most powerful and memorable was that of Heywood Broun, journalist extraordinary, who, up to that time, had expended his brilliance mainly on sports and the lighter side of life.

With a wide and avid following, Broun was one of the major attractions of New York's very attractive newspaper, the World. After distinguishing himself by going four years to Harvard without graduating, he started his career on the New York Telegraph at $20 a week. He was over six feet tall and two chairs broad; notoriously lazy, showily sloppy, and as full of quirks as an aging ballerina. But at his typewriter, especially when he was doing sports, he earned forgiveness for everything. He also earned, after moving in as World columnist from 1921 on, the then fabulous salary of $350 a week. Up to a point, he was allowed to write what he pleased, and he continued to write what he pleased beyond that point.

He went far and away beyond it in his effort to save the lives of Sacco and Vanzetti. His part in the protest on their behalf came as an explosive awakening out of the easy tenor of his literary way, a confrontation with evil which he had to fight, let the jobs fall where they may. As he recalled half a dozen years later, "The Sacco-Vanzetti case moved me to write the first violent newspaper pieces I had ever done. And pretty soon I was out of a job. Never since that time has it been possible to get back entirely into the mood of the kindly commentator on the less important phases of the passing show."

Here, from his column, "It Seems to Me," are the pieces to which he refers.

"It is death condemning life."

HEYWOOD BROUN (1888-1939)

August 5, 1927

When at last Judge Thayer in a tiny voice passed sentence upon Sacco and Vanzetti, a woman in the courtroom said with terror: "It is death condemning life!"

The men in Charlestown Prison are shining spirits, and Vanzetti has spoken with an eloquence not known elsewhere within our time. They are too bright, we shield our eyes and kill them. We are the dead, and in us there is not feeling nor imagination nor the terrible torment of lust for justice. And in the city where we sleep smug gardeners walk to keep the grass above our little houses sleek and cut whatever blade thrusts up a head above its fellows.

"The decision is unbelievably brutal," said the Chairman of the Defense Committee, and he was wrong. The thing is worthy to be believed. It has happened. It will happen again, and the shame is wider than that which must rest upon Massachusetts. I have never believed that the trial of Sacco and Vanzetti was one set apart from many by reason of the passion and prejudice which encrusted all the benches. Scratch through the varnish of any judgment seat and what will you strike but hate thick-clotted from centuries of angry verdicts? Did any man ever find power within his hand except to use it as a whip?

Gov. Alvan T. Fuller never had any intention in all his investigation but to put a new and higher polish upon the proceedings. The justice of the business was not his concern. He hoped to make it respectable. He called old men from high places to stand behind his chair so that he might seem to speak with all the authority of a high priest or a Pilate.

What more can these immigrants from Italy expect? It is not every prisoner who has a President of Harvard University throw on the switch for him. And Robert Grant is not only a former Judge but one of the most popular dinner guests in Boston. If this is a lynching, at least the fish peddler and his friend the factory hand may take unction to their souls that they will die at the hands of men in dinner coats or academic gowns, according to the conventionalities required by the hour of execution.

Already too much has been made of the personality of Webster Thayer. To sympathizers of Sacco and Vanzetti he has seemed a man with a cloven hoof. But in no usual sense of the term is this man a villain. Although probably not a great jurist, he is without doubt as capable and conscientious as the average Massachusetts Judge, and if that's enough to warm him in wet weather by all means let him stick the compliment against his ribs.

Webster Thayer has a thousand friends. He has courage, sincerity and conviction. Judge Thayer is a good man, and when he says that he made every effort to give a fair trial to the Anarchists brought before him, undoubtedly he thinks it and he means it. Quite often I've heard the remark: "I wonder how that man sleeps at night?" On this point I have no firsthand information, but I venture to guess that he is no more beset with uneasy dreams than most of us. He saw his duty and he thinks he did it.

And Gov. Fuller, also, is not in any accepted sense of the word a miscreant. Before becoming Governor he manufactured bicycles. Nobody was cheated by his company. He loves his family and pays his debts. Very much he desires to be Governor again, and there is an excellent chance that this ambition will be gratified. Other governors of Massachusetts have gone far, and it is not fantastic to assume that some day he might be President. His is not a master mind, but he is a solid and substantial American, chiming in heartily with all our national ideals and aspirations.

To me the tragedy of the conviction of Sacco and Vanzetti lies in the fact that this was not a deed done by crooks and knaves. In that case we could have a campaign with the slogan "Turn the rascals out," and set up for a year or two a reform Administration. Nor have I had much patience with any who would like to punish Thayer by impeachment or any other process. Unfrock him and his judicial robes would fall upon a pair of shoulders not different by the thickness of a fingernail. Men like Holmes and Brandeis do not grow on bushes. Popular government, as far as the eye can see, is always going to be administered by the Thayers and Fullers.

It has been said that the question at issue was not the guilt or innocence of Sacco and Vanzetti, but whether or not they received a fair trial. I will admit that this commands my interest to some extent, but still I think it is a minor phase in the whole matter. From a Utopian point of view the trial was far from fair, but it was not more biased than a thousand which take place in this country every year. It has been pointed out that the Public Prosecutor neglected to call certain witnesses because their testimony would not have been favorable to his case. Are there five District Attorneys, is there one, in the whole country who would do otherwise?

Again Prof. Frankfurter has most clearly shown that the prosecution asked a trick question in regard to the pistol, and made the expert seem to testify far more concretely than he was willing to commit himself. That was very wrong, but not unique. Our judicial processes are so arranged that it is to the interest of District Attorneys to secure convictions rather than to ascertain justice, and if it would profit his case, there is not one who would not stoop to confuse the issue in the minds of the jurymen.

Eleven of the twelve who convicted Sacco and Vanzetti are still alive, and Gov. Fuller talked to them. He reports somewhat naïvely that they all told him that they considered the trial fair. Did he expect them to report, "Why, no, Governor, we brought in a verdict of guilty just out of general depravity"?

By now there has been a long and careful sifting of the evidence in the case. It is ridiculous to say that Sacco and Vanzetti are being railroaded to the chair. The situation is much worse than that. This is a thing done cold-bloodedly and with deliberation. But care and deliberation do not guarantee justice. Even if every venerable college president in the country tottered forward to say "Guilty," they could not alter facts. The tragedy of it all lies in the fact that though a Southern mountain man may move more quickly to a dirty deed of violence, his feet are set no more firmly in the path of prejudice than a Lowell ambling sedately to a hanging.

I said of Calvin Coolidge that I admired his use of "I do not choose" [to run for the Presidency] but he was dealing with a problem wholly personal and had every right to withhold his reasons. For Gov. Fuller I can't say the same. These are the lives of others with which he is dealing. In his fairly long statement he answers not a single point which has been made against the justice of the conviction. The deliberations of himself and his associates were secret, and seemingly it is his intention that they shall remain secret. A gentleman does not investigate and tell.

I've said these men have slept, but from now on it is our business to make them toss and turn a little, for a cry should go up from many million voices before the day set for Sacco and Vanzetti to die. We have a right to beat against tight minds with our fists and shout a word into the ears of the old men. We want to know, we will know—"Why?"

"World readers were electrified by this flaming transfiguration of the normally easy-going, sometimes apathetic Broun," writes James W. Barrett, then city editor, in his book Joseph Pulitzer and His World. "Many were shocked at the attack on Harvard; others delighted. All were struck by its ferocity. Words of caution from R. P. (Ralph Pulitzer, then editor) and (Walter) Lippmann produced no assuagement of the tempest. In the next day's World Heywood followed up the attack with a still deadlier thrust at his Alma Mater."

August 6

Several points in the official decision of Gov. Fuller betray a state of mind unfortunate under the circumstances. It seems to me that the whole tone of Gov. Fuller's statement was apologetic, but this perhaps is debatable. There can be no question, however, that he fell into irrelevances.

"The South Braintree crime was particularly brutal," he wrote, and went on to describe the manner in which the robbers pumped bullets into a guard who was already wounded and helpless. Surely this is beside the point. Had this been one of the most considerate murders ever committed in the State of Massachusetts, Sacco and Vanzetti would still have been deserving of punishment if guilty. The contention of the defense has always been that the accused men had no part in the affair. The savagery of the killing certainly is wholly extraneous to the issue.

But these references of the Governor are worse than mere wasted motion. Unconsciously he has made an appeal to that type of thinker who says: "Why all the sympathy for those two anarchists and none for the unfortunate widow of the paymaster's guard?" But those of us who are convinced that Sacco and Vanzetti are innocent certainly pay no disrespect to the woes of the widow.

Again Gov. Fuller writes: "It is popularly supposed that he (Madeiros) confessed to committing the crime." Surely this gives the impression that no such statement ever came from the condemned criminal. The Governor may be within his rights in deciding that Madeiros lied, and for some self-seeking reason, but it is not only popularly supposed but also true that he did make a confession.

"In his testimony to me," the Governor explains, "he could not recall the details or describe the neighborhood."

This, I must say, seems to me a rather frowzy sort of psychology. Assuming that Madeiros took part in the crime, fired some shots and sped quickly away in an automobile, how could he be expected to remember the happenings in any precise detail? I have known men who ran seventy yards across the goal line in some football game and after this was over they knew little or nothing of what happened while excitement gripped them. I would be much more inclined to believe Madeiros a liar if he had been able to give a detailed and graphic account of everything which happened during the flurry.

And again, the Massachusetts Executive is far too cavalier in dealing with Sacco's alibi.

"He then claimed," says the Governor, "to have been at the Italian Consulate in Boston on that date, but the only confirmation of this claim is the memory of a former employee of the Consulate who made a deposition in Italy that Sacco among forty others was in the office that day. This employee had no memorandum to assist his memory."

In this brief paragraph I think I detect much bias. By speaking of the witness as "a former employee" Gov. Fuller seems to endeavor to discredit him. And yet the man who testified may be wholly worthy to be believed, even though he eventually took another job. Nor does the fact that his deposition was made in Italy militate against it. Truth may travel even across an ocean.

Assuming that Sacco did go to the Consulate as he has said, why should it be expected that his arrival would create such a stir that everyone there from the Consul down would have marked his coming indelibly? And this witness for the defense, according to Fuller, "had no memorandum to assist his memory." Why in Heaven's name should it be assumed that he would? There were other witnesses to whom the Governor gave credence who did not come with blueprints or flashlight photographs of happenings. Memory was all that served them and yet Fuller believed because he chose to.

One important point the Governor neglected to mention in dealing with the testimony of the Consulate clerk. The employee happened to fix Sacco in his mind by reason of a striking circumstance. The laborer, ignorant of passport requirements, brought with him to the Consulate not the conventional miniature but a large-sized crayon enlargement. And to my mind this should have been a clinching factor in the validity of the alibi.

Gov. Fuller has vindicated Judge Thayer of prejudice wholly upon the testimony of the record. Apparently he has overlooked entirely the large amount of testimony from reliable witnesses that the Judge spoke bitterly of the prisoners while the trial was on. The record is not enough. Anybody who has ever been to the theatre knows it is impossible to evaluate the effect of a line until you hear it read. It is just as important to consider Thayer's mood during the proceedings as to look over the words which he uttered.

Since the denial of the last appeal, Thayer has been most reticent, and has declared that it is his practice never to make public statements concerning any judicial matters which come before him. Possibly he never did make public statements, but certainly there is a mass of testimony from unimpeachable persons that he was not so careful in locker rooms and trains and club lounges.

Nor am I much moved at the outcries of admiration from the editorial writers who have expressed delight at the courage of the Governor of Massachusetts. Readily I will admit that in his decision he has exposed himself to the danger of physical violence. This is courage, but it is one of the more usual varieties. To decide in favor of Sacco and Vanzetti would have required a very different sort of courage. Such action upon Fuller's part might very possibly have blasted his political future.

I am afraid there is no question that a vast majority of the voters in the Bay State want to see the condemned men die. I don't know why. Clearly it depends upon no careful examination of the evidence. Mostly the feeling rests upon the fact that Sacco and Vanzetti are radicals and that they are foreigners. Also the backbone of Massachusetts, such as it is, happens to be up because of criticism beyond the borders of the State. "This is only our business," say the citizens of the Commonwealth, and they are very wrong.

Five times as many telegrams of praise as those of censure have come to the Governor, according to the official statement of his secretary. In such circumstances it seems to me that his courage in the business is of no great importance.

From now on, I want to know, will the institution of learning in Cambridge which once we called Harvard be known as Hangman's House?

"This was too much," City Editor Barrett recalls. "The World's Council-in-Dome was profoundly shaken. The business office demanded the suppression of Broun. Large advertisers were threatening to cancel contracts. 'The big department stores,' it was reported, 'do not desire the patronage of bomb-throwers.' Harvard alumni indignantly protested. Other readers telephoned, telegraphed, wrote letters. The uproar was terrific."
Pulitzer tried to induce Broun to stop writing about Sacco and Vanzetti. Broun went on writing about them. Pulitzer kept the copy out of the composing room. In the usual place of the "It Seems to Me" column on the World's

famous "op. ed." page he published an explanation that the World still considered Broun a member of its staff, "albeit taking a witch's sabbatical."

Five months later, writing for the Nation, Broun took the World to task, alleging that it "thundered on Thursdays and whispered on Monday mornings." Pulitzer, infuriated, fired him once and for all.

Three years later the World went out of existence. The name was bought by Roy Howard's New York Telegram.

It would be an exaggeration, perhaps, to say that the same severance that cost Heywood Broun his job cost the New York World its life. But certain it is that in firing Broun, Pulitzer dealt the paper a staggering blow. City Editor Barrett tried to belittle the effect. "Actually," he wrote, "the circle of admirers among World readers was not over 25,000—at least that was the drop in circulation that coincided with Broun's departure from the paper." But that was not the way to measure the total effect; it was only the beginning; the loss of Broun was a loss not only of immediate followers but of character in a great newspaper.

Broun moved over to the World-Telegram and stayed with it until a few months before his death. He wrote courageously and often in the cause of labor —against the use of strikebreakers; against New York State's rejection of the Child Labor Amendment in 1937, which he described as "the dirtiest day's work ever done in the New York State Assembly"; for the release of Tom Mooney; and for many trade union objectives.

In 1933 he organized the Newspaper Guild, the first collective bargaining agency ever set up to protect newsmen from abuses for which the publishers had long been notorious.

In 1938, on the anniversary of the execution of Sacco and Vanzetti, Broun wrote:

August 24

"The Good Shoemaker and the Poor Fish Peddler" were tried and sentenced eleven years ago.

For eleven years I have not written about Sacco and Vanzetti nor even talked much about the case. There have been meetings for commemoration, but it seemed to me there was small point in turning back the page. For all its ill the episode had ended.

Now I know that I was wrong, for in Washington I saw the shadow of the dead hand dance upon the wall. J. B. Matthews [then counsel for the House Committee on Un-American Activities] exorcised demons. His voice became shrill and fervent as he attacked the Youth Congress. And then upon a note of almost sheer hysteria he thrust out a thin arm and screamed that Shirley Temple [then ten years old] was a "stooge" of the "reds." The chairman of the House committee leaned forward eagerly and said, "Go on, professor."

The name of the chairman is Martin Dies. It might have been very funny, but I can assure you that it was not. Mr. Matthews is not a conscious humorist. It was death condemning life.

1922-33: "OUR OWN SAMUEL PEPYS"

CHICAGO-BORN FRANKLIN PIERCE ADAMS *began the diary he called "Our Own Samuel Pepys" in 1911 in the New York Evening Mail and from 1914 continued it in the New York Herald as part of his widely read column, "The Conning Tower." New Yorkers who didn't make news themselves enjoyed F.P.A.'s familiarity with those who did. "Whenever, for various reasons, I omitted it for a few issues," he recalls, "there were more protests than prayers of thanksgiving." So he kept it going and took it over with him to the New York World in 1922. Those were great days for newspaper readers, when they could enjoy F.P.A., Heywood Broun and Alexander Woollcott under one masthead; and it was in no small part because of these three that the folding of the World in 1931 was so deeply mourned. Adams carried on in the Herald Tribune and later in the New York Post, but eventually he gave up newspapering for broadcasting.*

"So finished my stint . . ."
FRANKLIN PIERCE ADAMS
(born 1881)

February 8 [1922]

So home, and with my wife to J. Wise's for dinner and then after to Mrs. Clare Sheridan's and sate near Mrs. John Barrymore, very beautiful, too, in a brown velvet dress, and she tells me she never reads any newspapers at all, nor ever has read any, which is as well, for she said it as who should say, There, that will put you in your place. Too there was Col. Repington, and all noted the presence of Mrs. Sheridan and him as that of two audacious diarists, but Lord, I do not see they are bolder than anybody else.

May 23

After dinner to see *Abie's Irish Rose,* which I thought the poorest, tawdriest play I could remember seeing.

November 4

To dinner, and thenafter Mr. Scott Fitzgerald and his wife come in, and we played at cards a little, but at five in the morning I grew weary of it, and so to bed.

February 1 [1925]

To Mistress Maud Fangel's to supper, and thence to a great party at S. Chotzinoff's, and Miss Alma Gluck there, and J. Heifetz and E. Zimbalist, and G. Gershwin, and Miss Grace Moore very pretty in a red and gold gown, and Miss Ruth Draper, who recited her piece about the children's party in Philadelphia, which I deem the finest piece of mimicry ever I heard.

March 25

Shocked this morning to see a picture in the publick prints of A. Woollcott smoking a cigarre [a commercial endorsement] in especiall when not only does he not smoke them save once or twice a year, but last night and the night before at his house he did not even offer me one.

At the office all day, and for a walk through the city, and bought some arbutus to take to the ailing poets of the town, Miss Edna Millay and Mr. A. Ficke. And I could not help thinking, I too am an ailing poet, yet no one giveth me so much as a pansy.

April 28

To the Republic to see *Abie's Irish Rose,* which I felt again to be a false, obvious, and cheap piece. [In a subsequent footnote the diarist informs us that Anne Nichols, the playwright, was said to have made $5,000,000 from the play.]

January 7 [1926]

Reading the tayles of how C. Mackay is wood-wroth that his daughter hath wedded I. Berlin, I was minded of a night last June, when G. Seldes the journalist come to my room in the Hotel Russie in Rome, and said, Do you know who this Mackay girl is? And I said Yes. And he told me that he had a cable from his journal, to the effect that the Vatican was considering at that moment the granting of a dispensation. And at that moment the band in the courtyard began to play, "What'll I Do?" and whether the Vatican was deliberating then none of us ever found out, but as I thought of the days when I. Berlin was a singing waiter on the Bowery, I thought it was dramatick enough.

February 24

Early up, and to the office and read with interest of a great party Earl Carroll hath given last night, and how it was said that there was a lady immersed in a bathtub of wine. And I thought, Lord! how much water hath flowed from bathtubs since the pre-Prohibition days, when an actress might immerse herself in a bathtub of milk and attain wide notoriety.

February 25

So finished my stint, with no great fervor neither, and thence home and read Theodore Dreiser's *An American Tragedy*, which is so far the best book I have read that I cannot recall aught I deem better. Lord! what tremendous power and feeling and sincerity he hath.

March 16

A. Woollcott come in, and I shewed him a game I invented, two-handed poker, but each player playing two complete hands, so that four separate hands are played separately, as interesting a game as ever I played and lost at, which is no faint praise for a game, neither.

April 3

To A. Woollcott's, and it being a misly day I did stop with him and had a game of our four-handed poker, and had a great argument with him as to which of us had invented the game, he having the hallucination that he had made it up. Which so angered me that I grew merciless, and won what he called an untidy sum.

April 15

Up by times, and read in the publick prints how Norman Thomas went yesterday to Garfield, N. J. and from an apple tree which was standing on private property the owner had given him permission to use, advised the persons in his hearing to be peaceable and to obey the law. Whereupon he was cast into jail. Nor would they let him have counsel. And they did hold him in $10,000 bail. Which made me so wroth I could not think of aught else. For the people who do such injustices are the ones who prate of respect for law, and the land of liberty and opportunity.

November 21

So to H. Swope's, and listened to this one and that one talk about the Hall-Mills case, each having his theory about it, and some thinking the whole affair dull, but I still think it is as interesting a case, trial and all, as there ever has been, it being vitally concerned with love, hate, money, jealousy, religion, and politicks.

[The diarist, in a footnote, gives this description of the enormously publicized case]: "On Sept. 16, 1922, in De Russey's Lane, New Brunswick,

N. J., the bodies of the Rev. Edward Wheeler Hall, 41, and his choir singer, Mrs. Eleanor Rinehart Mills, 33, were discovered side by side, dead from bullet wounds. The story attracted universal attention, and Middlesex County authorities investigated. The results were presented to the grand jury but no indictment was found. For nearly four years rumors and charges continued, and on Sept. 15, 1926, Mrs. Frances Stevens Hall, 59, wife of Dr. Hall, her cousin Henry Carpender, and her brothers William and Henry Stevens, were indicted for the murder of Mrs. Mills. A high light of the trial was the wheeling into court on a stretcher of Mrs. Jane Gibson, known as the 'pig woman,' who said she had been riding her mule Jenny, in De Russey's Lane on the murder night. Special prosecutor Alexander Simpson provided daily thrills for newspaper readers during the entire second trial which lasted until Dec. 3, 1926, when the jury found the defendants not guilty on the charge of having murdered Mrs. Mills. The other indictment, accusing them of having killed Dr. Hall, was nolle prossed."

March 2 [1927]

This morning Mr. George [Babe] Ruth come to town, and told the pressmen that he would not accept less than $100,000 a year, and I hope he gets it or more, as I think he attracts more money than that to the parks where he plays. But Lord! how weary it maketh me when petty persons compare this salary to the President's, or to their own, saying, "How hard I work, and how little I earn!" But this man chooseth to be a writer or a truckman, and that one a ballplayer, and if so be he is fortunate enough to have the qualities that a great public will pay to see displayed, who is anybody to complain of that? For all I would have to do, I tell myself, to get a larger salary than Babe Ruth's would be to be a greater ballplayer, and if I am not, I have no right to complain, nor do I, but say, "Huzzah for Mr. Ruth!"

Heard this afternoon that he hath accepted $70,000 a year.

April 6

Early up and to the office, and there read about the Nizam of Hyderabad, who is said to be wealthier than Mr. Ford or Mr. Rockefeller, and the accounts say he could buy and sell those gentlemen, but it might be a bad bargain, forasmuch as he might buy them and find that he was unable to dispose of them at a profit.

May 20

Early up, very weary, and to my office, and there learned how young Mr. Charles Lindbergh [The diarist's footnote: "Aviator, whom the day before, millions, including myself, never had heard of"] had started upon his aerial flight across the Atlantic Ocean, and I hope he is successful, or in any event that he cometh to no grief.

May 22

I read all the papers about the great success of Charles Lindbergh in flying his airplane across the Atlantic, and could not read enough of it, the whole story being the most thrilling and happy-endingest story I could imagine, and I doubt that any one ever will look upon its like again. And this is the first great thing I can recall when there is no dissenting or doubting voice, no one to whisper that perhaps it was "framed," or that it all was done by Wall Street men to further the interest of some stock or other. I saw no flaw in the entire proceeding, save what I imagine America, and especially New York, will try to do this young man in the way of making him listen to so much oratory that he will probably long for the comparatively unwindy stretches of the air above the Atlantic.

October 6

Hard at my work all the morning, and finished my stint by 1 o'clock, and Edna Millay the poet there, and made sport of me for having so great a sinecure that I could write a whole column in five hours, but Lord! if the truth were known, that should be long enough for me to write three columns. Save that Miss Millay may take two weeks to write a single line, and the chances are that it will be known a century from now, and that none of mine will.

October 24

So cometh a man to install our radio set, which I did bring with me last night and it worked very well, and I have ceased marveling at it, as I no longer at the telephone nor the electric light, neither of which I understand at all. And I heard some of the radio announcers, and could not believe that I was hearing aright, some of the advertising being pretentious and silly, as when one man spoke many times of the slogan of a company being "You might as well have the best," and I wondered how long it took that concern, and how many conferences were held, before they made that slogan up.

September 27

This day the Lord Mayor [James J. Walker] came home from his trip in Europe, where he is said to have studied problems of municipal importance, such as transit and the like, but I have misgivings about the profundity of his studying.

January 8 [1929]

Out, questing about here and there, and met J. Dempsey the former boxer, and he shook my hand for a short count, and seemed greatly delighted at meeting me, for he gave my hand a pressure that I can still feel, albeit I am writing this seventeen hours later.

May 27

I heard over the radio that Charles Lindbergh had been married to Miss Anne Morrow this afternoon at Englewood, and had outwitted the newspapers and the idiotically curious publick, too.

October 28

In the evening did some reading in E. Hemingway's *A Farewell to Arms,* abandoning myself to it, as A. Woollcott implored me to do, and I did like it far better than when I read it in the magazine, yet do have a hard time forgetting the style of it.

November 27

So to the office for a little to confer with Tom Smith the printer, and so home to work some more, words coming slowly to my paper, and I am filled with envy of H. Broun and A. Woollcott, the fluentest writers of great readability that ever I heard of. Lord! a thousand words an hour is dawdling for them.

March 20, 1930

Lay longer than I desired to lie, and so hurried to the office, and greatly astonished to read that the late Chief Justice Mr. Taft had said that he considered the result of Prohibition glorious. But all that I could think of was "Glorious! Glorious! One pint of wine among the four of us."

August 30

Early up, and hard at work in the cool of the morning, and last night I read about the "riding" of a baseball player, and wondered how old such a meaning of the word was, and this morning I found in Mr. Pepys's Diary, how he had gone to Greenwich, "where I find the stairs full of people, there being a great riding there to-day for a man, the constable of the town, whose wife beat him." For "riding," I learned, was serenading with kettle, horns, hand bells, and all manner of derogatory speech, somewhat as it is to-day. Except in those days it was generally a punishment for wife beating or husband beating, which there was a vast deal of in those days.

November 5

Up, and my wife telephones me that S. Lewis hath been given the great Nobel Prize for literature, chiefly for having written *Babbitt,* and he and Dot mighty delighted about it, and I too.

December 2

To the office and read Mr. Hoover's message to Congress, and thought that it was unique in its avoidance of any of the large controversial questions that beset the people, especially the prohibition matter, and all such things. The message reminded me of the girls in *Pirates of Penzance* who sing, "Let us shut our eyes, and talk about the weather."

April 30 [1931]

Lay long, being too weary to rise before nine o'clock, and read that 62 per cent of the Protestant clergymen, asked the question, said that they believed that the churches of America ought to go on record as refusing support or to sanction any future war. But think that means little, forasmuch as many of these clergymen would probably find that they did not mean that they would not sanction a war that was to liberate humanity, or free mankind, or whatever the poppycock phrase it is that we patriots will be able to think up by that time. And few clergymen will be brave enough, or foolhardy enough, to stand out against a great procession of bandwagons. And yet I think that the churches and the newspapers alone, if they had a united desire, could make future war impossible.

December 6

In the evening with my wife to Rob Lovett's, and Will Faulkner and his wife come there, too, and she tells us of life in the town of Oxford, in Mississippi, and I found Will a soft-spoken boy, but I would know him for a powerful one at a glance even if I never had read a word ever he had written.

December 10

Early up and to the office, and so read the recommendations made by Mr. Mellon about the exchequer, mighty sad reading, forasmuch as most of us have faced so many facts in the past twelvemonth that we are sick of the sight of another fact, and would not know an illusion if we met one in the street. Lord! there is nothing to be met on the street but another and another man that says that he is hungry, probably because hunger is the most direct appeal, but what seems worse to me is the night of no sleep, or of sleep in so unhallowed and foul a place, save it be in some park, as to be beyond the belief of most of us.

March 2 [1932]

Up and greatly shaken at reading of the theft of the Lindbergh baby last night, and I full of fear that the parents will not see him again, for no matter what the immunity offered to any kidnaper might be, it seems to me that he would be so ridden by fright of discovery later that his immunity would be limited. So took my boy Timothy to school, and he told me that I hurt his hand holding it too tight.

May 12

So after supper at my work, and then heard that little Charlie Lindbergh's body had been found, and that he had been murdered within a day or two after he had been kidnaped, and I think that the murder occurred within two hours of the kidnaping, and my feeling of insensate rage was so great that I felt like going out and killing the first person I met.

October 5

What aroused me more than any political thing that I had read in many years was that Mr. Al Smith went up to Mr. Roosevelt and said, "Hello, you old potato!" Which seemed to me to be one of the most electrically inspired bits of wording ever I heard in politicks, and I think in itself will make more votes for Roosevelt than a thousand campaign speeches would.

March 4 [1933]

Lay till past eight o'clock of a chilly windy morning, and so all the morning sate by the fire and worked at the assembling of some verses and prose; and then heard much of the Inauguration ceremonies by means of the wireless; and I thought what Mr. Roosevelt said was mighty good, and well said besides, he having a better feeling for words and their cadences than even Woodrow Wilson had, or so it seemed to me.

July 24

To my reading of the newspapers, and about the many codes [NRA] and maximum hours of labor, and minimum payments for them, and I suppose that there will be great dissatisfaction expressed by some, and great satisfaction by others; but I think the greatest thing of all is that Mr. Roosevelt hath emancipated the children from gainful labour. And I think the whole thing is a big step up, though I can well imagine the Communists saying that the President is truckling to Capitalism and the Capitalists saying that this man is nothing but an Anarchist.

To me it seems that his words are fairly spoken and that his deeds are more in consonance with them than hath been true of any other publick man in so long a time that I cannot cite the instance of one such.

August 14

I do hear men in filling stations and farmers whom I meet on the road talk about Mr. Roosevelt in a way that I never heard the people before talk about a President, which is to say that the cheering sections are crowded.

September 26

To a restaurant with my wife for breakfast, and read of the death of Ring Lardner, for whom I have the deepest and warmest affection in the world. There will be many to talk of his bitter hatred of the human race's selfishness and stupidity, but he was filled with a mighty compassion for the possessors of these qualities. But his loathing for pretensiousness and leering obscenity was uncompromising. And, as S. Walker [newspaper-man and author] told me, he had a great effect upon journalism, for he, more than anybody else, made it possible for reporters to write the words that people said instead of a lot of high-sounding, mealy-mouthed phrases and sentiments.

October 2

In the evening with Rose Feld to see E. O'Neill's *Ah, Wilderness*, which I liked and enjoyed better than any O'Neill play ever I saw, and as well as any other play ever I saw, it being full of tenderness and humor and some of the heart-breakingest scenes that ever I saw.

October 28

I to A. Woollcott's and met there E. M. Delafield and fell mighty much in love with her, but did not tell her so, partly because I feared that she would discredit my avowal, but mostly because it was not easy to interrupt A. Woollcott's rhapsody about the autumn foliage in Vermont.

--★

1924-35: A COWBOY LOOKS AT CONGRESS
--☆

"IN ALL THE AUTOBOGRAPHYS I EVER READ," wrote Will Rogers, "the first line was I was born at So-and-so on Such-and-such a Date. Now the thing that struck me was that if a feller could give a reason why he was born you'd be a novelty. Now that is what has been holding me up on this Autobography. I was born, but why? Now I've got it.

"I am the only known child in history who claims Nov. 4th as my Birthday, that is election day. Women couldent vote in those days so my Mother thought she would do something, so she stayed home and gave birth to me. The men were all away. I decided to get even with the Government. Thats why I have always had it in for politicians.

"I was the youngest and last of 7 children. My folks looked me over and said, "This thing has gone far enough, if they are going to look like this, we will stop."

Will's humor had a bite. His gibes at Congress were devastating. But the people loved them. At the height of his career his boxoffice attraction was greater than that of any other entertainer in America.

"There hasent been a Patrick Henry . . ."
WILL ROGERS (1879-1935)

May 11 [1924]

You wire the State or the Federal Government that your Cow or Hog is sick and they will send out experts from Washington and appropriate money to eradicate the Cause. You wire them that your Baby has the Diphtheria or Scarlet Fever and see what they do.

October 19

I have been trying to read the papers and see just what it is in this election that one Party wants that the other one don't.

November 2

Well, the publishing of the Income Tax amounts kinder knocked some of the big ones in the creek. It brought out many surprises. Few of us knew before that Jack Dempsey was as rich as J. P. Morgan. They both paid around 90 thousand dollars each. I thought Morgan made that much before breakfast every morning.

Don't feel discouraged if a lot of our well known men were not as wealthy according to their Tax as you thought they ought to be. This publication of amounts had nothing to do with their wealth. It was only a test of their honesty.

December 28

If Congress would just pass one law, as follows, they wouldn't need the 20th Amendment: "EVERY CHILD, REGARDLESS OF AGE, SHALL RECEIVE THE SAME WAGE AS A GROWN PERSON." That would stop your child labor.

February 17 [1925]

We have great fellows back from the War that can show you two Medals for every sack of Flour they have in the House.

February 22

Every Politician always talks about him [Abraham Lincoln] but none of them ever imitate him.

March 1

When a Gentleman quoted me on the floor of Congress the other day, another member took exception and said he objected to the remarks of a Professional Joke Maker going into the Congressional Record. Now can you beat that for jealousy among people in the same line?

June 28

If America is not good enough for you to live in and make money in, why, then you are privileged to go to some other Country. But don't ask protection from a Country that was not good enough for you. If you want to make money out of a Country, why, take out their Citizenship Papers and join them. Don't use one Country for Money and another for convenience.

Oklahoma City, October 29

The South is dry and will vote dry. That is everybody that is sober enough to stagger to the polls will.

Beverly Hills, November 3

Bureau of something or other in Washington announced that "America has reached the highest standard of living ever reached by any nation."

Yes, and if they will just cut down on the original payments we have to make from a dollar to fifty cents we will show you some living. It's an injustice to ask a hard-working people to pay a dollar down. It should be fifty cents down and fifty cents when they come to try and find it to take it back.

Course, we don't get meat as often as our forefathers, but we have our peanut butter and radio.

May 26 [1928]

We sure are a-living High.

Our Children are delivered to the schools in Automobiles. But whether that adds to their grades is doubtful. There hasent been a Thomas Jefferson produced in this country since we formed our first Trust. Rail splitting produced an immortal President in Abraham Lincoln; but Golf, with 29 thousand courses hasent produced even a good A-1 Congressman. There hasent been a Patrick Henry showed up since business men quit eating lunch with their families, joined a club and had indigestion from amateur Oratory.

Springfield, Mass., October 2

Al Smith unanimously nominated Franklin D. Roosevelt today for Governor of New York.

He is a Roosevelt by blood but a namesake politically. If he had retained his splendid qualities and stayed with the Republican end of the family he would have been President. But I doubt if he could have retained those qualities and been Republican.

Beverly Hills, June 28 [1929]

The tariff is an instrument invented for the benefit of those who make against those who buy. As there is more buys than there is makes, it is a document of the minority, but what a minority!

New York, October 29

When Wall Street took that tail spin, you had to stand in line to get a window to jump out of.

Los Angeles, October 31

Sure must be a great consolation to the poor people who lost their stock in the late crash to know that it has fallen into the hands of Mr. Rockefeller, who will take care of it and see that it has a good home and never be allowed to wander around unprotected again.

There is one rule that works in every calamity. Be it pestilence, war or famine, the rich get richer and the poor get poorer. The poor even help arrange it. But it's just as I have been constantly telling you, "Don't gamble"; take all your savings and buy some good stock and hold it till it goes up, then sell it.

If it don't go up, don't buy it.

Beverly Hills, December 22

You can't say civilization don't advance, for in every war they kill you a new way.

Los Angeles, November 2 [1930]

Come pretty near having two holidays of equal importance in the same week, Halloween and Election, and of the two, election provides us the most fun. On Halloween they put pumpkins on their heads, and on Election they don't have to.

Beverly Hills, February 22 [1931]

Here is what George Washington missed by not living to his 199th birthday. He would have seen our great political system of "equal rights to all and the privileges to none" working so smoothly that 7,000,000 are without a chance to earn their living; he would see 'em handing out rations in peace times—that would have reminded him of Valley Forge. In fact we have reversed the Old system; we all get fat in war times and thin during peace. I bet after seeing us he would sue us for calling him "father."

Beverly Hills, June 4

We used to always be talking and "sloganing" about "back to normalcy." Well, that's right where we are now, and where we are going to stay, so we might just as well get used to it. It's taught us one important fact, that we haven't got as many "big men" as we thought we had. We used to think every head of a big organization was a "big man" and he was, as long as everything was running in spite of him.

Beverly Hills, February 22 [1932]

You can't get a room in Washington; every hotel is jammed to the doors with bankers from all over America to get their "hand out" from the Dawes commission. And I have asked the following prominent men in America this question, "What group have been more responsible for this financial mess? The farmers? Labor? Manufacturers? Tradesmen, or who?" And every man, Henry Ford, Garner, Newt Baker, Borah, Curtis, and a real financier, Barney Baruch, and every one of 'em with out a moment's hesitation, said, "Why, the big bankers." Yet they have the honor of being the first group to go on the "dole" in America.

August 7

Our investigations have always contributed more to our amusement than they have to our knowledge.

Santa Monica, March 5 [1933]

America hasn't been as happy in three years as they are today, no money, no banks, no work, no nothing, but they know they got a man in there who is wise to Congress, wise to our so-called big men. The whole country is with him, just so he does something. If he burned down the capitol we would cheer and say "well, we at least got a fire started any-how." We have had years of "don't rock the boat."

San Francisco, May 2 [1934]

See where the U. S. Chamber of Commerce are gathered in Washington again. Its the caviar of big business, last time they met I happened to be in Washington and was the guest of Jesse Jones (head of the Reconstruction Finance) at their dinner. Now the whole constitution, bylaws, and secret ritual of that Orchid Club is to "keep the government out of business." Well thats all right for every organization must have a purpose, but here was the joke, they introduced all the big financiers, the head of this, that and the other. As each stood up, Jesse would write on the back of the menu card, just what he had loaned him from the R.F.C. (I got that menu card yet.)

Honolulu, August 1

You don't have to be warlike to get a real kick out of our greatest army post Schofield Barracks and the navy at Pearlharbor. If war was declared with some Pacific nation we would lose the Philippines before lunch but if we lost these it would be our own fault.

New Orleans, January 29 [1935]

In Louisiana they vote by electricity. Its a marvelous way to vote, but Huey [Long] runs the switchboard, so it dont matter which button the boys press, all the answers come out yes.

Santa Monica, February 17

See by todays papers Mr. Townsend appeared before the Senate Committee and they had a lot of fun and laughter at his plan, well they can have some fun with the amount, but they cant have much fun with the idea of paying a pension, you see its not just some idealistic cranks, or Bolsheviki idea, all the rest of the world are doing it but us, we thought we had a better idea, we called it a "Poor Farm" and everybody that could afford it or had any political influence, put their relatives there.

Beverly Hills, March 6

Our constitution protects aliens, drunks, and U. S. Senators. There ought to be one day a year (just one) when there is an open season on Senators.

March 13

Say, did you read about what Mr. Roosevelt said about those "Holding

Companies." A Holding Company is a thing where you hand an accomplice the goods while the policeman searches you.

March 16

Stay out of that Europe, that's a tough game to enter into. Their diplomats are trained, its their life business. Ours makes a campaign contribution and wakes up in Belgium, and don't know which ocean he crossed to get there.

June 30

A fellow can't afford to die now with all this excitement going on.

Fifteen days later Will Rogers was killed in an airplane crash in Alaska.

1933: FOR THE PEOPLE, A NEW DEAL

FOR THE FOUR ELECTIONS of Franklin D. Roosevelt, his adversaries had all kinds of explanations. He did it by demagogy. It was the "silver-toned voice." It was "tax-spend-elect." It was depression. War.

The one fact they could not shake off was that the people wanted him—overwhelmingly, in the face of opposition by very rich and very powerful men and by nine-tenths of the press.

At the time he came into office the air was electric with crisis. In the city streets, on the farms, in the tense neighborhoods of the mines and mills, America had 14,000,000 unemployed; and America had done nothing about them. In Washington they were a statistic in a bureau. The eyes of government were on the stock market.

Sound or unsound stock marketwise, the New Deal did something about the people, and let the blue chips fall—or rise—where they may.

Harold L. Ickes, Roosevelt's Secretary of the Interior, held his job thirteen years—longer than anybody else ever had. He kept a diary all that time. It was a secret. But it filled nearly a hundred volumes of closely typed copy—about 6,000,000 words.

The Ickes diary is in part the story of what the government did about the economic erosion which had penetrated the physical and moral fibers of the nation.

"Unless the situation improves . . ."

HAROLD L. ICKES (1874-1952)

April 13 [1933]

An earnest discussion of unemployment was had until half past ten.

I was struck with the pessimism of Senator Wheeler and Senator Thomas. They both think the economic situation is getting worse rapidly and they look for a very serious situation unless something is done speedily. In this connection, a very large and comprehensive public works program was suggested, and the immediate embarking on such a program was urged as of vital necessity.

Senator Thomas made the statement that the concentration camps now being set up for the men engaged in reforestation under the act recently passed might be found to have served as concentration camps for men marching against the government unless the situation improved rapidly. He also made the statement that in case of any serious outbreaks, those marching against the government would not be headed by rioters but by Ph.D.s and the educated classes. He pointed out that a great proportion of the educated classes were out of jobs at this time, more so than on any other occasion.

April 18

The Cabinet meeting this afternoon was given over entirely to a discussion of the economic situation. The President told of the drive that has been made on the dollar in Amsterdam, Paris, and London during the last few days.

At first he decided to throw enough gold in to maintain the dollar but finally concluded not to do so. This is to be the national policy from this time on unless changed. This may mean that the dollar will go down to ninety cents or thereabouts. It may also mean a fluctuating dollar for some time, but in the end it is thought that we will be better off, and the world will be better off, if the dollar is not artificially maintained at a value disproportionate to the rest of the principal currencies of the world.

The United States in effect went off the gold standard March 4, at the time of the banking crisis. There can be no doubt that we are definitely off the gold standard and that it will be so recognized.

May 4

I went to the annual dinner of the Chamber of Commerce of the United States tonight. The great and the mighty in the business world were there in force, and I couldn't help thinking how so many of these great and mighty were crawling to Washington on their hands and knees these days to beg the government to run their businesses for them.

August 12

There is one incident that I must record because it was so amusing, and the President on the way back [from inspection of the Civilian Conservation Corps camps in Shenandoah Park, Virginia] when I brought it up, laughingly said that I ought to include it in my memoirs but he couldn't.

The commanding general, while probably a very good officer, is just a little pompous. At the camp where we were having luncheon he began to tell what the Army is going to do in the way of educating the CCC boys while they were in camp. Apparently he didn't know, or chose to ignore the fact, that we are going to assign teachers to these camps, not on invitation of the Army, but in spite of the Army.

It gave him great pleasure to assure the President and all within hearing of his voice that any CCC boy could receive instruction on any subject. He told how someone was teaching trigonometry to one of the boys, how another was learning French, and he concluded with this gem: "There won't none of these boys leave these camps illiterate."

August 23

I went over to have a very personal and confidential talk with Louis Howe. A heavy barrage is being laid down to break my morale. My wife Anna is receiving a quantity of anonymous letters which naturally worry her. They must be deliberately planned because they are being mailed in such large numbers. Colonel Howe assured me that I was only getting my turn, and that the enemies of the Administration, having had no chance to attack the President himself, make attacks successively on those supposed to be close to him.

September 5

The President got back to Washington at noon [from a Labor Day weekend on Vincent Astor's yacht]. After the Council meeting I went into his office with him and arranged for an appointment for tomorrow to discuss public works. I have never seen him looking so well and I complimented him on his appearance. He said he had had three days of absolute rest where no one could get at him. He said that one night he had sat up until six o'clock in the morning playing poker and drinking beer, and I remarked that if it had the effect on him it appeared to have, he had better make a practice of it.

September 8

Toward the end of the [Cabinet] meeting, Secretary Roper remarked that some Chinese emperor back in the eleventh century at a time of depression had adopted the same measures for recovery that this Administration is now back of. The President laughingly inquired, "What happened to that emperor, was he beheaded?" Roper replied, "No, he wasn't beheaded; he was defeated."

September 28

Secretary [of the Treasury] Woodin was worried and frankly said so. He doesn't like the situation. He thinks the dollar ought to be stabilized and he doesn't care much at what point, provided only that it is stabilized. He said that the big financial men in New York are all down in the mouth and think that the NRA campaign will be a failure. As they look at it, it is going to put the country entirely in the hands of labor.

October 5

I took occasion to tell the President that if we only had a fair break of luck so that we didn't hit any more economic bumps and were able to hold our own and perhaps pull gradually out, his Administration would go down in history as one of profound and far-reaching social changes. I told him that there wasn't another man in the United States who could lead the country at this time along the paths that it ought to tread. Of course, he demurred to this, but I profoundly believe it to be true.

October 17

At nine o'clock I went to the Department of Agriculture to discuss with Henry Wallace and Harry Hopkins the purchase of surplus butter for the unemployed. We agreed to buy $10 million worth of butter and to make a bid for the surplus apple crop in the Northwest. It was also agreed to buy about $10 million worth of wheat.

October 20

He [President Roosevelt] read to me a letter from himself to President Kalinin, of Russia, and the latter's reply. The President in his letter proposed that Russia send a representative to talk with him and his suggestion was cordially received. This is undoubtedly paving the way to recognition, something that I have been in favor of for several years, and which pleased me very much indeed.

The Cabinet meeting was one of the most interesting we have had. The President repeated to the Cabinet what he had told me just before at luncheon about the Russian situation and what he said was received with varying emotions. Much to my surprise, both Secretary Wallace and Secretary Perkins seemed to doubt the wisdom of the move.

November 3

I had promised to make the principal address at the one hundredth anniversary of the Philadelphia Board of Trade. I had known that this was a very conservative group and perhaps there was some malice in the dose that I had prepared for them. The President of the Board of Trade seemed to me to be old almost to the point of senility, and the total age of the banqueters must have run into very high figures indeed. At the speakers' table were General Atterbury, president of the Pennsylvania Railroad; President Charles H. Ewing, of the Philadelphia and Reading Railroad; Samuel Vauclain, president of the Baldwin Locomotive Works; and Congressman James M. Beck, solicitor general under President Taft and one of the outstanding conservatives of the country. These were typical of the audience and I suspect that my speech must have convinced them that I am an extremely dangerous citizen.

In my speech I pointed out how ruthlessly we had exploited the natural resources of the country and then the human resources, including women and children. I went on to say that we were in the midst of a social revolution and that the days of rugged individualism and ruthless power were over forever.

November 7

Harry L. Hopkins and I lunched with the President to discuss Hopkins' plan of putting four million of the unemployed to work.

November 29

The President is always charming but he was delightful at Warm Springs. Everyone there loves him and crowds hang outside the gate, especially on Sundays, just to see him and cheer him as he drives in and out occasionally.

August 6 [On board train returning from site of Grand Coulee on the Columbia River]

The President sent word back, asking me to dine with him. He and his family and Louis Howe occupied a private car on the rear of the train.

At the dinner there were, besides the President and Mrs. Roosevelt, James Roosevelt, Franklin, Jr., and John Roosevelt; Senator Burton K. Wheeler, of Montana; Secretary of War Dern; Louis Howe; a friend of the younger Roosevelt boy; and myself.

This was a most interesting dinner. It resolved itself into a debate between the members of the Roosevelt family, with all of them frequently talking at one and the same time.

Mrs. Roosevelt precipitated the discussion by raising some social question and her three sons at once began to wave their arms in the air and take violent issue with her. She expressed belief in a strict limitation of income, whether earned or not, and the boys insisted that every man ought to have a right to earn as much as he could.

The President joined in at intervals, but he wasn't President of the United States on that occasion—he was merely the father of three sons who had opinions of their own. They interrupted him when they felt like it and all talked at him at the same time.

September 5

Lewis W. Douglas resigned as Director of the Budget two or three days ago. He has been out of sympathy all along with the fiscal policy of the President. Harry Hopkins told me that Douglas wrote an unpleasant letter of resignation to the President. Hopkins thinks the lines are forming for a test of strength between the conservatives and radicals, and he remarked plaintively that, outside of two or three of us, all of the men prominent in the Administration are conservatives.

October 2

Saturday morning we arrived at Atlanta to start the demolition for the first slum clearance program ever undertaken by the Federal government. There are two slum clearance projects for Atlanta, one for Negroes and one for whites.

October 26

It is surprising with what unanimity everyone, inside the newspaper profession and outside, says that the [Chicago] *Tribune* is the rottenest newspaper in the United States.

November 4

He [the President] seems to feel, as a result of information that has come to him, that big business is out on a deliberate policy of sabotaging the Administration.

November 19

We drove back to Tupelo [Mississippi] where another great crowd was gathered in a natural ampitheater to hear the President make a short extemporaneous speech. This speech was very significant in that it served notice on the power companies that have been obstructing the TVA program and upon the country at large that the Government is not only going ahead to carry out its TVA program but will undertake similar enterprises in different parts of the country. The President is a great believer in cheap power and rural electrification.

December 7

We did make very fast progress with this program [public works for 1935] because it is clear that the President has made up his mind to expend about $5 billion but Henry Morgenthau is always raising some childish objections. I have been puzzled to decide whether he is being obstructive or is trying to impress us with the profundity of his wisdom. I have really come to the conclusion that he is somewhat stupid.

The Vice-President [John Nance Garner] today made one or two statements that met with my cordial approval, as I told him afterwards. He took the position that fifty or sixty men in the United States, through interlocking directorates and holding companies, should not be permitted to control the economic life of the nation.

He expressed the utmost distrust of these men and told the President that, as he had urged on one or two other occasions, this was the time to put them in their place and keep them there. The Vice-President realizes that there are reactionaries in both parties and that when money and financial power are concerned, these men will show no consideration to anyone. He even doubts their patriotism when money is concerned.

March 12 [1935]

I ran into the Vice-President and he took me into his office. He locked the door and we had the most confidential talk that we have ever had. He told me very frankly that he was afraid. He said that if Roosevelt is not re-elected, a reactionary Republican will succeed him, and that then will follow either a fascist government or a communist one. He could actually foresee a revolution in certain circumstances. He spoke with deep feeling and with sadness.

May 10

I took occasion to say to Harry Hopkins the other day in the presence of Frank Walker that I did not believe the [work relief] program would work out. I said that as fast as men were taken off relief rolls, others would go on. People who have been able to keep off relief to date are gradually exhausting all their resources and sooner or later will have to turn to the Government for support. Moreover, the plan contemplates that only those on the relief rolls will be given employment under the new program and that will mean that if a man wants a job, he will have to go on relief rolls. I think this is bad psychology and bad politics.

June 1

Yesterday's Cabinet meeting was one of the most interesting we have had. Friday morning before Cabinet meeting the President had a press conference and he talked for two hours to the correspondents discussing the decision of the Supreme Court on NRA. He characterized that decision as an effort to put us back to the horse-and-buggy age and pointed out that national progress along economic and social lines would be impossible in the light of that decision and that it would be necessary to rely on the states for whatever advances along those lines might be hoped for.

We spent practically all the time at Cabinet meeting discussing the new issue that the President has raised. I think the issue is a sound one and one that would have to be raised sooner or later in any event. In fact, some years ago, in a speech that I made before the City Club of Chicago, I predicted that sooner or later the Supreme Court would become a political issue. Apparently that time has come and I, for one, am ready to meet it. Apparently the President is too.

June 19

While I was with him [the President] word came that the Security Bill had passed the Senate and that his message on taxation was being read. The President read this message to me. He told me that he thought it was the best thing he had done as President. He boldly demands a graduated increase in estate and gift taxes, an increase in taxes levied against incomes in the higher brackets, and a graduated income tax levied against corporations. Altogether the President takes an advanced stand on the question of taxation. At one place in the message he looked up at me with a smile and said, "That is for Hearst." I can imagine the clamor that will go up from Hearst and the big-money groups generally. But I believe the position he has taken on this question will go far to strengthen his position with the average man and woman.

August 23

I had a ten-thirty appointment with the President this morning. When I got up to his study, his valet ushered me into his bedroom, telling me that the President was shaving. He waved toward the bathroom and the President called out to me to come in. There he was, sitting before a mirror in front of the washstand, shaving. He invited me to sit on the toilet seat while we talked.

November 7 [1936]

Even believing as I did that the President would carry many more states than he needed to win, I was not prepared for the surprising results that came over the radio Tuesday night. It was soon clear that the President had not only won but that he had gone over by a tremendous popular and electoral college vote. Landon carried only two states—Maine and

Vermont. There has been nothing like it in the history of American politics. The President pulled through to victory men whose defeat would have been better for the country.

To my view, the outstanding thing about the campaign was the lack of influence of the newspapers.

1935: DIARY OF A SUBURBAN HOUSEWIFE

"I've always liked the word 'housewife,'" writes Dorothy Blake, "because it seemed to have a dignity and great depth of meaning. A really good housewife is, in my opinion, a pretty grand person."

We think her own life is pretty convincing proof of her statement. She is now in her nineteenth year as an editor of Woman's Day, the A & P magazine. There she conducts the popular column headed "Neighbors." Through these same years she has been as successful in her home-making career as she has in the world of writing. Diary of a Suburban Housewife came out as a book in 1936. A continuation under the title It's All in the Family was published in 1943.

In Manhasset, Long Island, the suburb where she is a housewife, she is Mrs. W. R. Robinson. Back in the days reported below, the Robinsons lived in what they remember now as The Big House. There the children grew up, three of them. Now all three are married and the Robinsons are, at this writing, seven-time grandparents. Ten years ago they moved from The Big House across the street to The Little House. Mrs. Robinson tells us her grandchildren are "especially wonderful" and adds that so are most people's grandchildren.

"At night . . . a feeling of peace."
DOROTHY BLAKE (born 1892)

Jan. 14 [1935]

Coasting is perfect down our side hill today and every child in Oakdale is out there. Funny to see them plod up time after time and never seem to tire. But ask one of them to walk the half-mile to the village for some useful purpose and they'd look abused.

Jan. 29

Brilliant sunshine and the air clear. Started out for a short drive and ended up by buying materials for a picnic at Long Beach! Corn on the cob, at a beach party, would remove the mystery from Garbo. I remember how Jim and I used to laugh, the year we lived in one capital city, to watch the exalted members of the legislature at the State Fair. Viewed from the gallery of the House they were fairly impressive, but viewed from the back of a log trestle table as they ate chili they were far from it. Their necks pleated and unpleated like some fleshy accordions. "In the name of the law" never meant so much to me after that. In fact I don't believe it ever meant much to me anyway. So many statutes are on the books because Bill Jones from Syracuse wants to do a favor for John Smith from Springfield. Then, at some future time, John Smith will do the same for him so they can both go back home and tell the dear constituents how active they have been in office.

Feb. 2

What a marvelous world this would be if all the children in it grew up as their fond parents hope they will! Just the same it is part of the thrill and compensation of that parenthood to watch your children take up where you left off.

Feb. 6

Came home this afternoon to find the living room floor filled with orange crates, grocery boxes, piles of books. No one in sight. I called Artie and heard a faint answer from the third floor, "Just a second, Mom, I'll be right down."

It seems that what I thought was the living room rug littered with trash —and our best books—was a new flying field and a hangar.

Feb. 10

Made scrapple this morning and dipped it in meal and fried it tonight. That is a grand dish when the thermometer is doing a little deep sea diving. And fried apples with their red skins changing to sort of a deep copper glaze as they cook. I tried shaving some maple sugar over them just before they were done, and, at the third helping, Jim reached over and took my hand, "Pretty good old world, honey, with you in it."

Why doesn't someone write a cook book stressing its spiritual values?

Feb. 24

Had an inspiration today to make a regular beef pie and tuck some oysters under the crust. Jim sat down to dinner and, before I brought it in, said brightly: "Say, I had something new for lunch today, beefsteak and oyster pie! It was great."

March 4

Went to a P.T.A. meeting in the school library.

The speaker's subject was, "Is Your Child a Norm?" Everybody answered Yes out loud and then questioned it inwardly.

March 7

Parents think children are bent on doing everything to annoy them and children think parents are bent on stopping anything they particularly enjoy doing.

March 16

My grandmother used to tell me how she'd kept grandfather's shirts in the same drawer in the same dresser for forty years—yet every time he wanted a clean one he called her.

April 19

Jim told me tonight he had seen Bill at lunch. I tried, as usual, to get some news of Beth and the children. He, as usual, said he couldn't remember that they talked about anything in particular.

July 9

We left for the beach at ten o'clock. I was fixing the lunch while Jim was getting the car ready. Then he came into the kitchen and stood watching me. "Gee, all those sandwiches? Who's going to eat them? Must think you're cooking for a re-forestation camp!"

I knew perfectly well that, before the day was out, he'd be asking me if I was trying to put him on a diet because the food had run out. He did.

Oct. 23

A perfectly windy autumn day with the leaves rushing around like women at a bargain sale. I'd like to turn the house inside out and upside down. In theory I'm all against twice yearly house-cleaning. But, in practice, I like nothing better than to air everything airable, wash everything washable, and polish and shine and set in order again.

Nov. 19

Took out the last extra blankets this morning as the paper predicted "Fair and much colder tonight." Every once in a while the weather man is right.

"Such a remark is simply childish," says Jim.

"So is the weather," say I. Whereupon I slip another section of apple pie onto his plate and we both feel better. We agree on practically nothing—except the essentials. We two aren't one, by any stretch of the imagination, but we are two working together toward the same goal. The road seems a little foggy these days and the goal of happiness and security for ourselves and education and preparation for our children seems a mirage.

But, one day at a time, we'll accomplish it somehow. Nice to stand together at night as we cover up the children the last thing before we go to bed. Blankets he has worked hard to buy, and I have worked hard to care for, keep them warm and well. They are bathed and fed and made content because we have pulled together and made a success of our marriage. There comes over us both a feeling of peace and satisfaction.

―――――――――――――――――――――――――――――――――――――★

1942:   BEHIND THE ADVERTISEMENTS
―――――――――――――――――――――――――――――――――――――☆

THEY DON'T HAVE an overly high opinion of the people of America in Ulcer Gulch, that bleak, barren, fluorescent-baked canyon of mid-Manhattan whose glass-and-chrome topsoil produces the billboards and commercials. James Webb Young, a native of Covington, Kentucky, started as an office boy, worked up to the vice-presidency of J. Walter Thompson Company, and later became a professor of business history and advertising at the University of Chicago. He was a founder of the Advertising Council of America.

"Lives of quiet desperation . . ."
JAMES WEBB YOUNG (born 1886)

July 8 [1942]

Romance in its broad sense is the most wanted product in the world. So many people lead lives of "quiet desperation" that any advertising which offers them escape, and any product which offers them utility plus color, performs a profound service.

August 27

Because words and phrases are regular Typhoid Marys of ideas, they have a power to inoculate us of which we are usually unconscious. When I was a boy we spoke of the retailer's occupation as "keeping store." That is, he *kept* the community's *store* of surplus goods until somebody needed them. And his whole business conduct was governed by this idea.

By what words was he changed into the aggressive merchant, and when? Only thirty years ago, in 1912, I had a part in the preparation of the first book on "sales quotas." These were new words then, and they, with other phrases, projected a new concept of making every man do his duty as a consumer; making every community toe an advancing consumption mark. Held up to manufacturers' salesmen, who in turn held them up to retailers, they changed the whole face of business; indeed, of life itself. Whether for better or for worse affiant saith not.

September 14

Sometimes under pressure, at white heat, you turn out the complete and perfect advertisement. At other times, with toil and trouble, rewrites and refinements, you finally get one to where it pleases you. In either case you send it off with some thrill of satisfaction and pride. Then in a week, two weeks, a month later you see it, suddenly in some publication. And you grimace and say, "My God. Did I do that?"

October 25

Every artist knows that sunlight can only be pictured with shadows. And every good biographer shows us, as Boswell did, that only the faults of a great man make him real to us. But in advertising we are afraid of this principle, hence less convincing than we might be. The most extraordinary response I ever got to an ad was when I offered a second-hand motor car for sale, and judiciously described its defects as well as its virtues.

October 27

Luncheon with a publisher; we talked about the rise and fall of different magazines over the last quarter of a century. Perhaps nothing else illustrates so well the economic maxim that "Wealth is a flow and not a fund." Successful publishing properties are built by men with dynamic instincts for the flow of things. Their decline begins when they fall into the hands of corporations controlled by counting-house brains, whose instincts are for preserving the funds. This stops the flow, and the wealth seeps away, no man knows how.

October 31

Returning from the movies this afternoon I thought how like they are in some ways to advertising. The exaggerations which people complain of in both are not so much due to an intent to deceive, as they are to a lack of skill in striking the true note. Camera men and ad men alike live too much on the surface of their callings, and lean too heavily on the tricks of their trade.

BEFORE HE TOOK COMMAND of the whole Asiatic mainland front against the Japanese in World War II, the late General Joseph W. (Vinegar Joe) Stilwell had spent ten years in China. He knew his soldiering. He also knew his Chinese. He could win with them if he could prevent their corrupt leaders, particularly Chiang K'ai-shek, from sabotaging his efforts. He gave himself the impossible assignment of trying to force this "ally" of the United States into an honest war against the Japanese, and met with inevitable failure. His diary, published two years after his death, keeps alive the memory of one of America's ablest and purest fighters.

"Bitched up by the Generalissimo . . ."
JOSEPH W. STILWELL (1883-1946)

Washington, January 16 [1942]

Chief of Staff sent for me at 2:30. Up there till 5:00 talking over China

Stimson didn't want to consider me, "because he had his head down." (Referring to the way I was sitting one day.) George [Marshall] told him the only reason I had my head down was probably because I was getting ready to butt something. So the Secretary [Stimson] said he'd see me, and I went up.

Are the chances for getting results good? I said yes if I have command. "What'll we do about that?" Ask Chiang if he'll do it. "O.K. Write out the question." So I went out and wrote it and he's sending it on to T. V. Soong. The angle is that I may be appointed chief of staff of Chiang K'ai-shek's joint staff, whatever that is, and in carrying out Chiang K'ai-shek's instructions, I exercise command. Well, there it is.

January 25

If we can hold on to Rangoon, and develop the bases in China, the bombers can be delivered, and along about summertime the Japs will begin to get it on the nose at home. What a pleasure that would be.

February 9

Our heavy bombers are piling up in India, unable to go farther. If we only had the ground crews, we could use them from where they are. Production is still the trouble, or rather distribution. For instance, for March, April, May, the U. S. gets 60-odd, 70-odd and 48 fighters. And the Limeys

598

get 400-odd, 325, and 300-odd. Kee-riste! Events are forcing all concerned to see the vital importance of Burma.

February 18

Singapore has surrendered—60,000 men. Christ. What the hell is the matter?

Calcutta, India, February 28

Wavell's plane late. Finally, at 5:30 it came in and they got off. Brereton slapping his fanny with his riding crop and darting around importantly. Finally we went up and introduced ourselves. Arranged a talk at 6:30 at Government House. He's [Wavell] a tired, depressed man, pretty well beaten down.

Chungking, China, March 6

Conference with Chiang K'ai-shek. It was a relief to find that the G-mo contemplates command in Burma for me.

March 9

Got word from Shang Chen he would be in with the staff setup. At 7:00 he came, with the expected abortion, making everyone equal and with me the chief of staff for Allied forces alone. Well, hell.

Lashio, Burma, March 14

I am amazed the way the Chinese accept me. At 11:30 decided to act. Told Lin Wei to start troops moving south. Die is cast.

Maymyo, Burma, March 25

Chiang K'ai-shek and his changeable mind had me worried. I was deadly afraid he would call off this attack. But the seed has apparently taken root, and as Tu says, now we can work my plan.

Pyawbwe, Burma, March 29

Called on him [Tu] for a real effort. Full of excuses as usual. It's all a bunch of crap. By Jesus, I'm about fed up.

March 30

To bed at 1:30 as usual. Alternatives now at hand. Let it ride and do nothing. Resign flatly. Ooze out and demand own force (make a statement "Now that command is unified [under Alexander] I believe it would unnecessarily complicate the situation if I or a third country national remain").

Shoved off at 9:30. Liao and Tu have dogged it again. The pusillanimous bastards. No attack at all. Front quiet, no Jap reaction. Just craven.

Liao [commander of 22nd division] moved command post back a mile. Tu ordered him not to attack till 96th and 55th get in.

Chungking, April 1

Through stupidity, fear, and the defensive attitude we have lost a grand chance to slap the Japs back at Toungoo. The basic reason is Chiang K'ai-shek's meddling. Had he not gone behind my back to Tu and Lin Wei, they might have obeyed my orders. He can't keep his hands off: Sixteen hundred miles from the front, he writes endless instructions to do this and that, based on fragmentary information and a cockeyed conception of tactics.

His constant interference and letter writing have the effect of completely nullifying my little authority. I have no authority to shoot anybody.

Shwebo, Burma, April 30

They will blow the bridge tonight. Last night word came that Lashio was taken.

An Associated Press dispatch from New Delhi, India, dated May 25, quoted General Stilwell as stating: "I claim we got a hell of a beating. We got run out of Burma and it is humiliating as hell. I think we ought to find out what caused it, go back and retake it."

Chungking, June 15

Talk with Chiang K'ai-shek about this and that. Fifth Army to stay in India. I to retain command, because that will make it easy for the Chinese; they won't have to deal with British. Tu to remain. (His face to be saved, the hell with mine.)

July 10

THE MANURE PILE: This is the most dreary type of maneuvering I've ever done, trying to guide and influence a stubborn, ignorant, prejudiced, conceited despot who never hears the truth except from me and finds it hard to believe. [Reference is to Chiang K'ai-shek.]

August 1

To office and worked through some poison. *Snafu* with Peanut [reference is to Chiang K'ai-shek]. No answer on anything. He's having a hell of a time with his face.

Calcutta, India, August 20

To movie. Wallace Beery as a cavalry soldier. Lewis Stone with stomach sticking out. Why don't they catch such things?

New Delhi, India, August 30

I'm too busy to mope, and I'm feeling O.K. again. And putting on some weight. If I could get some new teeth and eyes and some hair dye, I wouldn't look a day over seventy.

Chungking, September 14

We have been marking time. The Peanut is out of town, and of course the machinery of the government has shut down. A one-man dog is a grand institution, but a one-man government is something else.

Chungking, October 6

It was even worse than we thought. A bitched-up action at Ch'u Hsien, buggered completely by the Generalissimo, and then orders to retreat which were thoroughly carried out. The "reconquest" was merely reoccupation after the Japs had gone, allowing plenty of time to make sure. Peanut "directed operations" from Chungking with the usual brilliant result. The whole thing was a mess. Peanut ordered two armies to hide in the mountains and attack on flank when the Japs pass. The Jap simply blocked the exit roads and went on.

Chungking, November 19

We're rolling.

We have now gotten both the Limeys and the Chinese committed, and working at it. If we can keep a fire lit under Wavell and horn in on command and training on this side, the job is in a fair way to get done, bejesus.

January 3, 1943

The obstructioneers have been busy in the War Ministry. They delayed and delayed till X-Y [the Burma offensive] is damn near impossible and now of course the excuse is that there isn't time to put it on. Peanut screams that the British Navy hasn't appeared and the Limeys will use only three divisions instead of seven. The Limeys squawk that it "can't be done," and look on me as a crazy man, as well as a god-dam meddler stirring up trouble.

January 8

Black Friday. T. V. [Soong] gave Dorn the Peanut's answer to F.D.R. (Afraid to see me with it on account of probable blowup.)

Peanut says he won't fight.

January 14 [letter to Mrs. Stilwell]

You had better be prepared for a soured old pickle, if I ever get through with this shoveling.

Pappy's done his bit,
He shoveled all the ———,
He's just a sap,
He took the rap,
The wringer got his tit.

Pappy's now a wreck,
He got it in the neck,
He took a ride,
They tanned his hide,
They worked a phony deck.

Pappy's sore and lame,
He'll never be the same,
So yank the dub,
Put in a sub,
And let him play the game.

1944:   THE GIs INVADE HITLER'S EUROPE

ONCE THE Omaha and Utah beachheads were established on the French coast, an immediate and vital need of General Eisenhower's great cross-Channel invasion was to take the area lying between them. The key to that objective was the small but strongly fortified town of Carentan. Pfc. George Groh and his fellow-infantrymen suspected this was a red-hot assignment that would take them into the thick of the high-casualty "hedgerow fighting." They were right.

Groh, a long, slim Kansan, going on seven feet, left out the purple passages and the sentimentalism that ran through much of the paid writing of the time. His business was with the bayonet. But Yank Magazine liked his diary and published it. Other magazines since then have felt the same way about his work.

"Our only contact was Jerry . . ."
GEORGE GROH (born 1922)

D-Day [June 6, 1944]

While other regiments of our division (the 101st) swung the first liberation punch, we lay offshore in the [English] Channel in an LST. Our Company Commander predicted we were in for a tour of "light combat duty." He later revised his opinion.

D-Plus-One

We finally got our clearance and piled into assault boats. We came ashore with our first three days supplies on our backs. A few minutes later we hit the ground when four Messerschmitt 109s strafed us.

D-Plus-Two

In the afternoon we took off for the front, another traffic element in an already clogged roadway. A parachute captain, bicycling jauntily along, called to us, "They're a pushover, boys! You can take 'em!"

Our outfit was slated to relieve a parachute infantry unit holding down the left flank of the beachhead. Along the approach we were harassed by an 88mm. gun which caused considerable casualties. Then an artillery outfit plastered the Germans with a heavy barrage, and we moved out under cover of it to establish a new station under the bank of the Doove River. At nightfall we held one bank of the river, the Jerries the other.

D-Plus-Three

Lt. Werner and Pfc. Hatchel swam the river, taking across a rope. I crossed on that with Pvt. William Webb. Jerry had run a ferryboat aground, and we salvaged the boat, setting up a ferry service. Lt. Vynn went out with a combat patrol. Jerry ambushed the group, killing one man and wounding five. Our ferry system had bogged down. The rest of the patrol was ordered to recross the river under cover of improvised protecting fire. Two Pfc.s, though badly wounded, managed to make the swim unaided. Lt. Werner brought back the remainder of the men on a raft which he had made from two German signboards.

D-Plus-Four

We crossed the river in rubber boats. Briefing the mission, Maj. Hartford Salee told five of us we were to proceed to a certain bridge, avoiding a fight if possible, and establish contact with the VII Corps.

Rounding a bend, I came face to face with three bearded Heinies with machine-pistols. It was a case of mutual surprise. We decided it was "possible" to avoid a fight. We took off in what was probably a cross-country record. Jerry never fired a shot. I suspect he was busy setting records in the opposite direction.

Orders came to move on to Carentan. That was a red-hot assignment. German snipers worked on us all the way. Company A secured a large stone barn and two houses 100 yards further. From the barn to the houses we called "sniper run," later "machine-gun run," but Nazi fire was wild and served only to make dash-men out of a lot of slow Joes.

The two houses were inhabited by 20 Frenchmen—including a girl who would qualify as a pin-up in any league. The natives furnished a lot of moral support and cognac. Jerry took the OP [outpost] apart with mortar fire, knocked out our barn with hand grenades, and the forward element in our two houses was virtually surrounded. We collected our wounded and managed to leave under cover of darkness.

D-Plus-Five

We spent the morning outside Carentan exchanging fire with German emplacements. Jerry took a severe toll. His snipers and mortar fire were making it hard for us to get our wounded out. We went into a defensive around a tank park. Battalion issued two warnings—be careful of women snipers and of German combat patrols dressed in American uniform.

D-Plus-Six

I spent the morning with Lt. Werner, scouting. We walked right by one well-camouflaged machine-gun nest but the occupants turned out to be White Russians who didn't want to fight anyway and surrendered.

T/Sgt. Robert Graef led us on three successive bayonet charges. We dug in at dusk about 75 yards from the enemy. Pvt. Bill Robinson chased the Nazis out of a barn with a bazooka hit and Pvt. Jack Case gave them a little of their own back with a German machine gun which he'd been taught to operate by a PW.

I crawled along a hedgerow, needling the Nazis with a stock phrase from *Yank's* GI German lessons: "German soldiers, surrender or die." Jerry didn't like it, and a sniper began to needle me in return with his carbine. Since he had the better argument, I inched back to my own position.

When darkness fell, we were reduced to 88 enlisted men, our ammunition was low, and we'd lost contact with the right, the left and the rear. Our only sure contact was Jerry, just out in front. The enemy sprayed us with sporadic machine-gun fire. We felt better then, indications being that he was more concerned with his own defense than with infiltrating ours. All the same it was a long, long night.

D-Plus-Seven

At dawn we withdrew to a better defensive position about 300 yards to the rear. Jerry crept up and tossed a few grenades, and a sniper hit Pfc. Stephenson in the head. But he came up with one of those war miracles; his helmet turned the bullet and he escaped with a scalp wound.

By 11 o'clock that morning Allied tanks were rumbling up the road that was our front line and everybody relaxed. The first platoon—what was left of us—drew a mission just before dark to outpost and protect a bridge being built by some engineers of the 30th Division. We marched on past the bridge and set up our outposts, about two miles into German territory. Then, when the Nazis sprayed us after dark with machine-gun bursts, we fell back on time-honored tactics of "getting t' hell out of here."

We set up again 300 yards from the bridge and this time things were quiet. At dawn we went back to our bivouac area, the bridge having been completed. The 30th was to take over and swing some heavy blows with tanks, artillery and a fresh division of infantry.

We still had to go on and hold the base of the peninsula while other units drove north to Cherbourg. But our hardest work was done. And everybody was damn glad of it.

What Groh couldn't write for publication at the time was that his platoon was virtually wiped out twice.

1947: THE MAGIC OF MANHATTAN

To THOSE WHO never walk across Brooklyn Bridge or go to the top of the Empire State Building or visit the Statue of Liberty—that is, to the residents of New York City—the writings of foreigners about their neighborhood are often informative. Here is New York as seen by Simone de Beauvoir, noted French novelist, existentialist, and gifted reporter. In 1953 she published The Second Sex, a work on the status of woman which was so brilliant that it dazzled and quite overwhelmed the swarm of sociological hornets unnested by it. In 1956 there followed the best-selling novel, both in Europe and America, The Mandarins.

In 1947 Mlle. de Beauvoir made a nationwide tour of America, and a few years afterward published the diary of her trip.

"I couldn't quite believe it."
SIMONE DE BEAUVOIR (born 1908)

January 25

We were just waiting our turn: there is an airplane landing every minute at La Guardia Airport. Papers passed from hand to hand. A doctor vaguely examined our teeth as though we were horses up for sale. They were calling me; an official examined my beautiful visa printed on stiff paper and decorated, like a medieval chart, with red seals. He nodded his head. "You come from a beautiful country [France] but you're coming into a still more beautiful country." He asked for eight dollars. We followed the line of a river, crossed over an iron bridge, and suddenly my neighbor said, "This is Broadway." Then, at a glance I saw it—great luminous streets in which hundreds and hundreds of cars were moving, stopping and starting again with such discipline that they appeared to be controlled by some magnetic providence from the skies above.

We took a long time finding a place to park the car.

D.P. had booked a room for me in a huge hotel at the corner of Forty-fourth Street and Eighth Avenue.

I walked. Broadway. Times Square. Forty-second Street. I said to myself, "This is New York," but I couldn't quite believe it.

January 26

It was nine o'clock on a Sunday morning, the streets were deserted, light still lingered in the neon signs. There was not a person in sight, not a car in the street—nothing to break the rectilinear course of Eighth Avenue. The streets were all cubes, prisms and parallelograms—concrete abstract designs, their surfaces abstract intersections. The building materials had neither density nor structure; space itself had been poured into molds.

I drank orange juice at a counter and sat down in a chair in a shoeshine booth; little by little I came to life and the city grew more familiar. The surfaces had become façades; the solids, houses. In the roadway dust and old newspapers were raised by the wind. After Washington Square all mathematics went by the board. Right angles were broken; streets were no longer numbered but named; lines became curved and confused. I was lost as though in some European town.

The landscape changed. The word "landscape" suited this city abandoned by men and invaded by the sky—a sky that soared over the skyscrapers, plunged down into the straight streets, as if too vast for the city to annex—a mountain sky. I was walking in the depths of a canyon, between high cliffs that never saw the sun. There was the tang of salt in the air.

Man's history is not inscribed on these poised and knowingly calculated buildings; they are nearer to prehistoric caverns than the houses of Paris or Rome. In Paris, in Rome, history has filtered to the very roots of the soil; Paris stretches down to the center of the earth. New York's Battery does not have such deep roots. Beneath the subways, the drains and heating plants, the rock is virgin and inhuman.

This morning, between this rock and the open sky, Wall Street and Broadway, deep in the shadows of their gigantic buildings, belonged to nature. The little russet church, with its cemetery of flat tombstones, was as unexpected and as moving in the middle of Broadway as some Calvary on the wild seashore.

Here was the Bowery, and here were the drunks sleeping on the pavement.

January 27

The slightest act involved a problem. How was I to stamp my letters? Where should I post them? Those flutters of wings near the elevator, those white flashes, I almost took them for hallucinations. Behind a sheet of glass, letters were falling from the twenty-fifth floor to the depths of the basement. At the newsstand, there was a machine that spat out stamps, but the coins confused me. I tried for ten minutes to get a phone connection; all the telephones rejected the dime which I obstinately slipped in the slot designed for quarters.

Everything made me wonder, not only unexpected sights, but things I had foreseen. I did not know that in front of the apartment houses in fashionable neighborhoods there were green canvas canopies with large numbers projecting out over the sidewalks as if heralding some wedding. There were doormen on the threshold; each house looked like a hotel or a bar. Entrances, also guarded by uniformed men, were like palace halls. The elevators were worked by servants; it would be difficult to receive visitors in secret.

It was a fine sunny day, and I walked along the East River, but the drive—that wide raised road which runs beside the river—is reserved for cars. I tried to cheat, and I advanced, hugging the wall. But it is difficult to cheat in America; everything works like a machine which serves you so long as you fit in obediently. Cars driving at fifty miles an hour along this highway brushed past me dangerously. There is a park beside the water, and passers-by were strolling about in it, but it seemed impossible to reach them. I darted out and managed to reach the line dividing two traffic streams, flowing in opposite directions; but I had to stay there a long time, fixed like a street lamp, waiting for a sudden break in the traffic to gain the other side, and I still had to jump over a railing before I was safe. Weighed down by my winter coat, too heavy for the warm sun, I felt more tired than if I had climbed a mountain. I learned, a few minutes later, that there were passages under the drive for pedestrians, as well as connecting bridges overhead.

I walked for a long time. When I reached the bridge, the sun was crimson and the flaming sky was barred by the iron lattice-work of the bridge. One could see the towers of the Battery through a web of fire; the horizontal span of the bridge and the vertical flight of the skyscrapers were magnified in this atmosphere, and their boldness was fully rewarded by the glory of the light.

I had an appointment for six o'clock at the Plaza Hotel on Fifty-ninth Street. I climbed the stairs to the elevated. We traveled above the Bowery at second-floor level; we flashed past stations: here we were already at Fourteenth Street, then Thirty-fourth, Forty-second Street; I was watching for Fifty-ninth Street, but we shot past like a whirlwind; Seventieth, Eightieth Street, we no longer stopped. I had taken an "express." I got off at the first station and took a "local" back.

January 29th

I went to bed late again; but there is something in the New York air that makes sleep useless. Perhaps it is that the heart beats faster here than elsewhere. People with heart trouble sleep little, and many New Yorkers die of heart disease. At all events, I was delighted to be awake again. The days seemed too short to me.

Everything was a feast to me. Drugstores were things that fascinated me. They were both primitive and modern, a fact which gives them a peculiarly American charm. Everything has a family look: there is the same bright cheapness, the same modest gayety; books with glazed covers, tubes of dentifrice and boxes of candy, all have the same colors—you have the impression that reading these books will leave a taste of sugar, that the candy will have stories to tell. . . . And then one soon discovers that beneath the multicolored paper wrappers, all the chocolates taste of peanuts, all the best sellers tell the same story.

January 30th

What makes daily life so agreeable in America is the cordial good humor of the Americans. Of course, these qualities have their ugly side. I loathe those imperious invitations "to look at the best side of life," repeated in phrases and pictures as long as the day itself. On posters, for instance, what displays of shining white teeth before Coca-Cola, Lucky Strikes, and dishes of Quaker Oats; a smile like lockjaw. The constipated young woman smiles lovingly at the lemonade which eases her stomach. In the subway, in the street, on magazine pages, these smiles pursue me like obsessions.

You sense a hoax, but it does not prevent the fact that, owing to this personal consideration, the American does not have to be stuck-up to feel his dignity; businesslike, perhaps, but the friendliness of salesmen, employees, waiters and porters is, though not disinterested, none the less never servile; they are neither sour nor stiff, and their pleasantness is real. I was especially fond of taxi drivers. They talked throughout the entire ride, and it was often difficult to understand them.

February 3rd

I went to the top of the Empire State Building. We were directed to the express elevators, which shoot up nonstop to the eightieth floor. There, one must change elevators to reach the top; it is a single vertical expedition.

I saw Manhattan piled up to the south on the point of its peninsula. I saw Brooklyn, Queens, Staten Island, the islets, the land eaten away by the water and pierced by two rivers, the geography is so clear and the luminous water so vividly reveals the lay of the land that one forgets the houses, and New York appears to be a piece of virgin planet. The rivers, the archipelago, the curves of the peninsula, belong to prehistory: the sea is ageless; the capriciousness of the streets set at right angles gives them, by contrast, an air of extreme youth. The city is newborn; it covers with a thin crust rocks older than the flood.

And yet, when the lights go up from the Bronx to the Battery, from New Jersey to Brooklyn, the sea and the sky are only a decor: it is in the city that the true dominion of man asserts itself.

---★

1943:   THE ABUNDANT LIFE OF A BOY

---☆

DAVID KOGAN, of Yonkers, New York, kept up his diary almost to the day he died at 22. Above average in ability, he was in other respects pretty much like most boys, and that was what he wanted to be, what he tried very hard to be. In maturity he was tall and handsome. Here we meet him at the age of 14; and we leave him before he is stricken with lymphoma, not because his diary isn't just as appealing to the end of his lingering affliction but because death for such as David is beyond understanding. That abundance of life which he claimed for himself makes more sense.

"I wonder what is going to happen . . ."
DAVID S. KOGAN (1929-1951)

August 12 [1943]

This morning Grandma went down with Mother and Aunt Lilly to be sworn in as an American citizen. She resented being fingerprinted as an alien, and studied diligently for the forthcoming exam. She did quite well, until questioned whether she belonged to a subversive society.

Grandma, not understanding, nodded her head. The clerk inquired if she were a Communist, and Grandma exclaimed indignantly: "God forbid!"

She is very proud and happy.

August 20

Defense work has recruited labor, and domestic help is scarce. One of my subscribers [on his paper route] asked me whether my mother or sister could come out to clean her windows. She knows Mom from the [Jewish] Center Auxiliary, but cannot place me other than "the paper boy."

"Tell Mrs. Lindenbaum I have sixteen windows of my own to clean, but I'll think it over," Mom replied with a chuckle.

Being a paper boy is amusing and at times somewhat saddening. I feel sorry for those who cannot manage to pay for their paper week after week.

May 10, 1944

I guess I am one of the boys now. I've learned the facts of life, smoke, gamble, curse. Don't misunderstand me—I am able to do these things, but don't practice them.

I'm a fellow with so many faults. I know my faults too, and that's what gives me the conscience. The thing to do is to strike out and cut the forest around me. Unfortunately I pretend I'm lost and complacently sit on the ax—it'll cut a hole in my undersides yet.

After I did some homework, Gil came to my house. We went hunting for some really sexy book. Later we went over to Gil's house, where we listened to his swing records.

May 13

Tonight was the night of the A. S. C. [his club, of 21 members] anniversary dance. Strangely I had a pretty nice time. Hank took a liking to Bernice, and so, after I had him understand that his cutting in was welcome, I had a chance to look around and dance once in a while. Ken dropped in about eleven o'clock with a delicious piece of feminine pulchritude whom we nicknamed "Legs." What a face! And can she dance! There were a lot of other dames who couldn't exactly be called rotten tomatoes.

June 1

I have noticed that a breach has come between my parents and me. I don't tell them much and they resent it. I am sarcastic, which I shouldn't be; they use the same method and I can't take it. I know they are right, but I resent it, and they resent my resenting it.

Somehow I feel like a combo of the "Blues" and "Peck's Bad Boy." I feel I don't have a friend I can count on, who would help me in a pinch, who would wait for me. I also feel bad because Dad does not give me the freedom the fellers I go around with have. And to keep up with them I have to aggravate him, which burns. Then, too, although everybody likes to be liked, the girls do not like me enough to invite me anywhere.

June 7

Invasion [of France by the American forces] is the topic of the day, and the fog begins to clear. President Roosevelt, America's greatest president, and my personal hero (I still think he could do a lot of good that he does not do) addressed the nation last night. The D-Day Prayer which he wrote and delivered in his clear voice was simple and impressive.

September 2

We went to a girl's house. As usual, they listened to that lousy dance music, flirted, told corny jokes and happenings, and kissed a little. I'm always on the outside looking in. And yet, that and stags and meetings are practically the only ways I get together with my "friends."

Have decided to stop my evangelism for the causes for a while and learn more about them.

October 1

Mom came into the clubhouse early in the afternoon and found me playing cards with Mike (for fun). I told her I was playing for money, so that matters might come to a head. She chastised, but did not forbid.

I read a filthy document that described earthly love. I absorbed it intently. Might as well be informed for the future.

October 8

I feel self-conscious. I don't want to be handsome, but I hate my present appearance. Weak, pale, small ears, big nose, "peach fuzz," weak chin. Now my mouth is out of shape and I cannot smile, for Dr. Singer put my brace back yesterday.

October 14

Mike got the address of a disreputable firm in New York that sells the filthiest sex photos, stories and cartoons. He procured a book, *Ten Little Virgins,* and lent it to me. Frankly, it tells, but does not describe. I won't waste my time on those three hundred page spicy novels of the gay twenties.

I've been hanging around with Mike too much. His greatest thoughts are about sex.

November 7

Today was election day, and the politically minded Kogan was excited waiting for those returns. I awoke late and spent the morning gafoodling (that should be the term used for wasting time in the typical Kogan manner).

November 9

Miss Grant died today. It is not often that somebody whom I know dies, because I am young, and my acquaintance with older people is slight. It makes one pause and reflect on life and death, on death and life. Somehow I feel there will be no resurrection, and there is no Heaven. I realize it is a crime to waste a day. Everyone feels it when he steps into bed at night. Therefore it is my opinion that it is a crime to die without having lived. A man should not "gafoodle" a minute. He should not "ga-foodle" a day, so that he should not "gafoodle" his life.

November 12

My mother is not easy to get along with. She has brains, illogical woman's brains, and is unhappy. She does have remorse for a lot of things she does, nevertheless she never learns. She is a woman of many talents, a good artist, fair musician, and a pretty good cook. She dabbles here and dabbles there. She does, however, love me. A little change in her *weltanschauung* she might be a fine woman. I only hope that someday she might treat her family as well as her friends.

November 18

I went to Gladys's "Sweet Sixteen" party today. I had a fairly nice time. Danced, chatted, and ate. Saw "pretty little, witty little" D.B., still as charming and as unscrupulous as ever. I gave Gladys a nice "Sweet sixteen" kiss—it tasted good. It was the first kiss since my first party in December, 1941. The girls are beginning to look.

November 24

Stayed home at night. I am not going to my descent into the blues. I shall only state that I am very unpopular with family, fellow, and lass. If I would not use a lot of initiative, I would never be invited anywhere by anyone. I shouldn't be worried, but I am. It may be I am critical, but I am wet-blanketing myself.

December 12

I participated in something that was essentially a rowdy gang war. The

Rams "attacked" our clubhouse and we "defended" it. No one thought much of its consequences before the fight; now, afterwards, I view it with the feeling that the A.S.C. is continuing its course of self degradation; I also notice the disgusted looks of Gentiles and Jews in the neighborhood.

Well, to return to the struggle. Ed, Hank, and I manned the slanted roof, where a stiff battle ensued. I don't remember much, except being punched in the mouth. However, the whole school is giving me credit for pushing one of the attackers off the roof. After 35 min. the Rams left. We surveyed the damage: four broken windows, the work of six months of decorating and furnishing the clubhouse, cuts, bruises, and a broken arm. We rejoiced in our "glorious" victory.

January 16, 1945

I have indulged in a typical adolescent experience today. Was one of seven A.S.C. boys who piled into an old, smoking, bumpy '29 jalopy and toured around Yonkers for about a half hour. It's fun and thrilling, but I suppose quite dangerous. Nevertheless, everyone feels that *he* won't get hurt.

February 4

In my relations with the youth I am like an old man trying to act like a youth, and doing as well as a baby.

I took Sandra to the A.S.C. house party at the Horns' and had a lousy time. She's a teaser, and I don't mean strip. She is witty, cultured, but does not give a d———n about her date, as long as she has a good time. I could've kissed her goodnight, but I didn't. I knew she was disinterested. I hate that hypocritical "I love you" and the thrown kisses that go with it.

I'm in a melancholy mood. I'm beginning to think that I am repulsively ugly. I have a terrible voice, too.

February 7

Dr. Wilenky said that unless I feel terrible, I shouldn't stay home. Otherwise I would let fever, and only fever, be my guide. The doctor is a very learned man. However, in matters pertaining to medicine he can never make up his mind. In other words, he is a good doctor to have when you are well.

O! have I a genius for gafoodling. How can I ever hope to achieve success in my relations with other people if I am not successful in my relations with myself?

February 11

Nora, a most ugly girl, invited me to Irma's party last night. I went out of curiosity, hoping I won't be sorry.

It was the different type of affair. We got there at nine and found several couples. They talked for about ten minutes and then out went all the lights. The couples went into passionate positions. Ken had his hand under the brassiere of Dina for quite a while! I just sat there looking. Then I began kissing Nora; was she homely! The gang treated the affair so casually as with remarks like "Pull down your sweater, Audrey." I liked the indifference, the knowledge that the girls had not any modesty short of relations. It took a lot of the uncertainty and guessing out of it—the girls cooperated. Yes, I enjoyed the new experience, the action of others, but why did she have to be so homely!

February 15

We received word that Lester Smalheiser has been killed in Germany. The boy was only nineteen and was a good friend of mine. He gave his life before he lived. A good-natured American-Jewish boy, struck down by a Hitlerite bullet. The death of one individual helps one to make "40,000 killed" more meaningful.

February 24

Kogan and O'Grady got along quite nicely together, thank you. Acting on impulse, I called up Margery O'Grady, asking her to the A.S.C. party this evening. She is a very beautiful, proud, refined Catholic girl. I was scared, for I later learned that the party will be a "lights out" affair. After worrying almost all day, I got dressed and called for Margy. She looked beautiful, with her "Irish Eyes Smiling." Well, you can't touch her. I couldn't put my arm around her (I wonder if anyone else can). We danced and talked and ate. I had a nice time, because I didn't have any frustrated desires. We slowly walked home and talked.

February 26

I am "living an abundant life" with many outside activities ranging from studying the Bible to wrestling, and from saving pictures of famous personalities and semi-nude girls to preparing myself for a rabbinical seminary.

March 25

The boys had "game" tonight, and I could not resist the temptation to go. I really enjoyed myself, and find it interesting to watch people under pressure. I knew that Mom didn't want me to go (and Dad too), so I did not let them directly prohibit me, but waited until they went out. I quit at 11:20; Mike and I hurried home, and it seemed the folks beat me by about an hour. They said something about being home on school-days by 10:00 and went to sleep.

I'll say this: the parents say "no" a lot, but they don't know how to discipline me after I do something. However, they are good people (but nervous), and the storm shall pass.

April 12

President Franklin Delano Roosevelt is no more!

It is a great loss. As a matter of fact, his is the only administration which I have known in my span of fifteen years. (My political memory begins with the outlawing of the N.R.A.)

I wonder what is going to happen.

October 22

Mom had a real spat with me today. She said things like I'm throwing away my future; I never do any homework. I used my latest defense— look calmly sympathetic, and say that happiness is all that counts.

She calmed down beautifully, and then bent over backwards. Still, I know she's right in many ways.

October 26

This evening I was to attend Jill's party. Dina Brener clung to me, which greatly amused my friends, much to my discomfort. Toward the end of an evening of dancing and small-talk, I found myself in a dark room with Dina, engaged in necking, which I delighted in. The upshot of it was that I took the girl home. Before leaving, she kissed Lenny and Steve goodnight, altho hardly knowing them. Therefore, you see, it was no great tactical triumph.

November 7

I wonder if Mother ever reads this book? Or *anyone*—it is frightful to think that I mistrust people, but I would be permanently shaken if anyone did. The only thing—to go and buy a strong box with a lock. I don't want anyone reading these books.

December 5

I returned to school today—the day seemed most ordinary. The *Black-*

board our Y.H.S. yearbook, is becoming a "pain in the neck"! Joe Roth and I have definite ideas on the book. We wish its theme to be the United Nations. The hitch in all this is Miss Raftery—our adviser. She strongly feels that the theme should be the pagodas of China, which I think is the bunk.

December 21

Boy, am I having trouble getting a date for New Year's Eve. I know I'm no raving specimen of masculinity, nor personality plus prize package, nevertheless, no one including me wants less than he deserves. I'm out for the best, prettiest and most alive girl I'll feel comfortable with. Yet the going is tough. I waited too long and the field is limited.

I got a feelin' Dina Brener likes me. She's always moonin' around me, an' makes out as if she's awful interested in me.

December 25

I went to call on the Blind Date; in less time than it takes to write this she became Arlene Davidson, beautiful, laughing, intelligent, petite, a blond Sandra in every manner, but quieter. We clicked immediately, and fortune presented me with one of the happiest evenings my sad life has yet experienced.

The company was quite congenial. The Cafe Rouge, our destination, was a very nice place—a night club. We very maturely dined and boozed and danced to the strains of a name band. We loved it. Kogan was Cinderella, sparkling in conversation, with his native wit; Arlene Davidson became Arlene, someone to dream about. We waltzed 'n such. Before leaving I gallantly swiped an ash tray which she would always treasure. There were about eleven other couples from Yonkers. From there we went to a "bistro" on Fifty-second Street, where we ordered liquor and listened to Le Hot Jazz—pure jazz with no trace of swing. It is a worthwhile experience. A sidelight of the evening was my first cigar. I like 'em.

On returning to Yonkers, we agreed that Arlene would break her New Year's date and accompany me to the A.S.C. party.

January 1, 1946

I didn't make any resolutions yet!

Thought about the girl and the mistakes I made last night. One minute after midnight saw me in a beautiful romance with a lovely girl. It was the way I kissed her. It was the rude, weak, short, clumsy kiss of a coward. Of course I didn't realize it then but I do now. Gosh, but she's a swell kid.

Howie Lieber drove us home. Arlene was locked out and it was necessary to climb into a second-story window. I let Howie do it! That's what finished me.

January 19

Called up Arlene twice today and verified my date with her. Dressed in one of the prevailing men's fashions of the day, a white shirt and tie covered by a heavy colored flannel shirt. I got there about eight o'clock. She looked happy, pretty, intelligent and cold. I knew I shouldn't have taken her to the movies, but it was too late. Contrary to fond expectations, the time in the movies hung heavy. She was reserved and reticent. After walking her home, she quickly dashed upstairs, leaving me to ponder "ma chayenu"—what is life?

On the way home I dropped in at a "sweet sixteen" party in time to kiss the "sweet young thing" (look who's talking).

January 27

I know I am a failure in regard to Arlene. On the other hand, I know I hurt Dina Brener by constantly spurning her.

February 9

Why don't I let my parents in on the bleak, proud, lonely, and desolate castle high on the moor which is my social life—perhaps they would not understand—of course they wouldn't.

February 25

"Ring the bells!" We were awakened from the lethargy of our daily educational grind by the announcement that General "Vinegar Joe" Stilwell, Yonkers High's most distinguished alumnus, was visiting the school and would speak in the assembly.

We repaired thither and Frank L. Baker pulled out an introduction. Then Joe spoke, and quickly disarmed and won his youthful audience by his lack of oratory and his extensive use of the vernacular.

He told us of the "wind" he has to hear at dinners, how he was a lousy student in high school, always fooling around and playing pranks on the principal. He seriously said that this generation was better physically and mentally (didn't say morally) and urged us to work. All in all, it was a grand homecoming for this humble man who wore no decorations.

SOURCES AND
ACKNOWLEDGMENTS

Adams, Charles Francis: "Campaigning with Seward in 1860," edited by Theodore C. Blegen. *Minnesota History,* vol. 8 (1927).

Adams, Franklin Pierce: *Diary of Our Own Samuel Pepys.* New York, 1935. By permission of Simon and Schuster, Inc. Copyright 1935 by Franklin Pierce Adams.

Adams, John: *Works of John Adams,* edited by Charles Francis Adams, vol. 2. Boston, 1850.

Adams, John Quincy: *Memoirs of John Quincy Adams, Comprising Portions of His Diary from 1795 to 1848,* edited by Charles Francis Adams. Philadelphia, 1877.

Alcott, Amos Bronson: *Journals of Bronson Alcott,* edited by Odell Shepard. Boston, 1938. By permission of Little, Brown & Co., Odell Shepard, and F. Wolsey Pratt.

Alcott, Louisa May: *Louisa May Alcott: Her Life, Letters and Journals,* edited by Ednah D. Cheney. Boston, 1899.

Allen, James: Diary. *Pennsylvania Magazine of History and Biography,* vol. 9 (1885).

Anonymous Pilot in World War I: *War Birds: Diary of an Unknown Aviator.* New York, 1926. By permission of Elliott Springs.

Barron, Clarence W.: *They Told Barron,* 1930; and *More They Told Barron,* 1931; both edited by Arthur Pound and Samuel T. Moore. New York. By permission of Harper and Brothers. Copyright 1930, 1931 by Arthur Pound and Samuel Taylor Moore.

Beauvoir, Simone de: *America Day by Day.* New York, 1955. By permission of Grove Press.

Bell, James G.: "A Log of the Texas-California Cattle Trail," edited by J. Evetts Haley. *Southwestern Historical Quarterly,* vol. 35 (1931-32).

Black, William: Journal, edited by R. Alonzo Brock. *Pennsylvania Magazine of History and Biography,* vol. 1 (1878).

Blake, Dorothy: *Diary of a Suburban Housewife.* New York, 1936. By permission of William Morrow & Co., Inc. Copyright 1935, 1936 by Dorothy Blake.

Boit, John: *Voyages of the "Columbia" to the Northwest Coast, 1787-1790 and 1790-1793,* edited by Frederic William Howay. Boston, 1941. By permission of the Massachusetts Historical Society.

Booth, John Wilkes: *Report of the Committee of the Judiciary on the Assassination of Abraham Lincoln,* United States Senate, Washington, 1866.

Bradford, William: See "G. Mourt."

Breen, Patrick: Diary, edited by Frederick J. Teggart. *Publications of the Academy of Pacific Coast History,* vol. 1, no. 6. Berkeley, California, 1910. By permission of the Bancroft Library, University of California.

Brewer, William Henry: *Up and Down California in 1860-64,* edited by Francis Farquhar. Yale University Press, New Haven, 1930. By permission of University of California Press.

Broun, Heywood: *Collected Edition of Heywood Broun,* compiled by Heywood Hale Broun. New York, 1941. By permission of Harcourt, Brace and Company.

Brown, William R.: *Minnesota Farmers' Diaries,* edited by Rodney C. Loehr. St. Paul, 1939. By permission of the Minnesota Historical Society.

Burr, Aaron: *Private Journal of Aaron Burr.* William K. Bixby, St. Louis, 1903.

Cargill, James: "Hunting Indians in Massachusetts: A Scouting Journal of 1758," edited by Robert Francis Seybolt. *New England Quarterly,* vol. 3 (April 1930).

Carleton, James Henry: "Diary of an Ex-

618

cursion to the Ruins of Abo, Quarra and Gran Quivira in New Mexico under the Command of Major James Henry Carleton, U.S.A." *Ninth Annual Report of the Smithsonian Institution, Senate Miscellaneous Documents, Second Session, Thirty-third Congress,* vol. 1 (1854-55).

Catlin, George: *Letters and Notes on the Manners, Customs and Condition of the North American Indians.* London, 1842.

Chardon, Francis Auguste: *Chardon's Diary at Fort Clark,* edited by Annie Heloise Abel. Pierre, 1932. By permission of the State of South Dakota.

Chesnut, Mary Boykin: *A Diary from Dixie,* edited by Isabella D. Martin and Myrta Lockett Avary. New York, 1905. By permission of Appleton-Century-Crofts, Inc.

Clark, Bennett C.: "Diary of a Journey from Missouri to California in 1849," edited by Ralph P. Bieber. *Missouri Historical Review,* vol. 23 (October 1928).

Clark, William: *History of the Expedition under the Command of Captains Lewis and Clark to the Sources of the Missouri, thence across the Rocky Mountains and down the River Columbia to the Pacific Ocean,* edited by Paul Allen. Philadelphia, 1814.

Cleaver, Joseph, Jr.: "Diary of a Student at Delaware College," edited by William D. Lewis. *Delaware Notes,* Twenty-fourth Series (1951). Newark, Delaware. By permission of University of Delaware.

Colton, Walter: *Three Years in California.* New York, 1852.

Columbus, Christopher: *Journal of Christopher Columbus,* edited by Clements R. Markham. London, 1893. A translation of the "Historia del Signor Don Fernando Colombo" is included in *Churchill's Voyages,* London, 1752.

Cresswell, Nicholas: *Journal of Nicholas Cresswell,* edited by Samuel Thornely. New York, 1924. By permission of Dial Press, Inc. Copyright 1924, 1928 by Dial Press, Inc.

Crockett, David: *Col. Crockett's Exploits and Adventures in Texas.* London, 1837.

Dana, Richard Henry: *Richard Henry Dana, a Biography,* by Charles Francis Adams. Boston, 1891.

Danckaerts (Dankers), Jasper: *Journal of a Voyage to New York and a Tour of Several of the American Colonies, 1679-80,* translated and edited by Henry C. Murphy. Long Island Historical Society, Brooklyn, 1867.

Early, John: "Travels in the Cumberland Circuit," edited by Rt. Rev. Collins Denny. *Virginia Magazine,* vol. 33 (1925).

Edison, Thomas Alva: *Diary and Sundry Observations of Thomas Alva Edison,* edited by Dagobert D. Runes. New York, 1948. By permission of Philosophical Library.

Fithian, Philip Vickers: *Journal and Letters of Philip Vickers Fithian,* edited by Hunter D. Farish. Williamsburg, 1943. By permission of Colonial Williamsburg, Inc.

Floyd, John: *The Life and Diary of John Floyd,* by Charles H. Ambler. Richmond, Virginia, 1918.

Fontaine, William Winstan: *Diary. William and Mary College Quarterly,* vol. 16 (1907-08).

Forten, Charlotte L.: *Journal of Charlotte L. Forten,* edited by Ray Allen Billington. New York, 1953. By permission of Dryden Press. Copyright 1953 by The Dryden Press, Inc.

Fremantle, Arthur James Lyon: "Diary of an English Officer Present with the Confederate Army." *Blackwood's Edinburgh Magazine,* vol. 94 (1863).

Fuller, Elizabeth: *History of the Town of Princeton,* by Frances E. Blake. Princeton, Massachusetts, 1915. By permission of the town.

Greeley, Horace: *Overland Journey from New York to San Francisco.* New York, 1860.

Green, Ezra: *Diary of Ezra Green, M.D.* Boston, 1875.

Greenhow, Rose O'Neal: *My Imprisonment.* London, 1863.

Groh, George: "D-Day Diary of a Glider Infantryman." *Yank Magazine,* Continental edition, 1944.

Hamilton, Alexander: *Hamilton's Itinerarium,* edited by Albert Bushnell Hart. St. Louis, 1907.

Hamp, Sidford: *Diary,* edited by Herbert Oliver Brayer. *Annals of Wyoming,* vol. 14, no. 4 (October 1942).

Harrower, John: *Diary. American Historical Review,* vol. 6, no. 1 (October 1900).

Havens, Catherine Elizabeth: *Diary of a*

Little Girl in New York. New York, no date.

Helm, Edith Benham: *The Captains and the Kings.* New York, 1954. By permission of G. P. Putnam's Sons.

Hitchcock, Ethan Allen: *Fifty Years in Camp and Field,* edited by W. A. Croffut. New York, 1909.

Hone, Philip: *Diary of Philip Hone,* edited by Bayard Tuckerman. New York, 1899.

Ickes, Harold L.: *The Secret Diary of Harold L. Ickes.* New York, 1953. By permission of Simon and Schuster, Inc. Copyright 1953 by Simon and Schuster, Inc.

Jernegan, Laura: *Whaling Wives,* by Emma Mayhew Whiting and Henry Beetle Hough. Boston, 1953. By permission of Houghton Mifflin Company.

Johnson, William: *William Johnson's Natchez,* edited by Ransom Hogan and Edwin Adams Davis. Baton Rouge, 1951. By permission of Louisiana State University Press.

Kemble, Fanny: *Journal,* by Frances Anne (Kemble) Butler. London, 1835.

Kenny, James: Journal, edited by John W. Jordan. *Pennsylvania Magazine of History and Biography,* vol. 37 (1913).

Knight, Amelia Stewart: Diary. *Transactions of the Fifty-sixth Annual Reunion of the Oregon Pioneer Association,* 1928.

Knight, Sarah Kemble: *Journals of Madam Knight and Rev. Mr. Buckingham.* New York, 1825.

Kogan, David S.: *Diary,* edited by Meyer Levin. New York, 1955. By permission of Beechhurst Press.

Lanzit, Jacob Saul: *Memoirs of American Jews,* by Jacob Raeder Marcus, vol. 3. Philadelphia, 1956. By permission of The Jewish Publication Society of America.

Lee, John Doyle: *Journals of John D. Lee,* edited by Charles Kelly. Privately printed. Salt Lake City, 1938. *A Mormon Chronicle: The Diaries of John D. Lee,* edited by Robert Glass Cleland and Juanita Brooks. San Marino, California, 1955. By permission of the Huntington Library.

Lewis, Meriwether: See Clark, William.

Maclay, William: *Journal of William Maclay,* edited by E. S. Maclay. New York, 1890.

Macready, William Charles: *Macready's Reminiscences and Selections from His*

Diaries and Letters, edited by Sir Frederick Pollock. London, 1875.

Magoffin, Susan Shelby: *Diary of Susan Shelby Magoffin,* edited by Stella M. Drumm. New Haven, 1926. By permission of Yale University Press.

Morris, Gouverneur: *Diary and Letters of Gouverneur Morris,* edited by Anne Cary Morris. New York, 1888.

"Mourt, G." (William Bradford and Edward Winslow): *A Relation, or Journall, of the Beginnings and Proceedings of the English Plantation at Plimoth, in New England.* London, 1622.

Newberry, Julia: *Julia Newberry's Diary,* edited by Margaret Ayer Barnes and Janet Ayer Fairbank. New York, 1933. By permission of W. W. Norton & Co. Copyright 1933 by W. W. Norton & Co., Inc.

Newell, Timothy: *Journal. Massachusetts Historical Society Collections,* Fourth series, vol. 1 (1852).

Parkman, Francis: *Journal of Francis Parkman,* edited by Mason Wade. New York, 1947. By permission of Harper and Brothers.

Peirce, Clothier: *Whaling,* by Charles Boardman Hawes. New York, 1924. By permission of Doubleday & Co., Inc.

Ransom, John L.: *Andersonville Diary,* Auburn, New York, 1881.

Reed, James Frazier: Diary, edited by Carroll D. Hall. *Donner Miscellany.* San Francisco, 1947 (Book Club of California). By permission of Sutter's Fort State Historical Monument.

Reeder, Andrew H.: "Governor Reeder's Escape from Kansas." *Transactions of the Kansas State Historical Society,* vol. 3 (1883-85).

Rogers, Will: *The Autobiography of Will Rogers,* edited by Donald Day. Boston, 1949. By permission of Houghton Mifflin Company.

Russell, William Howard: *My Diary North and South.* Boston, 1863.

Sears, Joshua: *Shipmasters of Cape Cod,* by Henry C. Kittredge. Boston, 1935. By permission of Houghton Mifflin Company.

Sewall, Samuel: Diary, edited by Worthington Chauncey Ford. *Massachusetts Historical Society Collections,* Fifth series, vols. 5, 6 and 7 (1878).

Seymour, Silas: *Incidents of a Trip through the Great Platte Valley to the*

Rocky Mountains and Laramie Plains. New York, 1867.

Sheridan, Clare Consuelo: *My American Diary.* New York, 1922.

Sherwood, Elmer W.: *Diary of a Rainbow Veteran.* Terre Haute, Indiana, 1929. By permission of the author.

Smith, John: Diary, edited by Louise Rau. *Mississippi Valley Historical Review,* vol. 20, no. 2 (September 1933).

Stilwell, Joseph W.: *The Stilwell Papers,* edited by Theodore H. White. New York, 1948. By permission of William Sloane Associates. Copyright 1948 by Winifred A. Stilwell.

Strong, George Templeton: *Diary of George Templeton Strong,* edited by Allan Nevins and Milton Halsey Thomas. New York, 1952. By permission of The Macmillan Company.

Thacher, James: *Military Journal during the American Revolutionary War.* Boston, 1823.

Thoreau, Henry David: *The Writings of Henry David Thoreau,* edited by H. G. O. Blake. Boston, 1884-1898.

Tudor, John: *Deacon Tudor's Diary,* edited by William Tudor. Boston, 1896.

Ward, Lester Frank: *Young Ward's Diary,* edited by Bernhard J. Stern. New York, 1935.

Washington, George: *The Writings of George Washington,* edited by Worthington Chauncey Ford. New York, 1889.

Welles, Gideon: *The Diary of Gideon Welles,* edited by John T. Morse Jr. Boston, 1911. By permission of Houghton Mifflin Company.

Wetmore, Alphonso: *Senate Executive Document 90, Twenty-second Congress, First Session.* Washington, 1833.

White, John: Diary, fourth voyage, *Principall Navigations, Voiages and Discoveries of the English Nation,* edited by Richard Hakluyt. London, 1589. And diary, fifth voyage, *Principal Navigations, Voyages, Traffiques and Discoveries of the English Nation,* edited by Richard Hakluyt. London, 1600.

Whitman, Walt: *Complete Prose Works of Walt Whitman.* Philadelphia, 1892.

Winslow, Anna Green: *Diary of Anna Green Winslow,* edited by Alice Morse Earle. Boston, 1894.

Woolman, John: *Journal of John Woolman.* Philadelphia, 1774. Many later editions.

Young, James Webb: *Diary of an Ad Man.* Chicago, 1944. By permission of the author and Advertising Publications, Inc.

ABOUT THE EDITORS

JOSEPH BERGER *is the author of over ten previous books—Americana, history, and juveniles—under his own name and the pen name of Jeremiah Digges. He has also been a radio and television writer and speech writer for two Presidents of the United States, as well as a contributor to* The Atlantic, Esquire, Story, *and other magazines. Born in Denver in 1903, he has lived in Kansas City, New Orleans, Washington, and Provincetown, Massachusetts. He and his wife (and co-editor), Dorothy Berger, now divide their time between New York and their home in the White Mountains of New Hampshire.*

MRS. BERGER *is a professional illustrator and designer as well as a student of Americana. She traces her family back to their arrival in Salem, Massachusetts, in 1635. During the years of sifting and searching through libraries, archives, and private collections that went into the making of* Diary of America, *Mrs. Berger was delighted to encounter various of her ancestors.*

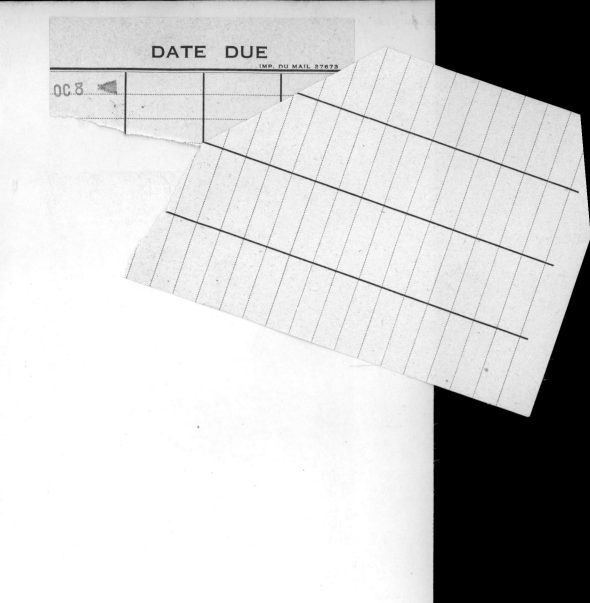